THE POLITICS OF NATIONAL PARTY CONVENTIONS

The POLITICS OF NATIONAL PARTY CONVENTIONS

By

PAUL T. DAVID

RALPH M. GOLDMAN

RICHARD C. BAIN

THE BROOKINGS INSTITUTION

Library of Congress Catalogue Card Number 60-7422

Printed in the United States of America
The George Banta Company, Inc.
Menasha, Wisconsin

THE BROOKINGS INSTITUTION is an independent organization engaged in research and education in the social sciences. Its principal purposes are to aid in the development of sound public policies and to provide advanced training for students in the social sciences.

The Institution was founded December 8, 1927, as a consolidation of three antecedent organizations: the Institute for Government Research, 1916; the Institute of Economics, 1922; and the Robert Brookings Graduate School of Economics and Government, 1924.

The general administration of the Institution is the responsibility of a self-perpetuating Board of Trustees. In addition to this general responsibility the By-Laws provide that, "It is the function of the Trustees to make possible the conduct of scientific research and publication, under the most favorable conditions, and to safeguard the independence of the research staff in the pursuit of their studies and in the publication of the results of such studies. It is not a part of their function to determine, control, or influence the conduct of particular investigations or the conclusions reached." The immediate direction of the policies, program, and staff of the Institution is vested in the President, who is assisted by an advisory council, chosen from the professional staff of the Institution.

In publishing a study the Institution presents it as a competent treatment of a subject worthy of public consideration. The interpretations and conclusions in such publications are those of the author or authors and do not necessarily reflect the views of other members of the Brookings staff or of the administrative officers of the Institution.

14054

Foreword

T H I S   V O L U M E presents an analysis of the convention system as a means of selecting nominees for the Presidency and Vice Presidency of the United States, based upon a review of the history and evolution of the major national parties as evidenced in and affected by their national conventions. The study was in part stimulated by and draws upon the five-volume study by Paul T. David, Malcolm Moos, and Ralph M. Goldman, *Presidential Nominating Politics in 1952,* which was conducted under the auspices of the American Political Science Association.

From a wealth of historical materials heretofore unanalyzed the authors have critically appraised the nominating process. The party out of power and the party holding office are examined as entities, each confronted with problems distinctive to its status. The leadership centers of out-party and in-party are described, with particular attention to the way various leadership elements have functioned in the nominating process since 1896.

The book may well lead to reconsideration of many widely held notions concerning the party system. It meets the hope of the Brookings Institution that the pioneering explorations of 1952 would lead to other and more fundamental research. This was also the hope of Dr. Will W. Alexander of the Edgar Stern Family Fund, who was a principal influence in the steps leading to the initiation of the 1952 study. The authors desire to dedicate this present book to his memory, since without his early interest the research would not have been possible.

A number of publications based in part on this study have already appeared. Among them are the lectures by Malcolm Moos and Paul T. David published in *Research Frontiers in Politics and Government* (Brookings Lectures, 1955); the book by Charles A. H. Thomson, *Television and Presidential Politics* (1956), and his paper "Television, Politics, and Public Policy," in *Public Policy: A Yearbook of the Graduate School of Public Administration, Harvard University* (1958); an article by Paul T. David and Ralph M. Goldman, "Presidential Nominating Patterns," *Western Political Quarterly* (September 1955); other articles by Paul T. David, "A New Role for the Opposition Party Leader," *New York Times Magazine,* September 18, 1955, and "The Changing Party Pattern," *Antioch Review,* Fall 1956; and a memorandum by Paul T. David, "Specifications for a Model State Presidential Primary Law," largely followed by the State of Florida in its enactment of 1955 and subsequently issued as Brookings Institution Reprint No. 11.

The investigation has also influenced three studies now in progress for Brookings publication: *Decisions and Voting Records of the National Party Conventions,* by Richard C. Bain; *The Presidential Campaign and Election of 1956,* by Charles A. H. Thomson and Frances M. Shattuck; and *Trends in National Party Leadership,* by Ralph M. Goldman of Michigan State University. (Tentative titles.)

The authors of the present book collaborated in the development of its analytical designs and in the exploratory research. Mr. David then assumed the principal responsibility for producing the consolidated draft of the book. Mr. Goldman has been an active collaborator in problem analysis and has served as reader and critic of the successive drafts. Mr. Bain was the project statistician and, besides contributing to the development of analytical theory throughout, was especially responsible for preparing the basic data of Chapter 7 and the major statistical analyses of Chapters 15 through 18.

Several others have made major contributions to the book. Final stages of the research were assisted by the helpful interest of George A. Graham, who became the Institution's Director of Governmental Studies on July 1, 1958. An early analysis of the leadership problems discussed in Chapters 4 and 5 was contributed by Malcolm Moos of Johns Hopkins University. The discussion of seating contests in Chapter 11 is based on materials prepared by John Ballard of Harvard University. Alice E. Robinson, now with the Democratic National Committee, served as a research assistant for more than a year, and prepared materials later used in Chapters 9, 10, and elsewhere. Frances M. Shattuck of the Brookings staff served intermittently as a research assistant over a five-year period and contributed to many portions of the book. F. P. Kilpatrick has acted frequently as a consultant on statistical problems since joining the Brookings staff a year ago. Warren E. Miller of the University of Michigan served as a general consultant on analytical and statistical problems in 1955 and 1956. The names of various others who have made specific contributions will be found noted at appropriate points throughout the book. David Cushman Coyle served for several months as editorial consultant. Kathleen Sproul edited the manuscript. The index was prepared by Jean Kyle.

The Interuniversity Summer Research Seminar on Presidential Nominating Politics held at Brookings in 1955 critically reviewed materials prepared for the study and contributed much to the book. Full-time participants and their connections at the time were Franklin M. Bridge, University of Arkansas; Harry R. Davis, Beloit College; Stanley Kelley, Jr., Brookings Research Fellow; Warren E. Miller, University of California; John H. Romani, Brookings Research Fellow; Lester G. Seligman, University of Oregon; Allan P. Sindler, Yale University; and, as consultants, James M. Burns, Williams College; David Easton, University of Chicago; Kenneth W. Hechler, American Political Science Association; Dayton McKean, University of Colorado; and Malcolm Moos, Johns Hopkins University.

To all of these who have contributed to the study, the authors and Brookings Institution are deeply indebted. To the authors themselves, who have shown imagination and perseverance through many difficulties, the Institution wishes to express its gratitude.

Throughout the study, the authors have had the benefit of consultations with an advisory committee consisting of Arthur N. Holcombe, chairman, Louis Brownlow, Richard S. Childs, Alexander Heard, Malcolm Moos, Peter H. Odegard, Louise Overacker, and James K. Pollock. The Institution, no less than the authors, is especially indebted to this group for its continued interest and helpful suggestions.

Special thanks are due the successive chairmen of the Democratic and Republican National Committees, who facilitated research by the authors and their collaborators at the national party conventions of 1952 and 1956, and were helpful in many other ways. The librarians and other staff members of the two national party committees have responded repeatedly to requests for assistance. The Institution is also grateful to the Librarian of Congress for assistance, especially during the years 1954-1957, when the Library's collection of national convention proceedings and related materials was being used most intensively.

Finally, on behalf of the Institution, I wish to express grateful appreciation to the John Randolph Haynes and Dora Haynes Foundation of Los Angeles for its generous grants in 1953 and 1955 in support of this investigation as a venture in the study of national problems. To Dr. Gordon Watkins and the Trustees of the Haynes Foundation, who saw the possibilities of such a study, we and all readers are deeply indebted. It hardly needs to be said, except for the record, that the conclusions and recommendations of this study have been reached wholly independently of the Haynes Foundation, which should not be understood as approving or disapproving the views expressed in this and other reports resulting from the investigation.

ROBERT D. CALKINS
President

November 1959

Table of Contents

1

Party Conventions and the Nominating Process

NATIONAL PARTY conventions entered the American scene during Andrew Jackson's first term as President. Uncertain and held irregularly at first, within a few decades they had developed the main features that have characterized them ever since. In a world of constant political change, they are among the oldest important political institutions to be found in any country.

Taken together as an interacting political system, the conventions of the two major parties provide widespread representation and make critical political decisions for the entire electorate. This high mission, however, is in strong contrast to the popular conception of them. It is also compromised by many aspects of their composition and institutional behavior.

Among political scientists, opinion on the technical effectiveness of the conventions is mixed. They have been described, for instance, as "unwieldy, unrepresentative, and less than responsible."[1] They have been regarded also as a serious obstacle to the establishment of responsible party government, because of the undue control exercised by the assembled party bosses.[2] On

the other hand, some scholars consider the conventions highly useful, because they provide the valuable service of testing the skill of competing politicians and developing party leadership.[3] A study of the present kind must necessarily devote attention to the practical question implied in such appraisals: are the conventions nothing more than meetings of party bosses hidden behind a noisy political circus, or can they be treated seriously as representative assemblies competent to decide the party's leadership and principles?[4]

An excellent way to understand the nature and utility of the American party convention is to recognize its similarity to what in certain other democracies is called a "parliament"—essentially, a place to talk (parley) that affords, to those duly chosen, appropriate privileges and immunities.[5] The party conventions have the important parliamentary characteristics of being masters of their own rules and subject to no written constitution, of exercising privileges of speech and action on the highest political questions, and of acting decisively on those questions that relate to their own leadership and that of the party they represent.

Whatever else it is, a party convention is primarily a forum for political decision-making. Convention decisions cut close to

[1] American Political Science Association, Committee on Political Parties, *Toward a More Responsible Two-Party System* (1950), p. 28.

[2] "Theoretically the national convention is the supreme governing body of the party. The local bosses, if they wanted to do so, could create a representative institution with great authority. Why has the convention failed to do so? The crucial fact about the national convention is not that it is controlled by the local bosses merely, but that the local bosses have no intention or desire to create an effective national institution." E. E. Schattschneider, *Party Government* (1942), pp. 157-58.

[3] Pendleton Herring, *The Politics of Democracy* (1940), p. 238

[4] Paul T. David, Malcolm Moos, and Ralph M. Goldman, *Presidential Nominating Politics in 1952* (1954), Vol. 1, p. 246.

[5] Cf. D. W. Brogan, *Politics in America* (1954), pp. 195, 214.

the great political concerns of any society: the allocation of political power, the purposes for which political power shall be used, and the further evolution of the political system. Perhaps no one is more reluctant to shatter precedent or to venture on dangerous innovations than the politicians who gather so thickly at the conventions, but they seldom lose sight of the fact that the decisions of the moment are only preliminary. Most of them know that the final decision is made in the election where their party will win or lose political prizes that cannot be disregarded.

When the moment for action arrives, a party convention can enter upon an executive mood of which few other representative political institutions are capable. Action, not deliberation, is the end product of a convention, and its most characteristic form is the selection of a new leadership for a political party that either is or hopes to become dominant in the affairs of the nation. The close of a convention is a time of victory for some contestants and their factions, of defeat for others, but for all it is mainly the moment of marching into battle against the common foe—the rival party.

The Convention as Representative Institution

Whether the conventions are "truly representative" institutions, worthy of respect in a democratic society, is a question—or tangle of questions—that may generate more heated theoretical argument than practical wisdom. Confusion on this subject stems from several characteristics of party politics and of the conventions themselves.

First, there is the fact that state party organizations are far more autonomous than state governments. They are united in a national party by rules and customs far less definitely federal than those that unite the states in a national government. Accordingly, a national party convention takes on some of the characteristics of an international conference of delegations from sovereign nations, some of which may be democracies, others autocracies of one sort or another. In one delegation to a party convention each member may have a direct relationship to a specific constituency of party voters; in another the members collectively may owe allegiance to a state committee or convention that is remote from the voters and little subject to their control. But each of these delegations represents its state party in one way or another, and the variation among them does not necessarily prevent the assembly as a whole from retaining its representative nature.

The uncertainties about the composition of a given party constituency provide a further source of confusion. How does one recognize those who are or should be considered members? The political parties in the states have seldom attempted to operate as dues-paying organizations with a clearly identified membership. In many states, to be sure, voters must identify themselves with a particular party when registering if they wish to vote in the primary elections, and this system seems to endow party affiliation with more substantial reality than it would otherwise have.[6] A convention is generally assumed to have the duty of representing only the party adherents, however they are defined, but the pressure to win votes is also a pressure in the direction of liberal standards of party membership. The public at large is always informally represented in each convention, in part because of the easy qualifications for taking a hand in local party affairs, but even more because of the efforts of each party to choose candidates who will attract the largest number of voters.

The behavior of conventions themselves makes it difficult to examine the representative nature of the institution. Many matters of importance seem to be settled without the taking of a record vote, or a

[6] Clarence A. Berdahl, "Party Membership in the United States," *American Political Science Review*, Vol. 36 (Feb. 1942), pp. 16-50; (April 1942), pp. 241-62.

vote, if taken, sometimes seems only to confirm a decision previously made elsewhere. The conventions undoubtedly fall short of what might be assumed as an appropriate ideal for their behavior:

... a nominating process in which an informed and involved party membership indicates its preferences among the contending candidates, and convention delegates ... meet peaceably and faithfully to register the result.[7]

But any representative institution may at times fall short of an assumed ideal for its behavior without entirely losing its representative character.

[It] may perform its functions on occasion by merely assenting, by confirming the acts of an existing leadership, or by accepting and ratifying a decision arranged at a different level. What happens in such a situation is that the principal function of the representative institution is to legitimize the previous decision.[8]

As legal entities, the conventions have been very nearly unrecognized in federal law until recently. Political parties are not mentioned in the federal Constitution, and only rarely and indirectly in federal statutes. The Supreme Court, however, had occasion in 1952 to refer to "a state political party, affiliated with a national party through acceptance of the national call to send state delegates to the national convention"; the Court upheld the authority of a state party committee to require would-be presidential electors to sign a pledge of support for the national party's candidates, still to be selected.[9] Recent proposals to establish a federal Presidential Primaries Commission seem to have been drafted on the assumption that the party convention is a type of representative institution. The establishment of such a commission would indirectly subject major features of the conventions to prescriptions of federal law.[10]

The argument over what the conventions ought to be has undoubtedly been complicated by a basic uncertainty: is nomination by a party organization proper at all? The most critical aspects of the nominating process arise from the fact that the alternatives of choice must be discovered as a part of the process. It is the function of the nominating process to reduce to finality the alternatives that can be made the subject of an election. The difference between the nominating process and the election process is nonetheless often misunderstood, because of a hasty assumption that the nominating procedures of the two major parties are limited to only two opposing possibilities—candidates will be chosen by a small inner circle of bosses unless they are determined in a national primary where all voters may take part.

Actually the party conventions occupy a middle ground. They can draw heavily on the voters for guidance, which they obtain formally in state primaries and informally by many kinds of grass-roots contact. They can also perform a service that is practicable only in a general parley—that of solving the problems of compromise, of combining first and second choices into some result that the whole party will support, thus maintaining party unity and avoiding disruption into splinter parties. This service of compromise is one of the essential differences between a major-party nomination and a general election, and one that makes it futile to judge the representative character of the nominations by the standards appropriate to an election.

---

[7] David B. Truman in *Political Science Quarterly*, Vol. 70 (June 1955), p. 311. The assumption was attributed to the editors of *Presidential Nominating Politics in 1952*, who in turn were attempting to apply such standards of legitimacy in political action as were assumed to be widely held among the American people.

[8] Malcolm Moos, "New Light on the Nominating Process," in Stephen K. Bailey, *et al.*, *Research Frontiers in Politics and Government* (Brookings Lectures 1955), p. 139.

[9] *Ray v. Blair*, 343 U. S. 214, 225.

[10] Such proposals have included bills introduced in recent sessions of Congress; for example, by Senator Paul H. Douglas of Illinois and Representative Charles E. Bennett of Florida, S. 1288 and H. R. 5004, 85 Cong. 1 sess. Discussion of these proposals as they were introduced in 1952 may be found in David, Moos, and Goldman, *op. cit.*, Vol. 1, pp. 217-24, 230, 242.

Nominating as the Recruitment of Leadership

Leadership is not simply a quality possessed by certain persons; in the main it is the product of a relationship among a number of people in which one is recognized as leader and the others as his followers. The leader not only influences the actions and attitudes of the followers but also as a rule acts as their representative in situations where they operate as a group. The question of who can serve as a leader is therefore related to the circumstances as well as the people—not only to the traits and qualities of the individuals, but particularly to the conflicts and problems in which they are involved.[11]

The recruitment of political leaders is ordinarily controlled or strongly influenced by the institutions through which political action takes place. These institutions include the constitutional and electoral forms embodied in law and also the customs and networks of influence through which informal political power is brought to bear. Students of political behavior have often assumed that in the selection of political leaders, whatever the formal aspects of the process, the actual determination of the outcome has been in the hands of an inner circle that somehow formed itself originally and then became self-perpetuating.[12] These students have, however, usually found it difficult to explain how the principal leader is selected or arises among a group of leaders, or how it is possible occasionally to find a leader coming to power who has been in opposition to what was considered the inner circle.[13]

If the presidental nomination is to be studied as a leadership recruiting process—which it undoubtedly is, whatever else it may also be—then the study must go far beyond an examination of stabilized inner circles, their formation and renewal. All the patterns of leadership ascent must be taken into account, and most of all those that occur when a post of top party leadership has fallen vacant with no definite heir apparent. Crises of this sort differ widely in the amount of conflict and freedom of choice that they engender, as well as in the breadth and characteristics of the groups that participate directly in the activities of choice.

In a previous study, *Presidential Nominating Politics in 1952,* a preliminary attempt was made to develop a general-purpose classification of patterns of leadership succession, including inheritance, inner group selection, and compromise or victory

---

[11] The manner in which the political community selects its leaders has always been a favorite subject for discussion among political scientists; it has also been receiving increasing attention from social psychologists, sociologists, and cultural anthropologists. Much of the early discussion was concerned with attempts to identify ideal personal traits that would qualify individuals for selection as leaders or that could be used in explanation of why particular individuals had been selected. More recently, greater emphasis has been given to the concept of leadership as a relationship. See Lester G. Seligman, "The Study of Political Leadership," *American Political Science Review,* Vol. 44 (Dec. 1950), pp. 904-15; Chester I. Barnard, *Organization and Management* (1948), pp. 39, 106-09.

See also the chapter on "Leadership" by Cecil A. Gibb, in Gardner Lindzey (ed.), *Handbook of Social Psychology* (1954), Vol. 2, pp. 877-920, for an excellent summarization and review of leadership theory and research in social psychology.

Political scientists interested in leadership have inevitably been attracted to the study of the Presidency. Insofar as a body of theory on leadership can be found in American political science, it appears mainly in the extensive and growing literature on the Presidency.

[12] Systematic studies of leadership recruitment within political parties, including particularly those of Ostrogorski, Michels, and Duverger, have tended to emphasize the formation and renewal of inner circles. See, for example, Maurice Duverger, *Political Parties* (1954), Chap. 3, "Party Leadership," pp. 133-202, in which the previous literature is summarized along with much new research.

[13] One excellent study of this kind exists—R. T. McKenzie's *British Political Parties* (1955), See also the articles on Canadian party conventions by John W. Lederle: "National Party Conventions: Canada Shows the Way," *Southwestern Social Science Quarterly* (Sept. 1944), pp. 118-33, "The Liberal Convention of 1919 and the Selection of Mackenzie King," *Dalhousie Review,* Vol. 27 (1948), pp. 85-92, "The Liberal Convention of 1893," *Canadian Journal of Economics and Political Science* (Feb. 1950), pp. 42-52; and the books on the New Zealand and Australian party systems: Leslie Lipson, *The Politics of Equality* (1948), and Louise Overacker, *The Australian Party System* (1952).

in factional conflict.[14] This classification system has been developed further in the present study and, as a basic step in the analysis, has been applied to all the major-party presidential nominations since the beginnings of the convention system.

The Cycle of the Nominating Process

The nomination that is "made" at a convention is actually the product of a long series of activities and decisions stretching back through the years. Because of the four-year term of the Presidency, there is in general a four-year cycle in the nominating process.[15] For about three years after the election the contest for the next nomination will generally be more or less latent. (This first phase of the cycle may last as long as seven years in the party of a newly elected President who will presumably be nominated for a second term without contest.) During this period the contest for the next presidential nomination lies hidden in the normal careers of outstanding political figures who are building up their reputations and attracting public attention as possible leaders. At the same time, the representatives of all kinds of special interests, sectional, economic, or ideological, are groping around for a handhold on the situation in the form of an attractive potential candidate, against the day when they may wish to take positive action. The potential candidates themselves and their friends and would-be managers are also groping around for the issues, factional interests, and combinations that might advance their potential candidacies. Toward the end of the phase of latency there is a marrying of forces by which the potential candidates and the factional sources of support come together. The factions in search of a leader and the would-be leaders in search of a faction become joined for the period of the second phase.

If there is to be a contest over the nomination, the second, or open, phase begins with the first overt announcement of candidacy—in recent times, often as early as October or November of the year before the election. Candidates who announce early incur the hazards of the "front-runner," much discussed quadrennially by political writers. But the mechanics of the presidential primaries in several states and the requirements for campaign fund-raising increasingly press for early announcements by willing candidates, thus producing many months of open campaigning when there is an active contest.

The nomination is, of course, not always contested, and when it is, not always as vigorously as in each party in 1952, or in the Democratic in 1956. Of the sixty-three major-party presidential nominations since the beginnings of the convention system, seventeen went to an incumbent President, and twenty others were made without much of an open contest.[16]

When the phase of open contest does occur, the situation becomes organized in terms of the respective contestants and their supporting cohorts and takes on many of the aspects of an election campaign. The moving tides of the struggle inside one or both of the parties often produce a public impression of the greatest confusion. In actuality, however, this phase is likely to be more simple in some respects than the phase of latency, when all possibilities had the appearance of being open. There are

[14] David, Moos, and Goldman, *op. cit.*, Vol. 1, pp. 11-14.

[15] The quadrennial character of the presidential nominating cycle is vividly illustrated in Roy V. Peel and George Snowden, "From Four Years of Politics the Candidates Emerge," *Public Opinion Quarterly*, Vol. 4 (Sept. 1940), pp. 451-64. Peel and Snowden use the "business review" technique of dividing the years 1936 to 1940 into quarterly summaries of high lights in presidential nominating politics. The preconvention campaign from 1936 to 1940 was particularly active in both parties in anticipation of the possibility that President Franklin D. Roosevelt would retire at the end of his second term.

[16] The total of sixty-three is an odd number because no Whig convention was held in 1836. Nominations by the bolting Democrats of 1860 and the bolting Republicans of 1912 were omitted in computing the major-party total. Further details appear in later chapters, especially Chapter 6.

seldom more than three or four candidates mounting active preconvention campaigns, though there may be "dark horse" candidates standing ready for an opening.

In the third phase the contest is by one means or another brought to its formal conclusion. The phase begins when all concerned realize clearly either that one of the contestants will win or that no contestant will hold an opening majority at the convention. Under the first contingency, both the second and third phases may be over when, or even before, the convention opens, even if the early contest has been an active one. This occurred, for example, in the Republican nominating contest of 1944, when Governor Thomas E. Dewey was sure of the nomination by mid-May, after a series of victories in the early primaries.

More often, the period of active contest, if it has occurred at all, extends into the opening days of the convention, with general uncertainty over the outcome. The third and final phase—resolution of the issue—then falls clearly to the convention itself, and is likely to involve difficult problems and much responsibility for the party leaders. Especially when there is a prospect of extended voting and the possibility of a stalemate, resolution of the contest becomes essentially a combination, on the one hand, of negotiation among candidates and other leaders and, on the other, of voting by the delegates in full convention assembled. The issue then frequently reaches settlement in the form of a divided vote.

Relationships to the Party System

The party conventions and the nominating process have had a most intimate relationship to the evolution of the American party system. The institutional origins of the national parties can be traced very largely in the evolution of the apparatus for dealing with presidential nominations, which occurred originally in Congress but did not remain there. Neither the party system nor the nominating process can be studied in isolation; the practical requirements of the party system have determined many aspects of the nominating process, and vice versa.

Such relationships exist because the nominating process is not an end unto itself. It is preparatory to an attempt to win an election, which in turn is preparatory to an attempt to operate a government. Presumably there are relationships between the manner in which a party nominates its candidates, the manner in which it campaigns for their election, and the manner in which it governs—or even the extent to which it can be said to govern—if it succeeds in electing its candidates. The various aspects of the nominating process thus need to be examined, not only in terms of their immediate consequences for the nomination itself, but with some regard for their effect on election campaigns and on the process of government in the widest sense.

Frequently the party conventions have been referred to simply as "the nominating conventions," on the obvious assumption that they have no other important functions. Other recognized functions do, however, exist. The adoption of a platform is one of the oldest; so is the use of the convention as a campaign rally. The convention has acted as the party governing body in some sense from the first, but the recognition of this function is relatively recent, if indeed it is recognized even now by members of the conventions in any self-conscious sense. A function may be latent for a long time or, nonexistent at first, emerge while an institution develops. In an institution as old as the party convention, it would be strange if all the functions that are manifest today had been so recognized from the beginning.[17]

The present book is concerned primarily with the nominating activities of the conventions. It deals with the other functions

[17] Ely Chinoy, *Sociological Perspective* (1954), pp. 37-41; Robert K. Merton, *Social Theory and Social Structure* (1949), Chap. 1.

in the context of their relationship to the nominating process, but in so doing does not intend to suggest that they are not important in their own right. Actually, they merit more attention than they could be given in this book, especially since suitable research techniques need to be developed for coping with their special aspects. The platform function, for instance, in view of the growing importance of all forms of public policy activity, particularly needs the kind of attentive and extended study that could fit it into the entire—and rather amorphous—process by which party positions are continuously developed and adjusted on issues of public policy. In this process the adoption of a platform at a convention may sometimes be merely an incident and not even a dominant one—unlike the controlling position of the nominating decisions among the phenomena to which they are most directly related.

So much of the present book is dependent on newly compiled data and the use of new analytical systems that it has not been easy to bring over-all integration to the treatment as a whole. Understanding of many aspects of this subject will doubtless be greatly enhanced through further use, adaptation, and criticism of the work by other scholars. But the job has to start somewhere, and any contribution to a better understanding of the presidential nominating process in its relationship to the party

system would seem sufficiently important to justify substantial efforts.

The main objective of all the research, accordingly, has been quite simply to achieve an improved perception of the process and its inner workings, preparatory to further efforts toward an understanding of the process as a whole and in its major parts. The important process elements are not equally conspicuous or equally accessible, even when their existence is known or suspected. A major concern has been to locate evidences of recurring pattern and long-term change wherever they can be found. These are likely to be phenomena of importance, whether or not they lend themselves at first to any easy or persuasive explanation.

Whether by conscious action or through the operation of unrecognized pressures, the conventions and the parties are sure to continue changing with the passage of time. The more clearly the operations of these institutions are seen and understood, the more readily it will be possible to devise efforts designed to improve their effectiveness in the general service of government— and the easier it will be to stave off changes that might be adverse to the general welfare. This, fundamentally, is the most weighty practical reason for pursuing the study of the details and the interrelationships of that central political operation, the choice of presidential candidates.

2

Origins of the National Convention System

HOW SHALL THE political community designate its leaders, invest them with special power, restrain their activities, and finally replace them? Many of the most fundamental issues of political philosophy are contained in that question. The problem was of great concern to the members of the Constitutional Convention of 1787, and one that they found far more difficult to solve for the executive branch of the government than for the legislature or the judiciary. The solution they provided remains largely unchanged in form, but there is no part of the Constitution where time and usage have done more to supply an unanticipated wealth of unwritten content. This is particularly true of the presidential nominating process, the principal subject of this book. Moreover, the usages that have grown up around the nominating process are not only of critical importance in the choice of a President but also have much to do with how he is invested with special power, restrained, and eventually replaced.

In the early years three systems of nomination and election were successively used in choosing a President. The first was that contemplated by the Constitution as written. The second grew up when party caucuses in Congress and popular elections in the states began to supplement the constitutional provisions. The third was provided when national party conventions were convened to make formal nominations in the name of the parties, to be presented for later choice by the whole electorate. This third system solidified in various ways over the course of a generation, along with

the two major political parties by which it has been operated since 1856, and continues in use today. Each of the three systems was the product of both an earlier history and the circumstances of the day, and each of the first two left an imprint on its successor, as undoubtedly the third will also do—*if* a fourth system is eventually created.

This is an area of constitutional practice in which there has always been an ample supply of proposals for change. In recent years the concept of a national presidential primary, coupled with electoral college reform, has had considerable support in Congress. Although this book is not concerned primarily with such proposals, past or present, the experience it deals with is relevant to consideration of their nominating aspects.

In view of the complexity of political institutions, a grasp of historical origins is essential if egregious errors are to be avoided in further attempts at study and analysis. This chapter reviews materials undoubtedly familiar to many students of American history, but it does so with special reference to aspects that will be the concern of the rest of the book.

The Constitution and the Problem of Executive Leadership

One of the most remarkable features of the American Constitution is the fact that it provides for a strong executive. This is not accidental. The provisions in question were the result of controversy that began in the earliest days of colonial history and that still continued when the Constitution was being written. Moreover, the adoption of the Constitution did not end the controversy.[1]

The structure of government under the Articles of Confederation as drawn in 1777 was a reflection of colonial sentiment. The only executive leadership at the head of the government for which the Articles provided was vested in the presiding officer of the Continental Congress, a post in which there was rotation from year to year. During the period of the Articles, nine men were chosen for this short-term presidency. But the conservatives in the Continental Congress never gave up their struggle for a stronger form of government. In 1786 they were able to secure authorization for what became the Constitutional Convention of 1787.

Most of the thirty-nine members of the Constitutional Convention who remained to the end and signed the final document were leaders of the conservative or nationalist wing of the "party of revolution." Well-read and politically knowledgeable, they were well aware of history's many records of conflict between executive and legislative organs. They knew at first hand the recent struggle between arbitrary colonial governors and protesting assemblies. They were also intent on the political necessity for national integration and the creation of a government able to govern. They decided that there should be a chief executive office in the new government, and that it should be filled by a single Head of State, rather than by a committee.

How, then, would this chief executive be chosen? The basic premise widely held among the Founding Fathers, themselves mostly bred in an aristocratic tradition, was that there exists a "natural aristocracy" of men imbued with such qualities as virtue, talent, wealth, distinguished descent, learning, and even physical strength. The problem was to devise a method for selecting "the best" from among this natural aristocracy to serve as chief executive of the United States.

The Virginia proposal was that Congress should choose the President. Many Virginians held in high regard the parliamentary model evolving in the mother country, in which the prime minister, the chief political executive, was chosen by the legislative majority.[2] The Virginia plan, however, would have violated the principle of separation of powers, to which the Founding Fathers were dedicated and which was their reason for establishing a separate executive. Nor was it possible to have the President chosen by the governors of the states, as proposed by a delegate from Massachusetts, since this would undermine the establishment of a national authority independent of the states. Nor could the President be chosen by direct election of the "people," since even the limited electorate of the day would not be able to employ the "proper" standards for soundly judging which one of the "natural aristocracy" was "the best."

The Convention finally settled upon the method of an *ad hoc* electoral college. Each state would convene separately its most capable individuals to serve briefly as presidential electors, and these electors in their wisdom would choose "the best" American for the office of President. The runner-up would become Vice President. Article II of the Constitution took care of the problem of large versus small states in presidential elections by providing that each state should have a number of presidential electors equal to the number of its senators and representatives in Congress. Each state legislature was left to work out its own method for choosing the presidential electors.

[1] Where other sources are not specifically cited on points involving original research, this chapter is based primarily on the historical material assembled by Ralph M. Goldman in "Party Chairmen and Party Faction, 1789-1900," unpublished doctoral dissertation, University of Chicago, 1951.

[2] This conception undoubtedly carried over into the early government when the "Virginia Dynasty," particularly Madison and Monroe, followed the route from congressional leadership to the secretaryship of state, then to the Presidency. It was also embodied for many years in the custom of presidential nomination by congressional caucus.

The Founders soon found themselves engaged in a hot national campaign to secure the adoption of the new Constitution. Calling themselves Federalists, these members of the "party of the Constitution" met almost overwhelming opposition in nearly every state, but they showed themselves to be expert in the art of circumventing established political institutions. They had wisely provided for ratification by a minimum of nine specially elected state conventions—not by the sitting state legislatures, most of which were under the control of agrarian, Antifederalist majorities, the former radicals of the "party of revolution." *The Federalist,* prepared by Alexander Hamilton, James Madison, and John Jay, was an encyclopedia of political philosophy and a campaign textbook rolled into one. By June 1788 the ninth state had ratified the document that presented a new structure of national government and leadership, including what was thought to be a strong but nonpartisan Presidency.

Leadership Recruitment from Washington to Jackson

The sixty-nine presidential electors who cast their ballots in February 1789 had no trouble making their unanimous choice of "the best." George Washington was not only the acclaimed military genius of a successful revolution. He had also presided over the Constitutional Convention, was one of the wealthiest men in the country, and was the leading citizen of Virginia—the state with the largest electoral vote.

In the brief span of Washington's first administration many political leaders came to realize that elections are critical occasions for change, even revolution, by constitutional means. They saw that the choice of governmental officeholders and the adoption of legislative policy on the basis of numerical majorities would automatically invite organized efforts to win those majorities. The recurring elections provided by the Constitution thus set in motion the

forces that produced, first, a Congress with the members divided into opposing groups; then the division of the state electorates into organized parties; and finally the organization of national parties with the power to make presidential nominations in preparation for the quadrennial contests in which one party or the other would win control of the executive machinery of government. Any incumbent of the Presidency, intended by the Founding Fathers to be a nonpartisan office, soon owed his position to the efforts of a political party.

From Washington onward, the procedures by which names came forward for consideration were important, but eleven presidential elections had been held and seven Presidents had occupied the office before the system of nominating in a national party convention began in 1831-1832. Every President since then, including Andrew Jackson for his second term, has been so nominated. During the years from 1789 to the early 1830's there was a steady expansion of the electorate, through growth in population, the admission of new states to the Union, and the extension of the franchise to new groups of voters by the state legislators. How to stabilize developing political institutions was a constant problem, and the provisions of the Constitution were frequently tested severely.

Emergent Partisanship and the Twelfth Amendment

The four principal figures in the opening years of the new government were President George Washington, Secretary of State Thomas Jefferson, Secretary of the Treasury Alexander Hamilton, and Representative James Madison. Washingon, although basically a Federalist, endeavored to remain neutral in the Hamilton-Jefferson feud, in which Jefferson and Madison were allies, and also kept himself clearly above the party battle that took place in Congress and the electorate. As President, he made all major, and many minor, decisions in matters of administration, but did tend to give preferment to the Hamiltonian program. Fundamentally, his nonpartisanship rested on the assumption of continued Federalist dominance in public policy.

In the opening session of the First Congress, Madison held the initiative in legislative business, speaking from the floor twice as often as the next most frequent speaker, pushing through the Bill of Rights amendments, winning the fight against the use of titles of honor for American public officials, and working hard to carry out his basic understandings of the new constitutional system. Hamilton, acting through his congressional friends, seized the initiative in the second session of the First Congress on behalf of the Federalist program. Party identifications in the First Congress were vague, but the supporters of the administration appeared to have a majority in each House as the situation stabilized. In the elections of 1790 for the Second Congress, the Federalists won small but definite majorities: 37 to 33 in the House of Representatives, 16 to 13 in the Senate.

Jefferson, after the lessons of these elections, began looking toward the general electorate for ultimate support of his philosophy of government. "The only corrective of what is corrupt in our present form of government," he observed in a letter to George Mason, "will be the augmentation of the number in the lower House, so as to get a more agricultural representation, which may put that interest above that of the stock-jobbers."[3] He promoted organizing work in many states through personal correspondence. New York State required special attention since it was Hamilton's main political base, and so, in May and June of 1791, Jefferson and Madison took their famous "botanizing expedition" up the Hudson Valley. The trip was credited with forging a political alliance between forces in New York and Pennsylvania, an alliance that shortly produced results in Congress and in the electoral college.

By 1792 the "Hamiltonians" and the

"Madisonians" were rapidly becoming political parties. Jefferson, eager to come out openly against the Hamiltonian program, several times offered his resignation as Secretary of State, but was also among those urging Washington to serve a second term. When Washington agreed to do so, the party struggle focused on the Vice Presidency and the congressional seats. Local campaigning was intense. An increasing number of Antifederalists, finally obliged to admit the success of the Constitution, dropped their party designation and began to call themselves "Republicans"—signifying that they were opposed to monarchy, which they accused the Federalists of trying to establish.

Washington received the unanimous vote of all 132 members of the electoral college. Of the second votes of each elector, the Republicans mustered 50 for George Clinton, not enough to beat the Federalist 77 for John Adams, who thus was re-elected Vice President. Four Republican votes went to Jefferson and one to Aaron Burr. The party balance in the Senate remained stable, but Washington entered his second term with the opposition in control of the House of Representatives.

Jefferson left the Cabinet late in 1793. The Republican opposition then proceeded to make itself heard in the press, in Congress, and occasionally from Monticello. In 1794 Hamilton left the Cabinet and devoted himself with increasing vigor to party politics. The Federalists continued their practice of publicly decrying partisanship in government while at the same time conducting secret caucuses in the state legislatures. Much of Hamilton's party effort was carried on through organized non-party groups such as the Cincinnati, the chambers of commerce, and the professional associations.

Party organizing activities continued to mount as the third presidential election year, 1796, approached. It was clear that the electoral college provisions of the Constitution were to receive their first real test. The Federalists were generally prepared to ele-

[3] Andrew A. Lipscomb (ed.), *The Writings of Thomas Jefferson*, Vol. 8 (1905), pp. 124-25.

vate Vice President John Adams to the Presidency. They were less concerned about the Vice Presidency, but most of them agreed, without taking organized action, that Thomas Pinckney of South Carolina would provide regional balance for their cause.

Article II of the Constitution, however, required each elector to vote for "two Persons" without indicating preference between them. Whoever won the largest number of votes, provided that the number was a majority of the total number of electors, would become President. In 1789 and 1792 the problem was simple, for all the electors gave one of their votes to Washington. The emphatic division of the vote for Vice President in 1792, however, indicated the effect of growing party activity. In 1796 there would be 138 electors, and with each of them having two officially nonpreferential votes it was possible that many different presidential candidates might win only a few votes each. It was also possible that many of the electors might share the same clear preference for a certain man as Vice President, and thus actually give him the Presidency when none of the intended first choices had mustered a majority. The fact that the electors voted in their own states and thus separately from each other made these possibilities all the more likely. In a contested situation, it seemed very evident that, if electors of like mind were to be mobilized in full strength, some influential leader or group was needed to unite them on a slate of clear first and second choices.

Throughout 1795 and early 1796, Madison and his Republican colleagues consulted frequently regarding the problem. To bring coordinated action to their own side, the Republicans in Congress held a caucus during the summer of 1796 and agreed to support Thomas Jefferson and Aaron Burr. This was the first congressional caucus to make an open presidential nomination.[4]

When the electors met in 1796, the cross-currents of constitutional design and party competition produced a confused outcome. Ballots were cast for thirteen candidates. The majority winner was Adams, with 71 votes, and the runner-up was Jefferson, with 68. Pinckney received 59 votes, and Burr, Jefferson's running-mate, 30. Thus a Federalist became President with a Republican Vice President. Twelve of the Adams electors had dissipated their second-choice votes, and at least one elector had voted for both Adams and Jefferson, since between them they received 139 votes in an electoral college of 138. Table 2.1 shows the leading states in the electoral college and the manner in which presidential electors were chosen in each. A change of 100 popular votes in Pennsylvania in 1796 would have lost that state's 15 electoral votes to Jefferson and resulted in Pinckney's election as Vice President. On the other hand, the Republican press taunted Adams with having won through the vote of the New York legislature, saying that the people would have voted for Jefferson—as indeed they did four years later.

The experience of 1796 emphasized the importance of pledging the electors to vote for *both* the presidential and vice-presidential nominations of their respective parties. This step in party planning, however, was subject to still another possible confusion— a tie vote between the two candidates of the

---

[4] Speculation as to the personnel included in congressional caucuses can be answered, at least in part, from two sources. John Quincy Adams, who had been elected to the United States Senate as a Federalist, reports in his famous *Diary* his attendance at the Republican caucus of 1808, presumably as a spectator. He dined beforehand with Senator Stephen R. Bradley of Vermont, who had called the meeting in his capacity of chairman of the preceding caucus of 1804. According to Adams, Bradley "said that he had issued his circulars to every republican member of both Houses; indeed, to every member, excepting *five* of the senate and twenty-two of the House of Representatives." These had not been invited because "they have never been in the habit of acting with us." Names of others active in the caucus included two senators and four representatives. See Allan Nevins (ed.), *Diary of John Quincy Adams, 1794-1845* (1928), pp. 51-52.

The last of the congressional caucuses, that of 1824, was reported in some detail in the *National Intelligencer*, Feb. 16, 1824; the account included a complete list of the fourteen senators and fifty-two representatives present.

same party if all electors should cast their ballots as instructed by the popular vote.

Between 1796 and 1800 increasing reliance was placed upon the congressional caucus to organize national and local party effort. The Republican caucus had little difficulty in uniting again upon a Jefferson-Burr ticket for 1800. Unity was not so readily achieved among the Federalists. President Adams' administration had alienated many of the members of his own party, particularly Hamilton, who considered Adams' re-election intolerable. Nevertheless most Federalists were constrained to support their incumbent President for re-election. They turned to another Pinckney of South Carolina—Charles C.—as their choice for second place.

Burr partisans for the state's full quota of presidential electors.

So perfect was Republican organization in 1800 that every one of that party's electors in the separate meetings in the states voted for Jefferson as his first choice and Burr as his second choice. The outcome was the ultimate arithmetical absurdity of the system: Jefferson and Burr, of the same party, tied for first place with 73 votes each. Adams received 65 votes, Pinckney 64, and John Jay one vote. The margin of victory, however, was close. A change of 214 popular votes in New York City would have resulted in a Federalist state legislature, 12 Federalist presidential electors from New York, and a Federalist majority in the electoral college.

TABLE 2.1. METHOD OF CHOOSING PRESIDENTIAL ELECTORS IN 1796,
SELECTED STATES[a]

State	Electoral College Votes	Method of Choosing
Virginia	21	Each on a district-wide basis by voters.
Massachusetts	16	Seven on district basis by voters; nine by majority in state legislature.
Pennsylvania	15	All on a single state-wide ticket by voters, popular majority winning all electors.
New York	12	All by majority of state legislature.

[a] Based on U. S. Bureau of the Census, *Historical Statistics of the United States, 1789-1945* (1949), p. 288.

As a part of the presidential contest, Aaron Burr led Tammany Hall of New York City in an unprecedented "get-out-the-vote" drive during the elections for the state legislature in 1800.[5] It was Burr who introduced the use of a card index file for names of voters, thereby enabling party workers to ferret out every possible supporter on election day. The Republicans carried a majority into the New York state legislature, which in turn selected Jefferson-

[5] Named for an Indian chief, the Tammany society of New York was formed in 1789 as one of a number of patriotic societies using the name. The New York organization alone survived; it early became a center for political activity among the partisans known then as Republicans, later as Democrats.

Burr, certain of at least the Vice Presidency yet eligible for the Presidency, did nothing to clarify the position as the election went into the House of Representatives for final decision. Ironically, the lame duck Federalist majority in the House had the power to frustrate the election of Jefferson merely by voting for Burr. But Hamilton, now that the hated Adams was safely barred from the Presidency, saw the issue as a choice between two lesser evils. Using every ounce of his influence, he convinced his Federalist colleagues that Jefferson, although "a contemptible hypocrite," was incorruptible, and therefore better than Burr.

The Republican victories of 1800 were

repeated in the congressional elections of 1802. Jefferson's personal popularity made his re-election in 1804 a matter of course, but he was uneasy about the ambitions of Vice President Burr. As early as 1802 he began to encourage the Clintons of New York to undermine Burr's political base in that state and prevent his getting another nomination. Jefferson next moved for an amendment to the Constitution that would separate the vice-presidential from the presidential electoral voting. On October 17, 1803, the opening day of the session, the proposed Twelfth Amendment was introduced into Congress.

The debate in Congress involved a complete reversal of party roles. The Federalists opposed the amendment on the ground that it violated states' rights, because it would diminish the possibility that presidential elections would be thrown into the House of Representatives, where each state, large and small, had one vote for President. The Republicans, traditionally strict constructionists, argued that the Constitution was "an experiment," to be amended whenever practical experience made it seem necessary. Nevertheless, within eight weeks, the proposed amendment had gone through the Congress and been sent to the states. Ratification was completed on September 25, 1804, just in time to free Jefferson from the electoral college risks he had encountered in 1800.

The events of 1804 ended a cycle in American political party development. The evidences included the rapid adoption, over Federalist opposition, of the amendment changing the mode of electing the principal officials of the national government; Hamilton's death in a duel of honor with Burr; and the enlargement of Republican majorities in Congress that initiated two decades of one-party government at the national level. Until 1801 the Federalists had retained a working majority in both houses of Congress, although a diminishing one. When the Seventh Congress opened session in 1801 the Republicans had majorities in both houses, and in successive Congresses their majorities became distinctly lopsided.

One-Party Rule

Jefferson was renominated by acclamation in 1804, when the Republican caucus in Congress met to perform its nominating function for the third time. Balloting was necessary on the vice-presidential nomination; George Clinton of New York was chosen. The election was a triumph for Jefferson and the Twelfth Amendment. The revised electoral college system produced 162 votes each for Jefferson and Clinton, and 14 each for Charles C. Pinckney and Rufus King, the Federalist candidates. In 1808, despite growing objections to the caucus system, the Republicans in Congress met again and, with Jefferson's support, nominated James Madison for President. Clinton was again nominated for Vice President.

"King Caucus" was never fully enthroned in the Federalist party. The system was unnecessary when the party was in power, and the congressional basis for it disappeared rapidly when the party had lost the Presidency. In 1804 the Federalist candidates, Pinckney and King, were nominated in a congressional caucus, but objection followed from the noncongressional Federalist leaders of Massachusetts and New York, who were more powerful in their home states than the party minority was in Congress. In 1808 the Federalists held no congressional caucus. Instead, at the instance of a committee of Massachusetts legislators, a delegate convention was held in New York. Although held without public notice and with its sessions closed to the public, this was in essence the first national nominating convention.[6] Eight of the seventeen states were represented, and the convention endorsed Pinckney and King. In the electoral college, Madison won by 122 votes to Pinckney's 47.

Nominating procedures in 1812 were carried on in the shadow of the outbreak of war with Great Britain. Madison received a unanimous renomination in the Republican

[6] S. E. Morison, "The First National Nominating Convention," *American Historical Review,* Vol. 17 (July 1912), pp. 744-63.

congressional caucus, but a group of bolting party members in New York backed De Witt Clinton. A secret Federalist convention met in New York and nominated Clinton as a fusion candidate. Madison won his second term, but the Federalist candidate received 89 votes in the electoral college to Madison's 128. The Federalists also gained in Congress, although still greatly outnumbered there.

By 1816 the war was over, and the Federalist party had been considerably discredited in the process. Madison's "heir apparent" was Secretary of State James Monroe, but Secretary of the Treasury William H. Crawford was popular—despite his disavowals of candidacy. Monroe was nominated by the most sharply divided caucus vote that had so far occurred, 65 to Crawford's 54. The Federalists held no organized caucus or convention; by common consent, their twice-defeated vice-presidential candidate, Rufus King, was given the empty honor of a hopeless race. He was the last of the Federalist candidates for President.

The Federalist party continued to have a small representation in Congress until 1824 and then disappeared—mainly the victim of its own incapacity to adapt to the organizational and leadership requirements of an expanding electorate. In 1802, Hamilton had developed an elaborate plan for a Federalist association to be called "The Christian Constitutional Society," with a dues-paying membership and an active organizational program. To this suggestion he had received the following reply:

An attempt at association, organized into clubs, on the part of the Federalists, would revive a thousand jealousies and suspicions. . . . Without any exertion on our part, in the course of two or three years [the Republicans] will render every honest man in the country our proselyte.[7]

Two years later, Hamilton was dead. In twenty-four years out of office, the party never recovered from the complacency of its other early leaders.

[7] Letter from James A. Bayard in John C. Hamilton (ed.), *The Works of Alexander Hamilton*, Vol. 6 (1851), p. 544.

The election of Monroe in 1816 inaugurated what became known as "the era of good feelings," a period in which there was neither an important opposition party nor a clearly defined set of divisions within the majority party. Several strong congressional leaders were competing with each other, and turbulence was growing among the various factions and cliques in Congress and the country. But in 1820 all welcomed a postponement of any showing of electoral force until 1824. Monroe was renominated by common consent and without formal action. No other party candidate was placed in the field against him. The electors gave him 235 votes, with 3 abstentions and one vote for John Quincy Adams. As might be expected, popular interest in the election reached a low ebb.

Monroe was the last of the "Virginia Dynasty," and toward the end of his second term it was clear that changes were becoming inevitable. Monroe himself had the makings of a strong executive. But, under the system of succession by which he had come to office, he had inherited a constitutional position that was in process of being stripped of its real power. The President owed his nomination to the members of his party in Congress, yet they had no feeling of dependence on him for their own electoral success, since there was no effective opposition party. As President, Monroe could preside but not rule, the end result of trends that had required two decades to unfold.

The Breakdown in Nominating Arrangements

In the country at large the political environment was changing rapidly. State constitutions were being overhauled and popular suffrage extended. The census was reflecting important population changes, shifting Virginia from first to third place and putting New York first and Pennsylvania second. The urban centers were becoming pivots of power, not only because of their wealth, but also because of their voting strength as more and more wage-earners gained the franchise. The frontier areas were also growing and were increasingly insistent on a greater voice in political affairs.

As 1824 approached, five major candidates emerged for the nomination of what was now called the Democratic-Republican party. John Quincy Adams of Massachusetts, son of the second President, was Secretary of State. William H. Crawford of Georgia was Secretary of the Treasury. John C. Calhoun of South Carolina was Secretary of War. Henry Clay of Kentucky was Speaker of the House. General Andrew Jackson of Tennessee was a national hero and was again sitting in the United States Senate.

The congressional caucus had not functioned at all as a nominating instrumentality in 1820, and there was opposition to its revival in 1824. Several proposals for a national Democratic-Republican nominating convention came to nothing. In the end, the several candidates were nominated mainly by the agencies most favorable to each of them, particularly the legislatures of their home states. The Georgia legislature favored Crawford, but declared that only a congressional caucus could legitimately make the nomination. On the other hand, the Tennessee legislature nominated Jackson, then issued a formal resolve that the caucus procedure was unconstitutional. A congressional committee ascertained that most members deemed the caucus method "inexpedient." Nevertheless, a minority attended a caucus at which Crawford was nominated. This was the last congressional caucus ever held for the purpose of nominating a presidential candidate.

In 1824 presidential electors were chosen in a variety of ways: by the legislatures in six states, by congressional districts in seven states, and on a state-wide ticket in eleven states. In only five states were Jackson, Adams, Crawford, and Clay all represented on the same ballot. Calhoun had found little support outside his own state for the Presidency, but was named by both the Adams and Jackson men as their vice-presidential choice. The total popular vote

in the eighteen states where the people voted for presidential electors was slightly over 350,000. Jackson won 99 of the 261 electoral college votes for President, not enough to elect; Adams 84, Crawford 41, and Clay 37. For the Vice Presidency, Calhoun led a field of six with 182 votes and was elected.[8]

The choice for President was thus thrown into the House of Representatives, to be made, as provided in the Constitution, from the top three. Clay, as the low man and as Speaker of the House, was put in the role of kingmaker and swung his influence to Adams. Each state delegation in the House had one vote. The vote was taken on February 9, 1825, and showed 13 states for Adams (a majority), 7 states for Jackson, and 4 for Crawford. When Clay subsequently became Adams' Secretary of State, Jackson and his managers immediately set up the cry "corrupt bargain." The Jacksonians, declaring that the people had been cheated by "the dynasty of the Secretaries," vowed revenge in 1828.

Thus the stage was set for the new party alignments: the Adams men versus the Jackson men. The outcome seemed predetermined, for President Adams professed opposition to political parties and made little effective use of his office and its prerogatives to organize for his own re-election. The Jacksonians, on the other hand, were willing organizers and turned expert hands to the creation of what was to become a new party—legislative and electoral, state and national.

In October 1825 the Tennessee legislature again nominated Jackson for President. Jackson accepted the nomination and resigned from the Senate to begin his campaign. In Washington, Senator Martin Van Buren of New York placed himself at the

[8] According to Wilfred E. Binkley, this was the first election in American history in which estimates of the popular vote for each candidate for President were widely publicized. These estimates indicated that Jackson led with about 42 per cent of the popular vote, an important factor in the subsequent popular outcry when he was denied the office. (Binkley, *American Political Parties, Their Natural History*, 3d ed., 1958, pp. 111-12.)

head of the anti-administration forces in Congress. In a statement on January 13, 1827, he proposed that a national convention be called to nominate candidates for President. No action followed the suggestion, but it was sufficient to prompt President Adams to call Van Buren "the great electioneering manager of General Jackson." Adams' own renomination for the contest of 1828 came out of a state convention in Maine, and was later endorsed by the legislatures of Vermont and Massachusetts and by state conventions in New York and Pennsylvania.

The methods for choosing presidential electors were still shifting in the direction of popular choice. Between 1824 and 1828, election by state legislature dropped from six to two and by congressional district from seven states to four, while election by state-wide general ticket went up from eleven to eighteen. The popular vote for electors rose to 1,155,000 in 1828, as against 350,000 four years earlier. The electoral college outcome was 178 for Jackson and 83 for Adams.

Jackson's election in 1828 brought with it a revolution in party politics that remains a favorite topic of comment for historians and politicians. It ended an era in the development both of the Presidency as an office and of relations between the Congress and the Executive. Jackson came to power as the result of a highly organized popular movement in which he owed nothing to those members of Congress who had refrained from becoming his announced supporters. Thereafter the Presidency could be and was to be occupied at times by incumbents who were notably independent of the Congress, and who entered office with at least some organized support from the political party by which they had been nominated.

It is easy to decry the congressional caucus as a nominating instrumentality in view of its evident weaknesses during the period in which it was used. But most of those weaknesses were probably the result of the imbalance in the party system as a whole, which in turn was the result of the disintegration of the Federalist party in Congress and in the country. If the Federalist party had maintained its position as an effective component in a two-party system, the congressional caucuses of the two major parties would each have been subjected to the discipline of competition in their selection of presidential candidates. The congressional caucuses might then have become as dependent upon the presidential candidates that they nominated as the candidates were upon them. In that event, the whole pattern of historical development might have been different, and in some respects it might have been a development more conductive to an integrated and effective national leadership than the one that actually occurred for a period of several decades.[9]

Early History of Party Conventions

The first national party convention in the modern sense was held by a short-lived party known as the Antimasons that sprang up in western New York and Massachusetts. Although some of its members were officeholders, its chance of nationwide growth and success depended on appealing mainly

[9] The relationship suggested is apparently the one that has come to prevail between British party leaders and members of Parliament; an analogous evolution can also be illustrated in American political history. Under the original provisions of the Constitution, members of the United States Senate were supposed to be selected by the state legislatures, with an implied responsibility to accept instructions from them. But any willingness to accept instructions had largely disappeared by the 1840's, and the practice was already developing by which senatorial campaigns were carried to the voters in the states with the object of controlling the election of state legislators. In the Lincoln-Douglas campaign of 1858, party slates of candidates for the Illinois legislature were formally pledged to the respective party candidates for senator. By the end of the century people were referred to the "election of Senators" in November, meaning the elections for the state legislatures. The Seventeenth Amendment was made possible because what it formalized was already largely in existence in more than half of the states. See William H. Riker, "The Senate and American Federalism," *American Political Science Review*, Vol. 49 (June 1955), pp. 452-69.

to voters in areas where the party had not yet won any elections. For this purpose a congressional caucus was obviously out of the question; an organization had to be built from the ground up, with recognition for adherents who had no representation whatever in public office. A party convention would answer this purpose.

Accordingly the New York State Antimason meeting in 1829 called a national convention to meet in Philadelphia on September 11, 1830. This was the first national party convention open to the public. It in turn called a nominating convention for September 26, 1831, at Baltimore, at which 116 delegates appeared and nominated William Wirt for the Presidency.

The Antimasons established four precedents that influenced other party conventions. Delegations were chosen in a manner determined by each state. Each delegation had as many votes as the state's representation in Congress. A special majority—in this case three fourths of the delegates—was required for nomination. Finally, an Antimasonic national committee was appointed to carry on between elections.

The party, however, did not survive to hold another convention. One of its two principal leaders, Thurlow Weed of New York, moved over into the Adams or "National Republican" wing of the Democratic-Republican party and later played a key role in founding the Whig party and then the Republican party. The other, Benjamin F. Hallett of Massachusetts, was to be the first national committee chairman of the Democratic party.

The second national convention was held by the National Republicans. By 1831 these conservatives had so few of their men in Congress that they, like the Antimasons, needed a device to give them at least a semblance of nationwide representation. Accordingly, they met in Baltimore on December 12, 1831, and nominated Henry Clay and John Sergeant. With Clay's overwhelming defeat in 1832, this attempt to form a conservative party from the dissi-

dent elements of the Democratic-Republicans was abandoned, and no further National Republican conventions were held.

On May 21-22, 1832, the Jackson supporters held a convention, also in Baltimore, of what was still called the Democratic-Republican party. The reason in this case was the bitter split in the administration between the supporters of Vice President John C. Calhoun and those of Secretary of State Martin Van Buren. The struggle was first brought into the open by the refusal of Washington society, led by the Calhoun faction, to receive Peggy O'Neale Eaton, the second wife of the Secretary of War. To Jackson the situation was reminiscent of the years of social difficulties suffered by his deceased wife Rachel; when he raised the issue at a Cabinet meeting, Martin Van Buren, a widower, was the only member to support Mrs. Eaton. Vice President Calhoun had a strong following in Congress, and Major William B. Lewis, of Jackson's "Kitchen Cabinet," therefore suggested the convention as an instrument for pulling the party together by drawing on Jackson's vast strength among the people. He also suggested the timing: the convention should be held after Congress had adjourned and gone home, so as "to prevent an improper interference by members of Congress."[10]

The Democratic-Republican convention followed the Antimasons in allowing each state to use its own judgment in choosing delegates; votes were allotted among the delegations on the electoral college basis; and a special majority of two thirds was required for nomination. To minimize public signs of disunity, each delegation was required to elect a spokesman to cast its vote. Jackson was unanimously nominated to succeed himself, and Van Buren was named for Vice President, 208 to 75, the Calhoun men failing to muster a third of the votes in opposition.

Thus the convention system was inau-

---

[10] "Origin of the Democratic Convention," *American Historical Magazine and Tennessee Historical Quarterly*, July 1902, pp. 267-73.

gurated by three parties in preparation for the 1832 campaign, as an agency for party representation independent of Congress. The underlying cause for this innovation was the matured dissatisfaction with the congressional caucus system of nominations. The immediate cause in all three parties was the manifest impossibility of obtaining a representation in the existing Congress that the party leaders could regard as acceptable. The two splinter parties died not long after birth, but the Democratic national convention, as it soon came to be called, has survived to become one of the most durable political institutions extant anywhere.

Some years were required to establish the authority of the national party conventions to determine the presidential nominations, with the party system itself in flux. Nevertheless, a second Democratic national convention was held in 1835, a third in 1840. The Whigs held their first national convention in 1839. Thereafter the nominating conventions of the leading national parties were uniformly held in the presidential election years.

The Jackson-Van Buren Succession

President Jackson's preference for Van Buren as his successor was known even before "the Little Magician" became Vice President, but this preference was strongly opposed by some of Jackson's own supporters. In preparation for 1836 the convention date was set for May 1835, to head off anti-Van Buren moves and clear the political atmosphere early. When the convention met, however, it was justified as a reform measure by its permanent chairman, who said:

. . . the democracy of the Union have been forced to look to a national convention, as the best means of concentrating the popular will, and giving it effect in the approaching election. It is in fact, the only defense against a minority president.[11]

[11] *Niles' Weekly Register*, Vol. 48, (May 23, 1835).

Van Buren received the presidential nomination without opposition, but the party's disharmony became evident in the choice of a nominee for Vice President. A motion to abolish the two thirds rule had previously been passed; just before the nominating ballots were taken, the action was reconsidered and, with the Virginia delegation reversing itself, the rule was put back into effect. Richard Johnson of Kentucky received a bare two thirds of the votes cast but, since many delegates abstained, less than two thirds of the convention. The Virginians, although agreeing to support Van Buren in the campaign, stated their refusal to support Johnson for Vice President under any condition. The convention nonetheless let the nomination stand.

Van Buren was duly elected in 1836, but no vice-presidential candidate received a majority. Johnson had 147 electoral votes to 147 for three others. Thus the Senate received its first and, so far, only opportunity to choose a Vice President. Johnson was the choice.

The calls for both the 1832 and 1835 Democratic-Republican conventions had been issued by the legislature of New Hampshire. In 1840 the call came from the New Hampshire state committee, which observed that the choice of a candidate for second place on a Van Buren slate might be left to the states. At the convention, a committee reported that it found no opposition to Van Buren's nomination for a second term, and that it seemed desirable not to nominate a single vice-presidential candidate. The adoption of this report constituted the entire nominating procedure. The convention also officially shortened the party name from Democratic-Republican to Democratic and adopted a statement of party principles called a "platform." Subsequently, three candidates for Vice President were named through the action of caucuses, conventions, and rallies in the various states. All three went down to defeat with Van Buren in the election.

The Whigs Adopt
the Convention System

Henry Clay's defeat as a National Republican in 1832 was followed by further attempts to form an opposition party. By 1834 the "Whig" party was spreading out of the South as the principal vehicle for the anti-Jacksonian forces. Thurlow Weed promptly became the outstanding Whig organizer in New York State. Clay was the leading public figure in the newly forming party, but it contained much other presidential timber. Weed, who had opposed giving Clay the Antimasonic nomination in 1831, remained doubtful about him as a vote-getter in a national election. Weed's skepticism about Clay was a continuing contribution to factionalism in the Whig party.

In 1835 and 1836 the variety of interests among the Whigs was too much for a united front against the Democratic-Republicans. Few of the new party's leaders believed that a national convention was capable of binding the fragments. The final strategy for the anti-Jacksonians was enunciated through the *National Intelligencer,* their major newspaper. The plan was to run several strong state and regional leaders for President in the areas where each was strong, thus preventing an electoral college majority for Van Buren and forcing the decision into the House of Representatives. Senator Daniel Webster would hold New England, the Northwest would unite on General William Henry Harrison, the Southwest would support Tennessee's Hugh L. White. Clay kept himself out of the race, awaiting the outcome of the Whig party's trial run on the national scene.

The Whig plan to win the election of 1836 very nearly succeeded. Van Buren's majority was only 25,688 in a popular vote of 1,505,290, with electors chosen by popular vote in every state except South Carolina. For the first time, a competitive two-party system had come into existence in most of the states, with the Whigs carrying 485 counties and the Democratic-Repub-

licans 557.[12] The electoral college vote, however, was 170 for Van Buren against a combined total of 124 for the other presidential candidates.

Harrison had made the best Whig showing in the electoral college. Soon after the election a political rally in New York City launched the Harrison candidacy for 1840, and Henry Clay followed with his own announcement. General Winfield Scott also drew large support. Thurlow Weed urged Clay to stay out of the 1840 race on the grounds that Harrison had a better chance of winning because Clay had made too many enemies. Clay would not agree, and his supporters laid plans for a Whig national convention. Many of the Harrison men preferred to leave the nomination to the state legislatures, where their forces were strongest, but Weed saw the possibilities for stopping Clay in a national convention and made ready his strategy. The call was issued by a Whig congressional caucus.

The first Whig national convention met on December 4, 1839, at Harrisburg. Shortly after its opening a Harrison delegate and a Webster delegate jointly sponsored the keystone of the Weed strategy: the unit rule. Under this proposal, a majority in each state delegation could commit the entire delegation's vote to its preferred candidate. The unit rule procedure gave Clay 103 votes, Harrison 94, and Scott 57 on the first nominating ballot. Twenty Scott votes in the New York delegation, however, were subject to Weed's control. When these and other Scott votes moved over to Harrison, the final result was: Harrison 148, Clay 90, and Scott 16. The Clay supporters were furious. An attempt was made to pacify them by giving a Clay man second place on the ticket, but they would have none of it. The vice-presidential nomination went instead to John Tyler of Virginia, a former Democrat whose Whiggery was of recent vintage. Finally, a letter from Henry Clay was read, in which

[12] W. Dean Burnham, *Presidential Ballots 1836-1892* (1955), pp. 17, 19.

he acknowledged the competence of the Harrisburg convention to make the nominations. The convention adjourned without preparing "an address to the nation."

The Whig "Tippecanoe and Tyler, too" campaign proved too much for the divided Van Buren machine. The popular vote jumped to over 2,400,000, a gain of about 60 per cent from the previous election—a rate of increase not since equaled, even after the adoption of women's suffrage.[13] The Whigs polled 53 per cent of the popular vote, and Harrison carried the electoral college by 234 votes to Van Buren's 60.

Two Parties in Precarious Balance

In the four successive elections from 1840 to 1852, the party in office was defeated in each election, which meant that the two parties alternated at four-year intervals. The ensuing problems of an unstable party system were accentuated by two cases of vice-presidential succession. Five Presidents held office during the twelve years.

President Harrison died one month after taking office in 1841, the first President to die in office. His death had many consequences. Vice President John Tyler took office as President on his own initiative, and in the face of views in Congress and Cabinet that he was only an acting incumbent of the office. Tyler's position on the interpretation of the Constitution was the one that prevailed, but the constitutional questions were grist for Henry Clay's mill. Before long, a Whig congressional caucus proceeded to read President Tyler out of the party he had so recently joined. Eventually, Tyler tried to create a middle-of-the-road party of his own, and in 1844 a pro-Tyler Democratic convention met on the same day as the regular Democratic convention and gave him a perfunctory nomination.

In the Whig party Henry Clay's principal opponents for the 1844 nomination were such perennials as Daniel Webster and Winfield Scott. To Clay's supporters, a na-

[13] *Ibid.,* pp. 22, 26.

tional convention seemed unnecessary, but one was held at the instance of the Whig congressional caucus. Clay was nominated by acclamation—in the absence of Thurlow Weed, who had encountered factional troubles of his own in New York. Weed's influence was credited with preventing Millard Fillmore of New York from receiving the vice-presidential nomination, and the later failure of Weed and his organization to get out the vote in the election may have cost the ticket New York's 36 electoral votes. With New York, Clay would have won.

In 1848 the Whig convention, again meeting at the call of a congressional caucus, considered another bid for the nomination from its titular leader, Henry Clay. The Mexican War had, however, produced a new crop of military heroes, including General Zachary Taylor. Thurlow Weed backed Taylor in an obvious repetition of the 1840 strategy, and Taylor won the nomination on the fourth ballot. The Clay forces retaliated in the nomination of Weed's archenemy, Millard Fillmore of New York, for the Vice Presidency. The Taylor-Fillmore ticket won the election, helped in part by the newly formed Free-Soilers, whose candidate, Martin Van Buren, split the Democratic vote. President Taylor died a year after taking office, and Fillmore was thus the second Vice President to become President through constitutional succession. The grim reaper had twice outwitted Thurlow Weed, quickly denying him access to the White House through the two Whig Presidents whom his strategy had nominated.

During the Tyler administration, the "regular" Democrats had divided on the issue of Texas annexation. The southerners generally were pro-annexationist; Andrew Jackson in retirement declared for annexation in 1843. In April 1844, Van Buren and Clay both published letters opposing immediate annexation, apparently by agreement and in the hope of removing the issue from the presidential campaign. The effect was to remove Van Buren from the campaign. When the regular Democratic national convention met in 1844, the annexationists immediately proposed readoption of the two thirds rule, as in former conventions. The critical vote was Virginia's. Virginia had come to the convention predominantly pro-Van Buren but was turning away from him as a result of his position against annexation. While the balloting on the rule proceeded, the Virginia delegation retired to consider its policy; the decision was to vote as a unit in order to conceal its growing anti-Van Buren sentiment. When Virginia returned to the floor, the vote stood 131 for and 116 against the rule. Virginia's 17 votes were added to the 131 rather than to the 116 as expected and the two thirds rule carried, as it had in 1832 and 1835.

On the nominating vote Van Buren held a simple majority for seven ballots. There was talk of nominating three presidential candidates. On the eighth ballot James K. Polk's name was proposed and received 44 votes. Polk turned out to be the middle ground upon which the annexationist and anti-annexationist extremists could land. On the ninth ballot, Polk became the first "dark horse" candidate in convention history and Van Buren the first titular party leader of the Democrats to seek renomination unsuccessfully. Polk carried fifteen of the twenty-six states, including New York, for 170 electoral votes to Clay's 105. The popular vote was again extremely close.

In 1845 a new federal statute was enacted, requiring that presidential electors be chosen on the same day throughout the United States, namely the Tuesday following the first Monday in November. Previously the elections had been held in different states on different days, with campaign managers concentrating their efforts first on one state and then another. The new election statute was a reflection of the growing intensity of the interparty struggle.

In 1848, President Polk was not a candidate to succeed himself, and was believed to favor Lewis Cass of Michigan.[14] As the Democratic convention approached, in response to a call by a congressional caucus, two preliminary issues became conspicuous. One was the two thirds rule, which the convention eventually readopted by 175 to 78 over the objections of the Cass supporters. The other was a problem of contesting state delegations. The New York Democrats had divided into the antislavery "Barnburner" contingent and the anti-abolitionist "Hunkers"; both sent delegations. The convention attempted to apply the wisdom of Solomon: it voted by 126 to 125 to seat both delegations, giving each one half of the state's vote. The Barnburners declined this compromise and walked out; three months later they held their own convention, which set up the Free-Soil party and nominated Martin Van Buren as its candidate.

After the Barnburners walked out of the Democratic convention, Cass was nominated on the fourth ballot and other important actions were taken. The convention adopted a platform and took note of the requirements for coordinated campaigning in view of the new uniform election day. It authorized that "a committee of one from each state, to be named by the respective delegations, be appointed to promote the democratic cause, with power to fill vacancies, and be designated 'The Democratic National Committee.'"

This was the first party national committee to serve until the following convention, for which it sent out the call. Thereafter the committee became a continuing body, with its membership renewed at each successive national convention. The first committee elected Benjamin F. Hallett, Antimason editor and lawyer of Massachusetts, as its chairman, thus completing the hierarchy of party officialdom that had previously come into existence in the form of state party committees and committee chairmen.

[14] Goldman, *op. cit.*, pp. 213-14.

The conventions of 1852 were held amid increasing strain over slavery. Both major parties adopted platforms accepting the Compromise of 1850—the program of legislation in which California was admitted as a free state, slave trade was ended in the District of Columbia, a stricter fugitive slave law was enacted, and the land won in the Mexican War was organized into territories without restrictions for or against slavery.

At the Democratic convention, Lewis Cass, the titular leader and defeated candidate of 1848, probably could have been renominated under a simple majority rule, although he made no strong efforts in his own behalf. Eventually Franklin Pierce of New Hampshire was nominated on the forty-ninth ballot, and William R. King of Alabama was nominated as his running mate.

At the Whig convention, its last as a major national party, President Fillmore was denied renomination, although his administration had a good record. General Winfield Scott was nominated on the fifty-third ballot. Thereafter the party rushed rapidly into limbo. President Fillmore refrained from supporting the party ticket. Henry Clay died the day that Scott's letter of acceptance of the nomination appeared. Daniel Webster, who had fought hard and unsuccessfully to secure his own nomination at the 1852 convention, died in October without having endorsed the party ticket. Thurlow Weed was in Europe, and the party's candidate, General Scott, was evasive on every issue. Pierce defeated Scott in twenty-seven of the thirty-one states.

Breakdown and Reconstruction in the Party System

The Democratic victory of 1852 was the most sweeping gained by the party between 1836 and 1892. The party received only 53.6 per cent of the two-party popular vote,

but this was high for the times and its electoral college majority was 254 to 42. Franklin Pierce was elected in the hope that the Compromise of 1850 could be maintained and the issues of slavery kept out of politics for at least a few years.

The opposite occurred. Stephen A. Douglas of Illinois, a leading Democrat in the Senate and a candidate for the Democratic presidential nomination of 1852, introduced the Kansas-Nebraska Bill early in 1854. In a deal for transcontinental railroad rights and a bid for southern nominating support in 1856, Douglas proposed, in effect, to repeal the Compromise of 1850 by permitting local disposition of the slavery issue in the territories not yet admitted to statehood. After a bitter debate involving many participants, the bill passed Congress by close margins and was approved by President Pierce, who thus became committed to the southern wing of the Democratic party. The result was civil war in Kansas by the spring of 1856, the destruction of any possibility that President Pierce could be renominated in a party convention under the two thirds rule, a considerable impairment of Douglas' prospects for nomination in 1856 and 1860, defections from the Democratic party in the North, and the final breakup of the Whig party everywhere.

Origins of the Republican Party

The Democrats held together in 1856 and eventually nominated James Buchanan of Pennsylvania, after rejecting Pierce, Douglas, and Cass. Buchanan was acceptable to all factions mainly because he had been out of the country—as Minister to England by Pierce's appointment—while the Kansas-Nebraska legislation was being debated.

The most immediate successor to the Whigs was the American or "Know-Nothing" party. Like the Whigs, the Americans were opposed to sectionalism in party organization and sought to find a basis for popular strength in every part of the country. They took over the anti-Catholic and anti-immigrant nativist elements of the former Whigs. The party became the major opposition to the Democrats in the South and also developed considerable strength in the North in 1853, 1854, and 1855. By 1856, however, it was on the decline, because it had begun to split on slavery issues and many of its antislavery adherents went over to the Republican party, the other successor to the Whigs.

The Republican party was highly sectional from the first. The organizing impetus came from radical northern and middle-western groups that were strongly opposed to the extension of slavery into the territories. These groups held a series of anti-Nebraska rallies in Wisconsin, Michigan, Vermont, Ohio, and Iowa in the opening months of 1854. By summer of 1854, Horace Greeley of New York was advocating a new party. In September 1855, New York Whigs and Republicans held simultaneous state party conventions at Syracuse, and Thurlow Weed led his (antislavery) "Woolly Heads" into the Republican camp. By this time, the Republicans had begun to gain strength in Congress, along with the Americans or Know-Nothings, and factional divisions among the Democrats and the remaining Whigs were steadily growing deeper. Supreme confusion in the party system was reflected in the selection of a Speaker of the House in December 1855; more than 130 ballots were taken before the candidate backed by Horace Greeley was victorious.

The first national meeting of the Republicans was held at Pittsburgh on February 22, 1856, with delegates, mostly self-appointed, from sixteen northern and eight southern states. A platform was written and a national executive committee was established, consisting of one representative from each state. A nominating convention was called for June 17, 1856, at Philadelphia,

where the party nominated Colonel John C. Frémont of California as its first presidential candidate. "Bleeding Kansas" became its principal campaign issue.

The Democrats won the election, with Buchanan polling 1,838,169 popular votes to Frémont's 1,341,264 and Fillmore's 874,534.[15] Fillmore carried one state, Maryland. Frémont carried 11 free states, including all of New England and New York, for an electoral college vote of 114. Buchanan, with only 45 per cent of the total popular vote, carried 14 slave states and 5 free states for an electoral college majority of 174. The Republican vote was almost all cast north of the Mason and Dixon line, but the "Know-Nothing" vote was polled in both North and South and hurt the Republican potentiality in many northern states.

The Four-Party Contest of 1860

Divisions within the Democratic party were opened wide in 1858 when Senator Douglas opposed and President Buchanan supported the admission of Kansas as a slave state on the basis of the "Lecompton" state constitution, the legality of which was in dispute. The Republican party made large gains in the mid-term elections of 1858, in the face of widespread southern threats of secession if a "Black Republican" were ever to be elected President.

The Democratic national convention of 1860 met first in Charleston, South Carolina. Southern "Ultras" pressed their views, but the Douglas men won a floor vote of 165 to 138 on the platform. Shortly after, the delegations of several southern states left the convention.

President Buchanan was not a candidate for renomination, bearing in mind the experience of his predecessor, Franklin Pierce, but was favorable to the aspirations of his

[15] U. S. Bureau of the Census, *Historical Statistics of the United States 1789-1945* (1949), p. 289. Burnham, *op. cit.,* has somewhat different major-party totals that are possibly more nearly correct, but no separate figure for Fillmore.

Vice President, John C. Breckinridge of Kentucky. Douglas was by far the leading contender, but after fifty-seven ballots the convention was still deadlocked. It adjourned, to meet again in Baltimore two months later. The seceders, who had been standing by, expecting to be recalled by the announcement of a compromise candidate, returned to their constituencies for a fresh mandate.

Public attention then turned to Congress. Senator Jefferson Davis repeated the demands of the southern extremists for passage of a "Congressional Slave Code." Douglas developed his own argument that only a majority in the national convention and not a minority in the Senate—referring to the southern extremists—could establish the tests of party fidelity. Meanwhile, in the states, the bolters were planning to go to the convention in Baltimore, and delegate fights in the constituencies foretold the critical importance of possible seating contests.

At Baltimore the credentials committee worked under extreme pressure. The Douglas men were ready to admit the bolters from South Carolina, Georgia, Florida, Mississippi, Arkansas, and Texas, but stood fast against admission of the delegations from Alabama and Louisiana, and their views prevailed by a vote of 150 to 100½. All attempts to delay proceedings in order to find time to negotiate were frustrated. Douglas' willingness to retire from the race was disregarded. The die was cast. Virginia led the exodus this time, followed by most of the delegates from North Carolina, Tennessee, Maryland, Kentucky, Missouri, and Arkansas. The Douglas men in these delegations remained seated. California and Oregon also walked out; both were free states, but their delegations were irrevocably opposed to the Douglas candidacy. Convention Chairman Caleb Cushing of Massachusetts was the last to depart. After the vice presidents of the convention chose a new chairman, Douglas was nominated.

Cushing became chairman of the "Seceders" convention, which claimed 231 "regularly elected" delegates from 19 states. Actually, full delegations were present from only 3 states, and most of the 58 northern delegates in the rump convention were Buchanan officeholders. Breckinridge was nominated for President by the seceders without difficulty.

The Republican party met in mid-May at Chicago and nominated Abraham Lincoln on the third ballot after discarding Thurlow Weed's candidate, William H. Seward of New York. A platform skillfully designed to attract all northern elements was adopted. It affirmed the right of each state to control its own domestic institutions, but denied the authority of Congress to give legal status to slavery in the territories.

The American party had already disappeared as an entity, but an opposition to the Democratic party still existed in southern and border states. Remnants of it and the erstwhile Whigs met in Baltimore as the Constitutional Union party and nominated John Bell of Tennessee for President. Thus the four-party contest was set up: northern Democrats and Republicans to compete in the North, southern Democrats and Constitutional Unionists in the South, with a mixed situation in the border areas.

The outcome was as follows:[16]

Lincoln: Popular vote, 1,865,593; electoral vote, 180; states carried—free, 18, slave, 0.

Douglas: Popular vote, 1,382,713; electoral vote, 12; states carried—free, 0, slave, 1.

Breckinridge: Popular vote, 848,356; electoral vote, 72; states carried—free, 0, slave, 11.

Bell: Popular vote, 592,906; electoral vote, 39; states carried—free, 0, slave, 3.

This was the only four-cornered election in American history in which each party and candidate had to be taken seriously and actually did win votes in the electoral college. Lincoln won with less than 40 per cent of the

[16] Burnham, *op. cit.,* pp. 246, 888.

total popular vote, but had popular majorities in states with a majority of the electoral vote. Douglas stumped the country and ran reasonably well in the free states, but carried only Missouri and 3 electoral votes from New Jersey; Breckinridge carried most of the South, and Bell took the rest. If the entire popular vote other than that for Lincoln had been combined for a single candidate, only 11 electoral votes would have been taken away from Lincoln, and he would still have been the victor.

By Inauguration Day in 1861, seven states had seceded. In a little over a month the Civil War began.

The Civil War and Its Aftermath

After hostilities began, the southern wing of the Democratic party was lost to the party and the nation for the duration of the war. The Constitutional Union party disappeared. The Republican party, only recently formed and in office for the first time, was in charge of fighting the war. The Democrats' northern wing, although split and in opposition, survived as an active political force. Its defeated candidate of 1860, Senator Stephen A. Douglas, completely supported Lincoln's policies after the outbreak of war. His death in June 1861 put the burden of national party leadership on national committee Chairman August Belmont, who proceeded to place the party officially behind the war effort. Opposing the "War Democrats" were Congressman Clement L. Vallandigham of Ohio, a former Douglas supporter, and Mayor Fernando Wood of New York City. Together they led the "Peace Democrats," also known as "Copperheads."

Divided though they were, the Democrats nonetheless won many state and congressional victories in the mid-term elections of 1862. Horatio Seymour's spectacular capture of the New York governorship gave the Democratic organization of that state a much-needed lift. The Republicans, divided in their own ranks, retained control of the House of Representatives, but by a reduced majority.

From the mid-term elections onward, Lincoln and the political leaders friendly to him realized that support for his conduct of the war would have to come from a combination of conservative Republicans and War Democrats. To facilitate such cooperation, the name "Union" party was employed in many places instead of "Republican." Meeting in February 1864, the Republican national committee took the responsibility of calling, not a Republican, but a "Union" national convention of "all qualified voters who desire the unconditional maintenance of the Union." The convention, which met at Baltimore, June 7, 1864, was friendly to the President, and renominated him by a vote of 484 to 22. To balance the ticket the convention chose a War Democrat, Andrew Johnson of Tennessee.

The effort to draw the Democrats into a Unionist coalition did not prevent the Democratic party from holding a national convention, which met uncommonly late, on August 29, 1864, at Chicago. Candidate potentialities were somewhat reduced by the fact that Vallandigham had suffered military arrest for treasonable activities and Governor Seymour had been successfully blamed for the New York draft riots of 1863. General George B. McClellan, removed from his command by Lincoln, was the most available Democrat.

Seymour acted as chairman of the convention. The "peace" faction managed to push through a plank demanding immediate cessation of hostilities, and the convention then nominated McClellan for President, although he still advocated vigorous prosecution of the war. With its "war" nominee and "peace" platform, the party was in an ambiguous position when the news came of spectacular Union Army victories. McClellan won only 21 electoral votes to Lincoln's 212, although the Democratic vote was 45 per cent of the popular total. The absence of the seceding states meant that 81 electoral votes were not cast.

Lincoln's assassination on April 14, 1865, brought a third Vice President to the White House under equivocal circumstances. As President, was Andrew Johnson a Republican or Democrat? He was soon detached from any important body of Republican support, while unable to return to the bosom of the Democratic party, where his welcome could not be wholly assured. Like John Tyler before him, Johnson tried to straddle the parties and to create his own following. He failed under attack from aggressive adversaries in Congress. The radical Republicans overrode Johnson's veto to make Negroes eligible to vote, and required the southern states to ratify the Fourteenth Amendment as a condition for readmission to the Union.

In an apparent effort to create a new political alignment supporting the President, the "Union" party held a mid-term "National Union convention" in Philadelphia on August 16, 1866. The Republican national committee chairman, Henry J. Raymond, and many conservative Republicans were present.[17] The radical Republicans countered by holding their own national convention on September 3 and, with some parliamentary roughriding, elected a new national chairman. Radical Republican victories in the mid-term election of 1866 led to passage of their "Congressional plan" for southern reconstruction. Ten southern states were placed under military rule. The finishing touch came with the impeachment of President Andrew Johnson in the spring of 1868. Although thirty-five

senators voted for conviction, he was saved, under the two thirds rule, by the votes of seven Republican and twelve Democratic senators.[18]

Both parties held regularly organized national conventions in 1868. The Republicans met at Chicago in May and gave General Ulysses S. Grant a unanimous nomination on the first ballot. The Democrats met at New York in July; Horatio Seymour again presided as permanent chairman. The party had gained in local elections in 1867, but was greatly divided on monetary policy. On the twenty-second ballot Seymour was nominated against his will as a compromise candidate.

In the election, three southern states, Virginia, Mississippi, and Texas were still excluded from voting. Eight others had been readmitted to the Union but were still under military rule, with registered Negro voters in the majority in South Carolina, Florida, Alabama, Mississippi, and Louisiana. Grant won by 214 electoral votes to 80; his popular majority of about 300,000 in a total of nearly 6,000,000 could be attributed to the southern Negro vote.

Grant's paper-thin majorities in 1868 showed the tenacity of the Democrats. They had been the principal political party for nearly half a century, but, as shown when they joined a Republican splinter movement in 1872 to nominate Horace Greeley, they were devoid of leadership at this time to match their popular support. The pre-Civil War Democratic leaders had suffered many discrediting misfortunes; no substantial new generation of Democratic officeholders had arisen to replenish the supply.

Grant's second-term victory in 1872 drew the Republican party's greatest popular majority during the nineteenth century. The *New York Times*, then a Republican news-

[17] War Democrats of Johnson's own stripe, moderate southerners who were attending a national convention for the first time in six years, and northern Peace Democrats were also present—including Vallandigham and Wood until they were persuaded to leave. The convention's importance in the rehabilitation of the Democratic party was one reason it became so vulnerable to factional attack in the Republican party. See Wilfred E. Binkley, *op. cit.*, pp. 273-74.

[18] He was saved in particular by the vote of one radical Republican, Senator Edmund G. Ross of Kansas, ostracized at the time but later regarded as the hero of the episode. See John F. Kennedy, *Profiles in Courage* (1956), Chap. 6.

paper, performed "last rites" over the Democratic party. But the moribund patient recovered with amazing rapidity when the panic of 1873 and the long depression that followed provided the setting for a party overturn. In 1874 the Democrats won a majority in the House of Representatives for the first time since 1858. In that year also, Democrat Samuel J. Tilden was elected to the governorship of New York as a "reform" candidate. The corruption of the second Grant administration was a natural target; by 1876, victory for the Democrats was in the air.

The result was the disputed Hayes-Tilden election of 1876, in which Tilden won the popular vote but was counted out in the electoral college under circumstances widely considered fraudulent.[19] Partisan activity in and around Congress, the Supreme Court, and the special electoral commission reached a high pitch during four months of uncertainty, with at least a possibility that there might again be a resort to armed conflict. In the end, the special commission gave Hayes the decision by a partisan majority of one. Tilden bowed to the decision, and so did the southern Democrats in the House, apparently after receiving assurances about the construction of a southern transcontinental railroad.[20]

President Rutherford B. Hayes brought the Reconstruction period to an end with the withdrawal of troops from South Carolina and Louisiana in April 1877. Republican and Democratic parties alike had survived the major crisis of postwar adjustment. The Democrats did not obtain the Presidency until they elected Grover Cleveland in 1884, but the party system had become stabilized, with the two national

parties that still continue as its major components.[21]

The Institutional Legacy of the Formative Years

The Civil War was as decisive as the War of the Revolution and the Constitutional Convention of 1787 in the formation and development of American institutions. No longer could it be argued that the United States was a mere confederation of independent sovereign nations, each of which might withdraw at will from the Union. On the field of battle it had been demonstrated that the United States was to be in fact "one nation, indivisible. . . ."

When the war came on, the country's political system seemed in the greatest confusion imaginable. Yet when the war was over, it was apparent that there would be a reversion to a two-party system that might be stronger but otherwise not greatly different from the one that had existed from 1840 to 1852.

Party bolting had been common for many years before 1860 as factions marched out of one camp and into another. The party bolts of 1860, however, were in major part the product of secessionist theory— the view that majority rule need not ultimately prevail. Dissident sectional elements claimed the right to depart not only from their political party but from their country as well. As long as this view was widely held, the authority of the national parties to deal firmly with their own affairs was always under challenge.

For the purposes of the present book, moreover, it is especially important to note that the institutional forms of the party

---

[19] There were ample opportunities for fraud on both sides; Hayes' popular vote doubtless would have been larger in several southern states but for a considerable curtailment in the Negro vote as compared to that cast for Grant in 1872. Hence the oft-quoted remark that "the Democratics stole the election in the first place and then the Republicans stole it back." Cf. Binkley, op. cit., pp. 305-07.

[20] C. Vann Woodward, Reunion and Reaction (1951), passim.

[21] For a review of party history since 1876 and a fuller account of the earlier period, see Binkley, op. cit. Other party histories are also noted, with evaluative comment, in V. O. Key, Jr., Politics, Parties, and Pressure Groups (4th ed., 1958), pp. 183-84, footnote.

A chronological listing of the presidential and vice-presidential nominees of the major parties since 1832 appears in Appendix A, Table 1.

system that had been established by 1860, and in most cases by 1852, were to survive. The national conventions had decisively replaced the congressional caucuses in making nominations for the Presidency. In the process a representative institution had been created within each of the national parties, for negotiating and deciding on the party's most important recurring concern, the nomination of its presidential candidate. This was probably the most limited activity through which a political party could achieve identity as a national institution, but it was sufficient for that result. Since 1832 the nominating process has been central to the creation of a national party system and to its further evolution.

Before the convention arrived on the scene, it had been repeatedly demonstrated that no caucus of a party's members in Congress could adequately represent all party elements. This was especially the case for the minority party; had the Federalist party developed the convention system of nominations more openly and effectively in 1808 and 1812, its chances of survival might have been enhanced. By 1852 the conventions were able to provide representation for the internal party constituencies, such as they were, in all of the states and in most of the congressional districts, and without depending on party fortunes in Congress. The conventions have remained pre-eminent ever since as the instrumentalities for giving representation within each party on a nationwide basis.[22]

Each of the four major functions of the conventions had been substantially developed by 1860. The nominating function had been stabilized for both Presidency and Vice Presidency after an interval of some years in which, because of difficulty in reaching agreement, there was a frequent temptation to leave one office or both to the mercy of other nominating agencies. After 1840 it was clear that failure to unite on a complete ticket at the convention would merely invite party defeat.

The platform-drafting function had evolved out of the occasional efforts to prepare "an address to the people," and had become accepted as a normal part of convention routine. Early platform-drafting, when it occurred at all, was usually deferred until after the nominations had been made. In 1852 both Democrats and Whigs adopted platforms before acting on nominations; this reflected deep fissures in each party over the Compromise of 1850, but it set a precedent in the ordering of the agenda that, with only a few exceptions, has prevailed ever since.

The campaign-rally function was recognized implicitly in the decision to hold the conventions as public meetings, the precedent established by the Antimasons in 1831. From the conventions of 1831-1832 onward, it was a function of growing importance, although seldom openly recognized as such.

The governing-body function, as exemplified particularly in the election of a continuing national committee, was estab-

---

[22] The changes in party history and the irregularity with which the conventions were held in the earlier years have presented certain minor problems for the analyses attempted later in this book. One question is that of whether the "Union" convention of 1864 should be treated as a Republican convention in statistical analyses and tabular listings; this has been done in accordance with the party's own custom. A more difficult question is the extent to which the National Republican convention of 1831 and the Whig conventions of 1839-1852 should be treated as conventions of parties predecessor to the Republican party. The National Republicans of 1831 were not identical with the Whigs of 1839, and the Whigs of 1852 were certainly not identical with

the Republicans of 1856, as the previous pages have sought to make clear. But in each case these parties formed the principal opposition to the Democrats and the predecessor relationship to the Republican party seems sufficiently valid to justify treating them as predecessors in tabular materials that seek to deal with the experience of the two major parties from 1832 onward. In the tables and related discussions, notably those beginning in Chapter 6, the table headings and other details are handled in terms of the election years for which the nominations were made in order to simplify the treatment, and the fact that the National Republican nominations for 1832 were actually made in 1831 is therefore usually disregarded.

lished as a characteristic of the national
conventions of both parties. The Whig convention of 1852 followed the Democratic
precedent in establishing a national committee; many of the Whig committeemen
were key figures who led their followers
into the Republican party in 1856 and then
helped to lead that party to victory in
1860.

The congressional caucuses that issued
the calls for the Democratic national convention of 1848 and the Whig national
conventions of 1848 and 1852 were the last
to perform this office. Thereafter the national party committees called the quadrennial party meetings, with the exception
of the first Republican nominating convention of 1856, which was called by a previous organizing meeting. Since 1852 the
presidential element in each national party
has been in a position to assert its independence of congressional control, even in
such matters as the determination of the
place at which the convention would meet.
All six of the Democratic conventions from
1832 to 1852 had been held in Baltimore;
of the four Whig conventions, two were
held in Philadelphia, one in Harrisburg,
and one in Baltimore. The choice of Baltimore was reasonable from the point of
view of delegate convenience at the time,
but its repeated recurrence was also a sign
of the extent of congressional involvement (and also a sign of presidential involvement in the party in power, as in
1835).[23] In 1856 the Democrats went to Cincinnati for their first national convention
away from Baltimore, while the new Republican party met in Philadelphia. There-

[23] In 1848 the attendance of senators and representatives at the conventions was so large that Congress
adjourned for both occasions at an estimated cost
in legislative salaries of $92,672. (*Washington Na-
tional Era*, June 15, 1848.) A check of the official
delegate lists of 1848 indicates that only 10 of the
56 senators and 26 of the 248 representatives were
delegates; undoubtedly a much larger number were
present as visitors. At the Democratic convention
there was a proposal to provide seats on the convention floor for the visiting Democratic members of
Congress, but the proposal was defeated. (*Niles'
National Register*, Vol. 74, pp. 324-25.)

after, Chicago, Philadelphia, and St. Louis
were the most favored convention meeting
places.

The voting methods by which candidates
were nominated reached early stability, but
with unsolved problems that still harass the
parties. The electoral college model was
adopted from the first for the apportionment of voting strength among the states
in the party conventions, but it obviously
over-represented the party elements in
states where the party concerned was weak,
as it still does. Democrats, Whigs, and Republicans simplified their record votes by
adopting the rule of calling the roll by
state delegations. This gave the conventions a much more federal aspect than even
the Congress, an aspect that still continues.
The unit rule, by which all votes in a
delegation are cast as determined by the
majority within the delegation, became an
early fixture in Democratic conventions,
where elements of it still persist.

Of all the rules with unanticipated consequences, the two thirds rule of the Democratic conventions was probably the most
important. As adopted at the first Democratic national convention in 1832 and not
abandoned until 1936, it specified that a
vote aggregating two thirds of the convention—sometimes interpreted as the entire
authorized voting strength, at other times
two thirds of those voting—was required
to nominate for President or Vice President. (See Chapter 9, section on The Two
Thirds Rule in Democratic Nominations,
and notes 45, 46). Yet the rule itself was
regularly adopted by simple majority votes,
since every convention had to begin by
adopting its own rules under a voting
formula that would permit business to proceed. The idea for the rule was taken over
in modified form and without much
thought from the Antimasons—whose own
successors, the Whigs and the Republicans,
never adopted it.

In 1844, the Democratic convention retained the rule even at the expense of its
majority preference, Van Buren; the result

was the dark horse Polk, whose candidacy was an original synthesis, wrought in a convention deadlocked by hostile factions. Moreover, the choice seemed to justify itself in the electoral results: Polk was accepted by the party, won the election, and proved to be one of the abler Presidents in an era of congressional ascendancy. What would have happened if the two thirds rule had never been adopted in the Democratic party? In that event, it seems probable that Van Buren would have been nominated for the third time for President in 1844, and the power of the slavery states in Democratic party affairs would have been markedly reduced. He might have won and resumed office, like Grover Cleveland in 1892; or he might have lost, in which case Henry Clay, previously defeated in 1832, would have become President in 1845. In either event the structure of national leadership and the form of the party system would have been different, perhaps in many notable respects.

This is merely one example, although one of the most striking, of the influence of institutional features on history. There have been many other occasions when the choice of a presidential nominee has hung on some party rule or its application in a party convention. No occasion of this sort can be unimportant in a political system that is so largely dependent on the personality of its President.

For all these reasons, the institutional features of the American party system take on a heightened importance as the country becomes larger, more powerful, and more involved in the problems of world order. The evolution of the American political system is not yet completed; it never will be as long as the country survives. As further evolution continues and the attendant problems arise, it is well to recall the origins of this country's political customs. The fact that these customs exist does not prove that they are beneficial, but it does suggest that they should be understood before changes are contemplated that might produce unanticipated effects.

3

Changes in the Party System and Their Consequences

THROUGHOUT triumph and adversity, each of the major parties has faced the problem every four years of nominating its candidates for President and Vice President of the United States. The process has operated under conditions so variable that its continuance since 1832 with so little overt change seems remarkable. Informality and flexibility in the major institutional elements of the process have probably contributed to its ability to withstand changing conditions. Yet it has undoubtedly been affected by the changes in the composition, behavior, and relative electoral strength of the parties. The party system itself has altered with the shifting balance of interparty relationships, although at times so slowly that periodic stocktakings are needed to gauge the amount and kind of change.

In the studies underlying the present book, a search was made for the dividing points in time that could be used most effectively in organizing historical data for the book's analytical purposes. Various considerations were applied in the search, including the facts and patterns of convention and party history in relation to other national events. The book's primary concerns begin with 1832, the first election contest between convention nominees, and end with 1956, the most recent presidential election year. For the earlier years, the Civil War seemed to produce a necessary division between 1860 and 1864. For the time span from the Civil War to World War I, it was easy to agree with many

analysts that 1892 was the end of one period of political history and 1896 the beginning of another. For more recent times, 1932 was a year of great historical change in politics, but in some ways the less noticed changes between 1924 and 1928 were more important for the inner workings of the party system. The periods 1832-1860, 1864-1892, 1896-1924, and 1928-1956 thus emerged; and, after testing them through repeated usage, it was concluded that they met most of the requirements.

The first period, 1832-1860, began with the first set of party conventions and ended with the last year in which the South participated in the making of presidential nominations on an ante-bellum basis. The period saw the evolution of national party institutions (traced in Chapter 2) and the development of what seemed to be a balanced two-party system. But neither party created a national leadership with strength and continuity in party affairs, and both came to grief on the issue of slavery. After 1852 the disintegration of the Whig party was so complete that it could be replaced in 1856 by the Republican party, full-blown in its first presidential contest. In 1860 the Democratic party divided; the war followed.

The period beginning in 1864 and ending in 1892 was a time of war and postwar adjustment, of close party balance and hair-thin victories after the re-enfranchisement of the South, of growing discontent with the existing major political parties, and of rising third-party movements, ending with the Populist upheaval of 1892. The Democratic party was somewhat in eclipse, but not nearly so much so as is generally assumed. Only the students of Civil War history remember that, in 1864, General George McClellan might have won the Presidency on the basis of the *northern* Democratic vote. From 1874 to 1894 the Democrats lost control of the House of Representatives only twice, in 1880 and 1888; Grover Cleveland's two victories in 1884 and 1892 involved substantial Democratic turnouts in the North. The two-party system was still a reality even for state politics in most states North and South, although it was frequently difficult to find any difference between the parties in either morals or economics.

It was between 1896 and 1924 that the Republican party came into its own as the party with a "natural" majority. The period began with the nominations of William Jennings Bryan and William McKinley and a hard-fought campaign over the fundamental issues of national monetary policy. The Republican victory was great; and the effect was to freeze the political pattern along sharply sectional lines for a generation. Thereafter the Republican party was predominant in more than twenty states, the Democratic in about a dozen. With this prolonged sectional imbalance, the Democrats won the White House in 1912 only through a split in the Republican party, and their victory in 1916 was by the closest of margins. Southern and western Democrats were dominant in their party throughout most of the period. In 1924 they deadlocked the convention until John W. Davis was nominated on the 103d ballot, and in the election the Democratic share of the national popular vote fell to its all-time low.

The break-up in the rigidity of a previously sectional pattern of politics was one of the profound changes that began to happen in 1928, with a pair of candidates who visibly offered alternative choices to the electorate—unlike the low visibility of the choice between Davis and Calvin Coolidge.[1] The competitive balance between the parties still appeared superficially about the same as in 1924, but the urban and industrial Democrats who finally achieved the nomination of Al Smith had a new base on which to build the power of their party in the electorate. The eastern wing of the Republican party also gained a new position in Herbert Hoover's nomination, and one that continued through the nominations of Wendell L. Willkie, Thomas E. Dewey, and Dwight D. Eisenhower. Since 1928, with the Democratic party in power nationally most of the time, state after state in the erstwhile "solid North" has become the scene of active party competition in presidential, gubernatorial, and senatorial contests. The South retains the appearance of solidity in state elections, but several southern states have voted Republican in each of the three elections since 1928 in which that party has won the Presidency —1928, 1952, and 1956.

Each of the four periods identified for study contains eight presidential elections and a time span of twenty-eight years. Or, if some intermediate point between elections is used to obviate a gap between adjoining periods, each of the periods would be about thirty-two years, and the most recent one could be thought of as extending into the year 1959. For various purposes, the first two periods may be combined as the longer period 1832-1892, and the more recent two as the period 1896-1956—between them dividing the total experience under the convention system into halves, each of which contains sixteen presidential election years. The identical length of the periods, whether thirty-two years or sixty-four, is convenient for many forms of

[1] V. O. Key, Jr., has emphasized the importance of the shifts in the 1928 election, while discussing generally the problem of critical election years, in "A Theory of Critical Elections," *Journal of Politics*, Vol. 17 (Feb. 1955), pp. 3-18. See also his *Politics, Parties, and Pressure Groups* (4th ed., 1958), pp. 568-83.

There would be room for a theory of critical nominations as well as critical elections, with the 1928 Democratic case as a leading example.

analysis, but they are also balanced in other respects. Each of the shorter, eight-election periods includes years in which each party held office, thus making it easier to concentrate on the broader aspects of system change, as distinguished from characteristics related to the incumbency in power of one political party alone.

As a unit in party history, each period has enough identity to lend support to the thesis that major turning points tend to occur at intervals of about a generation. This is so much the case that it lends interest to the question whether the country might not be moving past another turning point as it progressed from the conventions and elections of 1956 to those of 1960. The conjuncture of political circumstances during that period had many unique features that suggest further change, as will become apparent throughout the book.

It would be quixotic to press the idea of coincidence of past time divisions too far, except for convenience in making comparative analyses. A wide variety of historical and empirical data do nonetheless take on added meaning when arranged in terms of the periods specified, with many sharp contrasts between each one and those that preceded and followed it. In the following pages, some of the salient characteristics of each period are reviewed with particular attention to factors bearing on the status of

each party in relation to the other, institutional adjustments that tended to change the system, the nature of party organization, the amount of sectionalism, the character of interparty competition, the tendencies toward third-party movements, and broad shifts in the alignment of the parties at the end of one period and the beginning of another. The bearing of these matters upon the nominating process will be apparent throughout the book, but is also briefly reviewed at the end of this chapter.

The Ante-Bellum Years, 1832-1860

There is a frequent assumption that the two-party system did not really begin on a national scale until the founding of the Republican party in 1854. Yet the Whigs and the Democrats had alternated in power during most of the generation before the Civil War, and a Whig occupied the White House when the election of 1852 was held.

The most remarkable feature of the party system of the ante-bellum period is the relatively equal division of the major-party popular vote in the earlier years, followed by increasing unbalance and a rising tendency toward third-party voting. The figures for the eight elections are shown in Table 3.1.

TABLE 3.1. THE POPULAR VOTE FOR PRESIDENT, BY PARTIES, 1832-1860[a]

(in thousands)

Year	Democratic	National Republican, Whig, and Republican	Other
1832	707	329	255
1836	765	740	—
1840	1,128	1,275	6
1844	1,338	1,300	62
1848	1,222	1,361	295
1852	1,601	1,385	171
1856	1,833	1,340	872
1860	1,383	1,866	1,441

[a] Election returns for 1832 from Charles O. Paullin, *Atlas of the Historical Geography of the United States* (1932), p. 97; for 1836-1860, inclusive, from W. Dean Burnham, *Presidential Ballots 1836-1892* (1955), p. 246.

Until the Whig party broke up, each major party was truly national in its geographic distribution, even though each presented internally a picture of coalitions among divergent sectional forces. The cleavage line between the parties nationally was drawn mainly in terms of the economic conditions in local areas. Each major party could count on majorities in 400 to 500 agricultural counties spread throughout the nation. The counties that regularly went Democratic included predominantly the low-income rural districts in mountain, upland, and frontier regions. Whig counties were more likely to include the high-income, lowland, well-settled rural areas. Among the cities of the time, all still relatively small, New York, Baltimore, and Chicago were usually carried by the Democrats, while Boston, Philadelphia, St. Louis, and New Orleans usually went Whig.[2]

The total size of the electorate was not large by modern standards, with a popular vote in 1840 of about 2.4 million in a population of 17 million. Nevertheless, the era was the first to provide experience with mass electorates in the modern sense. The new situation began with the election of Andrew Jackson in 1828, which marked a tremendous change in this respect from the election of 1824 and all its predecessors. From 1836 onward, presidential electors were chosen by popular vote in every state but South Carolina, where the privilege was retained by the state legislature until after the Civil War. From 1848 on, presidential elections were held on the same day throughout the country, thus tending still further to make the election subject to the popular will on a national basis.

The district system of congressional elections was made uniform in all states during the 1840's.[3] The requirement that each representative in Congress be elected in a separately constituted district was first enacted in the federal apportionment act of 1842, and was re-enacted in most of the subsequent apportionment acts for many decades. Previously, most of the states had provided for the district system of elections, but there were several plural-member districts and New Hampshire, Connecticut, New Jersey, and Georgia preferred statewide election on a general ticket. It was not until 1846 that all members of the House of Representatives were elected individually from separate districts. Thereafter various exceptions were permitted from time to time and no general legislation is in effect at present, but the district system of single-member constituencies has been the predominant feature of elections to the House of Representatives for more than a century.

Majority and minority party leadership in Congress became more clearly defined and of greater significance during the period of the Whig-Democratic two-party system. The role of the party caucuses in the selection of Speaker of the House, President Pro Tem of the Senate, and minority leaders of each house presumably evolved considerably from the days of Jackson onward. (The role seems not to have been subjected to systematic historical study covering the first half of the nineteenth century.) Congressional elections in single-member constituencies, party elections of leaders in Congress, and the party contest every four years for the Presidency were all combining to strengthen the two-party mold of politics as the Whig party developed its strength.

At the same time, party organization in the nation at large was still extremely loose in almost every feature, even though hierarchies of party committees and party chairmanships had been created at county, state, and national levels by 1852. For party members and party officers the tradition of party loyalty had not yet achieved the emotional strength, even rigidity, that it was to attain by the end of the century. Members and officers alike could march out of one party and into another without much regret for the past or concern for

[2] The entire paragraph is based on W. Dean Burnham, *Presidential Ballots 1836-1892* (1955), pp. 55-59.
[3] The following is based mainly upon Charles O. Paullin, *Atlas of the Historical Geography of the United States* (1932), p. 105.

the future. Despite the perfection of symmetry in a two-party balance from 1836 to 1852 the situation was much more fluid than appeared on the surface.

A basic characteristic of the time was the fact that the legitimacy of a system of party politics was neither clearly understood nor fully accepted. The wide extension of the franchise had arrived as a fact, and massive electorates were the product; but there was little public acknowledgment that a mass electorate could become effective only through party organization. The practical necessities of political action, however, were given effect in the organization of the Democratic party and eventually, though belatedly and grudgingly, in the Whig. Like the Federalists before them, most of the Whigs began by abhorring publicly all partisan organization of any kind even when they could not avoid the use of tactics calculated to produce partisan success. Thurlow Weed was the most notable exception in this respect among the national leaders of the Whigs. Boss of a powerful machine in his own state for some decades, he was an unabashed believer in organization and a principal architect of the party's national apparatus, later carrying on the tradition into the Republican party which he helped to found.

Though national in name and in membership, and to some extent in appearance and behavior, both parties were essentially a collection of localisms. The Whigs in particular were not much more than an aggregation of several different sectional parties, all of which used the same name and were opposed to the Democrats, but for different reasons. In both parties the district system of elections for the House of Representatives, the state legislative selection for the Senate, and state party choice of national convention delegations, all emphasized state and locality rather than national party loyalties. Like the Congress, the national party convention was a nationalizing institution of a kind, but it was not yet supported effectively by any national system of communication. Political opinion itself was essentially a local phenomenon, led mainly by local discussion and with little reference to national leadership.

These aspects of the situation were enhanced by the absence of any important external threat to the security of the nation. The transatlantic disputes with the British over Oregon and other matters produced little risk of armed conflict. The Mexican War was won with relative ease, and served mainly to feed the fires of expansionism. Problems of external relations did not exercise any serious restraining or limiting influence within the arena of domestic politics.

Weakness of national political leadership was a continuing phenomenon during most of the period. A party turnover in the White House occurred every four years from 1840 to 1852. This rapidity in alternation, moreover, was a sign, not of the strength of the parties when in opposition, but rather of the weakness and inadequacy of either party when ostensibly in executive power.

Congressional leaders were almost all highly sectional in their followings and outlooks. With the reduced congressional influence on presidential nominations and elections that came with the convention system, friction between executive and legislative branches was on the rise. Meanwhile the conventions had not yet found means to discover or develop strong national leaders. For the time being, they were being used mainly to select weakness rather than strength for the presidential office.

Third-party movements were conspicuous in every presidential year from 1844 to 1860. They indicated forces working toward breakdown and party realignment over the issues related to slavery. Most of these third parties were essentially northern protest movements, demanding stronger resistance to southern demands than either major party was prepared to countenance before 1856. In 1844 the third-party vote evidently cost New York State for the

Whigs, in 1848 for the Democrats; in each case, it may have decisively affected the national outcome on the Presidency.

In 1860, however, when the third- and fourth-party vote was at its maximum, a different phenomenon was demonstrated. Party bolting and third-party voting did not decide the outcome. On the contrary, a partisan plurality of the electorate within a sectional majority of the states was able to demonstrate how a substantial majority could be polled in the electoral college with less than 40 per cent of the popular vote. The immediate result was the Civil War; a longer-term result was the discovery that a winning party did not have to be truly national in scope in order to win.

The Post-Civil War Period, 1864-1892

The general pattern of presidential election returns from 1864 to 1892 was oddly similar to that of 1832 to 1860, allowing for a reversal of Democratic and Republican roles, as the figures in Table 3.2 attest.

The Republican party was in power at the beginning of the period, as the Democratic party had been in 1832, and gave the appearance of being the stronger of the two parties during most of the time. It held the White House continuously for twenty-four years, from 1861 to 1885 (if Andrew Johnson is counted as a Republican Presi-

dent), yet the balance of the popular votes was nearly always close. At the end of the period the parties were alternating in power at four-year intervals, as they had under the Whig-Democratic two-party system.

After the Civil War the scene slowly changed from northern politics to national politics as southern states were progressively returned to participation in the affairs of the nation. There was also a march of new states into the Union with the spread of settlement throughout the West, culminating in the admission of six states in 1889-1890: North and South Dakota, Montana, Wyoming, Idaho, and Washington. These offsets to southern power in Congress, all admitted during the last Republican administration of the period, brought the number of states to forty-four. (Utah was to follow in 1896, Oklahoma in 1907, and Arizona and New Mexico in 1912, thus completing the extension of the franchise to all contiguous portions of continental United States except the District of Columbia.)

A vast expansion of the railroad network brought many changes in population movement, travel, and communication. Agricultural production was expanding rapidly, but so was industry. Immigration was still on the rise, cities were growing, and the strains of an industrial civilization were becoming important to a steadily rising proportion of the total population. National politics was still dominated by mone-

TABLE 3.2. THE POPULAR VOTE FOR PRESIDENT, BY PARTIES, 1864-1892[a]

(in thousands)

Year	Democratic	Republican	Other
1864	1,804	2,207	1
1868	2,707	3,013	—
1872	2,843	3,597	19
1876	4,284	4,037	85
1880	4,414	4,453	346
1884	4,919	4,850	283
1888	5,538	5,447	388
1892	5,555	5,183	1,323

[a] W. Dean Burnham, *Presidential Ballots 1836-1892* (1955), p. 247.

tary, tariff, and Civil War pension questions; there was little clarity on the new problems of labor, welfare, or the control of the economic system—which frequently gave the appearance of being dangerously unbridled, with new hazards for the party in power as a result.

Public policy during most of the period grew out of factional conflict in Congress. Presidential leadership reached its lowest ebb under Grant, but was rebuilt somewhat under Rutherford B. Hayes, James A. Garfield, and Chester A. Arthur. It remained for the two Cleveland administrations to demonstrate to the studious eye of young Professor Woodrow Wilson that the weaknesses of the American system of government were not as inevitable as he had thought.

The Democrats were effective in opposition but produced no great national leaders among their congressional representation. The party steadily lost respectability in the entire northern tier of states through the growing influence of the northern veterans' organization of the Civil War, the Grand Army of the Republic; and the party's increasing monopoly in the South tended mainly to strengthen its appearance of being only sectional in national affairs. If it had lacked the succession of Governors Horatio Seymour, Samuel J. Tilden, and Grover Cleveland of New York as its more effective candidates for the Presidency, its position would have been desperate indeed.

In the major parties and their followings, political activity was organized but at the same time increasingly devoid of issues. Party voting was becoming more and more traditional for most of the voters, who had inherited an attachment to one party or the other that they would not violate. Issues were fought out within each party; but, when the conflict was concluded, the presidential candidates nominated by each were so conservative as to offer little choice on election day.[4] This tendency reached an

extreme in the second election of Grover Cleveland. During his second term Cleveland himself was apparently much more conservative than during his first. The change was generally attributed to the connections developed during his four years of Wall Street law practice while out of the White House. However that may have been, the panic of 1893 and the depression that followed would have tested the skills of any President.

Rigidity within the major-party national organizations was accompanied by a steady rise in third-party movements from 1876 onward. The Greenback party polled over a million votes in the congressional elections of 1878 and was a factor in the presidential elections of 1880 and 1884. Intensification of agrarian and labor unrest led to the formation of the Populist or People's party, which held its first national nominating convention in 1892. The Populist platform advocated a soft-money policy—the free coinage of silver at 16 to 1; government ownership of railroads; direct election of senators; adoption of the secret ballot, the initiative, and the referendum; a shorter working day for labor; and restrictions on immigration. The party polled over a million popular votes and won 22 electoral votes in 1892. Aside from the vote transfers arising out of the death of Horace Greeley after election day in 1872, this was the first time since 1860 that more than two presidential candidates had received votes in the electoral college. Grover Cleveland's victory in 1892 was the Democratic party's greatest electoral college landslide in forty years, but the size of the Populist vote made the victory a hollow one.

Misfortune followed the Democrats during the second Cleveland administration. The panic of 1893 led Cleveland to insist on legislation to protect the gold standard;

[4] As a comment on the conservatism of the Democratic party during this period, Wilfred E. Binkley points out that Thomas Jefferson was unmentioned in Democratic party platforms from 1844 to 1892 and the Jeffersonian tradition was not actively revived in the Democratic party until after Bryan's nomination. (Binkley, *American Political Parties, Their Natural History*, 3d ed., 1958, pp. 273-74.)

he obtained the legislation, but the bitter fight had deeply split his own party in Congress. In the mid-term elections of 1894 the Republicans made striking gains in the House of Representatives. Previously the Republican proportion of the House had fallen in 1890 to 27 per cent of the two-party membership, then recovered to 37 per cent in 1892, the year Cleveland was re-elected; in 1894 it jumped to a majority of 71 per cent.[5] Now it was the Democratic party that showed signs of going the way of the Whigs in 1852, to be replaced by a new party that would give the voters of the West and the South a means for expressing themselves on the issues in which they were interested. But in 1896 the Democrats swallowed the Populists (or vice versa) and in name, at least, it was the Democratic party that survived.

Republican Dominance, 1896-1924

William Jennings Bryan, age 36, won the Democratic nomination of 1896; Governor William McKinley of Ohio was the Republican nominee. The Democrats were committed to the unlimited coinage of silver, the Republicans to the gold standard. Factional bolting occurred in both major parties: silver Republicans met in convention and endorsed the Democratic ticket, while gold Democrats met and nominated candidates of their own. McKinley won by 7,104,779 popular votes to Bryan's 6,502,925, with an electoral college majority of 271 to 176.

This ending of the twenty-year struggle by third-party interests was in striking contrast to what happened in the period ending in 1860. In the earlier period, neither party was willing to pay the price demanded by the party bolters and other third-party organizers. The later period led to the events of 1896, when the Democratic party paid the price involved in absorbing the Populists and the Republican party

[5] W. Dean Burnham, *op. cit.*, p. 155.

paid the price involved in consolidating its support among the monetary conservatives.[6]

The election returns of 1896 marked a re-alignment of the party electorates that was to endure for a considerable period.[7] In part the realignment was ideological, in part sectional, and in part it followed social and economic class lines, with the various divisions cutting across each other in a pattern of some confusion. Ideologically, the Democratic party was again identified as the party of radical soft-money agrarianism, as it had been in the days of Andrew Jackson, while the Republicans stood for sound money, high protective tariffs, and an active concern for the workingman's welfare and prosperity—"the full dinner-pail."

These ideological divisions were expressed in the sectional majorities of 1896. The Republican party carried every county in the six New England states, along with state-wide majorities in New York, New Jersey, Pennsylvania, Ohio, Indiana, Illinois, Michigan, Wisconsin, and nine other states. Bryan carried the South and most of the Plains, Moutain, and Pacific states, for a total of twenty-two states to McKinley's twenty-three.

[6] In a balanced voting situation the price of the tie-breaking pivotal votes goes up, but it has to be paid in one way or another. The experiences of 1832-1860 took place at a time when the major parties (before the advent of the Republicans) seemed to be incapable of arriving at either clear decisions or durable compromises; and the price was paid in the form of party breakup, unlike the way in which the price was paid in 1896. During the period ending in 1924, the Progressives of 1912 were unable to obtain their price but did impose a sanction in the defeat of the Republican party that year; in 1924, with the Republican party again dominant, the Progressives obtained neither price nor sanction. In the closer party balance of the present years, it remains to be seen whether the national conventions will be able to cope with dissident party factions without making excessive concessions for support and also without incurring excessive penalties when agreement proves impossible.

[7] For other views of the history and evolution of the party system since 1896, see particularly Binkley, *op. cit.*, Chap. 14-16; Key, 4th ed., *op. cit.*, Chap. 7; E. E. Schattschneider, "The Functional Approach to Party Government," in Sigmund Neumann (ed.), *Modern Political Parties* (1956), pp. 194-215; Samuel Lubell, *The Future of American Politics* (1952), Chaps. 10-11.

The social and economic cleavages must be inferred in the absence of survey data, but it can be assumed that conservative voters generally departed from the Democratic party, except in the South. The Republican party retained its previous sources of strength north of the Ohio and east of the Mississippi, while greatly enlarging its share of the working-class vote in that area.[8]

The vote was the most sharply sectional that had occurred since 1860. It ushered in a period in which the Republican party was dominant in the nation as a whole and in most of the northern states, while the Democratic party consolidated its control in the South. Previously, in the South, although the Democratic Party had polled substantial majorities from the end of Reconstruction onward, a significant opposition had continued to exist. The opposition consisted in part of southern white Republicans and of Negroes not yet disfranchised, reinforced by the various third-party movements, ending with the Populists. After 1896 the Democratic party was increasingly secure as the party of white supremacy throughout the South, and the various measures for the disfranchisement of Negroes were gradually tightened.

In northern states from Iowa and Minnesota eastward, the Republican party became entrenched with much more substantial majorities than it had previously enjoyed. After the end of Reconstruction the party had won its national victories by gaining narrow majorities in key states, with the Democratic party pressing hard in the presidential elections, and usually winning a majority in Congress even when it lost the Presidency. But after 1896 the Republican party consolidated its dominance in about twenty northern and western states. For a generation its position in these states was

[8] As a young lawyer, McKinley had risked his career by defending a group of striking workmen; his campaign manager in 1896, Mark Hanna, was one of the earliest capitalists to recognize and defend the rights of organized labor. The Democratic party, on the other hand, needed a long time to live down Cleveland's use of federal troops in the Pullman strike of 1894. Cf. Binkley, *op. cit.,* pp. 313, 325-26, 330-31.

to be nearly as secure as that of the Democratic party in the South; and, since the one-party Republican states had more congressional seats and more electoral votes than the one-party Democratic states, the Republican party could ordinarily assume victory in national elections. Republican control of the House of Representatives was unbroken from 1895 to 1911.

In 1912, Republican dominance was upset, but primarily by a split in the party's own ranks. Theodore Roosevelt, Republican President from 1901 to 1909, had become a leader of the insurgent Republicans in the party—the Progressives—and challenged his successor, President William Howard Taft, for the nomination. When Taft was nominated by the convention, the Progressives bolted, held their own convention, and nominated Roosevelt. The Democrats nominated Woodrow Wilson, but only after a long struggle of their own. The electoral college gave Wilson 435 votes, to Roosevelt's 88 and Taft's 8, but Wilson polled only 42 per cent of the popular vote. Wilson won again in the close contest of 1916. In the postwar election of 1920 the Democrats were decisively swept out of office.

Throughout the 1896-1924 period, in the states where one party or the other was dominant, the major opposition usually came from within the party, so far as state and congressional elections were concerned. Internal factional opposition to the party leadership was almost always present, and in some cases virulent. It provided most of the reforming energy that went into the adoption of primary election systems and the movement for the direct election of senators.

The first mandatory, state-wide, direct primary law was adopted in Wisconsin in 1903, and the Seventeenth Amendment, providing for the direct election of senators, came into effect in 1913. By 1916, gubernatorial and congressional candidates were being nominated in primaries in about two thirds of the states. A measure of democracy was thus restored, and boss rule sometimes circumvented, in states where one political party had already become so far dominant that the other no longer could provide an effective opposition. But the longer-term consequences were detrimental to the survival of two-party government in those states. A monopoly of the opposition is probably the most important asset of the minority party in a two-party system; when ample facilities for opposition are provided within a dominant party, the second party may tend to atrophy.[9]

At the national level, however, the convention system of nominations provided relatively strong party leadership during most of the period. William McKinley was an able practitioner of the arts of group diplomacy and an upholder of the powers and dignity of the Executive Branch. Although later overshadowed by his successor, Theodore Roosevelt, he nonetheless had done much to consolidate the Republican position as that of the party with a "natural" majority. Roosevelt in turn made the Republican party more hospitable to progressive elements and developed its popular following. Among the Democrats, Bryan filled what would otherwise have been a leadership vacuum for the sixteen years preceding the Wilson administration. Wilson developed the modern concept of the Presidency more fully than any of his predecessors, a concept that was to be carried forward in later years by a young member of his administration, Franklin D. Roosevelt.

The circumstances under which the Wilson administration came to power, stayed in power, and lost power nonetheless all pointed to the continuing fact of Republican dominance. Seemingly the minority party could not win except when the majority party was divided or ineptly led, and could hope at most for eight years in office. Yet the top-heavy Republican majorities of 1920 and 1924 were again accompanied by ominous agrarian discontent and the third-party movement of 1924.

Elements that traced their antecedents

mainly to the Progressives of 1912 coalesced in 1924 to nominate Senator Robert M. La Follette for President and Senator Burton K. Wheeler for Vice President. This ticket was endorsed by the Farmer-Labor party, the Socialist party, and officers of the American Federation of Labor. The "new" Progressives polled 13 electoral votes and almost 5 million popular votes, after surmounting the difficulties encountered in many states in suddenly placing a new party ticket on the ballot.[10] Although the Democratic party still held its place in the nation at large as the second party, its share in the popular vote was a meager 28.8 per cent. The Republican candidate, President Calvin Coolidge, won with 54.1 per cent of the popular vote.

For the Democrats, the fiasco of 1924 was the end of an era. (The year 1924 was an era's ending for the Progressives also, and their candidate and leader, Senator La Follette, died in 1925.) The defeated Democratic candidate, John W. Davis, was the last of the compromise nominees to be generated under the two thirds rule, but the rule itself survived until 1936.

Recent Times, 1928-1956

The realignment of the party electorates that occurred in the elections of 1928, 1932, and 1936 was at least as great as that of 1896. Cumulatively those elections reshaped the cleavage lines between the parties in terms of social and economic interests, with the Republican party becoming more clearly identified as representing the white-collar proprietary, professional, and upper-income classes, and the Democratic as standing for manual workers, organized labor, ethnic and religious minorities, and lower-income groups. In vast segments of the population the parties continued to

[9] V. O. Key, Jr., *American State Politics: An Introduction* (1956), Chap. 6, pp. 169-96.

[10] For details of these difficulties, which continue to inhibit the formation of a new major political party on a national scale, see Belle Case La Follette and Fola La Follette, *Robert M. La Follette, June 14, 1855—June 18, 1925* (1953), Vol. 2, pp. 1110-18, 1121-24, 1148.

overlap, but, as the years wore on, each party tended to assume more clearly the complex identity of group composition that it has borne in recent years.

One important result of this realignment was a considerable thawing out of the sectional patterns that had previously been frozen for a generation. Since 1928, with the Democratic party in power nationally most of the time, state after state in the erstwhile "solid North" has become the scene of active party competition in presidential, gubernatorial, and senatorial contests. The South has retained the appearance of solidity in local elections, but in the three presidential elections won by the Republicans—1928, 1952, and 1956—the southern vote split almost evenly in the presidential contest. Several southern states went Republican in each case; Virginia, Florida, and Texas have begun to take on the appearance of pivotal states in presidential politics.

The increase of competitive activity is indicated by the tabulation below, which shows the percentages of electoral college strength possessed by the respective groups of states, classified by their party alignment in presidential voting, in the two most recent periods. For tabular purposes, states

Categories of States	1896-1924	1928-1956
Democratic	29.2%	23.9%
Competitive	12.0	67.5
Republican	58.8	8.6
	100.0	100.0

that voted for the same party no more than five times in the eight elections of the period concerned are classified as competitive; those voting one way six times or more were classified as aligned with the party for which they had voted predominantly. (See Chapter 16 and Appendix A, Table 4.)

A generation ago the one-party states controlled over seven eighths of the electoral college vote; recently they have con-

trolled less than a third of it. The result of the increase in number of competitive states is indicated by the more even distribution of the electoral college votes polled by each party in the various regions, as shown below in percentages.[11] Obviously there has been

Region	Democratic		Republican	
	1896-1924	1928-1956	1896-1924	1928-1956
Northeast	8.8%	24.7%	44.4%	36.4%
Middle West	16.1	24.4	43.0	37.3
South	66.5	38.1	2.3	13.2
West	8.6	12.8	10.3	13.1
	100.0	100.0	100.0	100.0

a lack of regional balance in the electoral college strength of the two parties even in the most recent period, with the Democratic party still especially strong in the South. But the shift in the direction of greater regional balance *within* each party has been noteworthy.[12]

The period since 1928 has been like that of 1896-1924 and unlike the two earlier periods from 1832 to 1892 in two important respects, both of which are indicated in Chart 3.1: party overturn has been infrequent in presidential elections since 1896, and the amplitude of the swing in the major party vote has been far wider than before 1896. Before 1896 there were two periods of close party balance when the Presidency shifted every four years; no such condition has occurred since 1896. From 1832 to 1892 the difference in percentage points between the major-party shares in the presidential popular vote was often un-

[11] Throughout this book, the classification of states by regions is the same as that used in *Presidential Nominating Politics in 1952*, and that has been used in recent years by Dr. George Gallup and various other political analysts. The states are listed by regions in many of the later tables; see, for example, Chapter 8, Table 8.1.

[12] The regions are not of equal importance in the electoral college but the three older regions have been nearly equal at around 30 per cent each, with the West formerly around 10 per cent and now just under 15.

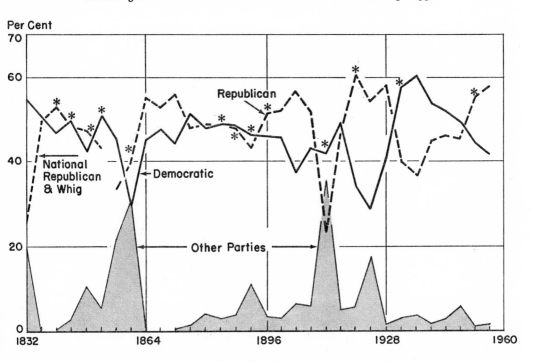

CHART 3.1. POPULAR VOTE AND PARTY TURNOVER, 1832-1956

The percentage of popular vote polled in presidential elections by Democratic, Republican, and other parties is shown above. The elections that resulted in a change of party administration in the White House are indicated by asterisks. Note the close votes and frequent overturns of 1840-1852 and 1884-1896, followed by the infrequent but wide vote swings and party overturns of 1896-1956. The chart is based on data for 1832 from Charles O. Paullin, *Atlas of the Historical Geography of the United States* (1932); 1836-1892 inclusive, W. Dean Burnham, *Presidential Ballots 1836-1892* (1955); 1896-1932 inclusive, Edgar E. Robinson, *The Presidential Vote 1896-1932* (1935); 1936-1956 inclusive, Bureau of the Census, *Statistical Abstracts,* 1936 to 1956.

der 5 per cent, and was never as much as 15 per cent except in 1832; since 1896 the spread has *averaged* 13.6 percentage points, and it fell below 5 points only in 1896, 1916, and 1948. The 1928-1956 period differs from all three earlier periods, however, in one respect: third-party movements have been relatively unimportant, posing a threat to either major party only in 1948.

The total popular vote for members of the House of Representatives usually provides majorities in the same direction as the presidential vote, but with important differences in amplitude. Since 1896 it has fluctuated much less widely than the presidential vote, despite the considerable fluctuations in the party composition of the House that have resulted from even these lesser shifts in popular vote. Since 1940 the divisions in the vote for the House have been very close; in 1956 they were the reverse of those in presidential voting, for the first time since 1848 in a presidential election year.

Sectional patterns of voting are reflected directly in the composition of the House of Representatives, which thus provides one of the best long-term indexes of the existence of one-party states and sections. There was much variation from election to election, but the general contrast between the periods 1897-1927 and 1929-1959 is indicated below by the summarization of the average numbers of members from each region during each period. (For the complete tabulation of numbers of members of each party from each region for the Congresses since the election of 1896 see Appendix A, Table 2.)

Still another indicator of sectional patterns and of the intensity of interparty competition in state politics is provided by the party affiliations of the three principal officials chosen in state-wide elections—the governor and the two senators. When one party is dominant in a state the three offices are usually held with considerable continuity by members of that party. In states where the parties are genuinely competitive, each party usually manages to occupy at least one of the three offices much of the time. This is a major factor in maintaining the competition, as well as a sign of having done so.

A summarization of the relevant data, brought together on a regional basis for each eighth year from 1897 to 1953 and for 1959, appears in Table 3.3. (For the complete tabulation of the data, see Appendix A, Table 3.) The summary figures show that, of the selected years, 1905 was the low point in the number of states in which the three offices were divided between the parties; it was generally representative of the situation from 1899 to 1909, when the Republican party was most dominant. The high point of Democratic ascendancy is reflected in the figures for 1937, with thirty states in which the Democrats held all three offices and only three states in which the Republicans did so. In 1959, when the number of such Republican states reached another low point of five, the number of such Democratic states was only twenty-one, while the states in which the three offices were divided stood at twenty-four, the highest figure for divided states in the table.

The national politics of the election years since 1940 have been dominated by the events and consequences of World War II and its aftermath. The new relationship of the United States to other parts of the world has had a heavy impact on the domestic political system. The Democratic party has been saddled with the reputation of being the war party, and apparently suffered therefrom in the presidential elections of 1952 and 1956, although the Republican party's revival and the popularity of its

Region	Democratic		Republican	
	1897-1927	1929-1959	1897-1927	1929-1959
Northeast	35	60	90	72
Middle West	37	51	98	80
South	107	114	8	6
West	6	24	18	23
Total	185	249	214	181

TABLE 3.3. PARTY DIVISION OF MAJOR STATE-WIDE OFFICES, BY NUMBERS OF STATES, SELECTED YEARS, 1897-1959[a]

Year	All Democratic	Divided	All Republican
1897	12	19	14
1905	13	8	24
1913	17	20	11
1921	10	17	21
1929	13	15	20
1937[b]	30	14	3
1945	18	18	12
1953	15	17	16
1959[c]	21	24	5
Average, 1897-1921	13	16	17
Average, 1929-1953	19	16	13

[a] Numbers of states in which the three offices—governor and U.S. senator—were held by members of the same political party or were divided between the parties. For sources, see Appendix A, Table 3.
[b] All three offices were held by the Farmer-Labor party in Minnesota in 1937, hence the 1937 figures do not add to 48.
[c] Includes Alaska and Hawaii.

candidate played the largest part in the Republican victory. The revival was also sufficient to win the congressional elections of 1946 and 1952. A considerable reshuffling of the party electorates occurred in the Republican victories of 1952, yet the previous patterns were notably restored in the congressional elections of 1954.[13] The Eisenhower victory of 1956 was largely unshared by his party, and there were strong signs of Democratic resurgence in the congressional, gubernatorial, and local elections of 1958.

Insofar as the experience in these recent elections provides any guide, the cleavages that have developed during the last generation between the major parties along social and economic lines do not seem likely to disappear soon. The development of this

[13] "The striking thing about the vote pattern of 1954 was its tendency to return to the pattern of 1948. . . .
"The Democratic victory of 1954 can most conservatively be attributed to the reassertion of the *natural majority* which the Democratic Party enjoys in this country." Angus Campbell, "1956—Return to Normalcy?" *New Republic,* Oct. 17, 1955, pp. 11-13. (Italics supplied.)

kind of stratification of the party electorates has been accompanied by a great decline in both sectionalism and traditionalism in voting. The decline in sectionalism seems likely to be permanent, in view of the continuing importance of economic and political issues that cut across the interests of all parts of the nation. Eventually the nationalizing tendencies of the present day, especially in economic development, may even erode the remains of sectional politics in the South.

The existing divisions between the parties along social and economic lines could provide a basis for a new traditionalism in voter alignments, but signs of its appearance have been slow in coming. Rather, the recent restless shifting of voting blocs and the increase in split-ticket voting both suggest that the current partisan attachments of a considerable part of the electorate are highly unstable. This is one of the major reasons for believing that the next ten years may be a period of change, bringing a further evolution of party institutions and the party system.

Party Competition and the Nominating Process

The manner in which the nominating process operates is always affected by the competitive status of the parties and their prospects for victory. A party with no hope of victory approaches the choice of a candidate in a spirit far different from that of a party that is certain of victory; and still different is the mood of each party when either might win but neither is overconfident. The problems of competitive status ramify out into many detailed aspects of the process (as will become apparent in later chapters). There are important differences, for example, between a situation of close competitive balance nationally that has its local impact in only a few pivotal states (because of a sectional alignment of the parties), and a situation of close balance that is broadly shared throughout each party because most of the states are themselves competitive. That is why the previous review of differences between the party periods has given so much emphasis to the levels of interparty competition and the kind of competition involved; it is also why expectations for the future are worth discussion despite the difficulty in clarifying expectations.

The fortunes of the two parties have been widely variable. For approximately sixty years, the position of the Democratic party was damaged by the aftermath of the Civil War; at its lowest ebb it was effective only as a vocal opposition and not as a competitor that could seriously hope to win. Then the position of the parties was reversed in the landslide of 1932, and for some years the Republican party occupied a minority position—as it apparently continued to do in the long-term voter alignments indicated by survey data in the late 1950's.

In the current situation of unstable balance the main thing that seems to be clear is that the Democratic party's Civil War legacy of subordination is gone. The future seems to hold several differing possibilities for the shape of the party system, but in none of them does it seem likely that the Democratic party will be the permanent inferior. More likely is the possibility that it would be the stronger competitor most of the time, or, alternatively, that the two parties would be so closely matched that either could hope to win the Presidency if it nominated a candidate capable of attracting the independent voters while retaining the party vote.

The possibility that the Democratic party may be the stronger competitor during the generation ahead is suggested mainly by two factors. First, for nearly a generation a much larger number of voters have considered themselves Democrats than Republicans, as shown repeatedly by many different types of survey evidence. Second, the Democratic party has demonstrated remarkable vitality on a broad front as it has moved up from a minority position in state after state during the last fifteen years—a kind of vitality that has recently been apparent in the Republican party only in isolated instances.

Against these factors is the persistent tendency of many Democratic adherents to be casual about actually voting, with the result that the Democratic turnout is usually a lower proportion of the party potential than the Republican turnout, thus offsetting the larger number of professed Democrats. The long-term position of the Democratic party may also be affected by a tendency toward party splitting that will probably become much more conspicuous in the South whenever the Democrats again win the White House. And there is the further possibility that the Republican centers of economic and social power may eventually find means to become politically more effective.

In any event, a more competitive relationship between the parties than has prevailed before on a long-term basis is a reasonable possibility. The major parties may come to compete much of the time within the 45-55 per cent range in presidential politics in states with about 90 per cent of the electoral college vote, with a presumption that governorship and congressional politics may become similarly competitive in those states. What would be the consequences of such a condition?

Professor E. E. Schattschneider has been the principal exponent of a theory about the potential consequences. He believes that current nationalizing tendencies in politics will maintain a high level of competition between the parties, with the prospect of a frequent alternation of the parties in power. In consequence, he anticipates the following:

1. A new kind of relation between the parties and the social structure.

2. A nationalization of pressure politics, with the pressure groups losing their neutrality and taking sides more definitely in party politics.

3. A shift of power within the parties toward the national level, with a decline in the power of local bosses, who cannot organize and compete on a wide scale.

4. A new attitude toward tighter national party organization, the opposite of the former situation in which sectionalism tended to depress efforts to organize nationally.

5. A movement of Congress into the focus of national politics.[14]

Each of these potential changes could have its own major effects on the presidential nominating process. If the parties become more cohesive and more clearly differentiated as elements in the social structure, the differentiation should become apparent in the characteristics of the delegates and leaders who attend the party conventions and the kind of candidates that they nominate. If the pressure groups lose their belief in the advantages of political neutrality, they will have more incentive to intervene directly in the nominating process, as organized labor has already done to a considerable extent. A nationalizing of power within the parties presumably would be reflected in less state boss control of delegate action at the conventions and more influence on the part of those most involved in organizing preconvention campaigns on a national scale. A new attitude toward tighter national party organization might be followed by more vigorous efforts to assure that those who are allowed to take part in convention action will be required to provide active assistance in the campaign that follows. An intensified party struggle for control of Congress could result both in more presidential involvement in congressional campaigning and more congressional involvement in the choice of presidential candidates.

The tendency toward a polarization of the parties along class and income lines, evident in the election returns and survey data of the last thirty years, has been welcomed by some as the basis for a more rational politics. Undoubtedly, to many other observers who prefer the more traditional patterns of American life and politics, the tendency seems sinister. For this group, there may be comfort in the probability that a close competitive balance between the parties would offer many protections to all interests.

No political party is likely to remain for long within striking distance of a national popular majority unless its own moderate elements remain firmly in control of the nominating process within the party. When both parties are competitive because neither can count on a continuing majority, both are forced to put up candidates who will cater for the votes of the party neu-

---

[14] These points have been adapted from Professor Schattschneider's unpublished paper for the 1955 annual meeting of the American Political Science Association. He has also expounded similar ideas in his contribution to Sigmund Neumann (ed.), *Modern Political Parties* (1956), and in other writings. See also Paul T. David, "The Changing Party Pattern," *Antioch Review*, Vol. 16 (Fall 1956), pp. 333-50 (also issued as Brookings Institution Reprint No. 15).

trals and of other independents who have no firm attachment to either party. A balanced two-party system is one of the clearest formulas for the organization of countervailing power, and historically it has offered strong protection for most democratic values.

The potential consequences of a more competitive party system have already been foreshadowed on a limited scale in the changing party patterns of the last thirty years. If there is a further intensification of the party struggle as more states become more competitive, the impact on the nominating process will become increasingly significant.

4

Leadership Centers of the Party in Power

WITHIN THE PARTY in power—the party on whose ticket the President in office was elected—there are many leaders for many purposes. The ostensible primary functions of some of these leaders are somewhat remote from nominating affairs. Nevertheless, the next party nomination for President is undoubtedly a matter of concern to every occupant of a leadership position of any kind. It would seem likely that a position of responsibility for any phase of party activity might be used on occasion as a base from which to become active in nominating matters.

The roster of such persons includes first and most obviously the President. It also includes the Vice President, the members of the Cabinet, the national committee chairman, the prospective chairmen of the convention, and the party leaders in the Senate and the House of Representatives.

Two other kinds of potential centers of leadership can also be identified. One consists of all the sources of candidates for the party nomination in addition to the various leaders previously listed. The other includes all of the various additional centers from which political and financial support can be put behind a potential candidate. The relative importance of such sources of candidates and of backing will be considered after reviewing the respective roles of the incumbents in the more continuing centers of party leadership.

Throughout the chapter it will become apparent that the chairmen and members of the national, state, and local party committees are not the only centers of party leadership on nominating matters, nor the most important. Public officials who have been elected to office on the party ticket have become relatively much more important than the holders of formal party office. The public officials claim their mandates directly from the voters on other matters, and this carries over into the nominating process. American officials are not unique in this respect; such a relationship between public and party officials is characteristic in most representative democracies.[1]

The President and His Associates

Presidents and their immediate associates were deeply involved in the procedures leading up to the nominating decisions of their party even in the days when a President was given little recognition as a party leader. In recent decades it has been taken for granted in the party in power that the President is the most important person to be consulted on the problem.

The first question is the availablity of the President for renomination. In recent decades it has been ordinarily assumed that a first-term President is available for renomination and that a second-term President is probably not. But the third-term

[1] Maurice Duverger, *Political Parties*, pp. 182-202; Sigmund Neumann (ed.), *Modern Political Parties; Approaches to Comparative Politics* (1956), pp. 30-32, 51-55, 71-72, but see pp. 93-94, 95-96, 97; R. T. McKenzie, *British Political Parties* (1955), pp. 184, 185, 188, 220-31, 242-44, 419, 452-53, 455-56, 582-85; R. T. McKenzie, "The Wilson Report and the Future of the Labour Party Organization," *Political Studies*, Vol. 4 (Feb. 1956), pp. 93-97.

tradition was not so sacred as to preclude all uncertainty at the end of a second term. Grover Cleveland was slow in renouncing third-term ambitions, and thereby further weakened an already weak leadership situation in preparing for the Democratic convention of 1896. There was far more uncertainty about the Vice Presidents who succeeded to the Presidency through death of the incumbent, served part of the term, and were thereafter nominated and elected for a full term in their own right. Previous tradition offered little guidance in such cases concerning a second presidential nomination. Theodore Roosevelt renounced third-term ambitions on the night of his election in 1904; in 1908 he adhered to his decision, although apparently with some regret. Calvin Coolidge, elected to the full term in 1924, took himself out of the running on August 2, 1927, with his statement, "I do not choose to run for President in nineteen twenty-eight." Harry S. Truman deferred his renunciation until March 29, 1952, after many months in which it had been widely assumed that he would be available.

The no-third-term tradition was eventually shattered by the acceptance of third and fourth terms by Franklin D. Roosevelt. The Twenty-second Amendment, ratified on February 26, 1951, prohibits more than two full terms for a President originally elected as such, or more than two and one half terms for a President who has succeeded from the Vice Presidency. Truman followed the rule laid down in the amendment when he withdrew, although it did not apply to him.

The effect of the amendment is to restore the previous tradition, but in a much more rigid form. Hereafter, only first-term Presidents will ordinarily have to decide whether they will be available for renomination. But even that decision can be a difficult one under some circumstances, as indicated by President Dwight D. Eisenhower when he announced his availability on February 29, 1956. This situation was a vivid reminder that, although the process of presidential nominations is mainly a collective activity in which many participate, certain questions along the way must be answered by the individuals who might be candidates. For them every such decision is a very personal one indeed.

Renomination Campaigns

Every first-term President, unless he enters office on an announced one-term basis—as no one has done since Rutherford B. Hayes—must give some attention to the problems of renomination from the day of his election onward. For the most part this activity blends into the other operations of the President and his staff so completely that it goes unnoticed as a separate element. A good record of performance in office is almost as important in running for renomination as in running for re-election, hence the most effective way to campaign is to do the job well—particularly those parts of the job, of which there are many, that are carried out under the eye of the public. These include opportunities for dramatic action in moments of crisis; the formulation and presentation of major legislation; on occasion, the exercise of the veto power; and the entire continuing round of public appearances, speeches on all subjects, press conferences, and addresses to the nation on radio and television. All of these opportunities are available to the President on a scale unapproached by any other officeholder. It is no wonder that for his office most of all, great advantages attach to the position of the incumbent.

In addition to the public duties, however, there are many special facets of the presidential routine that reflect the necessities of life in elective office. Callers are received whose presence on the official list is inexplicable except in terms of their contribution to the previous campaign and their possible utility in the next one. A tour around the country for any purpose involves usually a renewal of contacts with local political dignitaries by the hundreds. Much of the massive correspondence that pours through the White House daily is devoted to maintaining friendly relations with political supporters; they may write for a frivolous reason or no reason at all, but a cordial response is essential.

Other and more important elements of presidential activity are closely related to a possible renomination. One involves the decisions on public policy that vitally affect particular voting groups. The President cannot limit his concerns to decisions that benefit all or a majority of the citizenry; he is given many frequent reminders that particular minority groups—economic, racial, or religious—may be decisive in states that will have a critical influence on his political future. Sometimes he must decide between clear alternatives that reflect the general interest on the one hand, and the interest of some limited group on the other. More often, he must seek some appropriate formula by which all interests can be brought to a workable compromise; the skill he shows in this task will have much to do with how much enthusiasm his name will arouse at the next party convention.

A second area of direct political concern is the handling of patronage. The power to appoint must be used in the first instance to staff the administration. It is also used incidentally for a variety of other purposes, including the solidification of alliances that will be useful later. The conventions of the party in power are no longer made up so largely as in the past of the national administration's patronage appointees, but the general patterns followed in the distribution and administration of the President's appointments undoubtedly still do much to unify—or to dismember—the party he leads.

If the President handles his various political roles with skill, renomination at the end of the first term is likely to appear almost automatic. There was no visible challenge of any kind during the proceedings that led up to the renomination of McKinley in 1900, Wilson in 1916, Franklin D. Roosevelt in 1936, and, after he announced his availability, Eisenhower in 1956. Herbert

Hoover, to be sure, felt it necessary to work assiduously at his political fence-mending as 1932 approached. His party had lost control of Congress, economic conditions were becoming ever more disastrous, and victory in the election seemed doubtful. But the party had nowhere else to go, and in the end Hoover was renominated with 97.6 per cent of the convention vote.

Most onerous of all, in modern times, was the problem of William Howard Taft in securing renomination in 1912. Openly challenged by his predecessor and former mentor, Theodore Roosevelt, who early in 1912 announced his availability for the nomination, Taft was placed in a most difficult personal position. Probably only a popular and still young former President could have mounted so effective a challenge to a first-term President in full control of the regular party machinery. Faced by the challenge, Taft fought to the end and was renominated, with the help of the patronage-controlled southern Republican delegations that Roosevelt before him had not hesitated to use in 1904 and 1908. The resulting rupture left scars on the Republican party that endure to this day.

The three Vice Presidents who have succeeded to the Presidency since 1900 had no reason to think that a nomination for a full term as President would be automatic, in view of the experience of their nineteenth-century predecessors. But each had every intention of seeking the nomination and each achieved the goal. Theodore Roosevelt had nearly three years in which to consolidate his position after McKinley's death in 1901; he was helped also by his immense personal popularity and by the fact that the opposition of certain party chieftains collapsed with the death of Mark Hanna early in 1904. Coolidge, on the other hand, had only ten months in which to work between Harding's death and the Republican convention of 1924. In that interval, according to one biographer, he rebuilt the Republican party, taking convention control away from the national committee and congressional leaders who had successively nominated Taft, Hughes, and Harding.[2]

Truman had still a different problem. He inherited the coalition that Franklin D. Roosevelt had assembled, and was able to retain the support of its central elements. But he broke with Henry Wallace and leftist northern elements on issues of foreign policy and Soviet relations, and with James Byrnes and rightist southern elements on race relations and civil rights. Had his opposition been able to consolidate, he probably could not have been nominated in 1948, even by a simple majority, much less have won the expression of confidence implied by a two thirds vote. He entered the convention with a sound working majority and the support of the convention managers. An abortive effort to restore the two thirds rule was a failure, and in the end his nomination was opposed openly by only the die-hard southern faction.

The Franklin D. Roosevelt renomination of 1940 involved the breaching of the no-third-term tradition, and was disapproved by James A. Farley, Roosevelt's previous campaign manager, and John N. Garner, the Vice President. Roosevelt left his intentions in doubt until the final moment, and may well have been actually undecided, so far as his own conscious motivations and reasoning were concerned. Meanwhile, his staff and associates in effect conducted a renominating campaign, justified mainly by the worsening international situation. No potential competitor for the nomination was able to achieve a strong position. When it came to the vote, the renomination was easy, although control of the convention was difficult on other matters, notably the vice-presidential succession.[3]

In 1944, with no end to the war in sight, tradition was not a bar to a fourth term. Deeply involved in war management and the issues of a future peace, Roosevelt himself had much less hesitancy in deciding to be available than in 1940. His health did not become a significant public issue, and the available historical sources are in conflict on the extent to which other party leaders were actually dubious concerning his health. He was still relatively young—age 62. There was no significant opposition within the party; Roosevelt, in his efforts to lay the basis for congressional approval of postwar arrangements that would eventually be necessary, had been pursuing policies of utmost conciliation toward the other leaders of his own party and the congressional leaders of both parties.

The vital role a President plays in his own renominating campaign is clear. All other elements of leadership tend to be subordinate to it. This is true even when, for one reason or another, the President is much in need of special help from other powerful party figures. It is fair to say that the tradition of renominating a first-term

---

[2] William Allen White, *A Puritan in Babylon* (1938), p. 296.

[3] The complexities of Roosevelt's attitudes, motivations, and behavior both during the months before the convention and during the convention itself will doubtless continue to intrigue historians for many years to come. One recent student states, "I have concluded that he was not sure until the convention as to whether he would accept the nomination (even though all the while keeping

alternatives open). My interpretation of Roosevelt's personality, however, leads me to think that even if there had been no intensified international crisis, Roosevelt would have run again." (James M. Burns, *Roosevelt: The Lion and the Fox*, 1956, p. 532; see also pp. 409-13.)

A contemporary observer who worked with Harry Hopkins at the convention states, "I believe that Roosevelt did not finally decide to accept the nomination until late in the day following the actual voting of it by the 1940 convention of his party, and I think that the assembled evidence will point clearly to this conclusion." (Paul H. Appleby, "Roosevelt's Third-Term Decision," *American Political Science Review*, Vol. 46, Sept. 1952, pp. 754-65.) See also James A. Farley, *Jim Farley's Story: The Roosevelt Years* (1948), pp. 72, 78, 82, 109-11, 131, 142-43, 152-53, 190, 236, 238, 249, 258; Cordell Hull, *Memoirs* (1948), pp. 856-61.

Farley, Garner, and Hull would have been the principal alternatives for consideration by the convention if Roosevelt had removed himself. Of these, Hull was the only one who would have been acceptable to Roosevelt, and probably would have been nominated, quite possibly with Farley as his teammate. Hull was opposed to a third term, and was willing to accept the nomination, but unwilling to take any public stand as long as Roosevelt was apparently available. Burns, *op. cit.*, p. 413; Farley, *op. cit.*, p. 266.

president is at present so firmly established that only the President himself, by declination or through his own mistakes, can prevent it from operating.

But every such campaign, easy as it may appear on the surface, involves work and organization looking toward many goals, of which personal renomination is only one. The vice-presidential nomination may involve problems; and in preparation for the election campaign and for the further business of government if the election is won, a party platform must be skillfully planned and harmony established within the party on as broad a front as possible. An over-all goal—actually the means by which all the other goals are attained—is solid control of the national party organization. The pursuit of these multiple objectives is never simple, even when there is little reason to anticipate difficulty about the renomination as such; when the nomination is subject to challenge, achievement of the other goals becomes doubly difficult.

In modern times it has become normal for the President's own White House staff to carry on the most critical parts of the work and organization, maintaining liaison with such important leadership elements in the party as the national committee chairman, the congressional leaders, and the outstanding state governors. However, in preparation for the 1956 Republican campaign, an informal headquarters seems to have operated in New York from February 1955 on, with Thomas E. Stephens, President Eisenhower's former appointment secretary, as the principal person giving virtually full time to the activity. According to Joseph and Stewart Alsop, other members of what they termed the Commodore Regency included General Lucius D. Clay; former Governor Thomas E. Dewey; Attorney General Herbert Brownell; United Nations Ambassador Henry Cabot Lodge; Barak T. Mattingley of St. Louis; Senator James Duff of Pennsylvania; and Republican National Committee Chairman Leonard Hall, with the President's Assistant, Sherman Adams, in closest liaison. This group, again according to the Alsops, was originally concerned with the recruitment of "Eisenhower-type" delegates to the Republican national convention of 1956, particularly from southern states where Republican party organizations had previously been controlled by the Taft faction of the party, and also with the recruitment of "Eisenhower-type" Republicans to run in 1956 in the congressional districts that the party had lost by close margins in 1954. After the President's heart attack in September 1955 the group was largely concerned with the strategy of keeping open the possibility of an Eisenhower candidacy, and of stalling off possible rivals, particularly in the state primaries with early filing dates.[4] The President announced his availability on February 29, 1956. On March 2 the Associated Press reported from Sacramento, California, that Thomas E. Stephens had flown in from Washington and had deposited the President's signed statement of candidacy, as required by law for entry in the California primary. The delegation to be endorsed by the President was to be chosen jointly by Governor Goodwin Knight, Vice President Richard Nixon, and Senator William Knowland. After that, similar activities in other states moved rapidly.

Controlling the Succession

Campaigns to control the nomination of a successor, led by the President and his im-

[4] See syndicated columns by Joseph and Stewart Alsop carried in *The Washington Post and Times Herald*, particularly on Aug. 17, Dec. 19, 1955; Jan. 16, 25, 1956.

The critical meeting at which the President apparently went most of the way in deciding to run again occurred on January 13, 1956, and included only a small group, according to an account based on access to official records. (Robert J. Donovan, *Eisenhower: The Inside Story*, 1956, pp. 393-98.)

A dinner at the White House on March 8 that subsequently attracted considerable press speculation apparently included Stephens, Adams, Brownell, Dewey, and Clay in a total group of 18 or 20. ("White House Stag Party 'Just a Private Dinner'," *Washington Post and Times Herald*, March 10, 1956, p. 2.) Presumably this may have been an occasion for the discussion of campaign strategy and arrangements, since the decision to run again had already been announced.

mediate associates, are nearly as old as the convention system, with the succession from Andrew Jackson to Martin Van Buren in 1836 as the outstanding example. But the occasion for such activities was infrequent for many decades thereafter. The one-term Presidents who refrained from seeking renomination, James K. Polk, James Buchanan, and Rutherford B. Hayes, took no open role in connection with the succession. If they exerted influence behind the scenes, they were extremely discreet about it. Ulysses S. Grant, as the first President since Jackson to complete a second term, had some interest in third-term possibilities, as did Cleveland after his second White House occupancy, but neither was in a position to be effective in influencing the choice of his successor. Theodore Roosevelt, having renounced a third term for himself, was in an excellent position to take the initiative in the choice of a successor as 1908 approached. His personal choice of William Howard Taft, then serving in his Cabinet, is fully documented, and the dynamic Roosevelt was given most of the credit at the time for securing not only Taft's nomination but also his election.[5]

The next President to face the problem was Woodrow Wilson. Too ill to perform his presidential duties fully and with active dissension in his Cabinet, Wilson was in a poor position to control or even greatly influence the succession of 1920. Moreover, despite his strong view of the importance of the President's role as party leader, he was apparently opposed on principle to any presidential intervention in the nomination of a successor. He was reported by his secretary, Joseph P. Tumulty, as making the following statement:

We must make it clear to everyone who consults us that our attitude is to be impartial in fact as well as in spirit. Other Presidents have sought to influence the naming of their successors. Their efforts have frequently brought about scandals and factional disputes that have split

the party. This must not happen to us. We must not by any act seek to give the impression that we favor this or that man.[6]

Quite possibly this attitude was responsible for the fact that two members of the Wilson administration felt free to seek the nomination, Wilson's son-in-law, William G. McAdoo, and Attorney General A. Mitchell Palmer. Antipathy to any suggestion of nepotism may have prevented Wilson from favoring McAdoo, but there also is anecdotal evidence to the effect that Wilson did not consider McAdoo qualified.[7] More important is the suggestion that Wilson, notwithstanding his illness, actually wanted a third-term nomination for himself, in line with his insistence that the election ought to be made "a great and solemn referendum" on the League of Nations.[8] This view was credited by Governor James M. Cox, the final choice of the convention.[9]

Calvin Coolidge seemingly took little interest in the problem of the succession after his own withdrawal from candidacy in 1927. He showed no enthusiasm for the candidacy of Secretary of Commerce Herbert Hoover, but also did nothing to oppose it. Hoover was highly acceptable to the same groups that had supported Coolidge, and in effect inherited the nomination in the absence of overt action on Coolidge's part.[10]

From Coolidge to Truman the problem did not arise, except as Franklin Roosevelt gave it limited consideration in preparations for 1940, and presumably in his vice-

---

[5] William R. Thayer, *Theodore Roosevelt*, p. 314; Joseph B. Bishop, *Theodore Roosevelt and His Time* (1920), Vol. 2, p. 80.

[6] Joseph P. Tumulty, *Woodrow Wilson as I Know Him* (1925), p. 493.

[7] Josephus Daniels, *The Wilson Era* (1946), p. 553.

[8] According to Carter Glass, Wilson's physician was gravely alarmed by his third-term aspirations. (Rixey Smith and Norman Beasley, *Carter Glass: A Biography*, 1939, pp. 205-06.)

[9] James M. Cox, *Journey Through My Years* (1946), pp. 225-26.

[10] ". . . when convention time arrived, the entire block of southern delegates was 'in the bag' for Hoover. His ability to win this group of delegates showed that Coolidge was at least not standing in his way, as the southern Republican delegates, mostly negroes and recipients of administration favors, are easily directed by the incumbent of the presidential office if he so desires." Roy V. Peel and Thomas C. Donnelly, *The 1928 Campaign; An Analysis* (1931), p. 4.

presidential choice in 1944. When Truman confronted the problem in 1952 he brought to it a characteristically personal approach. According to his autobiography, he first sought to induce Chief Justice Frederick M. Vinson to become available. He then turned to Governor Adlai Stevenson of Illinois. When he met with Stevenson on January 22, 1952, Truman observed that every President was in a position to name his successor in the party nomination if he saw fit to do so; assured Stevenson of his support; and urged him to become an announced candidate. Stevenson declined, having already committed himself to run for re-election in Illinois. Truman eventually moved to Vice President Alben W. Barkley, after considering Mutual Security Administrator W. Averell Harriman along the way. But Barkley encountered opposition at the convention and withdrew his candidacy at the end of the first day. But for that, said Truman, he would have supported Barkley to the end, and "he would have been the Democratic nominee."[11] As it was, when Stevenson at last became a willing candidate Truman was free to support him.

Truman's personal doctrine on the prerogative of the President as party leader in dealing with the succession was stated more openly (after the event) and much more bluntly than that of any of his predecessors, even Theodore Roosevelt.[12] As a statement of prerogative, it is easily open to attack, although Truman probably referred mainly to the simple fact of political power. But the statement is also implicitly a doctrine concerning the responsibilities of party leadership; and it seems certain that, under modern conditions, a retiring President who has made no effort to find and support a worthy successor would be subject to criticism. Franklin D. Roosevelt was widely criticized for allegedly standing in the way of the development of appropriate successor candidacies in 1940. Dur-

ing the initial period of discussion that followed the Eisenhower heart attack in 1955, Walter Lippmann pointed out that even if President Eisenhower were unable himself to run again, it would be "virtually impossible for the President to escape the responsibility of party leader, at least as it affects the choice of his successor."[13] Perhaps there would be general agreement among public men of the present generation that a retiring President should avoid dictation to the party but should at the same time make every effort to assure the availability of at least one potential successor who is qualified and ready—insofar as such a distinction may be possible.

In some respects, the Twenty-second Amendment may be useful in clarifying the situation as a second-term President approaches the end of his tenure. Formerly, the second-term Presidents, in order to strengthen their hand in dealing with Congress, were encouraged to maintain the possibility that they might seek a third term. This had the almost automatic consequence that they could not or would not move with full effectiveness in finding and developing a successor. On the other hand, Truman demonstrated that it is possible for a retiring President to keep a firm hold on the party machinery by the very fact of actively looking about for a successor and using the powers of the Presidency and his position as party leader to that end. In the future, an active interest in the succession may become a substitute for third-term availability in maintaining the authority of a second-term President within his party. Moreover, the substitute might become more effective in some respects than the third-term possibility, since the President's motives in seeking a suitable successor are less open to question than those involved in seeking a third term.[14]

[13] Walter Lippmann, "On Marking Time," *Washington Post and Times Herald*, Sept. 29, 1955.
[14] According to James M. Burns, Franklin Roosevelt looked to his control of the 1940 nomination as an important means of maintaining his strength in dealing with Congress during his second term, deliberately spreading reports through his intimates

[11] Harry S. Truman, *Memoirs*, Vol. 2 (1956), pp. 489-97, *passim*.
[12] *Ibid.*, p. 492.

A President looking about for a successor may find the field rich or scanty. When he has made his choice, he may encounter the difficulty that a choice is not a command. It requires the consent and cooperation of the proposed successor, as Vinson, Stevenson, and Barkley successively demonstrated to Truman in their respective fashions.

The successful naming of a successor generally requires also the willing cooperation of other party leaders to a far greater degree than the securing of personal renomination. In the Truman-Barkley case, the national committee chairman and the congressional leaders were conspicuously present at the meetings at which the Barkley candidacy became definite.[15] Barkley himself was at the time Vice President and a former congressional leader. The composition of a meeting to advance the Stevenson candidacy, had Truman been able to reach the point of convening one after the conversation on January 22, 1952, might have been somewhat different, with more emphasis on other governors and party leaders. In any event, the composing of meetings to organize campaigns for the succession is likely always to be a delicate business, since the more representative the group, the more likely it is to include other possible nominees.

Presidential Control of Vice-Presidential Nominations

The convention system was installed in 1832 in the party in power largely because of Andrew Jackson's dissatisfaction with his first Vice President, John C. Calhoun, who had served in the same capacity in the

administration of John Quincy Adams. Jackson supported Martin Van Buren for the Vice Presidency, and obtained his nomination by overcoming the Calhoun forces in the convention. In 1840, President Van Buren secured his own renomination without difficulty, but neither supported nor openly opposed the renomination of Vice President Richard Johnson; no one, however, was nominated by the Democrats for Vice President that year. The election was won by the Whigs.

Thereafter, until the renomination of Vice President James Schoolcraft Sherman in 1912, the vice-presidential nomination of either party was never given twice in immediate succession to the same individual. Lincoln and Grant each served with two different Vice Presidents; neither took any open part in the convention to promote the replacement. Behind the scenes, Lincoln's role was probably decisive; Grant is not known to have taken much interest, but may have been consulted by the administration clique that moved to secure a replacement of Grant's first teammate.[16]

Cleveland ran with three different teammates. His first, Thomas A. Hendricks, who had also run with Samuel J. Tilden in 1876 but not with Winfield S. Hancock in 1880,

[15] Paul T. David, Malcolm Moos, and Ralph M. Goldman, *Presidential Nominating Politics in 1952*, Vol. 3, pp. 157-58; Alben W. Barkley, *That Reminds Me* (1954), p. 230; Truman, *op. cit.*, Vol. 2, p. 495.

that the 1940 nomination would go only to a Democrat "who met the tests of a New Dealer by the President's standards." Burns refers to this possibility as "a great countervailing force" through which the President could meet the political weakness from which most second-term Presidents have suffered, while noting that Roosevelt also never let third-term possibilities disappear. (Burns, *op. cit.*, p. 347.)

[16] Lincoln's official position was one of nonintervention. See Malcolm Moos, *The Republicans* (1956), pp. 108-09; John G. Nicolay and John Hay, *Abraham Lincoln*, Vol. 9, pp. 72-73. He was at work, however, behind the scenes early in 1864. He wanted to replace Hannibal Hamlin with a War Democrat in order to strengthen the ticket of his party, which had become the Union party for prosecuting the war. Lincoln's first choice was General Benjamin Butler, who refused; his second choice was Andrew Johnson. The President worked quietly through a number of trusted friends and political associates, including Simon Cameron and A. K. McClure of Pennsylvania; Leonard Swett of Illinois, Lincoln's former law partner; and Henry J. Raymond of the *New York Times*, who became Republican national chairman after the convention of 1864. The maneuver was carried through so skillfully that John G. Nicolay, Lincoln's secretary, was unaware of what was going on, and Hamlin himself did not learn that Lincoln had preferred Johnson until he was informed of it twenty-five years later. See A. K. McClure, *Abraham Lincoln and Men of War-Times* (1892), pp. 106-12, 425 ff.; J. G. Randall, *Lincoln the President*, Vol. 4 (1955), pp. 130-33; Eugene H. Roseboom, *A History of Presidential Elections* (1957), p. 197.

died in office; in 1888, Cleveland's running mate was A. G. Thurman; in 1892, Adlai Stevenson, who served the term and later ran with Bryan in 1900. Wilson's Vice President, Thomas R. Marshall, was the first since Calhoun and the origins of the convention system to be both nominated and elected to a second successive term.

In the present century it has been frequently assumed that the President can control the renomination of the incumbent Vice President, if any, or can arrange the nomination of a new man to suit himself. The historical record suggests, however, that this assumption is only partly justified. Three situations should be distinguished. Two of these arise when the President is running to succeed himself, the first when the Vice Presidency is occupied, the second when it is vacant. The third occurs when the President is retiring.

President and Vice President have simultaneously approached the occasion for renomination in five first-term cases since 1896, including Eisenhower and Nixon in 1956. In 1912, Taft considered the possibility of finding a new running mate who would give the ticket more balance in the liberal direction; but after the lines were drawn for a battle with T. R., he had little alternative but to continue with the conservative James S. Sherman.[17] In 1916, Wilson offered no objection to the renomination of Thomas R. Marshall, although there had been some earlier indications of friction and Secretary of War Newton D. Baker had been discussed as a possible substitute. In 1932, neither Herbert Hoover nor Charles Curtis supported the other in seeking renomination, although both were open candidates. The party, however, stood on its record and renominated both, although for a time it seemed possible that former Vice President Charles G. Dawes might be substituted for Curtis. In 1936, Roosevelt

and Garner were renominated as a team, apparently with little thought of change on the part of either, although some friction had developed between them. Garner had attended Cabinet meetings and had served actively as an intermediary between White House and Capitol Hill, at a time when the regular weekly leadership meetings had not yet been established.

In 1956, although Eisenhower refused to give an unequivocal endorsement to Vice President Richard M. Nixon and there was considerable speculation that the President might prefer a change, all his public comments gave high praise to his Vice President. When Harold Stassen, the President's adviser on disarmament, launched his move to replace Nixon with Governor Christian Herter of Massachusetts, the only known encouragement he received from President Eisenhower was permission to take a month's leave without pay to advance the cause. Stassen's eventual defeat for lack of other adherents was announced to the press by the President himself, who later told the convention that "it is a great satisfaction to me that the team of individuals you selected in 1952 you decided to keep intact for this campaign."[18]

It thus appears that, although in the nineteenth century no incumbent Vice President had been renominated in a party convention, all the twentieth-century Vice Presidents who came up as candidates in company with first-term Presidents have uniformly been renominated. But the uniform practice can be attributed more to the passive consent of the incumbent Presidents than to their favorable initiative and support.

The record was somewhat different in the Franklin D. Roosevelt third and fourth nominations. By 1940, Roosevelt and Garner were so completely at odds that a new

[17] Irving G. Williams, *The Rise of the Vice Presidency* (1956), p. 98. In view of the thoroughness with which Professor Williams has combed the biographical sources, his doctoral dissertation and his book on the same subject have been relied on extensively in the pages that follow.

[18] Republican National Convention, *Proceedings*, 1956, p. 348. (For an explanatory note on the usage in this book of the official convention proceedings, see Chapter 8, footnote 1.)
A detailed account of the "Nixon-replacement move" is given in Earl Mazo, *Richard Nixon: A Political and Personal Portrait* (1959), Chap. 11.

combination was necessary; Garner had also reached the age of 71. Secretary of Agriculture Henry A. Wallace was an early possibility in a field of more than a dozen availables. But Roosevelt's first choice was Secretary of State Cordell Hull, and he made at least three efforts to persuade Hull to run, the last on the day before Wallace was nominated. Under pressure from his convention managers for a decision, the President finally backed Wallace, only to discover that there was so much opposition among the delegates as to throw doubt upon the feasibility of the nomination. This so angered Roosevelt that he wrote out a refusal of his own renomination, which he had just received, and Wallace was then nominated.[19]

Early in 1944, Roosevelt considered the possible desirability of dropping Wallace from the ticket in the interests of party harmony and improved congressional relations. Substitutes were discussed in a conference at the White House that included Edwin W. Pauley, party treasurer and principal fund-raiser; Robert E. Hannegan, then chairman of the Democratic national committee; Frank Walker, a former chairman; and Edward J. Flynn, Bronx county leader and also a former national chairman. Senator Harry S. Truman emerged as the generally preferred name in this meeting, but no decision was made. In early July, Wallace received indications that the President had decided not to back him; but at his urging the President agreed not to repudiate him and gave him a letter praising his record but stating that the decision would have to be left to the convention. On the same day, however, Roosevelt gave a group of organization leaders, including Hannegan, a letter expressing his preference for Truman. On July 20, a Gallup poll was released showing that Wallace was the vice-presidential first preference of 65 per cent

of the Democratic voters. Roosevelt was renominated on that day, and Hannegan released the letter expressing preference for Truman, who had been firm in refusing to become a candidate and was managing a vice-presidential campaign for James F. Byrnes. An immediate vote on July 20 might have renominated Wallace; on the following day he led on the first ballot, but Truman was nominated on the second.[20]

Four of the Presidents seeking renomination since 1896 have done so in situations where the Vice Presidency was vacant. The first was McKinley, whose first-term Vice President died in office in November 1899. During early 1900 Governor Theodore Roosevelt of New York had been widely discussed as a vice-presidential possibility but was himself a reluctant candidate. President McKinley did not favor Roosevelt, but apparently had no candidate of his own and withdrew his opposition when the convention opened and the strength of the Roosevelt sentiment became apparent.

Roosevelt, Coolidge, and Truman all left the Vice Presidency vacant behind them when they succeeded to the Presidency. In 1904, Roosevelt accepted Senator Charles Warren Fairbanks as his running mate; Fairbanks was the choice of the erstwhile McKinley supporters and was not Roosevelt's preference, except to balance the ticket. In 1924, Coolidge's first choice as running mate was Senator William E. Borah, presumably in an effort to head off the third-party efforts of the La Follette Progressives. But neither Borah, the party leaders, nor the convention were willing. Coolidge's second choice, judging by the tactics of the national committee chairman at the convention, was apparently Senator Charles Curtis and his third, Secretary of Commerce Herbert Hoover, but the convention first nominated former Governor Frank O. Lowden of Illinois, who declined,

[19] Williams, op. cit., p. 179, based, according to the dissertation, on Ross McIntire and George Creel, White House Physician, p. 124; Robert E. Sherwood, Roosevelt and Hopkins, p. 178; see also Burns, op. cit., pp. 429-30.

[20] Williams, op. cit., pp. 200-01; 204-09; 213-18. See also Wallace's own account, U. S. News and World Report, "Henry A. Wallace Tells—How a Vice President Is Picked—Inside Look at U. S. Politics," Vol. 90 (April 6, 1956), pp. 86-89.

and then Charles G. Dawes. (After Dawes was elected he presided in the Senate but refused to sit in the Coolidge Cabinet.) In 1948, President Truman agreed to the selection of Senator Alben W. Barkley, but only after it had become apparent that Barkley was strongly the preference of almost the entire convention. Truman had previously searched widely for an alternative candidate and had attempted, unsuccessfully, to persuade Supreme Court Justice William O. Douglas to run with him.

The four cases just reviewed are alike in that the President was able to exercise only limited influence on the situation. In three of them the incumbent had been a Vice President who had succeeded to the higher office through death and who had a sufficient problem in securing his own nomination to succeed himself, but in all four it was apparent that more of a contest could develop than usually occurs in vice-presidential nominations. Seemingly the choice tended to be made by the convention, with other leaders exercising about as much influence as the President.

Vice-presidential nominations have been part of the problem of leadership succession in four cases since 1896, in which the President was retiring from office and both he and the new presidential candidate could be interested in the choice for second place. In the Roosevelt-Taft succession of 1908, James S. Sherman was nominated as Taft's running mate by the conservative congressional leadership in something of a revolt against the liberalism of the Roosevelt regime; others whom Taft himself would have preferred were unwilling to run. In 1920 the nomination of Franklin D. Roosevelt for the Vice Presidency was in the nature of a concession to the Wilsonians, who had clearly not controlled the presidential nomination. In 1928 the choice of Charles Curtis to run with Herbert Hoover was probably not the work of President Coolidge; as for Hoover's interest, Curtis had been in the forefront of the "stop-Hoover" movement. But Curtis had strong backing from Senator Borah and

other dissident agrarian forces, and no other candidate could have been nominated without a floor fight. Hoover accepted the situation without a struggle. In 1952 the possible vice-presidential candidacy of Senator John J. Sparkman on the Democratic ticket was privately under discussion in Congress and probably at the White House for some weeks before the convention. In the event, President Truman seemed to have more influence than the incoming presidential candidate, Adlai E. Stevenson.[21] Unlike his predecessors in similar situations, Truman was physically present at the convention and fully prepared to take a vigorous part in the choice.

The Vice-Presidency: Dead End or Stepping Stone?

Benjamin Franklin suggested that the Vice President should be known as "His Superfluous Excellency." Despite this estimate of inconsequence, the incumbents in the early days of the Republic were men of presidential stature and the position was a door to the Presidency.

From 1840 onward, however, the position and its occupants were the victims of a vicious circle. In each party the vice-presidential nomination was used mainly to secure the votes of an opposing faction for the presidential nomination or to placate them after that nomination had been made. As a result the presidential and vice-presidential nominees were almost invariably incompatible, factionally and personally. This necessarily impaired the usefulness of the Vice President as an assistant or a stand-in for the President and made it virtually impossible for him to succeed to the White House except through the death of the incumbent. Under the circumstances, if the ticket won, the new administration was likely to regard its vice-presidential teammate as an unwelcome outsider, to be iso-

---

[21] David, Moos, and Goldman, *op. cit.*, Vol. 1, pp. 155-56; Vol. 3, pp. 202-03; Truman, *op. cit.*, Vol. 2, p. 497.

lated as fully as possible in his minor role at the Capitol. If the President survived his term, the Vice President returned to the limbo from which he had come; the post had no value for purposes of career advancement. If the President was retiring, he did not favor the incumbent Vice President for the succession. If the President died in office and the Vice President succeeded, the result, usually, was that the Presidency had thus been entrusted to a secondary leader of a dissident faction of the party supposedly in power. The unworkable aspects of this formula in its most extreme form were vividly demonstrated during the administration of John Tyler. With Millard Fillmore and Chester A. Arthur the situation was less extreme in terms of the reversal of factional alignments that accompanied their accession to power, but the weakness inherent in their position was demonstrated by their inability to secure nomination to succeed themselves.

At the death of Abraham Lincoln, the accession of Andrew Johnson technically reversed the party hold on the Presidency, since Johnson was a War Democrat by origin, elected on a coalition ticket. But in fact Lincoln had chosen Johnson as a running mate because the two men were agreed on the chief question at issue between the White House and the dominant Radical wing of the Republican party—the question of southern reconstruction. In this case, since the President and Vice President did not represent opposing views, Johnson did not reverse the White House position. He carried forward the conflict much as Lincoln might have done, but without Lincoln's political skill and without benefit of an established position in the Republican party.

The Vice Presidency has recovered only slowly from the reputation it acquired between 1840 and 1900; nevertheless, the position has been on the upgrade most of the time since the turn of the century. Theodore Roosevelt took the nomination under pressure from Boss Tom Platt of New York, who was bitterly opposed to his continu-

ance in the governorship. He may have had a comforting hope of making something of the job.[22] At any rate his example, and the results, have encouraged many others. The Vice Presidents who obtained renomination to succeed themselves, with or without the willing cooperation of the Presidents with whom they had served—Sherman, Marshall, Curtis, Garner, and Nixon—were demonstrating that a Vice President can develop his own power base within his political party, one from which he is not easily challenged by any other influence. This lesson was probably appreciated sooner in the Senate—where the office is under close observation—than anywhere else. In the mid-1920's the office was being declined with contempt by prominent senators, but, for the last twenty years or more, Senate members have been showing an active interest in the Vice Presidency.

The office has been further strengthened with the gradual reversal of the custom of seeking factional balance on party tickets. The new doctrine is the one expounded by President Eisenhower in his press conference of May 31, 1955:

. . . unless the man . . . chosen were acceptable to the Presidential nominee, the Presidential nominee should immediately step aside, because we have a Government in this day and time when teamwork is so important, where abrupt changes could make so much difference.

If a President later is suddenly disabled or killed or dies, it would be fatal, in my opinion, if you had a tense period . . . not only to introduce now a man of an entirely different philosophy of Government, but he, in turn, would necessarily then get an entirely new Cabinet. I think you would have chaos for a while.

So I believe if . . . there isn't some kind of general closeness of feeling between these two, it is an impossible situation, at least the way I believe it should be run.

I personally believe the Vice President of the United States should never be a nonentity. I believe he should be used. I believe he should have a very useful job. And I think that ours has. Ours has worked as hard as any man I know in this whole Executive Department.[23]

[22] Williams, op. cit., pp. 3, 73.
[23] New York Times, June 1, 1955, p. 18.

This is the principle, at the time still unstated, that Franklin D. Roosevelt quite obviously was applying when he refused to run in 1940 unless Henry Wallace were also nominated.[24] Wallace, moreover, was far more active in the administration than any previous Vice President, although Coolidge and Garner had attended Cabinet meetings. He served for nearly two years as chairman of the Board of Economic Warfare, a full-time administrative post of Cabinet rank, and was also sent on various international missions. Under wartime conditions, these precedents were accepted without much notice at the time, but they clearly established new possibilities both in law and practice. They demonstrated that a Vice President could give his main time and attention to appointive duties in the Executive Branch,

[24] Wallace himself has expounded the doctrine in terms as clear and as strong as those used by President Eisenhower; in a lecture at the Harvard Law School Forum on March 30, 1956, he said in part:

"Now, with regard to the Vice President, it seems to me the first requisite is that he should stand for precisely the same policies as the President. He should come from the *same wing of the political party*, and, as soon as the National Convention names a man for President, that man should designate not more than three names—preferably only one—agreeable to him for Vice President. The great danger here is that the man just named for President will try desperately to heal the wounds and placate the dissidents in his party by naming a man or men from that wing of the party which the presidential nominee has just licked in a party battle. This means in case the President dies that many of the national policies wil be reversed by the Vice President who then takes over. . . .

"In closing let me say that I hope to see the day when no party will dare name a President from one wing of the party and the Vice President from the other wing. With a country as powerful as the U. S., we owe it to the world not to open the door to a sudden shift in our course as a result of the death of the President. No President should be burdened with a Vice President he does not respect and in whose ideas he does not believe.

"It is all-important today that the voters should chastise severely any party which runs for Vice President a man who disagrees on matters of policy with the President. My battle cry would be, 'No more deals—no more balancing of the ticket.' Let's warn both parties that we, the voters, hold them accountable for presenting men who like each other and who believe earnestly in the same policies.

"The old days passed forever with the coming of the hydrogen bomb and the domination of the world by two great powers." (*U. S. News and World Report, op. cit.*, pp. 87 and 89.)

if the President so desired. After all, the task of presiding over the Senate has been taken care of sufficiently well during the many periods when the Vice Presidency has been vacant for several years at a time; the protracted absences of Henry Wallace made little difference in the functioning of the Senate. In recent years the Vice Presidents have been under little compulsion to preside over the Senate except when they have found it convenient or important to do so, as when the possibility of breaking an important tie vote might arise.

The inherent strength of the policy of making vice-presidential nominations on a basis conducive to party continuity was demonstrated when Vice President Harry S. Truman succeeded to the Presidency in 1945. In 1952 and 1956, both major parties picked vice-presidential nominees who were acceptable to the respective presidential candidates, and who could probably have followed them successfully in office if necessary without a drastic shift in party direction and alignment.

The new conception of the Vice Presidency flowered with the accession of Richard M. Nixon to the office. He was immediately called on to attend the President's meetings with the congressional leaders, with the Cabinet, and with the National Security Council, of which he was a statutory member. All of these meetings require work in preparation and, frequently, in execution of the decisions taken. Nixon was invited to preside over meetings of the Cabinet in the President's absence, and frequently presided in the National Security Council. He was sent on various international missions, some of which were apparently more than ceremonial, although even the ceremonial missions have their importance for a possible future Chief of State. He carried a major part of the burden of partisan political campaigning on behalf of the Republican party, particularly in the congressional campaigns of 1954 and 1958. His political travels were seemingly about as extensive as those of the party's national committee chairman, and always in the role of a recognized national party spokesman. All of this was made possible because of the relatively high degree of compatibility, personal and factional, between the incumbent President and Vice President.

It remains to be seen whether vice-presidential nominations can or will be made in both parties in the future on a basis that will regularly permit this kind of a relationship between President and Vice President. The factor of geographical balance, implied in the Constitution itself, will undoubtedly continue to be closely observed in the composition of party tickets. It does not necessarily prevent personal and factional compatibility between the ticket leaders, but does restrict the field of potential candidates and complicate the choice.

What reasonably could be expected would be that the more glaring cases of incompatibility might be avoided in the future, at least insofar as they can be foreseen; and that the Vice Presidency will continue to evolve as a collection of duties in which the incumbent can serve actively and honorably without becoming too much of a nuisance to the President if some degree of conflict between them does arise. If this proves to be the case, it will be increasingly easy to recruit able and qualified candidates for the vice-presidential nominations. The post itself will also be increasingly recognized as one from which the incumbent might, on occasion, move on to the Presidency through the regular nominating and electoral processes. Should this happen, at least one office that can genuinely prepare a man for the Presidency, something that has been lacking for more than a century, will be restored to the American system of government.

The Cabinet

There have been Cabinets in American history in which several of the members were powerful political figures, who either were active leaders of party factions in their own right or had been prominent supporters of the President before his first election. The Cabinets of an incoming administration are still selected largely from among those who were identified as supporters of the winner in the previous campaigns, but factional leaders who are strong in their own right are no longer often appointed. The proportion of Cabinet members with previous experience as top elective officials has also declined substantially.[25]

Senators have become reluctant to enter the Cabinet except as they near the end of their careers; they can return to the Senate only if able to secure re-election in a possible contest with an incumbent successor, and then only with a complete loss of

[25] No complete tabulation has been found of the proportion of Cabinet members with previous service as governors, but this proportion has probably not increased. The proportion of Cabinet members with previous service in Congress has declined sharply since 1896. (Pendleton Herring, *Presidential Leadership*, 1940, pp. 164-65.)

Unpublished findings of Professor Joseph A. Schlesinger of Michigan State University provide data on the previous experience in public office of the 159 Cabinet members appointed between 1900 and 1959, including those incumbent in 1900 and up to Christian A. Herter's appointment in 1959. In percentage terms, that experience may be summarized as follows: Held elective office—0.6, Vice President of the United States; 20.1, members of Congress; 7.5, governors; 1.9, other state executive office; 15.7, state legislators; 11.9, local elective office; 7.6, defeated candidate for major office (President, Vice President, governor). Held appointive office—55.3, other Cabinet posts, sub-Cabinet officers, state and federal administration. Since selection for court office may be either elective or appointive, a separate category shows 10.7 per cent with service on federal, state, or local courts and another 25.1 per cent having held some public legal office such as district attorney. (Because of multiple experience, percentages do not add to 100 per cent.) The last office held prior to Cabinet appointment was in almost half the cases a non-elective, administrative position. Dr. Schlesinger's data reveal certain party differences. Democrats have made appointments more frequently from among persons holding high elective office; Republicans have appointed more often from persons holding no recent public office of any sort. Democratic appointees have usually held some public office in their careers; this has been less the case for Republicans.

For a comprehensive discussion of the political role of the Cabinet and its individual members, see Richard F. Fenno, Jr., *The President's Cabinet* (1959), and especially see pp. 68-77 for specific discussion of Cabinet appointments and their political implications.

seniority. There have been several recent instances of former Cabinet members seeking election to the Senate, but as a rule service in the Cabinet appears to lead nowhere except to a return to private life, an unattractive prospect for any political careerist. Cabinet members have tended to be regarded as departmental administrators rather than as political leaders, notwithstanding their important duties in developing and presenting proposed legislation, and in defending their administrative records before Congress and the public.

Nevertheless the Cabinet has functioned to some extent as an agency of inner group political communication almost from the first. Secretaries of the Treasury, Commerce, Labor, Agriculture, and Interior have long acted as advisers, negotiators, and channels between the President and important power-holding groups in the electorate. All Cabinet officers share this type of political role to at least a limited extent. In considering the President's legislative program, the Cabinet, with all its departmental interests, is still inevitably concerned with the over-all record of the party and its competitive relationship to the opposition party.[26] Every Cabinet member is involved in the problem of party patronage; typically, the Postmaster General and the Attorney General have been especially involved.

The members of the Cabinet are often involved directly in presidential nominating politics at the national level, and to some extent in their own states as well. This relation is most evident when the President is seeking renomination and re-election. In such cases it seems to be accepted that a loyal Cabinet member should do what he can to advance the President's cause. He may secure a place on the delegation of his home state at the national convention. He may be active in platform drafting and in negotiations with pressure groups concerning platform provisions. Most likely of all, the national committee may schedule him for campaign speeches—unless it is thought that he would hurt the party ticket more than help it, an attitude that may prevail at party headquarters even for Cabinet members that the President has no intention of replacing. But probably not more than one third to one half of the Cabinet members have been effective in any of these political capacities in recent decades.

When the nomination of a presidential successor is in prospect, members of the Cabinet may themselves be considered for the nomination. If one member is picked by the President, all or some of the others may support him—or may not. Contenders for the nomination are apt to accept the support of members of the Cabinet with gratification, but they seldom actively seek it.

Members and recent members of a retiring President's Cabinet have sometimes volunteered as candidates to succeed him, but the number is not large. William G. McAdoo and A. Mitchell Palmer were noteworthy in producing a contest between colleagues at the Democratic national convention of 1920; neither won the nomination. Averell Harriman, a member of Truman's Cabinet as Mutual Security Administrator, was an active candidate at the Democratic national convention of 1952.

William Howard Taft and Herbert Hoover are the only examples since 1896 of Cabinet members who obtained the presidential nomination of the party in power. The extent to which fellow Cabinet members worked for their election can perhaps be surmised by the number of them who were held over into the new administrations: Taft retained only James Wilson as Secretary of Agriculture; Hoover retained only Andrew Mellon as Secretary of the Treasury and James J. Davis as Secretary of

---

[26] The oncoming elections of 1954 apparently took a prominent place in the discussions of the Eisenhower Cabinet within a few months after it took office, with special reference to the role of the President and the presumed necessity for a Republican victory if the Eisenhower administration were to be a success. Vice President Nixon commented that the 1954 election could be won or lost in the congressional session of 1953; national committee Chairman Hall attended at least one meeting at which he reported that he agreed that the President should not actively campaign in 1954, a decision later changed. (Donovan, *op. cit.*, pp. 270-71.)

Labor. Mellon later came to be referred to in ironic jest as the only Secretary of the Treasury under whom three Presidents had served. His prenomination support was undoubtedly important to Hoover.

The fact that so few Cabinet members are considered for presidential nominations reflects an oddity of the American system of government; posts that seem to offer exceptional preparation for the executive office are largely disregarded in the search for candidates. The reason may perhaps be found in the modern tendency to regard Cabinet posts as more administrative than political, and certain of them as politically related to a specific interest-group clientele more than to the party as a whole, even though the secretary himself may have been appointed as a reward for general political work in the election of the President. The idea of party government will need to be brought into closer connection with federal administrative doctrine before the Cabinet can again become an important training ground for the Presidency. Such a merging may perhaps be in process.

President Eisenhower's Cabinet of 1953 included several members who had been active in the campaigns for his nomination and election. Secretary of State John Foster Dulles was closely associated with Thomas E. Dewey, one of Eisenhower's earliest backers, and had been active in the platform-drafting proceedings at the 1952 convention. Attorney General Herbert Brownell, Jr., had been one of the Eisenhower campaign managers at the convention and chaired the conference that recommended the selection of Richard M. Nixon for Vice President. Postmaster General Arthur E. Summerfield had been chairman of the Michigan delegation, one of the large uncommitted delegations that swung to Eisenhower at the critical moment. Secretary of the Interior Douglas McKay had been at the convention as Governor of Oregon and chairman of its delegation, solidly committed to Eisenhower. Secretary of Commerce Sinclair Weeks had been chairman of the Republican national finance

committee before the convention, served as an intermediary between Taft and Eisenhower groups in organizing the agreed slate of delegates at large from Massachusetts, was himself a delegate, and announced for Eisenhower after the delegation had been elected but before the convention. The Secretaries of the Treasury, Defense, Agriculture, and Health, Education, and Welfare were known Eisenhower partisans before the election, but had not been conspicuous in the prenomination campaigns.

Perhaps the most interesting recent straw in the wind was the decision to send Interior Secretary McKay to contest the Senate seat of Wayne Morse in their home state of Oregon in 1956. Cabinets that include a stable of former governors prepared to defend the party record, if necessary, by running for the Senate against their partisan opponents would be an interesting phenomenon and a striking change from past practice. This form of party service could of course be offered only when the secretary's home state had a senator of the opposite party who might be unseated. Of the eight members of the original Eisenhower Cabinet who were still serving in 1956, five others in addition to McKay were from states where the opposite party held at least one of the Senate seats. The prevalence of this situation reflects the spreading of two-party politics to a larger number of states in recent years, with a growing possibility of party reverses in the home states of members of the Cabinet, as well as in the constituencies of many members of Congress who had in the past been relatively secure.

National Committee and Convention Officers

The three party officers who stand successively at the apex of the official party hierarchy during the conventions are the national committee chairman, the temporary chairman of the convention, and the permanent chairman. The national committee chairmanship has existed continuously in each party for a century and in recent decades has usually been a full-time job. Each convention is called to order at the start by the national committee chairman. He presides until the temporary chairman has been installed. The temporary chairman presides while the convention committees are being organized and receives the report of the committee on permanent organization. This committee has the formal duty of recommending a slate of nominations for permanent chairman and other convention officers; but in both parties in recent years it has merely recommended the adoption of arrangements completed in advance by the national committee. The permanent chairman serves until the end of the convention.

In legal theory, every convention is an *ad hoc* body, unrestricted by any action of a previous convention and without authority to bind any convention in the future. Actually, the weight of precedent acts powerfully to preserve continuity from one convention to another. Those persons who according to precedent will probably be the officers at the next convention, and those who take part in appointing them, have a special influence on the course of party affairs that is usually well hidden from view but frequently of high importance. This type of influence, moreover, may be active long in advance of each convention and continue long afterward, in part because of the personal possession of strategically important information that is largely unavailable in written form. These persons are central links in a network of word-of-mouth communication that is one of the most extensive and complex in the body politic, and that normally centers in the national committee chairman.

The chairman of the party in power is assumed to be in continuous communication with the President as party leader and to be responsive to his wishes. The chairman acts not only as a channel through whom the President may convey his wishes to the party leaders but also as an important channel carrying information and party opinion

to the President. He is assisted in this capacity by the party's public relations advisers, its campaign organization specialists, its legal counsel, and its fund raisers. The fund-raising function is particularly vital in every political party; on some policies the chief contributors hold a considerable veto power unless the President and the chairman are prepared to develop alternative sources of funds.[27] In any event, the President usually works closely with the national committee chairman and his associates in preparation for a convention; this is one reason why, in modern times, the renomination of an incumbent President is usually achieved so smoothly that the outcome never seems in doubt.

The temporary chairman at a convention does not appear to hold great power, but his is nonetheless a post of some importance, especially when, as usual in recent decades, he delivers the "keynote address," proclaiming the chief points on which the party will base its appeal to the voters. From the President's point of view, it is obviously important that the keynote address of his party should present the record of his administration in the most favorable terms and give an emphasis consistent with his own preferences. Accordingly, it can be assumed that in the party in power the temporary chairman is selected either by the President or at least under his close supervision.

Since the turn of the century, as indicated in Table 4.1, senators have been chosen for the temporary chairmanship with considerable frequency in both parties, but there has been a recent tendency in both parties to appoint governors as keynote speakers and temporary chairmen. In 1952, General Douglas MacArthur was Republican keynoter but it was not considered appropriate that he serve as presiding officer in a party convention, so a different

---

[27] One conception of how this process operates was recently developed by Henry A. Wallace in presenting his view of how he was denied renomination for Vice President in 1944. (*U. S. News and World Report, op. cit.*)

temporary chairman was appointed. This separation of the tasks was repeated at the Republican convention of 1956.

The permanent chairmanship is by far the most important of the convention offices. The permanent chairman presides while the platform is being adopted, while candidates are being placed in nomination, and while the actual balloting on the nominations takes place. Throughout the period from 1832 to 1892, the post was usually filled by persons of prominence in state and local politics, but also usually not currently holding public office at any level. Since 1896 the permanent chairman, with only one exception, has been a member of the Senate or House of Representatives, and the exception was a former congressman.[28]

Since 1932 the Republicans have regularly appointed their party leader in the House as permanent chairman of their convention. The Democrats have followed the same practice since 1948, when Speaker Sam Rayburn was made permanent chairman. President Truman, in supporting this action, was probably influenced by his personal relationship to Speaker Rayburn and by the threat of a southern revolt, since Rayburn was firmly committed to holding the party together as an effective working organization in both North and South.

A balanced view of the relative power of these three posts—the national committee chairmanship and the temporary and permanent convention chairmanships—is not easily constructed. For some purposes, the posts are obviously much more powerful in

[28] For rosters of the incumbents of the committee and convention chairmanships since the beginnings of the convention system, see Richard C. Bain, *De-* *cisions and Voting Records of the National Party Conventions* (Brookings Institution, forthcoming).

TABLE 4.1. GOVERNMENTAL POSITIONS HELD BY MAJOR-PARTY NATIONAL CONVENTION CHAIRMEN AT THE TIME OF THEIR SERVICE

Governmental Position	Democrats		Republicans	
	1832-1892	1896-1956	1832-1892[a]	1896-1956
TEMPORARY CHAIRMEN				
Cabinet Member	–	–	–	1
Governor	1	4	–	3
U. S. Senator	–	5	1	9
Representative in Congress	1	2	–	1
State Legislator	3	–	–	–
Other or None	11	5	14	2
Total	16	16	15	16
PERMANENT CHAIRMEN				
Cabinet Member	–	–	–	–
Governor	2	–	1	–
U. S. Senator	–	9	1	7
Representative in Congress	2	7	–	8
State Legislator	2	–	–	–
Other or None	10	–	13	1
Total	16	16	15	16

[a] Includes predecessor parties and their conventions; see Chapter 2, footnote 22.

the out-party than in the party holding the White House, where the President is the acknowledged party leader. This aspect of the subject will be discussed further in the next chapter. In the party in power, no President who works at his job as party leader is likely to find his own renomination seriously threatened by opposition from these officials. But he will feel a greater need of cooperation in any campaign to control the succession or to deal with the vice-presidential nomination when the Vice Presidency is unoccupied. So far as other party business is concerned—drafting the platform, planning party strategy generally, and organizing the next election campaign—such matters are most apt to go as the President wishes if he can work with this group as a team and may go very badly indeed if he cannot.

The Congressional Leaders

Very little well-grounded historical information is available concerning the evolution of the posts of party leadership in Congress.[29] There is a substantial literature about the speaker of the House, but it is notably lacking in useful information on how the speakers have been selected or on the extent to which they have been amenable to influence by the party caucuses which, presumably, have selected them almost from the beginning.

The position of president pro tempore of the Senate corresponds in some respects to that of speaker of the House, but during the nineteenth century there were periods when the post was passed from hand to hand even during a single session of Congress. Early in the present century it seems to have taken on more importance as a post of majority leadership, but was superseded

[29] The best account seems to be that of Floyd M. Riddick, *Congressional Procedure* (1941), pp. 65-66, 68, 70, 311; see also W. F. Willoughby, *Principles of Legislative Organization and Administration* (1934), p. 551; D. A. S. Alexander, *History and Procedure of the House of Representatives* (1916), pp. 107ff.

when the position of majority floor leader became established as a separate post. The president pro tem has since come to hold little more than an honorary position, reserved for the dean of the majority in point of service, but with no substantial responsibility for organizing and leading the party in the Senate.

The situation has been complicated by the fact that the Vice President is constitutionally the presiding officer of the Senate, even when his party is not in power in that body. This and many other features of Senate organization have served to delay the development of arrangements for effective leadership in that body. It is only in recent years that the Senate has set up posts of both majority and minority floor leader, flanked by majority and minority whips and an apparatus of secretaries and staffs. Some part of this change may be attributed to the Legislative Reorganization Act of 1946; more of it may be due to the increasing competition between the national parties and the corresponding need for tighter party organization in all of the places where the parties are closely competitive.

The House has always had to be more highly organized than the Senate because of its greater size; but the beginnings of the present positions of majority and minority leadership seem to be lost in the mists of the early nineteenth century. Apparently for some decades the chairman of the Committee on Ways and Means functioned as a majority floor leader in addition to his other duties; after the Civil War the chairman of the Committee on Appropriations also frequently served in that capacity. Organization on the minority side was less fully developed, but the ranking minority members of the major committees often served as floor leaders. Most of the present formal leadership structure in the House has been created since 1918.

President Franklin D. Roosevelt began holding weekly leadership meetings at the White House, apparently in 1937 and perhaps as an aftermath of the Supreme Court fight.[30] This custom served to give greater importance to the congressional leaders of the party holding the Presidency. In Roosevelt's second, third, and fourth terms and with Democratic majorities in Congress, the "Big Four" consisted of the Vice President and the majority leader of the Senate, the speaker and majority leader of the House. During Truman's second term, with the Vice Presidency again occupied and Democratic majorities in both houses, the pattern was again the same. Eisenhower continued the pattern during the first Congress of his administration; this established the custom for the first time under a Republican President. During the Eighty-fourth Congress, with both houses under Democratic control, a larger group of Republican congressional leaders met regularly with the President. The additions included Senator Styles Bridges, who had been president pro tem of the Senate when the Republicans were in the majority; Senator Leverett Saltonstall, minority whip of the Senate; Senator Eugene Millikin, chairman of the Republican conference; Representative Leslie C. Arends, minority whip of the House; and Representative Leo Allen, ranking Re-

publican member of the House Rules Committee.[31] The President also adopted the practice, on occasion, of holding bipartisan meetings to which the Democratic leaders were also invited.[32]

Do the White House leadership meetings ever discuss nominating politics or national convention arrangements? Perhaps not in any systematic or organized way, since the primary purpose of the meetings is to review the legislative program. But the whole effect of such a review is presumably to establish a setting in which the concerns of the party as a whole tend to be brought into some kind of a continuing relationship to the forward planning of legislation, and vice versa. These meetings obviously cannot be unaware that the party's record in Congress will be argued by both sides in the next campaign when the President or his successor in the party nomination will be running for election. This would seem to have an important disciplinary effect for all concerned.[33]

[30] According to Floyd M. Riddick, no records are available concerning the origins of these conferences, but they were started soon after Sam Rayburn became floor leader in the House and represented an effort to improve relations that had been strained by the President's practice of sending controversial proposals to Congress, such as the "court packing plan," with little or no notice and without give-and-take consultation. (Riddick, "Sam Rayburn," in J. T. Salter, ed., *Public Men In and Out of Office*, 1946, pp. 161-62.) Rayburn became floor leader in January 1937, shortly before the episode of the court proposal, which suggests that the regular meetings may have been first held in the late winter or spring of 1937. Farley refers to such a meeting in 1937 on FDR's return to Washington from Warm Springs, where he had gone after sending up the court plan: "On his return to Washington, the President closeted himself with Vice President Garner, Speaker Bankhead, Majority Leader Robinson, and House Leader Rayburn to be brought up to date on the Court fight." (James A. Farley, *op. cit.*, p. 78.) When the Committee on Political Parties was writing its report in 1950, it had to content itself with referring to these meetings as having been going on "for more than ten years now." See American Political Science Association, *Toward a More Responsible Two-Party System* (1950), pp. 57-58.

[31] Based on information supplied at the time by the offices of Senator William F. Knowland and Representative Joseph W. Martin, Jr.

[32] President Eisenhower has been generally credited with developing congressional briefings for the advance presentation of his legislative recommendations more fully than any of his predecessors, particularly in connection with the messages that go up at the beginning of each session. See Richard E. Neustadt, "Presidency and Legislation: Planning the President's Program," *American Political Science Review*, Vol. 49 (Dec. 1955), pp. 980-1021.

[33] Republican national committee Chairman Thruston B. Morton stated, in response to a question when addressing the National Press Club on June 3, 1959, that he regularly attended the President's weekly meetings with the Republican congressional leaders. He said that he also had a standing invitation to attend Cabinet meetings, receiving the agenda paper in advance and deciding for himself whether it would be worthwhile to attend. He commented that the meetings with the leaders were more "political" and therefore of more interest to him; Cabinet sessions, by comparison, he found not very exciting.

Morton's entire performance on that occasion contained many clues to the closeness of his previous relationships with the President and the White House staff while serving from 1953 to 1956 as Assistant Secretary of State for Congressional Relations, thereby clarifying the background of his selection to serve as national committee chairman while also serving as a senator from Kentucky. The subjects to which he principally addressed himself were also a good demonstration of the kind of in-

The congressional leaders of the party that holds the White House are apt to have a personal interest in presidential nominating and election politics, for some of them may be potential candidates, and in any case they are likely to be among the leaders in the party's national convention. During the winter of 1955-1956, Senate Minority Leader William F. Knowland was an announced candidate for the Republican presidential nomination in the event that President Eisenhower should decide not to run. It was clear that Knowland was not the President's choice as his successor and that he was prepared to enter an open contest even if the President gave his support to some other candidate. When the President announced his availability, Knowland promptly withdrew and announced that he would support Eisenhower. In recent decades, congressional leaders of the party in power have seldom shown signs of being prepared to contest the succession; and seemingly never in recent decades has an incumbent President supported one of the congressional leaders for the nomination to succeed him.

In 1948, 1952, and 1956, as already noted, Joseph W. Martin, Jr., and Sam Rayburn, the top party leaders in the House, were the permanent chairmen of their respective national conventions. By 1956 this arrangement had apparently been accepted as a custom in both parties. The task of presiding officer during the critical period of a convention is obviously one requiring parliamentary skills of the highest order. Training in the House of Representatives, with its many members and the close similarity of its basic rules to those of the convention, may well be the best available preparation.

There are nonetheless two important limitations in the choice of a convention's permanent chairman: he should not oc-cupy a position elsewhere that would be incompatible with that post, and he should not himself be a candidate for either of the nominations. The positions of speaker and minority leader do not seem in any way incompatible with service as convention chairman; on the contrary, it could be argued that there is a certain affinity that makes the combination especially appropriate. If this is so, however, it has only recently been recognized, and for a reason probably growing out of the second limitation just mentioned. Speakers of the House of Representatives in the past have been figures too powerful to be overlooked in the perennial quest for presidential candidates; and every minority leader was a potential speaker. The party leaders in the House have often been mentioned as possible candidates, even though they have seldom polled any votes in the convention.

The comparatively recent custom of ordinarily choosing the House leaders as permanent chairmen could therefore be upset if at any future time one of those leaders should become a candidate for the nomination. The Republican leader who replaced Martin in 1959, Charles A. Halleck of Indiana, has not yet been tested on this issue. Sam Rayburn has repeatedly quelled presidential boomlets in his own favor, as did Martin during the years of his incumbency. The same factors that made them unavailable for the presidential or vice-presidential nominations may well be pertinent with their successors for many years ahead. If this proves to be true, candidacies such as those of Champ Clark in 1912 and John Nance Garner in 1932 may not occur often in the future.[34]

---

tegration that is always needed between current presidential and congressional concerns and the requirements of the next oncoming national election. See *New York Times,* June 4, 1959 (but not for the contents of the previous paragraph, since Morton's impromptu responses attracted little press interest).

[34] The factors referred to above as limiting availability would seem to include the following points. First, members of the House of Representatives are rarely allowed to come within striking distance of the speakership or minority leadership until after long service in the House. Martin had served 14 years and Rayburn 27 before they reached the highest posts; Halleck had served 24 years. The normal consequence is that the party leaders in the House come from safe districts if not from safe states, which in itself is adverse to availability for the presidential nominations.

Secondly, the disciplines of the House as a com-

Factional Candidates

Factional contests for the nomination of the party in power may arise under several different sets of circumstances: (1) when dissatisfaction with an incumbent President is so great that there is overt opposition to his renomination, (2) when there is factional opposition to an attempt by the President to control the nomination of a successor, (3) when the President is retiring but is unwilling or unable to deal effectively with the succession, with the result that the convention is more or less open. Whichever the type of case, the existence of an opposing faction does not always produce a contest, for the scarcity of available candidates is a greater limitation than any lack of dissatisfied groups. Factions with some kind of a continuing interest-group basis can suffer defeat repeatedly and live on to fight another day. This is much less true of candidates, who depreciate rapidly after even a single defeat.

---

munity militate against the kind of popular appeal that would seem to be essential in running for a presidential nomination. For the leader in the House, the emphasis is on regularity, and particularly on regularity as measured within the confines of each party's membership in the House. This is quite a different kind of a thing from regularity in the national party, although the two types of regularity may be coming closer together. Accordingly, party leaders in the House are unlikely to be considered except in a stalemate, such as the situation that led to James A. Garfield's nomination and election. Garfield had been a floor leader, although he had not reached the speakership; but convention stalemates and compromise nominations of the Garfield type are becoming increasingly rare.

Third, for all of these reasons, the type that emerges as speaker or minority leader is a radically different type from that shown by experience to be most highly eligible for a first-time presidential nomination—the glamorous and rapidly rising younger executive between 50 and 55 years of age with skill as a vote-getter in competitive two-party situations.

The leaders of the House of Representatives have good reason for pride of place in their own positions; they will have even more reason if the custom of regularly giving them the permanent chairmanships at the conventions becomes solidified in both parties. Paradoxical as it may seem, by abandoning presidential ambitions that were increasingly unrealistic, the party leaders in the House have been in a position to add substantially to their already considerable political power.

Since 1896 very few potential factional candidates have been willing to take on an all-out contest for the party nomination against the entrenched power of an incumbent President. The outstanding case is that of the party-splitting fight between Theodore Roosevelt and President William Howard Taft in 1912. In this case Roosevelt was the factional candidate, notwithstanding his eminence as a former President. Not quite so resounding was the contest between Senator Richard B. Russell and President Harry S. Truman for the Democratic nomination in 1948. Russell had little reason to hope for victory, but was prepared to lead a factional movement as a demonstration of southern solidarity in resisting Truman's civil rights position. The demonstration was impressive, and prepared the way for the third-party movement that followed.

The outstanding examples since 1896 of presidential campaigns to nominate a successor are those mounted by Theodore Roosevelt in 1908 and by Harry S. Truman in 1952. Factional opposition to the nomination of William Howard Taft in 1908 was latent in the situation, but the opposition found no outstanding candidate to provide a rallying point. In the end Roosevelt secured Taft's nomination with little trouble. Truman in 1952 had difficulty in finding a suitable and willing candidate to back; strong factional movements developed meanwhile behind Senators Estes Kefauver and Richard B. Russell.

The retiring Presidents since 1896 who made no overt effort to influence the succession have included Woodrow Wilson in 1920 and Calvin Coolidge in 1928. The result in 1920 was an open convention in which a Cabinet member, a former Cabinet member, and the incumbent governors of New York and Ohio were the main contenders, with Governor James M. Cox of Ohio winning the nomination. In 1928 the nomination of a recent Cabinet member, Herbert Hoover, was a foregone conclusion, although there was opposition and several other candidates received votes.

These cases contain recurring features that may be more than coincidental. It is noteworthy that where an incumbent President was providing strong party leadership in a nominating situation, all the main dissident factional candidates, except Theodore Roosevelt in 1912, were senators. It will also be recalled from an earlier section of the chapter that in most of the cases where incumbent Presidents had trouble with vice-presidential nominations, the opposition was usually led from the Senate and the nomination of a senator was a frequent result. On the other hand, incumbent governors, particularly those of the larger two-party states, have undoubtedly been frequent major allies of the incumbent Presidents who were seeking renomination or seeking to control the succession. Here the evidence is mainly negative; had the situation been otherwise, the usually harmonious course of nominating procedures in the party in power would have been much more often disturbed. But no governor of the President's party has appeared since 1896 as a factional candidate opposing the President or his choice. Governors and Cabinet members have been prominent as candidates in factional nominating contests in the party in power only in 1920, 1928, and 1952, when the President was not taking a strong position. And in 1952, Governor Stevenson made it a point to clear with President Truman before he finally agreed to accept the nomination.[35]

The sources of factional support for dissident candidacies in a party in power have followed no single pattern, but provide examples of most of the major types of factionalism within the national parties. The Bull Moose revolt of 1912 was an expression of the feuding between "Progressive" and "Old Guard" elements that had been going on for more than a decade within the Republican party. The Russell candidacies of 1948 and 1952 and the Dixiecrat revolt of 1948 were expressions of the sectional dissidence of the South. Midwestern agri-culture, finding expression as an interest group largely through its Republican representation in the Senate, was the source of most of the overt opposition to the Hoover nomination in 1928, and produced the Republican vice-presidential nominations of both 1924 and 1928. So far, neither big business nor big labor has visibly backed a minority candidate for the presidential nomination in a party in power, although both have helped in backing majority candidates. The support of business as an interest group was important to Herbert Hoover in securing the Republican nomination in 1928. Organized labor evidently provided a significant part of Henry Wallace's support in fighting for a second Democratic vice-presidential nomination in 1944, but labor also helped nominate Truman for Vice President instead in that year, Truman for President in 1948, and Stevenson for President in 1952.

The relative impotence of the minority candidates and dissident factions in the nominating procedure of the party in power is the main conclusion to be drawn from this review, yet their impotence is indeed relative rather than absolute. They undoubtedly retain a kind of veto power, under some circumstances, against other candidates and the policy preferences of other party leaders.[36]

Leadership Integration in the Party in Power

Unlike the political parties in major party systems abroad, the American national parties have been almost unique in their ability to go for long periods of time without any single continuing inner circle of central importance and governing power. Inner groups have always existed in the American parties, usually several of them, but the fact that they have been several

[35] Truman, op. cit., Vol. 2, p. 496.

[36] The Barkley candidacy was vetoed by organized labor in 1952, and the veto was effective because of Barkley's own reaction, if not for other reasons. See Chapter 5, section on Interest Groups and Their Leaders.

rather than one has been a basic characteristic of the system. This has been true for considerable periods even for the party in power when engaged in the tasks of government.

During most of the period from 1832 to 1892, in fact, the main inner groups of either party when in power consisted of the President and his immediate administrative and political associates of the same faction; the congressional leaders of the dominant faction of the party in Congress; the national committee chairman and his principal associates in control of the arrangements for the next national convention; and the leaders of the several major factions of the party in the country at large, centering mainly in the state party bosses of the major states. These groups all had a common interest in the election of the next presidential nominee of their party, and in the future of the party generally; but their impulse to work together was weak. Not one of the groups just named was necessarily prepared to admit or recognize the ascendancy of any other group as a matter of right, least of all in connection with matters pertaining to the next nomination.

The most important change affecting the nominating process since 1896 in the party in power has been the rising position of the Presidency and the increased recognition accorded the President as party leader. Other circles of influence continue to exist; but the group consisting of the President and his immediate associates has become the innermost inner circle; the others can now be regarded as a loose constellation of groups surrounding the White House as the center of power. As party leader, the President is in the most strategic position to deal with the next nomination. If available himself for a second nomination, this is usually assumed to settle the matter; and if another nominee must be found, there seems a general disposition to accord the President a right, even a duty, to advise the party—although if he were to try to dictate an unpopular choice there might be a quick rebellion.

A second important change that has taken place since 1896 has been in the status of the Vice Presidency and its relationship to other posts of leadership. This change has some importance for the presidential nominating process of the in-party, since it has brought the Vice President clearly within range of a possible presidential nomination when the succession is open. The change has been even more important for the vice-presidential nominating process itself. Before 1896, no first-term Vice President had ever been renominated in a party convention to succeed himself in the Vice Presidency, while since 1896, no first-term Vice President except Henry Wallace has failed of renomination. In the case of Henry Wallace, a third-term President took away, with some difficulty, what he had previously given with great difficulty. The Vice Presidents have become much more closely associated than formerly with the Presidents with whom they are elected, hold an office of increasing prestige and influence, and are increasingly used and useful. The Vice Presidency is still uniquely isolated in its constitutional status, but it has undoubtedly moved from an outfield to an inner position among the several power centers of the party in power.

Changes of lesser importance, but worthy of note, have overtaken the Cabinet and the relationship of its members to the President. Presidents no longer feel compelled, as Lincoln did, to tolerate openly dissident Cabinet members, and almost never appoint leaders of opposing factions to the Cabinet in the first place. Of late years the Cabinet members have been increasing their political activities as adherents and lieutenants of the President, and as party spokesmen on matters of public policy in their respective fields. To the extent that this development is occurring, it could be expected to strengthen the President in his political role as party leader, and to give him increasing resources through which to work.

Striking changes have taken place in the roles of the national committee and convention officers, and in their relationship to the President. For many decades after the creation of the first national committee chairmanship in 1848, the chairman was sometimes a factional leader in his own right, sometimes a neutral point of communication among factions, but only rarely the accredited agent of a fully accepted party leader. He did not necessarily maintain his office at the nation's capital, was likely to be chosen primarily for his connections as a fund-raiser, and was only intermittently in communication with the President. All this is changed in a situation in which the in-party national chairman is chosen by the President, occupies a full-time position in command of the party headquarters in Washington, and operates essentially as a member of the President's top political staff, with clearly defined functions for which he reports directly to the President in the latter's capacity as party leader.

Changes in the roles of the in-party convention officers are not as easy to document, but have undoubtedly moved in the direction of a firmer guardianship of the party's long-term interests, as distinguished from direct involvement in short-range factional conflict. This has been facilitated, it would seem, by a growing frank recognition of the President's role as party leader in the practices of in-party conventions. It now seems to be accepted that while the convention is in session, the President has the right to be informed, to give advice, and, on occasion, to take action through his own agents or by sending messages to it. To some degree, this existed in the conventions of the earlier period, but not overtly, and there was often a feeling that any presidential interference in the convention was illegitimate.

Several Presidents in modern times have done much to change this feeling: Woodrow Wilson by his open recognition of the role of party leader as one of honor and legitimacy; and Franklin D. Roosevelt, Harry S. Truman, and Dwight D. Eisenhower by their successive appearances at the conventions to receive nominations or to approve the nominations that have been made. On such an appearance, the chairman has found it a distinguished honor to introduce the President of the United States and to appropriate his prestige unto his political party. Nothing could be more symbolic of the present-day relationship between the President and the managers of an in-party convention.

The shifting relationships between the President and the congressional leaders of his party are in some respects the most interesting and significant of all. The inner circles of each party in the Senate and House of Representatives have undoubtedly been the party inner circles of greatest longevity and frequently of greatest power. For generations, they treated as equals— or more—with the Presidents on matters of legislative policy. They also undoubtedly had much influence on the nominations, even in the party holding the White House, although they were usually challenged and often defeated by other centers of power more firmly based in the state politics of the major states and regions. After 1896, as the Presidents came more firmly into control of the conventions of their own party, the congressional leaders also began to become more prominent as convention officers and direct participants in the convention proceedings. This may have been something of an offsetting response to the growing power of the Presidency.

Within the last twenty years, however, the relationship between the President and the congressional leaders of his party has become increasingly close. The calling of regular meetings *at the White House* to discuss the legislative program is an important symbolic recognition of the President's role as party leader for legislation as well as for other matters. (This custom was unknown in the days of Theodore Roosevelt and Woodrow Wilson, although they asserted the legislative prerogatives of the President as party leader more vigorously than any of their predecessors.) The meetings inevitably establish a close mutual relationship between the President and the congressional leaders in building the program and the record on which the party will nominate and campaign.

The practice of using the party leader in the House as the permanent chairman at the convention merely adds the capstone to this structure of relationships. Incumbent Presidents seeking renomination or seeking to control the nomination of a successor will no longer be in a position to select (or at least veto the selection of) the convention's top officer; he will have been picked, probably some years earlier, by the party caucus in the House of Representatives. At the same time, the party leader in the House, even though almost sure of appointment to the convention chairmanship, is not likely to become so powerful that he can disregard the President's wishes or openly defy the presidential wing of the party. The interaction seems rather strikingly symbolic of the forces that appear to be compelling the presidential and congressional wings of each party to work more closely together—even if sometimes reluctantly.

Aside from the top-ranking public and party officeholders of the party in power, there are numerous other party leaders who hold no national public or party office. Many of these are too powerful in the total party structure to overlook, but they form no single or cohesive group. In the past, they have included a variety of types: such widely different men as Thurlow Weed, Horace Greeley, and David B. Hill; the state bosses of the major states and the city bosses of the big-city machines; the former Presidents and former presidential candidates who became elder statesmen within their respective parties; the past and future candidates for the party nominations who had retained positions of active factional leadership; and the governors of major

states who were elected on the party ticket.

The sheer number and variety of these persons of possible influence has the effect of lessening the importance of each. In recent times, however, as organized labor has become predominantly attached to the Democratic party, and big business to the Republican, more definitely organized political leadership groups may arise outside the governmental and party structure, and might be capable of substantially influencing the behavior of the respective parties. Such a development for the future still remains largely speculative, and there is so far little clear evidence of positive influence on the presidential and vice-presidential nominations of the party in power, unlike the somewhat different situations in the party out of power.

Interest groups, minority factions, and individual political leaders can of course lobby the President and his associates to the extent that they can secure access for the purpose. In some instances they can doubtless threaten sanctions that may affect presidential and party behavior. But the record of the last sixty years shows few signs of effective interference with the nominating process when the President is seeking his own renomination. Even the nomination of a successor is largely under the President's control if he is in health, is prepared to devote himself to the leadership of his party, and is able to hold together the top leaders with whom it has become normal to maintain close working relations. Apparently either major party, when in power, has acquired the capacity to become a rather tightly-knit organization centering in the President, insofar as questions are at stake that would affect party survival and success in the oncoming presidential elections. From the viewpoint of that central group, every nominating decision is exactly such a question.

5

Leadership Centers of the Party Out of Power

EVEN MORE THAN the party holding the Presidency, the party out of power has its leadership scattered among a number of centers of influence, since there is no President to act as Chief with all the apparatus of the White House at his command. The position of titular leader is worth examining with some care, but under the present order of things it is not the central post in the out-party.[1] For certain limited purposes, the national committee chairman of the out-party can be thought of as occupying the central post, though the chairman has no definite responsibility for preparing the next nominations or for leading the party as an opposition in the government. The party leaders in the Senate and House do have that responsibility, but they are not often thought of as centers of leadership in other party matters, although they may sometimes act as such. Other members of Congress, governors, big-city mayors, state party officials, interest-group leaders, and many people of other types have significant leadership roles of one kind or another in the party out of power.

The relationships among the various centers of leadership in the out-party thus form a bewildering pattern, and one that is constantly changing in at least its minor features. Customs and usages are much more fluid than in the in-party, both in the con-

trol of the party machinery and in dealing with the problems of the succession. Candidates for the out-party nominations seemingly may come from almost any center of political activity; and any candidate who is strongly backed becomes for the time being, at least, a center of leadership. At the same time, there are other centers of leadership that have become somewhat institutionalized and relatively stable. Some of these, notably the party posts in Congress, are potential sources of presidential candidates; but even when this is not the case, all the major centers of party leadership may be expected to exert influence on the affairs of the party convention. A review of the various centers of out-party leadership may thus assist in gaining insight into the nominating process, even if the review raises more questions than it settles in attempting to assess the roles of the various participants.

Titular Leaders and Their Associates

The titular leader of the party out of power occupies no formal position in either the party hierarchy or the government. Nevertheless, he is the only one whose place in the out-party even faintly resembles that of the President in the party in power. The accumulation of custom and precedent for the out-party titular leadership takes on a corresponding importance.

In modern times, six defeated major-party candidates for President have made

[1] Although incumbent Presidents are sometimes referred to as "titular leaders" of their parties, the leadership role of a President under modern conditions is so different from that of the defeated candidate that for the sake of clarity the term "titular leader" throughout this book is confined to the defeated candidate.

substantial efforts to secure renomination at the next convention: Grover Cleveland (D), William Jennings Bryan (D), Alfred E. Smith (D), Wendell L. Willkie (R), Thomas E. Dewey (R), and Adlai E. Stevenson (D). The record of the titular leadership can be read most conveniently in the activities, experiences, and status of these men. In addition, however, some account must be taken of the record of the other defeated candidates from Bryan onward, who did not try for a second nomination.

The Record
of the Titular Leaders

Grover Cleveland left office as a defeated one-term President in 1889. He took up residence in New York City and resumed the private practice of law; not rich, he needed a suitable source of income. As an ex-President, he maintained a position of dignity, but he accepted many speaking engagements in which he continued to advocate the program of tariff reduction on which he had lost the election of 1888. He received many letters from friends and supporters throughout the United States, and made it a practice to answer all of them.[2] His position on the tariff was vindicated in the congressional elections of 1890, and it became increasingly apparent that he could become a strong candidate for the nomination in 1892.

Four main obstacles stood between Cleveland and a third presidential nomination. One was opposition in his own state of New York from Democratic Governor David B. Hill and the state party organization. A "snap" state convention was held on February 22, 1892, and elected an anti-Cleveland, pro-Hill delegation to the national convention. Another was the anti-Cleveland attitude of the national committee chairman, Calvin S. Brice, who predicted in April 1892 that Cleveland could

not obtain the necessary two thirds vote at the convention.[3] The two thirds rule itself, which had prevented Van Buren's renomination, was the third obvious obstacle. Finally, there was the unbroken practice of the two major parties since the origins of the convention system, in which no defeated presidential candidate of either had ever been renominated.

Cleveland's assets, on the other hand, included his record of previous success in the Presidency, the narrowness of his previous defeat (with an actual plurality in the popular vote), his great popular following, and the group of friends who organized to conduct his preconvention campaign under the skillful leadership of the wealthy William C. Whitney.[4] He was renominated on the first ballot by a bare two thirds majority and without the vote of New York. The Cleveland campaign managers had made no objection to the seating of the "regular" New York delegation—even though the "anti-Snappers" had sent a contesting delegation—and enough party harmony was eventually restored in New York so that Cleveland carried the state. He won the election, for his second term in the Presidency.

The circumstances under which William Jennings Bryan won the Democratic nomination of 1896 have been often related and are a sufficiently fabulous tale. Even more peculiar, however, is the fact that Bryan easily secured renomination in 1900 and again in 1908 in a party that still retained the two thirds rule. The precedent set by Cleveland's third nomination was doubtless helpful. Far more important, probably, was the broad fact that the Democratic party had been driven into a minority position in the nation with the solidification of one-party Republican regimes in most of the northern states. In state party systems where one party is typically dominant, the minor-

[2] Robert McElroy, *Grover Cleveland: The Man and the Statesman* (1923), Vol. 1, p. 313.

[3] Ralph M. Goldman, "Party Chairmen and Party Faction, 1789-1900," unpublished doctoral dissertation, University of Chicago, 1951, p. 563.
[4] *Ibid.*, pp. 563-66.

ity party often renominates its defeated candidates for governor. It is most likely to do so when it is short of potential candidates but is still hopeful of making a real fight. Bryan seems to be the only example of this phenomenon at the national level; he occupied the titular leadership at a time when the party was rarely able to elect governors outside the southern and border states. The two renominations were in part simply the result of his own availability and a lack of other outstanding candidates.

Bryan's continued availability, however, was no accident. As a young congressman, 1891-1895, he developed an interest in political activity that he never abandoned, whatever the current state of his political fortunes. For thirty years he was the most sought-after lecturer on the Chautauqua platforms of the period; this was a way of life that provided not only income, but also a perpetual rejuvenation of his local political contacts throughout the country, his personal knowledge of the course of sentiment, and his immense popular following. After his defeat in 1896, he retained a close grip on the party organization and left no doubt concerning his eagerness to accept renomination in 1900. He served briefly during the Spanish-American war, though without being given any opportunity for service under fire, and was influential with Democratic senators in the ratification of the peace treaty in 1899. After his defeat in 1900, he founded the *Commoner,* a weekly newspaper that kept his name and his views before the people. In 1904, he could not control the convention but was powerful nonetheless in platform matters. In 1908, he was again nominated. In 1912, he contributed significantly to Wilson's nomination; and he was still a figure in Democratic party affairs at the national convention of 1924, the last before his death.

For fifteen years, from 1913 to 1928, the post of out-party leadership in either party was almost completely vacant except during election campaigns. The precedents established by Cleveland and Bryan were not highly regarded in the Republican party when it left office in 1913. As a part of its continuing attack on Bryanism, the party had spent sixteen years in discrediting the notion that an out-party leader should be given any recognition. As an ex-President, however, William Howard Taft was influential in party matters between 1913 and 1916, particularly with the Old Guard Republicans who had gone down to defeat with him. His defeat—and Theodore Roosevelt's—had been so severe that there was no possibility of either of them being renominated, but in some respects this increased the capabilities of both men for influence by discouraging any renewal of their intra-party battle. Taft took an active part in the negotiations that led to the choice of Charles Evans Hughes as the next nominee.[5]

Hughes, in turn, adhered to what had become the standard Republican doctrine in rejecting any suggestion of renomination after his own narrow defeat in 1916. Furthermore, he specifically declined to act as a party leader, ridiculing the idea that a defeated candidate could successfully lead his party. His attitude apparently also reflected a deep reluctance to assume the burdens of another campaign—or of the White House if he should win. His contributions to the war effort of World War I were as a private citizen and not as spokesman for the opposition party. He refused to deliver the keynote address at the 1920 Republican convention or to allow his name to come before it, although he is said to have continued to be the first choice of the senatorial group that eventually succeeded in pushing forward the Harding candidacy.[6] Had he accepted renomination in 1920, it seems probable that he would have been elected, and much history might have been different.

[5] Henry F. Pringle, *The Life and Times of William Howard Taft* (1939), Vol. 2, pp. 856-57, 866, 870, 884-85, 890-92.
[6] Merlo J. Pusey, *Charles Evans Hughes* (1951), Vol. 1, 367-68, 403.

James M. Cox, the forty-fourth ballot nominee of the Democrats in 1920, was the first inheritor of the Bryan tradition in his party, but apparently accepted no personal responsibility for dealing with the problems of party reconstruction in defeat. He resolved "never again to seek or to accept a public office," and returned to newspaper publishing.[7] His role as titular leader was so minimal that it evidently seemed unworthy of mention in the following passage by Cordell Hull, who was national committee chairman from 1921 to 1924:

With the Party out of power and in the minority in both Houses of Congress, whoever occupied the office of chairman of the National Committee was in the highest position of Democratic Party leadership in the nation. This post, which at all times ranks near the top in a Party hierarchy, is at the very top when a Party is in the minority.[8]

Cox's own memoirs contain no reference to any significant action as titular leader until the point of breakdown had arrived at the 1924 convention. He then went to New York, and gave out the following statement:

I have come to New York at the urgent request of prominent members of the party, who have expressed to me the belief that a trying emergency has arisen and that the offices of the titular leader of the Democracy should be extended with a view to bring about harmony.[9]

Cox took credit for leadership in the compromise decision to nominate John W. Davis, while Hull reported that he (Hull) took no part other than by declining to be a compromise candidate himself.[10]

[7] James M. Cox, *Journey Through My Years* (1946), p. 285.
[8] *The Memoirs of Cordell Hull* (1948), Vol. 1, p. 113.
Hull had lost his seat in Congress in the Republican sweep of 1920. He served actively and effectively as national committee chairman until 1924, raising funds to meet a deficit of $300,000, leading the mid-term congressional campaign, organizing party clubs on a dues-paying basis, and putting up his own war bonds as collateral when a bank loan was necessary to meet the committee payroll. See *Ibid.*, pp. 114, 116.
[9] James M. Cox, *op. cit.*, p. 328.
[10] Hull, *op. cit.*, p. 122.

The defeat of Davis in 1924 was the most crushing suffered by any Democratic party nominee in the history of the party; the party was quiescent at the national level for some time thereafter. Davis did little as titular leader. His national committee chairman, an obscure West Virginian named C. L. Shaver, remained in office for the ensuing four years, during which time the amount of national organizing activity in the Democratic party probably fell to the lowest level since the period 1904-1908. The national committee office was moved from Washington, where it had functioned under Hull, to New York, and ran along at a low minimum level.

Alfred E. Smith, when he was defeated for the Presidency in 1928, was the incumbent governor of New York. His term expired at the end of that year and he resumed his residence in New York City. He was in need of an income-producing private occupation, and was soon elected to many boards of directors. Shortly after the 1928 election, he stated that he would never again run for public office; and this at the time was generally accepted as his intention. His wealthy friend John J. Raskob, however, continued to serve as chairman of the Democratic national committee from 1928 to 1932.

The 1928 campaign had ended with a party deficit estimated at $1,600,000. In January 1929, Smith made a radio speech in which he appealed for funds to lift the deficit, and over $100,000 came in immediately. Sales of 30,000 copies of Smith's campaign speeches brought in another $125,000, and, with further efforts by Raskob, W. F. Kenny, and other fund-raisers, the deficit was cut to $350,000 by May 1929. Smith was hailed as party leader after his successful fund appeal, but Franklin D. Roosevelt, the newly elected governor of New York, declined comment.

The establishment of a permanent headquarters in Washington for the national committee was discussed in April 1929, and it was agreed that Jouett Shouse would be in charge of the headquarters as chairman of an executive committee of the national committee. In June, Charles Michelson was retained as publicity director for the committee. Smith apparently participated actively in all of these arrangements. In August 1929 he became head of the company organized to build the Empire State Building, and thereafter was extremely busy with his new job, struggling to save a venture that encountered many difficulties after the onset of the depression. He traveled little outside the state, although he continued active in New York City politics. In September 1930, at the state party convention, he nominated Franklin D. Roosevelt for a second two-year term as governor, and at the end of October he made a national radio address under the auspices of the national committee on the program of the Democratic party, urging the election of a Democratic Congress.

Roosevelt, after his second election as governor in 1930, immediately came into increasing prominence as the most likely Democratic candidate for the next presidential race. Smith made no public comment on this prospect, and throughout 1931 there were frequent news stories indicating friction between the erstwhile friends and even more so between the camps of their supporters. Economic conditions were steadily deteriorating and prospects for a Democratic victory in 1932 were correspondingly improving. Toward the end of 1931 both Roosevelt and Smith were under increasing pressure to become open candidates; both postponed an open decision. Meanwhile, many of the previous Smith supporters had already made commitments to Roosevelt, on the assumption, which Smith himself is reported to have confirmed—probably as late as after the election of 1930—that he would not be available.[11] Roosevelt finally announced in late January 1932 and Smith about two weeks later,

after delegates favoring both had been entered in the New Hampshire primary. Roosevelt carried that primary, but Smith won in primaries or state conventions in Massachusetts, Rhode Island, Connecticut, and New Jersey. Roosevelt carried the Pennsylvania primary; Roosevelt and Smith were both defeated in California by John N. Garner. But Roosevelt entered the convention with well over a majority of the delegates and was nominated, under the two thirds rule, on the fourth ballot. Smith refused to comment and left the convention before Roosevelt arrived to deliver his speech of acceptance.

The defeated Republican candidates of 1932 and 1936, Hoover and Landon, made no strong effort to challenge their party's tradition against renomination, but both were undoubtedly more active as party leaders than their last previous Republican counterparts, Taft and Hughes. Hoover in his defeat retained the ardent loyalties of a hard core of personal and partisan followers; he was an active party spokesman in denouncing the policies of the Roosevelt administration, and received an ovation at the Republican convention of 1936.[12] Landon after 1936 retained greater control of the party machinery than Hoover had, took an active part in strengthening the Republican national committee headquarters, and devoted much effort and travel to maintaining the party following and organization throughout the country.[13] At the end of

---

[11] James A. Farley, *Behind the Ballots* (1938), pp. 59-62, 77-78, and *Jim Farley's Story* (1948), p. 6; Edward J. Flynn, *You're the Boss* (1947), pp. 85-86.

[12] "Discussed but never taken too seriously was the prospect that . . . Hoover . . . might still sweep the convention and be drafted at the last minute. Hoover carefully kept a discreet silence on this subject, maintaining always that he was not a candidate but never denying that he would accept the nomination in the remote and outside chance that it would be offered to him." Malcolm Moos, *The Republicans* (1956), pp. 396-97.

[13] According to Eugene H. Roseboom, the Republicans spent $9,000,000 in the campaign of 1936 and ended with a budget "badly out of balance." He mentions no dollar figure for the deficit. (Roseboom, *A History of Presidential Elections*, 1957, pp. 453-54.)

The more obvious sources have been searched for information on Republican campaign deficits since 1936, and what the respective titular leaders did about them, without finding much information of

1937 he took himself out of the running for 1940; by his own account, his sole purpose was to eliminate controversy that would otherwise impair his ability to serve the party.[14] He was a Kansas delegate at the 1940 convention, where he was thought to favor the nomination of Thomas E. Dewey, but promptly commented favorably on the Willkie nomination after it was made.

Wendell Willkie, the defeated Republican candidate of 1940, was both leader and instrument of a group of Republicans who were actively intent upon the reorientation of their party, and who had no intention of dropping the effort even in defeat. Willkie resumed the practice of law in New York in 1941 and became board chairman of 20th Century-Fox Film Corporation in 1942, but continued throughout to give most of his time to public affairs. His claims to recognition as party leader were actively opposed by the isolationist wing of the party and by some of its congressional leaders. In a Lincoln Day address in 1941, Senator Robert A. Taft declared flatly that Willkie "does not and cannot speak for the Republican party," and that there is "no justification in precedent or principle for the view that a defeated candidate for President is the titular leader of the party."[15] But Willkie was recognized as party leader nonetheless at a national committee meeting soon after, continued to be so recognized by many party officials during 1941 and 1942, and made a vigorous effort to assert the prerogatives of the position. He was especially concerned with New York State politics early in 1942, and opposed the nomination of Thomas E. Dewey for governor on the ground that Dewey was too isolationist. But he took little part in the mid-term campaigns of that year, choosing instead to make his famous "One World" tour around the world in a semiofficial status in September and October 1942.

In 1943, Willkie began actively preparing to seek the nomination in 1944, but was ever more clearly the leader of a faction within the party rather than of the party as a whole. Harold E. Stassen and John W. Bricker also announced as candidates. Dewey was the leading preference of Republicans in the Gallup poll, but he himself repeatedly stated that he would not run, and he attempted to take his name out of the Wisconsin primary in February 1944. The delegate-candidates favoring Dewey ignored his request and were elected in April, giving Willkie, who had stumped the state, a severe defeat. At that point Willkie abandoned his candidacy, after the most strenuous effort made up to that time by any Republican titular leader. He died on October 8, 1944, at the age of 52.

As a titular leader of the opposition party, Willkie was unique in the character and extent of the recognition he was accorded by the incumbent President, Franklin D. Roosevelt. Roosevelt, who actively sought bipartisan support for the conduct of the war, conferred with Willkie at the White House repeatedly, and facilitated his foreign tour in 1942. Willkie, in turn, gave vigorous support to the war effort and to Roosevelt's foreign policy. Undoubtedly this was one of Willkie's main handicaps in seeking his second nomination; the midwestern—largely isolationist—wing of the party, which had accepted his original nomination in part because of his German ancestry and Indiana origins, was the faction most violently opposed to his renomination in 1944, as indicated by the Wisconsin vote. Meanwhile, Willkie's own power base in New York, city and state, had been undermined by the impressive record and rising star of Thomas E. Dewey.

Dewey, after his own defeat in 1944, became the second titular leader of the Republican party actively to seek renomination. He was still firmly established in pub-

---

value. Inquiries have also been made at the Republican national committee. It has apparently been a standing policy of the party not to publicize its financial problems, unlike the opposite policy of the Democrats.

[14] *New York Times*, Dec. 11, 1937.
[15] *Newsweek*, Vol. 17 (Feb. 24, 1941), p. 17.

lic office (unlike Cleveland, Bryan, Smith, and Willkie) as governor of New York, where the state constitution had been amended in 1938 to provide a four-year term, staggered against the presidential term and without limit on re-election for successive terms.

Dewey's first problem in 1946 was to be re-elected to the governorship as a base for a try at the Presidency. Undue emphasis on presidential ambitions was obviously not likely to be helpful in his 1946 campaign. Nevertheless, he was actively involved in the reorganization of national party affairs after his defeat in 1944, and in spite of opposition, especially by supporters of Senator Taft, he was given some recognition as titular leader. In February 1945, Dewey was the featured speaker at a congressional Lincoln Day dinner in Washington. But the Republican congressional leadership gained in importance after Roosevelt's death in 1945 and Truman's accession to the Presidency, and in April 1946, Congressman Carroll Reece of the Taft camp was elected national committee chairman, replacing Dewey's associate, Herbert Brownell, Jr. Dewey won re-election as governor in November 1946, but the Republicans won control of Congress, and the position of their congressional leaders was thus still further strengthened. At the end of 1946, however, members of the national committee were said to favor Dewey, Taft, Bricker, and Stassen for the next nomination in that order.[16]

Throughout 1947 there was much jockeying for position by potential contenders for the next Republican nomination. Stassen opened headquarters in Washington in January 1947 and was continuously available. Taft was steadily gaining in eminence, but Senator John W. Bricker of Ohio was also frequently mentioned. Ohio Republicans eventually gave Taft their support and he announced his candidacy in October 1947. Governor Earl Warren of California

announced in November, but undertook little active campaigning outside his own state. A "draft-Eisenhower" movement took form, but Eisenhower declined to run and the movement was disbanded early in 1948.

Dewey meanwhile continued quietly building alliances. In July 1947 he made a "nonpolitical" tour of the western states. He announced in January 1948, and named Herbert Brownell, Jr., J. R. Sprague, and E. F. Jaeckle to manage his preconvention campaign. He won the New Hampshire primary in March, but lost badly to Stassen in Wisconsin and Nebraska in April after campaigning in those states. In May he defeated Stassen in the Oregon primary after both had stumped the state in a fashion that had seldom been seen in state presidential primaries. Dewey entered the convention as the favorite, with Taft as the runner-up, and won the nomination on the third ballot.

Dewey's election defeat in 1948 ended his career as a presidential candidate, at least for the time being, but not his status as the titular leader of the Republicans. The position, however, became increasingly "titular." He disclaimed further ambitions as a presidential candidate both publicly and privately. But he was again elected governor in 1950, retaining a position of great influence in his party, which he used in promoting the candidacy of Dwight D. Eisenhower. Meanwhile, Senator Taft gained the title of "Mr. Republican" by popular acclaim. Taft, Eisenhower, Warren, and Stassen all campaigned for the 1952 nomination; the choice of Eisenhower owed much to the strategic labors of Dewey and his allies.[17] In all of this activity, Dewey's public role was primarily that of a governor of New York, working within the party; but his ability to aid the Eisenhower cause was undoubtedly buttressed considerably by his previous experience in

[16] *New York Times*, Dec. 5, 1946.

[17] For an account of the preconvention campaigns of 1952, see Paul T. David, Malcolm Moos, and Ralph M. Goldman, *Presidential Nominating Politics in 1952*, Vol. 1, Chap. 2.

twice winning the presidential nomination, with all the relationships thereby established.

The Republican victory in 1952 returned the problems of a party out of power to the Democrats. Adlai Stevenson faced the situation with Stephen A. Mitchell, who had been his personal choice as national committee chairman. The campaign deficit was estimated at over $800,000, and there was the further problem of financing the regular operations of the national committee headquarters at Washington, with an operating budget of several hundred thousand dollars a year—a problem unknown in the days of Cleveland and Bryan. It was agreed that Mitchell would continue as national committee chairman and that Stevenson would help with the initial problems of party rebuilding, as he did at fund-raising dinners during the following winter.[18]

In the spring and summer of 1953, Stevenson went on a world tour. While abroad, he discovered that he was not only a celebrity, but also still a public figure with public responsibilities. Perhaps the British concept of an opposition party leader had traveled around the world ahead of him; at any rate, he was referred to in the dispatches as the "leader of the Democratic party," in a manner that would pass few copy editors in this country. After his return, he reported on his tour at a national committee meeting at Chicago in September 1953, and was generally acclaimed as party leader.

For more than a year thereafter, Stevenson devoted himself to the affairs of the Democratic party and the responsibilities of public leadership. The national committee met several times a year, rotating its meetings from region to region and holding

a fund-raising dinner in conjunction with each. Stevenson was the main attraction at most of these dinners, and took a strong line on many public issues. On July 2, 1954, he opened the mid-term campaign at Denver, and thereafter campaigned continuously in the critical states. The party won a remarkable number of governorships in the 1954 election, as well as recapturing control of both houses of Congress. Candidates whose victories were won with Stevenson help included Governors W. Averell Harriman (N.Y.), George M. Leader (Pa.), G. Mennen Williams (Mich.), and Orville L. Freeman (Minn.), and Senators Paul H. Douglas (Ill.), Hubert H. Humphrey (Minn.), and Richard L. Neuberger (Ore.). Throughout the country, Stevenson had renewed his contacts with the local political leaders, and profitably for all concerned.

With the mid-term elections won, the party entered a period of reorganization of its national leadership. Stevenson had already announced that he intended to resume law practice; after the election he hinted that he might retire from public life. Stephen Mitchell resigned as party chairman at a national committee meeting in New Orleans in December 1954 and was replaced by Paul M. Butler of Indiana after a divided vote, in which Butler was apparently the choice of Mitchell and other Stevenson supporters.

During most of 1955, Stevenson worked actively at his law practice, which included some foreign travel on behalf of corporate clients with foreign investments. He made only one major speech in the early months of 1955, an attack on the administration's foreign policy. He did not openly renounce the titular leadership, but was obviously not working hard at it, and he refused to clarify his intentions concerning the 1956 nomination. The public impression was that his mood was ambiguous; and if the reality corresponded to the public impression, it may well have reflected Stevenson's reaction to the treatment he was receiving not only from the Eisenhower administra-

[18] This account of Stevenson's record as titular leader was based primarily, when first written, on contemporary news reporting in the press and on feature articles in newspapers and magazines. The Stevenson biography by Kenneth S. Davis, *A Prophet in His Own Country* (1957), has since appeared and provides a fuller view of Stevenson's own thinking and personal relationships.

tion, but also from the Democratic leaders in Congress and the party's previous head, former President Truman.[19] Nevertheless, Stevenson announced as a candidate for the nomination on November 15, 1955; his decision was an open secret some weeks before the Eisenhower heart attack of September 24 had seemingly enhanced the Democratic party's chances of victory—while also enhancing the willingness of other Democrats to run for the nomination.[20]

Questions of campaign strategy arose as soon as Stevenson announced. Ordinarily a strong party leader seeking renomination could be expected to be available as a candidate in any state presidential primary where his presence on the ticket is desired by the local party organization. This is clearly the rule for an incumbent President seeking renomination, and it was also essentially what Dewey did in 1948. Furthermore, it is merely normal leadership tactics in any situation to accept a challenge with confidence, since reluctance is likely to be interpreted as an admission of weakness.

Stevenson was obviously a most reluctant candidate in the primaries. He hoped at first to confine his campaigning to those of Minnesota, Illinois, Pennsylvania, Florida, and California. This led almost inevitably to the poor showing of the Stevenson volunteer slate in New Hampshire, the first of the primaries. In Minnesota, Stevenson suffered a severe defeat by Senator Estes Kefauver. He recovered somewhat after a favorable showing in Illinois and Pennsylvania, and Kefauver's defeat in New Jersey; he then became a much more aggressive campaigner in the contests with Kefauver in Oregon, Florida, and California. Stevenson's victories in these three states, particularly his concluding landslide victory in California, made him again the strongest contender by far when the convention opened. Kefauver was virtually eliminated from the race, and conceded on July 31, two weeks before the convention. Governor Harriman had meanwhile announced and received the support of former President Truman at the convention, but was defeated and Stevenson was renominated.

Stevenson's election defeat in 1956 was more decisive than that in 1952.[21] It left him in the position of a twice-defeated candidate—a position previously occupied by Bryan and Dewey. After the election, Stevenson continued to be helpful in party matters and became a member of the newly formed Democratic Advisory Council, but was much less active as a titular leader than he had been in 1953 and 1954. He continued to be reported in the public opinion polls as a leading preference of Democrats for the next party nomination, but disclaimed any intention to campaign for it as 1960 approached.

The Present Status of the Titular Leadership

Notwithstanding the accumulation of experience that has so far occurred, the post of out-party leadership in America remains a nebulous one. As Stevenson commented,

[19] See discussions of these relationships in the signed stories by James Reston, *New York Times*, April 13, June 19, and Nov. 21, 1955. The main contentions were (1) that, unlike the Truman administration in keeping Governor Dewey informed on problems of foreign affairs while he was leader of the Republicans (and indirectly seeking his advice through John Foster Dulles), the Eisenhower administration accorded Stevenson neither recognition nor information, (2) that the Democratic congressional leaders, with their party again in the majority in both houses of Congress after a campaign in which Stevenson had actively participated, were not interested in hearing his views or in keeping him informed, although favorable to his candidacy in 1956 in a perfunctory sort of way, (3) that ex-President Truman was dissatisfied with Stevenson's behavior because of the moderation of his views and his inactivity in the leadership during much of 1955.

[20] According to Kenneth S. Davis, Stevenson made his decision to run again after a thorough job of checking to make sure that he would have general support from the governors and other party leaders and that there would probably be no serious opposing candidate for the nomination. After the Eisenhower heart attack, Kefauver announced, Harriman defected, and Truman favored an "open" convention; but Stevenson went ahead. (Davis, *op. cit.*, pp. 441-62.)

[21] For a post-mortem on the Stevenson campaign in 1956, with special reference to Stevenson's own behavior during the campaign, see *ibid.*, pp. 482-91.

The titular leader has no clear and defined authority within his party. He has no party office, no staff, no funds, nor is there any system of consultation whereby he may be advised of party policy and through which he may help to shape that policy. There are no devices such as the British have developed through which he can communicate directly and responsibly with the leaders of the party in power. Yet he is generally deemed the leading spokesman of his party.[22]

Despite its ambiguity, perhaps even because of it, the titular leadership has become a post that offers many opportunities for initiative, at least for a first-time incumbent. Like the present concept of the Presidency, far different from that held by Madison and Monroe, Buchanan and Grant, the present meaning of the titular leadership must be assembled from the contributions of the incumbents who have exercised initiative.

Cleveland and Bryan first gave vitality to the post by ending the tradition that a defeated presidential candidate is finished as a national party leader. Dewey completed the task on this first and most essential point by demonstrating that the Republican party, as well as the Democratic, could renominate a defeated candidate. Bryan and Dewey share another distinction: both demonstrated that it is possible for a twice-defeated nominee to exercise the critical weight of influence in the choice of the next successor nominee.

In perspective, Stevenson's impressive record in 1953 and 1954 can be seen as the further development and consolidation of a series of roles that had already been created. One role was that of leading the salvage operation: preventing the financial bankruptcy and disintegration of the national party apparatus, or its capture by dissident party factions, during the period immediately following defeat. Smith, Landon, and Willkie had each previously been effective in such a role.

A second role was that of leadership in re-building morale among the party rank and file, especially in those parts of the country where the party had been largely driven out of public office. Stevenson worked assiduously at this role, early signs of which had appeared in the activities of several of his predecessors, most notably Bryan and Landon.

A third role was that of a party spokesman in formulating and presenting a position on issues of public policy. For this task, Stevenson probably came closer to developing a shadow White House staff than any previous out-party leader, although the group surrounding Willkie in 1941 and the men around Dewey between 1944 and 1948 had some similarities to the volunteer Stevenson research group that was led by Thomas K. Finletter.[23] In 1953 and 1954 and in his foreign policy speech in the spring of 1955, Stevenson brought the spokesman role to a level seldom attained by his predecessors. Important party meetings were usually the forum from which he could speak as the representative of the whole party.

A fourth role was that of national party leader in fighting the mid-term campaigns. In extent and apparent success Stevenson's activity as chief mid-term campaigner in 1954 undoubtedly far exceeded that of any of his predecessors. It was a sign of the times, moreover, and perhaps a tribute to Stevenson's effectiveness, that the incumbent President found it necessary to take a more open and active part in the 1954 campaign than any of his predecessors.

Stevenson's record in 1953 and 1954 can thus be seen as the most substantial contribution to the development of the titular leadership that has thus far occurred. But by his own decision, he stopped short of consolidating the position between 1954 and 1956. His attitude was one of withdrawal during the preparations for the critical

[22] *What I Think* (1956), pp. ix-x. This statement was published before the formation of the Democratic Advisory Council, discussed later in the chapter.

[23] "I enlisted a small, informal group of experts in various fields to review and critically evaluate our major public policies." *Ibid.*, p. x. For descriptions of the composition and activities of this group, see *New York Times*, Oct. 25, 1955.

party meeting in New Orleans.[24] The transfer of the national committee chairmanship occurred under circumstances that led the new chairman to a policy of neutrality among candidates, thus making it difficult to continue using Stevenson as the principal party spokesman. At the same time there arose new and competing sources of leadership as the result of governorship victories in 1954, and the revived ascendancy of the congressional leaders, with the party again in control of both houses of Congress.

The net effect of the Stevenson experience between 1952 and 1956, therefore, was to establish a rather clear picture of what an able and willing out-party leader can do during the period leading up to the mid-term congressional elections, but not to clarify what might be usefully done in the critical period from mid-term to the next convention. This obscurity seems unlikely to be removed until another first-time defeated nominee goes through the cycle; and it may take several examples to make clear the possibilities, unless there should be some effort to remove uncertainties of status by formal action of the parties, as distinguished from the accumulation of practice and custom.

Meanwhile various elements of influence and power already seem to be established, at least potentially, in the titular leadership. Three categories of these elements can be distinguished: (1) those that are inherent in the position of the defeated candidate when defeated; (2) those that he can assemble by a vigorous course of action in defeat; and (3) those that depend mainly on availability for renomination on the next occasion.

A defeated major-party presidential nominee, at the time of his defeat, is an individual who has just experienced a tremendous deflation of prospects. Nevertheless, he continues to be one of the most important persons in the country. If he campaigned well, he still retains most of the qualities and attributes that made him available for the previous nomination. For some years, at least, he will be one of the very few political figures whose name will be recognized by over half of the voters.[25] Even if he retires from activity as a party leader, his public standing ordinarily will be such that he can make news of national interest merely by expressing his opinions on important issues of public policy. Unless he takes deliberate action to divest himself of the titular leadership, the symbolism of choice and the loyalties developed in the campaign will continue to give him a unique status in his party for the next four years.

Vigorous action to lead the party after defeat can further consolidate the position of the titular leader. As the record reveals all too clearly, there are various unwanted and backbreaking tasks to be performed in rebuilding a defeated party and its depleted treasury. The defeated candidate, and the national committee chairman whom he installed, have first call on these opportunities; by utilizing them, the former candidate can place all concerned under substantial obligation. Effective action in these matters builds up the complex of leader-follower relationships on a basis of reciprocity. The way to retain functions is to perform them; and, by taking the bitter with the sweet, it seems to be clear that an out-party leader can build a position from which it would be extremely difficult to oust him against his will, at any point short of the next party convention.

Availability for renomination brings into

---

[24] On his further remarks to the assembled party leaders at the meeting after going off the air, see Davis, *op. cit.*, p. 440.

[25] According to a Gallup poll published June 17, 1956, the following percentages of adult voters were able to recognize the names of the leading candidates for the Democratic presidential nomination: Stevenson, 88 per cent; Kefauver, 83; Harriman, 51; Lyndon Johnson, 32; Symington, 31; Lausche, 25. Four years earlier, when Stevenson was governor of Illinois, only 33 per cent of the voters were able to recognize his name, it was stated. As of 1956, 86 per cent of all adults were said to be able to identify Vice President Richard Nixon.

play a different but overlapping complex of forces. Availability for the nomination obviously does not assure it, as it normally does now for a first-term President; but unavailability excludes even the possibility. Titular leaders who are considered unavailable for the next nomination—Bryan after 1900 and again after 1908, Dewey after 1948, Hoover and Landon after their respective defeats—may exercise substantial influence on the basis of the factors enumerated in the previous two paragraphs. But actual availability for the next nomination is much more important.

The prospect of renomination is clearly the principal element of power that has become inherent in the position of a strong first-term out-party leader. Power involves the ability, actual or potential, to impose sanctions. Any person who is the most likely nominee of a major party in the next presidential election must be recognized as a possible incoming next President of the United States. In view of the sanctions that are always at the disposal of the President, any person who has the generally recognized possibility of becoming President within four years begins to acquire some of the elements of presidential power.[26]

[26] The argument here is obviously akin to that put forward by R. T. McKenzie in assessing the position of the opposition party leader in Britain. McKenzie concludes that in either the Conservative or the Labour Party, when in opposition, the power of the leader is overwhelmingly derived from the fact that he is potentially the next Prime Minister; although McKenzie also argues that this power is also based upon the consent of the followers in the parliamentary party and can be withdrawn by them at any time. See his *British Political Parties* (1955), particularly at pages 145, 298, 383-84. In a review, Leslie Lipson questioned whether McKenzie's two arguments as to causality are not in conflict. (*American Political Science Review*, Vol. 50, March 1956, pp. 227-29.) It would seem, however, that the two arguments could be reconciled with each other. In the British system, the sanctions may be very powerful for dealing with individual dissidents while almost worthless for dealing with intra-party majorities. Even where the formal position of the leader is subject to withdrawal at any time by party action, the power is real while it is retained with little sign of opposition. In the American case, the out-party leader cannot be formally deposed until the next convention, but his power would rapidly fade if his followers were visibly deserting him.

The position of the out-party leader is part of a mutual system of obligations embracing his own various roles and those of other members of the party. To the extent that he has served effectively in the campaign in which he was defeated, and also to the extent that he endured the burdens of leadership in adversity after defeat, the party becomes obligated to him. The position of the out-party leader is thus at its strongest when with these two factors of influence it combines, legitimately, the clear possibility of a renomination.

Stevenson's position throughout 1954 combined all three factors, since he had done nothing conclusively to remove himself from the prospect of renomination and was pursuing a course of action, until the end of 1954, that strongly suggested his intention to be available. Dewey's position as a first-term out-party leader, from 1944 to 1948, included all of the first and third groups of factors but relatively little of the second. His possible services as party leader were limited in part by his responsibilities as governor and even more by the activities of powerful opposing groups in the party. But his position as governor of New York provided other substantial elements of power—so much so, by contrast with the situation of Wendell Willkie four years earlier, that for a time the myth was current that only an incumbent officeholder could mount an effective campaign for a second out-party nomination. Yet, of the six titular leaders from Grover Cleveland on who thought their prospects were good enough to justify the effort, Dewey was the only one who continued throughout as an incumbent officeholder.

If the prospect of renomination supplies the main element of power in the position of a first-term out-party leader, any apparent indecision concerning availability can obviously lead quickly to erosion of the power base. This was illustrated in the deterioration of Stevenson's position between November 1954 and November 1955. It was illustrated even more forcibly in the case of Al Smith between 1928 and 1932, since Smith made statements of unavailability that seemed so positive as to lead many of his followers to transfer their allegiance to Roosevelt. Presumably Smith thought he had a right to change his mind, as eventually he did; but the awkward situation he thus created seems to have been at the bottom of the bitterness in a conflict that divided many previously close friends and associates. The presumption would seem to be that an out-party leader, like a first-term President, should never take his followers around a hairpin turn. He should at least leave the situation completely open until he has had time to know his own mind and is prepared to make a firm statement, to which he will then adhere thereafter.

To summarize, the out-party leadership has seemingly reached a status where it can be used to assure a high probability of renomination, if he so desires, for any first-term leader whose original nomination was adequately justified. The status of a twice-defeated out-party leader is obviously different and weaker; but it is not a negligible status in the hands of an incumbent who proposes to continue actively serving his party in the interim up to the next nomination. If he does so continue, he may retain a large measure of availability in his own right. In any event, he is likely to have a major voice in the choice of the next nominee if he chooses to play the game through to the end.

National Committee and Convention Officers

In form, the term of office of a national committee chairman is four years, running from the national committee meeting immediately after the convention until the similar committee meeting four years later. The chairman is elected by the committee, which also elects to fill any vacancy that arises during the term. In practice, the incoming chairman at the beginning of the term is customarily chosen by the presi-

dential candidate, and is then duly voted into office by the committee.

When the campaign is over, arrangements are often reconsidered. In the winning party, the chairman may move on to a Cabinet position, retaining the chairmanship, as frequently occurred in times past, or leaving room for a replacement to be chosen by the President and ratified by the committee. In the losing party, the chairmanship is subject to a different type of turnover. The chairman may return to private life on his own volition within a year or two, leaving behind the burdens of a relatively thankless office; or he may be forced out of office by a loss of majority support within the committee; or he may serve until the end of the next convention.

The Republicans have had a higher rate of turnover in the chairmanship than the Democrats. Relatively few Republican chairmen have served a full term, especially when the party was out of power. No Republican chairman has served longer than a full term since Mark Hanna, 1896-1904. The Democratic party has had four chairmen who served eight years or more, and has had fewer mid-term resignations while out of power than the Republicans.[27]

The fortunes of the titular leader and the committee chairman who goes through a campaign with him to defeat are inevitably linked. Early departure of the man whom the leader chose as chairman is usually interpreted as a sign of weakness in the position of the leader himself. Whatever the circumstances under which a new out-party chairman is selected as a replacement, the change frequently involves a contest and a divided vote in the national committee. Even if the new chairman is one favored by the titular leader, he is not likely to have the same relationship of allegiance as the previous one. He takes his mandate, more or less, from the national committee as a whole, or from the strongest faction within it, but ordinarily he is in a position of con-

[27] Rosters are provided in Richard C. Bain, *Decisions and Voting Records of the National Party Conventions* (Brookings Institution, forthcoming).

siderable freedom—subject to the desirability of remaining on good terms with all party elements and to the necessity of raising enough money to keep the party headquarters in operation.

The typical position of an out-party replacement chairman during the period preceding the next party convention is strikingly different from that of the in-party chairman. The differences, moreover, have an integral relationship to the conduct of preconvention campaigns for the next nomination, and to the position of the titular leader.

The most important difference is one of accepted doctrine in the chairman's relation to upcoming candidates. An out-party chairman, particularly a replacement chairman, is generally held to be acting improperly unless he holds himself neutral toward all comers who may decide to run for the next nomination. An in-party chairman, with an incumbent first-term President, is subject to a different rule. He is expected to regard the President as entitled to renomination and any opposing candidate as in effect an insurgent entitled to only a minimum of parliamentary courtesies at the convention. Under a second-term Presidency, the case becomes somewhat different, but the general body of established precedent indicates that the chairman is expected to follow the President's choice for the succession.

These in-party vs. out-party differences were illustrated in 1955 and 1956 by the public behavior of Leonard Hall and Paul M. Butler while serving as Republican and Democratic national committee chairmen. Hall repeatedly indicated his support for a second-term nomination, not only for Eisenhower but also for Nixon, holding the line for months after the Eisenhower heart attack in September 1955, while other candidacies, particularly that of Senator William F. Knowland, were developing. Butler, on the other hand, at no time gave direct or vocal public support for the renomination of the titular leader of the Democrats, Adlai Stevenson. Butler strongly urged neutral behavior as the only proper course for all members of the staff of the national committee.[28]

The experience of the Democratic party in 1955 and 1956 suggests the difficulties inherent in reconciling the doctrine of neutrality among oncoming candidates with the doctrine that the titular leader is entitled to serve as the principal party spokesman. This difficulty becomes particularly acute when the out-party finds itself in possession of an allocation of national network radio or television time, made available to the party without cost for the purpose of replying to a statement by the President. The question then arises as to who shall speak for the party; and it is the job of the national committee chairman to resolve the question.

During the active preconvention campaign period of early 1956 the question was settled by using someone other than the titular leader: the "official Democratic party reply" to President Eisenhower when he announced his candidacy in March was made by Senator John J. Sparkman, the party's former vice-presidential candidate; the reply to the Eisenhower veto of the farm bill was made by Senate Democratic Leader Lyndon B. Johnson.[29] In the spring of 1955, a year before, when Stevenson decided on his own initiative to take issue with the administration on foreign policy, he made his own arrangements for network time and told the party chairman he would speak "only for myself."[30] This attitude may have been a strategically useful concession to the sensitivities of other party leaders, but as a general operating procedure it tends to suggest that whenever a contest is in progress over the next nomination, the out-party has no recognized leader who can serve as its principal spokesman.

[28] Cordell Hull also expounded the doctrine of neutrality as a means of building harmony and cohesion in a divided party. (*Memoirs*, p. 149.) In state politics, this doctrine seems to be more common in the South and West than in the Northeast or Middle West.
[29] *Washington Post and Times Herald*, March 8 and April 24, 1956.
[30] *Newsweek*, April 18, 1955, p. 24.

Despite the national committee chairman's typical shortness of tenure, perhaps in part because of it, an out-party chairman himself has an unrivaled opportunity for the exercise of initiative. If no one else is prepared to speak for the party on questions of organization, party strategy, or even public policy, there is no one to prevent the chairman either from speaking or from finding a spokesman to express what he has in mind. If the out-party chairman feels that the party's leaders in Congress are failing to develop the issues and the party record in the form most useful for the next election campaign, he may urge them to take a stronger line in proposing alternatives to the President's program, as Paul Butler did in March 1956, when he specifically urged action on the Hell's Canyon dam and on the Niagara power project.[31] The unconventionality of this intrusion was commented on with enthusiasm by the official journal of the Republicans; the Democratic congressional leaders made no public response whatever, doubtless concluding that discretion was the better part of valor if they wished to occupy a satisfactory position at the next convention.[32]

The fortunes of candidates may in some cases be affected by the activities of the out-party chairman in a number of other ways in addition to those so far discussed.[33] The chairman is the center of planning and arrangements for the next party convention, including recommendations to the national committee on choice of convention city and temporary chairman, and he may personally decide many other lesser matters. The choice of convention city has seemingly been important on some occasions; for example, Lincoln might not have been nominated in 1860 if the Republican convention of that year had not been held in Chicago. The local political atmosphere is still taken into account in choosing convention cities, but no longer seems likely to have a decisive effect upon the nominations.

The successive convention presiding officers—national committee chairman, temporary chairman, permanent chairman—all have in turn some direct opportunity to influence action when they are in the chair. The means of exercising influence include the maintenance of order in the convention hall—or the failure to maintain it which can reach a level of "planned confusion" that may permit stratagems that would not otherwise be possible; the power of recognition in debate, giving access to the ears of the convention when several

[31] Butler's letter is said to have been dated March 16, 1956, but information concerning it did not reach the press until a few days later. See *Washington Post and Times Herald*, March 25, 1956, p. A2.

[32] Republican national committee comment was to the effect that "Democrat Congressmen were aghast at this unprecedented move on Butler's part." NBC Commentator Ned Brooks was quoted as reporting, "We're told that Butler was taken to task by Senate Leader (Lyndon) Johnson and others, at a Senate campaign committee." (*Straight from the Shoulder*, Vol. 3, April 1956, pp. 1, 16.)

The fact remains that the congressional leaders were evidently unable to take punitive action. There was ample reason to believe that Butler was voicing a widely held view in the party. Had the congressional leaders engaged in public controversy with him, they could easily have impaired their influence at the convention, even though their congressional positions remained unimpaired. Hence they simply ignored Butler and the position in effect was a standoff, leaving Butler with the honors, such as they were.

A similar and possibly more important flurry of events occurred in 1959, when Butler indicated dissatisfaction with the record of the party's congressional leaders during a television interview on July 5. After an exchange of recriminations by lesser members of both camps in which Butler's dismissal was actively demanded, Butler sought a conference with Speaker Sam Rayburn and Senate Leader Lyndon Johnson. The conference was held on July 24, 1959, and ended in various amicable statements to the press, in the course of which Rayburn predicted that Butler would serve out the remainder of his term as national committee chairman, while Butler made no comment on whether he would back Rayburn for the chairmanship of the 1960 convention. For summaries of this sequence of events, see *Congressional Quarterly Weekly Report*, July 10, 17, 24, 31, 1959, pp. 940, 967-68, 990-91, 1034.

[33] For a perceptive article on the functions of national committee chairmen, see Cabell Phillips, "Party Chairmen: Study in Feuds and Funds," *New York Times Magazine*, July 1, 1956, pp. 10-11, 28.

For comment on Paul Butler's record in particular, with special reference to his leading role in forming and preserving the Democratic Advisory Council, see *Congressional Quarterly Weekly Report*, Dec. 5, 1958, pp. 1497-99.

equally eligible delegates want to speak; the power of recognition for motions or new business, usually on the basis of arrangements made in advance—and not always with the knowledge of persons adversely affected; and the making of rulings on points of order, rulings which usually convey or withhold tactical advantages. Collectively, these various prerogatives of the presiding officer can make him a powerful figure, and especially so in the party out of power because of the typically high level of factional conflict in out-party conventions.[34]

At the same time, it must be recognized that as the activities of the national committee and convention officers come under closer public observation, especially on television, standards of appropriate behavior in these offices are probably rising. Intuitively the public tends to apply an ethical principle of judgment, holding that those who administer the machinery of choice have an obligation to insure fairness in the operation of the machinery. Overt or pronounced unfairness that appears motivated by candidate interests may even boomerang, operating to the detriment of the candidate whom it is intended to aid.

On the other hand, insofar as the presiding officers guard the interests of the whole party in dealing with internal factional conflict, it appears that much arbitrary conduct may be forgiven, or at least find continuing majority support. The situation is somewhat like that observed by many scholars in the evolution of the office of Speaker of the House of Representatives. The speaker seems to have come down a notch in power during the last half century, so far as opportunities for the abuse of his official position are concerned, while reaching new levels of moral authority when major issues of government are at stake. In the same way, the status of the convention officers may

well become more formidable as they are pressed by public scrutiny into devoting their powers to the task of enabling the party to debate and act along lines that clearly represent its best interests.

The Congressional Leaders

In the out-party the congressional leaders are especially conspicuous as power centers. By comparison with the titular leader, their positions have been institutionalized through a long evolution. They have an official, governmental status and are constantly occupied with public matters at the nation's capital. Often they serve for long tenures as leaders, although turnover in the leadership positions in the Senate has been relatively frequent in recent years. A strong party leader in Congress brings together elements of power that can be used for many purposes.

The congressional leaders operate at times in at least four different roles in relation to the presidential nominating process. They may serve as officers of the national party conventions. They may become candidates for the presidential and vice-presidential nominations. They may act as kingmakers, building up potential candidates. And finally, in their own principal and most official role, they are directly responsible for the legislative record on which the party will have to run.

Each of these roles is typically more important in the nominating process of the out-party than in that of the in-party. The role of the congressional leaders as convention officers, particularly the developing tradition by which the party leader in the House serves as convention permanent chairman, was reviewed in the previous chapter. Here the role is most clearly the same in both in-party and out-party, but the consequences of the possession of the role seem more important in the out-party, since it has no White House incumbent to dominate the nominating process. The same is

[34] For illustrations of almost all of the opportunities for influence by presiding officers, see the accounts of the two conventions of 1952 in David, Moos, and Goldman, op. cit., Vol. 1, Chaps. 3 and 4.

true of other roles at the convention that can be occupied by congressional leaders, such as the chairmanship of the committee on resolutions (platform).

Congressional leaders have often aspired to the presidential nomination but seldom with success even in the out-party. One of the characteristics of the American system of government is the fact that the posts corresponding to those of highest parliamentary responsibility in other democracies have served so rarely as stepping stones to the office of chief of state, or even to the nominations for it.

In the present century, speakers Champ Clark and John N. Garner have been the only party leaders in the House who were serious possibilities in a presidential nominating contest; both made their bids toward the end of a long period in which their party had been continuously out of power. If the House were to find some means of bringing to the top its ablest younger men from pivotal states, as it was able to do a century ago, it might conceivably put them again in a position to compete for the presidential nominations. The tendency to use the House leaders as convention chairmen is a tacit recognition that they are no longer likely to be available as candidates.

Markedly different trends have been operating in the Senate. During the last three decades the proportion of safe constituencies has become much smaller in the Senate than in the House and particularly so in the Republican party, with the declining number of one-party Republican states. When the number of safe constituencies is small, rotation is more frequent and the rising men can reach leadership positions more rapidly. Other features of Senate organization and tradition have also worked to the same end, with the result that it has become possible for senators from pivotal states to reach posts of majority and minority leadership within a few years after entering the Senate.

This was illustrated by the rapid rise of Senator Robert A. Taft of Ohio to the chairmanship of the Senate Republican Policy Committee and to recognition as the actual leader of his party in the Senate, long before he officially became a floor leader. Senator Lyndon B. Johnson of Texas was first elected to the Senate in 1948, became floor leader for his party after only four years of Senate service, and had already developed noteworthy characteristics of "availability" before his potentialities as a candidate were somewhat reduced by the heart attack he suffered in 1955. Senator William F. Knowland of California first came to the Senate in 1945, became floor leader for his party in 1953, and for a time seemed to have succeeded Senator Taft as the most outstanding presidential possibility among congressional Republicans.

The Senate leadership positions thus seem to be developing candidates who can compete with increasing effectiveness for the presidential nominations, particularly in the party out of power. The recent practice produces leaders who often share the attributes of the most available governors: the right age, origins in pivotal states, the glamour of a rapid rise in a public service career, and an "executive" type of personality—one that is trained by experience to operate across the board in all of the substantive problems of government, unlike other members of the legislature. Added to all this is the conspicuous, increasingly powerful, and well-publicized position occupied by the Senate leaders of both parties, a position that can well be envied by any governor. In an era of national issues cutting across sectional lines, the Senate leaders are more involved in the competitive aspects of national two-party politics than they have been for a century; and it is no wonder that this involvement has brought them to the forefront as potential presidential nominees.

The same factors that are developing the Senate leaders as candidates can also make them powerful as kingmakers. Each of the Senate party leaders occupies a special relationship to the other senators of his party. It would be an exaggeration to describe this relationship as simply that of leader and followers: a senior committee chairman, for example, does not often take orders from a relatively young floor leader whom he may have helped to install in an office that he did not wish for himself. A half-century ago, as noted in the previous chapter, these posts did not even exist in any regularized sense, and as recently as twenty-five years ago were not remarked as centers of positive coordination and influence. They have been filled by relatively young men in recent years, in part because many senior senators prefer the committee chairmanships, with their opportunities for legislative specialization, their more leisurely pace of activity, their longer tradition of autonomy and power, and their easier reconciliation of constituency and national party pressures. But with the constantly growing volume of important legislative business that must somehow be disposed of, the posts of formal leadership in the Senate become increasingly strategic. A Senate floor leader may not be able to command the cooperation of every other senator of his own party, but in most instances there is a close working contact and a developed awareness of mutual obligations on a give-and-take basis.

The result is that the leader of each party in the Senate is almost inevitably a center for the appraisal and discussion of the possible potential presidential candidates within his own party. From such discussion, it would be only a step to the building of coalitions of senators and their state party affiliates in support of particular candidacies. Thereafter, since the Senate leaders are prime news sources, they can easily bring into play the assistance of the Washington press corps in a developing build-up.

The Senate leaders, nonetheless, are under certain handicaps—not always apparent—because they receive so much of their information on state politics through other senators, whose perception of the situation in their own state may be somewhat different, for example, from that of the governor, even when they are of the same party and on friendly terms. Further, a Senate leader has little contact with local forces in the states that have sent no senators of his own party; but those states nonetheless have voting strength at the party conventions. Senators generally, including the leaders, probably tend to exaggerate their own political power and influence by comparison with the governors, who are rarely in a position to act collectively—except, however, during the vital days of the national party convention when most of them are present as chairmen of their state delegations. All these effects are accentuated during the preconvention period by the distorting effect of national political news reporting, which mainly emanates from Washington, where the ablest political reporters in the country rely largely on senators as political news sources. These factors are not readily measurable, but something of the sort must be at work, in view of the regularity with which senators have been boomed by other senators for nominations that they have almost never received.

The role of the congressional leaders as makers of the legislative record is directly related to the prospects for party success in the elections, but also may be their most important role in relation to the nominating process. It is by far the role that is most difficult to appraise in terms of its operations and consequences. Its importance in connection with the nominations derives from the fact that the out-party congressional leaders may confront their party convention with a choice between nominating a candidate who can run with pride on the party's congressional record, or one who will have to run somehow in spite of that record because he is quite obviously in disagreement with major portions of it. This is a phenomenon that has been recurrent throughout American political history, but that may be acquiring a new type of importance in the present era.

The phenomenon in its modern form was

illustrated in the Republican party between 1940 and 1952 and in the Democratic between 1952 and 1956, as it may be again in 1960. At the Republican national conventions of 1948 and 1952, Senator Taft was the champion of the party's congressional record in seeking the party nomination. Governor Dewey, the titular leader seeking renomination in 1948, had been little consulted on the development of the record in Congress between 1944 and 1948 and took virtually no responsibility for it. He was nominated nonetheless after a bitter contest and conducted a campaign in which he said as little as possible about the congressional performance of his party, which had been in control of both houses of Congress for the preceding two years. His opponent, President Truman, used the opportunity to direct his campaign primarily against the record of the Republican Eightieth Congress.

When Truman won, the Republican congressional leaders stubbornly drew the moral that their party had failed because of its unwillingness to nominate a candidate who could run on the party's own record. More convinced than ever, the congressional Republicans returned to the nominating contest of 1952 with Senator Taft again as their leader. After another bitter struggle, the party convention nominated Eisenhower, who had been personally associated with many policies long under attack by the party's congressional leaders. Eisenhower won in 1952 with only the narrowest of congressional majorities, including many Republicans who refused to support his policies. His party lost both houses two years later, and again in 1956 and 1958.

In the Democratic party between 1952 and 1956, the habit patterns arising from having carried the responsibility of government for twenty years were still in evidence. The relationship between the party record in Congress and the choice of a party nominee in 1956 was recognized as a problem. The problem cannot be said to have been solved, but the lines of discussion, and the composition of the decision-making group, were somewhat different from those in the Republican party during the previous years. There was little indication of any suggestion that, after the party's congressional leaders had made the party record, the party should then pick a nominee in terms of his accordance with that record. On the contrary, after the meeting in Texas in September 1955 between Adlai Stevenson, Senate Majority Leader Johnson, and House Speaker Rayburn, the Associated Press reported that the two congressional leaders, with Stevenson nodding approval, had "firmly pledged themselves to a congressional program which they hope will put a Democrat in the White House next year."[35]

Senator Johnson indicated that he thought it was his job to hammer out such a program. He later announced his proposals for the final congressional session of the first Eisenhower term, most of which could have been readily endorsed by any Democratic party national convention. But as a Texan he had to include the proposed natural gas bill. Later passed under Johnson's leadership, this was the subject of a damaging veto message by President Eisenhower. Still later, all three of the then leading candidates for the Democratic nomination—Stevenson, Kefauver, and Harriman—were reported as having stated, when interviewed by Elmer Davis, that if elected they would veto any such natural gas bill.[36]

Under present conditions, the congressional leaders of both parties will continue to be heavily involved in the presidential nominations even when they are unable to make their influence dominant—most of all when they are leading dissident party ele-

[35] *Washington Post and Times Herald,* Sept. 30, 1955.
[36] *ADA World,* June 1956, p. 3.
Differing views on how to develop the party record in Congress in preparation for the 1960 campaign were of course at the bottom of the friction between Paul Butler and the congressional leaders (noted in footnote 32 above). See also the discussion of the Democratic Advisory Council at the end of this chapter.

ments that have their principal power base in entrenched congressional positions. But aside from these special situations, the congressional leaders may devote their talents increasingly to the search for compromise solutions that will hold each party together sufficiently, even when out of power, to make a creditable race. The pressures in that direction arise from the party competition in an era of massive issues of public policy and the resulting close linkage between presidential and congressional campaigns. Certainly no end of these competitive pressures is currently in sight.

Other Members of Congress

Other members of Congress are seldom as much involved in the presidential nominating process as the party leaders, but instances of substantial involvement do occur. The principal roles that can be occupied by the other members are three in number: as candidates for the nominations; as candidate managers and active supporters; and as part of the communications network.

The Senate, unlike the House, continues to be a leading source of candidates for the presidential and vice-presidential nominations. Senators appear often as the favorite son candidates of their own states; and not all of the important senatorial candidates of recent years have been members of the official leadership groups or even approved by them. The differences between the candidacies of Senators Taft, Russell, and Kefauver in terms of their leadership status and relationships were especially noteworthy. Taft in 1948 and 1952 was running as a recognized leader of his party in the Senate. Russell was running in the same years to provide a rallying-point for a dissident sectional minority of the party in power. His candidacy was evidently not incompatible with his status as a senior chairman of one of the most powerful Senate committees. The Kefauver candidacy in

1952 and 1956 represented a different combination of factors. He was still a junior senator, particularly in 1952, was not a member of the official leadership group of his party in the Senate, and seems to have campaigned without their approval and in the face of their tacit opposition.

Kefauver's campaigns were almost unique in the extent to which they represented an attempt to use a Senate seat as the basis for developing a massive popular following in presidential politics, and to do so with relatively little support or encouragement from other senators or other political leaders.[37] The candidacy seems to have originated in the popular impact of the senator's widely televised crime-investigation hearings. In 1952, the strategy of entering all available presidential primaries demonstrated his wide appeal for the voters, in the absence of serious opposition in most of the primaries. Similar tactics in 1956 encountered heavy opposition and eventual defeat, although the vice-presidential nomination became available as a consolation prize.

The total showing, nevertheless, was an impressive one, and it raises obvious questions for the future. Granted the continued availability of the mass communication media, with relatively loose party organization in the Senate and presidential primaries that permit a direct appeal to the party voters, can it be expected that other senators will run without leadership support? Or will the party leaders be more successful in the future in fencing in the presidential ambitions of independently minded junior senators?

Obviously only time can answer these questions, but perhaps the answer will be determined in part by whether the parties are able to satisfy popular demands for leadership through other channels of leadership succession. The Kefauver candidacy of 1952 had much in common with the im-

[37] Historical parallels for the Kefauver candidacy are not easy to find and the parallelism is not close. Perhaps the nearest is that of Senator Robert M. La Follette, the elder, during the years when he was "available" for the Republican nomination.

portant third-party movements of an earlier time; it was a vehicle for dissent, unrest, and the criticism of existing leadership. When the creation of an effective third party no longer seems feasible, the presidential primaries can offer an alternative means of registering dissent. This may be one of their major functions in the future, with senators as the willing candidates.

The prospective Senate candidacies for the Democratic nomination of 1960 differ somewhat from those previously discussed, and seem to be a natural response to an open situation in which anyone can run, with or without the approval of the Senate leaders. They also reflect a growing sentiment at the nation's capital that seems to be shared by many governors, to the effect that senators have recently become much stronger than formerly in the perennial competition with the governors for the presidential nomination. This shift is attributed to the growing importance of the issues of war and peace—and of mass media attention to those issues at the nation's capital. The existence of such a change will remain unproved until a senator has won the nomination not merely once, but several times, but it may nonetheless be occurring.

The role of candidate manager or principal supporter is one in which members of Congress have appeared with some frequency in recent years. The members include a considerable part of the total supply of political managerial talent that is competent, motivated, and relatively available. Recent noteworthy examples of performance in the role include the activities of Senator Henry Cabot Lodge as Eisenhower preconvention manager in 1952 (which may, however, have been one reason for Lodge's defeat in his own Senate contest of the same year), and the 1952 activities of Congressmen Clarence J. Brown and Carroll Reece on behalf of Senator Taft. In 1956, Senator Hubert Humphrey was influential in persuading Adlai Stevenson to enter the Minnesota primary and in organizing his campaign in the state; and Congressman Robert L. F. Sikes served as Stevenson's manager for the Florida presidential primary campaign, in which Stevenson was supported by most of the Florida congressional delegation.

The role of members of Congress as part of the informal communications network in connection with the presidential nominating process is too intricate for much study here; it is also somewhat apart from the major concerns of the present chapter. Nevertheless, the role is too important to overlook, based as it is upon the following features: (1) the flexibility and multiplicity of the informal contacts among members of Congress, living as a single, highly organized community during the greater part of each year; (2) the continuous communication between the individual member and the party notables in his home state or district, by virtue of extensive use of air travel and the long-distance telephone, as well as other means of communication; (3) the intensity with which members of Congress seek to become well-informed on matters affecting the oncoming presidential nominations and elections, in view of possible consequences for their own career prospects; (4) the tendency of members of Congress to congregate at the national convention of their own party even when unable or unwilling to serve as delegates, with the corresponding extension of the communication function of Congress into and during the party conventions.

In most of these respects, there is no counterpart for Congress as a central element in the informal web of communication at the national party level, with the possible exception of the Washington press corps, which operates in conjunction with the congressional network and interacts with it. The effect of all this is difficult to assess; but the hypothesis might be ventured that information filtered through the congressional net tends to take on some coloration of congressional bias. Insofar as such information enters into the assessment of competing candidacies, it probably tends to inflate the appraisal of candidates with strong congressional appeal; and to the extent that an impression of strength is thus created for such candidates, it may increase their actual prospects.

More important is the fact that some such network of informal, pervasive, high-level communication would seem to be essential for the most effective operation of the presidential nominating process. It was the basis for the original functioning of the congressional caucuses as nominating instrumentalities; and it may still be the most important way in which Congress influences the nominations. It probably contributes substantially to the development of national consensus concerning the merits of candidates; if it does, it would inevitably become an important factor in the outcome.

The Governors

The history of the national parties has reflected a continuing tension between Presidency, Congress, and the governors as competing centers of influence on the presidential nominations. With the breaking of the power of the congressional caucus and the establishment of the party conventions in 1831-1832, the governors were able to take a direct part in the nominating process. They became somewhat prominent in national party affairs in both parties by the time of the Civil War. In the Republican party, Congress and the White House were the most formidable competing centers of leadership in selecting Republican nominees from the Civil War through 1932, although governors were occasionally nominated and were otherwise involved. In the Democratic party, where the practical necessity of nominating northern candidates was recognized throughout this long period, the party's northern governors were in a position of special importance and the congressional leaders were less influential than their Republican counterparts.

In recent decades the governors have become increasingly potent in the out-party, but the extent of their influence is dependent on their numbers, their relative cohesion, and the importance of the states they hold. Table 5.1 indicates how the number of incumbent governors of each political party has fluctuated since 1896 during the respective presidential years.

TABLE 5.1. INCUMBENT GOVERNORS BY POLITICAL PARTY, PRESIDENTIAL YEARS, 1896-1956

Year	Political Party		
	Democratic	Republican	Other
1896	17	26	2
1900	15	25	6
1904	19	26	
1908	20	26	
1912	25	23	
1916	28	20	
1920	21	27	
1924	27	21	
1928	21	27	
1932	27	19	2
1936	38	8	2
1940	30	18	
1944	22	26	
1948	24	24	
1952	23	25	
1956	27	21	

Shifts in the number of out-party governorships can provide important clues to out-party status and prospects. When the out-party has relatively few governors, it has usually been driven back into the predominantly one-party areas that rarely produce effective presidential candidates. Incumbent governors who look like presidential timber are at a premium if available at all. But when the out-party begins to win back an increasing number of governorships in contested territory, the prospects for presidential victory are on the increase; so is the number of governors who can actively contend for the nomination.

Not all governors are justified in entertaining presidential ambitions, but all can participate in the nominating process.[38] They can participate, if not as candidates for the nominations, possibly as convention officers or keynote speakers; as state party leaders and delegation chairmen; and as a "third house" for communication and collective influence within each party.

Governors and senators have provided the largest single categories of candidates, in terms of official status, since the beginnings of the convention system; but whereas before 1892 the governors seeking presidential nomination were only about one third as numerous as the senators, since that time the numbers have been about equal. Eight times as many governors as senators, however, have actually been nominated for the Presidency.

Despite the prominence of various governors and ex-governors in the early decades of the convention system, it was not until 1876 that either party nominated an incumbent governor for President. On that occasion both did so: Rutherford B. Hayes was governor of Ohio and Samuel J. Tilden of New York. Since then, the governors have provided a series of noteworthy names among the first-time nominees: Grover Cleveland, William McKinley, Woodrow Wilson, James M. Cox, Alfred E. Smith, Franklin D. Roosevelt, Alfred M. Landon, Thomas E. Dewey, and Adlai E. Stevenson. All of these were out-party nominees except Cox and Stevenson, both Democrats. The governors and former governors who have won election to the Presidency, moreover, have provided most of the outstanding Presidents since 1876.[39] The emergence of the

governors as a principal source of presidential candidates was in its way probably as significant for the development of the modern conception of the Presidency as the breaking of congressional control over the selection process when Jackson came to power.

No governor has served as a permanent convention chairman since McKinley in 1892, but governors have served repeatedly as temporary convention chairmen and keynote speakers in both parties since 1940. In 1956 the Democratic party had twenty-seven governors in office; it was said that nearly every one of them—outside of the deep South—was an active candidate for the convention's keynote role. The actual choice was Governor Frank C. Clement of Tennessee.[40]

The role of the governors as state party leaders and delegation chairmen is one that seems to have taken on increasing importance in recent years. The number and per cent of the governors of each party who have served as convention delegates is shown in Table 5.2 for selected years. In recent conventions, if a governor served as a delegate at all, he has been chosen delegation chairman in about three cases out of four. Whether this rule would hold for the historical experience is not known. In any event, the figures indicate a substantial increase over the years in the number of governors serving as delegates.

This trend undoubtedly parallels and reflects the growing importance of the gov-

---

[38] At the annual governors' conference at Bolton Landing, N.Y., in 1954, a popular story making the rounds recalled conversations with a youngster at a previous conference: "Do all governors want to be President?" "No, young man, some of them just want to choose him." (*New York Times*, July 18, 1954.)

[39] For specific comment making the comparisons

between governors and others as Presidents, see Wilfred E. Binkley, *President and Congress* (1947), pp. 297-98.

[40] Clement had been mentioned as a possibility for months and had managed, with some difficulty, to remain sufficiently neutral on the segregation issue to be acceptable to most elements of the party. He was chosen at a meeting of the arrangements committee at Chicago on July 9, 1956; the *New York Times* of that day had stated in a dispatch from Washington that Governor Edmund S. Muskie of Maine would be the choice. *The Washington Post and Times Herald*, in a Chicago dispatch published on July 9, stated that Senators Robert S. Kerr and Henry M. Jackson were being considered as leading possibilities.

TABLE 5.2. GOVERNORS SERVING AS DELEGATES TO NATIONAL
PARTY CONVENTIONS, SELECTED YEARS

	Democrats			Republicans		
Year	Governors	Delegates	Per Cent	Governors	Delegates	Per Cent
1848	20	0	0%	10[a]	0	0%
1860	20	1	5	12	0	0
1872	12	1	8	23	3	13
1884	25	4	16	12	1	8
1896	17	5	29	25	2	8
1908	20	11	55	26	9	34
1920	21	11	52	27	6	22
1928	21	9	43	27	12[b]	44[b]
1932	27	18[b]	67[b]	19	9	47
1936	38	23	61	8	4	50
1940	30	18	60	18	9	50
1944	22	18	82	26	14	54
1948	24	15	63	24	11	46
1952	23	19	83	25	13	52
1956	27	20[b]	74[b]	21	15	71

[a] Whig.
[b] One alternate delegate included.

ernor's office in the American political system. During most of the nineteenth century the governors in most states were relatively unimportant either as administrative officials or legislative leaders. Since the turn of the century, however, the state governments have had to struggle with a constantly growing volume of work. The governors have achieved greater independence as executives, have been recognized as the most effective centers for legislative leadership, and have largely replaced the old-time state political bosses in the control of the state parties. This is particularly true in the states where the major parties are effectively competitive, and in some others where there is a sharp factional division within a dominant party.

The governors, even those from the less important states, are effective as secondary power centers at the conventions in part because of their established relationships with one another. The custom of annual meetings to discuss matters of concern to

the state governments began about fifty years ago. Governors of each party are apt to caucus informally at the meetings, which have thus become an important annual source of political news.[41] The governors' conference in 1943 was employed by Governor Dewey as a sounding board for a bold pronouncement on foreign affairs. The conference in 1951 was used effectively to boom the Eisenhower candidacy for the following year. But the most dramatic exhibit of potent collective action by the governors of one party was the manifesto released by the Republicans at Houston in 1952. In this document, twenty-three of the twenty-five Republican governors recommended changes in the rules for seating contested delegations, a proposal that produced the first decisive vote at the Republican con-

[41] "Governors are usually the controlling powers in Presidential nominating conventions. Therefore the best political weather station in a Presidential year is the annual Governors' Conference, which comes before the conventions." Review of the Week, *New York Times*, July 1, 1956.

vention of 1952 and paved the way for the later Eisenhower nomination.[42]

In their collective role as developed at these conferences and elsewhere, the governors of each political party tend to act as a "third house" for high-level, informal communication. In this capacity, their role is somewhat analagous to that of the party members in Congress as a communications network. Since the governors do not often meet, their communication networks do not work as intensively as those in the Congress, and within each party they do not ordinarily extend to as large a number of states. But the governors operate on a higher level of political power, in view of their wide appointive and patronage authority, their continuous contact with the electorates in their own states, their relationships with state party chairmen (whom they often virtually appoint), and their very considerable influence with the national committee and the congressional members of their party.

It can also be surmised that governors, by comparison with senators and representatives, are often somewhat more directly in contact with the private individuals who are centers of political power in their own states but outside the formal party and governmental hierarchies. An effort to locate and describe some of these private centers of power is made in the remaining pages of this chapter.

Interest Groups and Their Leaders

The American social order contains many powerful and influential individuals in addition to those who hold public or party office, or who otherwise act as party leaders in one capacity or another. Many of these individuals become involved in the presidential nominating process at one time or another; some, according to reports, are almost continuously involved.

Systems of analysis for locating and classifying these influences and for studying their effect on the presidential nominations have not been extensively developed. What can be done here is merely exploratory in a field where there is an abundance of both historical and speculative material, but also a noteworthy absence of analytical research.[43]

A first distinction may be noted between the leaders of interest groups and other persons of power and influence. Interest groups and their leaders by definition are generally presumed to be concerned with particular issues. Other men of power who become highly involved in presidential nominating politics may in many cases be more interested in a candidate than in the issues, to the extent that such a distinction can be made. These other men of power will be discussed mainly in a later section; here we are primarily concerned with the interest groups and their leaders.

In the previous chapter, the conclusion was reached that interest groups and minority factions can sometimes threaten sanctions that may affect the nominating behavior of even the party in power; but that this kind of pressure will be relatively unimportant if the President and the central group of party leaders hold together. In the party out of power, the opportunities are much greater. Leadership is more dispersed and less able to present a united front; and the out-party leaders are more accessible to those seeking to influence them. The opportunities to be effective through direct participation are also greater; if organized labor controls a hundred votes in a party convention through delegates under its own discipline, for example, such a block of votes may be decisive in a hard-fought con-

---

[42] David, Moos, and Goldman, *op. cit.*, Vol. 1, p. 70-72.
For an interpretation of the influence of the governors, see the memorandum by Senator Robert A. Taft in Appendix F of the present book.

[43] "In view of the obvious significance of the nominating process, it is astonishing that we know almost nothing of a systematic character about how nominations are made, and about the role of groups in connection with them." David B. Truman, *The Governmental Process* (1952), p. 288.

test. Such a contest is more likely to occur in a party that is out of power. Finally, it is in the out-party that all the aspects of candidate build-up and preconvention campaigning usually reach their greatest importance; and it is here that there is the greatest opportunity for intervention from outside the party system.

In earlier times, the conspicuous examples of interest-group activity in the nominating process usually had a strongly sectional basis. The outstanding figures in the early party conventions were the local and regional party managers who were continuously active in party affairs but only rarely held public office. It was under such leadership in making nominations that both parties split over the issues of slavery before the Civil War. Sectional issues and sectional leaders were again prominent in the proceedings within each party that led to the Bryan and McKinley nominations of 1896. The McAdoo-Al Smith contest for the Democratic nomination in 1924 represented a strongly sectional division, with northern wets confronting southern and western drys. The leaders of the Anti-Saloon League and the anti-prohibition pressure groups were actively involved in the proceedings, as they were again in 1928. More recently, there has been a continuing sectional struggle within the Republican party between the middle-western "isolationists" and the eastern "internationalists." The sectional struggle within the Democratic party is over the issues of segregation and civil rights, with the South standing in embattled isolation within the party.

Most of the issues that have come to a sharp focus in the party conventions at one time or another—free trade and the tariff, bimetallism and monetary policy, woman suffrage, prohibition, civil rights— have produced an apparatus of organizations and pressure groups. The leaders of these groups have been much involved in the platform-drafting activities of the conventions, but have been less clearly active in the nominating proceedings. Influence,

when it has been overtly exerted, has generally been directed against candidates deemed unfriendly. Pressure-group leaders have rarely expressed a positive choice among candidates whose formal positions were satisfactory.

In modern times, agriculture, business, and labor are the three largest interest groupings that are continuously active in the forum of national politics. Each of these operates through a multiplicity of organizations and has its own complex formal and informal structures of leadership. The role of each in the nominating process deserves special consideration.

Organized agriculture speaks with a powerful voice on matters of national legislative policy, and both political parties have been intimidated in recent years by the drastic possible effects of a violent swing in the farm vote. Yet the major farm organizations and their leaders have generally continued to pursue a traditional policy of nonpartisanship and of nonintervention in the choice of candidates. In this they seem to reflect attitudes that have been deeply held by the farm population as a whole, and that may have been more serviceable in an earlier era than they are at present.[44]

In 1952, there was little evidence to sug-

[44] One student of agricultural politics has commented as follows:

"Farmers and agricultural leaders have gone on the premise that there was a nonpartisan approach to farm problems and that intense involvement in the political process was something to be avoided . . . The nonpartisan approach has not only dominated both party and group strategy but has influenced the way rank and file farmers have participated in their local political organizations. . . .

". . . agriculture's influence in the political party has dropped as the strength of other groups has risen. Farmer impact upon party policies and farmer access to party organization in recent years has been maintained largely through the influence of agriculture spokesmen in legislative bodies and not as a result of farm influence in the hierarchical levels of party organization. The rank and file farmer does not take party organization seriously, . . .

". . . farmers need to play a bigger part in party activity to offset agriculture's declining political influence." See Ernest A. Engelbert, "The Political Strategy of Agriculture," Journal of Farm Economics, Vol. 36 (Aug. 1954), pp. 376, 382, 383.

gest that the leaders of the major farm organizations were doing anything noteworthy about the presidential nomination in either political party. In 1956, the situation changed little in the Republican party, with no nominating contest; in the Democratic party, agricultural interests were apparently more than usually involved in the preconvention campaigning. Former officials of the Department of Agriculture in the Truman administration were reportedly intent upon securing the nomination of a Democratic candidate who could appeal effectively to the farm vote, and apparently opposed the nomination of Adlai Stevenson and favored that of Averell Harriman.

American business, industry, commerce, and finance cannot be said to have any one association or organization to speak for all of them. There are several hundred major corporations, every one of which is itself a center of economic power and is able to exert some political pressure if it decides to do so. Business corporations as such are subject to various legal restrictions that inhibit some forms of direct political activity, but the individuals of whom they are composed, and more especially their top officers and leaders, are in a position to be highly active politically.[45]

Since 1896, if not from its earliest origins, the Democratic party has been viewed with some suspicion by the greater part of the business community, and particularly by northern industries. The business community has thus taken a positive interest mainly in the nominations of the Republican party, although it has also attempted defensive action in connection with nominations of the Democratic party. Business interests, symbolized in the person of Mark Hanna, were predominant in the nomination of McKinley in 1896. The same interests were conspicuously influential in the

nominations of Hoover in 1928, Willkie in 1940, and Eisenhower in 1952. Business interests were not predominantly or unitedly opposed to the nomination of any of the Republican candidates from 1896 onward, although there was some question about Theodore Roosevelt in 1904. Divergencies within the business community, however, were undoubtedly a factor in the struggle between Governor Frank O. Lowden and General Leonard Wood in 1920, in which both lost, and in the continuing cleavages of the Republican contests from 1940 to 1952, between the "Taft" Republicans and the liberal wing of the party.

The assessments just made are in accord with an immense amount of well-informed political writing, but are nevertheless extremely difficult to support with more than circumstantial evidence. In 1952, for example, the titans of industry, commerce, and finance were not often found in person among the delegates or in other conspicuous positions at either party convention. No leading Wall Street figure served on either New York delegation in 1952, unless Averell Harriman and Herbert H. Lehman, both Democrats, should be so regarded—and both had left Wall Street for public service years before.[46]

[45] "Business in Politics: How Far You Can Go," Nation's Business, July 1956, pp. 25-27, 72-73. Reprints of this article were made available by the publisher, the Chamber of Commerce of the United States.

[46] A few cases of business leaders and wealthy industrialists can be cited. Prentiss Brown, board chairman of the Detroit Edison Company, was a Michigan Democratic delegate, in a delegation that also included at least seventeen labor union officials. Joseph N. Pew, Jr., board chairman of the Sun Oil Company, was a member and vice-chairman of the Pennsylvania Republican delegation. Thomas E. Millsop, president of the Weirton Steel Company, was a West Virginia Republican delegate. The Illinois Republican delegation included Colonel Robert R. McCormick, publisher of the Chicago Tribune; R. Douglas Stuart, treasurer of the Republican national committee and president of the Quaker Oats Company; and General Robert E. Wood, board chairman of Sears, Roebuck & Co. But more often the leaders of the business community remained in the background. An exception was the visit to Michigan Republican delegation headquarters by six top officials of the Ford Motor Company and the General Motors Corporation, including Henry Ford II and Charles E. Wilson, an event "watched with pleasure" by Eisenhower supporters. (The story was carried by the Detroit News,

One curiosity in 1952 was the presence at the Republican convention of H. L. Hunt of Dallas, possibly the wealthiest man in the United States, as a Texas delegate.[47] Despite his wealth, there is some question whether Hunt should be classed as a leader of the business community; at one point he was alone in the Texas delegation, and one of a handful of delegates in the entire convention, in casting his vote for General Douglas MacArthur. Hunt and some other similar cases provide evidence for the tentative hypothesis that members of the top business elites who feel confident of adequate representation do not themselves ordinarily seek places as convention delegates, whereas others, more insecure, wish to be in a position to cast votes directly and to exercise such influence as they may have. Yet many business men of considerable wealth but of less than national prominence undoubtedly seek places as delegates mainly because they enjoy the privileges of direct participation in the party conventions. This kind of representation of the business community has become much more extensive and perhaps more effective at Republican conventions than at the Democratic.[48]

Organized labor has been involved in politics since the earliest days of union organization in the United States. But in 1895, after a struggle over socialist control of the labor movement, the American Federation of Labor (AFL) amended its constitution to provide that "party politics shall have no place in the conventions" of the Federation.[49] Thereafter the Federation was technically neutral as between the major parties for many decades, although it supported Bryan in 1908 in what was regarded by Lorwin as "labor's first entry into a national political campaign."[50] The professed party neutrality of the AFL as such did not prevent its leading officers, and even more the leaders of the major affiliated unions, from taking strongly partisan positions. Some of these individuals were active in each of the major political parties.[51] With the coming of the Roosevelt New Deal and the formation of the Congress of Industrial Organizations (CIO) in 1935, both main branches of organized labor became increasingly associated with the Democratic party. The CIO endorsed the successive Democratic presidential candidates —Roosevelt, Truman, and Stevenson—and the AFL joined in endorsing Stevenson in 1952.[52] In 1956 the combined AFL-CIO endorsed the Stevenson-Kefauver ticket.[53]

The tempo of labor activity in party politics has been rising steadily for over fifteen years. The CIO set up its Political Action Committee (PAC) in 1943 in what has been described as "a hurried effort to save the fourth-term election for President Roosevelt."[54] The AFL created its Labor's League for Political Action in 1947. Labor campaign expenditures in recent election years, as reported to the Clerk of the House of Representatives and tabulated by *Congressional Quarterly*, were as follows:

1948	$1,291,343
1950	1,618,623
1952	2,070,350
1954	2,057,613
1956	1,805,482
1958	1,828,777

Labor rebuttal to criticism of these expenditures has taken the form of "broadcasting

July 9, 1952; see David, Moos, and Goldman, *op. cit.*, Vol. 4, p. 53.) According to Marquis Childs, syndicated columnist, "During the Republican convention one of the objects of scorn and anger for loyal Taftites was the box full of General Motors executives. There, muttered one of the Taft managers, are the people who are dictating this convention." (*Washington Post*, July 22, 1952).

[47] On Hunt's wealth, see C. Wright Mills, *The Power Elite* (1956), p. 104 and sources cited; also Charles J. V. Murphy, "Texas Business and McCarthy," *Fortune*, May 1954, p. 208.

[48] See Chapter 14.

[49] Lewis L. Lorwin, *The American Federation of Labor* (1933), p. 40.

[50] *Ibid.*, p. 92.

[51] *Ibid.*, p. 423.

[52] "Labor's Political Machine Goes to Work," *Nation's Business*, Feb. 1956, pp. 70-78. This article is a detailed discussion, from a business-oriented point of view, of labor participation in politics.

[53] *New York Times*, Aug. 29 and Sept. 13, 1956.

[54] "Labor's Political Machine," *op. cit.*, p. 73.

:he word that Republicans spent more in he last two elections than all Democratic ind labor groups combined"; for example, n 1954, "13 Democratic organizations spent \$2,224,210.93 and 41 labor organizations ipent \$2,057,613.06 . . . 27 Republican or- ;anizations reported . . . \$5,509,649.18 was ipent.[55] The merger that formed "The American Federation of Labor and Con- ;ress of Industrial Organizations" at the ind of 1955 was presumably inspired, imong other reasons, by a desire to in- :rease the political effectiveness of or- ;anized labor, and resulted in a joining of :he two previous political action arms as the Committee on Political Education (COPE).

At the party conventions of 1952 and 1956 organized labor was represented in itrength in the Democratic convention and ilmost not at all in the Republican. The Democratic convention labor caucus in 1952 included about one hundred votes dis- :ributed in some twenty-eight delegations. [n the Republican convention of 1952 two long-time Republican AFL officials, one of whom has since died, were delegates, but :he total number of labor votes was prob- ibly not over ten, mostly in the California delegation.[56] Moreover, as *Business Week* :ommented, "nowhere in the convention locuments or in the speeches was there a ;esture or overture to the union chiefs who, it least in their own belief, can influence a iizable number of their 15-million mem- bers."[57]

The labor group at the 1952 Democratic :onvention had able leadership and was ieemingly well organized. Jack Kroll of :he CIO and George M. Harrison of the Railway Clerks jointly led the attack on :he Barkley candidacy the day before the :onvention opened. This was probably the most conspicuous intervention by organized

labor in the nominating process that has so far occurred. Although the action was hotly attacked, by John L. Lewis among others, it evidently brought about Barkley's withdrawal in face of the fact that he had been assured of White House support.[58]

The labor leaders were not at first in agreement in 1952 on a positive choice among the available candidates for the Democratic nomination, dividing between Kefauver and Harriman as long as Steven- son seemed to be unavailable. But Walter Reuther was one of the earliest and most potent of the Stevenson supporters. He had much to do with swinging strategic delega- tions toward Stevenson after Kefauver had suffered his greatest defeat in the seating of the Virginia delegation.[59] When the labor-liberal bloc was unable to agree on a strategy at this point, "Jack Kroll, director of C.I.O.–P.A.C., thereupon instructed all the C.I.O. delegates to the convention to switch their votes to Stevenson as soon as they legally could."[60] In the end, Stevenson undoubtedly received the votes of most of the labor delegates. This probably occurred

[55] Robert C. Albright, in *Washington Post and Times Herald*, Dec. 9, 1955. The dollar figures were 'rom *Congressional Quarterly.*

[56] See Chapter 14.

[57] "Ike Can Get a Share of the Labor Vote," *Busi- ness Week*, July 19, 1952, p. 114.

[58] On Truman's role, see the discussion in the previous chapter and citation to his *Memoirs;* see also Barkley's own account in *That Reminds Me,* pp. 230-31, 236-43. An experienced political reporter commented on the latter as follows: "In his chron- icle of the events at Chicago, the Veep gives no indication that he recognized that the labor leaders had taken upon themselves the unpleasant duty of telling him what no Democratic politician dared— that he was too old to make a serious Presidential race. This was accepted at the time by most politi- cal reporters and verified privately by most Demo- cratic leaders. It still seems valid today. Mr. Barkley could have been nominated only as a sort of care- taker to hold the party together until 1956." (Jack Steele, "The Veep's Half Century," *Saturday Review,* Nov. 20, 1954, p. 40.)
Assuming that this interpretation is valid, it sup- ports the conclusion that organized labor was more insistent upon securing a strong candidate to head the Democratic party in 1952 than the party's own official leaders, who were prepared to see advantages in the installation of a member of their own group as a friendly caretaker in a year in which they had little hope of winning.

[59] David, Moos, and Goldman, *op. cit.,* Vol. 1, p. 150; Vol. 2, p. 284; Vol. 4, p. 189.

[60] David C. Williams, "Choosing the Presidential Candidates," *Political Quarterly,* Vol. 23 (Oct.-Dec., 1952), p. 377.

again in 1956, although, by their own decision, the leaders of organized labor were not as prominent as they had been in 1952.[61]

Bosses, Kingmakers, and Candidate Managers

Beyond the individuals, groups, and leaders so far discussed, still other types of men are frequently conspicuous in the presidential nominating process in the party out of power. These have been grouped together here as "bosses, kingmakers, and candidate managers"—a final catch-all of overlapping categories.

The political boss is defined in one dictionary as "A professional politician who controls a large number of votes in a party organization or who dictates unofficially appointments or legislative measures," and in another as "A politician who controls the machinery of his party, as in a particular district."[62] A political boss may occupy public office, but when he does so, it is usually supposed to be at his own choice. Basically his power is derived from control of a party organization, preferably one that can produce majorities in both primary and general elections. Firm control of such an organization provides a power base that is separate from the occupancy of public office and one that, in the past, has usually been much more enduring.[63]

There has never been a national party boss in the sense in which that term has been used repeatedly in state and local politics. Mark Hanna is usually thought to have come the closest to creating the role at the national level; but McKinley was his own man in the Presidency. It is one of the glories of the office, in fact, that no President has ever occupied a subordinate position in relation to a recognizable single individual acting as a party boss, unlike the positions that have been occupied at times by governors, senators, and big-city mayors.

In all periods of convention history, however, state and local bosses have figured prominently in the presidential nominating process. The state bosses of major states were probably at the zenith of their power in the period stretching from Grant to McKinley—when it could be said that "at the head of the ranks of those who really ran the country were great bosses like Conkling and Platt and Hill of New York, Randall and Cameron and Quay of Pennsylvania, Hanna and Foraker and Brice of Ohio."[64] These men, and others of similar type, were leaders in every national party convention of their time. Each could usually control the vote of a large state delegation. In situations where no one candidate was dominant, they could often control the outcome, provided they were able to reach agreement with each other. When they were not in agreement—which was often in an era of sharp sectional differences—they at least provided the main centers of organization and maneuver within the contesting factions, and inevitably had much to do with the outcome, whatever form it took.

State-wide bosses of the type of Tom Platt have largely disappeared. The leaders of the big-city machines, on the other hand, are still visible factors in Democratic conventions, although even here forces of change are at work. A coalition of Democratic city bosses is generally credited with much influence in securing the nomination of Harry Truman rather than Henry Wallace for the Vice Presidency in 1944; the influence of this group was felt by the President in deciding on his preference for running mate, by Truman himself in agreeing to become available, and by the convention

---

[61] See Chapter 14 and *New York Times*, Aug. 9, 15, 17, 1956.
Labor participation in the congressional elections of 1958 seemingly reached a new high in effectiveness. For a list of candidates for Senate and House of Representatives who received labor financial support—including about five Republicans in a list of over 200—see *Congressional Quarterly Weekly Report*, Nov. 7, 1958, pp. 1405-06.
[62] *Webster's New International, Unabridged; New Century Dictionary.*
[63] For a full discussion, see D. W. Brogan, *Politics in America* (1954), Chap. 4, "Machines and Bosses."

[64] S. E. Morison and H. S. Commager, *The Growth of the American Republic* (1937), Vol. 2, p. 216.

n the actual voting. In many of the big cities the once-strong political machines have fallen into a state of disrepair, with a corresponding decline in influence of their leaders in the national party conventions; out, in a country that is increasingly urban and metropolitan, it is difficult to see how big-city politics could long fail to be important in the conventions.

Party bosses may be kingmakers, and in the nineteenth century the bosses may have decided the presidential nominations more often then any other type of figure, partly because of their direct control of the big delegations in the conventions. But not all kingmakers are party bosses. Insofar as others who are not bosses succeed as kingmakers in American politics, they seem to fall mainly in two classes that have considerable overlap: one class includes the persons of wealth or strategic position, particularly in the publishing or mass communication industries, who take a continuing interest in presidential politics; the other includes the long-time friends and key personal supporters of potential candidates.

Harry Daugherty, who worked tirelessly for Harding's nomination for many years before it occurred, was of both classes.[65] More recently the presidential aspirations of Harold Stassen were promoted over a period of years by Amos Peaslee, a wealthy corporation lawyer, and Daniel Gainey, a jewelry manufacturer. The Eisenhower candidacy of 1952 seems to have been promoted by kingmakers and would-be kingmakers in all parts of the country, including the publishers of *Time-Life-Fortune,* the publishers of the *New York Herald Tribune,* other persons of wealth in New York City, millionaires in Texas, and various groups of business leaders in other centers.

Kingmakers who have no special strategic power of their own on which to trade, but who are personally attached to the candidate, have included such figures as Louis

McHenry Howe, who worked for many years to bring Franklin D. Roosevelt to the White House, David Ingalls, a cousin of Senator Robert A. Taft who worked for his nomination in successive campaigns, and the University of Chicago historian, Walter Johnson, who operated a "Draft-Stevenson" committee for months in advance of the conventions of 1952 with no encouragement from his candidate.

Bosses and kingmakers alike may act as candidate managers under some circumstances, but the role of the candidate manager is an increasingly specialized activity. In the more loosely organized politics of the nineteenth century, and in an era when candidates generally were supposed to refrain from overt efforts on their own behalf, the manager was not so clearly the appointed agent of his candidate as at present. But candidate managership has always been regarded as a serious business, one requiring great skill and adroitness before the convention and while the convention is actually in progress. The strategies and tactics of the successful managers are eagerly studied; the political experts of the press regularly hold morning-after quarterbacking sessions on the success or failure of the more conspicuous candidate managers.

Inevitably, a certain legendary lore builds up around the successful managers. Daugherty's feat in securing the Harding nomination was especially fabulous for the accuracy of his prediction, some months in advance of the convention, of the circumstances under which the nomination would occur. The most celebrated candidate manager of modern times was undoubtedly James A. Farley, who was given much of the credit for Franklin Roosevelt's nomination in 1932, and who has expounded the problems of candidate management with much perception in his two books. Herbert Brownell became nationally known as a behind-the-scenes operator in the Dewey campaigns of 1940, 1944, and 1948, and took an active part in the final stages of the Eisenhower campaign for the nomination of 1952, although Senator Henry Cabot Lodge

[65] Daugherty remarked to his crony Jess Smith when Harding was still a state senator in Ohio: "Gee, but he'd make a great-looking President; we'll put it over sometime, Jess!" See Mark Sullivan, *Our Times* (1935), Vol. 6, p. 26.

was the chief preconvention manager and continued as such during the convention.

In 1956 each of the three main contestants for the Democratic nomination was equipped with an experienced politician as campaign manager: Stevenson's was James A. Finnegan of Philadelphia, a state official and former president of the Philadelphia city council; Kefauver's was F. Joseph Donohue of Washington, attorney and a former commissioner of the District of Columbia; Harriman's was Carmine G. DeSapio, state official and leader of Tammany Hall. All three were relatively young and new to the national scene, but all had been long active in the local politics of their own areas, and each had been a delegate in 1952. All were named officially as managers shortly after their respective candidates announced.

An interesting feature of the 1956 proceedings was the formal recognition accorded the three candidate managers by the chairman of the Democratic national committee, Paul Butler, himself a very similar type of political leader. Butler called the three to Washington for an all-day meeting in late June, not only to discuss plans for the convention but also to arrive at agreements concerning the fall campaign that presumably would be valid whichever candidate received the nomination. A joint announcement was made concerning plans for the allocation of expenditures among campaign trains, television, and radio.[66]

Insofar as the bosses, kingmakers, and candidate managers are different rather than overlapping types, any final assessment of their relative importance in nominating politics is difficult. The manager role is obviously here to stay, but in some respects seems to become less important as it becomes increasingly professionalized. With long periods of open preconvention campaigning, active candidates are compelled to take responsibility for their own campaign decisions, and the manager's role becomes that of adviser, executive, and agent.

[66] *Washington Post and Times Herald,* June 22, 1956.

Kingmakers, on the other hand, are perhaps becoming more important, and particularly so in the Republican party, with its close affinity to the centers of financial power and to the leadership of the mass communications industries. Willkie's nomination in 1940 was largely the result of a strong initiative from power centers high in the business community but largely outside the formal apparatus of the Republican party. Dewey's two successful nominating drives of 1944 and 1948 were carried on by working politicians under his own active personal direction, but with a strong assist from the top leadership of the business community. The Eisenhower candidacy of 1952 was the product of the number of eminent persons who actively urged the General to run and the American people to support him.

Political leaders who make politics their business will undoubtedly continue to be important and will doubtless continue to receive the name of boss, regardless of the extent to which they may actually resemble the nineteenth-century bosses. They can and will continue to play an important part in the nominating process. Those at the state and local level probably will continue to be most important in the earlier stages of candidate careers, in connection with the screening process that helps to determine which of the possible candidates will be most worthy of national attention; but any state party leader may at some time acquire a strategic relationship that will carry through into the final stages of a presidential nomination. This would seem to be the inevitable and continuing consequence of a federal system in which leadership must perennially be renewed from below.

Leadership Integration in the Party Out of Power

The previous chapter reached the conclusion that either major political party, when in power, has acquired the capacity to become a rather tightly knit organization at the top, insofar as the nominating questions that most affect party survival are concerned. The informal structure of top party organization has come to center in the President in his recognized capacity as party leader. In the party out of power, a corresponding structure of informal organization does not exist—at least not yet. It is important, nonetheless, to examine whether there has been any significant long-term trend toward an integration of top party leadership in the out-party.

On the basis of the evidence assembled in this chapter, it can be concluded that there has indeed been such a trend, but that it is neither as strong, as clear, nor as far advanced as in the party in power. Furthermore, it might as well be said, the trend toward leadership integration, when in power or out of power, is not as far advanced in the Republican party as in the Democratic party. The Republicans' first renomination of a defeated presidential candidate came fifty-six years later than the Democrats'. The consequences of this long time-lag may continue to be felt for another generation, even if the Dewey renomination of 1948 comes in the end to be regarded as a kind of turning point in Republican party history.

The movement toward leadership integration in the out-party has taken the form of two different developments that are closely related to each other. First has been the strengthening of several centers of leadership that might or might not decide to work together; this development, described earlier in this chapter, is relatively clear and easy to document. Second has been the beginning of a tendency, tenuous and hard to pin down, for the several centers of leadership to cooperate more often than formerly in dealing with the over-all concerns of the party.

Both points can be illustrated in the recent history of the Republican party, but only to a limited degree in the case of the second point. During the long period from 1933 to 1953 when the Republicans were out of power, there was generally a fair degree of cooperation between the party's congressional and national committee leaders, and also a considerable degree of cooperation between the titular leader and the governors. But there was usually a situation of strained relationships, to say the least, between titular leader and congressional leaders.

In part this situation of strain reflected the differing voting structures of the party conferences in Congress, the national committee, and the convention. The conservative leaders of the Republican party in Congress were supported by majorities in their own conferences almost all of the time, in the national committee much of the time, and in the national conventions not at all, losing the contest on each successive party nomination from 1940 to 1952. It was natural, therefore, for the congressional leaders to disapprove of the party's choice of candidates. Their consequent reluctance to accord recognition to the titular leader was undoubtedly one of the main factors in the continuing weakness of the Republican party.

The period was climaxed, despite congressional opposition, by the two Dewey nominations and the first Eisenhower nomination and election. Since then, Eisenhower has again been nominated and elected, and many of the Republican conservatives were removed from Congress in 1958. It seems unlikely that there will be a complete reversion to past habits when the Republican party again finds itself out of power.

In the Democratic party the level of cooperation among the major centers of party leadership has clearly been higher since 1953 than it was between 1928 and 1932, and markedly higher than the level in the Republican party at any point during the twenty years it was out of power. The relative amicability with which all of the Democratic party leaders cooperated in fund-raising and campaigning activities between 1952 and 1956 was particularly noteworthy.

To a degree, this continued after 1956—
so far as the specifics of fund-raising and
campaigning are concerned. But a new situation of strain was initiated after the election of 1956 with the creation of what
became the Democratic Advisory Council.[67]

The Democratic Advisory Council

As soon as it became apparent that the
elections of 1956 had produced a Democratic
majority in each house of Congress, differences arose within the party over the legislative course to be pursued. Senate Majority Leader Lyndon Johnson and Speaker
Sam Rayburn, in firm control of a Congress
where the seniority system placed southerners at the head of most of the committees,
planned to wait for the Republican President to submit his legislative program,
upon which Congress would then act in accordance with the best interests of the nation as it saw them. This would mean the
kind of "moderation" that the two leaders
contended had brought the Democrats their
congressional victory. The procedure was
opposed by a group of liberal Democrats in
the Senate, who urged a sixteen-point "minimum program of liberal Democratic action" based on the party's 1956 platform;
they insisted that the congressional victory
meant popular approval of the platform as
a basis for legislature action.

Several members of the Democratic executive committee who came from northern and western urban centers agreed with
this approach. Three of them—Paul Ziffren
of California, David L. Lawrence of Pennsylvania, and Jacob M. Arvey of Illinois—
combined forces to effect the passage of a
resolution that (1) reaffirmed support of
the Democratic platform and called on the
party membership in both houses of Congress to "do all in their power to enact
legislation to put the platform into effect
as speedily as possible," (2) authorized the
national committee chairman to appoint an
advisory committee and provide it with
adequate staff, enabling it "to operate with
continuity during the next four years."[68]

The resolution specified "an advisory
committee of not more than 17 members
including Democratic members of the Congress, Governors, Mayors, and other outstanding Democrats to meet with the Executive Committee of the Democratic National
Committee from time to time at the call
of the Chairman to coordinate and advance
efforts in behalf of Democratic programs
and principles."[69] The authorized figure
was soon revised to twenty, and National
Committee Chairman Paul Butler issued
invitations to four groups: members of the
House of Representatives; members of the
Senate; governors and mayors; at large.

Each group included five names. Those
invited from the House and Senate were
chiefly the prospective leaders of the new
Congress: Speaker Sam Rayburn; Senate
Majority Leader Johnson; House Majority
Leader John W. McCormack; the two
Whips, Senator Michael J. Mansfield and
Representative Carl Albert; the chairmen
of the respective campaign committees
Senator George A. Smathers and Representative Michael J. Kirwan. The other
members of Congress invited were Senators Hubert Humphrey and John Kennedy, and Representative Edith Green. Governors invited were those of New York
Michigan, North Carolina, and Arizona
Mayor Raymond Tucker of St. Louis, Missouri, completed this group. The five members at large were former President Truman; the two recent party standard-bearers

[67] The account following is based on press releases
of the Democratic National Committee and the
Democratic Advisory Council; newspapers, particularly the *New York Times,* the *Washington Post and
Times Herald,* and the *Evening Star;* and interviews.
A good summary of the early stages of the Council
is in Hugh A. Bone, *Party Committees and National Politics* (1958), pp. 219-27. A shorter account is
included in Sidney Hyman, "Can a Democrat Win
in '60?" *The Reporter,* March 5, 1959, pp. 11-15. On
the Council's role as a shadow White House, see
Paul T. David and Ross Pollock, *Executives for Government* (1957), pp. 35-38.

[68] Democratic National Committee, Press Release
B-1458, Nov. 27, 1956.
[69] *Ibid.*

Adlai Stevenson and Senator Estes Kefauver; Mrs. Eleanor Roosevelt; and former Governor John S. Battle of Virginia.

All of the congressional leaders declined to join, on the ground that Congress was a body created by federal law, with functions for which it was responsible and that could not be shared with outsiders. Representative Green accepted, but reversed her decision as soon as she learned of the leadership's attitude. Of all the members of Congress invited to take part, only Senators Humphrey and Kefauver at that time accepted. The governors of North Carolina and Arizona did not accept, nor did the former governor of Virginia. Mrs. Roosevelt felt that her newspaper work would be in conflict with Council membership, but agreed to become a "consultant."

As finally constituted, the Advisory Council consisted of Chairman Butler, the fourteen members of the party executive committee, and seven others: Governors Averell Harriman of New York and G. Mennen Williams of Michigan; Mayor Tucker; Senators Humphrey and Kefauver; Stevenson and Truman. Former Senator Herbert H. Lehman became a member at large within a month or two, and took part in all but the very first stages of the Council's work. After the first year, there were other additions—Governors Orville L. Freeman of Minnesota, Foster Furcolo of Massachusetts, and Stephen L. R. McNichols of Colorado, and George M. Harrison, president of the Grand Lodge of the Brotherhood of Railway Clerks and a vice president of the AFL-CIO. In July 1959 the addition of Governor Edmund G. (Pat) Brown of California was announced; in November, Senators John F. Kennedy and Stuart Symington became members.

The Council held its organization meeting on January 4 and 5, 1957, coincident with the opening of the Eighty-fifth Congress. It entertained the congressional leaders at a two-hour breakfast meeting on the second day, and all appeared harmonious; nevertheless, it was obvious that neither side had yielded—the members of Congress intended to maintain their independence of action, and the Council would continue as a going body without them. Two attempts were later made to deprive the Council of power, the first in February, the other in May, at meetings of the Democratic national committee. Southern committee members opposed the Council, but both attempts were defeated, and the Advisory Council emerged with a clearly defined mandate to formulate and declare policy for the Democratic party between national conventions. The legal basis of this authority is the power conferred by the quadrennial party convention on the Democratic national committee to represent the party in the intervening years. In turn the national committee designates its executive committee to exercise most of its powers between national committee meetings.

The operating mechanism of the Council was substantially completed during the first half of 1957. A five-man steering committee was appointed in February, consisting of Stevenson, Governors Harriman and Williams, and two national committeemen, Camille F. Gravel, Jr., of Louisiana and Paul Ziffren of California. At the same time Charles S. Murphy, a former Truman staff member, was appointed general counsel. In April, Charles Tyroler, 2d, was named executive director. After the national committee's second endorsement in May, the Council set up an administrative committee of three—Paul Butler, Philip Perlman, and Thomas K. Finletter—to work with the executive director, and authorized Butler to establish four advisory committees: foreign policy; economic policy; methods of party financing; political techniques and development. A labor committee was added in 1958, and a committee on urban and suburban problems in 1959. Chairmen for the foreign and economic policy committees were announced during the summer of 1957—Dean Acheson and John K. Galbraith—and their labors were well under way by the fall.

Activities of the Council

From the very beginning, the Council, to effect its purposes, made policy statements on matters of current or long-term importance. There were brief "spot" statements on such timely items as the crisis at Little Rock and the launching of the first satellite by the Soviet Union. There were more lengthy documents dealing with aspects of foreign policy and of economic policy. Civil rights has been a recurring subject, separately and in conjunction with other topics. After the 1958 congressional elections, which greatly increased the party's majorities in both houses of Congress, the Council on December 8 issued its own State of the Union message, containing its own recommendations for the program to be adopted in the next two years.

The circumstances attending the establishment of the Council and an inspection of its membership roster lead inevitably to the conclusion that this group speaks for the so-called presidential wing of the party—the northern and western elements that are predominant in the quadrennial conventions, write the party platforms, and nominate the presidential candidates. These are the elements that have been conspicuously unable to control congressional action, especially when the party is out of power, by reason of southern possession of most of the positions of influence in Congress. The Council in its statements consistently attacked the Eisenhower Administration in a more aggressive manner than the southern Democratic leaders of Congress were willing to do and advocated many courses of action more liberal in cast than those leaders cared for—civil rights legislation and a Senate anti-filibuster rule, for example.

The Council meetings and statements were given press attention—frequently front-page space. The 1958 State of the Union message drew particularly wide coverage. Editorial writers and syndicated columnists took notice, and Republican leaders were occasionally goaded into making public responses, especially to the statements issued as the 1958 congressional election campaign got under way. Former President Truman and the titular leader, Adlai Stevenson, were not so conspicuous in the work of the Council as to dominate its public image, but there was no doubt that their presence and interest did much to give weight to the Council's deliberations.

*   *   *   *   *

The consequences—especially the long-range consequences—of a new type of party body such as the Democratic Advisory Council are not easily appraised. Policy statements alone, not implemented by either executive or legislative action, are merely words, which of themselves may neither influence government nor win elections. But the Council provided a forum through which the leadership of the presidential wing of one party, while out of power, had secured the opportunity to become more cohesive and to achieve greater continuity in developing and expressing a point of view.

The composition, the status, and even the existence of the new body remained uncertain beyond the 1960 Democratic national convention. The convention might disregard the Council's work and nominate an unsympathetic candidate; alternatively it might back the Council strongly and insist that it be made permanent. In either case, a new precedent has been created that seems likely to endure as a point of reference in connection with many unsolved problems. A number of the issues that center around alternative patterns of organization in this area are discussed further in the final chapter. Those issues are of great importance for the out-party nominating process, because of their potential impact, however resolved, on the leadership environment within which out-party nominations will be made in the future.

6

Main Patterns in the Nominating Process

IN THE STUDY OF presidential nominations, the analysis of recurring patterns can be most clearly understood by recognizing that the act of nominating a presidential candidate is primarily a choice of leadership—the formal act by which the organized political party selects or confirms the leader under whose banner it will campaign for the control of the government. In the first Democratic convention, in 1832, when Andrew Jackson was nominated to succeed himself, an existing party leadership was confirmed. When Martin Van Buren was nominated by the Democrats in 1836, a new leader was chosen to replace Jackson. When Abraham Lincoln was nominated by the Republican party in 1860, a leader was chosen to fill the void that had been left behind by the unsuccessful candidacy in 1856 of John C. Frémont, the new party's first presidential nominee.

The problem of apostolic succession has been solved in one way or another by every human organization that has managed to survive the loss of its first leader. The patterns of choice by which the succession may be achieved are not unlimited in number, even though previous attempts to establish classification that could be applied in the political field have been infrequent and have left much to be desired.[1]

Chapters 4 and 5 have described the principal centers of power that have been influential in recent decades in the choice of top leadership, for the party in office and for the party in opposition. Here it is proposed to classify all of the major-party presidential nominations since 1831 in accordance with the type of power center that in each case was most effective in determining the outcome. When this has been done, it will be evident that noteworthy comparisons can be made between the nominating patterns that have been common since 1896 and those of the earlier period.[2]

A Classification System for Presidential Nominations

There are three situations in which the presidential nomination has simply confirmed an existing party leadership: the renomination of a President who was elected directly to the office; the nomination for a full term of a President who, originally elected as a Vice President, succeeded to the Presidency through death of the incumbent; the renomination of a "titular leader" —a candidate who had suffered defeat in a previous election.

When a new leadership must be chosen, four major patterns of succession can be

---

[1] See, for example, Gardner Lindzey (ed.), *Handbook of Social Psychology* (1954), Vol. 2, pp. 912-13. An earlier version of portions of this chapter was published as an article: Paul T. David and Ralph M. Goldman, "Presidential Nominating Patterns," *Western Political Quarterly*, Sept. 1955, pp. 465-80. The classification concepts used here were originally developed in Paul T. David, Malcolm Moos, and Ralph M. Goldman, *Presidential Nominating Politics in 1952* (1954), Vol. 1, pp. 12-15.

[2] Early drafts of the present chapter, of the third section of Chapter 18 (then included in the present chapter), and of Chapter 7 were read in 1956 by Professor Gertrude Cox of the Institute of Statistics, University of North Carolina. She prepared helpful comments on the statistical methods employed and the problems of sampling discussed in footnote 16, below.

TABLE 6.1. SUCCESS AND FAILURE IN ACHIEVING RENOMINATION—
PRESIDENTS ELECTED DIRECTLY TO THE OFFICE[a]

Retired Voluntarily At End of One Term[b]	Sought Renomination Unsuccessfully	Renominated Once or More
DEMOCRATIC PARTY		
J. K. Polk, 1848	F. Pierce, 1856	A. Jackson, 1832
J. Buchanan, 1860		M. Van Buren, 1840
		G. Cleveland, 1888
		W. Wilson, 1916
		F. D. Roosevelt, 1936, 1940, 1944
NATIONAL REPUBLICAN, WHIG, AND REPUBLICAN PARTIES		
R. B. Hayes, 1880	None	A. Lincoln, 1864
		U. S. Grant, 1872
		B. Harrison, 1892
		W. McKinley, 1900
		W. H. Taft, 1912
		H. Hoover, 1932
		D. D. Eisenhower, 1956

[a] For full names of all presidential candidates of the two major parties, 1832-1956, see Appendix A, Table 1.
[b] In this column the year given is the one in which the incumbent President would have been required to seek renomination had he not decided to retire voluntarily, corresponding to years of action in the other columns.

TABLE 6.2. SUCCESS AND FAILURE IN ACHIEVING RENOMINATION—
PRESIDENTS ELECTED INITIALLY AS VICE PRESIDENTS[a]

Retired Voluntarily at End of One Incomplete Term	Sought Nomination Unsuccessfully	Nominated for a Full Term as President
DEMOCRATIC PARTY		
None	None	H. S. Truman, 1948
NATIONAL REPUBLICAN, WHIG, AND REPUBLICAN PARTIES		
None	J. Tyler, 1844	T. Roosevelt, 1904
	M. Fillmore, 1852	C. Coolidge, 1924
	A. Johnson, 1868	
	C. A. Arthur, 1884	

[a] For full names of all vice-presidential candidates of the two major parties, see Appendix A, Table 1

lentified, within each of which a number f variations occur:

1. Inheritance by an understudy whom ie previous leader has selected for the succession; or inheritance by someone whom ie party in general has already recognized s the natural successor.

2. Selection by an inner group either om within its own ranks when no single :ader had previously attained an unquesioned pre-eminence, or from outside its wn ranks.

3. Acceptance of the leader of a minor iction or a less prominent political figure s a compromise candidate after the leaders avored by the major factions have reached position of stalemate.

4. Advancement of the successful leader f an insurgent faction that wins in a conest with the faction previously holding the :adership; or advancement of the leader of ne of several factions, no one of which has een clearly in control but one of which ventually wins leadership of the party.

The various categories of leadership conrmation and succession, as just defined, iake up a classification system that can be pplied to the sixty-three presidential nomiations made in the period 1831-1956 by iajor-party national conventions. As in all iatters of classification, some cases can be ·laced much more easily than others. In iew of the important question: when did specific leadership cease to exist?—a quesion frequently surrounded by much ambiuity in American party history—the circumtances under which each previous leaderhip was terminated, abandoned, dissipated, r rejected were carefully considered. Often here is real doubt of the category to which case should be assigned; various doubtful ases are examined in footnotes throughout he chapter.

The tables that appear later in this chaper include all the cases of transfer in the op leadership of the present major parties hrough presidential nominations made in ·arty conventions. This is the only authoriative means by which the top party leaderhip has been transferred since 1832, except

for the constitutional succession of the Vice Presidents to the Presidency on the death of the President during his term of office. Seven Presidents have died in office—two Whigs, four Republicans and one Democrat —all since the beginnings of the convention system.

Patterns in Confirmation and Rejection of Leadership

The Presidents who seriously undertook to secure renomination and a second term were the first to give substance to the role of top national party leadership. Success in achieving the renomination was one type of proof of their effectiveness as party leaders. Vice Presidents who succeeded to the Presidency were obviously in a weaker position to assert party leadership than Presidents who had been elected directly to the office. Defeated presidential candidates, as titular leaders, were in a weaker position still. Nevertheless, from the beginnings of the convention system, all three types of party leaders have occasionally sought nominations to succeed themselves. When the instances in each category are examined, it becomes apparent that there have been significant long-term developments that are undoubtedly related to institutional change in the national government, in the posts of top party leadership, and in the Presidency.

Presidents Elected
Directly to the Office

As Tables 6.1, 6.2, and 6.3 suggest, incumbent Presidents who were elected directly to the office have generally been far more successful in obtaining renomination than either of the other two classes of party leader. At the beginning of the convention system, Jackson (in 1832) and Van Buren (in 1840) were renominated to succeed themselves; after that no further instance occurred until 1864. This was an era of one-term Presidencies and of frequent rejection of the President as party leader. The Whig platform of 1844 advocated a one-term limit. James K. Polk announced that he would not be a candidate for a second term; Franklin Pierce tried for the nomination and failed. James Buchanan found it expedient not to make the effort. The four-year limitation was accepted in principle to the point where Horace Greeley could use it editorially as a substantial argument against the renomination of Abraham Lincoln in 1864. With Lincoln and Ulysses S. Grant, however, the two-term tradition was restored. By 1892, even as weak a President as Benjamin Harrison was able to secure renomination in the face of factional opposition, although perhaps in part because the supporters of William McKinley expected a party defeat and wished to save their man for 1896.

For most of a century it has been assumed that a regularly elected President is entitled to his party's nomination for a second term. The tradition is so firmly established that contesting candidacies for the nomination of the party in power have rarely been discussed in recent decades, unless the President's own availability for a second term is for some reason in doubt. The conflict over the Taft renomination in 1912, with Theodore Roosevelt available as the alternative, is the only outstanding case to the contrary.

Vice Presidents
Succeeding to the Presidency

All of the seven Vice Presidents who became President through death of the previous incumbent sought party nominations for the next full term as President. Of the four nineteenth-century cases—John Tyler, Millard Fillmore, Andrew Johnson, and Chester A. Arthur—not one was able to secure the presidential nomination of the party by which he had previously been nominated for Vice President.

Tyler and Johnson had both been members of the opposite party before their vice-presidential nomination. They had been selected partly for that reason, in order to balance the ticket in a time when party lines were often crossed. After gaining the presidential office each discovered that any hope of a further nomination would have to come from their earlier associates. Tyler received a futile nomination from a splinter convention of his old party. Johnson, after his impeachment trial, hoped for vindication as a Democratic nominee. He actually received 65 votes on the first ballot in the 1868 Democratic convention, but was not taken seriously by the party leaders and soon disappeared from the balloting.[3]

Fillmore and Arthur belonged to minority factions in the Whig and Republican parties, and they too had been put on the ticket for balancing purposes. They were in no position to exercise strong party leadership after becoming President. Although each received substantial support for the presidential nomination in his respective party convention, both were defeated.

The change in practice was striking when it came; and the growing power of the Presidency was probably mainly responsible for the change. Each of the three Vice Presidents succeeding to the Presidency since William McKinley's election in 1896 easily won nomination to succeed himself, and won the election as well. The strength of Theodore Roosevelt as a popular leader was doubtless a factor in timing the change. But by 1924 even a Calvin Coolidge could be nominated for the full term without much opposition. In the Democratic party, where the problem has arisen only once, the claim to the nomination was successfully maintained by President Harry S. Truman in 1948.

If a Vice President succeeds to the office of President, political leaders, political writers, and the public generally now seem to agree that he automatically becomes the

[3] Charles H. Coleman, *The Election of 1868* (1933), pp. 159-60; Claude G. Bowers, *The Tragic Era* (1929), pp. 226, 229. Both authors cite various sources, including *The Diary of Gideon Welles* (1911), Vol. 3, pp. 383, 396, 398.

eader of his party and will be a strong candidate for the next nomination. A Vice President who succeeded very late in the presidential term might find himself at a tactical disadvantage, although there is some value under the Twenty-second Amendment in succeeding late enough to be eligible for two further nominations. Theodore Roosevelt and Truman both had ample time to consolidate their positions. Coolidge managed to do so with only ten months between Harding's death and the Republican convention of the following year, and in the face of the many scandals inherited from the Harding regime.

Titular Leaders
Who Had Suffered Electoral Defeat

The titular leaders have also gained strength in recent decades, and this development also is probably related to changes in the status of the Presidency, which confer a growing importance on any major-party candidate for the office. For a long period the possibility of renomination was remote for almost all defeated major-party candidates; in the present century the trend has been the other way.

Martin Van Buren was the first titular leader to seek renomination and to fail to

TABLE 6.3. SUCCESS AND FAILURE IN ACHIEVING RENOMINATION—
TITULAR LEADERS WHO HAD SUFFERED ELECTORAL DEFEAT

Did Not Seek Renomination in Party Convention Next Following Defeat[a]	Sought Renomination Unsuccessfully	Renominated Once or More
DEMOCRATIC PARTY		
G. B. McClellan, 1868	M. Van Buren, 1844[b]	G. Cleveland, 1892[b]
H. Seymour, 1872	L. Cass, 1852	W. J. Bryan, 1900, 1908
S. J. Tilden, 1880	A. E. Smith, 1932	A. E. Stevenson, 1956
W. S. Hancock, 1884		
W. J. Bryan, 1904,[c] 1912		
J. M. Cox, 1924		
J. W. Davis, 1928		
NATIONAL REPUBLICAN, WHIG, AND REPUBLICAN PARTIES		
H. Clay, 1836[d]	H. Clay, 1848	T. E. Dewey, 1948
W. Scott, 1856[e]	W. L. Willkie, 1944	
J. C. Frémont, 1860		
J. G. Blaine, 1888		
B. Harrison, 1896,[b]		
W. H. Taft, 1916[b]		
C. E. Hughes, 1920		
H. Hoover, 1936[b]		
A. M. Landon, 1940		
T. E. Dewey, 1952[c]		

[a] In this column the year given is the one in which the titular leader would have been required to seek renomination had he not decided to retire voluntarily, corresponding to the years of action in the other columns.

[b] Had served one term as President and had failed of re-election for a second term.

[c] Had previously been nominated and defeated twice when declining to stand for a third consecutive nomination.

[d] The National Republican party disintegrated after holding one convention and made no further nomination.

[e] The Whig party disintegrated after losing with Scott and held no national convention in 1856.

achieve it. Although he had been defeated in the election of 1840, he had the prestige of a previous term in the White House to sustain his candidacy for the party nomination in 1844. He was generally recognized as the party leader and his renomination was anticipated, but he failed to obtain the required two thirds vote. Henry Clay was twice nominated for the Presidency by major-party national conventions, but not by the same political party. The National Republican party, which gave him the honor in 1831, held no convention in 1836; in 1844 he was nominated by the Whigs, but, as their titular leader, failed of renomination in 1848. With the added obstacle of the two thirds rule, Lewis Cass likewise failed of renomination as the titular leader of the Democrats in 1852. Thereafter no defeated candidate of either major party sought renomination by his own party's national convention until Grover Cleveland's successful effort in 1892. Many of the former candidates dropped out of political life almost completely after their defeat. This was true of such relatively recent candidates as James M. Cox and John W. Davis. They had achieved only limited fame before their respective nominations; they were decisively defeated; and they took little interest in acting as party leaders without benefit of public office.

William Jennings Bryan was the first to achieve renomination in either party without benefit of a previous term in the White House; and he achieved it twice although not consecutively, in 1900 and 1908. In the Republican party, no defeated presidential candidate seems to have tried openly for a second nomination until the time of Wendell L. Willkie, whose attempt came to grief in the primaries of 1944. James G. Blaine probably considered the possibility after his defeat in 1884, and continued to have strong factional support, but he took himself out of the running early in 1888. Charles Evans Hughes rejected the role of party leader after his defeat in the election of 1916, notwithstanding his creditable

race and near-victory. But neither Willkie nor his successor, Thomas E. Dewey, suffered from similar inhibitions; and where Willkie failed in 1944, Dewey succeeded in 1948. In similar fashion, Adlai Stevenson won renomination in the Democratic party in 1956 after a period in which no one since Bryan had done so. In both parties the basis has thus been laid for the claim that a defeated candidate is entitled to another try if he has made a good race.

Patterns in Leadership Succession

When a previous party leader is unavailable, or is rejected, any one of several patterns of succession may operate, as previously noted. The instances are brought together in Table 6.4.

Inheritance

Inheritance by an understudy whom the outgoing leader has selected is a common form of succession in human organizations of all types, but it has not happened often in the making of presidential nominations under the convention system. The nominations of Van Buren in 1836 and of William H. Taft in 1908 seem to be the only two cases that can be clearly identified. In both a powerful second-term President was retiring from office and in his capacity as party leader took an overt interest in the succession.

An already outstanding member of the leadership group may also sometimes "inherit" the party nomination without a contest from other leaders, usually as the result of general agreement on his pre-eminent "availability" in a situation of relative party harmony. Clay's first and second nominations occurred in situations of this kind. Herbert Hoover's nomination in 1928 falls into this pattern rather than into that of inheritance as an understudy, since Coolidge had assumed a hands-off attitude toward the next nomination. By coincidence

Inheritance	Inner Group Selection	Compromise in Stalemate	Factional Victory
	DEMOCRATIC PARTY		
M. Van Buren, 1836	L. Cass, 1848	J. K. Polk, 1844	J. Buchanan, 1856
A. E. Smith, 1928	G. B. McClellan, 1864	F. Pierce, 1852	S. A. Douglas, 1860
	H. Greeley, 1872	H. Seymour, 1868	S. J. Tilden, 1876
	W. S. Hancock, 1880	J. W. Davis, 1924	W. J. Bryan, 1896
	G. Cleveland, 1884		W. Wilson, 1912
	A. B. Parker, 1904		J. M. Cox, 1920
			F. D. Roosevelt, 1932
			A. E. Stevenson, 1952
	NATIONAL REPUBLICAN, WHIG, AND REPUBLICAN PARTIES		
H. Clay, 1831, 1844	J. C. Frémont, 1856	R. B. Hayes, 1876	W. H. Harrison, 1840
W. H. Taft, 1908	U. S. Grant, 1868	J. A. Garfield, 1880	Z. Taylor, 1848
H. Hoover, 1928	C. E. Hughes, 1916	W. G. Harding, 1920	W. Scott, 1852
	A. M. Landon, 1936		A. Lincoln, 1860
			J. G. Blaine, 1884
			B. Harrison, 1888
			W. McKinley, 1896
			W. L. Willkie, 1940
			T. E. Dewey, 1944
			D. D. Eisenhower, 1952

[a] The period is treated as beginning in 1832 for the reasons noted in Chapter 2, footnote 22, although Clay's nomination for 1832 actually occurred in 1831, as related in Chapter 2.

l Smith's nomination in the same year fell into the same pattern also, when William G. McAdoo, his previous strong opponent, conceded the nomination by announcing that he would not again enter the contest.

Inner Group Selection

Processes of "inner group" selection can be said to occur at times in the American political parties at the national level, but only if the term "inner group" is given a rather special meaning. As noted in previous chapters, the American national parties do not ordinarily have any single or genuinely cohesive inner group that is dominant for all party affairs, except in the party in power when leadership has become firmly centered in the President. But there have been recurring occasions when the dominant leaders of the various groups have seemed disposed to work together informally on a sort of federated basis. Usually these occasions have arisen in preparation for a specific national convention and have not lasted long when the convention was over.

Selection by such an "inner group" from within its own ranks has occurred in some instances under circumstances akin to inheritance by an understudy or by a previously outstanding leader. Usually, however, a larger element of competition is involved, there being less of a previous consensus on the outstanding availability of any one possible nominee. Cass's nomination in 1848 had elements of inheritance, but there was a considerable amount of conflict at the convention even though Cass seemed to have the support of the incumbent Polk administration. Cleveland's first nomination in 1884 reflected the renewed ascendancy of the Tilden faction along with the strength of Cleveland's own position as governor of New York. He was the only nominee chosen by an inner group to win election and become an effective leader as President. Alfred M. Landon was something of an oddity as a nominee in 1936, but was a recognized leader within the party hierarchy, having a strong appeal as the only outstanding Republican governor in office at the time.

Selection by an inner group from outside its own ranks implies the existence of an inner group with power to dominate the party as a whole but containing no suitable candidate among its members. With the general election at stake, it sometimes becomes a better risk for such a group to run an "outsider" and perhaps win, than to maintain undivided control but probably lose the election. But the "outsider," if he runs and is defeated, usually finds himself soon rejected as a leader.

The pattern of selection by an inner group from outside its own ranks has been remarkably unsuccessful in recruiting candidates who could win or provide party leadership. Such selection has rarely occurred in the Democratic party except under conditions of extraordinary party weakness, as in the nomination of George B. McClellan in 1864, Horace Greeley in 1872, and Alton B. Parker in 1904. Winfield S. Hancock's nomination in 1880, however, was not an expression of weakness. Widely known as a military hero and outstanding Democrat, he was on active duty as the commanding general of the Atlantic Division of the Army when nominated in 1880. He continued in the post during the campaign and after his defeat. Whig and Republican cases of outsider selection by an inner group included those of Frémont in 1856, Grant in 1868, and Hughes in 1916. Of the seven "outsider" candidates chosen by major-party inner groups, Grant was the only one to be elected, and he was never

effective as a party leader even though h easily won renomination. Of the other si Greeley died immediately after his defea and Frémont, McClellan, Hancock, an Parker were virtually unrecognized as tit lar leaders. Hughes, by far the ablest the group, promptly took himself out the party leadership after his defeat.[4]

Compromise in Stalemate

Seven compromise candidates have bee chosen in stalemated conventions, fou Democratic and three Republican. Two the seven were the nominees of a party power: Rutherford B. Hayes, 1876, an James A. Garfield, 1880; both were in th Republican party and both won. In each these two cases, the incumbent Presiden refrained from making any noteworthy e fort to influence the succession, and th convention was badly split, with the stron est faction supporting a front-runner wh fell short of a majority. The "anti" grou started with several candidates and acu differences among them; in 1876, the fa tions opposed to James G. Blaine we eventually able to compromise on Haye and in 1880, those opposed to a third nom nation for former President Grant we able to compromise on Garfield.

In the other five cases, all of which o curred in a party out of power, the eve tual compromise candidate was acceptab to all of the major factions represented the convention. The nomination was th a major act of interfactional concilatio The first two such nominations, those James K. Polk, 1844, and Franklin Pierc 1852, occurred in the early years of th

[4] In the earlier version of this analysis, publish in the *Western Political Quarterly* (see footnote 1 this chapter), Parker and Hancock were regarded inner group selections from within. On further c sideration, the Parker case seems much closer that of Hughes, since Parker had been on the ben of the highest New York State court for ma years, had withdrawn from active politics, and, li Hughes, refused to campaign for the nominati prior to the convention. Hancock, as noted in t text, was on active military duty when nominat

emocratic party after attempts at the re-
omination of a previous titular leader
ad reached a position of stalemate. The
her three, Horatio Seymour, 1868, and
ohn W. Davis, 1924, in the Democratic
arty, and Warren G. Harding, 1920, in the
epublican, all occurred in factional situ-
ions where the previous titular leader
ad lost all standing or had specifically
ken himself out of the running.

Most of the seven compromise candidates
ist named have been considered "dark
orse" nominees, that peculiar appellation
 American politics. But there is no gen-
ally agreed definition of what constitutes
"dark horse" in the nominating contests.
n its face, the term seems to imply an
nanticipated or minor candidate whose
ctory was a surprise. According to Sidney
yman, the oral tradition of American
olitics holds that the authentic dark horses
ere only five: Polk, Pierce, Hayes, Gar-
ld, and Davis, to whom he would add
arding and Willkie.[5] But Willkie quali-
d as a dark horse, if at all, only because
 the extent to which his nomination was
surprise to many observers. He had been
mpaigning vigorously for several months
fore the convention, was the avowed
ndidate of an important aggregation of
irty supporters, and was certainly the
ost highly illuminated dark horse in his-
ry if he is to be accepted as such. In any
ent, he was not a compromise candidate
 a situation of convention deadlock.

If unexpected acceptance as a com-
romise candidate is a major criterion of
e dark horse species, there can be no
iestion about the inclusion of Harding
 the list—and Seymour must also be added,
 has been done here.[6] In Seymour's case,
e element of surprise and of compromise
ose out of his own determination not to

be considered for the nomination. He was
so highly esteemed within the party that
he probably could have been nominated
on an early ballot at the Democratic convention of 1868, if he had been willing to
run for the nomination in advance of the
convention. In the end, the nomination
was forced upon him after it had become
apparent that the convention was reluctant
to give even a simple majority to any other
candidate.[7]

Others sometimes mentioned as dark
horse candidates are Benjamin Harrison,
in 1888, and William Jennings Bryan, in
1896, both of whom are included in a
formal listing of the species by two eminent
scholars.[8] In the Republican convention of
1888 the confusion of the opening ballots
was mainly due to a hope that Blaine, who
was in Europe, would reconsider his previous decision not to run. John Sherman,
the early front-runner, was never near a
majority. Harrison, who had been a Blaine
supporter in 1884, became the runner-up
early in the balloting when much of the
Blaine faction consolidated behind him.
Eventually he became the winner, when
other factional elements moved to him, but
without any significant capitulation on the

[7] A close study of the convention voting, including
the shifts by states that came early in the critical
ballot, indicates that if Ohio had not broken for
Seymour when it did, Thomas A. Hendricks of
Indiana would have obtained a clear majority on
that ballot, after which he might have gone on to
secure the necessary two thirds. Hendricks was one
of the perennial candidates for the party nomination; after Greeley's death in 1872, Hendricks received most of the Greeley vote in the electoral
college; he was the Democratic vice-presidential
candidate in 1876 on the Tilden ticket that so
nearly won; he was elected with Cleveland in 1884,
and died in office as Vice President in 1885.

[8] Charles E. Merriam and Harold F. Gosnell, *The
American Party System* (3d ed., 1940), p. 313. In
addition, Merriam and Gosnell included the seven
nominations of the present tabulation. Their major
criterion in composing their list was that of compromise candidates, whom they also refer to as
"dark horses," candidates that came forward "only
after the others were deadlocked and evidently
unable to command the requisite votes for nomination."

Benjamin Harrison was included as a compromise
candidate in the version of this analysis published
in the *Western Political Quarterly*.

[5] Sidney Hyman, "Size-up of the Dark Horse
ecies," *The New York Times Magazine*, Nov. 6,
55, pp. 9, 67-69, 71-72, 76.
[6] Seymour has been classified as a dark horse
ndidate by many scholars, including Charles E.
erriam, Harold F. Gosnell, Edward M. Sait, and
ward R. Penniman.

part of the Sherman supporters. The nomination required eight ballots, but the convention was never deadlocked.

In a somewhat similar fashion at the Democratic convention of 1896, there was a main cleavage. The gold and silver Democrats were in sharp conflict, but the Silverites were so clearly in the majority that the contest for the nomination went on mainly within their ranks. Bryan was not the leader at the beginning, but he gained steadily and there was no deadlock. Hence there seem to be adequate grounds for excluding Harrison and Bryan from the group of compromise, or dark horse, candidates.[9]

Factional Victory

Factional victory can occur as a successful nominating pattern under conditions either of factional insurgency or of what can be called coordinate factionalism. The difference between the two conditions was not important in early decades of the convention system, but it has become important in the party in power and conceivably might become important in the party out of power. The respective groups of cases therefore merit some separate discussion, even though they have been consolidated in Table 6.4 and in the later tables of this chapter. For present purposes, a nomination occurs through successful action by an insurgent faction when the faction holding the leadership is overthrown.[10]

"The faction holding the leadership" denotes the supporters of a President in office or those of a titular leader expected to seek renomination. A nomination occurs under conditions of coordinate factionalism when "no one faction was previously in clear control of the party leadership and several factions were struggling to obtain it."[11]

Seven cases of nomination through successful insurgent factionalism can be identified.[12] Four of these cases occurred before the Civil War, two in the Whig party and two in the Democratic. In 1848, when Henry Clay, the outstanding Whig and the titular leader of his party, sought renomination, he was defeated and General Zachary Taylor was nominated instead.[13] In 1852, President Millard Fillmore, the second of the Whig Vice Presidents who had succeeded to the Presidency, sought the nomination. His nomination for Vice President on the Taylor ticket had been a sop to a minority faction, and he did not achieve recognition as a strong party leader while President. Although he led on the first convention ballot, he failed of nomination. General Winfield Scott was nominated after fifty-three ballots, thus eliminating Fillmore—while also destroying the party.

President Pierce sought renomination by the Democratic party in 1856 but lost the nomination to James Buchanan, his Minister to England, who had been a major contender for the nomination on previous occasions. With a further deepening in the split within the Democratic party, President

---

[9] The earlier version of the present analysis also included James M. Cox, the Democratic nominee of 1920, among the compromise candidates. Cox might be regarded as a compromise candidate in the sense that he was probably the most generally acceptable second choice for the supporters of William G. McAdoo, A. Mitchell Palmer, and Alfred E. Smith. Also, the convention was a sticky affair, since it took forty-four ballots to arrive at the nomination. But Cox was not a dark horse, although he did little to advance his own candidacy prior to the convention. His record as governor of Ohio was outstanding, he polled over 12 per cent of the convention vote on the first ballot, and he gained strength steadily throughout the convention.

[10] "Faction" has been defined as "a number of leaders and other adherents of a political party who are cooperating with each other for the purpose of controlling or influencing the formal behavior of

the party organization as a whole." David, Moos and Goldman, op. cit., Vol. 1, p. 11.

[11] Ibid., p. 9.

[12] The definition of insurgency that has been applied here reflects the present status of a President as party leader and the status that seems to be in process of achievement for the out-party titular leader; but that status existed much less clearly in the past. The definition has been applied to past experience partly to bring out the changes in attitudes and in practice that have occurred.

[13] In the earlier version of this analysis the nomination of Taylor in 1848 was treated as a case of inner group selection from outside its own ranks but this classification seems untenable in view of the fact that Henry Clay was actively seeking renomination.

Buchanan made no effort to secure his own renomination in 1860, but did attempt to act as party leader by opposing Stephen A. Douglas and giving at least tacit support to Vice President John C. Breckinridge. The Douglas elements eventually nominated their man at Baltimore in what continues to be regarded as the "regular" Democratic convention of 1860, though Breckinridge was nominated by bolting elements in a rump convention.

All four cases clearly represented successful insurgency, if a President or a titular leader is to be regarded as the leader of his party when he is actively attempting to function as such. But they also pointed to the disorder in the party system that preceded the Civil War, and to the weakness of the Presidency as a post of party leadership at the time.

The fifth case was that of President Chester A. Arthur in 1884. Arthur, who succeeded from the Vice Presidency, had difficulty in asserting his leadership in the face of opposing party elements strongly entrenched in Congress. He tried for renomination but, after four ballots, was defeated by James G. Blaine. Since his day, no President has sought renomination without getting it.

Important insurgent attempts to capture the nomination have occurred in both parties since the turn of the century, most notably in the Republican party in 1912, where the attempt was unsuccessful. Two attempts that can be considered insurgency and that were victorious, the sixth and seventh of the series, were those of Franklin D. Roosevelt in 1932 and Dewey in 1944, both of whom defeated titular leaders.

As these instances reveal, what has here been called insurgency has rarely been successful except when it was still unrecognized as such. Accepted notions of what constitutes "insurgency" in American presidential politics have undoubtedly gone through a lengthy evolution in reaching their present position. An attempt to un-

seat an incumbent President by preventing his nomination for a second term would currently be regarded almost universally as insurgency, regardless of whether the incumbent President was originally elected as such or not, but during past decades attempts of this kind were viewed with much tolerance within the parties. An attempt to prevent the second nomination of a defeated candidate who has served actively and effectively as party leader is beginning to be recognized as insurgency, but was rarely so regarded when Franklin D. Roosevelt and Thomas E. Dewey won their first presidential nominations. When a retiring President or titular leader is merely attempting to influence the succession, opposing candidates are seldom considered insurgents unless they are leading small dissident minorities that refuse to go along with the obvious sentiment of the majority within the party.

The field is open for the processes of coordinate factionalism when the retiring President declines an active role in the succession, or when his party faction has found no candidate to back. The field is also open in the out-party when there is no titular leader who is seeking renomination. This type of situation has occurred frequently. Sometimes the nomination has gone to the leader or candidate of one of the coordinate factions; on other occasions, the lines of factional warfare have been drawn so evenly that stalemate has compelled a compromise choice under the circumstances previously noted.

The first Harrison, in 1840, and Lincoln, in 1860, were both the nominees of new political parties, although Henry Clay was an important figure in the first case, and William H. Seward in the second. Samuel J. Tilden in 1876 was the nominee of a party whose last previous nominee had died before the electoral votes were counted. Cox in 1920 was the candidate of a party whose leader, President Woodrow Wilson, had been ill and was not inclined to take an active interest in the succession. Benjamin

Harrison in 1888, William McKinley in 1896, Wilson in 1912, Willkie in 1940, and Eisenhower in 1952 were each candidates of a party out of power at the time of their nomination and in which the previous nominee was generally regarded as out of the running. These were all cases in which processes of coordinate factionalism operated to give the nomination to the leader or the candidate of a major faction.

The Bryan nomination of 1896 and the Stevenson nomination of 1952 have also been treated as factional victories within situations of coordinate factionalism, although it might have been possible to define Bryan's nomination as a case of successful insurgency against the Cleveland faction, and Stevenson's as the successful defeat of insurgents Estes Kefauver and Richard B. Russell. But in 1896 the Cleveland faction had lost its position of leadership before the convention opened. Cleveland himself was belated in renouncing third-term ambitions, and his faction was defeated in the national committee on the choice of convention city and had no candidate with enough strength to deadlock the convention under the two thirds rule.[14] In 1952 the Truman faction was strong, but had been unable to find an adequate candidate before the convention, since Adlai Stevenson refused to serve as a Truman understudy. Hence it would seem too much to brand the Kefauver and Russell candidacies of 1952 as insurgency, although they may have been so considered by President Truman and his associates.[15]

The differing outcomes in the various factional contests, whether insurgent or coordinate, may be further illuminated by classifying the candidates according to their own relation to the faction by which they are put forward.

A candidate may himself be a faction leader, or he may be an outsider, or between these two extremes he may be a subordinate leader or a relatively inactive member of the faction. For example, McKinley, Wilson, and Dewey were faction leaders: there was no one more important in their faction nor more representative of its aims. William Henry Harrison, Taylor and Eisenhower, at least in the early stages of his candidacy, were outsiders recruited by a faction in search of a winner. Others are more difficult to classify, but insofar as their position in this respect was definite it called for a specific type of strategy.

A recognized factional leader must fight openly against the field; he is limited in the areas where he can be built up as a second choice, for as a rule he will have at least one unbending opponent. A candidate from the outside may have a better chance to pick up second-choice votes, especially in factions that are not diametrically opposed to the faction that is his particular sponsor.

Candidates who are factional leaders generally take an active part in the strategy of the campaigns. Those from outside are apt to be more in the position of passengers on a band wagon operated by the faction, while the activities of others in intermediate positions may vary from an appearance of abstention to overt participation.

Continuity and Change in the Patterns of Nomination

In the preceding pages of this chapter the major-party presidential nominations since 1832 have been classified as either the confirmation of the existing party leadership or a choice of new leadership through one or another of four different avenues of succession. The sixty-three cases are now recapitulated, in Tables 6.5 and 6.5, for the periods 1832-1892 and 1896-1956. The

[14] Ralph M. Goldman, "Party Chairmen and Party Faction, 1789-1900," unpublished doctoral dissertation, University of Chicago, 1951, pp. 585-87, 596.

[15] According to Alben W. Barkley, assurance of presidental support for his own candidacy was given him at a White House conference in which "the President . . . remarked that it had been traditional in this country that any outgoing President, if he so desired, could virtually nominate his successor." (Barkley, *That Reminds Me*, 1954, p. 230.)

TABLE 6.5. PATTERNS IN MAJOR-PARTY PRESIDENTIAL NOMINATIONS
SINCE 1832; BY MAJOR PARTIES[a]

Type of Nomination	Democratic		Republican[b]		Major-Party Total	
	1832–1892	1896–1956	1832–1892	1896–1956	1831–1892	1896–1956
A. Confirmation	4	8	3	7	7	15
B. Inheritance	1	1	2	2	3	3
C. Inner Group Selection	5	1	2	2	7	3
D. Compromise in Stalemate	3	1	2	1	5	2
E. Factional Victory	3	5	6	4	9	9
Total	16	16	15	16	31	32

[a] Data for Type A from Tables 6.1, 6.2, and 6.3; included are 14 cases of renomination of an incumbent President elected as such, 3 cases of nomination of a President who had succeeded from the Vice Presidency through death of the incumbent, and 5 cases of renomination of an incumbent titular leader. Other data from Table 6.4.
[b] Includes National Republican and Whig.

TABLE 6.6. PATTERNS IN MAJOR-PARTY PRESIDENTIAL NOMINATIONS SINCE 1832;
BY IN-POWER AND OUT-OF-POWER STATUS OF THE PARTIES[a]

Type of Nomination	Party in Power		Party Out of Power	
	1832–1892	1896–1956	1832–1892	1896–1956
A. Confirmation	6	11	1	4
B. Inheritance	2	2	1	1
C. Inner Group Selection	2	0	5	3
D. Compromise in Stalemate	2	0	3	2
E. Factional Victory	4	3	5	6
Total	16	16	15	16

[a] "In-power" and "out-power" status was determined in accordance with whether the currently incumbent President had been elected on the party ticket. The result is anomalous to the extent that it classifies the Whig party as holding power during John Tyler's administration, and the Republican party during Andrew Johnson's; but the result would be even more anomalous if the Democratic party were regarded as holding power in those instances.

periods divide the total experience under the convention system of nominations into two equal portions. The breaking point also coincides with the critical election year of 1896. The comparisons that can be made between the figures for the period ending in 1892 and those for the one beginning in 1896 therefore have special interest in connection with the study of long-term changes in the nominating process and the party system.

Interparty Comparisons

The various nominating patterns have occurred about as often in one party as the other since 1896. (See Table 6.5.) Differences were more apparent in the earlier period, probably the most notable being the greater number of inner group nominees among the Democrats before 1892, and the correspondingly greater number of nominations arising out of successful factional contests among the Whigs and Republicans during the same period. These differences, although not statistically significant, are consistent with the greater stability and continuity of the Democrats as the older party, and the turmoil that attended the breakup of the Whig party and the inception of the Republican.

From one period to the other, the number of nominations that confirmed an existing leadership or recognized inheritance rose from just under one third of the total to over one half. Other nominations that occurred without much of a contest and reflected inner group consensus followed an opposite trend; they comprised nearly one quarter of the nominations in the first sixty years and fell to one tenth in the second. Compromise nominations in situations of factional stalemate made up one sixth of the total in the first period, one fifteenth in the second. Nominations that reflected success in a vigorous intra-party contest, arising either from insurgency or coordinate factionalism, provided nearly one third of the cases from the beginning, with no apparent

trend toward either an increasing or a declining proportion of the total.

In-Party Versus Out-Party

When the cases are regrouped in terms of the "in-power" and "out-of-power" status of the respective parties at the time of each nomination (see Table 6.6), it becomes apparent that the "in-party" had a preponderance of the Type A nominations that confirmed an existing top leader, in its case the incumbent President, while the "out-party" less often confirmed its titular leader by giving him a second nomination. But in both in-party and out-party the number of confirming nominations was clearly on the upgrade. The in-party also had the preponderance of the Type B nominations that recognized a kind of inheritance of the party leadership; here the numbers are extremely small, but coincide in their lack of any indication of time trend by party status or in total.

Types C and D, inner group selections and compromise nominations respectively, again involve small numbers of cases, but are most remarkably coincidental in the closeness of pattern between the two types of nominations and between the two party statuses, with a downward shift in each of the possible comparisons between the time periods.

Type E, successful factional nominations, reveals relatively little difference by party status and by time period, but such differences as do appear are consistent with what might be expected: factional contests leading to factional victory in winning the nomination have been more common in the out-party than in the in-party—eleven cases to seven; and the number of such cases declined in the in-party while increasing in the out-party.

The Patterns of the Future

In all analytical work based upon small numbers of cases it is necessary to guard against inferences that may have no basis other than purely random variations in the numbers. There is also danger in projecting into the future the observed trends of the past, however well ascertained those trends may be. Both of these dangers are undoubtedly great in any effort to look into the future on the basis of the present data. But the data may be more persuasive than would ordinarily be expected by statisticians who are accustomed to dealing with large masses of figures.[16]

[16] If the 63 cases are considered as a sample, the sampling problem has two aspects: (1) if a larger number of nominations—say 500—had been made in the past 125 years under similar conditions, would the proportions be substantially the same as for the 63 that did occur; (2) could a long series of nominations in future years be expected to project the same rates of change that have developed in the first 125 years? To answer both questions in the affirmative would doubtless be in some degree invalid, but taken together the resulting assumptions would represent the closest approximation to a valid basis for future expectations.

In the use of the series in this way, with such small numbers of cases, the mathematical difficulties become acute. But some assistance can be found in qualitative judgments of the political sentiments and habits that appear to have caused various aspects of the changing pattern, and an attempt can be made to evaluate their present influence.

Four features add strength to the inferences that can be drawn from the data that have been collected in the present chapter. In the first place, all of the major-party presidential nominations made in party conventions have been included; 63 cases are not a large number, but in this instance they are all that have so far occurred over a period of a century and a quarter.

In the second place, numbers as small as 4 to 10 in a single cell of a table can be statistically significant when the relationships lean strongly in one direction. For example, if an event can happen in only one of two ways, the probability that 4 events will all happen in the same way by pure chance is approximately 6 in 100; for 5 cases, it is about 3 in 100. In most statistical work, results are considered significant when no more than 5 cases in 100 may be expected to deviate due to chance alone.

In the third place, there is every reason to assume interrelationship between the cells in the tables. This has the consequence that figures that might be lacking in significance when taken in isolation come closer to becoming significant in connection with each other. For some specific pairs of cases, the standard formula for testing the significance of a difference between proportions can be used and will demonstrate statistically significant results. More important, however, is the fact that the total set of interrelationships within each table is one that can be read intelligibly in almost any direction by

Any projection of trends on the basis of the figures alone would be hazardous indeed; but, in the total historical context, the figures mainly have the effect of clarifying and solidifying the largely qualitative estimates of what has already occurred that would otherwise be much more vague.

The figures derive much of their over-all interest from the importance of precedent in politics. All political observers are aware of the great difficulty of doing something in politics that has never been done before, compared with the relative ease of doing it again after it has been done once. In the same way, it is difficult to reverse a practice after it has occurred consecutively even twice, if it has the effect of producing a vested interest of some value. In this chapter, as well as elsewhere, it has been common to find strings of cases all going in one direction, ending in a point of reversal after which they go consistently in the opposite direction. One example of this is provided by the seven Vice Presidents who succeeded to the Presidency on the death of the incumbent: the first four uniformly failed of nomination for the next full term; the later three uniformly achieved nomination. When some such reversal, or any novel event, occurs in political behavior, there is a strong presumption that some powerful force has been brought to bear, such, for example, as the personality of Theodore Roosevelt in 1904.

The precedents established in the sixty-three nominations studied in this chapter probably give the previous experience more predictive value than it might have as a simple statistical sample of a process reaching into the future. But the precedent-setting events of the future must also be

any experienced political analyst. When so read, moreover, the figures cohere in a pattern of meaning that has a remarkable degree of over-all consistency.

In the fourth place, as a corollary of what has just been said, the figures have the effect of giving a concise, numerical form to a wide range of interlocking estimates of past behavior, interpretive hypotheses, and anticipations of the future in the making of presidential nominations.

taken into account. Unpredictable forces may enter at any time to change some aspects of the system, with unpredictable consequences. Accordingly, in the following comments on possible lines of future development, the materials assembled in Chapters 2 through 5 are highly relevant and the statistical analysis is merely a portion of the evidence to be taken into account. The predictions that are recorded here represent simply an effort to clarify the expectations that can reasonably be held at the present time.

Probably the simplest prediction that can be made is that first-term Presidents who have been elected directly to the office will, when willing and available, continue to secure party renominations with a high degree of unanimity, as they have since 1864, and that in the election they will continue to be extremely strong contenders. The latter part of this prediction is not as safe as the first part, since re-election for a second term implies eight years of continuous tenure by the same political party. As noted in Chapter 3, the United States may be moving into an era of closer party balance and more frequent party overturn than has existed since 1896.

Vice Presidents who succeed to the Presidency through death of the incumbent will probably continue to secure nomination for a second term with little difficulty, as they have since 1904, and will continue to benefit from the prestige of the office in their quest for re-election. Succession by the death of the President will cause less disruption of party and governmental affairs in the future than in the past, to the extent that increasing attention is given to factional and personal compatibility between the presidential and vice-presidential candidates of each party, rather than to "balancing" the ticket. But the Eisenhower doctrine on the selection of Vice Presidents has not yet been fully accepted.[17]

The future of the titular leaders as candidates for the Presidency is full of uncertainties and imponderables. The institu-

tional position of the titular leadership seems likely to continue to be strengthened, and this may be favorable to continued success in the pursuit of the party nominations. But these tendencies may be delayed or even reversed unless some titular leader eventually wins election as well as renomination.

In any event, incumbent Presidents cannot be renominated more than once under the Twenty-second Amendment if they win their second term, and not many titular leaders are likely to receive more than two consecutive nominations as long as the American party system retains its present form.

When a new leadership is to be chosen, the cases of factional contest hold special interest. Here the situation of the in-party must be sharply distinguished from that of the out-party. Factional conflict over the nomination, with a struggle and a divided vote, has become much less common in the party in power than in the party out of power. But factional conflict over the succession will probably continue to occur from time to time even in a party in power, as long as the parties are no more internally cohesive than they are at present.

Factional candidates in a party out of power can be expected to continue to achieve nominations with considerable frequency, unless the titular leadership is greatly strengthened, and probably even if it is. The successful factional candidates who drive through to the party nomination within ten years or less after they first become prominent on the national scene have a type of glamour that can be extremely useful in the interparty competition, particularly when it is necessary to face an incumbent President carrying the prestige of the office. If the factional in-fighting over the nomination does not become too severe, moreover, the contest itself may serve a useful purpose as a demonstration of party vitality and as a means of publicizing the eventual candidate. Such candidates will continue to have good chances for electoral victory.

[17] See Chapter 4, footnote 23.

Inner group nominations such as have occurred in the past are probably a type of limited importance for the future, unless there is return to a party imbalance so extreme that the out-party becomes a minority in which the recruitment of suitable candidates is difficult. If effective interparty competition is maintained in the future at the national level, as may well be desired for many reasons, inner group nominations caused by a shortage of suitable candidates are unlikely to occur.

What might develop would be a different type of inner group selection, arising out of a firmer establishment of the Presidency and the titular leadership as effective posts of party leadership. Should this occur, the retiring party leaders, President or titular leader as the case might be, might more often succeed in forming a representative inner party group of sufficient strength to compose internal differences and effectively pick the candidates long before the convention. Nominees coming out of this kind of background would be closer to the Type B cases of inheritance, and might expect a considerably greater measure of electoral success than has attended the inner group selections that arose out of weakness rather than strength.

The compromise or dark horse nominees have been reserved for final treatment because this group is in some respects both the most interesting and the most crucial for the appraisal of the nominating process. It is the group that is most generally cited when the convention system of nominations is under attack. The fact that even one Harding could be nominated under the convention system is to many critics a sufficient argument for the substitution of a national primary.

But all the other compromise candidates except John W. Davis, who was defeated, are figures of ancient history, when the parties were somewhat different; and some of them, in their day, may have served a useful purpose. It is easy to argue, as many scholars have, that they were the only possible solution—the price of union—at a time when politics was fiercely sectional and factional passions ran high. Undoubtedly each of the compromise candidates had the effect of preventing a sharper polarization of opinion between the major parties of the day, though by the same token they may have prevented the parties from performing an essential function—that of presenting the voters with viable alternatives through which to make progress in the solution of national issues.

Be that as it may, the dark horse candidate of the compromise-in-stalemate variety seems to be a vanishing type. The reasons for this can be readily inferred, but will be developed further in later chapters, in which it will become apparent that most of the conditions that were conducive to such candidacies have disappeared.

The nominating institutions of the major parties have developed over the years under the impact of changes in the structure of government, and in the kind of political issues at stake—and sometimes under the impact of personalities and personal decisions. There may also have been growth caused at times by the lessons of experience and by the arrival of an intelligent understanding of weaknesses and of opportunities for their correction. The main purpose of the convention system from the first has been to select candidates of each party in such a way as to unite the party for the election contest to follow. The various patterns identified in this chapter have grown up as the result of the tactics chosen by political leaders who sought to press for the results they desired and at the same time to avoid breaking up the party. Usually a consensus has been achieved; those who were disappointed were not so bitter as to walk out; the party has been held together; and the chance of victory in the election was not thrown away. On other occasions the consensus failed, and the party was split. Then the voters took a hand in the election and taught the warring political leaders the value of compromise, unity, and the integrity of the two-party system.

7

The Candidates for the Nominations

THE LEADING candidates for a major-party presidential nomination are generally recognized as centers of strategic action along the way to the final decision. The candidate who is chosen for a nomination exercises power equivalent to that of the convention when he accepts it, since no nominating decision is complete until it is accepted by the candidate.[1] Even the crudest descriptive information on characteristics of the candidates who are seriously considered for the presidential and vice-presidential nominations may thus throw some light on aspects of the nominating process and of government.

More important than simple description, however, is the possibility that data on candidate characteristics can be organized for various types of comparative analysis. Such questions as the following can be explored: Are there any notable differences between the types of candidates that are considered by the Democratic and Republican parties? Between candidates who win elections, those who merely win nominations, and those who win neither? Between candidates for presidential nominations and those for vice-presidential nominations? Have there been any changes in the characteristics that were typical of the candi-

dates before 1892 compared with those since 1896?

To the extent that noteworthy differences are found, it may be possible to draw further inferences about the nominating process and the party system. In some cases, the absence of any difference may itself be important. In any event, a review of the characteristics of the alternative candidates who were rejected may assist understanding of why the others were approved.

The number of names under consideration has fluctuated widely from convention to convention. Sometimes an incumbent President has been renominated without any competing name being placed before the national convention of his political party. At the other extreme, 60 different persons received votes for the presidential nomination at one time or another during the 103-ballot Democratic national convention of 1924. Table 7.1 reports a census of the situation by time periods, giving the number of candidates receiving over 3 per cent of the vote at any point in the convention balloting.[2]

---

[1] The latent power of a potential nominee is perhaps best indicated by General William Tecumseh Sherman's classic statement: "I will not accept if nominated and will not serve if elected." In three instances vice-presidential nominations were extended by the convention to men who promptly declined to receive them: Silas Wright (D, 1844); Benjamin Fitzpatrick (D, 1860); Frank O. Lowden (R, 1924).

[2] The 3 per cent cutoff level was selected after review of the data and consideration especially of 5 and 10 per cent levels as alternatives. As for the candidates who polled less than 3 per cent, it was apparent in most cases that they were receiving courtesy votes in situations of early balloting or other uncertainty. Even when they had some sort of favorite son status, they were from states too small to make them important—unless they were important for other reasons. It was also found that biographical materal for most of the candidates below the 3 per cent level was extremely scarce. Conversely, the 10 per cent level would omit favorite sons even from states as imporant as New

In both parties the number of aspirants for presidential nominations increased in successive periods up to and including 1896-1924 and declined noticeably in the period 1928-1956. More intensive preconvention campaigning, presidential primaries in certain states, and nationwide public opinion polling probably all have operated to reduce the number of candidates who reach the convention. With firm preconvention information about the strength of leading candidates, minor aspirants have more incentive to bargain for preconvention alliances and to avoid overt opposition in situations where they will lose.

The number of candidates for the presidential nominations has been considerably larger in the Democratic party than in the Republican. The difference appears in each of the four time periods, even in the recent period dominated by the four successive nominations of Franklin D. Roosevelt, although it is slight in that period.

The most important factor contributing to this long-term pattern may have been the influence of the Democratic party's two thirds rule before its elimination in 1936. In a convention under the two thirds rule in which a center of hard-core resistance approaches, but does not reach, $33\frac{1}{3}$ per cent of the total convention vote, the bargaining power of any other solid unit having from 3 to 10 per cent of the convention vote can be very high. In view of the stakes involved, it would be surprising indeed if the operation of the two thirds rule throughout most of the history of the Democratic party had not encouraged many state party organizations in the larger states to organize their convention delegations on a

basis for effective bargaining in so highly negotiable a situation. A strong favorite son candidate was obviously a very useful element in such an organizing effort.[3]

In the case of the vice-presidential nominations, the number of aspirants did not grow noticeably during the earlier periods, but has drastically declined in recent years. The Democratic party has had more aspirants than the Republican, but the differences are minor and the relationship has shifted from one time period to another. The two thirds rule was applicable to vice-presidential as well as presidential nominations in the Democratic party before 1936, but the instances in which it had any effect on the vice-presidential nominations seem to have been rare.

For the approximately 300 persons who

York when polling only the votes of their own state. The 5 per cent level, as of 1956 (see Chapter 8, Table 8.6), would include only New York, Pennsylvania, and California, while the 3 per cent level would typically include at least the favorite son candidates of the seven largest states when standing alone.

Candidates for the nominations who did not receive more than 3 per cent of the convention vote at their maximum for one office or the other will be disregarded in the remainder of this chapter.

[3] For a discussion of analogous situations in mathematical terms, see L. S. Shapley and Martin Shubik, "A Method for Evaluating the Distribution of Power in a Committee System," *American Political Science Review*, Vol. 48 (Sept. 1954), pp. 787-92.

In terms of practical politics, two examples may be cited of the situations before and after the elimination of the two thirds rule. In 1932, with the rule in effect, Franklin D. Roosevelt received about 57 per cent of the vote on the first ballot. Hard-core Smith delegates, who never shifted, were polling about 20 per cent of the convention vote. The decisive shift was made on the fourth ballot when the Garner delegates, mostly from Texas and California, shifted to Roosevelt. The Garner delegates had polled about 9 per cent of the vote on the third ballot and were thus in a position to give the nomination to Roosevelt. Garner was then nominated for Vice President.

In 1948, the hard core of resistance to the Truman nomination, mainly from the South, was in a position to poll about 25 per cent of the convention vote. Had the two thirds rule still been in effect, an additional unit aggregating about 10 per cent would have been sufficient to block the Truman nomination, either permanently or for trading purposes. The position of such a unit would have been quite secure throughout the trading process if the unit itself were sufficiently solid, since the southern opposition was in so adamant a mood that there was no danger of its disintegrating. On the other hand, if the vote on the Humphrey-Biemiller motion is an indication, the solid support for the Truman position on civil rights held about 53 per cent of the convention voting strength. On a simple majority basis, it was apparent soon after the convention opened that Truman's nomination was assured; it was therefore in the interest of all but the most extreme die-hards to get on the band wagon on the first ballot, as they did.

TABLE 7.1 NUMBERS OF CANDIDATES FOR MAJOR-PARTY PRESIDENTIAL AND VICE-PRESIDENTIAL NOMINATIONS WHO POLLED OVER 3 PER CENT IN CONVENTION VOTING, 1832-1956

Candidates	Democratic Party					Republican Party[a]					Total Both Parties[c]
	1832–1860	1864–1892	1896–1924	1928–1956	Total[b]	1832–1860	1864–1892	1896–1924	1928–1956	Total[b]	
Number of Presidential Nominees	8	8	8	8	32	7	8	8	8	31	63
Number of Candidates											
Presidential:											
At least one convention	18	29	36	22	101	14	23	25	18	76	177
Two or more conventions	8	10	8	6	29	4	8	10	6	24	53
Vice-Presidential:											
At least one convention	29	18	29	15	90	24	24	22	11	79	168
Two or more conventions	5	3	2	3	12	4	5	3	2	12	24

[a] Includes National Republican and Whig parties in early period; no convention for 1836 election.

[b] The figures in the total column are based on a direct count for the entire experience from 1832 to 1956 and thus eliminate duplication in the counting of individuals who are included in previous figures in more than one column.

[c] The separate party totals can be added to obtain the two-party totals in this column without duplication of individuals except in the case of the fourth line of figures, where the total is 168 rather than 169 because Andrew Stewart received over 3 per cent of the vote for the vice-presidential nomination in the Democratic convention of 1844 and in the Whig convention of 1848. Stewart is, however, counted twice in the totals of the two parties in some of the later tables of this chapter where the duplication could not be so easily removed. The presidential candidate totals exclude Andrew Jackson, because his 1832 nomination was made by the Tennessee legislature and merely confirmed by his party's first convention, which was called for the purpose of selecting for Vice President the man of Jackson's choice—Van Buren.

The net total number of individuals, eliminating duplications, who received 3 per cent of the vote in at least one convention for one nomination or the other is 306. This number cannot be obtained by merely adding 177 and 168 because of several kinds of duplication between these items: 16 individuals over the 3 per cent level for both nominations in the same convention; 21 for both nominations, but in different conventions of the same party; and two individuals, Daniel Dickinson and Andrew Johnson, who received over 3 per cent for the presidential nomination in Democratic conventions and for the vice-presidential in Republican conventions.

received 3 per cent or more of the convention vote for a presidential or vice-presidential nomination through 1956, an effort has been made to obtain the following biographical information:

Date of birth.
Place of birth.
Education.
Major occupation.
Age when considered by national convention.
State of residence when considered.
Public offices previously held at any time.
Public office, if any, when considered.
Age at death.

This information provides the basis for most of the remainder of this chapter. Data on religion and on parental occupation and parental political affiliations are unavailable for so many of the lesser-known aspirants that these items have not been collected.

Recurrence and Overlapping of Candidacies

Some of the candidates for party nominations recurred in the presidential part of the voting in two or more conventions, and some "overlapped"—that is, were candidates for both the presidential and vice-presidential nominations in the same convention.[4]

Recurrence

Three kinds of recurrence of the same candidates in convention voting have already been discussed in Chapter 6: an incumbent President, elected as such, is renominated to succeed himself; an out-party titular leader is renominated; and a Vice President succeeds to the Presidency through

[4] It is also possible to be a recurring candidate for the vice-presidential nomination, or to be a candidate for the vice-presidential nomination at one convention and the presidential at another, as indicated in Table 7.1. These types of recurrence and of overlapping seem to have relatively little importance, even though they have occurred with some frequency, and are not discussed here.

death of the incumbent and then seeks the presidential nomination to succeed himself. Other types of recurrence in the voting on presidential nominations are shown in Tables 7.2 and 7.3.

Before 1900 presidential nominations often went to candidates who had received more than 3 per cent of the votes in one or more previous conventions. In the present century the only conspicuous examples have been Alfred E. Smith and Thomas E. Dewey, though there had been small votes (under 7 per cent) for John W. Davis and Charles Evans Hughes in conventions before the ones in which they were nominated. Aside from incumbents and titular leaders who have been renominated, only a few nominees have reappeared in the balloting in subsequent conventions; as a rule, the nominee who lost the previous election and does not make a serious drive for a renewed mandate disappears completely from the balloting. (See Table 7.2.)

Perennials voted for in several conventions without ever winning a presidential nomination have not been numerous. (See Table 7.3.) The most persistent was Thomas A. Hendricks, who ran four times for the presidential nomination and twice for the vice-presidential, finally being nominated and elected Vice President under Cleveland in 1884. Of all the unsuccessful perennials, Senator Robert A. Taft was unique in the large though losing votes that he received—38 per cent in 1940, 25 per cent in 1948, and 41 in 1952.

The Taft record was undoubtedly a product not only of his own personality and skill as a political leader, but also of the strength and continuity of the faction that he led. Other instances of strong minority factions that were able and willing to rally behind a single leader for so long are extremely rare. James G. Blaine (who did achieve nomination in 1884) was somewhat comparable in the longevity of his influence as a potential presidential candidate, and John Sherman was an important factional leader. But no real counterpart

TABLE 7.2. RECURRING CANDIDATES FOR PRESIDENTIAL NOMINATIONS
WHO BECAME NOMINEES

Name of Candidate	Convention Years in Which the Candidate Received 3 Per Cent or More of the Convention Vote		
	Before Nomination	When Nominated	After Nomination
DEMOCRATIC			
M. Van Buren*	—	1836, 1840	1844
L. Cass	1844	1848	1852
F. Pierce*	—	1852	1856
J. Buchanan*	1844, 1848, 1852	1856	—
S. A. Douglas	1852, 1856	1860	—
H. Seymour	1864	1868	—
S. J. Tilden	—	1876	1880
W. S. Hancock	1868, 1876	1880	—
G. Cleveland*	—	1884, 1888, 1892	—
W. J. Bryan	—	1896, 1900, 1908	—
W. Wilson*	—	1912, 1916	—
J. M. Cox	—	1920	1924
J. W. Davis	1920	1924	—
A. E. Smith	1920, 1924	1928	1932
F. D. Roosevelt*	—	1932, 1936, 1940, 1944	—
A. E. Stevenson	—	1952, 1956	—
NATIONAL REPUBLICAN, WHIG, REPUBLICAN			
H. Clay	—	1832, 1844	1840, 1848
W. Scott	1840, 1848	1852	—
A. Lincoln*	—	1860, 1864	—
U. S. Grant*	1864	1868, 1872	1880
J. G. Blaine	1876, 1880	1884	1888, 1892
B. Harrison*	—	1888, 1892	—
W. McKinley*	1892	1896, 1900	—
T. Roosevelt*	—	1904**	1912, 1916
W. H. Taft*	—	1908, 1912	—
C. E. Hughes	1908	1916	—
C. Coolidge*	1920	1924**	—
H. Hoover*	—	1928, 1932	1940
T. E. Dewey	1940	1944, 1948	—
D. D. Eisenhower*	—	1952, 1956	—

* Elected President one or more times.
** Already incumbent when first nominated for President.

132

for Taft can be found in the Republican party, even in its earlier days. In the Democratic party, the nearest counterparts are William G. McAdoo and Richard B. Russell. McAdoo figured prominently in the voting in 1920 and 1924, would have been important in 1928 but for his withdrawal, and was still important as a factional leader in 1932. Russell was the sectional candidate of the South in 1948 and 1952.

some votes. Ulysses S. Grant was not running for President in 1864. James Buchanan was the only one of whom it could be said that perseverance conquered obstacles—and he was elected in 1856 when the opposition was split between the newly formed Republican and American (Know-Nothing) parties.

On the other hand, the ten candidates who failed of election after winning their

TABLE 7.3. RECURRING CANDIDATES FOR PRESIDENTIAL NOMINATIONS WHO WERE NEVER NOMINATED

Democratic Party		Whig and Republican Parties	
Name of Candidate	Years Receiving 3 Per Cent or More of Convention Vote	Name of Candidate	Years Receiving 3 Per Cent or More of Convention Vote
Daniel S. Dickinson	1852, 1860	Daniel Webster	1848, 1852
Joseph Lane	1852, 1860	George F. Edmunds	1880, 1884
Andrew Johnson	1860, 1868	John Sherman	1880, 1884,
Stephen J. Field	1868, 1880		1888
Thomas A. Hendricks	1868, 1876,	William B. Allison	1888, 1896
	1880, 1884	Charles Fairbanks	1908, 1916
Thomas F. Bayard	1876, 1880,	Philander Knox	1908, 1916
	1884	Robert M. La Follette	1912, 1924
Allen G. Thurman	1880, 1884	Frank O. Lowden	1920, 1928
Horace Boies	1892, 1896	Robert A. Taft	1940, 1948,
Oscar Underwood	1912, 1924		1952
William G. McAdoo	1920, 1924	Arthur H. Vandenberg	1940, 1948
John N. Garner	1932, 1936	Earl Warren	1948, 1952
Richard B. Russell	1948, 1952		

There are noteworthy indications in the data underlying the tables that candidates who fail of nomination on their first serious appearance before the convention have little chance of being elected President if later nominated. Of the twenty-seven candidates in both parties (not already incumbent) who were nominated on the first try, sixteen were elected; of the thirteen (not already incumbent) who attained the nomination after polling over 3 per cent in some previous convention, only three were elected. Moreover, these three were all exceptional in one way or another. William McKinley had disclaimed candidacy in the two previous conventions where he received

nomination on a second or later try included such hardy perennials as Scott, Douglas, Hancock, Blaine, Al Smith, and Dewey.

Overlapping

Instances have occurred in which the same candidate polls votes for both presidential and vice-presidential nominations in the same convention, but the total number of such instances is not large and candidates of the first rank have seldom been involved. Nine Democrats (one on two occasions) and seven Republicans since 1832 have received over 3 per cent of the vote

Table 7.4. Geographic Combinations on Major-Party Tickets, 1832-1956

(coded by major region: Northeast: N; Middle West: M; South: S; West: W)[a]

Year	Democratic — Presidential Candidate	Democratic — Vice-Pres. Candidate	Regions	Republican[b] — Presidential Candidate	Republican[b] — Vice-Pres. Candidate	Regions
	State of Residence	State of Residence		State of Residence	State of Residence	
1832	Tennessee*	New York	S–N	Kentucky	Pennsylvania	S–N
1836	New York*	Kentucky	N–S	(no convention)		
1840	New York	(no nominee[c])	N–X	Ohio*	Virginia	M–S
1844	Tennessee*	New York[d]		Kentucky	New Jersey	S–N
		Pennsylvania	S–N			
1848	Michigan	Kentucky	M–S	Virginia*	New York	S–N
1852	New Hampshire*	Alabama	N–S	Virginia	North Carolina	S–S
1856	Pennsylvania*	Kentucky	N–S	California	New Jersey	W–N
1860	Illinois	Alabama[d]		Illinois*	Maine	M–N
		Georgia	M–S			
1864	New Jersey	Ohio	N–M	Illinois*	Tennessee	M–S
1868	New York	Missouri	N–M	Illinois*	New York	M–N
1872	New York	Missouri	N–M	Illinois*	Massachusetts	M–N
1876	New York	Indiana	N–M	Ohio*	New York	M–N
1880	Pennsylvania	Indiana	N–M	Ohio*	New York	M–N
1884	New York*	Indiana	N–M	Maine	Illinois	N–M
1888	New York	Ohio	N–M	Indiana*	New York	M–N
1892	New York*	Illinois	N–M	Indiana	New York	M–N
1896	Nebraska	Maine	M–N	Ohio*	New Jersey	M–N
1900	Nebraska	Illinois	M–M	Ohio*	New York	M–N
1904	New York	West Virginia	N–N	New York*	Indiana	N–M
1908	Nebraska	Indiana	M–M	Ohio*	New York	M–N
1912	New Jersey*	Indiana	N–M	Ohio	New York	M–N
1916	New Jersey*	Indiana	N–M	New York	Indiana	N–M
1920	Ohio	New York	M–N	Ohio*	Massachusetts	M–N
1924	West Virginia	Nebraska	N–M	Massachusetts*	Illinois[d]	
					Illinois	N–M
1928	New York	Arkansas	N–S	California*	Kansas	W–M
1932	New York*	Texas	N–S	California	Kansas	W–M
1936	New York*	Texas	N–S	Kansas	Illinois	M–M
1940	New York*	Iowa	N–M	New York	Oregon	N–W
1944	New York*	Missouri	N–M	New York	Ohio	N–M
1948	Missouri*	Kentucky	M–S	New York	California	N–W
1952	Illinois	Alabama	M–S	New York*	California	N–W
1956	Illinois	Tennessee	M–S	Pennsylvania*	California	N–W

* Winning party.
[a] The assignment of states to regions is that followed in *Presidential Nominating Politics in 1952* and throughout the present book; see Chapter 8, note 26 and Table 8.1. For names of candidates see Appendix A, Table 1.
[b] Includes National Republican and Whig.
[c] The convention decided not to make any nomination for Vice President; see Chapter 2.
[d] Nominated but refused.

for each nomination in the same convention. Some were successful in winning the vice-presidential nomination.[5]

In some of these cases, it is probable that a man whose chance for the Presidency would at best be that of a dark horse in a stalemated convention, ran simply to show himself or to develop bargaining strength that could be of value in the vice-presidential contest. Examples of this possibility include Calvin Coolidge in 1920, Charles Curtis in 1928, John Nance Garner in 1932, and Earl Warren in 1948. Three of these were not only nominated but elected, possibly indicating that a ticket that includes a vice-presidential candidate who developed some strength for the Presidency, but was not the winner's most dangerous opponent, may have technical advantages for helping to win the election.

The principal losing candidate for first place on the ticket, however, has rarely been willing either to seek or to accept the second place, and the convention has been equally unwilling to offer it to him. Throughout the history of the Republican party, with its many sharply bifactional contests, there seems to be no instance in which the defeated leader of a major faction either sought or was offered the vice-presidential nomination. The record is more difficult to trace in the Democratic party—partly because the patterns of factional division have been more complex—but the case of 1956, in which Senator Estes Kefauver sought and received the vice-presidential nomination after having withdrawn from the presidential contest, was highly unusual if not unique. He had been the runner-up (and in some cases the winner) in the preconvention battles in the primaries, and might have been runner-up on at least the first ballot at the convention if he had not already withdrawn.

Presumably the former defeated candidates who were important factional leaders

were unwilling to accept the loss of prestige that was long inherent in a vice-presidential nomination; this aspect of the situation may be changing. Depending on the extent of the bitterness created by the prior contest, they may also have been reluctant to share the ticket and the election campaign with their winning opponent, who probably reciprocated the sentiment. The victors have found need to conciliate opposing interests in order to enhance their prospects for victory in the election, but have preferred to accept a lesser figure from the opposing faction as a gesture of conciliation rather than to seek out their late principal opponent as a teammate.

The Geography of Ticket Selection

Political analysts have long theorized about the importance of geography in the selection of presidential and vice-presidential candidates. Commonly it is held that a presidential candidate should be selected from a large state, in order that he may help to secure the state's large vote in the electoral college; and also that the state should be politically a doubtful one, since otherwise the nomination could not be used to pull a doubtful state into the winning column in the election. It is further held as a basic principle that after the presidential candidate has been picked, the vice-presidential candidate should be selected so as to balance the ticket geographically. Rudiments of this principle were imbedded in the Constitution by requiring the presidential electors to vote for two persons, "of whom one at least shall not be an inhabitant of the same State with themselves."

Actual practice in forming the geographic combinations that have been presented on the party tickets is reported in Table 7.4. As even a casual glance will make apparent, certain states and regional combinations appear in the listings much more often than others. The predominance of New York is evident, with a total of twenty presidential

[5] There was also the case of James K. Polk, who sought the Vice Presidency and won the Presidency in 1844.

nominations against Ohio's nine; Illinois ranks third, with seven, largely because of the two nominations each for Lincoln, Grant, and Stevenson.

were favorable or not. It is therefore desirable to look directly at the distribution among states of residence of the 40 individuals who have been nominated by a

TABLE 7.5. STATES OF RESIDENCE OF MAJOR-PARTY FIRST-TIME
PRESIDENTIAL NOMINEES, 1832-1956[a]

State[b]	Democratic Party		Republican Party[c]		Total, Both Major Parties	
	1832–1892	1896–1956	1832–1892	1896–1956	1832–1892	1896–1956
New York	5	3	—	4	5	7
Ohio	—	1	3	3	3	4
Illinois	1	1	2	—	3	1
Kansas	—	—	—	1	—	1
California	—	—	1	1	1	1
West Virginia	—	1	—	—	—	1
New Jersey	1	1	—	—	1	1
Nebraska	—	1	—	—	—	1
Pennsylvania	2	—	—	—	2	—
Virginia	—	—	2	—	2	—
Tennessee	1	—	—	—	1	—
Indiana	—	—	1	—	1	—
Maine	—	—	1	—	1	—
New Hampshire	1	—	—	—	1	—
Michigan	1	—	—	—	1	—
Kentucky	—	—	1	—	1	—
Total	12	8	11	9	23	17

[a] Omits incumbents who were already President when first nominated in conventions (Jackson, T. Roosevelt, Coolidge, and Truman).
[b] The order of ranking is based on (1) number of nominees since 1896; (2) numbers before 1896 if they have had none since; (3) the recency of the most recent nomination from the state.
[c] Includes National Republican and Whig parties.

In many cases, states have received more than one nomination merely because the same individual has been nominated twice; and this tends to distort the comparisons. Geography is undoubtedly much more important in choosing a regular first-time nominee than in renominating an incumbent or a titular leader who was defeated in a previous election; Vice Presidents who have succeeded to the Presidency have been nominated for another term with little regard for whether the geographical factors

major-party convention without being already incumbent in the Presidency, as shown in Table 7.5.[6]

[6] It seems clear that the characteristics of availability for a presidential nomination are likely to be somewhat different from those for a vice-presidential nomination. In any event, if differences are to be sought by compiling biographical characteristics of the respective groups of candidates, the two groups must be kept as distinct as possible. In the further analyses of this chapter, therefore (except for the recapitulation below of Table 7.4), Theodore Roosevelt, Calvin Coolidge, and Harry S. Truman are omitted from the category of first-time presidential

Presidential nominations have been increasingly concentrated in a small number of states. Between 1832 and 1892, when the number of states was smaller than it is now, first-time nominees were drawn from thirteen states, with at least two from each of five states, and no more than five from any state. Since 1896, first-time nonincumbent nominees have been drawn from eight states only, with more than one from only two states, and with seven out of seventeen from New York State alone. A smaller total number of individuals have been nominated in the more recent period, since it included more re-elections. The evidence of increasing concentration in recent decades appears to be unmistakable, but the trend is also one that might be reversed under some circumstances.[7]

The vice-presidential nominations have provided a means of giving recognition to some geographic region other than the one in which the presidential nominee is a resident. When the various tickets are coded for the regions of the two nominees, as was done in Table 7.4, it becomes apparent that certain regional combinations are much more common than others, and that there are sufficient evidences of pattern to deserve notice. For each of the four periods into which the table was divided, the combinations can be recapitulated as follows:[8]

Democratic	Republican
1832-1860	
3 N-S	3 S-N
2 S-N	1 M-S
2 M-S	1 S-S
1 N-X	1 W-N
	1 M-N
1864-1892	
8 N-M	6 M-N
	1 N-M
	1 M-S
1896-1924	
3 N-M	5 M-N
2 M-N	3 N-M
2 M-M	
1 N-N	
1928-1956	
3 N-S	4 N-W
2 N-M	2 W-M
3 M-S	1 M-M
	1 N-M

The South was an important source of presidential and vice-presidential nominees during the days of the Whig-Democratic two-party system before the Civil War. But after 1864, when Lincoln of Illinois and Johnson of Tennessee were teamed together on the "Union" ticket, no southerner appeared in either position on either party ticket until 1928. With sixteen possible combinations of the four regions among which to choose, the Democrats composed each of eight successive tickets from 1864 to 1892 on the same pattern: a northeastern leader and a midwestern teammate. In six of the same eight years, the Republicans composed party tickets that were the exact opposite: a midwestern leader and northeastern teammate. Between 1896 and 1924, the Northeast and Middle West continued to share the honors in both parties, but with no longer so strong a contrast between the

nominees, since they were already incumbent in the office and had obtained it by securing a nomination for Vice President. In the same way, Millard Fillmore, Andrew Johnson, and Chester A. Arthur are omitted from among the contenders for presidential nominations, since they were already incumbent.

Martin Van Buren, however, is included as a first-time presidential nominee in 1836; he was an incumbent Vice President, not President, when seeking the higher office in competition with others who had never held it. Andrew Jackson is omitted from the tabulations of first-time nominees for a different reason: he was already an incumbent President when the convention system was instituted.

[7] More states are becoming pivotal. If there is in fact an increasing tendency to nominate senators for President, as suggested elsewhere, the pivotal character of a state may also become less important as a factor in selection, with more tendency for the nominations to scatter.

The situation would be greatly changed if any of the various schemes for electoral college reform were to be adopted. The large states would become much less pivotal, and the tendency to seek candidates especially in those states might disappear.

[8] Nominees of predecessor parties are included in Republican; items in the 1832-1860 Republican group number seven because the Whigs held no convention in 1836. The letter X indicates the lack of a vice-presidential nomination by the Democrats in 1840.

parties in ticket arrangement. Since 1928, the South has received renewed recognition in the Democratic party, and the West in the Republican.

In five instances among the sixty-three pairs of major-party ticket mates, both came from the same region:

S-S 1852 Whig: W. Scott (Va.) and W. A. Graham (N.C.).
M-M 1900 Democratic: W. J. Bryan (Nebr.) and A. Stevenson (Ill.)
N-N 1904 Democratic: A. B. Parker (N.Y.) and H. G. Davis (W.Va.).
M-M 1908 Democratic: W. J. Bryan (Nebr.) and J. W. Kern (Ind.).
M-M 1936 Republican: A. M. Landon (Kans.) and F. Knox (Ill.).

All five of these tickets were defeated in the elections. In each case the inability or failure to compose a regionally balanced ticket was undoubtedly related to aspects of party weakness, including sectional antagonisms within the party. When Winfield Scott finally secured the Whig nomination in 1852 after fifty-three ballots, party leaders from sections other than the South were prepared to witness the defeat and dissolution of the party. In the case of Bryan's second and third nominations, there is ample reason to surmise that no outstanding Democrat of the Northeast was willing to be associated with him on the ticket; it would probably have been equally difficult to secure an outstanding ticket-mate from the Middle West when Parker was nominated in 1904. When Landon was nominated in 1936, the Republicans had already been swept out of office in most of the northeastern region, and the eastern Republicans of note had little desire to run for Vice President in a year of almost certain defeat. With the increasing political importance of the West and the restoration of a degree of two-party politics in the South, party tickets of the future can be expected to continue to show diversified patterns of regional balance, as they were doing during the period 1928-1956.

The period 1928-1956 was marked by one other feature of major interest. For the first time, a single state was predominantly the source of presidential candidates in both major parties. New York received five of the eight Democratic nominations, and four of the eight Republican.[9] In doing so, it returned to the role it had held in the Democratic party between 1864 and 1892, while also capturing the role that Ohio had held in the Republican party between 1896 and 1924.

The causes of this phenomenon presumably include more than the great size of New York as a state and the importance of New York City as the leading metropolis of the nation, since both of those factors were equally or even more important between 1896 and 1924, when only one of eight Democratic presidential nominations and two of eight Republican went to residents of New York State. Its return to a close competitive balance in state politics, after a lengthy period during which the governorship was generally won by the Republicans, undoubtedly made New York more effective as a source of presidential candidates in both parties.

This predominance may disappear during the years to come. When the census of 1960 has been taken, California will probably not be far behind New York in the electoral college. And—along with California—Pennsylvania, Ohio, Illinois, Michigan and Texas have become major fighting grounds between the parties in state and national elections, with governors and senators who find many opportunities to reach national prominence as party leaders. Many smaller states may also become able to compete more actively and effectively for the prize than could be the case during the long period of one-party dominance in state politics, North and South.

The Age Factor

Information on age is readily available for most high-ranking political figures. The

[9] President Eisenhower, although classed as a resident of New York when nominated in 1952, had become a resident of Pennsylvania before his nomination in 1956.

importance actually attached to age in the making of nominations is much more difficult to ascertain, while the question of the importance that *should* be given to factors of age is a complex set of practical and philosophic issues.

Statistics of average age of presidential and vice-presidential nominees when first nominated and of other candidates for the nominations for the time periods studied are shown in Table 7.6. The most important findings revealed by these statistics are: the relatively young average age of the major-party presidential nominees—an average of age 51 for the period since 1896; the close similarity between the two parties in the average age of their presidential nominees; and the decline of over three years in the average age of the candidates from the earlier period to the more recent one. In both parties and both time periods, the first-time nominees were younger on the average than the defeated contenders for

the nominations: 51 years against 58 for the period since 1896.

In both parties there has been a concentration of first-time presidential nominations in the bracket from 50 to 54 years during the period since 1896, as shown by the following distributions:

Age	Democratic 1832-1892	Democratic 1896-1956	Republican 1832-1892	Republican 1896-1956	Both Parties 1832-1892	Both Parties 1896-1956
35–39	1	1	–	–	1	1
40–44	–	–	1	1	1	1
45–49	4	–	2	2	6	2
50–54	1	5	3	4	4	9
55–59	2	2	2	1	4	3
60–64	2	–	1	1	3	1
65–69	2	–	2	–	4	–
Total	12	8	11	9	23	17

In the case of the vice-presidential nominees, as shown in Table 7.6, the average age has gone up rather than down since 1896, and especially so in the Democratic

TABLE 7.6. AVERAGE AGE OF PRESIDENTIAL AND VICE-PRESIDENTIAL NOMINEES WHEN FIRST NOMINATED, AND OF OTHER CONTENDERS, 1832-1956

	Democratic 1832–1892	Democratic 1896–1956	Republican[a] 1832–1892	Republican[a] 1896–1956	Both Parties 1832–1892	Both Parties 1896–1956
CANDIDATES FOR PRESIDENTIAL NOMINATIONS[b]						
Average Age of Nominees[c]	54.1	50.3	54.9	52.0	54.5	51.2
Number of Nominees	12	8	11	9	23	17
Average Age of Other Contenders[d]	58.6	56.7	56.8	59.0	57.9	57.6
Number of Other Contenders	31[e]	47	22	30	53[e]	77
CANDIDATES FOR VICE-PRESIDENTIAL NOMINATIONS						
Average Age of Nominees[c]	53.3	58.7	53.3	54.8	53.3	56.7
Number of Nominees	15	13	15	13	30	26
Average Age of Other Contenders[d]	51.4	52.3	52.3	56.0	51.9	53.8
Number of Other Contenders	32	28[f]	32	19	64	47[f]

[a] Includes National Republican and Whig candidates.

[b] Jackson, Theodore Roosevelt, Coolidge, and Truman are omitted as nominees, as in Table 7.5, and Fillmore, Johnson, and Arthur as other contenders (see footnote 6, above).

[c] As of time of first nomination if nominated more than once.

[d] Other candidates polling over 3 per cent in major-party conventions, as of the occasion on which they polled their highest vote and thus came closest to being nominated, if voted on in more than one convention.

[e] No information available for Sanford Church, 1868.

[f] No information available for Abraham W. Patrick, 1900; and Mrs. Leroy Springs, 1924.

party. Both parties selected relatively young vice-presidential candidates in 1952 and 1956, but both have nominated several candidates over age 60 since 1896. The complete list of those over 60 (without being limited to first-time nominees and including Frank O. Lowden, who refused the nomination) is as follows:

1896	Arthur Sewall (D)	61
1900	Adlai E. Stevenson (D)	65
1904	Henry Davis (D)	81
1916	Thomas R. Marshall (D)	62
1924	Frank O. Lowden (R)	63
1928	Charles Curtis (R)	68
1932	John N. Garner (D)	64
1936	John N. Garner (D)	68
1936	Frank Knox (R)	62
1940	Charles McNary (R)	66
1944	Harry S. Truman (D)	60
1948	Alben W. Barkley (D)	71

It is noteworthy that most of the cases on this list have occurred since 1928, with six successive presidential elections from 1928 to 1948 in which one party or the other nominated a vice-presidential candidate over 60.

It seems clear that the parties have not been disposed to worry much about the factor of age when selecting vice-presidential nominees, and especially so when the presidential candidate was relatively young. There have been three instances since 1832, however, in which both members of the ticket were over 60:

1916	(D)	Wilson and Marshall
1944	(D)	Roosevelt and Truman
1948	(D)	Truman and Barkley

All of these occurred in the Democratic party, all are of recent memory, and all involved an incumbent presidential candidate.

As the junior of the two offices and the one that may lead to the senior office by constitutional or electoral succession, the Vice Presidency presumably should be filled by an incumbent who would be young enough to serve effectively as President if called upon to do so, and to continue for additional periods of at least four years and possibly eight. If this reasoning is sound, the parties ordinarily would be wise to disregard candidates above the age of 60 in selecting vice-presidential nominees, as they did in 1952 and 1956.

Vice-presidential candidates who are conspicuously young present a different kind of problem. Obvious questions arise about their maturity; on the other hand, an active younger man who is nominated for Vice President automatically becomes eligible for later consideration for the presidential nomination, and may easily remain an important figure in the party for another quarter of a century. Theodore Roosevelt was 42 when he became President through constitutional succession; he was only 54 when he sought his third presidential term in 1912. Undoubtedly he would have been a less irksome problem to his party after leaving the Presidency in 1909 if he had been older and more inclined to retire. Franklin D. Roosevelt was 38 when nominated for Vice President in 1920. The vice-presidential campaign of 1920 was doubtless a useful preparatory experience; whether he would have been adequately qualified to serve as President at the time is another question.

In recent years, the death of President Franklin D. Roosevelt at the age of 63 and the heart attack suffered by President Dwight D. Eisenhower at the age of 65 have lent emphasis to the problems of age and mortality in the nation's highest office. At 67, William Henry Harrison was the oldest presidential candidate ever nominated; and he died in office at the age of 68. Much older men have often served in the chief executive positions of other governments, and in the Congress of the United States. But the Presidency is unique both in the burdens that it imposes on the incumbent and in the amount of governmental confusion, if not actual danger to the nation, that may arise when the President dies or becomes incapacitated during his fixed term of office.

The eleven Presidents who served between 1832 and 1892 and who escaped assassination lived to an average age of 68.6 years; the average for the Presidents of the 1896-1956 period may exceed this when the mortality experience of the period is complete.[10] For a time, the available statistical evidence seemed to suggest a considerable curtailment in the life expectancy of the Presidents because of the amount of stress inherent in holding the office.[11]

The factor of age at the time of nomination for President or Vice President is important for many reasons in addition to the possibility of death in office. The relationship between age and physical vigor may be at least equally important in a position so demanding as the Presidency.

Political parties, like other organizations,

must give thought to the age of their leaders if they are to retain vitality in a rapidly changing world. In some respects, political parties often have more difficulty than other organizations both in retiring the superannuated and in providing rapid advancement for the able young. In one of his most acute analyses Duverger writes of the problem as it affects the European parties. He notes "the fundamental conservatism of the masses and their fondness for the faces they know," as well as the opposition that comes from all ranks of the party hierarchy when advancement seems too rapid. He concludes that opportunity comes rapidly to the best qualified only in the parties that are sufficiently autocratic to disregard the sentiments of those who are passed over, or in those where the situation is so disorganized that a sort of free competition prevails at times. But in the Socialist parties of Europe, strongly organized and democratic in their ideology, he finds a general tendency toward an overaging of the leadership with stagnation throughout the organization as the result.[12]

Excessive age in the highest posts may be the product either of a long continuation in high office or of advanced age when first attaining the office, or both. In the case of the Presidency the two-term tradition (long before the Twenty-second Amendment) had imposed a limit on service in the highest office, once a man is elected. Similar customs have had the same effect even more strongly in the office of governor in many of the states. But there is no fixed custom or constitutional provision to prevent aged candidates from being nominated for President and Vice President; and there are many sectors of the American political system from which such candidates may come. Any candid observer of an important state or national political meeting is likely to find a substantial quota of persons of advanced years, many of whom are still potential candidates for office. This situation prevails

[10] For the six deceased Presidents of the 1896-1956 period (omitting Cleveland, whose term ended in 1897, and McKinley, who was assassinated) the average age at death was 63.2. But of the three Presidents still living as of fall, 1959, former President Herbert Hoover was 85 on August 10, 1959; former President Harry S. Truman was 75 on May 8, 1959; President Dwight D. Eisenhower was 69 on October 14, 1959.

[11] A statistical study stimulated by President Roosevelt's death found that the Presidents who took office before 1850 outlived their expectation of life at inauguration by an average of 2.9 years, while those who served between 1850 and 1900 fell short by an identical figure, an average of 2.9 years. For the Presidents who held office between 1900 and 1946 and who were deceased at the time of the study, the deficit of actuality against life expectancy when taking office was an average of about 8 years. Six of the first ten Presidents outlived their life expectancies by many years, but from Abraham Lincoln to Calvin Coolidge, no President did so. ("Does the Presidency Shorten Life?" *Statistical Bulletin of the Metropolitan Life Insurance Company*, Vol. 27, Oct. 1946, pp. 1-3.)

An earlier but more elaborate study, published in 1940, arrived at similar findings for the Presidents, while discovering that the mortality experience of Vice Presidents, Cabinet members, and Supreme Court justices had improved substantially since 1865. (Frank L. Griffin, Jr., "Actuarial Note: Mortality of United States Presidents and Certain Other Federal Officers," *Transactions, Actuarial Society of America*, Vol. 41, 1940, pp. 487-91.)

It seems likely that the Presidents have been better protected against assassination in recent years than was the case between 1865 and 1940, and that both Presidents and ex-Presidents are getting better medical care then formerly. The longevity of the living ex-Presidents suggests that a change in the mortality experience of these officials may be occurring, even though the number of individuals involved is so small that it has no statistical significance.

[12] Maurice Duverger, *Political Parties* (1954), pp. 160-68.

TABLE 7.7. EDUCATIONAL LEVELS ATTAINED BY PRESIDENTAL AND VICE-PRESIDENTIAL NOMINEES WHEN FIRST NOMINATED, AND BY OTHER CONTENDERS, 1832-1956

Level Attained	Democratic		Republican[a]		Both Parties	
	1832–1892	1896–1956	1832–1892	1896–1956	1832–1892	1896–1956
PRESIDENTIAL NOMINEES[b]						
Law School	—	6	2	7	2	13
Other College or University Only	7	—	5	2	12	2
Secondary School Only[c]	4	—	2	—	6	—
Elementary School Only[d]	1	2	2	—	3	2
Number of Persons	12	8	11	9	23	17
OTHER CONTENDERS FOR PRESIDENTIAL NOMINATION[e]						
Law School	2	14	3	17	5	31
Other College or University Only	14	23	11	8	25	31
Secondary School Only[c]	9	3	4	2	13	5
Elementary School Only[d]	6	7	4	3	10	10
Number of Persons	31[f]	47	22	30	53[f]	77
VICE-PRESIDENTIAL NOMINEES						
Law School	2	7	—	9	2	16
Other College or University Only	10	3	9	3	19	7
Secondary School Only[c]	3	—	3	—	6	—
Elementary School Only[d]	—	3	3	1	3	3
Number of Persons	15	13	15	13	30	26
OTHER CONTENDERS FOR VICE-PRESIDENTIAL NOMINATION[e]						
Law School	—	18	4	7	4	25
Other College or University Only	24	6	14	7	38	13
Secondary School Only[c]	6	2	8	1	14	3
Elementary School Only[d]	2	3	6	4	8	7
Number of Persons	32	29[g]	32	19	64	48[g]

[a] Includes National Republican and Whig candidates.
[b] Jackson, Theodore Roosevelt, Coolidge, and Truman are omitted, as in previous tables.
[c] Includes high school, academy, and private tutoring.
[d] Includes some with no formal schooling.
[e] Other candidates polling 3 per cent or more in major-party conventions; Fillmore, Johnson, and Arthur are omitted from the contenders for the presidential nomination.
[f] No information available for Sanford Church, 1868.
[g] No information available for Abraham W. Patrick, 1900.

at the national party conventions as well as elsewhere.

Apparently the chief influences that may correct a tendency to the nomination of average candidates must come from experience of the success of younger candidates put forward by one party at times when the other is clearly recognized as suffering from feeble leadership by older men. Competition between the parties may thus be the most reliable corrective. There is little evidence, however, that the parties give much conscious thought, under ordinary conditions, to the age of their candidates.

The observed experience in regard to age seems to be the by-product of the career channels that bring men to the point of active consideration for the Presidency. Those who arrive between the ages of 50 and 54 are the product of a special type of career pattern, as will become apparent later in the chapter. The fact that the career patterns that are normally most successful in producing presidential candidates also produce them at a relatively young age is a special feature of the American political system. This is a feature that may have its own advantages, but it is not one for which any system architect can be given credit—unless it might be the founder of the convention system, Andrew Jackson.

Education and Occupational Background

Information on education and occupational background is of some interest for what it may reveal of both qualifying preparation and social status.

Education

Educational data representing levels attained but not necessarily completed, are shown for the candidates for presidential and vice-presidential nominations in Table 7.7. All the Republican presidential nomi-

nees from 1896 to 1956 and six of the eight Democrats had received some college training. The nominees differed little from the other candidates for the presidential nominations in this respect. Vice-presidential nominees during the same period had also received college training with rare exceptions; differences between the averages for the various groups do not seem important. Of the twenty-three major-party first-time nominees for President up to 1892, all of whom had completed their education before the Civil War, only three had attended law school; but of the seventeen since 1896, thirteen had done so, as had also the three Vice Presidents who won election after succeeding a deceased President. The change undoubtedly reflects the greater extent to which training for the legal profession has been provided in law schools in recent decades, instead of by the older custom of reading law in an attorney's office, as the later statistics on occupations help to make clear.

Nominees and other candidates for the nomination with postgraduate education in fields other than law have been extremely rare. President Eisenhower is a graduate of what is now the Industrial College of the Armed Forces, one of the senior institutions of military education. Woodrow Wilson was the only nominee of either party with an earned doctorate in political science—or any other subject.

In general, the educational preparation of the presidential candidates has compared favorably with that of the governors and of members of the Senate, but has not been conspicuously higher.[13]

Occupations in Private Life

Careers leading to the Presidency, insofar as they have involved governmental experience, have usually included experience

[13] Some comparative data, and a discussion of its significance, can be found in Donald R. Matthews, *The Social Background of Political Decision-Makers* (1954), pp. 28-29.

TABLE 7.8. PRINCIPAL OCCUPATIONS IN PRIVATE LIFE OF PRESIDENTIAL NOMINEES WHEN FIRST NOMINATED, AND OF OTHER CONTENDERS, 1832-1956

Principal Occupations in Private Life (sometimes more than one per individual)	Democratic		Republican[a]		Both Parties	
	1832–1892	1896–1956	1832–1892	1896–1956	1832–1892	1896–1956
PRESIDENTIAL NOMINEES[b]						
Practice of Law	9	6	4	5	13	11
Publishers, Editors, and Journalists	1	2	1	1	2	3
Other Professional Occupations	2	—	2	2	4	2
Business Proprietors and Executives	2	1	—	1	2	2
Farmers and Ranchers	—	—	—	—	—	—
Other	—	2	—	—	—	2
None (because principally occupied in military or other public life)	1[c]	1	6[d]	1[c]	7	2
Number of Cases[e]	12	8	11	9	23	17
OTHER CONTENDERS FOR PRESIDENTIAL NOMINATION[f]						
Practice of Law	26	30	17	20	43	50
Publishers, Editors, and Journalists	1	6	1	5	2	11
Other Professional Occupations	1	4	—	5	1	9
Businesss Proprietors and Executives	5	14	3	7	8	21
Farmers and Ranchers	1	4	2	—	3	4
Other	1	—	—	—	1	—
None (because principally occupied in military or other public life)	1	—	2	—	3	—
Number of Cases[e]	31	47[g]	22	30	53	77[g]

[a] Includes National Republican and Whig candidates.
[b] Jackson, T. Roosevelt, Coolidge, and Truman are omitted, as in previous tables.
[c] Soldier.
[d] Five soldiers.
[e] Sums of columns may exceed number of cases due to inclusion of some candidates in two or more categories.
[f] Other candidates polling 3 per cent or more in major-party conventions; Fillmore, Johnson, and Arthur are omitted.
[g] No information available for Abraham W. Patrick, 1900.

high elective and appointive office. These are types of office that are frequently ill paid in relation to the burdens that they impose, and that always involve substantial elements of career risk. Most of the individuals who have eventually become candidates for the presidential and vice-presidential nominations have entered upon public careers only after becoming established in some private occuption. Usually they have also found it necessary to maintain some occupational status in private life to which they could retreat when not occupied in public life.

The principal occupations in private life of the candidates for the presidential and vice-presidential nominations are shown in Tables 7.8 and 7.9. The overwhelming importance of the practice of law as the occupational background of most candidates, even in the earlier period, is apparent. Publishers and editors, business proprietors and executives, and the professions other than law occasionally find representation among the nominees and among the other aspirants, but even collectively the other occupations are outnumbered by the law.

The main thing that all of these occupations have in common is a moderately high social and economic status, providing a base of operations from which to campaign for high public office and to which to return when necessary. As an occupation, law is especially suited to the combining of public and private careers; fortunately, it also ranks high in the preparatory training that it can give for the holding of public office.[14]

Governmental Experience and Position

In most political systems, individuals are not advanced to the highest posts until they have served an apprenticeship in other high public offices. In parliamentary forms of government, it is usually necessary to be a member of the legislature in order to be appointed to a junior cabinet post; and it is only when a new political party is coming to power for the first time that anyone is likely to become prime minister without having previously served for some years as a prominent member of the cabinet—and at the same time of the legislature. There is a strong presumption that such experience has value as training for those who eventually reach the top. But service in high office is not merely a useful preparatory experience; it also gives the individual a status from which to compete more effectively for the higher posts on the political ladder.

The American political system is much more open than most others, and less characterized by rigidity in the channels of political advancement. There are many roads that may lead to the Presidency; and in the competition for the office, an existing position as a governor or senator is more likely to be regarded as a power base from which to campaign than as an opportunity to obtain a type of qualifying experience. But both aspects of the situation are important. Accordingly, the record of the candidates for the nominations will be examined first in terms of the variety and extent of governmental experience, and the channels of advancement along the way, before turning to the official positions, if any, that they were holding at the time they were considered for the presidential or vice-presidential nomination of their political party.[15]

[14] For a further discussion and survey of the literature on the relationships between legal practice and officeholding, see Matthews, op. cit., pp. 30-32; also Joseph A. Schlesinger, "Lawyers and American Politics: A Clarified View," Midwest Journal of Political Science, Vol. 1 (May 1957), pp. 26-39.

[15] The basic research and most of the analysis for this chapter were carried out in 1955 and 1956, and therefore preceded the publication of a somewhat comparable piece of research on the governors: Joseph A. Schlesinger, How They Became Governor (1957). The analytical methods developed by Professor Schlesinger would deserve further consideration in connection with research on presidential career patterns. His findings are also relevant to the career patterns of the governors who eventually became candidates for presidential and vice-presidential nominations, and to the changes over time in the career patterns of elective officials.

TABLE 7.9. Principal Occupations in Private Life of Vice-Presidential Nominees When First Nominated, and of Other Contenders, 1832-1956

Principal Occupations in Private Life (sometimes more than one per individual)	Democratic		Republican[a]		Both Parties	
	1832–1892	1896–1956	1832–1892	1896–1956	1832–1892	1896–1956
VICE-PRESIDENTIAL NOMINEES						
Practice of Law	14	9	10	12	24	21
Publishers, Editors, and Journalists	—	2	3	1	3	3
Other Professional Occupations	—	—	—	1	—	1
Business Proprietors and Executives	1	2	2	1	3	3
Farmers and Ranchers	—	1	—	—	—	1
Other	—	1	—	—	—	1
None (because principally occupied in military or other public life)	1	—	1	—	2	—
Number of Cases[b]	15	13	15	13	30	26
OTHER CONTENDERS FOR VICE-PRESIDENTIAL NOMINATION[c]						
Practice of Law	26	23	28	8	54	31
Publishers, Editors, and Journalists	—	2	3	1	3	3
Other Professional Occupations	1	2	—	2	1	4
Business Proprietors and Executives	3	5	4	6	7	11
Farmers and Ranchers	2	3	—	—	2	3
Other	1	—	1	—	2	—
None (because principally occupied in military or other public life)	1	—	—	2	1	2
Number of Cases[b]	32	29[d]	32	19	64	48[d]

[a] Includes National Republican and Whig candidates.
[b] Sums of columns may exceed number of cases due to inclusion of some candidates in two or more categories.
[c] Other candidates polling 3 per cent or more in major-party conventions.
[d] No information available for Abraham W. Patrick, 1900.

146

Previous Governmental Experience

Tables 7.10 and 7.11 summarize the previous governmental experience of the candidates by major types of officeholding. The data do not provide any direct measure of the number of years of previous governmental experience on the part of the nominees and other candidates; such data would be difficult to compile from the usually available biographical materials. But the tables make it apparent that most of the candidates have previously occupied at least two or three different governmental positions before they were actively considered for the nominations.

Only one presidential nominee, Wendell Willkie, and four other contenders for the presidential nomination were classified as having had no governmental experience. The other four were Jesse Jones (1928) and John R. McLean (1896) on the Democratic side; Henry Ford (1916) and Frank E. Gannett (1940) on the Republican. Willkie was a career executive in big business, although he had started as a lawyer; as a successful candidate for a major-party presidential nomination, he was unique. No vice-presidential nominee was classified as lacking any governmental experience. Candidates without such experience have rarely sought the vice-presidential nomination of either party.

The normal channels of political advancement frequently include experience in local government and in state and federal legislative and executive positions. Local government has provided a beginning point for many political careers, but has not been of major importance in careers leading to the presidential and vice-presidential nominations. Of the forty presidential nominees, nine had experience in local government; of the fifty-six vice-presidential nominees, twenty-one. The indications of change over time are not very clear and, in view of the small number of cases and the absence of more precise categories within the general field of local government, are of doubtful importance.

Big-city mayors are local political figures of unusual importance, but they do not appear in the present figures to any significant extent. No mayor or former mayor of a city of 500,000 population or more ever polled over 3 per cent in convention for either Republican nomination, and the Democratic cases have been rare. A former mayor of Cleveland (Newton D. Baker) appeared in the balloting for the Democratic presidential nomination, and a former mayor of Philadelphia and incumbent mayors of Baltimore and New York for the vice-presidential. (When Grover Cleveland was mayor of Buffalo, New York, in 1881-1882, it had not yet attained its present big-city status.) The infrequency of these cases doubtless reflects the historical forces that have given a rural bias to almost all American politics other than the politics of the big cities themselves. This is an aspect of political evolution that is not confined to the United States; that it will continue into the indefinite future even in this country may be unlikely. The 168 metropolitan areas with a central city of 50,000 or more now contain half of the total population of the United States.

The state legislatures, like some phases of local government, provide relatively easy beginning points for some types of political careers, but presidential careers seldom begin there. For this type of experience, moreover, the time trends have been clear. In each of eight pairs of possible time-period comparisons—nominees and other contenders for both offices in both parties—the trend was sharply downward from 1832-1892 to 1896-1956. In most cases the drop in the proportion with state legislative experience was about one half. Only four of the seventeen first-time major-party presidential nominees since 1896 had any state legislative experience. State government executive positions other than governor have provided a stepping stone to about one third of the Republican presidential and vice-presidential nominees since 1896, but to none of the Democrats.

TABLE 7.10. GOVERNMENTAL EXPERIENCE OF PRESIDENTIAL NOMINEES WHEN FIRST NOMINATED, AND OF OTHER CONTENDERS, 1832-1956

Experience[a]	Democratic 1832–1892	Democratic 1896–1956	Republican[b] 1832–1892	Republican[b] 1896–1956	Both Parties 1832–1892	Both Parties 1896–1956
PRESIDENTIAL NOMINEES[c]						
No Governmental Experience[d]	—	—	—	1	—	1
Local Governmental Experience	3	1	2	3	5	4
State Legislature	8	3	5	1	13	4
State Executive Other Than Governor	3	—	—	3	3	3
House of Representatives	5	3	6	1	11	4
Senate	5	—	5	1	10	1
Governor	5	5	2	4	7	9
Federal Appointive Office[e]	4	3	3	2	7	5
Vice President	1	—	—	—	1	—
General, Regular Army	2	—	3	1	5	1
Federal and State Judiciary	1	1	—	2	1	3
Number of Items of Experience	37	16	26	19	63	35
Number of Individuals	12	8	11	9	23	17
Average Number of Types of Governmental Experience	3.1	2.0	2.4	2.1	2.7	2.1
OTHER CONTENDERS FOR PRESIDENTIAL NOMINATION[f]						
No Governmental Experience[d]	—	2	—	2	—	4
Local Governmental Experience	11	14	5	10	17	24
State Legislature	22	14	10	8	32	22
State Executive Other Than Governor	7	6	8	5	15	11
House of Representatives	19	16	10	10	29	26
Senate	18	19	12	14	30	33
Governor	10	17	6	12	16	29
Federal Appointive Office[e]	9	10	9	10	17	20
Vice President	1	2	—	2	1	4
General, Regular Army	—	—	—	1	—	1
Federal and State Judiciary	7	5	3	1	10	6
No Information	1	—	—	—	1	—
Number of Items of Experience	104	103	63	73	167	176
Number of Individuals	32	47	22	30	54	77
Average Number of Types of Governmental Experience	3.3	2.2	2.9	2.4	3.1	2.3

[a] Experience as of the time of first nomination if a nominee; for other contenders, experience as of the time of the convention in which the largest percentage of convention vote was received.
[b] Includes National Republican and Whig candidates.
[c] Omits Jackson, T. Roosevelt, Coolidge, and Truman, as in previous tables.
[d] Military service has been disregarded in determining governmental experience, except in the case of the generals of the regular army.
[e] In the Executive Branch, other than military.
[f] Omits Fillmore, Johnson, and Arthur, as in previous tables.

148

With its many members, the United States House of Representatives could be expected to be a seed bed for all types of national political talent. It corresponds to the lower chambers from which national political leadership is drawn in most of the parliamentary democracies. But the House of Representatives in this country has never been a gate through which all presidential and vice-presidential candidates must pass, and in this respect it is no longer even as important as it was a century ago. Only a quarter of the first-time presidential nominees from 1896 to 1956 had served in the House, and only a third of the contenders for the nomination.

With its smaller and presumably more select membership, the United States Senate might be expected to be more important than the House in the career patterns of the candidates. Actually, the differences between Senate and House as sources of previous experience are not striking, partly because many of the senators seeking presidential nominations had previously served in the House.

Of the three categories of high civil executive positions shown in Tables 7.10 and 7.11, the two main ones are governor and federal appointive office in the Executive Branch of the government, usually as a member of the President's Cabinet or sub-Cabinet or as head of a diplomatic mission. The third—Vice President—is necessary to complete the table in the case of presidential nominations; Martin Van Buren (D) had acquired experience as Vice President when first nominated for President, and so had several others who sought the presidential nomination without achieving it.[16]

The office of governor has become so well known as an important source of candidates for the presidential nominations that the statistics shown here on previous experience as governor will occasion little surprise. Since 1896 over half of the presidential nominees and about one third of the vice-presidential nominees have been governors or former governors. Governors and ex-governors have also been prominent among the other candidates for both nominations, but are not as conspicuously so as might be expected. The implication would appear to be that in a field of contestants for the nominations, governors do not run without success as often as others.

Federal appointive office has provided a type of experience possessed by fewer than one third of the presidential and vice-presidential nominees since the beginnings of the convention system, and has been about equally important in the experience of the other contestants. The proportion among presidential nominees has been remarkably stable since the beginning. In the Democratic party, the figures for vice-presidential nominations suggest a marked decline in eligibility for that nomination (or in interest in receiving it) on the part of possible candidates with experience in federal appointive office.

Generals of the regular army have been nominated for President by the conventions of each major party, though President Eisenhower is the only one since 1880. The complete list is as follows:[17]

Zachary Taylor (W), 1848
Winfield Scott (W), 1852
George McClellan (D), 1864
Ulysses S. Grant (R), 1868
Winfield Scott Hancock (D), 1880
Dwight D. Eisenhower (R), 1952

---

[16] Succession from lieutenant governor to governor by nomination and election has been common enough in some states to become a recognized pattern of career advancement in elective politics. It has apparently occurred mainly in states where competition between and within the parties was minimal and where there was also a tradition or requirement of rapid rotation in the governor's office, with the choice of lieutenant governor taking on the characteristics of a choice of governor-elect. See Joseph A. Schlesinger, *How They Became Governor,* pp. 22-28.

[17] Andrew Jackson is omitted for reasons noted previously. William Henry Harrison (W), 1840, who is also omitted from the list, held high military rank only as a major general of volunteers during the War of 1812, although his military service was the principal reason for the fame that made his nomination possible. Several other nominees had derived at least part of their fame from some prior period of military service, as in the case of Colonel Theodore Roosevelt.

Table 7.11. Governmental Experience of Vice-Presidential Nominees When First Nominated, and of Other Contenders, 1832-1956

Experience[a]	Democratic		Republican[b]		Both Parties	
	1832–1892	1896–1956	1832–1892	1896–1956	1832–1892	1896–1956
VICE-PRESIDENTIAL NOMINEES						
No Governmental Experience[c]	—	—	—	—	—	—
Local Governmental Experience	5	6	4	6	9	12
State Legislature	11	5	10	3	21	8
State Executive Other Than Governor	4	—	2	4	6	4
House of Representatives	10	4	9	3	19	7
Senate	9	6	8	4	17	10
Governor	4	3	4	5	8	8
Federal Appointive Office[d]	6	3	5	3	11	6
General, Regular Army	—	—	—	—	—	—
Federal and State Judiciary	1	—	1	1	2	1
Number of Items of Experience	50	27	43	29	93	56
Number of Individuals	15	13	15	13	30	26
Average Number of Types of Governmental Experience	3.3	2.1	2.9	2.2	3.1	2.2
OTHER CONTENDERS FOR VICE-PRESIDENTIAL NOMINATION						
No Governmental Experience[c]	2	3	—	—	2	3
Local Governmental Experience	3	10	8	7	11	17
State Legislature	19	12	15	4	34	16
State Executive Other Than Governor	3	3	7	2	10	5
House of Representatives	15	11	19	10	34	21
Senate	12	11	8	6	20	17
Governor	6	5	8	7	14	12
Federal Appointive Office[d]	13	1	8	4	21	5
General, Regular Army	—	—	1	1	1	1
Federal and State Judiciary	9	3	3	2	12	5
No Information	—	1	—	—	—	1
Number of Items of Experience	80	56	77	43	157	99
Number of Individuals	32	30	32	19	64	49
Average Number of Types of Governmental Experience	2.5	1.9	2.4	2.3	2.4	2.0

[a] Experience as of the time of first nomination if a nominee; for other contenders, experience as of the time of the convention in which the largest percentage of convention vote was received.
[b] Includes National Republican and Whig candidates.
[c] Military service has been disregarded in determining governmental experience, except in the case of the generals of the regular army.
[d] In the Executive Branch, other than military.

Among the other contenders for the presidential nomination, the only regular army general was Leonard Wood, who polled 32 per cent of the vote on the fourth ballot in the Republican convention of 1920. No general ever received the vice-presidential nomination; James Harbord (R, 1932) was the only contender for that honor that ever passed the 3 per cent level in the voting.

Men who have served as judges in federal or state courts have only occasionally been candidates for the presidential nomination. The four first-time presidential nominees with judicial experience were: Stephen A. Douglas (D), who had served on the Illinois supreme court; Alton B. Parker (D), who was chief justice of the highest New York state court when nominated in 1904; William Howard Taft (R), who had served some years in state and federal courts before he left the bench in 1900 for other appointive office; and Charles Evans Hughes (R), the best-known case of all, who was a member of the United States Supreme Court when he was drafted for the Republican nomination in 1916. At least three members of the United States Supreme Court were active but unsuccessful candidates for major-party presidential nominations between 1836 and 1880: John McLean (W, R), Salmon P. Chase (D, R), and Stephen J. Field (D). In the table, McLean and Field are counted among the "other" candidates; Chase did not exceed the 3 per cent level in the voting after becoming a justice.

Since 1880 the tradition has gradually strengthened that high court judges should leave politics behind them when they enter the judiciary, although Justices Vinson, Douglas, and Warren were mentioned prominently in speculation concerning presidential nominations after they had become members of the Court.[18] The total number of candidates for presidential and vice-presidential nominations who have come forward from the judiciary has declined markedly in the present century. Most of those who have attracted attention had extensive political experience in the background; otherwise they would probably not have been considered.

Most of the nominees for both the Presidency and the Vice Presidency and most of the other contenders, from the beginning, have been men who had previously held two or more governmental positions, as indicated in Tables 7.10 and 7.11. If the experience is compared for the two periods of the tables, however, it is apparent that in each of eight possible comparisons between separate categories of individuals, there was a decline from the earlier period to the more recent one in the average number of governmental positions previously held.[19] The amount of the decline is slight in some instances, but the consistency of the pattern is so clear that it is unmistakable. The average decline (computed directly from the table without adjusting for duplications) was from about 2.8 previous government positions to 2.3.

The circulation of officeholders among the various types of public office was apparently both more rapid and more extensive (in terms of variety of governmental experience) in the earlier period. Long tenure was relatively rare in either house of Congress, and a period of federal service was often followed by a return to state office. Such men as Henry Clay saw no loss of dignity in returning to the state legislature after a term in the United States Senate. Before the direct election of senators, it was the state legislature that retained the privilege of returning them to the Senate. James K. Polk, the only ex-Speaker of the House who was ever elected to the Presidency, had returned to his home state to run for governor after fourteen years in Congress; and he had served one term as governor of Tennessee and been defeated twice when finally he was nominated for President and elected in 1844.

---

[18] For a review of the historical evolution of thought and practice on the point by a legal scholar, see Alexander M. Bickel, "Chief Justice Warren and the Presidency," *New Republic,* January 23, 1956, pp. 8-10.

[19] The eight categories result from the splits by party, by office, and by whether nominated or not. The same differences are apparent in the two-party totals, but these overlap the other categories.

TABLE 7.12. GOVERNMENTAL POSITIONS HELD BY PRESIDENTIAL NOMINEES WHEN FIRST NOMINATED, AND BY OTHER CONTENDERS, 1832-1956

Governmental Position[a]	Democratic		Republican[b]		Both Parties	
	1832–1892	1896–1956	1832–1892	1896–1956	1832–1892	1896–1956
PRESIDENTIAL NOMINEES[c]						
No Governmental Position[d]	4	2	5	1	9	3
State Executive Other Than Governor	—	—	—	—	—	—
House of Representatives	—	—	1	—	1	—
Senate	2	—	1	1	3	1
Governor	2	5	1	3	3	8
Federal Appointive Office[e]	1	—	—	2	1	2
General, Regular Army	2	—	3	1	5	1
Federal and State Judiciary	—	1	—	1	—	2
Vice President	1	—	—	—	1	—
Number of Cases	12	8	11	9	23	17
OTHER CONTENDERS FOR PRESIDENTIAL NOMINATION[f]						
No Governmental Position[d]	13	10	5	8	18	18
State Executive Other Than Governor	—	—	1	—	1	—
House of Representatives	3	5	1	3	4	8
Senate	10	16	9	11	19	27
Governor	3	11	2	7	5	18
Federal Appointive Office[e]	—	2	2	—	2	2
General, Regular Army	—	—	—	1	—	1
Federal and State Judiciary	2	1	2	—	4	1
Vice President	—	2	—	—	—	2
No Information	1	—	—	—	1	—
Number of Cases.	32	47	22	30	54	77

[a] Governmental position held at the time of first nomination if a nominee; for other contenders, position as of the time of the convention in which the largest percentage of convention vote was received.

[b] Includes National Republican and Whig candidates.

[c] Omits Jackson, T. Roosevelt, Coolidge, and Truman, as in previous tables.

[d] Military service has been disregarded in determining governmental experience except in the case of the generals of the regular army.

[e] In the Executive Branch, other than military.

[f] Omits Fillmore, Johnson, and Arthur, as in previous tables.

Different types of political career pattern have become common in recent decades. Election to the House of Representatives without prior governmental experience has become relatively common. From there the road leads mainly to the Senate, only rarely back to the state governorship, and almost never directly into the President's Cabinet, although House members received Cabinet appointments with some frequency between 1888 and 1920. Governors typically arrive at the State House without prior federal experience, are rapidly rotated out of office under limitations on tenure, and then typically move either to the Senate or back into private life, after a possible brief interlude of consideration along the way as presidential hopefuls. Senators hate to go back home, even to run for governor, although they occasionally do both. Seemingly they are increasingly reluctant to enter the President's Cabinet or else they are less often invited, or both. Incumbent senators who could appropriately be considered for Cabinet appointment would almost invariably suffer a marked loss in seniority and security without any countervailing gain in long-term futures.[20] Cabinet members usually go back to private life and disappear without ever being seriously considered for the presidential or vice-presidential nominations; but there may be an increasing tendency for them to seek seats in the Senate, in view of the increasing prestige and attraction of that body for those who have continuing political interests.

Positions Occupied When Considered

Tables 7.12 and 7.13 indicate the governmental positions occupied at the time when the candidates were first nominated or were

most actively considered for the nominations.

The category "No Governmental Position" is parallel to the category "No Governmental Experience," in Tables 7.10 and 7.11, but far from the same. Many of the presidential and vice-presidential nominees were currently occupying no governmental position at the time of their first nomination; most of them, however, had previously acquired extensive experience in government, as the earlier tables have suggested. There was a marked decline after 1896 in both parties and for both offices in the proportion of the first-time nominations that went to candidates who were out of office at the time. The only cases among presidential nominees from 1896 to 1956 were William Jennings Bryan (D, 1896), John W. Davis (D, 1924), and Wendell Willkie (R, 1940). All were defeated.

No one in local government or a state legislature ever ran (above the 3 per cent level) for the presidential nomination in a major-party convention. And with the exception of three mayors on the Democratic side, the story is similar for the vice-presidential nomination: Mayor James Preston of Baltimore was a candidate for that nomination in 1912, as were John F. Hylan and Robert Wagner, mayors of New York, in 1924 and 1956. Only two incumbent state executive officials other than a governor ever ran above the 3 per cent level for either nomination; one of these, Millard Fillmore, then New York State comptroller, was nominated for Vice President on the Whig ticket of 1848, was elected, and became President on Zachary Taylor's death in 1850.

The only incumbent member of the House ever to achieve a major-party nomination for President since the beginnings of the convention system was James A. Garfield, elected in 1880. He had been serving as majority floor leader in the House of Representatives and had just been elected to the Senate by the legislature of Ohio at the time of the nomination. All the other fourteen presidential nominees with ex-

[20] A tabulation of Cabinet members from 1861 to 1940 indicates that 37 per cent of the members from the first Lincoln administration through the second Cleveland administration had served previously in House or Senate or both; but from the first McKinley administration to the second Franklin D. Roosevelt administration the proportion dropped to 18 per cent. See Pendleton Herring, *Presidential Leadership* (1940), pp. 164-65.

TABLE 7.13. GOVERNMENTAL POSITIONS HELD BY VICE-PRESIDENTIAL NOMINEES
WHEN FIRST NOMINATED, AND BY OTHER CONTENDERS, 1832-1956

Governmental Position[a]	Democratic		Republican[b]		Both Parties	
	1832–1892	1896–1956	1832–1892	1896–1956	1832–1892	1896–1956
VICE-PRESIDENTIAL NOMINEES						
No Governmental Position[c]	7[d]	3	7	4	14	7
Mayor	—	—	—	—	—	—
State Executive Other Than Governor	—	—	1	—	1	—
House of Representatives	2	1	2	1	4	2
Senate	3	5	3	4	6	9
Governor	2	2	—	4	2	6
Federal Appointive Office[e]	1	2	2	—	3	2
Federal and State Judiciary	—	—	—	—	—	—
Number of Cases	15	13	15	13	30	26
OTHER CONTENDERS FOR VICE-PRESIDENTIAL NOMINATION						
No Governmental Position[c]	13[f]	13	17[g]	6	30	19
Mayor	—	3	—	—	—	3
State Executive Other Than Governor	—	—	—	—	—	—
House of Representatives	4	2	4	4	8	6
Senate	6	8	5	3	11	11
Governor	1	3	2	3	3	6
Federal Appointive Office[e]	4	—	3	2	7	2
Federal and State Judiciary	4	1	1	1	5	2
Number of Cases	32	30	32	19	64	49

[a] Governmental position held at the time of first nomination if a nominee; for other contenders, position as of the time of the convention in which the largest percentage of convention vote was received.

[b] Includes National Republican and Whig candidates.

[c] Military service has been disregarded in determining governmental experience, except in the case of the generals of the regular army.

[d] Includes William Butler, who was holding a commission as a temporary general officer in the Mexican War.

[e] In the Executive Branch, other than military.

[f] Includes John Quitman, who was holding a commission as a temporary general officer in the Mexican War.

[g] Includes Benjamin F. Butler and L. H. Rousseau, who were holding commissions as temporary general officers in the Civil War.

perience in the House had ended their tenure before they were nominated, in most cases moving on to a governorship or to the Senate, or, as in the cases of Lincoln and Bryan, returning to private life. Of the twenty-six vice-presidential nominees who had served in the House, six were incumbent when nominated. Only two of these six were in the 1896-1956 period: James S. Sherman (R), who had served in the House for many years when nominated and elected as Taft's running mate in 1908, and Speaker John N. Garner (D), nominated and elected in 1932.

Incumbent senators have been major contenders for the presidential and vice-presidential nominations since the beginnings of the system, and incumbent governors were becoming so well before 1892. The basic figures for nominees with incumbency or previous experience as senators and governors (as compared with total nominees of all origins) in the two periods are:

	Presidential Nominees		Vice-Presidential Nominees	
	1832–1892	1896–1956	1832–1892	1896–1956
Total Nominees, All Origins	23	17	30	26
Incumbent				
Senators	3	1	6	9
Governors	3	8	2	6
Total	6	9	8	15
Former				
Senators	7	–	11	1
Governors	3	1	6	2
Total	10	1	17	3

Several points stand out in this brief array of figures. Incumbency in high office, by comparison with previous experience, has become relatively much more important than formerly for success in the pursuit of the nominations for the two highest offices. This is clear for all of the combinations of incumbent officeholding and office-seeking in the tabulation except senators seeking presidential nominations. Incumbent senators were less successful in the second period

than the first, but no former senator, not currently incumbent, was successful at all in the second period, although seven had been in the first. Governors were much more successful than senators in winning presidential nominations between 1896 and 1956, while senators were somewhat more successful than governors in winning vice-presidential nominations during that period.

The category "General, Regular Army" in Table 7.12 includes the same individuals as in Table 7.10. The six generals of the regular army who received presidential nominations were all on active duty when the preconvention campaigns for their nomination were started. General Eisenhower seems to be the only one of the six who resigned from active duty before the nomination had been consummated at the convention. Winfield Scott Hancock (D, 1880), the most recent before Eisenhower, retained his commission and remained on active duty, conducting a front-porch campaign from his command post at Governors Island, New York.[21]

Tables 7.12 and 7.13, even more clearly than Tables 7.10 and 7.11, show the tendency toward elimination of the members of the judiciary from active consideration for the national party nominations. Alton B. Parker and Charles Evans Hughes were the only high court judges actually serving as such when nominated. During the period ending in 1892, nine incumbent judges polled 3 per cent or more for one nomination or the other. From 1896 to 1956, there were only three such cases other than Parker and Hughes.

[21] No indication has been found that either Zachary Taylor or Winfield Scott resigned during their election campaigns. McClellan had been relieved of command in 1863 and told to await orders, which he never received. Grant held the post of Secretary of War for a short time simultaneously with that of senior General of the Army—was, in fact, his own boss: Secretary Grant issuing orders to General Grant. In accepting the Presidency, he lost the security of a pension in return for what was presumed to be at most eight years in the White House.

Candidate Sources and Electoral Success

What political offices have been most important as the final stepping stone to presidential or vice-presidential nomination? And to success in the election that followed? In Table 7.14 the information basic to these questions has been organized on an in-party—out-party basis. Each cell of the table contains a fraction indicating the number of winners in relation to the number of nominees in the category—for example, only one governor (Hayes) was nominated for President before 1892 in the party in power, but he was a winner.

The table provides a thought-provoking array, even though the figures in most of the items are much too small to be satisfactory for statistical analysis.[22] Naturally enough, the principal patterns revealed by the table are in accord with how the presidential system might be expected to operate, since sophisticated expectations have been derived from the experience summarized in the table. But there are various relationships, somewhat elusive, with what might be anticipated from the observation of other elective systems and administrative organizations.

One striking feature is the small total number of first-time nominees for President from 1896 to 1956 in the party in power, and the even smaller number of these nominations in which the election was won. The only winners (Taft and Hoover) came directly out of the administration of the party in power; when an in-party administration went outside of its own ranks for a new nominee or was unable to control the choice (Cox, Stevenson, Bryan), it lost the election and went out of power. One can speculate that any hierarchical or-

ganization that is too weak or too divided internally to deal smoothly with the problems of succession in the headship will also find its competitive problems difficult until its leadership situation is stabilized.

The special patterns of in-party nominations do not become very clear in the table for the period before 1892, but have been traced in the historical studies of Arthur Holcombe for the entire period from George Washington on. Holcombe argues that the "ins" have always tended to pick candidates closely associated with the administration in office, and have had their greatest electoral success with such candidates. When an administration has been conspicuously weak or unpopular, another type of candidate has sometimes been nominated, but this strategy has rarely proven successful in winning the election. On the other hand, according to Holcombe, the "outs" have usually found it expedient to look away from the leaders of the official opposition in Congress; there seems to be a natural principle of the American political order that handicaps these men when they seek to serve as presidential candidates, as demonstrated by American history from the earliest days.[23]

For the out-party, the relative predominance of the governors during the period 1896-1956 is clear—as is the lack of any such predominance during the earlier period in either in-party or out-party. Three out-party governors won both nomination and election (McKinley, Wilson, and F. D. Roosevelt); three were nominated but lost (Smith, Landon, and Dewey).

The record of the six generals in winning election was merely average. Ulysses S. Grant was the only in-party nominee in the list—if he can be called that with Andrew Johnson in the White House—who won. Winfield Scott, the other in-party nominee, was a spectacular loser. Winfield Scott Hancock lost as an out-party nominee, as did George B. McClellan. Zachary Taylor and

---

[22] See Chapter 6, footnote 16, and Chapter 18, footnote 30, for discussions of the problems of statistical significance in dealing with small numbers.

In the context of the present discussion, it should be clear that, in considering the relationships between governmental position when nominated and electoral success, there is no assumption of any simple pattern of one-way, one-factor causation.

[23] Arthur N. Holcombe, *Our More Perfect Union* (1950), pp. 82-87.

Dwight D. Eisenhower were the out-party winners, one in each period.[24]

Incumbent senators lost their elections on the occasions when nominated for President prior to 1892 (Clay, Cass, and Douglas); in

(Van Buren and Garfield), and two who lost (Parker and Hughes).

As for candidates holding no governmental position at the time when first nominated for President, the respective in-parties

TABLE 7.14. SOURCES OF FIRST-TIME NOMINEES AND THEIR ELECTORAL SUCCESS, BY PARTY STATUS, 1832-1892 AND 1896-1956[a]

Governmental Position of Nominee	Party In Power		Party Out of Power	
	1832–1892	1896–1956	1832–1892	1896–1956
PRESIDENTIAL NOMINEES				
Governor	1/1	0/2	1/2	3/6
Federal Official[b]	1/1	2/2	—	—
Army General	1/2	—	1/3	1/1
Senator	0/2	—	0/1	1/1
Other[c]	2/2	—	—	0/2
None	0/1	0/1	5/8	0/2
Total	5/9	2/5	7/14	5/12
VICE-PRESIDENTIAL NOMINEES				
Senator	1/3	4/5	2/3	1/4
Representative	3/3	1/1	0/1	1/1
Governor	—	1/1	1/2	2/5
Federal Official[b]	1/2	1/2	0/1	—
Other[d]	0/1	—	1/1	—
None	3/6	2/3	4/7	1/4
Total	8/15	9/12	8/15	5/14

[a] In each cell of the table, the denominator is the total number of nominees in the category and the numerator is the number who won in the ensuing general election.
[b] Appointive officials in the Executive Branch.
[c] One Vice President, one representative in Congress, and two judges.
[d] One army general and one state official (Butler and Fillmore).

the period 1896-1956 the only one (Harding) was a winner. The candidates holding "other" positions included two who won

[24] As noted earlier in the chapter, this list is limited to generals of the regular army winning first nominations after the beginnings of the convention system, and thus does not include Andrew Jackson or William Henry Harrison. Civilians publicized as military heroes on the basis of some earlier period of service, such as Harrison or T. Roosevelt, have done relatively well in the electoral competition. See Albert Somit, "The Military Hero as Presidential Candidate," *Public Opinion Quarterly,* Vol. 12 (Summer 1948), pp. 192-200.

lost with James G. Blaine in 1884 and William J. Bryan in 1896, and thereafter made no such nomination. The out-parties did relatively well before 1892 with non-incumbents in public office (the two Harrisons, Polk, Pierce, and Lincoln); between 1896 and 1956 both such out-party candidates (Davis and Willkie) lost. This showing further confirms an earlier comment on the need for incumbency in some high office in seeking the Presidency in modern times.

The vice-presidential nominees have differed notably from the presidential in the offices they were holding when first nominated and in their patterns of electoral success. The frequently noted predominance of senators is again clear, but in this table it becomes apparent that since 1896 the in-party senatorial nominees for Vice President have been on winning tickets much more regularly than out-party senators. In the in-party group, 1896-1956, John J. Sparkman (D, 1952) was the only loser, while in the out-party group Richard M. Nixon (R, 1952) was the only winner.

In all categories for the period 1896-1956 the high proportion of in-party first-time vice-presidential nominees who were winners is noteworthy. In most cases they were sharing the ticket with an incumbent who was seeking a further term; all the losers were on an in-party ticket headed by a first-time nominee. Conversely, on the out-party side, 1896-1956, all five of the winners were on a ticket with a winning first-time presidential nominee. Senators, governors, and nonincumbents in any office were equally available for service as running mates on out-party losing tickets after 1896: three in each category are apparent in the table. Throughout convention history, however, representatives in Congress, always up for election at the end of a two-year term, have shown little eagerness to share a possibly losing presidential ticket; George H. Pendleton, who ran with McClellan in 1864, was the only one to do so. In 1932, John N. Garner hedged his bet by running for both offices; after winning both, he resigned his House seat.

Less tangible differences between the vice-presidential nominees and the presidential can also be surmised, even if they do not become visible in the present table. On the basis of all of the material in the present chapter relating to states of residence, age, occupation, governmental experience, and the sequences of officeholding, as well as a wide variety of impressionistic evidence, it seems clear that the career patterns of the vice-presidential nominees have on the whole been much more "political," in a semi-derogatory sense, than those of the presidential.

A party war horse or a party hack has rarely if ever been nominated for President, even in a party that could reasonably expect to lose; party hacks (and old party war horses) have often been nominated for Vice President under such circumstances. Considerations akin to patronage have seldom influenced a presidential choice; they have often been of the essence in a vice-presidential nomination, especially when a party in power was filling a vacancy on a prospectively winning ticket.

All of this may be changing under the impact of an intensified party competition and the other factors noted in Chapters 3, 4, and 5; but for past experience the effects of such practices become somewhat apparent even in the statistical records.

Is There a Type That Emerges?

Popular writing in almost every presidential year includes efforts to define the personality characteristics and other qualifications of "the perfect President" or "the ideal nominee."[25] The data of the present chapter do not lend themselves easily to this kind of judgment, except perhaps for a few salient criteria within which there is much room for personality variation. Perhaps the most important suggestion that the data convey is that there is no single pattern of characteristics for presidential nominees that the conventions will invariably choose. The conventions may be guided to some extent by some unconscious ideal that has already had its effects in screening out those

[25] For example, Eugene Burdick, "The Perfect President," *This Week Magazine*, Jan. 1, 1956, pp. 7-9, 14; Cabell Phillips, "What Makes a Presidential Candidate," *New York Times Magazine*, Jan. 8, 1956, pp. 9, 59, 62, 65. The first is a popularization of the "father image" approach in much recent social science research, and was prepared at the Center for Advanced Study in the Behavioral Sciences; the second is an appraisal by an experienced political analyst.

who are clearly unavailable, but the conventions are mainly seeking to choose among those who are still available; and the system seems to throw up a wide range of types for choice, although not always a very wide range in any one year.

The situation was different in the early days of the Republic. As James Bryce pointed out, the early Presidents from Washington to John Quincy Adams were all men who were well known for their previous participation in national affairs, and who had many qualities in common. The congressional caucuses in picking most of the nominees stayed largely within the circle of their own observation and acquaintanceship.

The previous channels of advancement were disregarded when Andrew Jackson came to power as a people's hero. During his administration the convention system was installed, in part to prevent any restoration of the previous channels. Within a decade the new system had effectually broken the tendency to pick presidential nominees from a small circle of nationally known statesmen. It gave scope to the campaigning efforts of the sectional leaders, made room for factional candidacies, and provided machinery for selecting a compromise candidate when the leading factional candidates had defeated each other. The field was open to state government officials as well as federal, to legislators as much as executives, and to persons with no previous governmental experience, if for some other reason they had developed that intangible quality known as "availability."

The conventions have not easily solved the problem of defining the standards for choosing between the aspirants who may be available. Some of their difficulties are suggested by the diversity of the data patterns indicated in the present chapter. But with all of the cumbersomeness of the process, a sort of "natural selection" has always gone on, with the result that various negative standards have generally been applied in the determination of "availability." These

have been discussed at length by Sidney Hyman, who summarized his analysis as follows:

The natural aristocracy from which our Presidents are chosen is the residue of what is left when we subtract (1) all females from the total population, (2) all males who do not fall into the age group of 35 to 67 years, (3) all who were not born as American citizens, (4) all whose ethnic strain is not compatible with that of the English alliance, (5) all men who are ill, (6) all who have experienced spectacular marital difficulties, (7) all colored peoples, (8) all non-Protestants, (9) all Southerners, (10) all who come from small states, (11) all who have been conspicuously identified with big-city life, (12) all whose family origins cause unease to our middle and upper classes, (13) all lawyers conspicuously identified with a specialized clientele, (14) all individuals conspicuously identified with a special segment of the economic community, (15) all without some experience in major offices of government, whether at the international, national, or state and local level. If these rules of exclusion are applied to the entire population—with millions lopped off at each turn—the minority that can pass all these tests at any one time is probably in the neighborhood of one hundred men.[26]

The criteria just summarized are a good picture of the total historical experience. Recently it has seemed that some of these criteria may be occasionally subject to re-

[26] Sidney Hyman, *The American President* (1954), pp. 231-32 (quoted, courtesy of Harper & Brothers). For a revisionist approach to his own theories in the light of further developments, see also Hyman, "Nine Tests for the Presidential Hopeful," *New York Times Magazine*, Jan. 4, 1959, p. 11, 47, 48, 50.
The possibility that the religious factor might work in reverse, beginning with the nominations of 1960, was noted by Joseph Alsop in his syndicated column, July 15, 1959 (*Washington Post and Times Herald*). He reported that it was generally assumed in Democratic circles that at least one place on the 1960 ticket must go to a Catholic, and that Vice President Nixon was planning on a Catholic running mate in 1960 unless the Democratic ticket was led by Senator Kennedy, in which case an all-Protestant ticket was thought likely to be more advantageous to the Republican party. The concept of a religiously balanced ticket thus seems to be coming to presidential politics, as Alsop noted.

consideration, and in the future some of them may be abandoned. But, to the extent that criteria such as these are controlling, it can be suggested that most of the controls are usually exercised at lower levels of the political system. The controls have already operated, in most cases, long before candidates are within striking distance of a presidential nomination, by limiting access to the points of advancement along the way. Rules of eligibility such as these do not explain why governors are more often preferred than senators, or why the governors of certain states are especially preferred, or why there is a high preference, in making first-time nominations, for presidential candidates in their early fifties, or why the patterns of qualification for the vice-presidential nominees seem to be so notably different from the presidential. For the most part, it is necessary to look directly at the political system for elucidation on these points, as was done in the two chapters on centers of leadership in the nominating process.

Insofar as the data of the present chapter can be helpful in suggesting what kind of person a party is most likely to nominate, they probably help most as guides to what has clearly been untypical and to some elements of what is perhaps becoming typical.

In the case of the eight first-time Democratic presidential nominees during the period 1896-1956, for example, it would seem relatively easy to conclude that William Jennings Bryan, Alton B. Parker, and John W. Davis were all notably untypical in major respects.[27] Bryan was young, inexperienced, and from a small and predominantly Republican state. Parker was a high court judge, long withdrawn from active politics, a vigorous supporter of the gold standard that had been opposed by previous convention majorities of his own

[27] Here, as in the relevant tables throughout the chapter, the Vice Presidents who succeeded to the Presidency through the death of the incumbent are omitted from the category of first-time nominees.

party. Davis was a Wall Street lawyer whose previous political career had included two elections to the House of Representatives from West Virginia, followed by appointive positions in the Wilson administration.

The other Democratic presidential nominees of the period were Woodrow Wilson, James M. Cox, Alfred E. Smith, Franklin D. Roosevelt, and Adlai E. Stevenson. When first nominated, each of these men was the active and able governor of a populous, hard-fought, two-party state. Their ages respectively were 55, 50, 55, 50, and 52. Although they were all relatively young and new to the national scene, each had already achieved great distinction in a public-service type of career. Among the five, Cox was somewhat untypical in being a businessman and publisher, and Smith was certainly untypical because of his religious affiliation and highly urban origins. But all five were typical of much that has seemed best in the American political system: the rapid elevation of able political leaders who are still in the prime of life, and who have come up through elective executive office in states where politics is vigorous and competitive, without necessarily having as yet taken on the characteristics of a "father image." This appears to be the type that has been preferred by the Democratic party in its first-time presidential nominations of recent decades when the type was available. And the two who were elected (Wilson and Roosevelt) were highly exemplary of that preferred standard. The type was in conspicuously short supply when Bryan and Parker were nominated; and probably Davis would not have been nominated in 1924 if Al Smith had not been so conspicuously lacking in certain qualities of availability, even though pre-eminent in others.

The Republican party, on the other hand, seems to have had a fondness for "untypical" nominees. Wendell Willkie was probably the most outstanding example of untypicality, with his total lack of previous governmental experience. Dwight D. Eisenhower, with all of his eminence as a five-star general and in other respects, was a reversion to an earlier pattern of American politics and was one of the most untypical of the possible choices when first nominated. Charles Evans Hughes, remote and Olympian, was untypical as the only Supreme Court justice in history who has been nominated for President, notwithstanding his previous experience as a successful governor of New York State. Warren Gamaliel Harding, the only incumbent senator who had been nominated for President since Stephen A. Douglas in 1860, was untypical in a sufficient number of respects.

The other five first-time Republican nominees of 1896-1956 were William McKinley, Alfred M. Landon, and Thomas E. Dewey, who were incumbent governors when nominated, and William Howard Taft and Herbert Hoover, who served in the Cabinets of the Presidents that they succeeded. These five come closest to offering possibilities for the construction of a composite pattern of a typical Republican first-time presidential nominee in modern times. All were able executives whose affiliations with the business community were close and well known. Their ages respectively when first nominated were 53, 49, 42, 51, and 54. Their careers had included various elements of distinguished public service and evidences of capacity for the cultivation of the electorate. With the exception of Landon, their origins lay in the populous, two-party states where presidential elections have generally been won or lost. With the exception perhaps of Dewey, they were not characterized by the same kind of dynamism in their approach to public problems that seemed somewhat generally characteristic of the five governors who have been taken collectively as the Democratic type. They were therefore less likely to become the kind of "strong" President that, since Lincoln, seems to have been regarded by the Republican party as objectionable in the White House.

What has been adjudged here the preferred type—preferred by the conventions when they had an adequate opportunity for choice among alternatives—has provided the more successful Presidents of recent decades. On the Democratic side, it provided Wilson and F. D. Roosevelt, both of whom were rated among the great Presidents in a poll of fifty-five historians, conducted in the late 1940's by Arthur M. Schlesinger. On the Republican side, it provided McKinley, Taft, and Hoover, all of whom were rated by the historians' poll as at least average in their performance in the White House. Among the untypical nominees on the Democratic side, none won his election. Among the untypical Republican nominees, two were elected—Harding and Eisenhower—of whom only the former was rated by the historians, since the latter was not yet in office; Harding was classed as one of the two outright failures as President, the other being Grant. The entire set of ratings (as published in *Life* in 1948) is given in Table 7.15, in which the Presidents have been classified as to nominating system and political party by the authors of this book.[28]

Previous identification with public office as a governor rather than senator, one of the conspicuous attributes of the typical nominee group, takes on added importance against the background of the historians'

[28] Although the rankings contained in the table are an expression of one type of authoritative opinion, there could be considerable disagreement with some of them. The authors of the present study, in particular, would be inclined to wonder whether Grant was as great a failure as either Buchanan or Pierce. Buchanan presided over the final sequence of events that made the Civil War inevitable. Pierce was equally ineffective in providing the kind of presidential leadership that was needed during the period that culminated in the war, and in addition has the distinction of being the only President elected as such who openly sought renomination and was unable to achieve it. Grant, of course, was renominated and re-elected with ease, a pragmatic test that is highly respected by most politicians; on that count, at least, he was not a failure. He also was President at the time of the Hayes-Tilden affair; and although he was in a remarkably convenient position to organize a military intervention in the succession of the kind that has occurred frequently under the presidential system in other countries, he did his part in maintaining the integrity of the system and in preserving the Union.

TABLE 7.15. THE PRESIDENTS UP TO 1945 AS RATED BY HISTORIANS[a]

(adapted here to categories of nominating systems and political parties)

Category Assigned by Poll of 55 Historians	Presidents Selected Prior to Convention System	Presidents Nominated in National Party Conventions	
		Democratic	Republican[b]
Great	2. G. Washington 5. T. Jefferson 6. A. Jackson	3. F. D. Roosevelt 4. W. Wilson	1. A. Lincoln
Near Great	9. J. Adams	8. G. Cleveland 10. J. K. Polk	7. T. Roosevelt
Average	11. J. Q. Adams 12. J. Monroe 14. J. Madison	15. M. Van Buren	13. R. B. Hayes 16. W. H. Taft 17. C. A. Arthur 18. W. McKinley 19. A. Johnson 20. H. Hoover 21. B. Harrison
Below Average		26. J. Buchanan 27. F. Pierce	22. J. Tyler 23. C. Coolidge 24. M. Fillmore 25. Z. Taylor
Failure			28. U. S. Grant 29. W. G. Harding

[a] Arthur M. Schlesinger, "The U. S. Presidents," *Life*, Vol. 25 (Nov. 1, 1948), pp. 65-66, 68, 73-74. Based on "an informal presidential rating poll which I conducted not long ago among my colleagues in American history and government. . . . There was a large measure of agreement among the 'experts' within the important categories of great, near great, and failures. The six greats . . . had no close runners-up, although Lincoln was the only one to get all 55 votes for the top rank" (p. 66). William Henry Harrison and James A. Garfield were omitted because of the brevity of their life in office. Harry S. Truman was omitted because his record was not complete at the time of the poll. (Rating material used by courtesy of Professor Schlesinger and *Life*.)
[b] Includes Whig (Tyler, Fillmore, and Taylor) and War Democrat (Johnson).

ratings of the Presidents. Among the great Presidents, only Jackson had served in the Senate, and his brief service there was one of the least important parts of his career. As Wilfred Binkley points out,

Returning to the verdicts of the jury of historians, not one of the six "great" presidents had served a full term in the Senate. Nor had one of the four "near great" ever sat in the Senate. The former senators cluster near the foot of the class. Three of the eleven "average" presidents, three of the six "below average" presidents, and one of the two "failures" had been senators. Half of the "great" presidents had been state governors, three-fourths of the "near-great," and five of the eleven "average" presidents had been governors. There was only one governor among the eight presidents rated still lower.[29]

Withal, it is necessary to remember for both parties that, at any given time, it is possible to choose only from among those who are available. If the preferred type, at least in a party out of power, is a vote-getting governor in an important two-party state, still in his early fifties after an aggressive climb to the top in his own locality and with a clean record of distinguished public service activities along the way, the number of such persons currently in office

[29] Wilfred E. Binkley, *The Man in the White House* (1958), p. 93 (quoted, courtesy of The Johns Hopkins Press).

in both parties together is not likely to be more than a dozen at any one time. It may not be more than three or four. If the tide of one party's fortune has ebbed throughout the country, the available governors may all be of the other party—in which case the party that finds itself in that difficulty will have to start looking for a different type of candidate, along with an appropriate set of rationalizations with which to justify his selection.

In the current era, however, the problem seems to be taking a somewhat different form. Governors and former governors are in ample supply in both parties under the present conditions of party competition and the increasing number of pivotal states. But the growing importance of the federal government, of the issues of national policy, and of American involvements with the world at large may be shifting the whole political spectrum in a way that increases the availability of senators (and of others with international experience) by comparison with the governors. This is a possibility that became apparent in the earlier chapters on the centers of leadership in the nominating process. The data of the present chapter give a concise overview of past practice; it remains to be seen whether the picture will remain closely similar in the future.

8

Apportionment of Votes Among the States

THE RULES THAT determine how many votes each state delegation shall have in the national convention are in some respects the most basic rules of all, since they determine how units of power are to be shared and can influence how every significant decision will be resolved.

Theoretically the delegations might be chosen on some other basis than by states and congressional districts. They might be made up predominantly of public and party officeholders appointed ex officio, and also might include delegates directly chosen by farmer, business, and labor organizations. But the fact that elections are held on a territorial basis has naturally led to the adoption of a similar basis for the definition of delegations and apportionment of their voting power. This chapter is concerned with the evolution of the present apportionment rules and with recent proposals for their amendment. It does not undertake to examine fundamentally different alternatives, such as the abandonment of the states as delegation units or the introduction of proportional representation.

Informally, however, the network of influence in the conventions is far more complex than the apportionment of delegate votes would suggest. Many public and party officeholders are in practice given places in the state delegations, where they exert the weight of their position much as if they were ex officio members. Moreover, the delegates are not the only participants in the conventions. Others who directly affect the results include the convention officers, headed as a rule by party leaders in Congress; the members of the national committee; the distinguished guests, including ex-Presidents and other dignitaries; and the representatives of pressure groups who are officially invited to submit proposals to the platform committee and who unofficially lobby among the delegates.

But the voting power lies in the delegations, and inevitably the apportionment of voting strength among the states favors some interests at the expense of others. Any change involves some shifting in power relationships and will be resisted by those who are threatened with relative loss of power—as well as by the characteristic inertia of all generally acceptable institutions. Informal practices may therefore be important for modifying the effects of rigid formulas that cannot be formally amended.

Evolution of Apportionment Rules

The basic allocation of voting power from the start of the convention system in the 1832 campaign was the same as that in the electoral college—equal to the total of senators and representatives from each state. The principle of allowing every state two votes, plus a number proportionate to its population, had been thoroughly debated and agreed upon by the Founding Fathers in designing the structure of the United States Congress. It was intended to give a special advantage to the small states in recognition of their equal sovereignty, and the principle involved was carried over into the national party organizations without question. Later, when the electoral college basis for apportionment was questioned, it was not so much the sovereignty votes as the validity of allotting votes in proportion to population that came under attack. In Congress the allocation of House seats according to population was acceptable, but in a party convention an anomaly arose with the appearance of "one-party" states, in which the minority party had an abnormally small constituency. Before the Civil War both parties were widely distributed and the one-party states were hardly a problem; but more recently this problem has affected the apportionment policies of both parties.

The size of delegations sent to the conventions has often varied with little regard to the number of votes allotted to the delegation, and as a result the delegates have often had fractional votes. The chief cause of this phenomenon was the pressure to find seats for all the influential party members who desired to attend. In general, the party in each state has retained the right to elect its delegation, subject at times to state laws, while the convention holds the right to apportion the voting strength among the states.

Variable Delegations
in the Democratic Party

Delegations of variable size caused some confusion in early years, and in 1848 the Democratic convention tried to limit the delegations to a ratio of one-man-one-vote, but without success.[1] In an effort to relieve

the pressure, the convention of 1852 voted to allow each state twice as many delegates as it had votes, and no more, giving each delegate a half vote. In 1872 the number of votes was doubled so that each delegate might have a whole vote.[2]

In 1924, after the adoption of women's suffrage, the Democrats split up the four places of delegate at large from each state—corresponding to its senatorial quota of two electoral votes—into eight places with a half vote each, "to give adequate representation to women as delegates at large, without disturbing prevailing party customs."[3] These efforts to determine the number of delegates did not, however, prevent the continued appearance and seating of oversized delegations with corresponding fractional votes.

The Republicans'
Century of Controversy

In the Republican party the apportionment rules have had a more complex history. At the convention of 1856, the first for the newborn party, each state was allowed six delegates at large, and three for each congressional district. This was changed in 1860 to four at large and two for each district, an apportionment that remained in effect until after the convention of 1912, despite growing dissatisfaction.

In 1856 the new Republican party was entirely northern; no delegations from south of the Potomac appeared in response to its call. But in 1860 there came delegations from Virginia and Texas. The Texas delegation was challenged, since the party had no significant membership there. The credentials committee suggested seating the Texans with a reduction in voting strength from eight to six, and this was approved—the first instance of recognition that lack of

---

[1] DNC, *Proceedings*, 1852, p. 3, quoting a resolution passed in 1848. Another resolution of 1848 was later read, stating the entitlement of each state to only its electoral college vote, regardless of the number of delegates in attendance; see *ibid.*, p. 27. The official proceedings of the national party conventions have varied considerably in precise title, format, and publishing auspices. In this work, they are cited simply by year and by "DNC" for the Democratic National Convention and "RNC" for the Republican. Convention debates on the rules will be summarized and actions reported in detail, in the forthcoming book by Richard C. Bain, *Decisions and Voting Records of the National Party Conventions* (Brookings Institution), which will also include

bibliographical details on the proceedings as variously published.

[2] A search of the proceedings for 1868 and 1872 has failed to locate any formal action on this point; but in 1868 the total number of votes was 317 while in 1872 it was 732.

[3] DNC, *Proceedings*, 1924, p. 5. The authorized half votes were frequently used for other purposes.

party strength would not require total exclusion but might involve a penalty in the apportionment of convention votes.[4]

In 1864, however, for the Republican National Union convention, Tennessee, Arkansas, and Louisiana—where the Union armies were in sufficient control to enable unionist governments to be established—sent delegations that were seated with full voting rights. During Reconstruction and thereafter all the southern states sent delegations, and they were given their full apportionment, though after 1876, with the growth of devices for disfranchising the Negroes, the number of Republican voters shrank drastically.

With the emergence in 1880 of the "Solid South" controlled by white Democratic majorities, the "rotten borough" Republican delegations, often composed mainly of federal officials when the party was in power, were an embarrassing feature of the Republican conventions. The southern delegate problem was discussed by the Republican national committee in preparation for the 1884 convention, but no change in apportionment was made. Efforts in the conventions of 1884 and 1892 to reduce the representation of the South were unsuccessful. In 1896, with the party out of power, there was talk of widespread bribery among these delegates.[5]

In 1900 another reform proposal was introduced, apparently for the principal purpose of putting pressure on President McKinley. It was withdrawn when he agreed to accept Theodore Roosevelt as his running mate.[6]

In 1908 a minority report of the rules committee proposed that for the 1912 convention each state should have four delegates at large and one additional delegate for each 10,000 Republican votes or major fraction thereof in the last preceding presidential election.[7] This proposal came to a floor vote and was narrowly defeated, 506 to 471. The bulk of the opposition came from the South and the more thinly settled of the western states; however, a large part of the margin came from Ohio, which voted against the proposal 38 to 8.[8] Ohio's system of delegate election by congressional districts would have been disturbed had the rule change been successful. But the Ohio delegates doubtless had other less-mentioned reasons for voting against the proposal, including the need for southern support in securing the 1908 nomination for William Howard Taft of Ohio and his prospective need for control of the convention in 1912 if he was elected in 1908, as he seemed likely to be.[9]

Had the proposal been adopted, southern representation in the 1912 convention would have been cut in half, and Roosevelt

---

[4] RNC, *Proceedings*, the first three Republican conventions, pp. 124-25. This and following passages are based in part on Phillip E. Daum, "Delegate Apportionment in Republican National Conventions, 1856-1956" (April 20, 1953), unpublished senior thesis, on deposit in the Library of Princeton University. This 152-page manuscript appears to be the most complete single source on the history of the recurring debates over Republican apportionment rules.

[5] There was a comment on the means by which "all but six" of the Negro delegates from the South were brought around to the support of the gold standard: Dr. Courtney of Massachusetts was commended for the "able and honourable work" by which he succeeded in "intellectually persuading the Negro delegates to accept gold," while credit was also given to a former carpetbag governor of Louisiana "whose arguments were believed to have been of another kind." See Anon., "The Republican National Convention," *Outlook Magazine*, Vol. 53 (1896), p. 1182.

[6] For an account of the political maneuver, see Harold F. Gosnell, *Boss Platt and His New York Machine* (1924), pp. 121-22; for the actual proposal, together with complete tabulations of the effect of three alternative plans of apportionment, see RNC, *Proceedings*, 1900, pp. 96-98.

[7] RNC, *Proceedings*, 1908, pp. 95-96.

[8] RNC, *Proceedings*, pp. 95-110; Daum, *op. cit.*, pp. 76-77.

[9] Presumably the T. Roosevelt forces that were supporting the Taft nomination in 1908 were opposed to the change in the apportionment rules, and a defection on the part of the Ohio delegation would have been a serious break in administration strength. The delegations supporting Taft, who voted 98 per cent for his nomination, voted 72 per cent against the change in the rules. Conversely, the delegations opposing Taft, who voted 83 per cent against his nomination, voted 91 per cent for the change. See Chapter 17, Table 17.8.

would probably have been nominated instead of Taft. The 11 formerly Confederate states had 252 votes in that convention, or 23 per cent of the total, though they had supplied less than 7 per cent of the Republican popular vote in 1908. Taft won the first test vote in 1912 by 558 to 501, with 256 contested delegates voting. Of the 256, 176 were from the 11 southern states, and these gave Taft more than enough votes to assure victory. His nomination was then steamrollered through. Roosevelt's Progressive faction bolted, and the election was thrown to Wilson.[10]

Reacting to the disaster of 1912, the Republican national committee, with no delegated authority to act, stepped into the breach. It offered a plan for the 1916 convention that would become effective if approved before the end of 1914 by state conventions in states having a majority of the electoral votes.[11] According to the new plan, each state would retain its four delegates at large, along with one delegate for each congressional district. One additional delegate in 1916 would be allowed to each district in which 7,500 Republican votes had been cast for President in 1908 or for congressman in 1914—since the debacle in 1912 was not deemed a proper measure of Republican strength.

By October 1914 the plan had been ratified by twenty-two states, including Arkansas, North Carolina, South Carolina, Oklahoma, and Tennessee.[12] Under the new rules, eleven southern states lost seventy-eight delegates in 1916 and seven more in 1920. The only northern states affected in those years were New York, which lost three

delegates in 1916 and two in 1920, as compared with 1912, and Massachusetts, which lost one in 1920.[13]

For the 1924 convention the requirement for the second district delegate was raised from 7,500 votes to 10,000, taking some account of population growth and the advent of women's suffrage, and a system of bonus delegates was adopted for the first time. Three bonus delegates at large were allotted to each state carried by the party in the last preceding presidential election, a provision favoring the northern states. The provision also favored the small states at the expense of the large, since the number of bonus votes was in no way related to state size, but this aspect of the problem does not seem to have figured in the debate.

In 1940, effective 1944, a congressional district was required to have produced 1,000 Republican votes in the last preceding presidential or congressional election in order to qualify for even one district delegate; in 1952, effective 1956, the figure was raised to 2,000.[14] The 10,000-vote requirement—instituted in 1924—for the second district delegate remained unchanged. In 1956, however, the rules were amended to make it clear that votes for the Republican candidate for President would be recognized even where the candidate had received those votes as an "independent" (as in Mississippi and South Carolina in 1952).[15]

The provisions on bonus votes have been repeatedly expanded. In 1940, effective 1944, it was provided that a state that the party failed to carry in the presidential election could still have its three bonus votes if it should elect a Republican senator in the following off-year election.[16] Alaska and Hawaii were also authorized to receive two bonus delegates for the election of a Republican delegate to Congress. In 1948, ef-

---

[10] The first test vote by roll call occurred on the temporary chairmanship, and was not tabulated in the proceedings; each delegation was polled. (RNC, *Proceedings, 1912*, pp. 61-88.) The number of contested but seated delegates was computed from Republican Party, National Committee, *Statement Related to Contests Over Seats in the Republican National Convention, 1912* (Washington, 1912), pp. 69-72. Only five delegates on the temporary roll failed to vote.
[11] *New York Times*, Dec. 18, 1913; RNC, *Proceedings*, 1916, p. 9.
[12] *New York Times*, Oct. 26, 1914.

[13] Howard R. Penniman, *Sait's American Parties and Elections* (5th ed., 1952), p. 400.
[14] RNC, *Proceedings*, 1940, pp. 102-03; 1952, p. 290.
[15] *Ibid.*, 1956, p. 162.
[16] *Ibid.*, 1944, p. 21.

fective 1952, the number of bonus delegates for party victory in a state was raised from three to six and the bonus was made available for success in the last preceding presidential, senatorial, or gubernatorial election.[17] The Republican national committee ruled in January 1952, for example, that the State of Washington was entitled to bonus votes under this rule because it had elected a Republican governor in 1948, even though it had been carried by the Democratic candidate for President in 1948 and for senator in 1950.[18] In 1952, effective 1956, the bonus for electing a Republican territorial delegate to Congress was increased from two to four, but there was no change in the bonus vote provisions for the states.[19] No further change was made in 1956.

Recent Changes in Democratic Apportionment Rules

Bonus votes came later in the Democratic party than in the Republican and until recently were less freely distributed. In 1936, as a concession to the South in connection with the repeal of the two thirds rule, the national committee was directed "to formulate and to recommend to the next National Convention a plan for improving the system by which delegates and alternates to the Democratic National Convention are apportioned," taking into account "the Democratic strength within each state."[20] The 1940 convention approved a rule, effective in 1944, by which two bonus votes would be allotted to each state going Democratic in the last preceding presidential election.[21] In 1944 the convention again directed the national committee to continue its consideration of the problem, and authorized it to modify the apportionment in

calling the 1948 convention. The committee then increased the bonus to four votes for states going Democratic in the previous presidential election. This change was included in the call for the 1948 convention, was confirmed in seating the delegates, and remained unchanged in the convention of 1952.[22]

In making the apportionment for 1952, the Democratic national committee encountered a problem resulting from the congressional reapportionment after the 1950 census. The states gaining seats in Congress were of course given corresponding recognition in the convention by the operation of the usual rules. But nine states were in process of losing congressional seats because of the reapportionment, and in some, notably New York, the necessary redistricting had not yet been completed. Faced with the same problem, the Republican party authorities took no action and left the individual states to adjust to their loss of delegate votes as best they could. But the Democratic national committee yielded to the pressures inherent in the situation, and adopted a special rule providing that for the 1952 convention no state should lose convention votes by reason of the congressional reapportionment. Similar actions had been taken by the Democrats in 1912 and 1932, when conventions followed close on congressional reapportionment, but with a return to the normal convention rules in 1916 and 1936.[23]

In the preparations for the 1956 convention, however, the committee provided that every state should receive *all* of the votes previously allotted to it in the 1952 convention and four *additional* votes if it had either cast its electoral votes for the Democratic nominees of 1952 or had elected a Democratic governor or senator on or after November 4, 1952.[24] This had the effect of

---

[17] *Ibid.*, 1948, pp. 85-86; 1952, pp. 16-17.
[18] Paul T. David, Malcolm Moos, Ralph M. Goldman, *Presidential Nominating Politics in 1952* (1954), Vol. 5, p. 163.
[19] RNC, *Proceedings*, 1952, pp. 289-90.
[20] DNC, *Proceedings*, 1936, p. 190; also quoted, 1948, p. 398.
[21] *Ibid.*, 1940, pp. 201, 341-56.

[22] *Ibid.*, 1948, p. 13; 1952, pp. 7, 556.
[23] *Ibid.*, 1912, pp. 1-2; 1916, p. 12; 1932, pp. 15-16; 1936, p. 26; 1952, pp. 6-7.
[24] Call for the 1956 Democratic National Convention, December 21, 1955, as contained in Clarence Cannon, *Democratic Manual* (1956), pp. 12-17.

carrying over into 1956 the compensatory votes for the congressional reapportionment of 1950, thus establishing a precedent under which the votes corresponding to lost congressional districts might be indefinitely continued from census to census by states otherwise losing ground.

In the case of the bonus votes, the effect was even more extraordinary. The basis for bonus votes was broadened to include gubernatorial and senatorial elections, for the first time in the Democratic party. Many of the states credited with bonus votes in 1952 and again in 1956 for their Democratic presidential vote in 1948 were thus given a like number of additional bonus votes in 1956 for voting Democratic in 1952 or 1954 for President, governor, or senator. These states then each had received a total of eight bonus votes in 1956; and a new precedent was established for the accumulation of bonus votes from convention to convention. The states were also authorized to send either one or two delegates for each vote, thus putting most of the delegates on a half-vote basis (see Chapter 9, footnote 71).

In preparations for the 1960 convention, national committee Chairman Paul M. Butler led an effort to end the bonus system, which he said had "grossly distorted representation" at the 1956 convention. Butler's initial plan would have compensated many of the states for their loss of bonus votes by increasing the number of regular votes allotted to every state, but fifteen states would have suffered some loss in their total number of votes. After discussion in the meeting of the national committee on September 16, 1959, compromise rules were adopted that retained major elements of Butler's plan, but that also provided that no state should suffer any reduction in the number of votes that it had received in 1956. For the first time it was also provided that the national committee members should be seated as delegates on an ex officio basis, with one half vote each. The additional vote for the two members was not to be charged against the regular quota or the bonus votes

carried over from 1956, with the result that every state received at least one more vote than previously. The total number of votes was increased to 1,521, and the states were again authorized to send either one delegate or two for each vote; thus there was the prospect of approximately 3,000 delegates at the 1960 Democratic convention.[25]

Apportionment in 1956 and 1960

The practical effect of the apportionment rules as they stood in 1956 and as they are planned for 1960 is demonstrated in Table 8.1 for the Democratic party and in Table 8.2 for the Republican party. In these tables the states are listed in the standard geographic pattern developed originally for the tables in *Presidential Nominating Politics in 1952*.[26]

Among the major regions, the Northeast, Middle West, and South are nearly the same in total population; they were accorded approximately the same voting strength in the 1956 conventions of both parties. The South, however, was in this position in the Republican convention of 1956 because it had profited greatly in convention voting strength from its previous increases in Republican presidential voting.

In total population, the West is much the smallest of the four major regions, with less than half the population of any one of the three others in 1950. Accordingly, its voting strength in both party conventions has been markedly less than that of the other regions, but in recent years had been

(Text continued on page 174)

[25] See Associated Press article by D. Harold Oliver, carried in *Washington Post and Times Herald*, Sept. 13, 1959; Publicity Division, Democratic National Committee, "Resolution 'G,' Adopted . . . Sept. 16, 1959"; *New York Times*, Sept. 17, 1959; *Democratic Digest*, Oct. 1959, pp. 6, 11-12.
[26] David, Moos, and Goldman, *op. cit.*, Vol. 1, p. 82. The basic principle of the pattern is as far as possible to move from one contiguous state to another in making the listing, moving generally from north to south and east to west, thus producing a pattern in the tables that facilitates comparisons between nearby states.

TABLE 8.1. VOTING STRENGTH IN THE DEMOCRATIC NATIONAL CONVENTION OF 1956, AND AS PLANNED FOR 1960, BY STATES AND REGIONS

	1956				1960			
	Votes at Large		Congressional District Votes	Total Votes	Basic Allotment		Holdover Bonus Votes[b]	Total Votes
Region and State	Regular	Bonus			Regular Votes	Nat. Com. Votes[a]		
Northeast								
Maine................	4	4	6	14	13	1	1	15
New Hampshire.......	4	—	4	8	10	1	—	11
Vermont[c]............	6	—	—	6	8	1	—	9
Massachusetts........	4	8	28	40	40	1	—	41
Rhode Island.........	4	8	4	16	10	1	6	17
Connecticut[d].........	6	4	10	20	20	1	—	21
New York[e]...........	8	4	86	98	113	1	—	114
New Jersey...........	4	4	28	36	40	1	—	41
Delaware[c]...........	6	4	—	10	8	1	2	11
Maryland.............	4	—	14	18	23	1	—	24
Pennsylvania[e]........	10	4	60	74	80	1	—	81
West Virginia........	4	8	12	24	20	1	4	25
	64	48	252	364	385	12	13	410
Middle West								
Ohio.................	4	8	46	58	63	1	—	64
Michigan.............	4	4	36	44	50	1	—	51
Indiana..............	4	—	22	26	33	1	—	34
Illinois[e]..............	6	8	50	64	68	1	—	69
Wisconsin............	4	4	20	28	30	1	—	31
Minnesota...........	4	8	18	30	28	1	2	31
Iowa................	4	4	16	24	25	1	—	26
Missouri[e]............	8	8	22	38	33	1	5	39
North Dakota[f]........	8	—	—	8	10	1	—	11
South Dakota.........	4	—	4	8	10	1	—	11
Nebraska.............	4	—	8	12	15	1	—	16
Kansas...............	4	—	12	16	20	1	—	21
	58	44	254	356	385	12	7	404
South								
Virginia.............	4	8	20	32	30	1	2	33
North Carolina.......	4	8	24	36	35	1	1	37
South Carolina.......	4	4	12	20	20	1	—	21
Georgia.............	4	8	20	32	30	1	2	33
Florida.............	4	8	16	28	25	1	3	29
Kentucky[e]...........	6	8	16	30	25	1	5	31
Tennessee[e]...........	6	8	18	32	28	1	4	33
Alabama.............	4	4	18	26	28	1	—	29
Mississippi[e]..........	6	4	12	22	20	1	2	23
Arkansas[e]............	6	8	12	26	20	1	6	27
Louisiana............	4	4	16	24	25	1	—	26
Oklahoma[e]..........	8	8	12	28	20	1	8	29
Texas[g]...............	6	8	42	56	60	1	—	61
	66	88	238	392	366	13	33	412

	1956				1960			
	Votes at Large		Congres-sional District Votes	Total Votes	Basic Allotment			
						Nat. Com. Votes[a]	Holdover Bonus Votes[b]	
Region and State	Regular	Bonus			Regular Votes			Total Votes
West								
Montana............	4	8	4	16	10	1	6	17
Idaho..............	4	4	4	12	10	1	2	13
Wyoming[c]...........	6	8	—	14	8	1	6	15
Colorado............	4	8	8	20	15	1	5	21
Utah...............	4	4	4	12	10	1	2	13
Nevada[c].............	6	8	—	14	8	1	6	15
New Mexico[c].........	8	8	—	16	10	1	6	17
Arizona.............	4	8	4	16	10	1	6	17
Washington[h].........	6	8	12	26	23	1	3	27
Oregon..............	4	4	8	16	15	1	1	17
California...........	4	4	60	68	80	1	—	81
Alaska	6	—	—	6	8	1	—	9
Hawaii	6	—	—	6	8	1	—	9
	66	72	104	242	215	13	43	271
Non-State Areas								
District of Columbia....	6	—	—	6	8	1	—	9
Puerto Rico..........	6	—	—	6	6	1	—	7
Virgin Islands........	3	—	—	3	3	1	—	4
Canal Zone..........	3	—	—	3	3	1	—	4
	18	—	—	18	20	4	—	24
Total..............	272	252	848	1,372	1,371	54	96	1,521

[a] Votes for national committee members serving ex officio as members of state delegations.

[b] Votes authorized to prevent reduction from the number of votes held in 1956, exclusive of the added vote for national committee members.

[c] Only one representative in Congress at large, hence all 1956 delegates at large.

[d] Connecticut has five congressional districts and one representative at large.

[e] Nine states lost congressional seats following the 1950 census, but were given votes on the basis of the previous number of seats, by virtue of a special Democratic national rule that no state should have its delegate voting strength reduced by reason of the congressional reapportionment. The additional votes for all nine states are included under "Votes at Large" for 1956.

[f] Two representatives, both at large, hence all delegates at large in 1956.

[g] Texas had twenty-one congressional districts and one representative at large.

[h] Washington had six congressional districts and one representative at large.

	1956				1960[a]			
	Votes at Large		Congressional District Votes	Total Votes	Votes at Large		Congressional District Votes	Total Votes
Region and State	Regular	Bonus			Regular	Bonus		
Northeast								
Maine................	4	6	6	16	4	6	6	16
New Hampshire.......	4	6	4	14	4	6	4	14
Vermont[b]............	6	6	—	12	6	6	—	12
Massachusetts........	4	6	28	38	4	6	28	38
Rhode Island.........	4	6	4	14	4	6	4	14
Connecticut[c].........	6	6	10	22	6	6	10	22
New York	4	6	86	96	4	6	86	96
New Jersey...........	4	6	28	38	4	6	28	38
Delaware[b]...........	6	6	—	12	6	6	—	12
Maryland............	4	6	14	24	4	6	14	24
Pennsylvania.........	4	6	60	70	4	6	60	70
West Virginia........	4	—	12	16	4	6	12	22
	54	66	252	372	54	72	252	378
Middle West								
Ohio................	4	6	46	56	4	6	46	56
Michigan............	4	6	36	46	4	6	36	46
Indiana.............	4	6	22	32	4	6	22	32
Illinois.............	4	6	50	60	4	6	50	60
Wisconsin...........	4	6	20	30	4	6	20	30
Minnesota...........	4	6	18	28	4	6	18	28
Iowa................	4	6	16	26	4	6	16	26
Missouri............	4	6	22	32	4	—	22	26
North Dakota[d].......	8	6	—	14	8	6	—	14
South Dakota........	4	6	4	14	4	6	4	14
Nebraska............	4	6	8	18	4	6	8	18
Kansas..............	4	6	12	22	4	6	12	22
	52	72	254	378	52	66	254	372
South								
Virginia............	4	6	20	30	4	6	20	30
North Carolina.......	4	—	24	28	4	—	24	28
South Carolina.......	4	—	12[e]	16	4	—	9	13
Georgia.............	4	—	19	23	4	—	20	24
Florida.............	4	6	16	26	4	6	16	26
Kentucky............	4	6	16	26	4	6	16	26
Tennessee...........	4	6	18	28	4	6	18	28
Alabama............	4	—	17	21	4	—	18	22
Mississippi..........	4	—	11[e]	15	4	—	8	12
Arkansas............	4	—	12	16	4	—	12	16
Louisiana...........	4	—	16	20	4	6	16	26
Oklahoma...........	4	6	12	22	4	6	12	22
Texas[f]...............	6	6	42	54	4	6	44	54
	54	36	235	325	52	42	233	327

	1956				1960[a]			
	Votes at Large		Congres-sional District	Total	Votes at Large		Congres-sional District	Total
Region and State	Regular	Bonus	Votes	Votes	Regular	Bonus	Votes	Votes
West								
Montana............	4	6	4	14	4	6	4	14
Idaho..............	4	6	4	14	4	6	4	14
Wyoming[b]..........	6	6	—	12	6	6	—	12
Colorado...........	4	6	8	18	4	6	8	18
Utah...............	4	6	4	14	4	6	4	14
Nevada[b]............	6	6	—	12	6	6	—	12
New Mexico[d]........	8	6	—	14	8	6	—	14
Arizona............	4	6	4	14	4	6	4	14
Washington[g]........	6	6	12	24	4	6	14	24
Oregon	4	6	8	18	4	6	8	18
California..........	4	6	60	70	4	6	60	70
Alaska	4	—	—	4	6	—	—	6
Hawaii	6	4	—	10	6	6	—	12
	64	70	104	238	64	72	106	242
Non-State Areas								
District of Columbia....	6	—	—	6	8	—	—	8
Puerto Rico..........	3	—	—	3	3	—	—	3
Virgin Islands........	1	—	—	1	1	—	—	1
	10	—	—	10	12	—	—	12
Total..............	234	244	845	1,323	234	252	845	1,331

[a] Based on a publication issued by the Research Division, Republican National Committee, *The Process of Delegate Selection for the Republican National Convention of 1960* (mimeo, Sept. 1959), Foreword.
[b] Only one representative in Congress at large, hence all delegates at large.
[c] Connecticut has five congressional districts and one representative at large.
[d] Two representatives, both at large, hence all delegates at large.
[e] The "Independent" vote for Eisenhower in South Carolina and Mississippi in 1952 was recognized as a basis for apportioning delegates in the Republican national convention of 1956.
[f] Texas had twenty-one congressional districts and one representative at large.
[g] Washington had six congressional districts and one representative at large.

helped considerably by the operation of the various systems of bonus votes. In 1956 bonus votes provided nearly one third of western strength in each party convention. From 1960 on, western influence in the conventions and elections will be increased by the addition of Alaska and Hawaii as states.

Most states (as shown in the tables) were able to qualify for bonus votes in the conventions of both parties in 1956; the main effect of the bonus system therefore was simply to penalize the few states where the party was most unsuccessful—eight in each party, as it happened in 1956.

In 1960, there will be no newly authorized bonus votes at the Democratic national convention, but there will be 96 holdover bonus votes that reflect the effects of the previous system, with the beneficiaries mainly found among the southern and western states. The major portion of the apportionment will be provided by giving each state $2\frac{1}{2}$ votes for each of its senators and representatives in Congress, rounding off to the next higher vote when necessary to avoid a fraction. At the Republican convention, there will be only minor changes from 1956. Missouri will lose its bonus votes, while West Virginia and Louisiana gain bonus votes; South Carolina and Mississippi will each lose three district votes, while Georgia and Alabama each gain one. Alaska, Hawaii, and the District of Columbia will each gain two votes.

Voting Power Under the Apportionment

In actual convention votes in 1956, the state delegations ranged between 6 and 98 in the Democratic convention, 12 and 96 in the Republican. The variation in delegation size and voting strength is accentuated by the tendency of delegations to vote as units. In some cases delegations are required to vote as units under state law or under a unit rule imposed by state party authorities. Even where this is not the case, a considerable amount of cohesion is the normal rule in delegation voting, as will be demonstrated in Chapter 15.

All of this emphasizes the conspicuou position of the larger state delegations notably those of New York, Pennsylvania Ohio, Illinois, California, and Texas. Th suspicion that these delegations are exer cising overwhelming power is undoubtedl a continuing source of frustration to th smaller delegations and their leaders—de spite the obvious fact that party constitu encies are overrepresented to the greates extent in the small delegations. The pres sure for bonus votes has no doubt arisen i part from the feeling of the smaller stat delegations that such distributions merel offset, and not sufficiently, the excessiv power (from their point of view) of th large states in convention voting.

The question of relative power is fa more complex than appears on the surface Fortunately, students of the mathematica theory of games have recently develope methods for analyzing the mathematica distributions of power in voting systems in volving unequal distributions of votin strength.[27] Such an analysis has been ap plied to the voting composition of the elec toral college by a team consisting of Her man Kahn, I. Mann, and L. S. Shapley. Th resulting distribution of power indices i shown in Table 8.3. The data reported i the table support the conclusion that th power indices of the states in the electora college are *not* out of accord, to any note worthy extent, with the voting strength ac tually accorded them.[28] With appropriat qualifications for variable cohesion withir

[27] L. S. Shapley and Martin Shubik, "A Metho for Evaluating the Distribution of Power in a Com mittee System," *American Political Science Review* Vol. 48 (Sept. 1954), pp. 787-92.

[28] The estimated anomalies range between plu and minus 5 per cent of the actual percentages o voting strength, as Table 8.3 indicates. The anom alies fluctuate in response to the extent to which a particular amount of voting strength happens t affect the possibility that the state may be critica in the attainment of a majority under all of th possible combinations of state quotas of votes tha might enter into a majority. In some combinations for example, six votes may be as good as eight in achieving a majority (and thus equally powerful) while other combinations could be devised in which three votes, say, would never be enough t make the difference, and the votes would there fore be worthless (in those combinations).

delegations in place of the rigid unit rule of the electoral college, and for variable amounts of coalition among delegations, the same statement can evidently be made for the distribution of voting power in the conventions. The basic point seems to be one forecast in the article by L. S. Shapley and Martin Shubik on voting in a committee system :

If there are two or more large interests, the power distribution depends in a fairly complicated way on the sizes of the large interests. Generally speaking, however, the small holders

are better off than in the previous case [of one large interest and many nearly equal small interests]. If there are two big interests, equal in size, then the small holders actually have an advantage over the large holders, on a power per share [vote] basis. This suggests that such a situation is highly unstable.[29]

The type of situation just referred to was graphically illustrated in the Republican national convention of 1952, when two strong voting coalitions of nearly equal size were supporting the respective candi-

[29] *Op. cit.*, p. 791, footnote.

TABLE 8.3. STATE POWER INDICES IN THE ELECTORAL COLLEGE[a]

Electoral Votes of Individual States		Per Cent of Total Voting Strength, Each State	Estimated Power Index
Number of Votes Per State	Number of States		
45	1	8.47%	8.92
32	2	6.03	6.21
27	1	5.08	5.17
25	1	4.71	4.70
24	1	4.52	4.53
20	1	3.77	3.82
16	2	3.01	3.02
14	1	2.64	2.62
13	2	2.45	2.44
12	3	2.26	2.18
11	3	2.07	2.03
10	4	1.88	1.87
9	2	1.69	1.66
8	7	1.51	1.48
6	3	1.13	1.12
5	1	0.94	0.95
4	9	0.75	0.72
3	4	0.56	0.54
531	48	99.95	99.84

[a] The table was transmitted to Paul T. David by L. S. Shapley in a letter dated March 12, 1959. In an earlier letter, he made the following statement concerning its derivation: "The present results were obtained by means of a 'Monte Carlo' computation devised by Herman Kahn, of The RAND Corporation, and carried out on one of RAND's high speed computers. Since an exact determination of the indices is quite out of the question (there are something like 10^{60} cases to consider), this statistical technique, which examines several thousand sample cases chosen at random, was used instead. Even then, a good deal of ingenuity was required to keep the amount of work within bounds."
As indicated by its title, the power index is an estimate, but each of the estimates is independent of the others and the statistical probability that any given one of them is off by as much as 3 per cent of its own value is less than one in fifty. The table is based on the 1950 electoral college apportionment.

dacies of Taft and Eisenhower. In that situation, disproportionate amounts of the balance of power were held by the uncommitted delegates and delegations. Relatively small delegations, such as those of Maryland and Minnesota, were in a position to be of critical importance.[30]

More often, in contested situations the coalitions have been more variable in size and less strongly organized. The conditions under which votes of pivotal importance could be contributed have fluctuated widely; but there seems little reason to think that the large states have generally had power in these situations disproportionately greater than their manifest voting strength. Almost by definition, when there is a contest the big state delegations will be found in opposing groupings. In each such group, they may provide much of the leadership, tactical skill, and sheer mass for the battle; but they nonetheless tend to offset each other, thereby offering important deciding powers to the uncommitted delegations, both small and large. On the other hand, it is obvious that there can seldom be a contest when the large states do happen to be in agreement, unless the small and middle-sized ones are closely united in opposition.

Issues in Present Systems of Apportionment

Vigorous controversy over convention apportionment seems to have receded into the past, but the existing rules are seldom praised and often criticized. In each party, there has been a tendency to tinker with details of the rules in recent years, particularly in allotting bonus votes. Moreover, there has been some recent consideration of legislative proposals for a national presidential primary, as well as less fundamental forms of federal intervention in the nominating process. Several of these proposals involve the problem of allocating nominating power among the states, whether or not party conventions are held for the purpose.[31] The differential effects of such proposed legislation upon existing parties and prospective third parties are among the serious complications in the consideration of such legislation.

Issues involving alleged deficiencies in the present rules necessarily involve the problem of defining a just distribution of voting power; and it is not a problem that is easily solved. As Alfred de Grazia has pointed out, "No system of apportionment and no system of suffrage, balloting, or counting is neutral. The process of apportionment . . . is a point of entry for preferred social values." Any system of apportionment "institutionalizes the values of some group in society."[32]

Equal Representation of Sovereign State Units

The principle of equal representation of sovereign states rather than of human voters has been widely accepted in international bodies and federal unions. It reflects the values of independence that are embodied in the concept of sovereignty; it is the only basis on which relatively weak but independent units of government can usually be persuaded to join with more powerful units in a voting system. As such, it is currently reflected in the General Assembly of the United Nations, where every member nation has one vote, and in the Senate of the United States, where each state has two votes.

The party conventions, in adopting the electoral college apportionment in its original and unmodified form, had an appearance of giving the same weight to state sovereignty that was given in Congress and in the electoral college. Neither party can

[30] See David, Moos, and Goldman, op. cit., Vol. 1, pp. 91-94.

[31] Ibid., Vol. 1, pp. 196-98, 211.

[32] Alternative systems of representation and apportionment are reviewed by Alfred de Grazia both in his longer works and in a brief article, "General Theory of Apportionment," Law and Contemporary Problems, Vol. 17 (Spring 1952), pp. 256-67. The quotation is from p. 257.

be assumed to have given much conscious thought to any alternative when the system was first adopted for the conventions. It could be supposed, however, that the system would not have survived in party apportionment rules as long as it has—in this country of broadening suffrage and massive electorates—if it had not reflected values that are both important and widely held. The same can be said concerning the durability of the electoral college itself, despite its obvious shortcomings.

Should aspects of state sovereignty continue to be reflected in composing the national party conventions? Most political leaders would probably answer this question with an unqualified yes, on grounds that such composition is probably desirable and in any case inevitable, in view of the established power relationships among the states. Whenever plans for apportioning most of the delegates on the basis of the party vote have been debated, the equal quota of regular delegates at large for every state has seldom been questioned, and never impaired, except as it has been muddied by the unequal addition of bonus votes.

Some political scientists would undoubtedly contend, nonetheless, that the argument for recognition of state sovereignty in a national political convention is specious. The superficial resemblance between a sovereign state, having certain rights among its sister states and in relation to the federal union, and the state organization of a political party in its relation with the party's national organization, becomes thin when the state political party is weak or practically nonexistent. A national party may be strong enough to win elections in some states without even existing in others, as was proved by nationally organized third parties in 1892, 1912, and 1924. The alleged existence of the Republican party in some southern states has not been much more than a fiction over long periods of time; to a lesser extent the same has been true of the Democratic party in some northern states. In the "one-party" states, north and south, obviously the handful of minority party adherents cannot logically be regarded as capable of maintaining rights and duties toward their national party analogous to those of a sovereign state toward the federal government.

A national political party has its federal aspects, such as its dependence on state victories to give it the electoral votes necessary for winning a presidential election. But in its national convention its chief business, the nomination and election of a President, is an operation more national than federal. If, for instance, the party organization in any state chooses to bolt, there is no enforceable federal constitution to impose sanctions, legal or military. In such case the national party can enter the state and do whatever the law allows to put its candidates on the ballot. The logic of the relationship points toward giving no sovereignty votes to state party organizations in states that show no foreseeable prospect of contributing electoral votes to the party's national ticket.

Despite all this, the limited recognition accorded state sovereignty by the electoral college system would retain great appeal for national convention apportionment in all political parties that are important in national elections—if there could be assurance that two conditions would be met: (1) that there will be no apportionment problem for some new political party that is so largely sectional that the electoral college basis would be completely inappropriate, and (2) that the existing major national parties will become and remain sufficiently competitive through loyal party organizations in every state to justify giving the same kind of recognition to every state in the national conventions of each party. As indicated at the end of Chapter 3, there is some reason to think that departures from these conditions may be exceptional in the future, but the specified conditions cannot be depended upon as a certainty.

Meanwhile, under existing conditions of

variable state size and unequal party strength in many states, those aspects of the system that give equal representation to every state and to each party in the same state will continue to produce anomalies. The small states will continue to be over-represented in the party conventions of both existing major parties; and those states, large or small, in which one party is weak or nonexistent will be overrepresented in the conventions of that party.

Apportionment
Related to the Party Vote

Apportionment according to the number of voters has wide appeal in the modern democracies. It reflects a system of moral values in which all individuals are held to have equal political rights, whether commoners or gentry, rich or poor, white or colored, male or female, rural or urban. In the United States, the legal prescriptions for one house of a bicameral legislature usually run in terms of territorial surveys that are intended to provide representative districts of equal population. Frequently there are great discrepancies in the districts actually provided; but the moral rightness of apportionment on the basis of equal numbers is seldom attacked directly. Moreover, a "flagrant contradiction between law and practice, such as exists . . . in a number of American states, causes great moral uneasiness and discontent."[33]

In a party assembly total population is not directly relevant. The principle of apportionment on the basis of the number of party adherents finds expression most easily by using the party vote as recorded in some previous election, since the major American political parties do not have a definite, dues-paying membership. Party registration statistics, another source of information on the number of party adherents, are dependent on varying systems of registration as provided by state law and cannot be readily compared from state to state. Even where

available, registration figures are notoriously different from voting records and the actual votes are of far greater validity as a definition of the number of persons adhering to a political party.

The principle of apportionment on the basis of the party vote has long been widely followed in state political conventions.[34] For many decades it has been a formal requirement—for state conventions electing national convention delegates—in the national rules of the Republican party. The practice has been equally common in Democratic state conventions. In both parties the survey of experience in 1952 found conspicuous exceptions mainly in Rhode Island, Connecticut, Delaware, and Maryland, states with long records of rotten borough arrangements in their legislatures. In addition, convention apportionment was found to be related to state legislative apportionment in one way or another in Mississippi, Montana, and Wyoming. But the typical kind of arrangement can be illustrated by the Indiana state political conventions, where state law apportioned the 1952 state convention delegates among the counties, townships, and wards on the basis of one delegate per 400 party votes in the preceding election for state secretary of state.

The extent to which apportionment in the national conventions in 1956 departed from the principle of equal representation of party voters is indicated by Table 8.4. On the basis of this criterion, Nevada Democrats were more heavily represented proportionately than the party voters of any other party or state, with 11 votes in the convention for every 25,000 party voters in the state. Wyoming Democrats placed next, and Nevada Republicans third. At the other end of the scale, New York, Illinois, and California Republicans were the party voters most underrepresented in the respective conventions, with six tenths of a delegate vote for every 25,000 party voters.

[33] Alfred de Grazia, op. cit., p. 262.

[34] David, Moos, and Goldman, op. cit.; see items indexed in each of the four regional volumes under "Apportionment in state conventions."

In general, the apportionment rules tend to overrepresent the small states and underrepresent the large; and to overrepresent the areas of low voter turnout and underrepresent the areas of high voter turnout. In states where one party is much stronger than the other, the rules tend to overrepresent the voters of the weaker party and underrepresent the voters of the stronger party.

Numerous examples of all three types of anomaly can be found in the table. They are primarily the result of the basic principle of apportionment according to the electoral college system, which gives weight to the states as sovereign units, together with various more or less accidental effects of the patchwork bonus systems. In the South in 1956, however, the relationships were highly confused because of the variable impact of the Republican gains of 1952 and the differences between the bonus vote systems of the two parties. Several southern states received a double bonus at the Democratic convention although they had gone Republican in the presidential election of 1952.

Reward as an Apportionment Criterion

The problem of incentives and rewards has seldom been discussed in connection with criteria for legislative apportionment, but it has been continuously present in most active discussions of apportionment in party assemblies. Rewards for previous party victories and incentives for future campaigning efforts, together with penalties for apathy, are the manifest purposes of the existing systems of bonus votes.

Probably every partisan would agree in principle that, so far as possible, any system of representation within the party should be designed to encourage party growth and success, and in any event not to discourage it. More generally, anyone with a civic interest in maintaining a competitive party system might agree that systems of party apportionment should be appraised at least in part in terms of their probable effects upon the long-term development of the respective parties. In the state party conventions the systems of apportionment based upon the party vote have undoubtedly held their own not only because they meet elementary standards of fairness, but also because they obviously contain a built-in system of rewards and penalties, one that appears likely to encourage party growth.

On the other hand, the recent systems of bonus votes given for party victories are highly deficient as procedures for providing rewards and incentives, and almost equally so in both parties. They give easy rewards where victory is automatic, as in the dominant party in a one-party state. They frequently fail to provide rewards where they may be deserved, a situation that occurs often in heavily contested states where national "political tides" may push the state from one party column to the other regardless of local party effort. Moreover, by 1956 the bonus vote requirements had been relaxed in both parties to the point where most states could qualify so easily that the incentive feature had virtually disappeared.

The Republican rule for conditioning congressional district delegate votes on the achievement of minimum party votes in the districts has been a useful approach to the problem. It will not continue to be useful, however, unless the minimums are kept high enough to discriminate between active and apathetic districts. The present minimums —2,000 party votes for the first district delegate vote, and 10,000 for the second—are too low to have such an effect under present conditions.[35]

The bonus vote system is arbitrary and unsatisfactory for another reason, that it gives a uniform reward for victory in a

[35] According to the presidential vote as tabulated by congressional districts for the Republican congressional campaign committee, there were *no* districts in either 1952 or 1956 in which the Republican presidential vote fell below 2,000. The Republican presidential vote fell below 10,000 in only three districts in 1952 and seven in 1956.

Region and State	Democratic		Republican	
	Voters per Delegate Vote[a]	Delegate Votes per 25,000 Voters[b]	Voters per Delegate Vote[a]	Delegate Votes per 25,000 Voters[b]
Northeast				
Maine......................	8,486	2.9	14,522	1.7
New Hampshire...............	13,333	1.9	11,878	2.1
Vermont....................	7,226	3.5	9,143	2.7
Massachusetts.................	27,088	.9	34,009	.7
Rhode Island.................	12,706	2.0	15,067	1.7
Connecticut..................	24,082	1.0	27,773	.9
New York...................	27,427[c]	.8	41,175	.6
New Jersey..................	28,220	.9	36,174	.7
Delaware...................	8,332	3.0	7,505	3.3
Maryland...................	21,963	1.1	20,809	1.2
Pennsylvania.................	29,004	.9	34,511	.7
West Virginia................	18,899	1.3	26,248	1.0
Northeast Average...........	24,230[c]	1.0	30,579	.8
Middle West				
Ohio.......................	27,592	.9	37,508	.7
Michigan...................	27,969	.9	33,729	.7
Indiana....................	30,828	.8	35,508	.7
Illinois.....................	31,468	.8	40,955	.6
Wisconsin...................	22,221	1.1	32,658	.8
Minnesota..................	20,282	1.2	27,258	.9
Iowa......................	18,813	1.3	31,112	.8
Missouri....................	24,469	1.0	29,982	.8
North Dakota................	9,587	2.6	13,694	1.6
South Dakota................	11,303	2.2	14,561	1.7
Nebraska...................	15,671	1.6	23,422	1.1
Kansas.....................	17,081	1.5	28,014	.9
Middle West Average........	24,963	1.0	32,250	.8

[a] Number of votes for the party's candidate in the 1952 presidential election for each delegate vote at the 1956 party national convention.
[b] Number of delegate votes at the 1956 party national convention for each 25,000 votes for the party candidate in the 1952 presidential election.
[c] Excludes Liberal party votes.

Region and State	Democratic		Republican	
	Voters per Delegate Vote[a]	Delegate Votes per 25,000 Voters[b]	Voters per Delegate Vote[a]	Delegate Votes per 25,000 Voters[b]
South				
Virginia.....................	8,396	3.0	11,635	2.1
North Carolina...............	18,133	1.4	19,932	1.3
South Carolina...............	8,650	2.9	10,505	2.4
Georgia......................	14,276	1.8	8,651	2.9
Florida......................	15,891	1.6	20,924	1.2
Kentucky.....................	16,524	1.5	19,040	1.3
Tennessee....................	13,866	1.8	15,934	1.6
Alabama......................	10,580	2.4	7,106	3.5
Mississippi..................	7,844	3.2	7,531	3.3
Arkansas.....................	8,704	2.9	11,072	2.3
Louisiana....................	14,376	1.7	15,346	1.6
Oklahoma.....................	15,391	1.6	23,548	1.1
Texas........................	17,308	1.4	20,424	1.2
South Average...............	13,660	1.8	15,774	1.6
West				
Montana......................	6,638	3.8	11,242	2.2
Idaho........................	7,923	3.2	12,908	1.9
Wyoming......................	3,424	7.3	6,754	3.7
Colorado.....................	12,275	2.0	21,099	1.2
Utah.........................	11,280	2.2	13,871	1.8
Nevada.......................	2,263	11.0	4,209	5.9
New Mexico...................	6,604	3.8	9,441	2.6
Arizona......................	6,783	3.7	10,860	2.3
Washington...................	18,956	1.3	24,963	1.0
Oregon.......................	16,911	1.5	23,379	1.1
California...................	32,317	.8	41,390	.6
West Average................	16,682	1.5	23,415	1.1
United States Average............	20,043	1.2	26,165	1.0

small or large state, thus adding to the existing overrepresentation of the small states. In both parties, several states were given as many bonus votes as other votes in 1956: Rhode Island, Montana, New Mexico, and Arizona in the Democratic party; Vermont, Delaware, Wyoming, and Nevada in the Republican. Under the Democratic bonus rules of 1956, Wyoming and Nevada actually received more bonus votes than regular votes, eight to six in each case. The extent

sweep of that state, would wield far more persuasive power than the shamefaced delegation from New York. Similarly in the Republican convention, the New Yorkers were expected to exert more influence than the Californians, out of all proportion to their formal voting strength.[36]

But if bonus votes are to be given at all, there would be advantages in bringing form into accord with reality. There is nothing inherent in the concept of such votes that

TABLE 8.5. VOTING STRENGTH OF THE STATES IN 1956, BY POPULATION GROUPINGS

(in percentage of total)

States by Population Groupings	Population, 1950 Census[a]	Electoral College Vote	Democratic		Republican	
			Popular Democratic Vote[b]	Convention Votes	Popular Republican Vote[b]	Convention Votes
Twelve Most Populous States	58.5%	52.2%	64.0%	46.5%	65.4%	46.9%
Twenty-Four Middle States	34.9	39.5	31.8	41.1	29.8	39.2
Twelve Least Populous States	4.2	8.3	4.2	10.2	4.8	12.1
Non-State Areas[c]	2.4	—	—	2.2	—	1.8
Total	100.0	100.0	100.0	100.0	100.0	100.0

[a] Population of continental United States, plus outlying areas represented at national party conventions: Alaska, Hawaii, Puerto Rico, Virgin Islands, Canal Zone.
[b] Major-party popular vote for President in 1956.
[c] As of 1956; includes Alaska and Hawaii.

to which the small states are overrepresented, and the large state underrepresented, is apparent in Table 8.5.

These aberrations may be offset somewhat by the fact that aside from formal recognition of party success through apportionment, there is at times an even more effective informal bonus in the relative influence wielded by delegations from conspicuously successful state parties. For example, after the 1958 election many commentators pointed out that in the 1960 Democratic convention the California delegation, owing to the spectacular Democratic

requires the same number to be given to all states that qualify. Bonus votes could have been given, for example, at the rate of one bonus vote for every three votes contributed by the state party in the most recent voting of the electoral college. On that

[36] See, for instance, Arthur Krock in the *New York Times*, Nov. 6, 1958, p. 36. "The power of the California delegation in the Republican National Convention will be sharply reduced. . . . Conversely the California delegation in the next Democratic National Convention . . . will increase in power." I.e., an informal "party strength" formula operates when the differences are spectacular, and its operation correspondingly relieves the pressure for a more logical formal allocation of the voting power.

basis, the small states rating three electoral votes could have qualified for one bonus vote each, while New York, with its forty-five electoral votes, could have qualified for fifteen in the next convention of the party carrying the state. The basis for bonus votes could also be limited to votes in the electoral college, disregarding other elections, such as those of senator and governor, which are of markedly less relevance to the functions of a national convention.

Alternatives to Present Systems of Apportionment

The previous review of controversies over the existing systems of apportionment suggests that there might be considerable sentiment for reform if there could be agreement on what changes would constitute improvement. Hence it seems appropriate to attempt a systematic review of alternative systems of apportionment that would give effect to principles that have been advocated at one time or another in previous discussions of the problem. There seem to be four major alternatives for consideration:

a. A return to the straight electoral college system of apportionment.

b. Equal representation of party voters.

c. Equal representation of each state, plus equal representation of party voters.

d. Representation based on "party strength" in the states, i.e., the electoral vote of each state multiplied by the party percentage in the last presidential election.

Some of these alternatives involve the use of numerical formulas somewhat similar to those that have been developed in various schemes of electoral college reform. Hence it should be noted at the outset that, while there is a complex interrelationship, it should not be assumed that formulas for electoral college reform will necessarily operate the same way or have similar consequences if carried over into formulas for convention apportionment. This is especially the case if the electoral college system itself remains unchanged in the elections.

The relationships between big states and small states, pivotal states and one-party states, are quite different in the conventions from those that prevail in the electoral college. Moreover, the active proposals for electoral college reform have largely arisen because of the practice of unit voting by each state in the electoral college, and one of the major proposals would consist simply in restoring the congressional district system of voting separately for presidential electors. But in the conventions, district autonomy in the election of delegates is widely prevalent and unit voting by state delegation has been dying out; where it still exists, it gives rise to a different set of problems, as will be discussed in Chapter 9.

Electoral College System

The electoral college system of apportionment, unmodified for convention use except for a doubling or tripling of the number of votes accorded each state, was followed by both of the major parties until 1916. To return to this system, all that would be necessary would be the abandonment of provisions for bonus and ex officio votes and the special Republican rules that restrict the representation of congressional districts where the party is weak.

Conceivably an electoral college system might be reimposed on the parties by congressional action. Senator George A. Smathers (D, Florida), for example, has proposed constitutional amendments for a national presidential primary (replacing the convention system of nomination), under which each state would be given the same proportion of voting strength in the primary of each party that it has in the electoral college.[37] The votes allotted each state in the

[37] S. J. Res. 9, 84 Cong. 1 sess.; S. J. Res. 14, 85 Cong. 1 sess. For discussion of this and related proposals for constitutional change affecting the nominating process, see David, Moos, and Goldman, *op. cit.*, Vol. 1, pp. 196-211; also see statement of Paul T. David in Hearings . . . Committee on the Judiciary, U. S. Senate (1955), *Nomination and Election of President and Vice President*, pp. 207-17.

primary would be distributed among the aspirants for each party nomination in accord with the popular vote of the party voters for each aspirant in the state—a formula somewhat like the so-called Lodge-Gossett plan of electoral college reform. For the Republican party, this would have the effect of again giving the southern states the same weight in Republican nominations that they had before the reforms of 1916. The Smathers proposal also would have included any third party within its scope that achieved a membership of 10 per cent or more of the registered voters of the United States—a definition that could include a sectional third party under some circumstances. Such a party would be required to follow the electoral college system of apportionment in voting on nominations without regard to the distribution of its own membership.

If success were eventually to attend the efforts to create a sectional third party in the South, serious problems would arise, under the proposed amendment, for all three parties. Such a party would presumably replace major portions of both the Democratic and Republican parties in several southern states. In that event, the new sectional third party presumably would need to find some basis of representation and apportionment for nominating purposes in which representation would be denied or restricted in the case of the states where it was weak. Moreover, both the Republican and Democratic parties might find it highly uncomfortable to be forced back into their old system of apportionment with its exaggerated overrepresentation of the states controlled by the new party.

Equal Representation of Party Voters

Those who criticize the conventions for their failure to give equal representation to the party voters in all states presumably would favor the alternative by which this objective would be achieved most directly

and completely. The technical problems involved in devising a formula for the purpose would not be difficult. The national committees could be directed to apportion the votes at the next convention on the basis of the party vote in the previous election. Conventions of approximately the present size could be produced by giving each state a delegate vote for every 25,000 or 30,000 party voters in the previous election in the state. The result would be a severe curtailment of the votes allotted the smaller states: Nevada, Wyoming, Vermont, and Delaware, for example, would receive no more than three or four delegates apiece in the respective conventions. Regions with low voter turnout would also be penalized in both parties, and the change in power relationships within the conventions would be drastic.

Equal Representation of States and Party Voters

An apportionment giving equal representation of party voters could be modified by adding a limited amount of equal representation for each state. This could be done, for example, by giving each state a quota of votes at large and in addition to an allocation based on party vote. As noted earlier, such plans were agitated in the Republican party for a generation, and one of them had strong support in the Republican national convention of 1908. If the plan considered at that time had been modified so that the congressional districts could maintain the right to select district delegates, it might have been approvd.

Plans of this kind have been given little attention in either party since 1908 so far a convention apportionment is concerned, but a similar arrangement has recently been proposed as a compromise method of electoral college reform.[38] The Humphrey plan, as it is called, retains the total

[38] Ralph M. Goldman, "Hubert Humphrey's S. J. 152," *Midwest Journal of Political Science*, Vol. 2 (Feb. 1958), pp. 89-96.

strength of both houses of Congress, 537 votes, as the numerical basis for determining the election of Presidents. Each state retains two senatorial electoral votes; these go to the presidential candidate winning the popular plurality in the state. The remaining block of 437 votes is then divided according to the proportion of popular vote received by each candidate on a nationwide basis. Thus, for example, Eisenhower carried 41 states and received 36 million of the 62 million votes cast for President in 1956. Under the Humphrey proposal, he would have received 82 senatorial electoral votes and about 250 of the remaining 435 votes (before admission of Alaska and Hawaii), for a total of 332 electoral votes to Stevenson's 196—a substantial majority but one much less inflated by the counting system than the 457 electoral votes that he actually received to Stevenson's 73. (The other vote was cast in Alabama for a States Rights candidate.) In a close election, of course, the outcome might be changed under the proposed plan from what it would be under the present system—the basic reason for considering reforms.

The Humphrey plan retains the equality of states principle in its senatorial electoral votes, while the method of dividing the other 437 electoral votes is in accord with each state's contribution to the total popular vote of each party. This would have the effect of giving states with high voter turnout a relatively larger voice in the decision. In 1956, for example, California would have produced 23 votes for Eisenhower and 17 for Stevenson, the equivalent of 40 electoral votes instead of its actual 32. Virginia would have produced only 7 electoral votes instead of its actual 12— 5 for Eisenhower and 2 for Stevenson.[39]

The general principles of the Humphrey plan could be adapted with slight modification by either party to its national convention apportionment. Total convention voting strength would be based on the total number of votes in the electoral college, that is, 537 votes, or on some multiple thereof: 1,074 if the multiple is two, 1,611 if the multiple is three, etc. Each state delegation would receive the same number of senatorial votes in the convention, preserving the basic idea of the federal equality of state parties. The remaining 437 votes, however, would be apportioned according to each state party's contribution in popular votes to the national party's total national popular vote in the preceding presidential election. For example, California Republicans gave Eisenhower about 8.6 per cent of his total national popular vote in 1956; 8.6 per cent of 435 (the figure applicable in 1956) would give California 37 votes, in addition to its 2 senatorial votes, in the 1960 Republican convention. These 39 votes (or 78, if a multiple of two is used) would compare with the 70 held by California Republicans in 1956.[40]

For a precise comparison of the results of this plan with the planned apportionment for 1960, it is necessary to express the results of each in terms of the percentage of total convention voting strength allotted to each state. This has been done in Table 8.6. The

[39] *Ibid.*, p. 91, Table 1. These computations are based on the turnout that actually occurred in 1956, although the plan would provide incentives for an increase in turnout in the low turnout states.

[40] Under this plan, or any other plan under which state quotas lose their direct relationship to the number of congressional districts in the state, it is necessary to be somewhat inventive in dealing with the problem of apportionment within states if congressional district autonomy in the choice of delegates is to be maintained so far as possible. The issues involved in district representation and apportionment within states are discussed in Chapter 9. Here it may be noted that if the plan for equal representation of states and party voters were to be adopted, the further problem of district representation could be left completely to the states, or some policy line could be laid down for execution by the states, or national rules on the question could be adopted as part of the plan. Under the latter course, the national committee could be directed to set the quota of votes that would be used in determining the number of delegates to which each district would be entitled. For example, each district might be authorized to elect one delegate for every 25,000 popular votes for the party candidate for President in the previous election; balances above this figure or from districts left out under

(*Footnote continued on page 188*)

TABLE 8.6. HYPOTHETICAL APPORTIONMENT OF DELEGATE VOTES IN 1960

(in percentages of total convention voting strength by states)

Region and State	Electoral College Strength[a]	Democratic National Convention			Republican National Convention		
		Expected Official, 1960	Hypothetical 1960 Based on States and Party Voters[b]	Hypothetical 1960 Based on "Party Strength"[c]	Expected Official, 1960	Hypothetical 1960 Based on States and Party Voters[b]	Hypothetical 1960 Based on "Party Strength"[c]
Northeast							
Maine............	.9%	1.0%	.7%	.6%	1.2%	.9%	1.2%
New Hampshire...	.8	.7	.7	.7	1.1	.8	1.1
Vermont.........	.6	.6	.5	.4	.9	.6	.7
Massachusetts....	3.0	2.8	3.4	2.9	2.9	3.6	3.2
Rhode Island.....	.8	1.1	.9	.9	1.1	.9	1.0
Connecticut......	1.5	1.4	1.6	1.3	1.7	2.0	1.7
New York........	8.5	7.7	9.0	6.9	7.4	10.4	9.2
New Jersey......	3.0	2.8	3.0	2.4	2.9	4.1	3.5
Delaware........	.6	.7	.6	.6	.9	.6	.6
Maryland........	1.7	1.6	1.6	1.6	1.8	1.7	1.8
Pennsylvania.....	6.0	5.5	6.6	6.1	5.4	6.3	6.1
West Virginia....	1.5	1.7	1.6	1.6	1.7	1.4	1.5
Total........	28.8	27.7	30.2	26.0	29.0	33.3	31.6
Middle West							
Ohio............	4.7	4.3	4.9	4.3	4.3	5.6	5.1
Michigan........	3.8	3.4	4.7	3.9	3.5	4.3	3.7
Indiana.........	2.4	2.3	2.8	2.3	2.5	3.1	2.6
Illinois.........	5.1	4.7	6.0	4.8	4.6	6.4	5.4
Wisconsin.......	2.3	2.1	2.2	2.0	2.3	2.6	2.5
Minnesota.......	2.1	2.1	2.3	2.2	2.1	2.0	2.0
Iowa...........	1.9	1.8	2.0	1.8	2.0	2.0	2.0
Missouri........	2.4	2.6	3.3	2.9	2.0	2.5	2.2
North Dakota....	.8	.7	.7	.7	1.1	.7	.8
South Dakota....	.8	.7	.8	.7	1.1	.8	.8
Nebraska........	1.1	1.1	1.0	.9	1.4	1.3	1.3
Kansas.........	1.5	1.4	1.3	1.2	1.7	1.7	1.8
Total........	28.9	27.3	32.0	27.7	28.6	33.0	30.2
South							
Virginia........	2.3	2.2	1.2	2.0	2.3	1.3	2.2
North Carolina...	2.6	2.5	2.2	3.1	2.1	1.7	2.3

Florida	1.9	2.0	1.9	1.9	2.0	1.9	1.9
Kentucky	1.9	2.1	1.8	2.0	2.0	1.7	1.8
Tennessee	2.0	2.2	1.8	2.4	2.1	1.4	1.8
Alabama	2.0	2.0	1.3	2.8	1.7	.8	1.5
Mississippi	1.5	1.6	.8	2.1	.9	.5	.6
Arkansas	1.5	1.8	1.1	1.9	1.2	.8	1.2
Louisiana	1.9	1.8	1.1	1.7	2.0	1.1	1.8
Oklahoma	1.5	2.0	1.6	1.6	1.7	1.5	1.5
Texas	4.5	4.1	3.1	4.7	4.1	2.9	4.5
Total	27.5	27.9	20.6	31.3	25.1	17.0	23.1

West

Montana	.8	1.1	.8	1.1	.7	.8	.8
Idaho	.8	.9	.7	1.1	.8	.8	.8
Wyoming	.6	1.0	.5	.9	.5	.6	.6
Colorado	1.1	1.4	1.2	1.4	1.3	1.2	1.2
Utah	.8	.9	.8	1.1	.9	.9	.9
Nevada	.6	1.0	.5	.9	.5	.6	.6
New Mexico	.8	1.1	.7	.9	.7	.8	.8
Arizona	.8	1.1	.7	1.1	.8	.8	.8
Washington	1.7	1.8	1.8	1.8	1.8	1.8	1.6
Oregon	1.1	1.1	1.2	1.4	1.3	1.3	1.1
California	6.0	5.5	8.0	5.4	7.4	6.3	5.9
Total	14.9	17.1	17.2	15.0	17.3	16.7	15.1
48-State Total[d]	100.0	100.0	100.0	100.0	100.0	100.0	100.0

RECAPITULATION BY POPULATION CATEGORIES OF STATES[d]

Twelve Most Populous States	52.2%	48.2%	57.0%	50.6%	47.0%	58.3%	53.7%
Twenty-Four Middle States	39.5	41.0	35.1	41.7	40.7	33.3	37.0
Twelve Least Populous States	8.3	10.8	7.9	7.7	12.3	8.4	9.3

a Same for both parties. Due to rounding, the sums of the detail figures do not always agree with the totals or subtotals.

b The apportionment upon which these percentages are based assigns two votes at large to each state, plus the state's share in a total further apportionment of 435 votes, computed by applying to 435 the state's percentage of the national popular vote of the party in the 1956 presidential elections.

c The apportionment upon which these percentages are based is computed by multiplying the electoral college strength for each state by the percentage of popular vote polled in the state for presidential electors of the party concerned in the 1956 election. For most states, the two "party strength" figures in Columns 4 and 7 when added are approximately twice the electoral college figure in Column 1; but they fall short in the case of those states where the third party vote was important in 1956.

d Non-state areas of 1956 are not included in the table. It is assumed that apportionment for these areas would be made on an arbitrary basis, as in the past. In 1956, non-state areas comprised 2.2 per cent of the voting strength in the Democratic convention and 1.8 per cent in the Republican, as shown in Table 8.5. If one or other of these hypothetical plans were to be placed in effect in time for use at the 1960 conventions, it would be necessary to make some arbitrary adjustment for Alaska and Hawaii, since they were not allowed to vote in the presidential election of 1956. In a plan effective in 1964, however, presumably they could be treated in the same manner as other states.

table also shows a second hypothetical apportionment for 1960, discussed below.

As will be apparent from the table, the formula for combining equal representation of states with equal representation of party voters would reduce the representation of the small states now receiving bonus votes, would increase the representation of most of the large states, would have little effect upon states of average size and voter turnout, and would substantially reduce the representation of the states in which voter turnout is low. All of the southern states would lose votes in both party conventions, mainly because of small turnout, unless they took steps to increase turnout rates.

*Representation
on Basis of "Party Strength"*

The fourth alternative listed previously, representation on the basis of "party strength" in the various states, refers to a new proposal that has not had much public discussion. It seems to have arisen among senators and others who were involved in discussions of electoral college reform.[41] The proposal, not previously spelled out in detail in any available source, seems to include the notion that states should retain their relative political importance on the

electoral college basis in the convention system of both parties taken together, but should be given representation in the national conventions of *each* political party on a basis proportionate to the strength of that party in each state. If a state, for example, is currently entitled to twenty votes in the electoral college and is one where the Democratic party polled 45 per cent of the vote and the Republican party 55 per cent in the most recent presidential election, it might be given nine votes (45 per cent of twenty) in the next Democratic national convention and eleven in the next Republican.[42]

The results of this formula, converted to state percentages of total convention voting strength, are shown for 1960 in Table 8.6. As the table shows, under present conditions a change to apportionment on the basis of party strength would not have major consequences for states of average size. Small states would lose the special advantages they have had under recent systems of bonus votes, while most of the large states would gain correspondingly. States where one party has been markedly stronger than the other would have correspondingly large delegations in one convention and small ones in the other.

The formula for apportionment on the basis of party strength would produce relatively little change in regional relationships in either convention under recently pre-

this rule could be used to increase the number of delegates at large from the state.

In the text above and previous discussion, the electoral college is referred to as including 537 votes in recognition of the admission of Alaska and Hawaii as states. It is probable, however, that, under permanent legislation long in effect, as well as under the specific provisions of the statutes admitting Alaska and Hawaii (Public Laws 85-508 and 86-3), the House of Representatives will be reapportioned after the 1960 census on the basis of its accustomed 435 seats. In that event, the Senate would still continue with 100 seats and the size of the electoral college would shift to 535.

Table 8.6 was computed on the basis of an electoral college of 531, and 435 House seats, since it was constructed on a 48-state basis before the admission of Alaska and Hawaii.

[41] Senator Kefauver, for example, included a reference to the proposal in an article published in 1952; see Estes Kefauver, "Indictment of the Political Convention," *New York Times Magazine,* March 16, 1952, pp. 9, 59-61, 63.

[42] On this basis, the two conventions together would aggregate 537 votes, aside from any representation of non-state areas. A multiple of two might be used to produce conventions averaging the same size as the electoral college, a multiple of five to produce conventions of approximately the 1956 size, including bonus votes. Incidentally, such multiplication would increase proportionately the accuracy with which voting percentages could be transferred into convention votes.

In the illustration given in the text, the two major parties divided the total vote. Where third-party voting occurs, the apportionment base for each of the major parties would still be simply its fraction of the total popular vote, applied to the state's electoral college quota. The system could be used to apportion voting strength at the conventions in a three-party system, and would automatically adjust for sectional imbalance in the impact of third-party voting.

vailing conditions, unlike the formula for giving equal weight to states and to voters, with its strong reflection of relative voter turnout. The most pronounced regional effects under either plan would be felt by the South, which would lose representation markedly in both party conventions under the formula for giving equal weight to states and to voters, and would lose somewhat in Republican conventions and gain in Democratic under the formula based on party strength. Specifically, the relative percentage weight accorded the thirteen southern states under the three plans presented in Table 8.6 would be as follows:

	Democratic Convention	Republican Convention
Planned apportionment of 1960	27.9%	25.1%
Hypothetical equal representation of states and voters, 1960	20.6	17.0
Hypothetical equal representation of "party strength," 1960	31.3	23.1

The party strength plan finds its intellectual origins in the so-called Lodge-Gossett plan of electoral college reform, but would apply a similar type of numerical formula to the convention system as a whole, rather than to each party separately—as would be done under the previously cited Smathers plan.[43] States where there is a lack of party balance would tend to gain strength in one party convention to the extent that they lost it in the other—Georgia, for example, would lose relative strength in the Republican convention but gain it in the Democratic. There is nothing in the party strength

[43] Actually, existing arrangements within the conventions are closer to the Smathers plan and the Lodge-Gossett plan of electoral college counting than to the present operations of the electoral college, since every state is given something like its electoral college weight in the convention and most states are free of the "unit" rule; that is, each can divide its votes among the several candidates at the convention in accord with local preferences.

formula, however, that makes it inherently incapable of adoption by either party alone and without regard to what the other is doing. Within each party there are strong and obvious pressures to cut down the representation of areas where the party is weak and to increase the representation of the areas where it is strong. This, in effect, is what the party strength plan would do by comparison with an unmodified electoral college plan; and it would do it with far more precision and effectiveness than the bonus schemes with which each party has modified the electoral college plan in recent years.

The possible disadvantages of the party strength plan seem to be mainly twofold. By giving no weight at all to the factors of voter turnout, it would seem to accept the existing practices that restrict voting in the low turnout areas as legitimate, although many of those practices are clearly out of accord with the values and ethical standards of the American people. By increasing the voting strength in each party of its areas of one-party dominance, the party would be subjected to greater influence from its more conservative elements. As will become apparent in the analyses in Chapter 16, there are many reasons for doubting the wisdom of an increase in convention strength for such areas, because of their frequent disinterest in finding the kind of nominee that seems necessary for victory in the states where the party faces competition.

Prospects for Change

Apportionment problems being what they are, any change in the present rules that would serve more than parochial interests may seem unlikely. It is hard to see what sources of leadership would be likely to undertake the arduous efforts required for success with any of the far-reaching proposals. Nevertheless, there are two aspects of the situation that suggest opportunities for change. One is the possibility of congressional intervention in connection with proposals for constitutional amendments. The other is the increasingly self-conscious attitude of both parties toward their own central institutional arrangements.

The proposed constitutional amendments repeatedly introduced in Congress for creating a national presidential primary or regulating the party conventions in some way (as mentioned earlier in this chapter and in Chapter 1) have usually been associated with parallel proposals for electoral college reform, and often with little regard for the major differences between the two problems. The nominating process, however, has so central a relationship to the organization of the national party system that it might at any time attract amending attention on its own merits. Should this occur, the apportionment problem for nominating purposes would take on new interest in the drafting of proposed constitutional amendments.

Most of the alternatives previously discussed would seem highly unsatisfactory for incorporation into any form of public law. The existing systems of the two parties, with their bonus votes and other oddities, are much too jerry-built for that purpose. The unmodified electoral college system has already been included in proposed constitutional amendments, as previously noted. It might be an improvement over the existing situation, if it could be assumed that the existing two major parties will become and remain strongly competitive in all parts of the country. But, as a minimum, any proposed system should promise to be satisfactory even with a greater degree of imbalance than at present between the existing major parties. And presumably no system should be adopted by amending the Constitution that would not be reasonably satisfactory for any third party that might qualify.

Apportionment directly on the basis of the party vote alone has strong claims in principle. For those who believe that one

party voter is as good as another, and equally entitled to representation in party affairs, this is the plan that should be approved. But because of its effect on existing power relationships, as well as the continuing respect for the principles of federalism, it seems unlikely to win adoption. Its prospects are probably no better than those of the long-standing Norris-Langer proposals for direct election of the President by popular vote.

The plan for combining equal representation of states with equal representaton of party voters clearly recognizes principles of federalism—not only in the Union at large but within each political party. But, even if a stable two-party system is assumed, the adverse effect upon the states with low voter turnout is probably too great for political feasibility if congressional action is required, although the plan would have more favorable prospects for direct adoption by the party conventions under some circumstances. Another obstacle to the adoption of this proposal by law is that it would seem to place unreasonable obstacles in the way of any sectional third party— unless the law applied only to parties that had qualified under some formula limiting it to major parties of national scope.

The plan for representation on the basis of party strength remains as perhaps the only solution that could safely be written into a constitutional amendment to regulate the national conventions or to establish a national system of presidential primaries. The small states would still be overrepresented in relation to population or the party vote, but not as much as at present. They would retain the same relative strength that they hold in the electoral college and no more. The plan takes account of the principles of federalism and attempts no change in the existing power relationships among the states. In the system as a whole, each state would have the same weight that it is accorded in the electoral college. The plan would be workable for any political party without regard to the degree of sectional balance or the lack of it within the party. On the average, moreover, the senatorial portion of the apportionment would be given the same weight in one party convention that it is given in the other. In general, the plan could be expected to give a relatively balanced effect to the most important criteria of apportionment under widely variable conditions.

The congressional approach to apportionment reform is one that under some conditions might lend itself to comprehensive plans and long-range considerations; no other approach is appropriate in dealing with proposals for constitutional amendments. By contrast, action by the parties themselves can be much more flexible. This is in part the reason for some of the oddities in the existing rules, and it suggests that the opportunities for flexibility that have sometimes been perverted might also be used for the achievement of at least minor improvements.

Modest efforts at improvement in either party might attempt to lessen the irrationalities of the existing systems. The Republican rule for conditioning district delegate votes on the party vote in each district could be strengthened by raising the limits, and something like it might well be considered in the Democratic party. The Democratic failure to follow through with the effort to eliminate the bonus votes might be redressed by action based on a greater regard for the long-term interest of the party in the development and enforcement of its rules.

Collectively, changes of this kind would have a considerable importance and would merit serious attention and effort. The basic difficulty, however, probably lies in the fact that many elements in existing practices have become so entrenched in both parties that it will not be easy to reform them, except by going forward to some new type of plan that can attract wide support because of its own positive virtues.

Changes in party rules seem most likely to occur when a proposal of seeming general merit happens to coincide with the factional interests of a potential majority group that needs an issue. Situations of this kind may arise at any time, but none is apparent at present on the horizon of the Republican party. At the meeting at which the Democratic national committee adopted the apportionment for 1960 (as reflected in Table 8.1) the chairman was authorized to establish a special commission to make recommendations before the end of 1961 on reapportionment in 1964.[44] Action might also be taken at the national convention of 1960, where the existing voting strength of the large states could be used more effectively than in the national committee in voting on changes in apportionment rules.

The current situation in the Democratic party is obviously one of some factional strain between the southern and non-southern elements of the party. Should the strain become more acute, something like the "states and party voters" plan might be brought forward, since its effect would be to reduce southern representation. The same considerations that would limit its political feasibility as a subject for congressional action might even enhance its potentialities, under such circumstances, within a setting of sectional conflict in the convention. Conversely, should sentiment develop for a rationalization of the Democratic apportionment rules in a setting of desire for intra-party harmony, there might then be some opportunity for consideration of the "party strength" formula, with its tendency to strengthen the convention position of the South.

Speculation of this kind should be taken as illustrative of possibilities rather than probabilities. Undoubtedly, the major probability is that both parties will continue to muddle along with something like their present apportionment systems. The highly privileged position that has been conferred upon the small states could be dangerous if those states were capable of acting as a bloc in either convention, and if they were also strongly deviant from the national norm. Fortunately, they have shown almost no capacity for bloc action either in party conventions or in Congress, and their average behavior has long been close to the national norm. The problem of deviant states is essentially the problem of the South; but the southern states are mostly of such average size that they will do well under any system of apportionment other than one that directly penalizes low voter turnout. The introduction of any reflection of turnout into apportionment formulas would touch a sensitive spot and raise the possibility of bitter resistance if ever the delegations from the high turnout states should come to feel strongly that the representation accorded the low turnout states is excessive.

9

The Voting Structure Within the Conventions

THE APPORTIONMENT of votes among the states is only one part of the system of rules by which each party determines the distribution of voting power and how the vote shall be counted. The two most important features of the voting system inside the convention are: the possible use of a unit rule under which the majority of a delegation may cast the entire vote regardless of the preference of the minority; and the possible requirement of more than a simple majority to effect a nomination. Closely related to the unit rule, in turn, is the question of apportionment within states; specifically, whether each congressional district shall be separately represented on some basis or whether the whole delegation shall be elected or appointed on a state-wide basis without any formal regard to the preferences of the districts.

These three issues have always been closely interlocked; any change in regard to one tends to affect the others. In addition, there are the more diffuse problems of fractional votes, the status of alternate delegates, and other factors related to excessive size. Now that the public is able to watch the conventions on television, unattractive performances such as argument over the casting of fractional votes have become not only tedious but politically embarrassing, and public criticism of the visible aspects of the convention drama may be an added factor in discussions of the voting system.

The Apportionment of Votes Within States

There are many different ways in which a state's quota of votes can be assigned or distributed within the state, and there is a further issue in the extent to which the state parties are allowed to exercise authority in the matter. From the beginning the Democrats have been more inclined than the Republicans to leave freedom to the state parties in these matters. The presidential primary movement, however, brought in new considerations. State legislatures have repeatedly imposed rules upon the state party organizations during the present century. This in turn has had consequences for the national parties.

Under the electoral college system of apportionment, the states were given a clear guide to the distribution of the seats (1) between delegates at large and district delegates, and (2) among the congressional districts. Both of these problems become much more acute under any system if the number of seats assigned to each state changes from one convention to the next. This would especially be the case if the national apportionment system were no longer to allot to every state at least as many votes as it has congressional districts.

The recent systems of bonus votes have introduced a substantial element of uncertainty and fluctuation. This has been met, almost invariably, by permitting the number of delegateships at large to fluctuate while holding the number of district delegateships constant.[1] Presumably the distribution would merit some reconsideration in terms of the functions served by one class of delegates by contrast with the other, and the relative need for each.

The Number and Uses of Delegates at Large

The places for delegates at large are frequently occupied by individuals of special status: the state party's principal public officeholders, notably the governor and senators, if they are of the party; the state party chairman and vice chairman; the national committee members for the state; retired party leaders of major stature; and other prominent party members. Thus the delegateships at large often represent a special form of patronage and recognition. They also provide leaders who can represent the delegation in negotiations with other delegations, convention managers, and candidates.

The extent to which these purposes can be served is related to how the delegates at large are selected. Where all of the delegates are selected by a state party convention or committee, the slate-making process is usually such that appropriate party dignitaries are included, unless there is fac-

[1] When bonus votes were first provided in the Democratic party, a district scheme of bonus votes was proposed but not adopted. Montana provided for an apportionment of three delegates to each congressional district in an abortive primary law, adopted in 1954 and repealed before use. This apportionment could have been met by reducing the number of regular delegates at large, but may have resulted in part from an anticipation that bonus votes would ordinarily be available. Utah Democrats assigned all delegate seats, including bonus seats, to their two congressional districts in selecting their 1952 delegation. See Paul T. David, Malcolm Moos, and Ralph M. Goldman, *Presidential Nominating Politics in 1952* (1954), Vol. 5, p. 93.

Montana has since enacted another presidential primary law, used it in 1956, and repealed it in 1959, but let stand the provision for three district delegates from each congressional district, to be elected in state party conventions. See *Revised Codes of Montana, 1947*, Sec. 23-1006, as successively amended, including amendments of 1959.

tional conflict on a winner-take-all basis. In the states with presidential primaries, practice is more variable. In some states there seems to be a tradition to the effect that leaders who already hold high public or party office should not run for delegate, especially in a primary that will be contested. But in the states where party organization is strong, the process of slate-making is likely to be about the same for a primary as for a state convention. New York, Pennsylvania, and Illinois, moreover, have all provided by law for the selection of delegates at large by party committees or conventions, although other delegates are elected in primaries held in the districts.

In many states the number of distinguished party members with claims for recognition has been so great that there has been constant pressure to increase the number of delegates at large. This has undoubtedly stimulated the development of the bonus system. It may have been a factor when the Democratic party doubled the number of delegates at large in 1924 by placing them on a half-vote basis—which had the somewhat ironical result that the district delegates, although supposedly of lower status, were technically more powerful because each was given a full vote.[2] These pressures suggest that there may be a genuine need in many states for more than the traditional allotment of delegates at large, a need that is considerably easier to meet under some systems of apportionment than it would be under others.

The Issue of District Representation

The electoral college basis of apportioning votes among the states carried with it the implication that the delegates corre-

[2] The Utah Democrats recognized these distinctions in 1952 by reversing the usual procedure and giving their four full-vote district places to their highest ranking delegates, leaving the rank and file to occupy the sixteen seats of delegates at large with half a vote each. See David, Moos, and Goldman, *op. cit.*, Vol. 5, p. 93.

sponding to senators might represent their states at large, while the delegates corresponding to members of the House might represent congressional districts. The delegates to the earliest conventions were selected with little regard for this distinction, but in the Democratic convention of 1840 at least two large states, New York and Pennsylvania, sent delegations divided between delegates at large and district delegates. In 1844 nineteen of the twenty-five states apparently sent district delegates to the Democratic convention. Thereafter district delegates were usually selected and identified as such if a state contained more than one or two congressional districts. The so-called district delegates were, however, usually elected in state party conventions. A relationship of individual delegates to particular districts was not emphasized, since the unit rule was widely in effect in the Democratic party until after the advent of the primaries.

The calls for the first two Republican national conventions made the distinction between delegates at large and district delegates, although many of the smaller states sent only delegates at large. Republican practice thereafter tended to maintain the congressional district as the basic constituency unit for as many delegates as possible. At the Republican convention of 1880 the issue became controversial in conjunction with conflict over the unit rule. A majority report by the credentials committee opposed any unit rule and favored the principle of separate congressional district representation. The report referred to district representation as having "had its origin with the birth of the Republican party," and stated that "the right of the Congressional district to two members residing within it and representing its sentiments, has been treated as sacred." It was further argued that the purpose to be secured in nominating a President is the election of a winning candidate, and the nearer the party could get to the popular feeling, in the manner of selecting delegates,

the wiser and safer would be its nominations. If a state convention were to be allowed to overrule the delegate preferences of the congressional districts, the report concluded, this purpose would be defeated.[3]

Contrary views were presented in four minority reports. These took generally a states' rights position, arguing that the state conventions had usually chosen the delegates, and, though they had allowed the districts to select in some cases, they generally treated the district selections as no more than recommendations. Finally, argued the minority, the whole body of party voters of a state had the right through their state convention to instruct the state delegation to vote as a unit and the power to make that instruction "effectual and binding."[4]

The minority views were rejected 449 to 306 in a test vote on the seating of the Alabama delegation. The convention later passed a resolution instructing the Republican national committee to prescribe rules for electing delegates to the convention of 1884, "*Provided,* that such methods or rules shall include and secure to the several Congressional districts in the United States the right to elect their own delegates to the National Convention."[5] The call for 1884 accordingly provided that delegates at large "shall be chosen by popular State conventions" and district delegates either "at separate popular delegate conventions" in the congressional districts or "by subdivisions of the State Conventions into District Conventions." The call directed the use of the latter method when district delegates had not yet been chosen at the time of the state convention.[6] Thereafter the rule was reworded from time to time, but the Republican party still continues to favor district representation wherever possible.

With the origin of the movement for presidential primaries, there came the possi-

[3] RNC, *Proceedings,* 1880, pp. 49, 50.
[4] *Ibid.,* p. 51 ff.
[5] *Ibid.,* p. 160.
[6] RNC, *Proceedings,* 1884, p. 4.

bility of conflict between state law and the Republican national party rules. In 1911, California adopted a primary law requiring that all delegates should be elected at large on a winner-take-all basis. The issue was debated actively before the law was adopted. Statewide election of all delegates was favored on grounds that this was the manner in which presidential electors were chosen, and that it would give the state a more united and more powerful delegation at each party convention, that is, it would favor voting comparable to that under a unit rule. It was opposed on grounds that the ballot would be clumsy because of the length of the delegate lists, voters would be unable to pass on the qualifications of so many candidates, machine politics would be facilitated, and only the majority faction of a state party would be represented, notwithstanding sharp sectional differences.[7] The adoption of the law seems to have resulted largely from the support of the dominant Hiram Johnson faction of the Republican party, which wanted a solid delegation to use against the renomination of President Taft and in favor of Theodore Roosevelt. In the first primary under the law, in 1912, two Taft delegates carried a San Francisco district even though in the state as a whole the Taft slate was defeated by the Roosevelt slate. The national convention upheld its own rules for district representation and seated the two Taft delegates in direct opposition to the provisions of the state law.[8]

Four years later, however, the Republican convention of 1916 bowed to state legislative action. Although the national party did not directly concede that state laws could have any binding effect on it, the convention passed a resolution providing that "all delegates from any State may be chosen from the State-at-large or part from the State-at-large and part from the Congressional Districts, in conformity with the laws of the State in which the election occurs."[9] Both parties thereafter accepted state legislative action as controlling until the members of the Democratic national committee added themselves to the forthcoming 1960 convention delegations without regard to state legislative provisions.

In the states where delegate selection is left to the party machinery, the situation retains its traditional form in both parties. The Democratic party held no separate congressional district conventions in 1952, but there was much caucusing on a district basis at the state party conventions and the caucus recommendations were seldom disregarded. In the Republican party in 1952, district delegates were elected through final action in autonomous district conventions in at least seventeen states.[10]

Among the states with presidential primary laws, the separate election of district delegates has usually been favored. Only California and South Dakota continue to elect all delegates as delegates at large on state-wide slates. In South Dakota, with only two congressional districts, the issue is unimportant. For California, the consequences of its law have apparently been substantial. The winning California delegations have had the voting unity intended by the statute, but they have frequently been united behind a losing cause, as will become apparent in later analyses. The California experience suggests that the consequences of the practice may also be especially undesirable in a contest among three or more candidates, when there is danger of an unrepresentative plurality victory such as the one that committed the California Democratic delegation to John N. Garner in 1932.

Methods of Apportionment Among Districts

Under the apportionment rules as they became stabilized in the two parties after

[7] Louise Overacker, *The Presidential Primary* (1926), pp. 49-51.
[8] *Ibid.*, p. 54, citing RNC, *Proceedings*, 1912, pp. 202-12.
[9] RNC, *Proceedings*, 1916, p. 74.
[10] David, Moos, and Goldman, *op. cit.*, particularly Vol. 1, p. 163.

he Civil War each congressional district vas automatically considered entitled to wo delegates. After the Republican party idopted its new rules in 1916, a minimum varty vote was required in each district in order to qualify for two delegates and later a minimum was required for even one, with obvious consequences for state voting trength and the apportionment within he state. The Democratic party in 1956 authorized each state to send four delegates per district on a half-vote basis, retaining the state quota at two votes per district.

Some new system of apportionment among the districts would be required under at least three of the alternative plans discussed at the end of Chapter 8. Any new approach to the distribution of seats between delegates at large and district delegates would also be likely to involve reconsideration of the distribution of district delegateships. If the present national rules were to be amended—but with the states still retaining authority for their own internal apportionment—the state parties would be likely to find most of their purposes best served by some system of assigning delegates to the districts in accordance with district voting records. The state party could reserve enough places for delegates at large to meet its state-wide needs, and might also give every district a minimum of one vote, using the rest for allocation by rules designed to provide rewards and incentives.[11]

All-or-None vs. Proportional Representation

Some contests, political and otherwise, are conducted with either total victory or total defeat as the only alternatives in the payoff. Other contests proceed according to rules that permit a sharing in the payoff by all, both winners and also-rans. If a single delegate is elected by a district in a contest between two factions, only one person can be the indivisible victor in the election contest. The faction represented by the loser will then have no delegates, unless elsewhere in the state there may be a district that gives that faction a majority of its vote. Definite provision for sharing the payoff, on the other hand, is the main characteristic of proportional representation plans, found most often in the governmental arrangements of countries on the continent of Europe.

In convention experience, it soon became apparent that apportionment of the delegates to congressional districts was of little importance if state delegations were to be voted as units without regard to the district constituencies. Hence the conflict over the unit rule and over the election of all delegates on an at-large basis, as in California. But similar effects can occur without a formal unit rule and even in the absence of state-wide choice of slates, if, for example, one national candidate should have even a slight majority in an election in every district.

The issue is one frequently argued as a question of policy in delegate selection at state party conventions: should the delegates all be committed to a single candidate, giving no representation to the minority choice, or should there be some informal distribution of delegateships among all the candidates that have appreciable support in the state? This question arises most often in the choice of delegates at large, where it may be overladen by a desire to find places for state party leaders without regard to their candidate sympathies. But it may also arise for slates of district delegates when these are composed through some unified procedure at a state convention.

The issue was especially acute in the Republican party in 1952.

In several states, party leaders were deeply stirred over whether the party's inner conflicts should be fought out on a winner-take-all basis or instead should be compromised by awarding delegate seats to each faction on an agreed

[11] But see also footnote 40 in Chapter 8, commenting on what might be involved if the plan for equal representation of states and voters were to be adopted.

basis. The struggles in Vermont, Rhode Island, Connecticut, Utah, and Washington were fought on a winner-take-all basis, although that result was not completely achieved in all cases. In many states, the desire to maintain party unity in the interests of the general election campaign led to varying degrees of moderation and restraint, often when one faction or the other was clearly predominant and in a position to make its own terms. The most common type of compromise was a decision not to instruct the delegation, sometimes accompanied by the naming of several delegates who seemed to be truly uncommitted and undecided. Concessions on rules changes and on the naming of individual delegates were often obtained even where major battles were lost.[12]

The issue of balanced representation versus winner-take-all was acute in Republican proceedings in 1952, not only because the contest was heated, but also because there was a sharp division between two factions that were closely balanced in the nation as a whole. In many states either Taft or Eisenhower supporters could hope to dominate the proceedings through solid working majorities at district or state levels. The natural impulse was to exploit their advantage to the fullest in view of the prospective close division at the national convention. But all-or-none tactics on behalf of one candidate in a situation where he was winning tended to provoke a like response on behalf of the other where *he* had the upper hand, as was documented time after time in the unfolding chronology of the struggle. There were some states, however, where both candidates were short of a majority and uncommitted elements occupied a strategic position, leading to some form of compromise. In Oklahoma, for example, the state convention finally appointed a special committee on delegates made up of four Taft supporters, four Eisenhower supporters, and three neutrals. This committee eventually chose a balanced slate of delegates, who were then elected without instruction.[13] The Iowa conven-

tion, following a record of equally divided results in the election of district delegates, appointed a balanced nominating committee for delegates, composed of four Taft and four Eisenhower supporters, to propose delegates at large. But it was known that the Eisenhower supporters could probably muster a majority on the floor of the state convention. A slate was eventually selected and approved in which seven delegates at large were for Eisenhower, two neutral, and one for Taft—and the one Taft delegate was a party official who had been particularly objectionable to the Eisenhower supporters.[14]

Drives for balanced slates and party harmony are most likely to prevail when three or more candidates are in the field, with no one far in the lead. Attempts to pursue all-or-none tactics were rarities in Democratic state party conventions in 1952; an effort of this kind was mounted on behalf of Kefauver only in the state convention of Washington, where a motion to instruct for Kefauver was defeated 544 to 286 on a roll call vote.[15]

The uses and consequences of all-or-none *vs.* proportional representation have been argued interminably in connection with the designing of general election systems. There is some question whether the arguments in that context merit transfer when proportional representation is considered for use in a presidential primary, and still more so when something like proportional representation is already provided informally within the setting of party processes for the selection of delegates. In the latter instance, a balanced or proportional representation of all interests can be part of the process of factional accommodation, since it can be tailored to meet the situation of each case with the usual purpose of rendering factional divisions temporary and looking to future party unity as a means of victory. On the other hand, formal proportional representation election systems

[12] David, Moos, and Goldman, *op. cit.*, Vol. 1, p. 168.
[13] *Ibid.*, Vol. 3, p. 300.
[14] *Ibid.*, Vol. 4, pp. 203-04.
[15] *Ibid.*, Vol. 1, pp. 169-70; Vol. 5, p. 177.

seem to have the opposite effect of encouraging the growth and persistence of factional conflict by giving each major faction an assured position on a continuing basis. It is, incidentally, a notable feature of the American electoral college system that its unit method of counting seldom gives a splinter party any electoral score whatever, thus helping to maintain the two-party system desired by most Americans.

In the multiple candidacy situations that are typical of nominating contests, state parties that compose a balanced slate of delegates are able to avoid committing their entire strength on the basis of a plurality sentiment that may be substantially less than a majority. They also avoid staking all of a state party's interests on a single outcome at the convention, while maintaining potentially friendly relations among opposing factions in preparation for the later, and presumably more important, general election contest, where in union there is strength.

The general development of contests for delegate support on a state-wide all-or-none basis, as in the California primary, would probably intensify the degree of mobilization undertaken by the contestants. With the stakes in the contest heightened, weak contenders (other than favorite sons in their own states) would generally be frightened off. By alliance and defection as all-or-none contests proceed, the number of contestants would tend to narrow down until only two or three, possibly only one, remained for choice by the convention. This might expedite decision in the convention, but it also seems likely to increase the burden of primary campaigning, to embitter the divisions within the parties, and to obstruct the restoration of party unity for the general election campaign.

The selection of district delegates through procedures that maintain district autonomy has the effect of permitting a series of small all-or-none contests, whether in primaries or party conventions, without necessarily leading to rigid commitments that may be costly later on. Separate district elections avoid the high stakes inherent in state-wide winner-take-all contests, but offer potential rewards for those who mobilize and campaign actively. They provide direct representation for relatively small subunits of party opinion in the country at large, and occasionally they result in the election of mixed delegations made up of supporters of two or more different candidates. They can thus be viewed to some extent as intermediate between all-or-none and proportional representation systems for the state as a whole; and they can exist regardless of the use of either type of system for the selection of delegates at large.

The Unit Rule

In one form or another, the unit rule has been used to some extent in the Democratic party throughout its history. It was never adopted as a part of the national rules of the Republican party, though it was an issue in that party for a time.[16]

The Unit Rule in the Democratic Party

In the Democratic party, the unit rule originated as a matter of practice rather than of formal decision. It has been a perennial source of conflict within individual delegations, with requests for rulings by the chair at almost every convention. Only infrequently, however, has the rule become broadly controversial within the party as a matter of principle; on a number of those occasions it has been associated

---

[16] The impression that the unit rule was a normal feature of the procedure in both political parties in their early years was given currency by statements in a book by Frederick W. Dallinger, *Nominations for Elective Office in the United States*, published in the Harvard Historical Studies, 1897. These statements are quoted and refuted at length, in so far as the Republican party is concerned, in Carl Becker, "The Unit Rule in National Nominating Conventions," *American Historical Review*, Vol. 5 (1899), pp. 64-82; see especially pp. 65, 75-80.

with argument over the two thirds rule.

The party's first convention in 1832 established that each delegation should designate a spokesman by majority vote, and that he in turn should report the vote of the delegation. Most of the delegations were reported as casting unanimous votes at that convention; informal unit rule practices may have been in effect in many of them. In 1835 the winning candidate for the vice-presidential nomination, Richard M. Johnson, benefited from the existence of a unit rule in the Ohio delegation, where he had majority support, and from its absence in the Massachusetts delegation, where he was favored by only a minority. Had the voting procedure been reversed in either delegation, Johnson might have failed to achieve his two thirds majority. In each case the decision on voting procedure, after protest and discussion, was left to the delegation concerned.[17] Practice continued to harden on a states' rights basis in subsequent conventions. The 1852 rules included a clause to the effect that "the manner in which said vote is to be cast [is] to be decided by the delegation of each state by itself."[18]

In 1860 minority interests within delegations were given limited relief in a new rule, adopted by a vote of 197 to 103½: "That in any State which has not provided or directed by its State Convention how its vote may be given, the Convention will recognize the right of each Delegate to cast his individual vote."[19] But the main result was a strengthening of the unit rule where it was backed by the state convention. In subsequent conventions, also, the right of minority delegates to be heard was gradually evaded. The delegation chairmen were given increasing authority to report the delegation vote as they saw fit, with the chair declining to recognize challenges by dissident members of delegations.

After the Civil War, however, the Republican emphasis on the rights of district delegates began spreading to some parts of the Democratic party. A motion to abolish the unit rule, in part with the purpose of promoting district representation, was made unsuccessfully in 1868.[20] A more substantial effort occurred in 1884. The defeat of an attempt to introduce the unit rule in the Republican convention of 1880 figured in the debate, but the Democratic attack on the rule in 1884 was sparked primarily by the large minority within the New York delegation that opposed the Cleveland nomination. The delegation had been bound to a unit rule by its state convention; the minority sought to amend the national rules so as to nullify the state's action. In the debate and the vote many of the defenders of the unit rule were obviously influenced by the fact that it would help Cleveland, but the independent support for it was also so strong that historian Carl Becker found it impressive: "the question of the unit rule was also a real question and the resolution was not supported or opposed simply because it might aid in defeating or nominating a certain candidate."[21] Retention of the rule was sustained by a vote of 463 to 332 after an extended debate in which the states' rights position was summed up by a Wisconsin delegate:

I know, Mr. President, that in the Republican party—a party which believes that Congress and the Federal Government have every power which is not expressly denied, and that the States have hardly any rights left which the Federal Government is bound to respect—they can adopt in their Convention this idea that the State does not control its own Delegation in a National Convention. Not so in the Convention of the great Democratic party. We stand, Mr. President, for the rights of the States. We do not, by declaring ourselves in favor of the rights of the States, declare that the Federal Government has not its rights also; and the Federal law and the Federal Constitution have provided that the votes for President shall be by States, and the voice of the State shall be obeyed by its Delegates.[22]

[17] Niles' Weekly Register, Vol. 48, p. 229; Baltimore Republican and Commercial Advertiser, May 25, 1835.
[18] DNC, Proceedings, 1852, p. 9.
[19] DNC, Proceedings, 1860, pp. 10-15, 18-20.
[20] DNC, Proceedings, 1868, p. 138.
[21] Becker, op. cit., p. 71.
[22] DNC, Proceedings, 1884, p. 16.

The defeated proposal of 1884 included a provision for the polling of delegations when the vote as reported by the spokesman was challenged, as well as for the revocation of the unit rule. The new Republican rule of 1880 had specifically authorized the polling of delegations, and the practice was common in Republican conventions from then on. As late as 1892 presiding officers in Democratic conventions refused to go behind the vote as reported, but in 1896, a year of change, the practice was changed without debate or warning at the instance of national committee Chairman William F. Harrity, who was presiding during the opening procedure of the convention. The vote of the Iowa delegation was challenged during a vote for temporary chairman. Harrity directed the secretary to call the roll of the delegation. When this action was challenged, Harrity agreed that the delegation was subject to the unit rule, but added:

The Chair further holds that if a delegate from any given State challenges the accuracy or integrity of the vote of the State as announced that then the list of delegates from that State shall be called for the purpose of verifying the vote as recorded.[23]

The ruling was maintained by other presiding officers who followed Harrity, and delegation polling has continued on occasion in Democratic conventions to this day.

In 1912 the conventions of both parties faced new issues arising from the presidential primary laws adopted in many states. The Democratic convention had the problem of deciding whether to recognize the authority of a state party convention in Ohio to impose a unit rule on delegates who had been elected in separate congressional district primaries, regardless of their own preferences or those of their constituents. A majority report of the rules committee, somewhat ambiguous, would have allowed state convention instructions to prevail, "so long as a majority of the delegates from such State are of the opinion that such in-

[23] DNC, *Proceedings*, 1896, p. 94.

structions are applicable."[24] But a minority report, signed by nineteen members, proposed that:

The Chair shall recognize and enforce a unit rule enacted by a State convention, except in such States as have by mandatory statute provided for the nomination and election of delegates and alternates to national political conventions in Congressional districts, and have not subjected delegates so selected to the authority of the State committee or convention of the party, in which case no such rule shall be held to apply.[25]

After debate in which the unit rule and the two thirds rule were jointly defended as necessary to preserve the rights of the states, with counterargument to the effect that the party should not encourage a state convention to nullify a state statute, the majority report was rejected and the minority report was adopted by a vote of 565½ to 492⅓, with 36⅙ not voting.[26]

The rules and practice as thus amended in 1912 have been carried forward in subsequent Democratic conventions with little further change. The unit rule continues to be enforced when imposed by a state party convention in the absence of a primary. If the vote is challenged, the delegation is polled to ascertain the majority view, which then controls. If the vote is tied within the delegation or split several ways with no majority, the divided vote is recorded. On the other hand, if the delegates are elected in a primary, with or without instructions on the basis of the state-wide or district vote, no unit rule is applicable so far as the convention is concerned. Moreover, the delegate is not required by the rules to follow any preference vote that may have been recorded in the primary:

. . . the Convention declines to assume responsibility for instructions imposed in a primary. Such instructions may be disregarded at will as a matter between the delegate and his constituency.[27]

[24] DNC, *Proceedings*, 1912, p. 59.
[25] *Ibid.*, pp. 59-60.
[26] *Ibid.*, pp. 61, 76.
[27] Ruling by the chair, DNC, *Proceedings*, 1952, pp. 464-65.

The unit rule has continued to be controversial and has been abandoned by a number of states that formerly practiced it.[28] It was a constant issue in the 1924 convention, with efforts to revoke it following the seventy-third, seventy-seventh, ninety-sixth, and ninety-seventh ballots.[29] In 1932 the voting involved eight challenges of votes cast by unit rule states, and in 1952, seven. The Michigan delegation, bound in 1952 by a unit rule through a routine and little-noticed action at the end of its state convention, attempted repeatedly to secure rulings permitting it to disregard the rule, which had little support in the delegation itself.[30] Michigan abandoned the rule in preparing for the 1956 convention, as Montana and South Carolina did also.

The Unit Rule
in the Republican Party

Among the predecessors of the Republican party, the unit rule concept gained no strong foothold. The Whigs did adopt a unit rule at their first national convention in 1839; this was a part of Thurlow Weed's successful strategy for the nomination of William Henry Harrison (as noted in Chapter 2). But in most of the Whig conventions the delegates voted as individuals, and the

Free Soil conventions in 1848 and 1852 also adopted rules that were intended to give each delegate an uncontrolled vote.[31] This precedent was followed in organizing the Republican convention of 1856: each delegation chairman was required to report the number of votes given to each candidate by members of his delegation.[32] But about half of the states were unanimous in their balloting on the nominations; some of these delegations may have followed a unit rule in practice.

In 1860 the Maryland delegation came to the Republican convention with instructions to vote as a unit, and so announced on the first ballot. The question of its duty to follow such instructions was put to the convention, which promptly rejected it on a voice vote.[33] Thereafter the question was not again raised as a major issue until 1876, when the Pennsylvania delegation arrived with unit voting instructions which it sought to enforce. The vote was challenged, and the chair ruled "that it is the right of any and of every member equally, to vote his sentiments in this convention." The ruling was appealed and sustained. On a motion to reconsider, the chair was again sustained after debate, by a vote of 395 to 353.[34] During the course of the debate a Kansas delegate stated the theory behind the Republican practice:

The principle which is involved in this controversy, is whether the state of Pennsylvania shall make laws for this convention; or whether this convention is supreme and shall make its own laws. We are supreme. We are original. We stand here representing the great Republican party of the United States, and neither Pennsylvania nor New York nor any state can come in here and bind us down with caucus resolutions. More than that . . . the great principles of the Republican organization demand that each man shall have his vote himself, and not be bound up by some party or power that is behind him. . . . The convention . . . has the right, and it is its duty, its beholden duty, to let each delegate here represent the sentiments of

[28] The convention proceedings have been searched for announcements that a unit rule was in effect, anl also for instances of state delegations that voted unanimously on all roll call votes in more than half of the conventions since 1896. On the basis of this kind of fragmentary and indirect evidence, it appears that about twenty-two states may have made frequent use of the unit rule since 1896. But the rule seems to have been abandoned by a number of these states some time ago, notably Iowa, Washington, Wyoming, Utah, New Jersey, Minnesota, and Maryland.
Reversions to the unit rule could occur on the part of states previously abandoning it; past practice has doubtless included cases of states that adopted the rule intermittently for use only in conventions where more conflict than usual was anticipated. But the weight of sentiment seems increasingly opposed to such reversion where the rule has once been abandoned.

[29] DNC, *Proceedings*, 1924, pp. 756-62, 783-86, 915, and 923.

[30] David, Moos, and Goldman, *op. cit.*, Vol. 4, pp. 60-63, 68-70.

[31] Becker, *op. cit.*, pp. 73-75.

[32] RNC, *Proceedings*, 1856, p. 27.

[33] RNC, *Proceedings*, 1860, pp. 150-51.

[34] RNC, *Proceedings*, 1876, pp. 88-99.

is constituents, and not compel him to vote as anybody shall dictate.[35]

Despite the action in 1876, further attempts were made in 1880 to develop some form of unit voting. Leaders of the New York and Pennsylvania delegations believed that they could secure a third-term nomination for Grant if they could win the right to vote their own delegations, and a few others, as units. Lacking the strength to secure the direct adoption of a unit rule by the national convention, they sought to achieve the same result through a combination of state convention instructions and favorable rulings from the chair.[36] But the main result was a redrafting of the convention rules, again rejecting the unit rule and in addition clarifying the right of any delegate to have his delegation polled. The language thus added to the Republican rules in 1880 has survived to the present day almost without change, and the unit rule has not since been an issue in that party at the national level. Occasional instances of unit rule voting still occur in Republican conventions when all the members of a delegation defer to state party instructions—as, for example, in the case of the Idaho delegation in 1952.[37] But these instances do not have the sanction of the national convention and can be voided whenever any minority delegate sees fit to avail himself of his rights under the national party rules.

Merits and Consequences of the Unit Rule

The merits of the unit rule have been argued in terms of theories of federalism, of party organization, of representation, and of majority rule. States' rights have always figured prominently in the debate, with heavy emphasis upon the fact that in the electoral college state votes are "always" cast as a unit. The unit rule gives effect, in theory at least, to majority sentiment within a state party, and assists in maintaining the federal nature of a national party organization. The unit rule is said to help maintain the integrity of state party organization, since dissident elements can be simply overridden and voted with the majority without having to resort to other forms of pressure and persuasion.

Against these arguments, delegates with a direct relationship to a district constituency have argued that mandates originating in smaller territorial units are closer to the popular will and more likely to be expressive of popular sentiments within the party. Minority factions in unit rule delegations have also argued that fair play, willing consent, and freedom to vote as they see fit would be more conducive to harmony in state party organizations than any rule binding delegates against their will. Delegations frequently act with a high degree of unanimity even when no unit rule is in effect and even when delegate selection has been highly decentralized.[38] Such unanimity is doubtless often an expression of the individual delegate's need for the reassurance of group support, and of his desire to enhance his state's influence. A similar cohesion is often apparent in the state party delegations in Congress.[39]

Undoubtedly, state parties have often imposed a unit rule with the purpose of keeping intact their greatest possible weight in the voting at the national convention. If a delegation is allowed to divide its vote, part of the delegation merely cancels the votes of

---

[35] Ibid., pp. 97-98.

[36] Becker, op. cit., pp. 78-79; Gordon S. P. Kleeberg, The Formation of the Republican Party as a National Political Organization (1911), pp. 158-60.

[37] David, Moos, and Goldman, op. cit., Vol. 5, p. 32.
The California Republican delegation of 1956, composed of elements chosen by Governor Goodwin Knight, Vice President Richard Nixon, and Senator William Knowland, reportedly adopted the unit rule in order to give its unanimous support to Nixon for renomination. See New York Times, August 22, 1956.

[38] For a comparative discussion of the factors tending toward unanimity in the California and New York delegations, see David, Moos, and Goldman, op. cit., Vol. 2, pp. 181-82.

[39] David B. Truman, "The State Delegations and the Structure of Party Voting in the United States House of Representatives," American Political Science Review, Vol. 50 (Dec. 1956), pp. 1023-45.

another part. The state's influence on the
eventual outcome is visibly reduced and may
become inconsequential, with a weakening
of its bargaining position in national party
councils. Hence it is easy to argue in any
state party situation that it is foolish not
to impose a unit rule as long as other state
parties are allowed to use it—essentially the
same argument that led long ago to bloc
voting in the electoral college, although
such voting was not prescribed by
the Constitution. This type of argument
suggests that the unit rule should either be
followed universally in a party convention
or not be used at all. The fact that some
states are allowed to take advantage of the
rule seems unfair to the others that refrain
from doing so.

The existing mixed situation in the
Democratic party, with some states using the
rule and others not, has repeatedly been a
source of confusion and conflict within delegations. The rule has the effect of creating
a procedural structure that may either almost double or eliminate entirely the influence of a faction or group within a delegation. Thirteen votes, for example, may decide how the entire vote of a delegation
of twenty-five shall be cast. In this case,
each of thirteen votes is worth one thir-
teenth of twenty-five, or slightly more than
one and nine tenths votes each. Conversely,
each of the twelve votes submerged by the
majority becomes worth exactly zero. The
constituency of one delegate finds its mandate multiplied, while that of another finds
its mandate dissipated. Frustration is further compounded when there is a possibility that the submerged minority votes within individual delegations may mean the
difference between victory and defeat in a
vote of the convention. It is typically in
such close contests that the controversies
over unit voting become most heated.[40]

The charge has been made repeatedl
that the unit rule can be used to nominate
candidates with a minority of the delegates
If a dozen large delegations with hal
the convention voting strength could al
vote the same way as units, they might con
trol the nomination even if nearly half the
members of those very delegations were op
posed. This type of possibility has ofte
been referred to as a threat, but with fe
attempts to demonstrate that it has eve
occurred.

To estimate the actual consequenecs o
the rule is in fact an extremely difficult mat
ter. Perhaps William Henry Harrison wa
really a minority candidate when nomi
nated by the Whig convention of 1839
despite the size of his recorded majority. In
any event, the use of the rule may have
made it possible to shift a larger number
of votes from Scott and Clay to Harrison on
the critical ballot than would otherwise
have been possible.[41] In the Democratic
party, the unit rule may have helped or
hindered various nominations in conjunction with the two thirds rule, as in the previously noted case of the vice-presidential
nomination of Johnson in 1835. With the
two thirds rule no longer in effect, the
Democratic party has nominated a number
of candidates since 1940 with narrow majorities. In most of these cases it is not readily possible to tell what effect the unit rule

[40] The actual size of these submerged minorities
does not ordinarily become public knowledge except under circumstances of extreme controversy.
In the published Democratic convention proceedings from 1896 to 1952, however, there are at least
forty-four instances in which the size of the submerged minority became a part of the record

through one means or another. Of these instances,
twelve occurred in 1896, eleven in 1912, and eight
in 1924, these being the most contested conventions
of the period. In 1896 the submerged minorities
ranged from 6.3 to 42.9 per cent of their respective
whole delegations, averaging 26.8 per cent; in 1912
they ranged from 16.7 to 50 per cent, averaging
33.2 per cent; in 1924 from 15.4 to 50 per cent,
averaging 38.5 per cent. The Oklahoma, Kansas,
and Iowa delegations were repeatedly shifted from
one candidate to another in 1924 by small voting
shifts across the 50 per cent mark within each of
these delegations. Delegations that became conspicuous for their submerged minorities frequently
came from state parties characterized by a sustained factionalism, where adoption of the unit
rule inevitably took on punitive overtones.
[41] However, the unit rule was merely one part of
a procedure designed "to give the greatest possible
opportunity for combinations and intrigue . . . the
culmination of a shrewd scheme to defeat Henry
Clay." Becker, op. cit., p. 74.

TABLE 9.1. UNIT RULE VOTING ON THE CRITICAL BALLOT (THIRD BALLOT PRIOR TO VOTE SWITCHING), DEMOCRATIC CONVENTION, 1952[a]

Region and Delegation	Votes Cast Under the Unit Rule			
	Russell	Stevenson	Barkley	Kefauver
Northeast, Middle West, and West				
Connecticut................	—	16	—	—
Delaware..................	—	6	—	—
Michigan..................	—	40	—	—
North Dakota..............	—	8	—	—
Kansas....................	—	16	—	—
Montana..................	—	12	—	—
Idaho.....................	—	12	—	—
Arizona...................	12	—	—	—
South				
Virginia..................	28	—	—	—
South Carolina............	16	—	—	—
Georgia..................	28	—	—	—
Kentucky.................	—	—	26	—
Tennessee................	—	—	—	28
Mississippi...............	18	—	—	—
Louisiana................	20	—	—	—
Oklahoma................	—	—	24	—
Texas....................	52	—	—	—
Non-State Areas				
District of Columbia........	—	6	—	—
Puerto Rico..............	—	6	—	—
Alaska...................	—	—	—	6
Total Under Unit Rule	174	122	50	34
Other Votes..............	87½	491	17½	245½
Grand Total[b]............	261½	613	67½	279½

[a] The voting statistics are from David, Moos, and Goldman, *Presidential Nominating Politics in 1952*, Vol. 1, pp. 152-53. The states voting under the unit rule were determined primarily from the delegation reports in other volumes (see items indexed under unit rule), supplemented by announcements and rulings as found in the convention proceedings.

[b] Omits 8½ votes for other candidates or not voting. All totals are prior to the switch of 4½ Utah votes that completed Stevenson's majority. See *ibid.*, p. 153. footnote c.

may have had—it may have worked against the winning candidates as much as, or more than, it worked for them.

Better information is available on unit rule voting at the 1952 and 1956 conventions than for any other recent cases. The delegations known to be voting under a unit rule in 1952, and their votes on the critical ballot for Stevenson, are shown in Table 9.1. In most of these delegations the votes recorded were undoubtedly supported by overwhelming majorities; it may therefor be assumed that without the rule the results would not have been much different. So far as Stevenson's victory is concerned, it appears that with individual voting he might have been 15 or 20 votes short of a majority at the end of the critical third roll call, instead of merely 2½.[42] But, since many delegates were ready to switch and the other major candidates were already prepared to concede, it would be difficult indeed to attribute the Stevenson victory to the rule or to consider him the choice of only a minority of the delegates.

At the Democratic national convention of 1956 the number of delegations operating under the unit rule was smaller than in 1952. Michigan and Montana had abandoned the rule and divided their voting on several of the ballots. Among the thirteen southern states, Florida and Alabama continued to elect delegates in separate district primaries, precluding the imposition of unit voting. North Carolina continued to allow individual voting, and was joined by South Carolina. Arkansas continued to select its delegates by means that assured unanimity without a formal rule. So far as is known, the other eight southern states continued to impose a unit rule on their delegations; all were voted unanimously on all votes in 1956.

The closest vote at the convention, and the one in which unit voting might have had the greatest influence, occurred on the second ballot for the vice-presidential nomination. At the end of the roll call no candidate had a majority, but Senator John F. Kennedy was leading, with a vote of 618 to Senator Estes Kefauver's 551½. After the vote switching had been completed, Kefauver was nominated with a vote of 755½ to Kennedy's 589. The unit rule votes as they stood at the end of the ballot and prior to switching are shown in Table 9.2. The indication is that the net effect of unit voting was to hinder Kefauver and help Kennedy—assuming, in the absence of information, that splinter votes were distributed somewhat at random among the delegations involved.

In the large northern states, except Michigan, the unit rule is no longer available to the Democratic party organizations, because the district delegates are elected in primaries. In most of the other northern states, including Michigan, the rule has been abandoned on grounds that it is unfair, undemocratic, and in the long run contrary to the best interests of the state party organization.[43]

The rule has been criticized in recent years by leading southern Democrats on grounds that when the two thirds rule was abolished, the unit rule was retained as a device for control of the conventions by northern urban states—this despite the fact that Massachusetts, New York, New Jersey, Pennsylvania, Ohio, and Illinois have long elected their district delegates in primaries and have frequently divided their votes at

[42] In the Michigan and District of Columbia delegations, which were polled at the time, 7 and 2¼ votes respectively would have gone to other candidates in the absence of the unit rule. See DNC, *Proceedings*, 1952, pp. 512, 534.

[43] In the District of Columbia primary, where all delegates are elected at large, the 1956 ballot carried a referendum question on whether the delegation should be instructed to operate under the unit rule. The delegation was so instructed by action of the voters, who no doubt hoped thereby to increase the influence of the disenfranchised District of Columbia, which had no election other than a presidential primary.

Region and Delegation	Votes Cast Under the Unit Rule			
	Kennedy	Gore	Kefauver	Wagner
Northeast, Middle West, and West				
Connecticut..................	20	—	—	—
Delaware....................	10	—	—	—
North Dakota................	—	—	8	—
Kansas......................	—	—	16	—
Idaho.......................	—	—	12	—
Arizona.....................	—	—	16	—
South				
Virginia....................	32	—	—	—
Georgia.....................	32	—	—	—
Kentucky....................	—	30	—	—
Tennessee...................	—	32	—	—
Mississippi.................	22	—	—	—
Louisiana...................	24	—	—	—
Oklahoma....................	—	28	—	—
Texas.......................	56	—	—	—
Non-State Areas				
Alaska......................	—	—	6	—
Puerto Rico.................	—	—	—	6
Total Under Unit Rule......	196	90	58	6
Other Votes...............	422	$20\frac{1}{2}$	$493\frac{1}{2}$	$3\frac{1}{2}$
Grand Total[b].............	618	$110\frac{1}{2}$	$551\frac{1}{2}$	$9\frac{1}{2}$

[a] The delegations voting under the unit rule were identified on the basis of announcements recorded in the stenographic transcript of the proceedings, consultation with staff of the Democratic national committee, and other sources.
[b] Omits 82½ votes for other candidates or not voting.

the conventions.[44] The actual fact seems to be that at present the unit rule is used chiefly to concentrate the voting strength of the southern faction that has been in chronic disagreement with the national Democratic party. It seems reasonable to suspect that the rule as restricted in 1912 was allowed to survive in 1936 at least in

[44] For a remarkable example of this kind of political sophistry, see the pamphlet by Allan Shivers, *Restore the Two-Thirds Rule* (published by the American Good Government Society for distribution in the early months of 1956). On pages 14-15 of the pamphlet, Shivers, who was then governor of Texas, states: "So we come to the core of the matter—the fact that in the absence of the two-thirds rule, we are in constant danger of a minority choice for President and Vice President—dictated by the big city political machines." He then goes on to use New York and Illinois as the basis for his hypothetical unit rule examples, with no reference to the existence of primaries in those states. The pamphlet was introduced and recommended in a foreword by Senator Harry F. Byrd. See also the presentation of similar arguments in the minority rules report in 1948 by Wright Morrow of Texas and the supporting statement by Edgar A. Brown of South Carolina. (DNC, *Proceedings*, 1948, pp. 110-12.) As Tables 9.1 and 9.2 indicate, Texas was the largest state retaining the unit rule in 1956.

part as a concession to the southerners. Elimination of the remaining remnants of the rule might bring to light a minority of votes not in agreement with the leadership in some southern delegations.

The Two Thirds Rule in Democratic Party Nominations

For more than a century, the nominating procedures of the Democratic party were governed by variations of the rule adopted in 1832: "that two thirds of the whole number of votes given be required to a nomination."[45] This wording was followed by subsequent conventions until 1860.

Early Experience Under the Rule

In its origins, as noted in Chapter 2, the two thirds rule was favored by the Jackson men, who argued that it would make a more impressive showing of party unity than a mere majority vote. Many historians, however, have attributed other motivations of a factional sort. They believe that the Jackson men were fearful of a Calhoun maneuver to control the vice-presidential nomination; under the two thirds rule, Jackson partisans were sure they had the votes to block any unfriendly nomination.

If this interpretation is correct, the Jackson men were remarkably blind to the strength of the weapon they were offering to their opponents. They had called the convention primarily to nominate Martin Van Buren for Vice President, and he was nominated with very few more than a two thirds majority.

In further Democratic conventions during the formative period, the two thirds rule was often under attack yet continued to be adopted at each convention on mo-

tions that were passed by simple majorities. The fortunes of individual candidates were obviously linked to the arguments, but the rule was also hotly debated on its own merits. Over the years it developed its own body of powerful supporters, strongly wedded to states' rights, party federalism, and the Calhoun doctrine of concurrent majorities. The objective was to make it certain that no candidate could be nominated except with the concurrent approval—or at least the passive consent—of most major factions within the party.

The consequences of the rule were clearly apparent on several occasions. In 1844, the rule was a direct cause of Van Buren's failure to secure the presidential nomination; he polled a majority for seven ballots before the convention shifted to Polk. In 1848, with Polk not a candidate to succeed himself, Cass was nominated on the fourth ballot under the two thirds rule, which had been adopted as usual but over the objection of some of his supporters. In 1852, the rule probably prevented a second nomination for Cass, the titular leader; Pierce was nominated on the forty-ninth ballot. By 1856, it was apparent that Pierce could not be renominated under the two thirds rule (or perhaps any other rule); Buchanan was nominated on the seventeenth ballot. In 1860, Buchanan followed the example of Polk in declining a second nomination, rather than that of Pierce in seeking it unsuccessfully; Douglas was eventually nominated at Baltimore.

In 1860, the rule was a major factor in the strategy of the southern die-hards and others favoring a compromise candidate, such as Horatio Seymour. The rule was proposed in a form that required a vote equal to two thirds of the whole electoral college instead of merely two thirds of the delegates present and voting in the convention. It was objected that this constituted a change in the rules, as it clearly did. But the chair ruled that it did not constitute such a change, and was sustained by a vote 144 to 108 on appeal, after which the rule was

---

[45] DNC, *Proceedings*, 1832, p. 6. In *Niles' Weekly Register*, May 26, 1832, the ruling was reported thus (pp. 234-35): ". . . two thirds of the whole number of votes in the convention shall be necessary to constitute a choice."

dopted by a vote of 141 to 112.[46] In the
alloting thereafter, Douglas held a solid
majority of those actually voting for fifty-
even ballots, without being able to reach
he number required under the rule. After
he convention had adjourned and later re-
onvened in Baltimore, the previous rules
were continued in effect, but in preliminary
oting the total vote in the convention was
ever higher than 251½, as compared with
he full electoral college strength of 303,
equiring 202 to nominate under the rule
s adopted at Charleston. On the first nomi-
ating ballot, 190½ votes were cast in all,
f which Douglas received 173½. On a
econd ballot he polled 181½ out of 194½
otes. The convention then extricated itself
y passing a resolution in which Douglas
vas "unanimously" declared the nominee
in accordance with the uniform customs
nd rules of former Democratic Conven-
ions."[47]

The record from 1832 to 1860, taken as a
vhole, suggests that the two thirds rule
vas a major factor in producing the weak
xecutive leadership of the period, since its
ormal effect was to eliminate anyone with
ufficient character and record to have
roused serious opposition. In an era when
nly one political party had any substantial
xperience in holding Executive responsibil-
ties, the rule was used in 1844 to cut down
he party's titular leader on the first occa-
ion for a renomination after defeat. There-
fter, there was no renomination of an in-
umbent President or titular leader of the

party until after the Civil War. As sectional strain increased, the party's nominees
became progressively weaker, most notably
in the case of Pierce and Buchanan. Douglas obviously was not a weak nominee, but
his nomination occurred in spite of the rule
and under circumstances tending to prove
the point. Both at Charleston and Baltimore, the bolting southern factions apparently expected that the Douglas faction
would give up and accept a compromise
choice. Instead, the party was split and the
election went to the Republicans.

In the period before the Civil War, the
Whig party came to power twice. While not
saddled with a two thirds rule, the Whigs
had an openly avowed preference for a
weak Executive and a one-term Presidency,
as stated in their 1844 platform. Both Whig
Presidents who had been elected as such
died in office and were succeeded by Vice
Presidents who had no adequate political
support within the party on whose ticket
they had been elected. Thus the weaknesses
in the party system and in the Executive
were doubly compounded during a period
that led in the end to armed conflict involving the whole nation.

*Later Experience
and Revocation of the Rule*

From 1864 to 1908 there were unsuccessful efforts to revoke the two thirds rule in
the Democratic conventions, but it was relatively much less important than it had been
previously. The rule may have had something to do with the twenty-two ballots required to find a nominee in 1868, but it did
not prevent the nomination of Tilden in
1876, the three successive nominations of
Grover Cleveland, or the three nominations
of William Jennings Bryan. Throughout
this period no candidate who reached a
simple majority in the balloting ever failed
to go on to the two thirds. After Tilden's
nomination in 1876, a resolution was
adopted that called the rule "unwise and

---

[46] DNC, *Proceedings*, 1860, Charleston portion, pp.
1-74. On two previous occasions, nominations were
made in which the candidate received less than two
thirds of the whole electoral college; in neither case
did the Proceedings record any question of the
nomination on the two thirds rule basis. In 1835,
with three states unrepresented, Richard M. Johnson
received one vote more than two thirds of the votes
ast, but substantially less than two thirds of the
uthorized convention strength. In 1848, with the
arge New York delegation refusing to vote, Lewis
Cass received two thirds of the balance, but less than
wo thirds of the total convention if New York were
ncluded. None of the early rules mention a requirement for a quorum.

[47] DNC, *Proceedings*, 1860, Baltimore portion,
. 169.

unnecessary" and suggested its abandonment in 1880. But the 1880 convention thought otherwise, as did other conventions where revocation was attempted.[48]

In 1912, the proceedings that led to the Wilson nomination constituted a reversal of long-standing practice under the rule. This time it was the minority faction that proved more enduring. Speaker Champ Clark was denied the nomination after holding a majority from the tenth to sixteenth ballots, and Wilson was nominated on the forty-sixth ballot. The result was to encourage minorities to hang on in hope of a reversal, as was evident in 1920 and 1924. In 1920, it took forty-four ballots to nominate Cox in a mixed field of candidates. In 1924, Davis was nominated on the 103d ballot after McAdoo and Smith had defeated each other.

There had been efforts to abolish the two thirds rule in advance of each of these conventions. A motion to recommend abolition was tabled in the national committee on January 20, 1920.[49] In 1924, the McAdoo forces came to New York, the convention city, a week before the opening day prepared for an all-out attack on the rule. During the previous eight months, discussion of abrogation had appeared to be a major factor in McAdoo strategy. But the pending move was apparently aborted when Senator Carter Glass of Virginia visited McAdoo to inform him that the South would never surrender the power it held under the rule.[50] The report of the rules committee at the convention suggested no change and was adopted unanimously. As the balloting on the nomination dragged on, attempts to abolish the rule were made after the seventy-third, seventy-seventh, and ninety-seventh ballots, all unsuccessful.[51]

In the aftermath of the 1924 convention further proposals for abolition of the

rule were made in 1926.[52] But there were n[o] concrete results in 1928, perhaps becaus[e] Governor Al Smith at last seemed assure[d] of the nomination and was attempting t[o] conciliate the South. The two thirds rul[e] was specifically included in a motion re adopting the rules of the previous conven tion.

The successful drive to terminate the rul[e] began as part of the preconvention cam paign for Franklin D. Roosevelt's nomina tion in 1932. Four days before the conven tion opened, a meeting of about 150 Roose velt supporters adopted a resolution pre sented by Senator Huey Long, pledging th[e] group to do all within its power to abolis[h] the rule.[53] The adherents included severa[l] figures who had been active in previous at tacks on the rule. But the other contenders particularly Al Smith, Newton D. Baker and Harry F. Byrd, were vehement in thei[r] protests against any strategy that would ob viously make it harder to block the front runner. The move was further denounce[d] by John W. Davis, James M. Cox, Carte[r] Glass, former Senator John Sharp William[s] of Mississippi, Senator Pat Harrison of Mis sissippi, and others. Some members of th[e] Texas delegation began talking of a pos sible bolt; Sam Rayburn warned James A Farley that if Roosevelt wanted to win th[e] nomination he would have to play accord ing to the rules of the game.[54] Some of th[e] opposition came from Roosevelt's own sup porters, who deplored the charges of unfair ness because of the timing of the effort. Stil[l] others thought it unfair to abolish the tw[o] thirds rule while retaining the unit rule, ap parently failing to recognize that the south erners, if they should lose the advantage[s] of the former, would be all the more in clined to cling to the latter as an instru ment of minority action.[55]

---

[48] DNC, *Proceedings*, 1876, pp. 166-69; 1880, pp. 8-9; 1884, pp. 192-93; 1896, pp. 317-18, 322; 1912, p. 212.

[49] DNC, *Proceedings*, 1920, pp. 569-70.

[50] *New York Times*, June 22, 1924.

[51] DNC, *Proceedings*, 1924, pp. 756-57, 783, 923.

[52] *New York Times*, May 24, July 29, and Sept 17, 1926.

[53] *New York Times*, June 24, 1932.

[54] *Ibid.*, June 25-26, 1932.

[55] Robert H. Jackson, a Roosevelt supporter, was quoted as saying, "The unit rule was devised with the two thirds rule. Andrew Jackson devised it so

On the Sunday before the convention Roosevelt and Farley both seemed determined to press the issue; a majority of 701 to 453 was claimed in favor of the change. On the basis of its own poll, however, the *New York Times* reported a much smaller majority for the change, 584 to 565, with only 5 votes in a total of 1,154 doubtful or unknown.[56] At this point, prospective members of the rules committee began discussing a compromise proposal, under which majority rule would be substituted only after six ballots had been taken under the two thirds rule without a choice. This was approved in the Rules Committee on the Monday of the convention opening by a vote of 30 to 20, but meanwhile sentiment among the delegates had shifted to the point where, according to another *New York Times* poll, even the compromise was certain to be defeated by a vote of 601 to 545.[57] On Tuesday the Roosevelt forces accepted defeat, and Farley came before the rules committee to oppose any change in the rule.[58] The committee recommended the following resolution, which was adopted by a voice vote in the convention:

We recommend to the next National Convention of the party that it shall consider the question of changing the two thirds rule now required for the nomination of President and Vice President of the United States so as to make the nomination by a majority vote of the delegates to the convention with a further declaration that that convention is to be the sole judge of its own rules.[59]

In 1936, nearly 900 delegates came to the convention committed to changing the rule.[60] With White House backing, Senator Bennett Champ Clark of Missouri had

worked since 1932 to achieve repeal. He was joined by Representative Robert L. Doughton of North Carolina in leading the movement. The rules committee voted 36 to 13 for the change after assurances had been given that the convention apportionment rules would be modified to give greater recognition to the solidly Democratic states.[61] The opposition to repeal was led by James A. Allred of Texas, Representative Eugene E. Cox of Georgia, and Senator Harry F. Byrd of Virginia, who stated that the southerners did not expect to prevent abrogation of the rule, but that they hoped to secure abolition of the unit rule as a corollary provision.[62] When the committee's report finally came to the floor of the convention, the repeal of the rule was moved by Senator Clark, whose father had lost the nomination in 1912 through the operation of the rule. The action was then taken by voice vote and without a floor fight.[63]

The South has frequently been credited with responsibility for preventing the rules amendment until 1936, but the actual situation was complicated. The South undoubtedly provided most of the active leadership in defending the old rule, but the southern delegations were actually split deeply on the issue in 1932, as they had been in other years. According to the *New York Times* poll in 1932, the delegates from thirteen southern states were *for* the change by a margin of 167 to 141 on Sunday, June 26, and were *for* the compromise by 162 to 146 on Monday, June 27.[64] The opposition, both southern and non-southern, consisted largely of those who were trying to stop the Roosevelt candidacy; but the states' rights philosophy of the opposition came largely from its southern leadership.

When the action finally came, the unit rule was left untouched. The constant linkage of the two issues in previous discussion was probably intended merely to complicate

---

as to make the fulfillment of the two thirds requirement possible. If the new rules proposed by our side are adopted, they should, in my opinion, release to act individually all delegates who have not been chosen in a primary held pursuant of statute. Otherwise we should be pressing a double advantage." *Ibid.*, June 25, 1932.

[56] *Ibid.*, June 27, 1932.
[57] *Ibid.*, June 28, 1932.
[58] *Ibid.*, June 29, 1932.
[59] DNC, *Proceedings*, 1932, p. 140.
[60] *New York Times*, June 26, 1936.

[61] *Ibid.*
[62] *Ibid.*, June 24, 1936.
[63] DNC, *Proceedings*, 1936, pp. 189-92.
[64] *New York Times*, June 27, 28, 1932.

the issues and avoid any change. Once the two thirds rule was abrogated, there was no further pressure for action on the unit rule. Presumably most of the state delegations that had the unit rule desired to retain it, and were prepared to regard the issues as separable. There were probably at least as many non-southern as southern states using the unit rule at the time, and both groups may have influenced the decision not to disturb it in 1936.

Majority Nominations and Efforts to Restore the Rule

Under the present rules, Roosevelt was nominated for a third term in 1940 with a vote of 86 per cent. Wallace received the vice-presidential nomination from a reluctant convention with less than a two thirds vote; he was denied it in 1944, though a minority of more than one third favored his renomination on the first ballot. Stevenson was nominated in 1952 with a bare majority and as titular leader won renomination with 66 per cent of the vote in 1956. Kefauver won the vice-presidential nomination in 1956 with less than a majority before vote-shifting and in the face of determined opposition.[65]

Any or all of these majority decisions might have been prevented or given a different form under the two thirds rule. The negotiations and adjustments that are necessary to accumulate and retain any majority undoubtedly would have proceeded with greater difficulty and under more pressure. Thus, for example, while it may seem difficult to believe that the third Roosevelt nomination could have been prevented, yet, if the two thirds rule had still been in effect, the whole complex of previous events leading up to that nomination would have been colored by a greater feeling of strength on

the part of the opposition within the party, and by more uncertainty on Mr. Roosevelt's own part. The die-hard believers in the rule are entitled to their view that if it had been retained it might have prevented the violation of the two-term tradition—and much else.[66]

Proposals to restore the two thirds rule have been a favorite rallying cry in the South since 1936. It is hard to tell which of these proposals, if any, have been put forward for more than trading purposes. The strongest effort occurred at the 1948 convention. Senator Claude Pepper of Florida acted as spokesman of a group pressing for application of the old rule on the first three nominating ballots.[67] This proposal was not accepted by the rules committee, but a minority report, signed by seven members, recommended full restoration of the old rule. In thirty minutes of debate in the full convention, the discussion never became heated, and the minority report was rejected on a voice vote.[68] In 1952 and 1956 the efforts for restoration seem to have been confined to preconvention propaganda, without pressing for formal action or debate when the conventions actually met.

The values that men live by are deeply involved in both sides of the historic controversy over the two thirds rule. It was and is defended by many public men who have strongly favored action to accommodate the views of respectable minorities. Allen Shivers cited such northern Democrats as James M. Cox, Newton D. Baker, and Al Smith in defense of the rule.[69] If the rule had always operated as it apparently did between 1864 and 1908, it might still be in effect.

The difficulty with the rule is the extent to which it can permit an embattled minority to frustrate the will of a respectable majority. If the two thirds rule is used in con-

---

[65] All references are to the critical vote, as defined in Chapter 16. For the percentages, see Tables 16.4, 17.13, and 17.14.
See also the discussion of the two thirds rule in Chapter 7, first section, in connection with its apparent effects upon the numbers of candidates for the nominations.

[66] "I firmly believe that retention of the two thirds rule would have prevented these developments and others which have sprung from them." Allan Shivers, op. cit., p. 23.
[67] New York Times, July 13, 1948.
[68] DNC, Proceedings, 1948, pp. 109-17.
[69] Shivers, op. cit., pp. 20-21.

unction with the unit rule, a nomination could be vetoed by a cohesive minority faction with far less than one third of the voting strength of the entire convention, if it were distributed in the form of working majorities within delegations that did aggregate one third.

Yet nominating decisions must be made, or the party dies. If accommodation proves impossible, the only alternative to majority rule is minority rule. In the Republican party, which has had a rather clear bifactional form throughout much of its history, the two thirds rule would have endangered if not prevented such nominations as those of Lincoln and Eisenhower. There was never any substantial support for the two thirds rule in the Republican party, although Republicans have sometimes seemed to favor it for the Democratic party.[70] In the Democratic party, it seems clear that those who continue to advocate a return to the two thirds rule desire it for use primarily in the frustration of the majority within the party. If it were to be so used, as it often was between 1840 and 1860, the effect once more would be to favor the nomination of weak men for the Presidency, in the face of the evident preference of the American public for a strong Executive. The fact that the majority of the Democratic party is aware of the frustrating effects of the rule is the main reason why it seems unlikely to be readopted, despite agitation to that end that may continue for another generation.

Massive Size and Its Consequences

In its origins, a national convention was intended to be a delegate body approximating the size of the Senate and House of Representatives when sitting in joint session. In 1832 this would have produced a conven-

tion of 286 members; in 1956, 531. Parliamentary bodies of this size are large enough to encounter many awkward problems, but the party conventions have repeatedly moved in the direction of even greater size.

Oversize Delegations, Fractional Votes, and Alternates

The pressure to provide convention seats for distinguished or deserving party members, together with the adoption of patchwork bonus systems, has led to a vast expansion of the conventions. In the 1956 Democratic convention this expansion had gone to such an extreme that 2,477 delegates were seated, with an authorized voting strength of 1,372.[71] The Republican convention of the same year contained 1,323 delegates, with all delegates on a full-vote basis.

The delegates, whether full-vote or fractional, are not the only official members of the conventions. Each party authorizes alternate delegates. In actual practice the lists of alternates are sometimes incomplete, but the authorized number has usually been the same as that for delegates. In 1956, however, when putting the whole convention on a half-vote basis, the Democrats refrained from increasing the number of district alternates. For 1960 they authorized only one alternate for each vote, except those of the national committee members.

The ostensible or manifest function of the alternates is to act as substitutes for the delegates who never arrive, leave early, or are absent during the proceedings. This, however, is not a function requiring so many substitutes, or so imperative that it has to be performed at all. In most legislative bodies there is no provision for replacement of absentees, who merely reduce the

---

[70] Senator Karl E. Mundt, for example, has frequently commiserated with southern audiences on the disappearance of the two thirds rule in the Democratic party, without suggesting that it be adopted in the Republican.

[71] Florida, Illinois, Minnesota, Nebraska, New Hampshire, New York, Ohio, Oregon, and West Virginia sent district delegates to the Democratic convention on a full-vote basis. All of these states elected their district delegates in presidential primaries. Other states with primaries mostly shifted to the half-vote basis.

total voting strength of the body except as they may arrange for pairs. In the conventions, the use of alternates has the effect, usually, of maintaining voting strength at the maximum level authorized, but at the cost of many complications in procedure.[72] Evidently the continuing custom of having a body of alternates serves another purpose than merely to assure substitutes for missing delegates. In fact, such seats provide a convenient way of giving places on the floor to local party dignitaries who failed to achieve selection as delegates, to wives of delegates, and to miscellaneous others who wish to be present at the convention with official privileges. These latent uses are often somewhat frustrated when the state primary laws require the alternates to be elected.

Other Convention Participants

In addition to the delegates and alternates, eight other classes of persons are important in swelling the total size of the conventions.

1. The convention officers, from permanent chairman to the assistant sergeants at arms. Even the chairman is not necessarily required to be an accredited delegate, and many convention officers do not have delegate status.

2. The members of the outgoing national committee, whose terms expire at the end of the convention. They are treated as officials of the convention, even when they lack status as delegates, although they perform no important special functions after the convention has opened.[73]

3. The distinguished guests: party dignitaries other than delegates who are of sufficient importance to claim special recognition, including living ex-Presidents of the party, former national committee chairmen and other present and former high elective officials, notably governors and senators who have failed to achieve delegate status.[74]

4. The members of the convention staff partly taken over from the national committee but also expanded by temporary recruitment.

5. The representatives of organized interest groups, who appear at the public hearings of the platform committees and otherwise attempt to influence convention action; at recent conventions these have numbered well into the hundreds. Many of them have obtained status as delegates or official visitors in order to enhance their access to convention proceedings.

6. The representatives of press, radio and television and their staffs, a group estimated at 2,500 in the immediate convention environment at Chicago in 1956, and about 1,700 in San Francisco in the same year.

7. The official visitors who receive the courtesy of a reserved seat in the galleries through any one of several channels: quotas assigned to state delegations through the national committee members, a quota allotted to the host city committee that assisted on financial arrangements for the convention, and a quota administered directly by national party officials, including provision for the afore-mentioned distinguished guests and for foreign diplomats visiting the convention.

8. Other visitors. The 1956 edition of Cannon's *Manual* still reported (page 8) a general admission provision: "Seats unoccupied one half hour after scheduled time

---

[72] A considerable body of parliamentary law has accumulated on the subject of which alternates may be substituted for which delegates and under what conditons. Cf. Clarence Cannon, *Democratic Manual* (1956), pp. 28-30.

[73] They are also accorded many other perquisites, including an assigned car and driver for each member during the convention by courtesy of the automobile industry, and a quota of tickets for guests. Usually the committee members share these facilities with the delegation chairmen and state party officials from their respective states, but lame-duck

committee members may cause friction within delegations by an arbitrary use of perquisites on a personal basis.

[74] It should not be assumed from this listing that all such persons are automatically provided with seats. Recognition as a distinguished guest is discretionary; hence the pressure to secure formal title to a seat as delegate or alternate, which also provides greater access to others seated on the floor of the convention.

of opening of each session are thrown open to the public." But even general admission, so-called, has been rigidly controlled by ticket in the recent conventions of both parties, with no actual admission of the general public.

With this aggregation of elements, each of which has tended to grow, the party conventions have become massive affairs indeed. If the distinguished guests, the staff, the interest-group representatives, the press, and the official visitors are included as active members of the convention institution, in the sense that all are involved in its action and decisions, the mass of involved persons in the immediate convention environment usually exceeds 5,000, and was closer to 10,000 at the Democratic convention of 1956. If, however, attention is directed only to the delegates, alternates, and convention officers who take part in the action in some formal or official sense, the participants in the Democratic national convention of 1956 numbered about 4,500; in the Republican convention of the same year, about 2,700.

The Consequences

Massive size has many consequences for an institution in which various forms of debate and deliberation are attempted, and in which decisions are taken or authenticated by a formal vote. One of the first is the limited choice among cities at which any convention can be held. Halls, hotels, and other facilities for a convention as large as that held by the Democrats at Chicago in 1956 are available at only two or three locations in the entire country. Moreover, the delegations from New York, California, and Pennsylvania in 1956 could not hold a full delegation meeting in a space accommodating fewer than about 250 persons. In that year more than 20 Democratic and 7 Republican delegations required meeting space accommodating 100 persons or more.

The decision-making process within delegations is hampered by factors of size in many different ways. Greater size means less privacy in any discussion where all members take part. More formality is necessary; parliamentary procedures that would be ridiculous in a delegation of 12 become imperative is one of 250. Large unwieldy delegations are more dependent upon their leadership for information, for estimates of the situation, and for clarification of alternatives. Inevitably they tend to leave decision-making to the leaders on all matters other than those that can be adapted to settlement through a cumbersome voting process. Individual delegations, as well as the convention as a whole, provide apt illustrations of Madison's principle:

. . . that in all legislative assemblies the greater the number composing them may be, the fewer will be the men who will in fact direct their proceedings.[75]

The states that were prevented by their primary laws or other technicalities from doubling the size of their delegations to the Democratic national convention of 1956 were probably fortunate, so far as the effectiveness of their representation at the convention was concerned.

In the action of the convention proper while in session, massive size has other consequences, some of which are more obvious than others. Disorder, confusion, and a high noise level are not necessarily the direct result of size, but great size makes it more difficult to deal with these traditional aspects of convention behavior, themselves enhanced by size. All forms of debate and deliberation are influenced by the noise level and other physical aspects of the situation inside the hall. The formal proceedings tend to consist of a series of set speeches from the rostrum, beating against the background of noise throughout the hall. Sometimes members of the convention follow speeches from the rostrum with close attention, and sometimes the give and take of debate between rostrum and floor is closely followed. These occasions comprise a relatively small portion of the total period during which any convention is in session, although they can be of critical importance.

[75] *The Federalist*, No. 58.

During the rest of the time, the only obviously effective forms of deliberation are the small group discussions in which the active members of the convention seem to be continuously involved, on the floor and off.

Small group discussions and delegation deliberations are linked together during a convention through a complex network of informal communication. Most of the time, the leaders and other individuals who need to keep in touch with each other are able to do so; but size and congestion frequently lead to breakdown in communication between them at critical moments. Floor leaders resort to signaling devices. Messages are sent by runners, who may or may not succeed in getting through to their objectives. Even the telephone was pressed into service as a means for communication between floor and rostrum at the conventions in 1956.

The consequences of excessive size are especially apparent in the voting practices of the conventions. Questions are settled as often as possible by taking the "ayes" and "noes," but the voice vote is a hazardous instrument of decision in so large and noisy a meeting. Routine matters and some not so routine are often gaveled through, one after another, with the hall in disorder and no one listening or actually voting. On controversial questions put to vote during the course of debate, a voice vote does in fact occur, but unless the vote is strongly one-sided, including the galleries, the outcome is apt to be in doubt. The chair then decides the issue, subject to an appeal for a roll call which may or may not be obtained, even if desired by the requisite number of delegations.

Roll call votes remain as the recourse when it is essential to obtain a vote that will be accepted as valid. Even these involve special problems in achieving accuracy—when some delegations have fractional votes, when the issue put to vote is unclear, and when the hall is in disorder. All of these conditions have repeatedly occurred in Democratic conventions, with the result that the votes as eventually announced were in some instances undoubtedly incorrect, although not so incorrect as to change the outcome.[76] Even in the recent Republican conventions, smaller in size, with no fractional votes, and on the whole somewhat more orderly, the process of securing an accurate roll call vote remains a difficult one. Many delegations have their own internal troubles in securing an accurate vote to report. Delegation polling occurs frequently, with argument over which alternates are replacing which absent delegates. All of the problems are magnified by size and noise, and in some cases disproportionately.

All of the various categories of individuals who participate in the total complex of convention activity have some personal or institutional reason for being present. Probably all contribute in some degree to the operations of the nominating process and of the party system. The work of the conventions involves so many people so directly that it would be difficult indeed to prevent these gatherings from taking on massive size.

Admitting all this, it would seem that in 1952 both conventions were so big as to be pushing close to the limits of operational feasibility, in part because of the new pressures for television working space and the intensity of popular interest in that year. At the Democratic convention of 1956 the problems of massive size were rather clearly out of hand. Hence it would seem that both parties need to give thought to all of the various means by which they might clarify the various classes of representation at the conventions, while improving the internal structure of the convention as a working organization. Many suggestions could be made, of which perhaps four proposals may merit mention here:

Authorize each delegation to appoint from three to five delegation consultants, to be seated with the delegation on the floor of the convention.

Return the Democratic convention to a

[76] See, for example, David, Moos, and Goldman, op. cit., Vol. 1, pp. 143, 148.

delegate strength no larger than its recently authorized voting strength by eliminating all provision for delegates carrying only a fractional vote.

Eliminate all provision for alternates except as replacements for delegates-elect who fail to appear at the convention, and who are thereupon replaced for the duration of the convention.

Allocate to the states the space previously required for seating the alternates to be used for official visitors, under control of the delegations through their chairmen.

The reasons for these suggestions are probably self-evident. In regard to the first proposal, however, it should be noted that while much of the pressure for delegation enlargement comes from state politicos who are seeking places, mere enlargement of authorized quotas does not necessarily have the effect of including the persons who are most likely to be needed for actual advice when questions arise. An open provision for delegation consultants would seem more likely to have this effect, since it avoids the complications of state primary laws and other limitations on slate-making that apply to the voting members of a delegation. As to the third suggestion—the complete elimination of alternates who are not actually replacing delegates—it is submitted that the surplus alternates are for the most part supernumerary visitors and observers from the state. But the formal selection machinery for alternates, especially when they must be elected in the primaries, generally fails to assemble the visitors who could be most useful to the delegation and to the state.

In each national party, there seems to be a growing discrepancy between the necessities of long-term institutional integrity and survival, on the one hand, and on the other the pressure of expediency and short-range gains, with dangerous over-expansion as the result. The forces of expediency have many arguments at their disposal: the importance of the campaign-rally function of the conventions; the desirability of involving as many active party workers and con-

tributors as possible; the usefulness of having ample patronage available in the form of convention seats for distribution to the faithful; the desirability of compromising state party fights by taking both factions to the convention and having both of them seated; and no doubt others.

But there are limits, presumably, beyond which the practical operation of the conventions cannot be impaired without endangering institutional success or even survival. In recent decades the Republican party has clearly done a better job in protecting the integrity of its central party institutions than the Democratic, where the actions in preparation for the 1956 convention were in especially flagrant disregard of practical needs. But in neither party is the record good enough to deserve commendation.

Most political institutions that survive and become long-lived develop their own core of elder statesmen who guard the institutional traditions. It is the function of such men to remind those of shorter memories of what will be sacrificed if concessions are made to the expediency of the moment. By such means a degree of equilibrium may be maintained; without it, survival becomes doubtful.

The conventions are especially in need of this kind of service in view of their complexity, short duration, and characteristic intermittency. They have indeed benefited greatly from a core of presiding officers, parliamentarians, and sergeants at arms, many of whom have occupied these critical posts successively in as many as three or four conventions after an earlier career of regular convention attendance. But the parties do not seem to have developed the kind of farsighted leadership that was responsible for stabilizing the size of the House of Representatives at 435 members and holding it at that level for nearly half a century. More of this kind of leadership would seem to be needed in the future if the conventions are to continue to perform their present functions and to endure as permanent features in the American political system.

10

Presidential Primary Systems and Their Effects

AS REPRESENTATIVE institutions, the party conventions raise the classic issues, theoretical and practical, on the relationship between a representative and his constituents. Is the delegate a mere agent, carrying a mandate of detailed instructions to which he is firmly committed in advance? Or is he supposed to embody the conscience of a certain constituency, with a mandate to exercise his judgment in accordance with his own view of his constituents' best interests? Or, if he finds himself in a minority position, at what point, if any, does it become permissible or obligatory to submerge the desires of his constituents, and possibly his own, for the sake of the unity of the whole body?

All of these issues were apparent in the early years of the national conventions, but they took on a new and sharper form with the invention of the presidential primaries. The primaries originated in an effort to bring the presidential nominating process under the fullest measure of popular control. Carried to its conclusion, the impulse behind certain types of primary would have turned the party conventions into rubber-stamp devices as mechanical as the electoral college.

Presidential primaries have been shaped in response to many conflicting motivations as they evolved. They still have the effect of binding many delegates with specific mandates for convention voting, but they also have other effects. It is possible to suspect that their indirect and even unintended effects may be more important in placing bounds on convention action than the results that are most overt and conspicuous. In any event, if the nominating process as a whole in its present form is to be understood, some effort must be made to understand the effects of the primaries. They add greatly to the complexity of the process, even though primaries were held in only nineteen states in 1956.

Part of the reason for this complicating effect is the fact that, at one time or another and in one place or another, primaries have embodied almost all known theories for mandating a representative—even to the frequent inclusion of inconsistent theories in the same statute. Hence, although the present chapter is concerned primarily with the evolution, operation, and present status of the presidential primary laws, it seems desirable to begin with some exploration of the theory of mandates and its applications to the presidential nominating process.

The Nature of Mandates and Delegate Commitments

Mandates are the instructions, express or implied, that are given by an authoritative constituency to its chosen representative. Some mandates are affirmative in content, others take the character of a veto. But basically the term "mandate" refers to the obligations laid on a representative by his relationship to his constituents. Those obligations, however, must be understood and weighed with full regard for how clearly they may have been expressed by the constituency and accepted by the representative.

A mandate may be express or implied. In

the presidential nominating process, express mandates often take the form of resolutions adopted in a state party convention or of statutory instructions arising out of a presidential preference primary. Implied mandates, on the other hand, may be read into the situation in which a would-be delegate has made known informally his presidential preference while campaigning for a place on a delegation, or even has run as a known "conservative" or "liberal." If elected, the delegate can treat his electoral success as an implied mandate to stand by his previously indicated preference. Whether express or implied, mandates are relatively easy to interpret—so long as the situation to which they apply remains unchanged. After a change, such as an unexpectedly poor showing by the preferred candidate or a shift in his position on some important issue, the mandate is often either voided or made difficult to interpret.

A mandate is affirmative when it directs the delegate to seek a specific goal. A candidate for delegate in California, for example, is required by law to declare his presidential preference and to pledge his support for that preference, if elected, to the best of his judgment and ability. A mandate is negative when it directs the delegate to take an attitude of firm opposition in the convention, such as voting to the end *against* a particularly unacceptable candidate or measure. In 1948 the Democratic state convention of Mississippi imposed a clearly negative mandate when it instructed its delegates to withdraw from the national convention "unless they secure an unbroken and complete assurance that the Party and its nominees for President and Vice President will fight against the wilful invasion of States' rights as urged by President Truman in his Civil Rights message to the Congress."[1]

A mandate may be definite and specific or broad and general. In the national conventions, delegates must act on a considerable variety of questions, not all of which can

[1] DNC, *Proceedings*, 1948, pp. 102-04.

be clearly seen in advance; constituencies obviously cannot instruct their representatives ahead of time on all the possible decisions that may have to be made. But the presidential nominating act has a special pre-eminence as the main feature of convention business, and here specific instructions are common. On any other subject definite mandates are infrequent. When they do occur they indicate the high priority that the constituency is placing on the issue in question. Southern delegations in recent years have repeatedly arrived at Democratic national conventions with overriding instructions on the issues of civil rights. There have been other historic occasions on which great popular issues have produced mandates that dominated convention proceedings.

Mandates also vary in the degree to which they may be considered valid or invalid. In any ultimate sense, no mandate is valid unless it represents an intentional act of informed judgment by the constituency and clearly conveys that judgment to the representative. Mandates may be binding in a purely legal sense without meeting either of these tests. One of the important faults of certain types of presidential primary is the frequency with which they seem to give more or less accidental mandates that are legally binding, but that do not necessarily represent an informed constituency judgment or may even be inconsistent with it.

Historical Evolution of Legislative Mandates

The idea of the mandate is an ancient one. It has been much debated throughout the history of representative institutions, so much so that there is almost no aspect of the problem as it arises in connection with the party conventions that has not been previously considered in some other context. The experience in other times and places may not all be relevant to the peculiar situation of the political convention, but it would seem impossible to disregard that experience without examining it at least briefly.

Theories of strict representation were common in the early days of European parliaments and their prototypes. The Spanish Cortes of the Middle Ages, for example, had what was known as the "imperative mandate." But an opposite doctrine, emphasizing the representative's duty to the whole nation and the incompatibility of following instructions from the individual constituencies, was proclaimed in the French revolutionary assembly of 1789. Throughout the nineteenth century European liberal thought leaned heavily in the direction of a principle of "free" representation—freedom, that is, from the specific instructions of particular constituencies.

A similar evolution occurred in British parliamentary institutions. The House of Commons was originally regarded as a group of loyal subjects assembled to petition the Crown on behalf of local interests. The members were thought of as "delegates," bound to their constituents by firm instructions wherever feasible. This concept, moreover, was stated in increasingly rigid terms during the seventeenth century as the doctrine of the radical Puritans, the "Levellers." They believed that the constitution should restrict the powers of the representatives rather than the powers of the people; that any position of power ought to be elective; that the popular majority was the best indicator of the will of the people; that a representative ought to follow the instructions of his constituents; and that representatives should therefore be subject to frequent election and to the referendum and recall. These doctrines, brought to America by some of the earliest colonists, were of great importance during the formative years of the republic, were central to the Populist thought of the late nineteenth century, and are still widely held.

In England, however, representatives of the landed nobility and of the commercial classes were busily engaged throughout the eighteenth century in developing a legisla-

tive oligarchy acting through the ministers of the Cabinet. Their object was to challenge the Crown as the chief spokesman and interpreter of the national will. It was in this vein that Edmund Burke addressed the voters of Bristol in 1774, when he spoke of Parliament as "a deliberative assembly of *one* nation, with *one* interest, that of the whole." He opposed the tide of radicalism that had taken up the Levellers' conception of strict instructions. He favored the idea of *virtual* representation in these words:

It ought to be the happiness and glory of a representative, to live in the strictest union, the closest correspondence, and the most unreserved communication with his constituents. . . . To deliver an opinion, is the right of all men; that of constituents is a weighty and respectable opinion, which a representative ought always to rejoice to hear; and which he ought always most seriously to consider. But *authoritative* instructions; *mandates* issued, which the member is bound blindly and implicitly to obey, to vote and argue for, though contrary to the clearest conviction of his judgment and conscience; these are things utterly unknown to the laws of this land, and which arise from a fundamental mistake of the whole order and tenour of our constitution.[2]

The Burkian principle was of great importance during the nineteenth-century evolution of British parliamentary institutions. Similar principles were advocated in America, but never obtained so dominant a place. In fact, several of the early state constitutions, including that of West Virginia as late as 1872, contained provisions looking to the direct instruction of members of the legislature. Jefferson, Madison, and Hamilton debated the issue during the formative years of the federal government, with Jefferson on the side of the Levellers and Madison and Hamilton opposed. In the First Congress, a proposal to include the right to instruct as one of the provisions in the proposed Bill of Rights was voted down 41 to 10.[3] Federalist theory from the first held to the principle of virtual representation for members of the House of Representatives.

[2] "Speech to the Electors of Bristol" (1774), in Edmund Burke, *Works*, Vol. 2, p. 12.
[3] Alfred de Grazia, *Public and Republic* (1951), pp. 99, 123.

Senators, however, were considered the ambassadors of the states whose legislatures had elected them; for several decades, the right of the state legislatures to instruct was generally recognized and frequently used. Eventually the Whig party opposed the doctrine of instruction for senators, and it gradually fell into disuse.

By the end of the nineteenth century, political organizations and pressure groups were affecting the theory of legislative representation. Members of legislative bodies seemed to have been freed from the direct instructions of their constituencies only to surrender their personal judgment to other and more unsuitable masters. As the twentieth century opened, public resentment was rising against the "machines" and the "interests." The primary election, the initiative, the referendum, and the recall came into vogue as devices for the restoration of a measure of direct democracy. After trial, all of these devices were found somewhat wanting; and the present status of the legislator's relationship to his constituency is not easily summarized.

The modern legislator evidently lives in a pluralistic universe in which the implied or overt mandates of his political party, of his own faction within the party, of the interest groups that may defeat him if he defies them, and of the constituency that he represents—all may press upon him at once. In the end he has to make his own decisions on what mandate, if any, to follow; and there seems to be a general hope that he will be guided by conscience, good judgment, and a sound view of the national interest. But the Puritan theory of strict representation, with the corollary that the constituency should hold meetings to adopt specific instructions, seems in legislative matters to be about as far removed from the present era as the imperative mandate of the Spanish Cortes. It is still present in the attitude of many state parties toward their delegates to their national convention.[4]

[4] Much of the previous discussion is based upon the previously cited work by Alfred de Grazia, which is in some ways the most generally useful study of

Precedents of the Electoral College

While the problem of mandates and of representation has been debated mainly in connection with legislatures, it arises in many other situations, among them constitutional conventions and the elections of executives—Presidents, governors, or mayors. For present purposes, the analogies and precedents of the electoral college have a special importance.

The electoral college was not originally intended as an instrument of direct democracy. It was designed as an institution for the *virtual* representation of the people in the choice of a President. As Alexander Hamilton put it:

. . . a small number of persons, selected by their fellow citizens from the general mass, will be most likely to possess the information and discernment requisite to so complicated an investigation.[5]

The Constitution did not specify which "fellow citizens" would choose the requisite "small number of persons," but it was generally assumed that they, like the senators, would be elected by the state legislatures. But even in 1792 five of the fifteen states chose all their presidential electors in popular elections. By 1828 all but two of the then twenty-four states were doing so.[6]

The theory of virtual representation in the electoral college, with the electors exercising their personal judgment, was a dead letter from the first. There was an early period of confusion in the vice-presidential part of the voting, which made necessary the Twelfth Amendment of the Constitution. But the first two groups of electors were clearly intended to elect George Washington to the Presidency; and by the time

the theory and history of representation for Americans; see also, in the *Encyclopaedia of the Social Sciences*, the articles "Constituency," by William Seal Carpenter, and "Representation," by Francis W. Coker and Carlton C. Rodee; and Alice M. Holden, "The Imperative Mandate in the Spanish Cortes of the Middle Ages," *American Political Science Review*, Vol. 24 (Nov. 1930), pp. 886-912.

[5] *The Federalist*, No. 68.

[6] U. S. Bureau of the Census, *Historical Statistics of the United States 1789-1945* (1949), pp. 283, 288.

of the third election the party system was well enough established to produce an ordered choice between alternative candidates, with all electors firmly committed in advance.

The only occasion on which presidential electors in any substantial number have used their own judgment was created by the death of Horace Greeley in 1872, after his defeat in the election and before the electoral college had met. The Democratic party was badly disorganized, and the Greeley electors received no authoritative guidance. They scattered their vote among four candidates, with some votes not cast. In 1912, when the Republican vice-presidential candidate, James S. Sherman, died a few days before the election, the Republican national committee named Nicholas Murray Butler to the vacancy. The eight electors of the defeated Republican party accepted their mandate accordingly and eventually cast their ballots for Butler. This type of case, in which the electors might suddenly be called upon to exercise great responsibility in the choice of President or Vice President, has not so far occurred in a winning party.

In 1876 the outcome of the disputed Hayes-Tilden election hung upon a single electoral vote. James Russell Lowell, chosen as a Hayes elector, was urged to resolve the dispute by casting his vote for Tilden. He declined, saying:

In my own judgment I have no choice, and am bound in honor to vote for Hayes, as the people who chose me expected me to do. They did not choose me because they had confidence in my judgment, but because they thought they knew what that judgment would be. If I had told them that I should vote for Tilden, they would never have nominated me. It is a plain question of trust.[7]

Of the many thousands of presidential electors who have cast their ballots since the adoption of the Twelfth Amendment in

[7] Letter to Leslie Stephen in Horace E. Scudder, *James Russell Lowell* (1901), Vol. 2, as cited by Ruth C. Silva, "State Law on the Nomination, Election, and Instruction of Presidential Electors," *American Political Science Review*, Vol. 42 (June 1948), p. 527, footnote 24.

1804, only a few have failed to vote for the presidential candidates to whom it was assumed they were committed, and none of these affected the outcome. State election laws now generally assume a strict mandate binding the electors. This is so much the case that the ballot in about half the states carries, not the electors' names, but only the names of the presidential and vice-presidential candidates to whom the electors are committed. Yet within recent years the Supreme Court has reaffirmed the legal right of the elector to vote as he sees fit.[8] The elector's mandate thus remains essentially a matter of moral obligation, notwithstanding the express provisions of some state laws.[9] If the electors were ever to exer-

[8] *Ray* v. *Blair,* 343 U. S. 154, 214 (1952). In this case, the Court upheld the right of the elector to vote as he saw fit *if elected;* but it also upheld the right of the Democratic state committee of Alabama to require a loyalty pledge of Democratic candidates for elector before placing them on the primary ballot. It was this pledge that was taken, and violated, by the Alabama Democratic elector who failed to vote for Stevenson in 1956.

[9] According to Professor Ruth C. Silva, writing in 1948, "The last time an elector failed to follow his 'instructions' was in 1820, when William Plumer of New Hampshire cast his electoral ballot for Adams and Rush instead of voting for Monroe and Tomkins." *Op. cit.,* p. 527, footnote 24. Writing in 1955, Ralph M. Goldman stated: "Out of the 12,463 votes cast in the electoral college between 1820 and 1952, inclusive, only 5 have been cast contrary to instruction: by 1 New Hampshire elector in 1820 (for Adams instead of Monroe), by 3 New York electors in 1824 (for Clay's opponents), and by 1 Tennessee elector in 1948 (for Thurmond instead of Truman)." See Hearings . . . Committee on the Judiciary, U. S. Senate (1955), *Nomination and Election of President and Vice President,* p. 461. In the 1956 case noted in footnote 8, an Alabama elector cast his vote for Walter B. Jones instead of Adlai E. Stevenson.

A systematic review of presidential election returns, popular and electoral, will turn up a number of cases in which the electoral vote is divided, with some portion inconsistent with the reported popular vote. These cases seem to have resulted, in most instances, from election systems in which the names of all candidates for elector were printed on the ballot and were voted on separately, with minor variations in the vote for different members of the same electoral slate. The Republican party is credited with carrying Maryland in 1904, for example, but actually elected only a single Republican elector, the Democrats winning seven electors in an election reportedly decided by 51 votes. Similar instances happened repeatedly in California before it changed its ballot system. See E. E. Robinson, *The*

cise their constitutional rights on any scale sufficient to affect the outcome of an election, the foundations of the government would be shaken and the movement for electoral college reform would probably become irresistible.[10]

The doctrine of popular election of electors, rigid instructions, and strict representation has thus become so firmly established for the electoral college that in general it results in election of the President by a vote of the people. But the operations of the system are still controversial, and mainly because of another feature, not required by the Constitution, but of early origin. This is the practice of electing the slates of electors on a state-wide, winner-take-all basis. This seemed natural enough when the election was by the state legislature, but the practice was carried over into the many states where the electors were elected by the people. Three states in 1792 provided for the election of electors separately by congressional districts, thus allowing representation for any minority interests that might be strong in particular localities. For about forty years a few states continued this practice, but it

was never popular and eventually disappeared entirely.[11]

The result is that every state usually votes as a unit in the electoral college. The majority sentiment within every state is thus over represented, while the minority sentiment receives no representation at all. This adds to the distortion of the popular vote in the electoral college; there would be some distortion in any event because of other features. The unit voting aspect of the situation is generally held to enhance the importance of the largest states in electoral college voting.[12] Recent attempts to amend the constitutional provisions on election of the President have been largely concentrated on efforts to change this feature of the system.

Relevance of the Analogies

Customs already established in the Congress and the electoral college were powerfully influential in the original formation of the party conventions. Within each party, for example, each state was given the same relative voting strength in the party conventions as in the electoral college, which in turn was the sum of the votes previously allotted to it in the Senate and House.

There were some inescapable differences. Congress and the electoral college were designed to be representative of the national population as a whole. But neither party convention could hope to be representative of more than a part of the population—a part, moreover, that was likely to be inde-

---

Presidential Vote, 1896-1932 (1934), p. 13, footnote, and Tables 2 and 10; W. Dean Burnham, *Presidential Ballots, 1836-1892* (1955), Tables 4 and 6. Robinson and Burnham include notes explaining the discrepancies between popular and electoral votes in some instances but not all. For 1892, see George Harmon Knoles, *The Presidential Campaign and Election of 1892* (1942), p. 229. These sources suggest that at least one of the North Dakota electors voted contrary to his instructions in 1892. A sufficient amount of searching might find other instances that have been overlooked.

[10] Schemes for using the electors in this way have nonetheless been actively debated in southern Democratic circles in recent years. What was said to be a South-wide plan would free the electors of several states from their obligation to a party candidate when the action of the convention in choosing a candidate was displeasing. The basis for the plan was provided in Georgia, Alabama, and South Carolina by legislation under which the ballot would carry merely the lists of presidential electors under their respective party labels, without putting the names of the presidential and vice-presidential candidates on the ballot, presumably leaving the electors subject to instruction by the party authorities in their respective states. See "The Blank Ballot —South's Secret Weapon for 1960," *U. S. News & World Report,* April 11, 1958, pp. 67-69.

[11] Michigan provided for separate district elections of presidential electors in 1891 and split its electoral vote 9 to 5 in 1892. The law was later changed to return to the present system. See Silva, *op. cit.,* p. 526, footnote 21.

As noted in our footnote 9, a state may divide its electoral vote even when all electors are elected by state-wide vote, if electors are voted on individually. This is the result of minor amounts of split-ticket voting or of failure by some voters to mark their ballots completely. At least ten states have recently permitted split-ticket voting for presidential electors. (*Ibid.,* p. 527.)

[12] It also tends to enhance the apparent popular mandate of the President by generally giving him a much higher per cent of the electoral college "score" than of the actual popular vote.

terminate in size, shifting in composition, and unequally distributed throughout the nation. The conventions also have lacked the public, authoritative character of Congress and the electoral college. Notwithstanding their importance, they are still the product of informal action by loosely constituted, voluntary associations, unregulated and to a large extent unrecognized in federal law. From this point of view they lack the formal legitimacy of the constitutionally established parts of the political system. Yet they have a legitimacy of their own because of their antiquity, the stability of their basic procedures, and their authoritative position in the nominating process.

In view of the pre-eminence of the nominating function, the conventions are obviously closer to the electoral college than to Congress. But there are at least three major differences.

First, the electoral college has been able to operate under a system of strict mandates, in part because it has an escape clause from the deadlock that results when no candidate has a majority: the decision is simply transferred to the House of Representatives. The party conventions do not have this option; if the party is to stay alive, its convention *must* choose, however difficult the choice may be.

Second, even if the electors were to attempt the solution of a deadlock, the fact that they meet separately in the several states would prevent the kind of negotiation that is essential for a final choice when mandates, strictly interpreted, prove unworkable. The conventions were organized to make possible just such negotiation and abandonment of unworkable mandates, and on the assumption that this would be necessary on at least some occasions.

Third, the electoral college has usually been presented with a choice between only two candidates with electoral votes, one of whom was certain to have a majority if all votes were cast. The conventions, whenever the nomination is not a foregone conclusion, usually begin their balloting with sev-

eral candidates; the choice, in fact, may never be clearly limited to two leading candidates, and frequently there are good reasons why it should not be. When two leading candidates do appear, it may also become apparent that if either is nominated the party will be so split as to lose the election. It then becomes necessary, if the party is not to throw away its chance of success, to find a third candidate and nominate him.

For all of these reasons, it would seem likely that strict mandates would often prove unworkable in the party conventions; and this in fact has been the case. In this respect, the party conventions resemble legislatures more than they do the electoral college. Moreover, in addition to the nominations, the conventions take action on other matters much like the action of a legislature.

Evolution toward implied rather than express mandates and toward virtual rather than strict representation may be almost as characteristic of the conventions as of the legislatures. But if the tendency does exist for the conventions, it exists in spite of a widespread desire for popular control and it is mainly caused by the difficulty of imposing such control. The conventions are not unique in this respect. The dilemma is one that has been characteristic of most representative institutions.

Origins of Presidential Primary Laws

Most, but not all, of the elections that have come to be known as presidential primaries involve both the choice of delegates and some opportunity for an expression of preference among presidential candidates. When a primary includes both features, the relationships between them are complex and variable.

The first known occasion on which national convention delegates were elected in a public primary occurred in Florida in 1904, under general legislation empowering party authorities of any recognized political party to hold primary elections. Democratic delegates in that state were thereafter elected in primaries.[13] In 1906, Pennsylvania enacted general legislation on primary elections and provided for the election of district delegates; the provision was disregarded in 1908 but used in 1912.[14]

The first law directed mainly at the election of delegates, however, seems to have been the one enacted in Wisconsin in 1905. It made no provision for any form of presidential preference, but the victory by followers of Senator Robert M. La Follette sent a delegation to the Republican national convention of 1908 with a strong set of implied mandates: they fought hard for the entire Progressive credo in the platform proceedings. In 1910, Oregon enacted a measure providing both for the direct election of all delegates and for taking a presidential preference vote for their guidance. This statute was hailed as part of the Progressive movement of the times. It also provided a formula that was seized upon by the supporters of ex-President Theodore Roosevelt in their campaign to unseat President Taft. The result was a wave of legislation that made it possible to hold some form of presidential primary in fourteen states in 1912.

By 1916 the number of states holding presidential primaries had grown to at least twenty-two.[15] Thereafter the number de-

clined, to around sixteen in the period 1936-1948. Six of the states that had authorized presidential primaries by 1912 or 1916 actually held them for only a few years, thereafter repealing their laws or letting them fall into disuse. In 1956 some form of presidential primary was held in nineteen states, Alaska, and the District of Columbia. Three of these states and Alaska held only preference polls. Two states, Minnesota and Montana, repealed their presidential primary laws in 1959.[16]

Nearly half of the states have never enacted any presidential primary law. The evolution of the laws has thus gone on mainly through the amending process in the states where the movement started. Minor amendments have been common, and several states have made major changes in their laws. But, so far, there has been no apparent tendency toward uniformity as the result of these changes, although studies of state experience may eventually lay the basis for greater uniformity. Meanwhile, the existing laws differ among themselves so much that it has been difficult to develop any satisfactory classification under which to discuss them.

As a first step, however, it seems desirable to distinguish between the systems in which delegate election is the major feature and those that emphasize a presidential preference poll. Even this distinction is not without its difficulties, as will become apparent, but it provides a basis for grouping the state systems for discussion in the two sections that follow.

Delegate Election Systems

Delegates were elected in presidential primaries in sixteen states and the District of Columbia in 1956.[17] In one of these states

---

[13] Manning J. Dauer (with others), "Toward a Model State Presidential Primary Law," *American Political Science Review*, Vol. 50 (March 1956), pp. 138-53, at p. 143. Prior to the publication of this article most authorities were under the impression that the first presidential primary was held in Wisconsin in 1908. On the matter of continuity since 1904, a letter from Professor Dauer (April 3, 1958) cited the *Florida Times Union* (Jacksonville) for May 11, 30, June 27, 1908, April 29, May 10, June 7, 1912, June 6, 1916, and the *Report of the Secretary of State of the State of Florida* (1916), p. 331, and subsequent reports of Florida secretaries of state. Runoff primaries for delegates were held in some cases in 1908 and 1912.

[14] Louise Overacker, *The Presidential Primary* (1926), p. 11.

[15] *Ibid.*, p. 209, for 1912-1924 lists. Florida should be added to these lists on the basis of the previously cited researches by Dauer. Georgia should be added for 1912, 1920, and 1924, and it also held a primary in 1932, in each case only in the Democratic party; see Lynwood M. Holland, *The Direct Primary in Georgia* (1949), pp. 100-10.

[16] See Appendix B for lists of states with primary laws, past or present.

[17] For a brief review of the experience in each of these states and in the others conducting presidential preference polls in 1952 and 1956, see Richard M. Scammon, "The Road to 1960," in *American Government Annual, 1959-60* (1959), pp. 23-43.

—Oregon—the mandate derived from a presidential preference poll. In the systems of the other fifteen and the District of Columbia the delegates obtained their mandates principally through the process by which they were elected; for these systems the authors of this book have concluded that the set of categories below provides the most generally useful classification.

Category One

The earliest form of presidential primary listed the would-be delegates without letting them identify themselves on the ballot as supporters of a particular presidential candidate. This form was used in 1956 in New York, Pennsylvania, Illinois, West Virginia, Alabama, Nebraska, and the District

CATEGORY ONE: Ballot *must not* show the delegate's preference among candidates; delegates *must* run on a "no-preference" basis so far as the ballot is concerned.
In 1956: New York, Pennsylvania, Illinois, West Virginia, Alabama, Nebraska, District of Columbia.

CATEGORY TWO: Ballot *may* show delegate's preference *if* the candidate consents; delegates may also run on a "no-preference" basis.
In 1956: South Dakota, Massachusetts, New Jersey.

CATEGORY THREE: Ballot *may* show delegate's preference, whether or not the candidate consents; delegates may also run on a "no-preference" basis.
In 1956: New Hampshire, Florida.

CATEGORY FOUR: Ballot *must* show delegate's preference for a candidate who has given consent; delegates *must not* run on a "no-preference" basis.
In 1956: California, Ohio, Wisconsin, Minnesota.

The main differences among these four types of primary are in the extent to which the delegates are permitted or required to run as supporters of a specific candidate, and the extent to which leading candidates are permitted and encouraged to take a hand in the primaries. The types also differ in the amount of information given the voter who may wish to express a choice between presidential candidates, and in how strong a mandate the voting imposes on the chosen delegate.[18]

[18] The categories can be tested for completeness as a classification system by using the method of dichotomous division, dividing first in terms of whether the delegate does or does not have discretion in securing association on the ballot with a preferred candidate. If he has discretion, it may be subject to exercise either with or without the candidate's consent. If he does not have discretion, he may be required either to associate (in turn, with or without consent) or not to associate. Five categories thus result: may with, may without, must with, must without, must not. The four numbered categories in the text include all of these except "must without" —a category that does not exist in practice, but that might have strong appeal for a state in search of a system that would assure strict mandating, strong

of Columbia. (For details of the primary laws in these states, see Appendix C, Category One.) In Pennsylvania, Illinois, West Virginia, and Nebraska there was also a

representation, and wide-open competition in preconvention campaigning.

Despite the self-evident plausibility of the categories, they were not discovered until after several years of intermittent consideration of the problem. While working on the 1952 survey of delegate selection, for example, two of the present authors were involved in an attempt at a new classification of presidential primaries. This was developed in a paper presented at the 1953 meeting of the American Political Science Association. It was a step in the direction of the present classification, but met with no more than a lukewarm reception, perhaps because of the failure to achieve homologous criteria for differentiating the categories. For lack of anything better, however, the same approach, somewhat simplified, was followed in the survey report. (David, Moos, and Goldman, *Presidential Nominating Politics in 1952*, Vol. 1, pp. 173-86.) The present classification produces similar groupings of state systems in most instances, but differs in associating the South Dakota system with the Massachusetts and New Jersey systems and the Ohio system with California's and Wisconsin's. This occurs in each case despite differences that are conspicuous but relatively unimportant in their effects on critical aspects of system behavior.

preference poll in which presidential candidates could be entered. This poll had somewhat more importance in Nebraska than in the other three states, but in none of them did it provide a mandate that the delegates felt bound to observe. When delegate voting at the conventions coincides with the outcome of the preference poll, as it often does, it also seems probable that the winner of the poll was a candidate who had been encouraged to appear on the ballot in the state because he already had the support of the party organization and the prospective delegates. For all six states and the District of Columbia, the more important mandates appear to be those implied by the process through which the delegates were elected.

In New York, Pennsylvania, and Illinois, the party organizations usually nominate the candidates for district delegate, and these candidates are frequently elected in their respective districts without a contest. When contests do occur, they reflect local factionalism more often than any relation to national candidates. This does not mean, however, that these delegates arrive at the conventions with no mandate. They mainly derive their mandates from their party organization or factional connections, which means that in some cases they arrive at the conventions firmly committed to a candidate, while in others they are firmly occupying a position of noncommitment.[19] In general, these delegates have the same kind of implied mandate that is normally attached to an elected representative who has won without making binding commitments to his constituents, but who owes his election to a political party or faction in a competitive situation.

Delegates at large are named directly by the party organizations in these three states —in New York and Pennsylvania by the state committees, in Illinois through state conventions. They include political figures of some note, drawn mainly from the offi-

[19] They are subject, in other words, to nonstatutory processes of instruction of the kind discussed in Chapter 11, with reference mainly to delegates elected in state party conventions.

cial party hierarchy but also including governors, senators, and big-city mayors. Groups so composed frequently include supporters of more than one presidential candidate, since they may give representation to divergent elements in the leadership of the state party.

In Alabama, West Virginia, and Nebraska, the party organizations are relatively much weaker and have less control over delegate selection in the primaries. Contests are the rule in most districts and often occur state-wide for the seats at large, but the delegates win their places mainly as the result of personal and factional influences. The result is that the delegate is largely on his own with no express mandate.

In the District of Columbia in 1956 the unofficial making of slates and distribution of sample ballots served to identify the would-be delegates and gave an opportunity for campaigning on behalf of the presidential candidates. The slate-making activity also provided an early opportunity for delegation leadership to emerge and become identified. The total result in the Democratic primary amounted to a clear and specific mandate in favor of Stevenson.

By contrast, similar opportunities have rarely been used in West Virginia, Alabama, or Nebraska, and not very often in New York, Pennsylvania, or Illinois, presumably for lack of sufficient incentives to undertake the amount of state-wide campaign organization and slate-making activity that would be involved.

Category Two

In South Dakota, Massachusetts, and New Jersey in 1956 would-be delegates could run on a "no-preference" basis, or they could show a candidate preference on the ballot if the candidate gave his consent. (See Appendix C, Category Two.) The South Dakota primary was like California's and unlike that of any other state in the fact that all delegates were elected at large; but the distinction made little difference in

South Dakota, since it had only two congressional districts. The South Dakota ballot was also simpler than that of Massachusetts or New Jersey, since delegates were not voted on individually.

The chief differences between the systems of the three states are clearly the result of differing public and party organization attitudes. Contests between delegations supporting leading national candidates have been more welcome in South Dakota than in Massachusetts or New Jersey and have occurred more frequently. In the latter states, the systems have operated most of the time like those of Pennsylvania and Illinois, although providing greater opportunities for national candidates and their avowed supporters when they are willing to enter a direct contest for delegate votes in the state. In all three states, delegation commitment to a stand-in or favorite son candidate has been rare. The use of the device is never imperative under their systems, since a "no-preference" ballot is permissible, and none of the states has been very productive of favorite sons who were serious contenders for a presidential nomination.

Massachusetts and New Jersey, unlike South Dakota, have each provided a renewed opportunity for a separate presidential preference vote in recent years. The Massachusetts system for this purpose consists solely of providing designated blank spaces on the ballot in which the voter may "insert" his choice of a presidential candidate for his designated political party. No candidate names appear on this part of the ballot, and there is no problem therefore of filing dates, petitions, and candidate consent. There is also no problem in assessing the relative merits of write-in votes by comparison with votes for a named candidate. The insertion of the voter's choice may be either by write-in, with enough clarity to show intent regardless of spelling, or by applying a sticker carrying the preferred candidate's name. Under the sticker system, Eisenhower was a two and one half to one choice over Taft in Massachusetts in 1952.

New Jersey's preference poll requires

entering the candidates, but the system is relatively simple; names may be entered without the candidate's consent but do not go on the ballot if he objects. Eisenhower, Taft, and Stassen were rivals in the Republican poll of 1952, with Eisenhower a heavy winner.

The preference polls result in the possibility of dual mandates that are inconsistent with each other. An instance of this occurred in New Jersey in 1956: Senator Estes Kefauver was entered in the preference poll, which he won against write-in votes for Adlai E. Stevenson, but only one member of a full slate of Kefauver-identified delegates was elected in a contest with a regular-organization, uncommitted slate headed by Governor Robert B. Meyner. This type of outcome is less probable under the Massachusetts system, where the preference poll can operate independently of candidate filing. In both states the party organizations seem disposed to tolerate the preference polls only because they are purely advisory.

In practice, a delegation from any of the three states has usually carried no more of an express mandate than a New York delegation. Less often, there has been an express mandate resulting from the election of delegates who have indicated their presidential preference on the ballot with the candidate's consent. Such delegations are clearly committed but are not required by law to be pledged in any formal sense. In some instances, what is technically a "no-preference" delegation may be equally committed. The implied mandate of the "no-preference" Eisenhower delegation from Massachusetts in 1952 was clearly as strong as the express mandate of the ballot-identified Taft delegation from South Dakota in the same year. In each case there had been a contest with a clearly defined victory.

Category Three

In 1952 and 1956, New Hampshire, Florida, and Oregon permitted would-be delegates to identify their preferred presidential candidate on the ballot without his consent. Oregon also provided for a separate presidential preference poll which committed the delegates without regard to their stated preference, a feature of such peculiar moment that Oregon is separately discussed in the section on mandatory preference polls. In past years New Jersey and Wisconsin also had the Category Three type of primary. (See Appendix C, Category Three, for details of the systems in New Hampshire and Florida, and for the past experience of New Jersey and Wisconsin.)

The experience of these states indicates that, when would-be delegates can freely identify their candidate preference on the ballot, popular preferences can usually be given effective expression through the delegate elections. This was in general the case in Florida in 1952 and in Wisconsin and New Hampshire over a long period of years —even though in these cases every delegate had to be voted on individually on a long ballot, with rotation of the names of would-be delegates and no segregation of slates on the basis of candidate preferences.[20] The main limitation arose from the fact that, with the New Hampshire and Wisconsin primaries coming so early in the year, would-be delegates often had trouble finding out whether their preferred candidate would be available. But where delegates were elected on a preference basis they were given a clear mandate to proceed with the execution of their stated intentions at the convention if this course of action proved feasible.

The Florida system effective in 1956 greatly simplified the task of the voter. By requiring every would-be delegate to be-

come a member of an organized slate in order to get on the ballot, by increasing the visibility of the relationship between slates and their preferred candidates, and by concentrating the attention of the voter upon the candidates, the system became a more powerful instrument for popular choice— and also one that was capable of putting greater pressure on the serious candidates to come into the state and campaign. Stevenson apparently found it impossible to escape going to Florida in 1956, though he tried to stay out of the New Hampshire primary and did no campaigning in that state. But the Florida primary of 1956 differed only in degree from that in New Hampshire, and the earlier ones in Wisconsin and Florida, in the pressures on the candidates and the opportunities offered the voters. The Dewey-Willkie and Dewey-Stassen contests in Wisconsin in 1944 and 1948 and the Kefauver-Russell contest in Florida in 1952 went far to prove this point.

Category Four

This category included four states in 1956, California, Ohio, Wisconsin and Minnesota (as described in detail in Appendix C, Category Four). Minnesota repealed its law in 1959 and went back to the party convention system of selecting delegates.

In their formal aspects, the four mandating systems of these states differed distinctly. California required delegates to pledge themselves in writing to support their candidate to the best of their judgment and ability. Ohio exacted no written pledge. Wisconsin and Minnesota both required written pledges that delegates would vote for their candidate, unless released, on the first ballot and thereafter until the candidate's vote dropped below 10 per cent of the total convention vote. The more pertinent fact, however, seems to be that under all four systems in actual operation, would-be delegates were obliged to have the approval of a presidential candidate in order to get on the ballot.

In its origins, this aspect of the systems

---

[20] In such cases, the candidates for delegate at large were carried in one section of the ballot, the candidates for delegate from the particular district in another. The long-ballot aspect of the problem applied particularly to the delegates at large; in Florida in 1952, for example, thirty-two candidates were running for eight seats at large (David, Moos, and Goldman, *op. cit.*, Vol. 3, p. 136). When electing half-vote delegates in the districts, however, with four seats to fill, any contest would normally involve considerable numbers of candidates for the district seats.

was rarely the result of any single or clearly thought-out logic; conflicting motivations and accidental factors had much to do with it. In Ohio, where the system was frozen in this form before 1916, the demand that delegates invariably declare their candidate preferences on the ballot was presumably inspired by theories of Progressivism. The further requirement that the delegates secure the written consent of the candidates may have been suggested by party organization people who wished to discourage mavericks and irresponsibles from running for delegate. Initially it may have been assumed that any serious candidate would readily give consent.

California's system was formed by decisions over a period of years. The major influences leading to the elimination of "uninstructed" delegations were probably progressive in intent, but it also seems to have been taken for granted from the first that delegations favoring a candidate should not be permitted to run without the candidate's tacit approval; the requirement for written approval merely formalized the previous relationship. In Wisconsin the change to a requirement for consent was promoted by the supporters of a willing candidate, Harold E. Stassen, who had been alarmed by the near success in 1948 of a slate of volunteers who sought to draft General Douglas MacArthur.[21] In Minnesota the legislature intended to permit delegate slates to use the name of a preferred candidate without his consent, but then wrote further provisions attempting to limit the candidate's right to withdraw; these were thrown out by the state attorney general and the courts.[22] Thus, in the end, the candidate's consent became a requirement.

In any event, as the systems have actually operated in all four states, would-be delegates, for lack of a serious candidate willing to enter the primary, were often forced to run under the name of a mere stand-in or undistinguished favorite son, who often

[21] David, Moos, and Goldman, op. cit., Vol. 4, p. 130.
[22] Ibid., pp. 162-63.

won with little or no opposition. Under such circumstances, delegates so elected were unlikely to take their statutory mandate seriously; a mandate validly reflecting the views of the party voters had not been produced. They voted for their ostensible candidate at the convention only when it was strategically desirable to do so on early ballots, as a holding operation pending clarification of the situation. Often, however, they voted for one of the serious candidates on the first ballot.

Delegations pledged to favorite son candidates with enough strength to merit national attention are another matter. Such delegations, even when elected without a contest, take their mandate seriously and rarely leave their candidates until definitely released.

The mandate becomes even stronger under these systems when the successful delegation is elected after a sharp contest in which it has defeated a favorite son, the party organization, or an opposing candidate of national stature. In these cases, the would-be delegates and their candidate have usually campaigned together in the state and have risked their fortunes together at the polls. Whatever the situation at the convention, delegations of this kind usually stay with their candidate to the bitter end, and sometimes even after being released. The California Champ Clark delegation of 1912, still voting almost solidly for their candidate on the forty-sixth ballot, was an example. The California delegation of 1932, elected by a plurality in a three-cornered race, was another, staying with Speaker John N. Garner until released under terms of the trade that put Garner into the Vice Presidency.

Systems of this kind have obviously favored the entry of favorite son and stand-in candidates, while rarely placing more than one of the serious national contestants before the party voters. For the future, however, it should be noted that these systems may be peculiarly susceptible to the effects of new styles of national campaigning. Willing candidates who are prepared to enter a state even if they have to challenge a favorite son can find substantial opportunities in these systems. Harold Stassen and Estes Kefauver have each demonstrated the point, sometimes to the discomfiture of the favorite sons and party organization concerned. Moreover, when an aggressive candidate is seeking to enter all available primaries, other serious candidates may have little choice except to do likewise. State party organizations may also have to look for a candidate of national stature who can win in their state, when they find that an organization slate backing a nonentity can no longer keep other candidates out of the state. California, especially, may be too much of a prize to be allowed to lock up its convention strength very often behind a favorite son without a challenge, unless he has genuine national strength.

Comparative Analysis

Within these major categories of primary election systems each state has its own peculiarities with their special effects, but it still is possible to describe types of system behavior that are characteristic of each category. The similarities within categories are recapitulated below; for the differences, see the comparative analyses of state systems in Appendix C.

CATEGORY ONE. Where, as in New York for example, the would-be delegates are not allowed to state a candidate preference on the ballot, they rarely campaign in the primary as supporters of a preferred candidate. The candidates, in turn, rarely take any direct part in the formation of delegate slates or in their campaigns for election. The voters are seldom given a choice between presidential candidates, although often permitted to choose between would-be delegates on the basis of factional alignments or personal characteristics.

Such mandates as may be created through this process are implied rather than express, general rather than specific. To the extent that they do become specific, they are apt to be negative—delegates know that certain candidates would not be acceptable to their constituency, but usually have considerable freedom of choice among acceptable alternatives.

Mandates that are both specific and affirmative are sometimes given through these systems when the organizing impulse is strong enough, but they are not encouraged or especially facilitated. On the other hand, mandates that are specific but invalid are seldom produced.

CATEGORY TWO. Where, as in Massachusetts, the would-be delegates are allowed to name a preferred candidate on the ballot, but only with his consent, "no-preference" delegations are frequently elected without a contest or with only scattered opposition. This may occur even when a lively contest is in prospect at the convention: if the state party organization prefers to send an uncommitted delegation with freedom to maneuver; if dissident factions see little reason to expect success with a contesting slate; if out-of-state candidates prefer to avoid being involved. In such cases, these systems operate in much the same way as those in Category One.

Under other conditions, however, the systems in Category Two can offer a focused contest between opposing slates and candidates. When thus challenged, even an ostensibly "no-preference" slate is likely to publicize its candidate preferences in the effort to attract votes. The voters are then given a meaningful choice, and the resulting mandates, even if only implied, are likely to be affirmative and specific. They are also likely to be executed with considerable vigor at the conventions.

CATEGORY THREE. Where, as in Florida or New Hampshire, the would-be delegates are allowed to name their preferred candidate on the ballot without his consent, "no-preference" delegations have sometimes run and been elected, when candidate availabilities were not clear at the time of filing, or when the choice among available candidates was viewed with apathy in the state. Under other conditions, these systems have usually resulted in the election of delegations that had previously announced their choice and carried it on the ballot. Such delegations when favoring the renomination of an incumbent President have often been elected without a contest. In open nominating situations, however, the primaries are usually contested, and would-be delegates have been strongly impelled to seek association with a popular candidate who will help them win. Candidates have been permitted and encouraged to campaign in these primaries. No initiatives have been required of candidates who were reluctant or unwilling—though even some of these have been handed the fruits of victory. In critical years, the voters have usually been offered a meaningful choice. The resulting mandates have been express, affirmative, and specific, have given effect to popular preferences in the state, and have been executed at the conventions almost without exception.

CATEGORY FOUR. Where, as in California, the would-be delegates are required to name a preferred candidate on the ballot and are further required to obtain his consent, it is customary for slates that would otherwise run on a "no-preference" basis to run in the name of a favorite son or stand-in. Frequently these slates are elected. In some instances this results in a formal mandate of limited validity that is nonetheless followed at the convention. In other instances the formal mandate is so patently invalid that it is disregarded, and the delegation is practically as free as one elected on a "no-preference" ballot under other systems.

Serious candidates who might enter a state have on the whole been even more reluctant to challenge a favorite son slate than an organization-sponsored "no-preference" slate. A paradoxical result has therefore been achieved. Where the law requires the would-be delegate to find a candidate who will lend his name, it is particularly hard to persuade any genuine candidate of national importance to enter the state.

But when any of the serious candidates have been willing to lend their names for a contest in one of these states they have also usually been willing to campaign actively in the state, and contests of considerable importance have resulted. In these contests the voters have been given a somewhat meaningful choice, but a less complete range of alternatives than they might have had if candidate consent had not been required for every slate. When not all the principal candidates are on the ballot, the validity of the resulting mandates is open to question. Such mandates have sometimes been executed at the conventions with more rigidity than seemed warranted under the circumstances.

THE INFLUENCE OF OTHER FACTORS. Despite the similarities of pattern within each of the four categories, the total experience also suggests that other recurring factors have been influential. Three of these merit special attention.

The relative strength of party organization in the state and party concerned is important in assessing how any of these systems has operated in the past and is likely to operate in the future. It also has much to do with the kind of system that can come into existence and survive in a particular state. Party organizations apparently fear the divisive effects of vigorous primary campaigns, and, whatever the system, a strong organization will usually seek to discourage any state-wide mobilization of opposing slates in support of nationally important candidates. The systems of Category One seem to serve best from this point of view, while those of Two and Four are tolerated because of the opportunities they provide for achieving the same objective. Systems of Category Three have rarely survived where state party organization was strong, a fact that seems to be more than mere coincidence.

The size of a state also has an effect on

the type of primary, if any. Party organization seems more likely to be strong in the larger states, which are also the ones most likely to produce favorite son candidates of real strength. The larger states are thus more difficult than others for out-of-state candidates to enter. The systems of Category Four, for example, seemed to produce contests involving out-of-state candidates more often in smaller Minnesota and Wisconsin than in larger California and Ohio.

Finally, styles of campaigning of the various candidates have had different effects in the different types of systems. Candidates who are anxious to stay on good terms with state party organizations and their favorite sons adopt one style of campaigning. Those who are willing to challenge state organizations or favorite sons or both adopt a different style. If the latter type of candidate were to become more usual, marked changes would probably occur in the typical behavior patterns of Categories Two and Four, where candidate consent is required for the use of his name by would-be delegates. Organized contests between the supporters of different candidates might become more common even in the states of Category One, especially where the party organizations are relatively weak.

Presidential Preference Polls and Their Effects

The term "presidential preference poll" is used to denote a vote on the candidates, separate from the election of delegates. It is not customary, for example, to refer to the California or Wisconsin primary election as a preference poll, even though the voting in these states is concerned almost entirely with candidates for presidential nominations, to whose names favoring slates of delegates are attached for election.

In terms of the intent of the statutes creating them, the preference polls may be either advisory or compulsory in the resulting mandates. In either case, the delegates for whose guidance the mandates are provided may be elected in public primaries or may be chosen by the party organization, usually in a state convention.

Advisory Preference Polls

Seven of the states in which delegates are elected in primaries—New Hampshire, Massachusetts, New Jersey, Pennsylvania, West Virginia, Illinois, and Nebraska—also have preference polls that are treated as advisory.

In the early fervor of 1912, it seems to have been widely assumed that the outcome of any preference poll would control the delegates from the state, at least in the early stages of voting at the conventions, and regardless of how the delegates were selected. Disillusionment followed. The distinction between polls that are admitted to be merely advisory and those that are intended to be mandatory has been gradually clarified in law and practice.[23]

The validity of the advice given by any poll depends mainly on whether the voters have had a chance to express themselves on the candidates who are likely to be voted upon at the convention. This in turn may depend upon whether candidates can be entered in the poll without their consent, whether they remain on the ballot if they object, and whether voters may write in the name of a candidate not on the ballot. Write-in opportunities are generally provided in advisory polls, but they create the

[23] Alaska has provided the only recent example of a preference poll that was merely advisory while leaving delegate selection to party conventions. Under a statute adopted in 1955, such a poll was conducted in 1956. Eisenhower defeated Knowland on the Republican side, and Stevenson defeated Kefauver on the Democratic.

According to George Sundborg, administrative assistant to Senator Ernest Gruening (responding to an inquiry on June 24, 1959), the first session of the Alaska state legislature changed the date of the general primary election from April to September. This change will also apply to the presidential primary and will have the effect of making it inoperative in 1960 even if the provision for such a primary is not repealed. But Sundborg anticipated that the repeal would occur when the legislature next met—in January 1960.

problem of weighing the importance of the write-in votes in comparison with votes for candidates whose names are on the ballot. As noted, this problem is avoided in Massachusetts, where no names of presidential candidates appear on the ballot and a sticker system is available for inserting names.

Advisory polls always create the possibility of conflicting mandates: one expressed by the poll and the other expressed or implied through the process of delegate selection. The mandates provided by the advisory polls may still be useful, but only if the poll itself so clearly expresses an informed popular judgment that it has to be treated with respect. In the period of nearly fifty years since these polls were invented this clear result has been achieved only rarely in any state. As a rule the advisory polls have not been effective, either as a means of measuring popular sentiment or of mandating the delegates.[24]

Mandatory Preference Polls

In four states—Oregon, Maryland, Indiana, and Montana—polls were in effect in 1956 that attempted specifically to control the action of the delegates. (See Appendix D for details of the polls.) The delegates were elected separately in the primary in

[24] The advisory preference polls can be compared with advisory referenda on proposed legislation. In a study of such referenda, it was found that they hold some promise as a means for educating the voters on public matters and for improving the communication between the electorate and its representatives. But it was further concluded that "as a device for authoritative popular participation in public policy-making upon a non-legislating basis, the usefulness of the advisory referendum has yet to be demonstrated fully." See Ralph M. Goldman, "The Advisory Referendum in America," *Public Opinion Quarterly*, Vol. 14 (Summer 1950), pp. 303-15.

The advisory polls on presidential candidates have also probably contributed more to voter education and the formation of public opinion than to authoritative decision-making. In the voting on legislative issues, however, a full array of alternatives can be submitted to the voters, without having to obtain consent from one or more of the alternatives. The preference polls on candidates are presumably as defective for education as for decision-making when the array of alternative candidates presented to the voters is conspicuously incomplete.

Oregon, in party conventions in the other three states. Montana repealed its law in 1959, thus abandoning the attempt to instruct delegates through a preference poll.

Oregon has revised its presidential primary laws repeatedly, and has gone farther than any other state in attempting to find means for the expression of the popular will. By various devices it has sought to secure the presence on the ballot of all of the principal candidates, whether they are willing or not, and has made the outcome binding on the delegates who were elected in the same primary. Maryland, Indiana, and Montana adopted the form of mandatory instructing primary that is least onerous from the point of view of the party organizations, since delegate selection was left to the party conventions.

Even so, the four states had in common in 1956 the fact that their systems had the possibility of giving instructions to delegates who might be not only indifferent, but even actually opposed to the mandate they were receiving. This is the natural consequence of the separation of delegate selection from the mandating process. In such cases, delegates disliking their mandates have often sabotaged their ostensible candidates on procedural votes even while dutifully voting for them on the first and other early nominating ballots. This characteristic behavior of reluctant delegates was obvious in the earliest days of the primary system and was still observable in 1952 and 1956.

Open vs. Closed Primaries

Presidential primaries, like other primary elections, are usually open only to the registered voters of the political party concerned. Some states, however, notably Wisconsin and Minnesota, have had what is known as the "open primary," in which there is no requirement for party registration and the voter can vote in the primary of either party (but not both) whenever a primary election is held.

Systems of this type frequently lead to statements that the primary of one party has been invaded by voters who belong in the other party, for the alleged purpose of nominating the candidate who would be easiest to beat. An alternative explanation also usually offered for such voter migration is that voters who are dissatisfied with their traditional party sometimes move into the primary of the other party to support the kind of nominee they want, and will then vote for him in the general election if he is in fact nominated, whether or not they have any serious intention of changing their party affiliation permanently. Some students have concluded that the latter type of explanation is more often correct than the former, at least in ordinary types of primary elections.[25]

In Wisconsin in 1952 there was some evidence of Democrats moving into the Republican presidential primary in support of Warren against Taft.[26] Much more important accusations followed the Minnesota primary of 1956, in which Kefauver defeated Stevenson for most of the Democratic delegation at a time when there was no important contest on the Republican side. Stevenson campaign leaders promptly charged Republican collusion, by which 125,000 voters had crossed party lines to stop the strongest Democratic candidate. Independent observers later assessed the evidence as indicating both a substantial bona fide Republican farm vote for Kefauver and a considerable Republican crossover in other areas that appeared to be deliberately intended to confuse the issue within the Democratic party. In the absence of the crossover, it was thought, Stevenson would have won the primary by about a 55 to 45 per cent vote.[27] All of these circumstances

were widely discussed in Minnesota and undoubtedly had their part in discrediting the primary law, which was repealed in 1959.

Presidential primaries that produce a focused race between candidates for a presidential nomination seem especially hazardous when conducted on an "open" basis. When an exciting contest is going on in one party, voters of the other party may become almost as much involved emotionally as the voters of the party directly concerned. Secondly, cases of this kind are most likely to occur when the contest in one party is far more important than that in the other, or when one party has no contest at all, as often happens in presidential politics. The voters of one party can then migrate into the presidential primary of the other with impunity, and may have strong incentives to do so. This suggests that states that insist on an open primary for other purposes might better refrain from attempting the more complex types of presidential primary, as Minnesota has now done by repealing its law.

The Problem of Plurality Voting

Presidential primary elections have been settled almost without exception on the basis of plurality voting: the leading delegate candidate, delegate slate, or presidential candidate has been declared the winner without regard to whether he polled an actual majority. So far as is known, there has been no provision for a runoff type of election in any presidential primary system, except for delegate elections in Florida under an early statute since amended. The only known experimentation with any form

[25] V. O. Key, Jr., *Politics, Parties, and Pressure Groups* (4th ed., 1958), p. 428.

[26] David, Moos, and Goldman, *op. cit.*, Vol. 4, p. 138.

[27] Stevenson for President Committee (New York State), press releases of March 21, 1956, comments of Thomas K. Finletter; *Washington Post and Times Herald*, March 25, 1956, using some of this material; text of broadcast by Eric Sevareid, May 3, 1956, mimeo, as issued by CBS, in which Sevareid referred

to studies by "one of the most reputable statistical research organizations in the country" (unnamed); Doris Fleeson, *New York Post*, May 8, 1958, in which it was reported that, at a private dinner attended mainly by Republicans, John (Tex) McCrary made a speech in the course of which he referred to the persons present who had raised the money to get Kefauver nominated over Stevenson in the Minnesota primary.

of preferential voting was tried only once, in Oregon in 1912.[28]

Elections that can be won by a plurality always run the risk of producing a minority choice, if there are three or more alternatives, as happens often in nominating contests. Plurality voting would present serious national hazards if types of presidential primary were to become widespread under which the delegates were committed to a definite choice before they arrived at the convention. But even in the present diverse and chaotic system of primaries, plurality voting has substantial capabilities for the production of unsatisfactory electoral mandates.

One example was provided by the Republican side of the Oregon primary in 1920. The ballot carried four strong candidates, who split the vote as follows: Hiram W. Johnson, 38 per cent; Leonard Wood, 37 per cent; Frank O. Lowden, 13 per cent; Herbert Hoover, 12 per cent. The whole delegation was thereby legally committed to Johnson, but it gave him only limited support at the convention. In another example, the California Democrats in 1932 divided their vote as follows: John Nance Garner, 41 per cent; Franklin D. Roosevelt, 33 per cent; Alfred E. Smith, 26 per cent. The delegation was thereby committed to Garner, but eventually swung to Roosevelt after one of the most publicized deals in convention history. The Wisconsin statewide Republican vote in 1948 divided approximately as follows: Harold E. Stassen, 40 per cent; Douglas MacArthur, 36 per cent; Thomas E. Dewey, 24 per cent.[29] In 1952, also in Wisconsin but after revision of its law, the state-wide Republican vote divided as follows: Robert A. Taft, 41 per

cent; Earl Warren, 34 per cent; Harold E. Stassen, 22 per cent; others, 3 per cent. Taft thereby won all the delegates at large, as Stassen had in 1948, and won fourteen of the district delegates against Warren's six.

In each of these cases a runoff primary might have produced a different outcome, possibly even replacing the plurality leader with the candidate who had previously run second. In any event, a runoff would have had the effect of putting the outcome on a majority basis, thereby clarifying the mandate and increasing its validity as an expression of voter choice.

Time, expense, and added complication will no doubt continue to militate against any frequent provision for runoff primaries in this field. The problem could probably be solved, however—at the expense of creating some other problems—by adopting some form of either proportional representation or preferential voting with a transferable vote.

Proportional Representation

The application of proportional representation in this field was suggested by R. S. Boots in 1920.[30] Mr. Boots proposed that, in each state, there be a simple contest between the candidates for the presidential nomination of each party, with no election of delegates; when the election returns were in, each candidate would be permitted to select as many members of the state delegation as he would be entitled to on the basis of his proportion of the state-wide vote in the primary. In a somewhat more complicated form, the same idea appears in the draft outline of a model state presidential primary law, circulated since January 1955 as one of a set of tentative election laws issued for criticism by Richard S. Childs, of the National Municipal League.[31]

Under Mr. Childs' proposal, the state party committee in each state would file a

[28] Overacker, *op. cit.*, pp. 55-56.
[29] In each case the ballot carried seven would-be delegates at large who were identified as preferring the named candidate. The average vote of the Stassen delegates, who all won, was approximately 228,000; of the MacArthur delegates, 203,000; of the Dewey delegates, 137,000. The top MacArthur delegate came within about 3,000 votes of defeating the bottom Stassen delegate. Of the twenty district delegates, Stassen won twelve and MacArthur eight. This was the last election before revision of the statute to require candidate consent before a slate using his name could be entered; see Appendix C.

[30] Boots, "The Presidential Primary," *National Municipal Review Supplement*, Sept. 1920, as cited by Louise Overacker, *op. cit.*, pp. 190-91.
[31] Nine pages, mimeo., free, 47 East 68th Street, New York 21. For a brief published description, see also Richard S. Childs, "The Model State Presidential Primary Law," *Women Lawyers Journal*, Vol. 41 (April 1955), pp. 9-10.

slate of "uninstructed" delegates, whose respective allegiances to presidential aspirants could be freely avowed or withheld, as they chose, but would not appear on the ballot. Any aspirant for the presidential nomination would also be authorized to file a slate of proposed delegates; if there was no challenge of the organization slate by any such aspirant, no primary would be held. In the event a slate was filed by each of one or more aspirants, the several slates would appear on the ballot under their appropriate labels, each slate consisting of a numbered list. Delegates would then be elected at large from the state in the numbered order as far down each list as justified by the proportion of the total vote cast for the list. Major features of this plan were incorporated in a draft bill prepared for possible enactment in Nevada.[32]

This method of electing a state delegation would presumably give accurate representation to the degree of popularity generated by each candidate among the party voters. In a year of contest among several candidates, it would also automatically divide each delegation into several clearly identified groups. Each of these groups would largely consist of persons with a heavy commitment to their candidate, these being the ones most likely to be given a place at the top of his delegate list. Presumably their loyalties would be mainly to their candidate, rather than to the entire party following in their state, and collectively they would form blocs extending throughout the convention and cutting across the state delegations. Convention behavior under such conditions would be difficult to predict, but the potentialities both for deadlock and for an unsatisfactory type of compromise choice would seem to be so great as to make the plan dangerous.

The Alternative Vote

Preferential voting with a transferable vote, one form of which is frequently known as the alternative vote, is often considered a type akin to proportional representation, but it can also be developed as an instrument for achieving a majority choice in a geographically defined constituency. This has been the case since 1919 in elections for the Australian House of Representatives, where the members are elected from single-member constituencies similar to the congressional districts of this country. The ballot often carries as many as three candidates for each seat, not infrequently five or six. The voter marks his ballot by indicating his order of preference among all the candidates: he is required to put a number, 1, 2, 3, etc., against *each* name on the ballot, thus making an exhaustive choice and indicating the candidate he likes least as well as the one he prefers most.

When the ballots are counted, any candidate who receives an absolute majority of first preference votes is thereupon declared elected. If no candidate has a first preference majority, the lowest ranking candidate is eliminated and his ballots are redistributed in accordance with their indicated second choice. This procedure is repeated as long as necessary until a candidate is found with a valid majority; he is often the plurality leader on the first count, but this does not always happen. In the Australian election of 1943, for example, second or even third preferences were counted in about half the districts, and the original plurality leader was defeated in seven of the thirty-two districts where it was necessary to go beyond the first preference count.[33]

[32] Nevada Legislative Council Bureau, "A Study of the Presidential Primary," *Bulletin No. 32*, Dec. 1958. See especially p. 83.

[33] Louise Overacker, *The Australian Party System* (1952), pp. 28-29, and see pp. 221-22, 280, 304-5. See also Clarence G. Hoag and George H. Hallett. *Proportional Representation* (1926), pp. 19-20, 480-85; Harold F. Gosnell, *Democracy—The Threshold of Freedom* (1948), pp. 167-70, 302-04.
For a special study of an election in which second and third preferences became important, see Henry Mayer and Joan Rydon, *The Gwdiyr By-Election* (Canberra, Australian National University, 1954).
The system just described is usually known in Australia as "preferential voting with an exhaustive choice"; in Britain, it is frequently referred to simply as "the alternative vote." American writers have referred to it as the single-member system with alternative vote or as the single transferable vote system of majority preferential voting, and in other ways. The insistence upon an exhaustive choice if the voter's ballot is to be valid is what distinguishes the Australian system from the type of preferential

This type of preferential voting with an exhaustive choice was favored in Australia as a compromise between plurality elections in single-member constituencies, on the one hand, and proportional representation from multi-member constituencies, on the other. It is probably not as favorable as proportional representation for the development of a stable multi-party system; but neither is it as favorable to a two-party system as plurality elections. The preferential system was adopted in Australia as the outcome of a bargain whereby minority interests made common cause against the Australian Labor Party, which they then jointly defeated in the election of 1919. The system seems to be partly responsible for the success with which a coalition of two parties has since been able to survive and frequently win as the opposition to the Labor Party.[34]

Comparative Analysis

For those who prefer a two-party system in the nation at large, plurality decisions in the general election can be defended because of their presumed long-range effects in the elimination of third parties. But plurality decisions in primary elections, by the same reasoning, would tend to keep each party split into two warring factions. This may be thought desirable in a one-party state, and it has been speculated that plur-

ality decisions in the primaries do have that effect.[35] But when a state already has the advantage of a relative balance between two major parties, such as has generally prevailed in the national party system, there is no apparent reason why electoral institutions should be designed to foster bifactionalism within each of those parties, or to restrict the choice within the party to only two candidates.

The requirement of an absolute majority in the national convention, where only one candidate can win, produces its own pressures in the direction of bifactionalism—all the more reason for trying to establish offsetting pressures in the activities that occur before the convention. Paradoxical as it may appear, the conclusion seems plausible that preferential voting like that used in Australia could advantageously be used in the primaries for exactly the reasons for not adopting it in general elections: to foster a loose, multiple, and shifting factionalism inside the parties, while seeking to maintain a sharp, focused, and persistent competition between two parties in each state and in the nation.[36]

[35] Duverger, *op. cit.,* pp. 219-20; V. O. Key, Jr., *Southern Politics in State and Nation* (1949), pp. 416-23.

[36] In the above analysis, it is not intended to imply that the form of an electoral system is inevitably controlling of the structure of party and factional interests and the nature of the competition between them. What is implied and is believed by the present authors is that the electoral system exerts a continuing influence that tends to move the larger party system in a determinate direction, although other and sometimes more powerful influences may also be at work that tend to push in other directions. There is doubtless merit in the view that schemes of proportional representation have been the product of a multi-party system more often than a multi-party system has been produced by a pre-existing system of proportional representation. See, for example, John G. Grumm, "Theories of Electoral Systems," *Midwest Journal of Political Science,* Vol. 2 (Nov. 1958), pp. 357-76. Grumm produces considerable evidence in support of the thesis just stated, and then begins his final paragraph by stating, "Of course, it should not be inferred from any of the foregoing that the electoral systems have *no* effects on party systems."

For a strongly argued statement of the disintegrating effects of proportional representation and the integrating effects of majority representation, see Ferdinand A. Hermens, *The Representative Republic* (1958), pp. 163-69, 201-10, 465-78. His discussion of the experience in India is especially striking.

voting tried and discarded in some American cities; with an exhaustive choice, an absolute majority will inevitably result for some one candidate.

[34] Cf. Overacker, *op. cit.*; Maurice Duverger, *Political Parties* (1954), pp. 217-18.

The results of the Australian election of November 1958 are analyzed by George Howatt in "Australia Elects Senate by P.R.," *National Civic Review,* Vol. 48 (March 1959), pp. 144-48. In the elections for the House of Representatives, the Labor party polled 42.8 per cent of the vote and won 36.9 per cent of the seats; the Liberal and Country parties together polled 46.4 per cent of the vote and won 63.1 per cent of the seats; a splinter party known as the Democratic Labor party polled 9.6 per cent of the vote and won no seats at all; others polled 1.2 per cent of the vote and won no seats. In the elections for the Senate, with a form of proportional representation at work, a similar split in the popular vote gave the Labor party fifteen seats, the Liberal and Country parties sixteen seats, and the splinter party one seat. This was apparently considered a commendable outcome by the author of the article.

Applied to the situation of the state primaries that frequently produce a clear contest between several presidential candidates, preferential voting with an exhaustive choice could be used state-wide in the election of slates of delegates at large, and it could be used in each district to elect the delegates from that district. It would be necessary to centralize the counting of the ballots in each congressional district, in order to manage the redistribution of the ballots of each low man until district and state-wide majorities were attained, and other complications would doubtless arise. But the use of such a voting plan would greatly reduce the danger of victory by cohesive minority interests in situations where the majority point of view had developed several strong candidates.

Situations of this kind may happen often in primary campaigning, judging by the examples cited earlier and by other evidence. It may not be an important problem as long as only a few states maintain primaries that seem to encourage contests between three or more candidates and their supporting slates of delegates. Adopted on a national scale, however, any such type of primary could lead to a minority choice, with disastrous results for the party concerned, if not for the nation. If the voting plans that would avoid this risk also seem undesirable—or at least unduly complicated—the New York type of primary for unpledged district delegates and the state convention system of delegate election may each hold somewhat greater merit as alternatives than has been generally realized.

Effects of the Primaries on Participants

The various forms of presidential primary were intended to provide opportunities for voter control of the presidential nominating process. But while the primaries affect most notably the fortunes of the presidential candidates, they affect other classes of participants as well, including the would-be delegates, the party organizations,

and the state governments. All of these interests have been considered to some extent in the legislative processes by which the primary laws were passed. Much of the variation in the laws undoubtedly represents differing conceptions of the treatment to which the several classes of participants were considered to be entitled. It may therefore be worth while to look again at how the primaries have in practice affected the interests of the participants.

Presidential Candidates: Actual and Potential

Several different types of presidential candidates may be separately considered: Presidents who are available to succeed themselves, out-party titular leaders if available, other willing candidates, and other potential candidates.

THE PRESIDENT. Many of the primary elections initiated in 1912 had the immediate purpose of pulling down an incumbent first-term President, William Howard Taft. Presidents Taft and Herbert Hoover both ran badly in the primaries that occurred toward the end of their respective first terms, and conceivably they each might have been denied renomination if certain types of primary system had been more widespread. President Coolidge, on the other hand, was a beneficiary of the primaries in 1924; he entered and won most of those that were available, demonstrating his popular appeal at a time when he was not entirely confident of organization support. In 1940, President Roosevelt's waiting tactics on a third-term nomination were assisted by a series of primary victories. President Truman's record also was impressive in the primaries of 1948.

The party organizations generally assume that a first-term President will be available to succeed himself; they usually enter him in the available primaries unless he objects, and expect to use the primaries as part of the mechanism for beating down dissident candidates and party factionalism. For Presidents who find their political support in a massive popular following, the primaries can be helpful in solidifying a second-term nomination. But to the extent that the primaries are instruments of the popular will, they can harass an unpopular President.

OUT-PARTY TITULAR LEADERS. The experience of the titular leaders in seeking renomination was reviewed in Chapter 5. Alfred E. Smith was indecisive in preparing for the primaries in 1932, but finally permitted use of his name in several. The results were mixed but not sufficiently adverse to end his candidacy before the convention. In 1944, however, Wendell Willkie's candidacy was ended in the primaries after he had actively campaigned in an effort to develop and demonstrate popular strength. In 1948, Thomas E. Dewey prepared for and entered most of the available primaries, other than those pre-empted by favorite sons. After losing to Harold E. Stassen in Wisconsin and Nebraska, he defeated him in Oregon and was able to enter the convention as the favorite. In 1956, when Adlai E. Stevenson announced his candidacy, he indicated that he was reluctant to do extensive primary campaigning. But after losing in New Hampshire and Minnesota, he had to recognize that he could not win at the convention if he suffered further serious defeats in the primaries. With changed tactics and intensified campaigning he gained victories in Oregon, Florida, and California, which did much to win him the nomination.

The accumulated experience tends to suggest that any titular leader who is willing to run should make himself available in any primaries where his presence on the ticket is strongly desired, either by the local party organization or by factional elements capable of putting up an effective slate. This is obviously the rule followed by incumbent Presidents when seeking renomination. Any reluctance shown by a candidate who already occupies the exposed position of titular leadership is likely to be interpreted as a public admission of weakness—one that

will encourage other candidates to contest the nomination and assist their supporters in fund raising for the purpose.

OTHER WILLING CANDIDATES. These include both the candidates who seek the active cooperation of the state organizations and those who prefer or must accept a more independent style of campaigning. Most candidates come in the former category; they usually negotiate carefully to assure a welcome before entering a primary, stay out of contests with favorite sons, and avoid other contests unless the chances of victory are reasonably good.

For such candidates, the distinctions between the different types of primaries are of vital importance in campaign planning. They are apt to avoid delegate contests where would-be delegates are unidentified on the ballot. But in an organized contest between candidate-supporting slates, they may be involved by their local partisans, whether willing or not. Where their consent is required for the use of their names on the ballot, they usually withhold it unless the state party organization either desires their sponsorship for its own slate or is at least prepared to be neutral.

The Florida, New Hampshire, and Oregon systems present special problems for a candidate of this kind. His name can be involved without his consent in an election that he might prefer not to enter. In Florida and New Hampshire, his main protection is the fact that any slate using his name without his authority is under such a handicap that it is not likely to take the risk unless it has high hopes of success or remarkably strong feelings of conviction. In Oregon, not even this protection is available, since the delegates are elected separately from the preference poll by which they are instructed and in which the candidate's name can be entered without his consent. In all three states, a strong candidate is given little chance to escape having his name placed in competition. A strongly affirmative attitude is therefore likely to be the safest course he can adopt. But if defeat seems inevitable because of special conditions in any one of these states, the candidate can disclaim all responsibility, refrain from any form of campaigning, and thereby limit somewhat the effect on his own prestige if he is defeated.

For willing candidates who are prepared to enter any and all primaries, with or without the cooperation of the state party organizations concerned, the Florida, New Hampshire, and Oregon systems are as useful as any others. Candidates of this type, especially such insurgents as Stassen and Kefauver, have attempted to exploit all the available primaries as a means of both developing and demonstrating popular support. Stassen and Kefauver each came to national attention as presidential timber largely because of their striking victories in some of the primaries. In the end, both began to suffer defeats even in the primaries, but they had meanwhile forced the party organizations and the other candidates to take the primaries more seriously.

OTHER POTENTIAL CANDIDATES. The primaries in most states are not designed to bring forward the name of a potential candidate who is available only in response to a genuine draft or who is reluctant or unwilling. A candidate requiring a draft cannot be placed directly on the ballot in California or Ohio, because his specific consent is concerned, and every delegate elected in these states is committed to a named candidate. Such a delegation can help in a draft if it is led by a favorite son who favors the reluctant candidate, but otherwise the general effect is to delay the delegation's support for a draft in the early ballots at the convention. The South Dakota-Massachusetts-New Jersey type of primary is less adverse, since so-called "no-preference" delegations that actually have a preference can run effectively in these states—as demonstrated by the "no-preference" slates for Eisenhower in South Dakota and Massachusetts in 1952. The New York-District of Columbia type is neutral on the point: it does nothing to facilitate reluctant candidacies, but neither does it do anything to prevent them.

The Florida, New Hampshire, and Oregon primaries are exceptional in the extent to which they can be used to promote a reluctant candidate when the situation is appropriate. If the candidacy is merely potential and requires either a draft or a substantial showing of popular support to make it actual—as that of Justice Charles Evans Hughes in 1916 and of General Eisenhower in 1952 before his decision to return from Paris—the Florida and New Hampshire laws permit a slate of favoring delegates to get itself organized and perhaps elected without any action whatever by the candidate. The Oregon law has a similar effect through different mechanisms. The potential candidate has no reason to feel embarrassed by the use of his name, for the would-be delegates and other supporters are merely expressing their own views, not his. The would-be delegates, moreover, are making a substantial investment of effort at considerable risk in organizing a slate and mounting a campaign in a situation full of unpredictable contingencies. In addition to all of the usual possibilities of defeat and the hazards of factional retaliation, there is always the possibility that the preferred candidate may at any time utter a statement of unavailability so positive that it will be taken at face value by the voters, with defeat for the slate as the almost inevitable result.

A somewhat different situation was presented by such candidacies as Dewey's in the early months of 1944 and Stevenson's in 1952. Both men were potential candidates of high availability who could well have had their own reasons in those particular years for preferring not to run until four years later. But partial slates were organized for Dewey in New Hampshire and Wisconsin early in 1944. In each state Dewey withdrew his name from the preference poll and requested would-be delegates not to use it. Nevertheless, the delegate candidates went ahead, with the result that two delegates pledged to Dewey were elected in

New Hampshire, and most of the Dewey slate was elected in Wisconsin, decisively defeating the Willkie delegates. A few weeks later Dewey announced his active candidacy. Something similar might have happened to Stevenson in 1952 if the same type of primary system had been available in the states where he was best known (it was no longer available in Wisconsin), but the situation was complicated by the lateness of Truman's statement of unavailability, Kefauver's campaigning energy, and Stevenson's repeated efforts to discourage his own supporters. No slate openly favoring Stevenson went on the ballot in any state in 1952.

If the Florida, New Hampshire, or Oregon primaries were to be copied more widely, it would still be possible to draft a Hughes or an Eisenhower on occasion. But a general extension of the California-type primary might make it impossible to do so.

Delegates: Actual and Potential

In the absence of a public primary in which delegates are elected, their selection usually falls to the state or district party organizations in one way or another. There may be varying degrees of factional and personal infighting, with or without directly involving the interests of presidential candidates. A public primary usually provides a somewhat greater opportunity for an independent would-be delegate or group to challenge the organization. But the actual consequences depend upon such variations in primary systems as have been previously discussed, the strength of party organization, and the situation of the would-be delegates themselves: whether party regulars or party dissidents, whether heavily committed to a particular candidate or faction, and whether politically or otherwise prominent. The effect of such factors is illustrated in detail in the report on delegate selection in 1952.[37]

One further point of public policy, how-

[37] David, Moos, and Goldman, *op. cit.*

ever, may merit attention here: the consequences of ballot forms that make it possible for an individual delegate to run by himself, compared with those that encourage or require organized slate-making. The first form of ballot is based on the doctrine that the voter should be permitted or required to pick his representatives as individuals and that those desiring to serve as representatives should be encouraged to run independently. In a presidential primary, this results in multiple candidacies for multiple offices. The voter may be required to select twelve or more individuals as delegates at large, out of an alphabetical list of forty or fifty names. On the other hand, where only organized slates may file, no one can become a delegate unless he is willing and able to secure membership in an organized group, constituted on whatever basis is required for getting on the ballot. The first type of system often permits party mavericks to appear on the ballot—and sometimes they are elected—but they are rarely effective at the conventions. The second type produces delegations that are more likely to be unified and cohesive, whether the slates are organized by the party leadership or by a successful factional or candidate organization.

The Massachusetts and New Jersey systems represent a compromise on this issue, since organized slates can be filed and appear together on the ballot, even though delegates must be voted for individually. Other would-be delegates can file without becoming members of slates. The experience in these states indicates that the privilege of running as an individual for delegate at large is worth little in a contest with an organized slate. In district delegate elections, however, where the voter has a more manageable problem of choice, persons of prominence can win when running as individuals.

Party Organizations

The overt effects of presidential primaries on the national party organizations have not been numerous or clearly important

The national conventions of both parties had to adjust their rules in 1912 and 1916 to accommodate to primary laws, as noted in Chapter 9. The weakening of the unit rule in the Democratic party was the most important result.

Whether other and more diffuse effects of the primaries on the national party organizations could be identified is a question. The primaries, in their present state of development at least, do not seem to have deprived the national organizations of any of their functions. The national convention retains its vitality as the nominating authority and as the forum where coalitions are organized for victory in the national election. The impact of the primaries on party organization has so far been felt mainly in the states.

If it is true that deprivation of function leads to atrophy, all the primaries that have transferred the election and instructing of delegates away from the state party organizations have presumably tended to weaken those organizations.[38] But the extent to which this transfer has actually occurred has obviously been extremely variable.

An uncomplicated direct election of district delegates, as in New York, may do little to prevent the effective nomination of the delegates by a strong organization if it exists. On the other hand, where there is no strong organization, a system like that of New York or the District of Columbia will do little to promote one, on behalf of either a candidate or the party.

Wherever would-be delegates can be identified with a candidate on the ballot, the state organizations face the threat of invasion by a Stassen or a Kefauver. A party-splitting fight is likely to be the minimum consequence of such an invastion. If the invasion is successful, the party organizations lose control of delegate selection for the time being unless they have made terms in advance for a compromise with the in-

vader. But the systems that permit use of a candidate's name on the ballot differ considerably in the problems they present to the organizations.

If the delegates *must* be ballot identified, as in California and Ohio, a manipulative type of favorite son politics seems to be encouraged that in most years has almost automatically played into the hands of the organizations. On the other hand, the New Jersey-Massachusetts type systems permit great flexibility of organization strategies in dealing with any external threat, while usually allowing the organization to obtain an uncommitted delegation able to trade freely in the national convention.

The problems under the Florida and New Hampshire systems are somewhat different. The opportunity of the party leaders of the state to send an uncommitted delegation is undoubtedly reduced substantially when a slate favoring a popular candidate can go on the ballot easily without the consent of either the party leaders or the candidate. Under systems of this type the organization has four main options that are likely to be useful.

(1) If it is relatively easy to pick the winner, the organization can pick him first and climb on board the band wagon by committing its own slate and running it on a preference basis.

(2) If the situation is hopelessly confused or all of the available candidates are weak, an organization slate can be run on a "no-preference" basis and probably win.

(3) If the national situation is developing into a contest between two or more strong candidates, the organization can pick its preference, back him strongly with an organization slate, and let the chips fall where they may.

(4) Under some conditions, the organization may be able to run a favorite son slate with success, but the necessary conditions do not seem likely to occur often in states where preference slates can easily secure access to the ballot. What the organization cannot do with much hope of success is run a "no-preference" slate when one or more

[38] For a development of this theory in regard to primaries in general, see V. O. Key, Jr., *American State Politics: An Introduction* (1956), pp. 130-32, 167-68, 169-96, 287-89.

strong candidates are certain to have their slates on the ballot.

A successful invasion by an out-of-state candidate may set off a conflict that divides friend from friend within the party organization, leaving it seriously weakened both for the purposes of state politics and for the oncoming presidential campaign after the nomination has been made. This seems to be the basic reason why the party organizations in such states as New York, Pennsylvania, Massachusetts, New Jersey, and Illinois all tend to favor systems that limit the possibilities for organizing sharply divisive contests between candidates within the state. The organizations in these states have a strong interest in their own internal cohesion because of the rigors of the interparty competition. They can claim with some justice that a primary that gives maximum popular control may tend to weaken the party and is therefore not desirable in any state where there is a strongly competitive two-party system.

This line of argument is largely irrelevant in all the states where one party or the other is dominant, although a party faction within such a state may be equally reluctant to see its own position compromised by a conflict between out-of-state candidates for a presidential nomination. In general, however, in many states where state-wide party organization is weak, it has not been the opposition of the organizations that prevented the introduction of effective presidential primaries. More often it has been a combination of inertia, the possible cost of a separate presidential primary, and a variety of opposing factional interests, not all of them necessarily rational. It might well be that in some of these states the adoption of a Florida-type statute would lead to a more organized politics than has prevailed in the past—and might even contribute to the development of more effective party organizations.

As a final point on the type of law used in Florida in 1956 and for a much longer period in New Hampshire, by comparison with all those where the candidate's consent is required for the use of his name on the ballot, it should be noted that the pressure for including consent features in the laws of various states has almost certainly come much more from the party organizations than from the candidates and their friends. Candidates are sometimes outraged when they discover that they can be subjected to the risks of a state campaign without their consent. Candidates in general, however, have rarely been effectively represented at the legislative sessions where state primary laws were being adopted, and when such representation has actually occurred, it has been on the part of the more eager candidates rather than those who might want the right to forbid the use of their names. The party organizations, on the other hand, have undoubtedly been aware that to require the candidate's consent usually has the effect of requiring the state organization's consent—since a prudent candidate is apt to be unwilling to enter a state where the organization does not welcome him. This is probably the real reason that, in all of those states where the candidate's consent is required, the selection offered the voters has typically been so unsatisfactory.

State Governments

Legislators, governors, attorneys general, and state election officials, with an occasional assist from the judiciary, are the elements of the state governments that have an active part in adopting and administering presidential primary laws. These authorities tend to be responsive to party organization attitudes, but also on occasion to candidate interests and to voter opinion. The state governments thus tend to reflect a composite of many interests in varying proportions. But some degree of special interest of their own may arise from two facts often overlooked: expense and trouble are involved in the holding of every public election; and, on the other hand, state elections concerned with national issues can attract attention and enhance the state's public reputation in the nation at large.

The average state or local expense involved in holding a separate presidential rimary was estimated at between seventy-ive cents and a dollar a vote at a time when rice levels were markedly lower than at resent.[39] Iowa repealed its early statute fter a single use in 1916 in which an election involving no contest between presidential candidates in either party, and not nany contests between would-be delegates, ad cost the state approximately $130,000.[40] Presidential primaries held in the spring in onjunction with other primary elections re much less expensive and usually draw a greater turnout; but many of the states hold heir regular primaries for state offices in August and September. This timing provides a shorter campaigning period between rimary and general election, but it is too ate for the election of delegates to party onventions held in July or August. In 1956 ight states that do not hold presidential rimaries could conveniently have done so n connection with other elections: New Mexico (May 8), North Carolina (May 26), Iowa (June 4), South Carolina (June 12), Maine (June 18), North Dakota (June 26), Oklahoma (July 3), and Virginia (July 10).[41] States that have become habituated to the holding of separate presidential primaries absorb the expense with little objection rom anyone and consider it well justified, but the expense seems to be a significant deterrent to the adoption of primary legislation in states that do not have it.

States with primaries that attract leading candidates for active local campaigning inevitably become centers of national attention. New Hampshire is wedded to its primary because of the conspicuous role it gives the state; not only is it the first in the series of all state primaries, but it has often involved an exciting contest. In 1952, the New Hampshire primary's finest year, not only did an Eisenhower slate defeat Taft and Stassen slates, but Estes Kefauver handed a stinging defeat to the adherents of President Truman. Minnesota revived its primary in 1952, also in March, partly, it would seem, for the purpose of competing with New Hampshire for national attention—an effort that was remarkably successful in 1952 and 1956. Oregon has long enjoyed the attention attracted by its primary, which is strategic in part because it is one of the last as well as one of those most likely to produce a contest. Motivations of this sort help to sustain the primaries that foster contests, and may lead to changes in some of the states that have other types of primary.

Voters in Relation to Other Participants

From a voter point of view, the primaries are usually assumed to be most effective when they produce a colorful contest. Undoubtedly, if there is to be any visible and direct voter control, there must be at least occasionally a contest. But contests, and voter control as well, are likely to be welcomed only in moderation, if at all, by candidates, would-be delegates, party organizations, and state governments. Moreover, the voters themselves, as loyal party members, often share the interests of these other participants in the avoidance of unnecessary contests, in stabilizing the party leadership for appropriate periods of time, and in maintaining the cohesion and vitality of their party as it faces its enemy in the general election.

Functional Effectiveness

This whole chapter has been concerned with what is essentially a functional analysis, conducted mainly from a voter point of view, but also from other points of view.

[39] Louise Overacker, *The Presidential Primary*, (1926), p. 147.
In Nevada, the cost of the regular primary held n 1956 was an average of $1.39 per vote, ranging between $0.77 and $3.34 in the various counties. Nevada Legislative Council Bureau, "A Study of the Presidential Primary," *Bulletin No. 32*, Dec. 1958, p. 69.
[40] Overacker, *op. cit.*, pp. 149, 228-29.
[41] Seven other states without presidential primaries actually held regular primaries before the conventions met in 1956, but at dates so close to the convention as to be inconvenient for the selection of delegates; and, of course, the conventions were unusually late in 1956. In 1952 both conventions were held in July.

This final section turns to a summary of the previous analysis in terms of the functional effectiveness of major systems and provisions.

Many specific features of existing primary systems can be identified as self-defeating. Some of the basic types are more effective than others, but there appears to be a rather broad range of effectiveness within which what is lost from one point of view may be gained from another. Within this range, the total effects of the various systems involve so many imponderables that any final assessment of net comparative advantage is not easy to make.

Ineffective Systems and Provisions

All of the systems that are built on preference polls, separated from delegate election, appear to be gravely deficient in terms of performing their own ostensible functions. They are fundamentally incapable of assuring that the elected delegates will be in sympathy with whatever mandate is provided through the preference poll. Any form of separate preference poll also tends to distract the attention of voters and other participants from the processes by which delegates are elected—although it is the delegates who will vote in the convention, with or without heeding any mandate coming from sources outside their own election.

The purely advisory polls produce unrepresentative results so frequently that they seem inherently undesirable. In a contest where the outcome is purely advisory, no one can be sure that victory would be worth the amount of effort required to win it—even if the voters may have actually been given a choice between two or more genuine candidates. Hence the indecision and erratic impulses that typically characterize both the filing for the advisory polls and the organization of campaigns to make a showing. In an era when so many other devices for measuring opinion are available, official preference polls that are merely advisory and generally incomplete would seem unnecessary in any event. Their elimination would remove an element of confusion in a process that will remain sufficiently complex.

Preference polls that attempt to give a compulsory mandate to delegates elected through some other procedure sometimes depend upon candidate consent and sometimes not. Where consent is required, this type of primary frequently fails to operate at all and often produces an unrepresentative mandate when it does operate. Where consent is not required, the resulting mandate is more likely to be representative and it is therefore more likely to be treated with respect by the delegates. But such systems have substantial elements of unfairness for candidates who find themselves on the ballot without their consent. Typically, the candidates are threatened with the risk of defeat without being effectively assured of the fruits of victory if they win.

In Oregon the relative success of the system, in terms of the respect the delegates have accorded its mandates, seems to be due to the somewhat unusual political traditions of the state. But the state's own purposes would probably be served better by the New Hampshire or Florida type of primary which is about what Oregon would have if it were to abolish its mandatory preference poll while retaining its other provisions for delegate election. The Maryland and Indiana systems, in which delegates are chosen by party conventions, represent compromises between the forces favoring and those opposing some more effective type of system. In these instances, the forces favoring a primary were given an instrument so defective because of the general reluctance of candidates to enter, that they might better have preferred no primary at all.

Among the principal categories of delegate election systems, those of Category Four, permitting would-be delegates to run only under the name of a candidate who gives consent, appear to be inherently ineffective—at least by comparison with other readily available systems. This type of system prevails in California, Ohio, and Wisconsin. The purpose of the primary is often frustrated by the unwillingness of potential leading candidates to enter it. When this occurs, the delegates may be precluded from obtaining, and the voters from giving, the only specific mandate that would be of any value in the circumstances. An invalid mandate is then given because the system requires a specific mandate.

The other source of ineffectiveness in these systems is the prohibition against running on a "no-preference" basis. This prohibition is especially unrealistic when slates must be organized in January or February of the presidential year, when important future candidates are not yet running. Systems of this kind, however, are worse than unrealistic. They work specifically against the development of representative mandates by fostering a tradition of favorite son and stand-in candidacies. The result is that other candidates of national stature are influenced to stay away from such states even when they are actively running in other parts of the country. On the other hand, in states where "no-preference" slates are permitted to run in competition with preference slates, the record seems to show no noteworthy abuses and it is almost entirely uncluttered with stand-ins or undistinguished favorite son candidates. The attempt to compel would-be delegates to declare a preference when they have not yet had any fair chance to form one, or when they can be refused permission to specify their actual preference by the candidate himself, has been a failure and merits repeal.

Effective Systems and Provisions

Categories One, Two, and Three would all appear to be basically effective—at least if stripped of the extraneous advisory preference polls that clutter them in some cases. They differ in the types of mandate that they provide, but in no case do they present serious hazards of confusing the voters, offering one-sided choices, or formalizing mandates that are inherently invalid.

The most successful type of system for developing valid popular mandates and making them effective is that of Category Three, found in New Hampshire and Florida, in which delegates can identify their candidate preferences on the ballot without obtaining consent. In several respects, the Florida statute is the most advanced of the existing presidential primary laws. It goes far to satisfy the various interests of voters, candidates, would-be delegates, party organizations, and state governments.

The voters are given the possibility of a campaign in the state in any open nominating situation, followed by an opportunity to vote a meaningful choice on a short ballot. The candidates are given a mechanism by which a maximum of responsibility is placed upon their supporters in the state who wish to organize a campaign and win places as delegates. The would-be delegates are compelled to work within a framework of organized effort in which casual individuals running as mavericks are ruled out; and in return they form an organized slate and are given a relationship to each other and to their candidate, if they have one, that is superior for campaigning purposes. Moreover, if they win they go to the convention as an experienced and well-knit team. The party organizations are offered a system that recognizes the need for organizing effort of the kind in which they are supposed to be proficient; although some of the alternatives previously open to them are eliminated, new opportunities are created. The state governments are given a type of election to administer that is almost immune to frivolous candidacies, while readily open to genuine candidates who find support in the state, with an uncluttered ballot and a vote that is easy to count—a type of election that should do credit to any state.

The intermediate systems of South Dakota, Massachusetts, and New Jersey, in Category Two, where delegates may identify their preferred candidate on the ballot if they wish to do so and are able to obtain consent, are functional in a different way. They avoid the difficulties of the California system because slates can be run on a "no-preference" basis. This feature also makes it largely unnecessary to determine whether the requirement of candidate consent is a good or bad feature in these systems. From the point of view of the voters, the requirement does not necessarily keep them from having realistic alternatives for choice in critical years. From the point of view of the party organizations, the requirement is useful in giving them greater control over slate-making and good relationships with out-of-state candidates who may seriously consider campaigning in the state.

The Category One systems of New York and other states for the direct election of delegates unidentified with a candidate are of value in still a different way. By comparison with the situation in two thirds of the states, where there is no public election of delegates, these systems bring in those aspects of legitimacy that under the American political system seem to be recognized only in public elections. Not only have the elected delegates incurred all the obligations involved in a public election, but, in particular, their relationship to a defined constituency of party voters has been made manifest, with many consequences, including the fact that no unit rule can bind the state delegation. The system as a whole is consonant with the nature of the party conventions as representative institutions; there is no statutory attempt to provide express mandates of any kind. If the voter in these states does not like the way his implied mandates are carried out at the convention of his party, he can always vote for the candidate of the other party in the November election; and this is an option that the voters sometimes exercise with devastating effect in a number of these states, by virtue of the close margin of party competition.[42]

Something like a political earthquake would be required to secure the adoption of the Florida system in New York, Pennsylvania, or Illinois—three states that between them elect about one sixth of all the convention delegates. It is not clear that any major public interest would be served if that system were to be adopted by any one of these three. But in a number of other states its adoption as a substitute for their present systems would undoubtedly be a substantial improvement for almost all of the affected interests.

[42] When an attempt was made in the Council of State Governments to develop a recommended form of presidential primary, it was decided that no recommendation should be made, but that interested states might well give consideration to the Florida and New York plans. See Council of State Governments, *Suggested State Legislation, Program for 1957*, p. 179.

11

Other Systems for Mandating Delegates

ABOUT 45 PER CENT of the national convention delegates of 1952 and 50 per cent of those of 1956 were elected or instructed through the presidential primary systems described in the previous chapter. The other delegates came from party conventions and other party organization processes. These older methods of selecting and instructing delegates retain many features that have come down from the earliest days of party organization. Most of them are built on local *ad hoc* meetings of the party voters, held to select representatives who will attend higher-level party meetings.

There is much variation in how many levels of party meetings there are and how direct is the representation that results. In the most common pattern, local party meetings elect the members of county conventions, who elect the members of state conventions, who in turn elect the delegates to the national convention. If congressional district conventions are held to elect the district delegates, a common practice in the Republican party, the delegates to the district and the state party conventions are usually elected through identical procedures. Often they are the same individuals, serving first as members of their district convention and then of the state convention.

When primary elections were invented, presidential primaries were substituted in a number of states for the entire apparatus just described. In some other states the state party organization continued to select the national convention delegates, but the base of the organization rested on the party voters acting in primaries instead of in local party meetings. In a few of these states delegates to state conventions are elected directly in primaries; in a larger number the members of county conventions or committees are elected in primaries, and in turn elect the members of the higher party bodies.

The various systems can be classified on the basis of how the organization is related to the rank and file of the party. The differences between the systems affect the extent to which the respective national convention delegates receive mandates from the voters that are relatively direct and specific, but in operation other features may be equally or more important. The systems do not easily lend themselves to the kind of classification and analysis used in the previous chapter for the presidential primaries. In the primaries, the forms of action required by law often seem to have a controlling influence; through these forms, persisting from one election to another, some aspects of the experience in each primary system become a matter of public record, as data on candidate filings and electoral results.

In the non-primary systems the informal and unrecorded aspects are much more important. Field work on a national scale to capture and record some of this experience has been attempted for only a single presidential election year, 1952. The central problem of what to look for in making field surveys of political behavior within the party organizations is one that has so far been studied only in a rudimentary way. For the 1952 survey it was handled provisionally by seeking data that would permit the application of the same standards of judgment to both the primary and non-primary systems, on the assumption that both existed mainly as means for choosing and sometimes mandating the national convention delegates.

But it seems possible that while these manifest functions of the primary and non-primary systems are the same, the latent functions are not. The latent functions of the primaries might be thought to include campaigns to educate the voters; the arousing of political interest; and a strengthening of the bonds between the party rank and file and their chosen national leader, who may become President and will need their support if he does. The latent functions of the non-primary systems, on the other hand, may be said to include the renewal and strengthening of the internal bonds of party organization; the recruitment of more party activists who will participate in party meetings and then work in general election campaigns; and a strengthening of the bonds between the working members of the party and their chosen national leader, who will need their special support, as well as that of the voters, if he becomes President.[1]

The alternative sets of latent functions involve differing conceptions, ideals, and values. They are not easily commensurable with each other, although to some extent they overlap, and it might be possible to design methods of delegate selection that would serve most elements in both sets of functions most of the time. Great caution must therefore be used in making comparative assessments of the relative effectiveness of the primary and non-primary systems, especially when making comparisons that go beyond what the record shows in regard to their success in their ostensible main purposes.

After an introduction to the classification of the systems, the present chapter reviews the party processes for mandating delegates on the presidential nominations and on platform issues and questions of party policy. The problem of seating contests and their effect on mandates is then taken up. It appears in this chapter primarily because the problem seems to be confined almost entirely to delegates who are selected and instructed by a party organization rather than in primaries. The chapter then concludes with a comparative analysis of mandating systems.

Popular Origins of Party Bodies Electing Delegates

In more than two thirds of all the states national convention delegates are elected in party bodies of one sort or another. These bodies differ widely; all, however, are representative institutions within the state parties, and all rest their claims to political legitimacy on some connection with the rank and file. In effect, they claim to produce delegations that represent the mass of the party adherents within the state.

If such claims are to be weighed, it is necessary to examine the various methods by which the party bodies obtain their popular sanction. When this is done it appears that the various systems for electing national convention delegates in party bodies can best be arranged for examination in classes as given below, moving from the most formal to the least formal. (For details of these state systems, see Appendix E.) The classification is based primarily on what was found in the 1952 survey, but updated for known changes since that year.[2]

[1] This paragraph should be considered a preliminary formulation that needs further discussion, both on the distinctions between manifest and latent functions in this area and more importantly on the essential differences in function, if any, between primary and non-primary systems. On the basic concepts of manifest and latent functions in this type of analysis, see Robert K. Merton, *Social Theory and Social Structure* (1949), Chap. 1; Ely Chinoy, *Sociological Perspective* (1954), pp. 37-41; Marion J. Levy, Jr., "Some Aspects of 'Structural-Functional' Analysis and Political Science," in Roland A. Young (ed.), *Approaches to the Study of Politics* (1958), pp. 52-66.

[2] For the 1952 data, see Paul T. David, Malcolm Moos, and Ralph M. Goldman, *Presidential Nominating Politics in 1952* (1954), Vol. 1, pp. 162-73, and relevant state chapters in the other four volumes

CLASS 1: Party bodies derived from primary elections.
(a) State party committee members elected in primaries: Louisiana, Georgia, Arkansas (Democratic only); New York, Pennsylvania (delegates at large only).
(b) State and district convention delegates elected in primaries: Delaware, Maryland, Indiana.
(c) State and district convention delegates chosen by local bodies elected in primaries: Michigan, Rhode Island, North Dakota, Wyoming, Arizona, Montana; Illinois (delegates at large only).

CLASS 2: State and district party conventions derived partly from primaries and partly from *ad hoc* meetings.
(a) Idaho, Kansas, Washington.

CLASS 3: State and district party conventions derived from *ad hoc* meetings.
(a) Delegates elected directly in *ad hoc* meetings: Maine, Vermont, Connecticut; Virginia, Kentucky, Tennessee; Georgia, Alabama, Arkansas, Louisiana (Republican only).
(b) Delegates chosen by county conventions derived from local *ad hoc* meetings: North Carolina, South Carolina, Mississippi, Oklahoma, Texas, Minnesota, Iowa, Missouri, Colorado, Utah, Nevada, New Mexico.

The differences among state systems on which this classification is based undoubtedly have consequences for system behavior, as noted in Appendix E and at various points in the present chapter. Other factors, however, are often so much more important that precise appraisals are difficult.

Party Processes for Mandating Delegates on Nominations

Where delegates are selected by the party organization, the procedures of selection do not always provide mandates as explicit as those in some primary systems. Nevertheless, the act of selection, however performed, always has mandating implications. Moreover, when it occurs in a party meeting, it can easily be accompanied by advice or instruction that may become highly specific.

These possibilities were illustrated long ago in the preparations for the Democratic national convention of 1844, for which an unusually full record of delegate commitments is available.[3] Ex-President Martin

Van Buren was seeking a third nomination. Delegate pledging was intended to develop a band-wagon movement for Van Buren as much as to bind the action of the delegates. In all, instructions favorable to Van Buren came from about fourteen state party conventions, four congressional district conventions, and one Democratic caucus in a state legislature, producing a total of 159 votes ostensibly committed to Van Buren—only 18 votes short of the two thirds needed to nominate.

After most of these instructions were given and before the convention met, Van Buren published a letter opposing the annexation of Texas. Many of Van Buren's supporters were alienated by this action. The two thirds rule was adopted again at the convention, and many Van Buren delegates voted for it. On the first nominating ballot 29 of the 159 Van Buren delegates failed to vote for him, though he gained 16 votes not previously committed to him. His losses were mainly in Alabama, Mississippi, and Louisiana; his gains were mainly in northern and border states. The net effect left him with more than a majority but far short of the necessary two thirds; eventually James K. Polk was nominated.

This experience illustrated many phenomena that were to recur again and again

[3] *Niles' National Register*, Vol. 66, pp. 211-13.
The outcome of the 1844 convention may have had something to do with the fact that no similar record of delegate commitments in advance of a national convention was available for many years thereafter.

in later conventions. Large numbers of delegates were committed at the time of their selection, months before the convention and on the basis of incomplete information. In other cases there were equally firm refusals to mandate the delegates at the time of selection. Later there was some reinterpretation of mandates, whether express or implied, in the light of changing events and additional information about the candidate. Express mandates were much more closely followed on the actual nominating vote than on earlier procedural votes that might be of critical importance to candidate success. Thus the Van Buren majority might have voted down the two thirds rule, but that rule also involved other interests in the continuity of party customs and in the defense of state and sectional interests.

The instructing formulas in 1844 varied from state to state, as they still do. The Democratic caucus of the Massachusetts legislature followed a practice of earlier years and actually placed Van Buren in nomination, "subject to the decision of the democratic national convention to be holden in Baltimore in May next."[4] At least eight state conventions and several district conventions simply instructed their delegates to vote for Van Buren. Vermont delegates were further instructed to "use all honorable means" to procure his nomination, Pennsylvania delegates to "use all their influence," Alabama delegates to "use every practical effort." Connecticut refrained from a direct instruction but expressed "decided preference" for Van Buren. Arkansas simply "recommended" him.

In Georgia, John C. Calhoun was the favorite and the delegates were so instructed, but the Georgia convention resolved:

. . . whatever may be the prepossessions of the members of the democratic party of this state in favor of any one of the distinguished republicans whose names have been connected with the contemplated nomination, they will as a party sustain and support the nominees of said convention.[5]

North Carolina gave no instructions but pledged itself to support the outcome. Several other states sent uninstructed delegations. Tennessee was unusual in that it avowed no preference for the Presidency, but for the Vice Presidency it strongly recommended its favorite son, Polk—who in the end became the presidential nominee and President.

Express Mandates of Commitment

State conventions and other party bodies selecting delegates have exercised the right to instruct throughout the history of the national convention system. Where a system of instruction through a primary has been imposed by law, the authority of the state convention is correspondingly limited, but even here the party bodies may offer supplementary advice.

References to instructions are scattered throughout the proceedings of the national conventions, but provide little basis for any estimate of how often express instructions have been given. The data collected in 1952, however, make it possible to classify the delegates of that year in terms of their instructions and commitments, as well as the manner of their selection. These data are presented more fully in a later chapter, but the essential facts about the proportions of delegates subject to one type of candidate commitment or another are summarized in Table 11.1.

The table indicates the range of variation that is possible in the proportions of delegates who receive instructions in open nominating situations, and in the character of those instructions. Relatively small numbers of delegates in either party were elected in public primaries that gave them a binding instruction to support one or another of the leading candidates—under 10 per cent in the Democratic party, under 5 per cent in the Republican. Known preferences were

---

[4] *Ibid.*, p. 211.
[5] *Ibid.*, p. 212. It will be recalled that in 1844

Democrats were still sometimes called Republicans, while most of the future Republicans were called Whigs.

apparently a factor in the election of more than half of the Republican delegates elected in primaries, but this was also true of those selected through party processes, and pointed mainly to the heat of the Taft-Eisenhower struggle in 1952. In each party and through each method of selection, some delegates were committed to "non-leading" candidates—favorite sons and others who failed to make much of a showing in the actual balloting. In the Democratic party, confusion and indecision were reflected in the high proportions of delegates, how-

the delegates in early balloting. Delegations chosen by party conventions, however, usually have a part in writing their own instructions, and if conditions change they usually feel competent to decide how far and how long their mandates apply.

Implied Mandates of Commitment

When delegates are selected because of a known candidate preference or without objection to it, an implied commitment results. Usually it is assumed that implied

TABLE 11.1. ADVANCE COMMITMENT OF NATIONAL CONVENTION DELEGATES, 1952[a]

(in per cent of each convention)

Type of Commitment by Statutory or Party Action	Democratic Delegates		Republican Delegates	
	Elected in Public Primaries	Selected by Party Processes	Elected in Public Primaries	Selected by Party Processes
Firmly Bound to a Leading Candidate	9.4%	5.0%	3.5%	7.7%
Preferring a Leading Candidate	4.8	5.8	23.3	34.3
Committed to a Non-Leading Candidate	3.9	11.3	8.0	2.9
Preference Undecided or Unknown	26.2	33.6	9.4	10.9
Total	44.3	55.7	44.2	55.8

[a] Derived from Appendix A, Tables 8 and 9, in which the footnotes indicate the criteria used in assigning delegates to the several categories. Since these tables were constructed primarily on the basis of majority status within delegations, the minority elements in each delegation were reassigned among the major categories in accordance with the distributions indicated in the tables. Other summaries of the same data appear in Chapter 15, particularly Tables 15.2 and 15.3.

ever selected, whose preferences were undecided or unknown when they were chosen.

Formal instructions, however given, may vary in intensity of commitment, conditions of applicability, and duration. When given by resolution of a state party body, the strongest form includes an instruction not only to vote for the preferred candidate, but also to work for his nomination in all possible ways. The weakest form is the resolution of commendation or preference, without direct instruction to the delegation. Weak resolutions of instruction usually reflect some uncertainty, indecision, or conflict in the instructing body, but any express mandate is likely to be respected by

mandates leave the delegates in a position of greater freedom than express mandates, but the opposite may be the case. An express mandate is often a merely formal commitment to a favorite son whose chances will never become serious. Implied mandates, on the other hand, take on substantial meaning when they involve a clear commitment to a genuine candidate.

Implied mandates are most clearly evident as the end product of a public contest between well-defined factions over candidate preferences. Many examples of this occurred in the Taft-Eisenhower struggle of 1952. Local factional struggles often involve the use of competing presidential candidacies. The Republican "young Turks" of Delaware, for example, won representation in the state organization in 1952 as supporters of General Eisenhower against the pro-Taft "old guard." Incidents of this kind took place in other states in 1952 as "new Republicans" sought to use the Eisenhower candidacy in their drive for greater recognition in party affairs. The Eisenhower managers gave aid and comfort to the development of insurgent movements in a number of states where party regulars were mainly for Taft. In some instances these conflicts were settled by all-or-none victory for one side; in others by compromise agreements dividing the available seats in the convention. In either case the factional alignments of the delegates carried over into their presumed mandates and usually into their actual voting behavior.

Whatever the balance of local and national interests, a strong factional contest usually produces strong mandates if the opposing factions are clearly identified with competing national candidates. In other cases, however, factional conflict over delegate seats may run high without involving candidate interests, either because the competing factions all prefer the same candidate or because they have no preference and are preoccupied with the local power struggle. Instances of this were common in the selection of Democratic delegates in 1952.

Implied mandates of some strength can develop with a minimum of open conflict in situations where the official party organization is strong and cohesive. The commitments of the delegates may become apparent through the public statements and the preconvention activities of party leaders; and this can occur as easily in a state with a primary as in one without if the delegates are technically left unpledged. In New York, for example, with Governor Dewey publicly supporting Eisenhower as early as 1950, and with the Taft forces in the state making little effort to elect delegates, there could be small doubt about the implied commitments of the New York

delegates who had been endorsed by the organization. Early in 1952, Rhode Island Democratic leaders publicly agreed on Governor Stevenson as their first choice if available; any would-be delegate who had organization backing could be assumed to be willing to go along with this preference.

State conventions and other party meetings may indicate strong predispositions, if not commitments, by their choice of guest speakers or convention officials. Senator Taft gave the keynote address at the Arkansas Republican state convention in 1952, and the delegation chosen there gave him most of its votes at the convention. Montana and Utah Republican conventions chose pro-Taft delegations after hearing strongly pro-Taft guest speakers. Missouri Republicans chose a full slate of pro-Eisenhower state convention officers; the delegation chosen by this convention gave Eisenhower 21 of its 25 votes at Chicago. In each of these four states, the delegations were formally unpledged and uninstructed, but they carried a strong implied mandate arising out of a public display of preference for one candidate or the other in the proceedings through which they had been selected.

Frequently the total absence of opposition in the state convention, or primary as the case may be, to the slate of delegates proposed by the party leaders seems to imply that there is tacit agreement on the delegation's mandate. This was true of the Utah Republican delegation cited above, which gave its unanimous vote to Taft. Georgia's Democratic delegation of 1952 backed Senator Richard B. Russell to the last man. Just as often, however, the unopposed "organization slate" reflects the end product of negotiation among the leaders to compose a delegation representing the different regional, jurisdictional, and factional interests. In 1952, Delaware, New Jersey, and North Dakota Republican and Michigan and Connecticut Democratic "organization slates" of this kind were elected unopposed, or practically so. Taken alone, therefore, the fact that the organization slate is unopposed provides no assurance that the delegates are all for the same candidate. Before jumping to that conclusion it is well to look for additional evidence—perhaps the background details of the electing state convention or primary—to confirm or modify such an evaluation of the delegation's mandate. But when there is no open conflict in the selection of a delegation there is a basis for the presumption that, when the time comes, the delegation will be able to reach agreement in its own ranks on the candidate it prefers and will unite in his support.

Procedures Leading to Conflicting Mandates

The practice of electing a representative through one procedure and instructing him through another inevitably introduces the possibility of conflicting mandates; it has few rivals as a source of confusion in representative institutions. In the primaries this type of confusion is apt to be created when district delegates are elected by the voters of the district, but are advised or instructed by the outcome of a state-wide preference vote. A similar situation may arise even in a party convention—for example, when a mandate is implied by the selection of delegates who are openly committed to one presidential candidate, and they are then instructed by resolution to vote for a different one.

In the Democratic party formal conventions are rarely held at the congressional district level. Where delegates are not elected in primaries, plenary authority to elect and instruct them rests with the state party conventions or committees. But district caucuses are usually held in advance of the meetings of the state conventions. These caucuses agree informally on the choice of district delegates, and often undertake to instruct. Such a grass-roots mandate, which is likely to correspond closely with the delegate's own preference, may in turn be overridden in the state convention, either by overt resolutions of instruction or

by adopting a unit rule under which the majority vote in the delegation will be binding on all the members.

In the Republican party the national rules have long favored the election of district delegates in district party conventions. In 1952 these were held separately from the state conventions—in both time and place—in about a dozen states, mainly southern.[6] Under those circumstances, they may instruct and, according to Republican practice, are not subject to being overridden by the state convention. In other states, Republican practice is like the Democratic: district conventions or caucuses are held in conjunction with the state convention and these are more liable to overriding in the state convention. One such case occurred in Indiana in 1952, when the state convention passed a resolution instructing the entire delegation for Taft. Two district delegates who had been elected as known Eisenhower supporters refused to recognize the authority of the state convention; they afterward obtained assurance from national convention officers that they would be allowed to vote as they saw fit.[7]

The position of the district delegates would be clearer if it were more nearly like that of members of the House of Representatives (on which these posts were modeled), as it would be if all district delegates were both elected and instructed by district party bodies or electorates, without overriding by any unit rule or state convention.

Mandates of Noncommitment

Mandates of noncommitment are as possible as those of commitment. Noncommitment is a deliberate postponement of decision, either because the basis for decision does not yet seem adequate or because of a desire to enhance its effect when it comes, i.e., to be in a position to make a good

[6] David, Moos, and Goldman, op. cit., Vol. 1, p. 163.
[7] Ibid., Vol. 4, pp. 84-86.

trade. Governor John S. Fine's followers in the Pennsylvania Republican delegation of 1952 deliberately assumed an uncommitted posture to strengthen their position at the convention. Michigan Republicans chose a delegation broadly representative of all candidate factions in order to maintain friendly relations within the party at home. But to maintain a common front at Chicago the delegation withheld all commitments until a strategic moment in convention developments. The New Jersey Democratic delegation of 1952, unpledged, uninstructed, and unbossed for the first time in twenty years, decided in May to take no stand on candidates at that time. At a meeting in June it adopted a resolution commiting the delegates not to make public any preference until they met again in Chicago five weeks later.

A mandate of noncommitment may sometimes be the consequence of sheer stalemate among competing factions. At other times it may reflect indecision because the preferred candidate seems to be unavailable. The situation of the Indiana Democrats in 1952 typified that of many others who favored Stevenson but were doubtful of his availability and uncertain about supporting anyone else. They went to Chicago "uninstructed," but were for Stevenson "when the time came." Noncommitment may also be an expression of political courtesy to a powerful party leader who is himself undecided. The Maryland Republican delegation awaited the word of Governor McKeldin, the state's favorite son, before a majority of the delegation went for Eisenhower in 1952. Other motivations for noncommitment are apparent when several candidates are attractive but none is overwhelmingly so. In such cases the desire to avoid getting on the wrong band wagon is a powerful incentive to delay.

Conflicting Pressures
on the Timing of Commitment

In the various types of organized noncommitment, conflicting pressures on the

timing of decision are apparent. As in most complex organizations, there is a normal tendency not to make decisions sooner than necessary and in any event to withhold public announcement until the last possible moment. These tendencies arise both from the difficulty of reaching a decision involving major interests and from the risk inherent in taking a stand—still more in announcing it—in a situation that may change before the decision is to be given effect. Since a delegate cannot cast his vote until the convention meets, and since the situation may easily change between the time of selection and the convention, the long-range interests of the party organizations mainly work to postpone commitment until the convention voting is about to begin.

Other strong pressures, however, work for early commitment. First of these is the normal human impulse to end the frustration of long periods of indecision and reach at least some interim working conclusion, so as to get started on plans for action. It can be supposed that most would-be delegates have a tentative scale of candidate preferences in mind at a rather early date, even if they are unwilling to reveal it. Second are the pressures applied by the enthusiastic followers of a preferred candidate, who seek to take their state party organization into camp.

The organizations can see advantages as well as risks in an early commitment. The advantages, in addition to any possible satisfaction of an actual preference, include the prospect of easy access to the White House if the organization commits itself early to a candidate who wins both nomination and election. By waiting, a delegation may be able to get a good price for a negotiated commitment at a strategic moment, but, on the other hand, the band wagon may start to roll too soon and the delegation may then have to scramble for a place on it. A last-minute commitment strategy that waits too long and misses the band wagon is one of the nightmares of all politicians. It leaves only the possibility of trading on the candidate's need for support in the general election; and no form of delayed support is likely to produce the intimate access to the seats of power that can be built by helping in the early stages of a successful campaign. This is the lesson of Jim Farley's regard for those who were "For Roosevelt Before Chicago"; and it helps to point up the complexity of the pressures that affect the timing of decisions by organizations, factions, and delegates.

"Independent Delegates" and Problems of Group Affiliation

In the broadest sense, every delegate to a national convention must be subject to pressures and sooner or later must make commitments, since in the end he must vote as an individual. Most often, to be sure, the individual's conception of his mandate becomes explicit or is implied in his association with some party faction, group, or movement. Informal obligations within the delegate group lend force to the public's conception of the group mandate.

Occasionally, however, an individual delegate finds it appropriate or expedient to hold himself independent. He may have given his support informally, through public statements along the way, to a candidate not favored by the majority of his delegation. Or he may remain uncommitted up to the time of the actual voting.

An independent delegate may have been elected in a public primary because of personal popularity or stature with the party electorate. This was clearly the case for most members of the Alabama Democratic delegation of 1952. If chosen in a state convention he may, on the one hand, be the party's "grand old man" or a former "war horse"; or, on the other, a party dissident in a strong bargaining position. Either way, he may be given a place without reference to his candidate preference or his willingness to work with other members of the delegation.

The number of such delegates obviously is not likely to be large, but in the Republican convention of 1952 there were one-man splinter votes in sixteen state delegations on the first nominating roll call. Most of these were cast by delegates who had previously become identified as isolated within their delegations. A number of other delegates who went along with delegation majorities or minorities in the actual voting had been equally independent in behavior up to that point. A few of the one- and two-man splinter groups were, strictly speaking, not independent, being bound by explicit mandates from district constituencies or local party organizations that happened to differ from the sentiment in the state at large.

An independent delegate presumably carries only an implied mandate to represent his constituents to the best of his own judgment. He feels free to interpret his own mandate as he sees fit, and with small risk of later sanctions because of the speed with which minor incidents in the voting are forgotten. On the other hand, those delegates who are closely affiliated with a delegation or some part of it rarely feel free to reinterpret their mandates as individuals. The discipline of the electing constituency or party body may be far away, but that of the delegation as a group is close at hand. When the delegation as a whole moves, its motion is news at home, and any sudden defection would not be overlooked. Thus any reinterpretation of mandates, express or implied, is a matter for group decision, and frequently for some public announcement or explanation when it occurs.

Mandates on Non-Nominating Issues

Since the main business of the convention is the choice of candidates, there are many devices and pressures for developing mandates on the nominations. Corresponding devices and pressures for instructing on other issues can be found and illustrated, but they only occasionally become important. In the conventions of 1896, for example, particularly the Democratic, free silver, bimetallism, and "16 to 1" were the rallying cries, and most of the delegates undoubtedly arrived with mandates on these issues. Often they had been instructed by specific resolutions in state party conventions, and mandates could also be implied from sentiments widely held and voiced in party constituencies.

In the 1948 Democratic convention most of the southern delegations arrived with specific instructions to oppose the civil rights policies advocated by President Truman. Some were also instructed to bolt the convention if necessary in order to make their opposition felt. Northern delegations were less well prepared for the issue. They had no specific instructions from any source, and no clear point of view of their own, on how far to go in dealing with southern revolt. While relatively clear in their support of the President on the substantive issues, they fumbled the problem of maintaining party discipline.

Mandates may be needed and are sometimes provided in regard to questions of changes in the rules. The reduction of southern representation in the Republican national convention of 1916 was prepared for by elaborate consultation with state party organizations. In effect, mandates were developed for the 1916 convention by which the changes were put in line for formal approval. Even more extensive preparatory work preceded the revocation of the two thirds rule at the Democratic convention of 1936.[8]

At the Democratic convention of 1956 important changes in the rules, including a substantial clarification of the obligations of state party organizations to the national party, were adopted unanimously and with relatively little controversy even behind the scenes. This was the result of a four-year effort going on from the loyalty oath controversy of 1952. It was apparent that no delegation had any express mandate, or even a strong implied mandate, to oppose the recommendations formulated by the

Mitchell committee.[9] The committee's report had been widely circulated a year before the convention, and its principal recommendations had been incorporated into the convention call.

Instructions on issues other than the nominations are usually given in the form of resolutions adopted by state conventions or other party bodies. The state conventions may also adopt party platforms for the state. These platforms may be regarded as guidance by the national convention delegates insofar as they happen to be both relevant and current, particularly if they were adopted at the same convention at which the delegates were elected.

More often than not, however, it appears that delegates elected in party conventions are given a free hand on substantive issues on the assumption that they will have the same attitudes as the convention that selected them. Delegates elected in primaries are rarely given any specific instruction on non-nominating issues, and seldom have occasion to campaign in a way that would result in specific policy commitments. It thus seems safe to conclude that delegates rarely bring express mandates on any question outside the nominations. When they do have mandates on such matters they are generally no more than implied and advisory.

Seating Contests and the Problem of Mandates

Occasionally two competing delegations from the same state appear at a national convention and demand seating. Individual delegates and small groups may also be challenged, but these lesser cases rarely involve major issues or delay convention ac-

[8] See Chapters 8 and 9.

[9] Democratic National Committee, *Interim Report of Special Advisory Committee on Rules of the 1956 Democratic National Convention* (1955). Also see commentary and excerpts in Harold Leventhal, "The Democratic Party's Approach to Its Convention Rules," *American Political Science Review*, Vol. 50 (June 1956) pp. 553-68; Clarence Cannon, *Democratic Manual* (1956).

tion. A seating contest between entire delegations usually reflects a serious disorder in the party processes of the state, sometimes involving party bolting and the holding of a rump convention to elect a contesting delegation. Accusations of irregular procedure are almost invariably made.

The causes of such irregularities are discussed more fully in the later sections of this chapter. Their importance may be seen by looking at the problems they create for the convention.[10]

The Development of Seating Procedures

The first Democratic national convention inaugurated the practice of appointing one delegate from each state to form a committee to report a list of the delegates. At the second convention, in 1835, the committee was faced with two "setts" of delegates from Pennsylvania. It reported both without recommendation; after debate both were seated, with voting rights divided between them. In 1840 the committee was "vested with power to ascertain who were entitled to seats in this convention, and also to report their names."[11] In 1848, faced with the contesting delegations of Barnburners and Hunkers from New York, the committee adopted a resolution by a majority of one refusing to open the discussion of the contest "until each party shall pledge themselves to abide the decision of said Convention, and agree to support, by all honorable means, the nominees of this Convention."[12] The Barnburners refused to comply, insisting on unconditional admission or none, while the Hunkers accepted the pledge. After floor debate, the convention voted, 126 to 124, to seat both delegations, but this decision was not acceptable to either. The Hunkers remained to the

end but did not vote; the Barnburners withdrew after the nomination of Lewis Cass, and later took part in a separate convention that nominated Martin Van Buren.

The first national party committee was elected by the Democratic convention of 1848 and issued the call for the convention of 1852. Over 700 delegates appeared to fill the authorized 296 seats; the new national committee was accordingly authorized to specify in 1856 the number of seats to which each state was entitled and to "secure the same to the delegates elect."[13] This began the practice of having the national committee make up the temporary roll. As the committee explained in 1856, they

... regarded all papers which on their face bear *prima facie* evidence of the regular election of the person presenting them, as entitling those persons to seats in this hall. They considered it their duty to issue tickets to all delegates who presented themselves with such *prima facie* evidence of election by the people.[14]

In the case of two contesting delegations from Missouri, the committee gave tickets only to the one presenting evidence of election in the better form. In the case of two New York delegations, both of which carried *prima facie* evidence of their election, the problem was referred back to the two delegations; eventually both were seated by the convention.

By 1856 the Democratic party had three successive forums for handling seating contests: the national committee, the convention committee on credentials, and the full convention. The full convention acted as the final authority, but not as an entirely autonomous one. At this early stage of its proceedings its voting membership was determined by the temporary roll prepared by the national committee which had been elected in the previous national convention.

In the Republican party, similar procedures were adopted at its first convention in 1856, so far as credentials committee and floor action were concerned. Until 1884 the

---

[10] The following discussion of seating contests is based largely on materials prepared by John Ballard while serving as a member of the staff of the Brookings Institution in the summer of 1954.

[11] DNC, *Proceedings*, 1840, p. 3.

[12] *Baltimore Sun*, May 24, 1848.

[13] DNC, *Proceedings*, 1852. p. 42.

[14] DNC, *Proceedings*, 1856, p. 10.

temporary roll was drawn up by the secretary of the national committee, who also received notice of contests for convention action; from 1884 onward, the national committee itself heard contests and acted on them in preparing the temporary roll.

Contest Exploitation and Convention Control

The potentialities of controlling a convention by means of seating contests became apparent at the two Democratic national conventions held in 1860. At the Charleston convention, in April, contesting delegations appeared from both New York and Illinois; in each case the national committee made a choice and seated only one on the temporary roll of the convention. The credentials committee upheld the delegations already seated and the convention concurred. But the convention broke up after the walkout of many of the delegations, and a new meeting was called in Baltimore.

At Baltimore many of the delegations that had withdrawn from the earlier convention returned with new credentials. Contesting delegations were also present from four southern states, and all seats that had been made vacant by the Charleston secession were referred to the credentials committee. The committee recommended the seating of new delegations from Alabama and Louisiana that favored the nomination of Senator Stephen A. Douglas, and against the seating of the former seceding delegations from those states. It recommended seating the seceding delegations from Delaware, Mississippi, and Texas, and both seceding and contesting delegations from Georgia and Arkansas. A minority committee report opposing parts of these actions was submitted on behalf of nine state delegations that had voted against Douglas at Charleston but had remained in the convention. The convention upheld the majority, and the southern anti-Douglas delegations again began leaving the convention.

Douglas was eventually nominated by the delegates who remained.

In the Republican party the problem of seating contests was linked almost from the first with the problems of apportionment and rotten borough representation. In 1860 there was opposition to the seating of delegates from a number of slave states and from the territories and the District of Columbia. David Wilmot of Pennsylvania voiced arguments that were to become familiar in succeeding Republican conventions:

This is not a mass convention, in which a mere numerical majority of all who choose to attend control the result, but this is a Convention of delegates representing a constituency, and having constituents at home to represent. Now sir, can it be possible that those gentlemen who come here from states in which there is no organized party, or from states in which they cannot maintain an organized party—is it possible that they are to come here and by their votes control the action of the Convention? I can see nothing better calculated to demoralize a party, and to break it up, than just such a proceeding.[15]

But Wilmot's position was defeated and the delegates he opposed were seated.

The basis was thus laid for what was later to become known in Republican parlance as the "steamroller," which operated as follows. The faction controlling the national committee would sponsor contests against delegations committed to its opponents. Then its majority, voting in the national committee, would seat the faction's delegations on the temporary roll. The convention majority thus created could then vote itself onto the permanent roll in preparation for controlling the nominations. This game could be played easily with the delegations from the southern states, which after the Reconstruction period owed no responsibility to any substantial constituency.

Throughout much of its history the Republican party has been marked by sharp conflict between well-matched factions and

[15] RNC, *Proceedings*, 1860, p. 111.

by close convention majorities at critical moments. This feature has lent added importance to the seating contests. In 1876, for example, two Republican delegations claimed the twenty convention votes of Alabama; the one that eventually voted for Governor Rutherford B. Hayes of Ohio was seated by a vote of 375 to 354. In 1880 the partisans of former President Grant were defeated when twenty-four delegates from Illinois who supported Senator James G. Blaine were seated by a vote of 387 to 353. In 1892 an Alabama delegation favoring Benjamin Harrison was seated by a vote of 463 to 423½, aided by a ruling that sitting delegates on the temporary roll could vote on all but their own contests.

Mark Hanna is credited with the dubious honor of bringing the Republican steamroller to its highest point. The convention of 1892 had been marked by contests from seven southern states. In 1894, Hanna began his drive to win control of the national committee and also to gain the support of party leaders in the South.[16] At the national committee contest hearings before the convention of 1896, a total of more than 150 seats were contested. In the contests where the interests of Governor William McKinley of Ohio were involved, the committee apparently awarded 32 seats to anti-McKinley or uncommitted delegates and 78 seats to those favoring McKinley.[17] The credentials committee voted 29 to 17 to adopt the temporary roll and to hear only certain contests, involving 10 seats, on which the national committee had reached no decision. It settled these cases in favor of McKinley. On the convention floor the opposition was flattened by a vote of 551½

to 359½ on a procedural issue. On the first nominating ballot, McKinley was an easy victor.[18]

At the Republican conventions of 1900 and 1904, with a sitting President seeking renomination in each convention, smaller numbers of contests, mostly from the South, were disposed of without difficulty. In 1908, however, the struggle to prevent the nomination of Secretary of War William Howard Taft was fought mainly through seating contests, and the steamroller again operated. In all, 221 seats were contested, including 202 from the South. In the end, only 5 anti-Taft contestants were seated on the temporary and permanent rolls. Most of the delegates who were seated were as representative as those who were rejected, but in most cases neither group had much of a constituency.

The climax came at the convention of 1912. The actual manipulation of seating contests in 1912 was not much more scandalous than in 1908 or 1896, but the issues were more fully tested and public opinion was much more clearly aroused.

Altogether, 260 seats, 198 from the South, were contested before the national committee, which gave all but 14 to Taft supporters. The test vote came at the opening of the convention on the election of the temporary chairman. All challenges of the temporary roll were ruled out of order by the national committee chairman, Victor Rosewater, who held that an unorganized assemblage could not pass upon credentials. He refused to entertain any appeal from this ruling, and proceeded with a roll call in which every delegation was individually

---

[16] Herbert Croly, *Marcus Alonzo Hanna: His Life and Work* (1912), pp. 175 ff; Arthur Wallace Dunn, *From Harrison to Harding* (1922), pp. 171 ff.

[17] On the basis of the summary carried by the *New York Times*, June 15, 1896, and previous daily dispatches. The actual figures as reported by this anti-McKinley newspaper would seem to imply that the steamrollering on behalf of McKinley was not as flagrant as the Hanna biographers have suggested, although it probably increased what might otherwise have been a relatively thin majority.

[18] An accumulating record of malpractice in party affairs was doing much to discredit the parties by the turn of the century. It led to the reformist literature of the period and gave strength to the party factions that sought the installation of primary elections in the states. For descriptions of steamroller tactics on the state level during this period, see Harold F. Gosnell, *Boss Platt and His New York Machine* (1924), pp. 89-92; and M. Ostrogorski, *Democracy and the Party System in the United States: A Study in Extra-Constitutional Government* (1910), p. 122.

polled, in order to insure voting by the specific delegates named on the temporary roll. By this means Senator Elihu Root was elected temporary chairman by a vote of 558 to 501, with 72 contested but seated delegates providing the margin of victory.[19]

A further motion to prevent contested delegates from voting on the report of the credentials committee was tabled by a vote of 567 to 507. Challenges of the credentials committee report were lost by similar margins, with contested delegations voting on all but their own contests. The closest vote came on a contest involving the new California primary law, which the Roosevelt forces lost 529-542.[20]

Roosevelt then denounced the convention as "in no proper sense any longer a Republican Convention representing the real Republican party," and asked his supporters to refrain from further voting. Taft was nominated by 561 votes, with 107 for Roosevelt, 349 present but not voting, and 66 scattered. Roosevelt bolted; he became the nominee of the Progressive party; and in November the Republican split placed Woodrow Wilson in the White House. The steamrollers of 1896 and 1908 had faced little effective opposition, but in 1912, with two closely matched and strong candidates each trying to operate his own steamroller, the stage was set for party division and defeat.

[19] It should not be assumed that the forces of ex-President Theodore Roosevelt were necessarily entitled to the delegate seats they contested. They were attempting to operate their own steamroller, and had undoubtedly created contests for the purpose in some states where they would not otherwise have occurred. Many of the contests probably were created merely to improve Roosevelt's apparent prospects during the early period of his preconvention campaign. Of the 246 contests decided for Taft by the national committee, the Roosevelt forces challenged only 72 on the floor of the convention. This figure seems to have been selected at least in part with regard for the number of votes that would have been necessary to change the convention majority. See the chapter on 1912 in Richard C. Bain, *Decisions and Voting Records of the National Party Conventions* (Brookings Institution, forthcoming).

[20] See Chapter 9.

Origins and Frequency of Recent Seating Contests

A summary of the numbers and percentages of convention seats involved in contests since 1872 is provided by Table 11.2. Because many of the data underlying the table are of dubious accuracy for any given year and state, the totals and averages contained in the table should be considered only approximate, but they probably give a trustworthy picture of the general pattern.

The data on regional origins make it clear that most of the contests have been a by-product of southern politics in both parties since 1928, and in the Republican party for a much longer period. The Democratic party's record before 1928 involved a lower proportion of contests in the South than in other regions.

On the Republican side, every South Carolina and Mississippi delegation from 1916 to 1948 was involved in some sort of contest, and the delegations from Georgia, Florida, and Louisiana were disputed in most of those years. Texas delegations were contested from 1916 to 1928, but not from 1932 to 1948. Most of these contests arose out of local factional fights in extremely weak minority parties. The campaign managers of national candidates made some efforts to manipulate contests, but there is no reason to conclude that the settlement of the contests had any significant influence on the nominations or on other convention outcomes from 1916 to 1948.

The 1952 Republican convention was much more complicated. Taft and Eisenhower managers had both worked hard in the South, but the Taft forces had closer relations with the party leaders in several states. The most flagrant steamrollering occurred in Louisiana, where clear majorities of Eisenhower supporters were repeatedly overridden by presiding officers in party meetings that only registered Republicans could attend. In Texas, on the other hand, the situation was confused by the absence of any registration system and by ambiguities in the state laws on party membership. Eisenhower majorities were frequently counted out or disregarded in local meetings, but often the majorities given this treatment consisted of "new Republicans." Still a different situation prevailed in Georgia, where rival Republican parties

the Texas delegates in accordance with a formula suggested by Senator Taft.

In the convention the first test vote came on the so-called "Fair Play" amendment, suggested by the Republican governors' "manifesto" at the governors' conference at Houston, to restrict the voting rights of dele-

TABLE 11.2. SEATING CONTESTS IN NATIONAL PARTY CONVENTIONS, 1872-1956[a]

Period	Democratic				Republican			
	Non-Southern States	Southern States[b]	Non-State Areas	Total	Non-Southern States	Southern States[b]	Non-State Areas	Total
AVERAGE NUMBER OF SEATS CONTESTED PER CONVENTION								
1872–1892	18.2	3.7	.7	22.5	9.5	26.2	1.0	36.7
1896–1924	30.6	8.0	6.8	45.4	18.0	110.0	3.5	131.5
1928–1956	8.5	27.5	5.3	41.3	1.5	45.4	2.9	49.8
AVERAGE PER CENT OF SEATS CONTESTED PER CONVENTION								
1872–1892	3.2%	1.6%	40.0%	2.8%	1.7%	11.3%	42.9%	4.6%
1896–1924	4.3	2.8	28.1	4.4	2.5	43.0	34.2	13.2
1928–1956	1.0	8.5	15.2	3.5	.2	18.9	19.3	4.5
PER CENT OF TOTAL CONTESTED SEATS BY AREA CATEGORIES								
1872–1892	80.7%	16.3%	3.0%	100.0%	25.9%	71.4%	2.7%	100.0%
1896–1924	67.5	17.6	14.9	100.0	13.7	83.7	2.6	100.0
1928–1956	20.6	66.7	12.7	100.0	3.0	91.2	5.8	100.0

[a] The seating contests reported in this table include those considered by the national committees in the preparation of the temporary roll for each convention and any additional contests considered by the credentials committees; many were considered in both forums but are counted only once when this occurred. The basic data were obtained from the convention proceedings so far as possible, but many contests disposed of by the national committees and some by the credentials committees were not reported to the conventions and remained unrecorded in the proceedings. Data concerning these were compiled mainly from the *New York Times* and in some cases from other newspapers and books. Reports frequently disagree on the number of seats involved. Many of the underlying data are undoubtedly inaccurate, but the errors are probably offsetting in the aggregates used in the table. The basic data were compiled by John Ballard; Richard C. Bain completed the table.
[b] Virginia, North Carolina, South Carolina, Georgia, Florida, Kentucky, Tennessee, Alabama, Mississippi, Arkansas, Louisiana, Oklahoma, Texas.

had existed for several years; in 1952 the one previously recognized by the national committee was dominated by Taft supporters, the other by Eisenhower supporters. When these contests reached the national committee, it voted, by majorities of approximately 60 to 40, to seat the Taft delegates from Georgia, to seat most of the Taft delegates from Louisiana, and to split

gates on the temporary roll if they had been seated by less than a two thirds vote in the national committee. On this, the Taft forces lost by 658 to 548, despite the inclusion of 47 challenged votes within the 548. The credentials committee supported the national committee on the Georgia and Texas delegates, but the Taft forces conceded in the Louisiana contest. Then on the floor of the convention Taft lost the Georgia delegation and conceded the Texas delegation after debate—with the result that he was deprived of a number of Texas delegates to whom he was probably entitled by the sentiment among the party voters in the districts. The compromise settlement suggested by Taft had apparently been not far from the merits, but had come too late in a campaign that had previously been fought on an all-or-none basis by both sides.[21]

In the Democratic party, Minnesota sent contesting delegations in 1932 and 1936, and until 1940 the non-state areas produced a flow of minor contests. All other contests between 1912 and 1956 involving rival delegations were from southern states. Since 1944, in most of these contests, a faction that proposed to bolt the national party, if dissatisfied with the platform or the candidates, was fighting another faction that proposed to remain in the party even if platform and candidates proved unpalatable.

In 1948 a Mississippi delegation with restricted credentials was seated despite protests. In 1952, on the basis of this precedent, six states sent delegations that were prepared to challenge the authority of the national party in one way or another. Those from Mississippi and Texas were faced by contesting delegations from rump conventions, who challenged them on disloyalty grounds. Eventually, the regular Mississippi and Texas delegations were seated after they had given limited assurances of good behavior, but by that time a controversy over a so-called loyalty oath had called in question the seating of those from Virginia, South Carolina, and Louisiana. Eventually these also were given full seating rights, but under circumstances making it clear that their willingness to bolt was nearly equaled by the willingness of other party elements to see them go. In all of these

conflicts there was little disagreement over facts or technical rules. The basic question was the extent to which it was proper or expedient for the national party to enforce majority rule at a time of great internal disagreement.[22]

The events of 1952 in the Democratic party led to the previously noted work of the Mitchell committee between 1952 and 1956, for the purpose of reaching agreement on the minimum obligations to the national party assumed by the delegations and the state parties that send them. The result was a substantial reduction in the number of delegations that arrived in 1956 with restricted credentials. Delegations from Mississippi and South Carolina were again contested, and the organization delegations were seated.[23]

At the Republican convention of 1956 the main seating problem was how many seats to give to Mississippi and South Carolina, where in 1952 most of the Eisenhower vote had been cast for presidential electors who were running as "Independents for Eisenhower" rather than as Republicans. In the end, the entire popular vote for Eisenhower in both states was recognized as a basis for apportioning seats to delegates who had been accredited by the respective Republican organizations. The decision was made by the national committee in establishing the temporary roll and was accepted by the convention without discussion.[24]

Problems of Legitimacy

Two generalizations about seating contests can be made that throw considerable light on the situations in which they arise. The first is that no delegation elected in a primary has been the subject of a seating contest of any significance since 1912.[25]

---

[21] For the 1952 Republican contests, see David, Moos, and Goldman, op. cit., Vol. 1, pp. 52-55, 68-85, 166-68, 234; Vol. 3, particularly Chaps. 5, 12, and 14.

[22] For fuller details, see ibid., Vol. 1, Chap. 4; Vol. 3, Chaps. 2, 4, 5, 10, 12, and 14.
[23] New York Times, Aug. 12 and 14, 1956.
[24] Ibid., Aug. 15 and 16, 1956.
[25] On the immunity of delegations elected in primaries against seating challenges, see Louise Overacker, The Presidental Primary (1926), pp. 166-68.

Even delegations elected in open primaries that were apparently raided by members of the other party have been seated without comment on the questionable nature of their credentials.[26] It would be difficult to mount a seating contest after a primary election without the active cooperation of the would-be delegates who could claim to have been defeated as the result of raiding. But losers have rarely been willing to face the political unpopularity that would result at home in a state enamored of an open primary system. The fact that apparently no such effort has ever been pressed is a tribute to the legitimacy with which primary elections are endowed by public attitudes, so long as the state's own procedures have been duly followed, and even when the vote is not confined by law to members of the party.

The other generalization is that for many years past, even when delegations are chosen by party bodies, seating contests have been extremely rare in strongly two-party states. The pressures of competition in such states make it necessary to safeguard the public reputation of each party even when internal conflict is deep and bitter. Hence, codes of appropriate political behavior are apt to be better observed; and, even when they are not, the victims hesitate to bring the issue to public attention by creating a seating contest.[27]

These factors help to explain why seating contests have originated mainly in the one-party South in recent decades, and why they occur more often in some southern states than in others. Seating contests have rarely come up to either convention from Virginia, North Carolina, Kentucky, or Tennessee— all states in which the Republican party has had a certain strength and continuity. On the other hand, the states where the party balance is most lopsided have had most of the contests.

Althought a seating contest ordinarily questions who is legitimately entitled to represent a given party constituency, the legitimacy or even the existence of the constituency is itself often questionable. But when candidate interests are involved in the seating contests, they tend to dominate the voting to the exclusion of concern for the ostensible merits. Accordingly, a reform of national party practice in these matters is often considered wildly impractical. Yet the fact is that the parties have already reformed their own behavior in handling contests to a considerable degree, and they would probably find it feasible to go even farther in cleaning up situations that impair their public reputations.

Not all seating contests are dominated by candidate interests, and there are important variations of degree among those that are. In general the problems of legitimacy in preventing and settling contests are directly related to the extent of candidate involvement. A few contests are merely frivolous or mainly involve the personal idiosyncrasies of leading participants.[28] Prudent candidates rarely become involved in such broils if adequately informed, and, as a rule, contests of this kind can be disposed of quickly.

Historically, contests involving major portions of delegations have usually arisen out of a continuing struggle between factions for control of a state party organization. Recognition by the national party, including control over federal patronage in the state when it is available, is an important asset to any faction in such a struggle.

[26] Proof of raiding is always difficult, particularly because it involves questions of motivation. Democrats who voted for Governor Earl Warren on the Republican ballot in the Wisconsin primary of 1952 were generally regarded in the state as "one-day" Republicans; but many of them may have voted for Eisenhower in November. (David, Moos, and Goldman, *op. cit.*, Vol. 4, pp. 133, 138-39.) The Minnesota Republican farmers who apparently were partly responsible for Kefauver's victory over Stevenson in the Minnesota Democratic primary of 1956 may have been prepared to vote Democratic in 1956 *if* the party nominated a candidate whom they liked. See Chapter 10, footnote 27.

[27] Cf. David, Moos, and Goldman, *op. cit.*, Vol. 1, pp. 167-68, 172.

[28] Cf. *ibid.*, Vol. 3, pp. 121-30, on the Florida Republican contest of 1952.

The faction that wins the seats at the national convention can usually name the national committee members from the state; this in turn usually carries national party recognition automatically for the next four years.

When there is active competition for the presidential nominations, the state factions engaged in any such continuing struggle are likely to become attached to alternative national candidates, either at the suggestion of a candidate manager or on their own initiative. The resulting seating contest is not easily settled on its merits. But contests involving the same state factions often arise in years when candidate interests are relatively minor and when the basic problem is to strengthen the national party for the general election campaign and for the future. When this occurs, it would seem far more likely that seating contests could be settled on their merits. In the past these opportunities have rarely been grasped effectively in either party. Instead, when contests were practically free of candidate interests, they have usually been handled on the basis of other considerations of immediate expediency, with the result that further factional discord is encouraged, the state party remains weak, and a similar contest is likely to recur four years later, when it may again be tangled with the claims of rival candidates.

Both parties have been conscious of this problem; the result has been an occasional impulse toward more care in handling seating contests and greater effort to prevent them. In 1916 and 1920 the Republican national committee went to considerable lengths to assure fair settlements but also sought to badger the contesting groups into unifying as consolidated delegations representing all factions. The apparent success of some of these efforts was largely due to the skill of Charles B. Warren as special counsel to the committee.

In recent years both parties have increased their provision for hearings and investigations in advance of the conventions.

Potentially more important, however, are the efforts that can be carried on in the intervals between conventions to develop unified, loyal, and active organizations in the states. The Republican party was able to improve its organization in a number of southern states between 1928 and 1932, and has again had some success in that regard since 1952.

In the Democratic party most of the recent contests have involved questions of state party loyalty to the national party. The new rules adopted in 1956 seem likely to restrict opportunities for bolting without penalty. If further bolting occurs, however, the national party could enforce the rule requiring replacement of national committee members who fail to give active support to the national ticket. If loyal and effective members are then appointed, the national party will be in a better position either to bring the bolting state party organization into line if possible or to maintain active relations with any loyal faction in the state.

This in turn may result in further seating contests at the next national convention, but in that event the national party will at least be able to seat a loyal delegation from the state if it wishes to do so. The possibilities in this kind of strategy were illustrated in the Mississippi and Texas contests of 1952, where the availability of contesting loyalist delegations for possible seating had a marked restraining effect upon the insurgent tendencies of the regular state party delegations that were eventually seated.[29]

Further procedural reforms could perhaps be devised that might be of some help in guarding against the hazards of seating contests in the rare years when they occur in extreme form. In the main, however, it would seem that the more effective solutions will have to come through building competitive state systems in which each state party is sufficiently in accord with national sentiment in its party to accept

[29] *Ibid.*, Vol. 3, Chaps. 10 and 14.

majority rule at the national conventions, and sufficiently strong and cohesive to deal with its own membership and factional problems at home. This is a problem for both national parties, and one that goes far beyond the immediate questions involved in the contests for seats at the national conventions.

Comparative Analysis of Mandating Systems

Formidable difficulties stand in the way of any comparative analysis of the mandating systems that operate through presidential primary elections and those that operate through what are here called party processes. Accordingly, the provisional nature of the present analysis should be emphasized.[30]

[30] The term "party processes" has been used in this chapter for all of the systems other than those usually called presidential primary elections. This terminology is not entirely satisfactory, but a more satisfactory or less confusing one has not so far been discovered.

In a strict sense, party processes also obviously operate within and through the presidential primary systems. The party organizations often put slates of would-be delegates on the ballot in every form of presidential primary, and often these slates are elected unopposed or with no substantial opposition. When voters are given a ballot choice between contesting slates, each slate may represent the organizing efforts of a party faction. After the election, the winning slate has a mandate not only from the party voters who elected it but also from the party groups that helped to put it on the ballot in the first place; and the latter may be its most influential mandate.

The nature of the mandates conferred, and especially how valid and specific they will be, is largely controlled by the several units that comprise a mandating system. For the presidential primary systems, the principal units include such elements as (a) public polling places, (b) public election officials, (c) definitions of the voters who may vote in the primary of each party, (d) the ballot, (e) formal procedures by which the alternatives are determined and entered on the ballot, and (f) informal procedures that precede the formulation of these alternatives.

For the party process systems built on *ad hoc* meetings, the counterpart units include (a) semipublic party meetings, (b) party officials rather than public officials in charge of the meetings, (c) little clarity in the definition of the "party voters" who may participate (sometimes defined in law or formal

Like the presidential primaries, the party processes built on *ad hoc* meetings plainly embody the theory that party voters should be given an opportunity to impose a relevant mandate through an election at an appropriate time and place. But the validity of the popular mandate may become blurred by the party processes as it moves up through the hierarchy of meetings and representation.

The semipublic meeting can readily become a very private meeting, held at an inappropriate time and place. The party official presiding, with his own vested interests, may be prejudiced in the procedural and other decisions that he will be called upon to make. The definitions of the party voters who are allowed to attend, while probably no more variable than the definitions that have been written into public law for the primaries, are open to question both in what they say and how they are interpreted. The procedures for taking and recording the votes readily become faulty. The system as a whole is capable of raising innumerable questions about the legitimacy of the decisions throughout its lower levels, which may then be passed up for review in higher-level meetings that have inherited the same infirmities.

Despite all this, the observers who participated in the 1952 study were impressed with the respectability of these procedures generally in most of the states where they are used. Party meetings at all levels were conducted most of the time in a manner that appeared to be compatible with the cultural and ethical standards that are generally held throughout American life. Aside from the few states where seating contests arose, the results were generally accepted as legitimate. Voter apathy was judged to

party rules, but subject in practice to the discretion of presiding officers), (d) further party meetings of the representatives selected in the lowest level meetings, (e) voting usually by voice votes and show-of-hand voting with little use of a written, printed, or secret ballot, (f) use of parliamentary procedures in formalizing the alternatives for choice, (g) informal procedures that precede the final choice of the alternatives.

be more responsible than any other single factor for the inadequacy of mandates.

Where the lower-level party representatives are elected in primaries, the problems of *ad hoc* meetings are avoided. The units of which these systems are built up are similar to those of the presidential primaries in some respects, to those of the purely party process systems in others. In general, however, unlike both the presidential primaries and the *ad hoc* meetings, they offer the party voters no opportunity to provide relevant mandates through their votes. Instead, it seems to be assumed that the party organizations will provide representation at the national convention, and that the party voters, if they have anything to say, should say it at the proper time to the representatives who have been provided, rather than making it a basis for choice among competing delegates at some earlier time.

Obviously this is the system least open to active control by voters interested in a particular candidate. But it is not necessarily unresponsive to voter opinion that is strongly held. The mandates of the party voters of Michigan, the largest state where this system exists, were seemingly at least as well executed at the party conventions of 1952 as those of most other states.

Perhaps the most basic difference between the party processes and the presidential primaries is in the timing and the other features that depend on timing. In the party process systems the selection and mandating of the delegates remain largely open until near the final moment of choice in the responsible party body. Voter opinion may then be assessed in terms of its current manifestations, as well as of manifestations that may have occurred in earlier stages of the process. It can be flexibly taken into account both in the choice of delegates and in the related decisions on whether to instruct formally and to what extent.

In the presidential primaries, by contrast, there is a tendency to cut arbitrarily into early phases of the campaign and often to compel premature decisions as to who shall go on the ballot. This is conspicuously so when presidential candidates must be named on the ballot with their own formal consent. On a lesser scale, the same problems are involved when would-be delegates with known preferences must decide long in advance whether or not to file.

The presidential primary systems assume that by the date of the primary the voter can make an informed choice among candidates for delegate if not among candidates for President. It is for this reason that the various systems for associating delegates with presidential candidates, or for avoiding such association, are so important in distinguishing among the various categories of primaries. But the party process systems make no assumption about how soon the party voter will make up his mind. If his mind is made up, he may come to a meeting or express his opinion to a party committeeman. If he is undecided or indifferent, the process will still operate, and in the end will give consideration to his views at least by trying to estimate the prospects for victory with one candidate rather than another.

The party process systems are similar in major respects to those presidential primary systems in which delegates are not allowed to name a preferred candidate on the ballot. Would-be delegates are seldom compelled by the party organizations to associate themselves publicly with a national candidate when they are running for election by a party convention. The systems, in fact, rarely provide them with special facilities, such as ballot identifications, through which to do so.[31] Candidates for the nominations

[31] The Republican state party convention in Vermont in 1952 used a printed ballot in the election of the national convention delegates; presidential preferences of the would-be delegates were indicated on the ballot. (David, Moos, and Goldman, *op. cit.*, Vol. 2, pp. 59-60.) An Australian ballot was used in one of the Republican congressional district conventions in Maine. (*Ibid.*, p. 15.) The present authors have had occasion to be aware of the use of printed ballots in county mass meetings near Washington, D.C.

are not encouraged to campaign among the voters in the hope of securing the election of supporting delegations, and they almost never undertake such campaigns on their own initiative.

In the party process systems typically, the informed choice is made in the convention or committee that selects the delegates. In preparation for that decision, the would-be delegates may become identified informally with preferred candidates. The local managers for the national candidates, on their part, may work behind the scenes for the selection of a favorable delegation. Members of state conventions are usually well informed on such involvements, and also on other circumstances that may arouse conflict in the election of the delegates. When such conflict occurs, it may be concerned not only with candidates, but also with issues, state party factions, and the personalities of would-be delegates.

The correct interpretation of the outcome may be relatively unknown to the public, but it is usually understood from one point of view or another by the active participants, including the delegates who win election. It forms an essential part of their mandate.

Adequacy of the Mandates

As ordinarily conceived, an adequate mandate is one that is both valid and specific. Where it is difficult or impossible to be both valid and specific, presumably it is more important that the mandate be valid (or at least not invalid) than that it be specific. Some discretion to deal with contingencies must always be left to the delegate if representative processes are to be used. It would seem that a valid mandate can always be given if, but only if, the instructing constituency is willing to be sufficiently general in instructions to leave room for this essential discretion. Invalid mandates are the usual result of attempts to be specific under circumstances that make valid specificity impossible.

Any state presidential primary in which the delegates are invariably required to pledge themselves to a named candidate before the filing date for the primary is thereby capable of producing an invalid mandate. This is the inevitable consequence of the fact that no early ballot can surely place before the party voters the principal alternatives to be considered months later by the respective conventions, since the list of available candidates as well as their relative standing will often change during the period before the convention. The existing primaries differ widely in the frequency with which they are likely to produce invalid mandates in an open nominating contest, but it is easy to recognize situations in which no state primary can hope to produce a valid mandate for a specific candidate in a given year. This apparently was the situation in the Democratic party in 1952; in that year, probably the only Democratic primaries that produced valid mandates were those like New York's, in which the delegates were given discretion without being committed to any specific candidate.[32]

Party processes that commit the delegates to a specific candidate at the time of delegate election also run the risk of producing invalid mandates. They are, however, much less vulnerable than the primaries to this danger. Party bodies are free to look over the entire field of possible candidates. They are never required by law to name a specific choice, and if they do they rarely go beyond a favorite son unless the circumstances appear to be such that clarity of choice is possible.

[32] Perhaps an exception should be made for the Florida primary, since its mandate for Senator Richard B. Russell was probably a valid expression of the views of Florida Democrats, both at the time of the primary and at the time of the convention. The New Hampshire mandate for Senator Estes Kefauver also had a strong presumption of validity, since he defeated an incumbent President who was still presumed to be in the race. In all the other mandates given for Kefauver through the primaries, the validity of the result was open to question because Stevenson's name was not before the voters in any effective way, and neither was that of any other candidate behind whom the leaders might have rallied, such as Barkley.

Although instructions for a favorite son are common, they are often simply a gambit to avoid premature commitment in a time of uncertainty. The designation of a favorite son is unlikely to hobble the proper discretion of a delegation elected in a state party body. A full allowance for the informal aspects of the situation, as well as for the contingencies that will doubtless arise, is usually assumed to be implicit in any instructions given by a party body. Delegates elected in primaries, by contrast, sometimes appear to feel that they have no substantial discretion to reinterpret a specific mandate when the situation changes.

A party body, in validly instructing the delegates according to its own preferences, may still be imposing a mandate that is invalid as a representation of rank-and-file opinion. For the state convention or committee is generally made up of organization regulars whose preferences among candidates may be quite different from those of the voters of their own parties. The evidence concerning the differences in attitudes has frequently been clear and well documented. Senator Robert A. Taft's popularity with Republican party workers, for example, ran well ahead of his popularity among Republican voters for a long period of years, if the public opinion polls can be trusted on that point. Party regulars appear to be typically more conservative than the voters, and less receptive to candidates who talk about a need for change in the old ways. They look for candidates who will work harmoniously with the organizations, and dislike those who run primarily as independents.

On the other hand, the party regulars are usually intent on finding and nominating candidates who can win, and they may sacrifice some of their feelings to that end. Much can be forgiven a candidate who looks like a winner if he will at least refrain from openly attacking the organization. What seems to happen is that popular mandates are distorted in the direction of organization attitudes whenever the regu-

lars either feel certain of victory or have no hope of it. In close elections, the state organizations, even when they are deeply hostile to their national party organization, are under pressure to support the candidate who will be most preferred by the voters of their own party—and who can pull votes from the other party and the independents.

The creation of valid mandates is particularly complex when the choice has to be made from among alternatives that cannot be well known to the voters. The party voters throughout the country are rarely in a position to know, for example, which five of the party's upcoming governors are most deserving of consideration for the next presidential nomination. For this kind of problem, it can be argued that the party process systems are usually far superior to the primaries in which delegates are required to become committed.

Mandates that are merely implied and sometimes even those that are express may call for a type of candidate rather than a particular individual. This kind of mandate sets bounds to the discretion of the delegates while leaving freedom of action within those bounds. Such mandates are probably most often given by the party process systems and by primaries of the New York type. Their adequacy is difficult to appraise, but it would seem that they are rarely invalid. Often they may be much more specific than is commonly supposed.

It was noted of the New York Democratic delegation of 1952, for example, that

. . . there was a strongly crystallized conviction among the delegates, overriding the personal preferences of many, that only a certain kind of platform and a certain kind of candidate would be acceptable to the voters of New York.[33]

To the extent that party competition or other factors produce definite and similar attitudes throughout the mass of the party voters in a state, the delegates will know of such attitudes and so may find themselves

[33] David, Moos, and Goldman, op. cit., Vol. 2, p. 176.

clearly provided with mandates that override personal preferences.

Possible Improvements

It seems unlikely that party processes can be so reformed as to bring masses of voters into action in the presidential nominating contests. If this is the objective, it would be necessary first of all to provide conditions under which contests will develop and engage public attention, and then to make it relatively simple for the voters of each party to have their say. Both specifications would seem to call for something like the Florida or New Hampshire type of primary, since it is unlikely they would be met by the party process systems, however improved.

A different objective, and one to which party processes are better adapted, is to avoid invalid mandates and provide valid ones with some degree of definiteness wherever possible. Here, as previously noted, the major hazards are the biases that tend to accumulate in party organizations that remain too long undisturbed by infusions of a principled insurgency.

In many states the party process systems have nonetheless developed considerable ability to respond to waves of voter interest, such as the signs of insurgency noted among the "new Republicans" of 1952. Relatively modest amounts of public pressure, applied under appropriate circumstances, might help to make the systems in other states more open and more responsive to the popular will.

In many of these systems fairly simple changes in procedure could bring the voters into closer touch with the party organization. In the systems built on *ad hoc* meetings, there is still a frequent need for better scheduling and more accessible locations of meetings. If all such meetings throughout a state are held on the same date, late in the spring of the presidential year, it becomes easier to focus public attention on them and to encourage attendance. If they thus become subject to public attention, including the attention of the press, malpractice in the conduct of the meetings is also less of a hazard.

The systems built on the election of precinct representatives in the off-year primaries would attract more popular interest if shifted to the spring of the presidential year. In a state that is not too large it might be desirable for the voters to elect representatives directly to the state conventions, without going through an intermediate level of county conventions; but in the large states this might involve excessive size either in the state convention or in the local units of representation.

It may also be worth while to inquire whether the states that have attained order by using primaries in the lower levels of party organization may have paid too high a price. A return to *ad hoc* party meetings in the spring of the presidential year might prove useful in enlisting the interest of the party voters in the nominating campaigns and in the general election campaign to follow.

Even if the number of voters coming out were to be no higher in the *ad hoc* meetings than in the precinct primaries—and it could hardly be lower—attendance at a meeting may lead to recruitment into some greater form of party activity, whereas voting in a primary seems less likely to do so. Moreover, a meeting with no ostensible purpose except to elect a precinct representative may still lead to the discussion of party policy, the development of views, and the expression of a mandate—none of which could well happen in a precinct primary.

In some states improvements in the party processes might have important consequences. It seems likely, however, that questions of procedure are far more important in the primary systems. Every feature included in a primary is in effect a formalization of procedure by public law. Many of these formalizations may limit the effectiveness of the system in ways discussed in Chapter 10. All formalization, moreover, probably tends to reduce effectiveness merely by making the system more rigid. Formalization may also prevent the consideration of underlying disagreements that would have aroused argument and attracted voter attention. The informality of the party processes is at the root of most of the allegations of malpractice, but it may also be their greatest strength because of leaving room for open contention, adaptation, and change. If this is so, proposals for drastic reform in the party processes, and especially those that look toward further formalization by law, should be regarded with caution.

The more effective utilization of party processes will depend on changes going well beyond matters of procedure. The skill and the wisdom with which the party processes are used would seem to be related first of all to the health of the party system as a whole. This can be impaired by faulty procedures, and procedural reform may therefore be a worthy first step in dealing with situations that are clearly unhealthy. But far more basic would seem to be the ideals and objectives with which political activity is undertaken, the tone of the surrounding social order, and the energy and readiness with which great public causes are pursued. These are questions that cannot be avoided in dealing with the problems of nominations for the highest political office in the United States; it is well to keep them in mind most of all when dealing with procedural issues whose total effect may indeed seem minor against this larger background.

12

The Changing Character of Nominating Campaigns

THE TWO PREVIOUS chapters have been concerned with the evolving apparatus of the presidential primaries and other mandating systems. How that apparatus will work on any given occasion, however, is largely dependent on the changing modes of behavior of the candidates and their managers, the party activists, and the ordinary voters.

Over the long run, there has been an increasing tendency to mount nominating campaigns that look toward the development of a popular choice, along with a marked rise in voter participation in the nominations. Candidates seem to feel an increasing need to prove in one way or another that they have popular support. Some of the primaries give room for such demonstrations, but in their present form their importance comes mainly from their interaction with other methods for developing and giving effect to public and voter opinion.

In a striking review of these developments Professor William G. Carleton has argued that there has been a revolution in how nominations are made.

Party methods of nominating presidential and vice-presidential candidates are yielding, without much formal or structural change, to twentieth-century mass democracy. Delegates to national conventions, even the biggest of the "big shots," are in the process of being reduced to popular rubber stamps, very much as presidential electors were reduced to nullities during the first decade of our present federal Constitution. Increasingly a national nominating convention is merely choosing its nominee from among popular national favorites; increasingly it is being forced to pick *the* national favorite.[1]

This view puts the case in extreme terms and rests upon evidence that has been somewhat overstated.[2] Nevertheless, it does appear that real and significant changes have occurred. To the present writers, those changes—so far as they can be traced to specific influences—appear to be mainly due to the combined effect of the primaries, the public opinion polls, and the mass media of communication. Other factors, more general and more remote, were no doubt also influential. The growing power of the Presidency, a heightened concern for the position of the United States and its leadership in the world at large, and the many pressures toward centralization in a mass society—all have had their impact on the presidential office and on attitudes concerning how it should be filled. But the primaries, the polls, and the mass media have in effect become parts of the nominating process that must be taken into account.

[1] William G. Carleton, "The Revolution in the Presidential Nominating Convention," *Political Science Quarterly*, Vol. 72 (June 1957), pp. 224-40.
[2] For example, Governor Adlai E. Stevenson had not become a "national name" (as that term was used in the article) nor was he leading the public opinion polls at the time of his nomination in 1952. According to a Gallup Poll two months before the convention, only a third of the voters could identify Stevenson; in the last preconvention poll, he was running a poor third among Democratic voters, polling 12 per cent against Vice President Alben W. Barkley's 18 and Senator Estes Kefauver's 45. See George Gallup, "Stevenson Draft Foreshadowed," *Washington Post*, July 13, 1952.

They are very much taken into account by the strategists who plan nominating campaigns; and a review of some of the changing features of those campaigns may help to reveal how and why this has come about.

Styles of Campaigning and Their Influence on Mandates

In the days before presidential primaries were invented, the aphorism was current that the office should seek the man, and not the man the office. No doubt this doctrine was honored in the breach, even a hundred years ago, but it had a marked restraining effect upon the overt behavior of potential candidates.

It was not customary to make an open announcement of a candidacy for the nomination nor to stump the country before the convention met. On the contrary, anyone mentioned for the nomination was expected to respond with modest deprecation, to continue his previous pursuits with a minimum of ostentation, to avoid the appearance of campaigning, and to refrain from coming to the convention city unless required to be there for some other reason. Flat disavowals of candidacy were common. The candidates who were actually nominated in national party conventions during the nineteenth century had made their availability clear mainly through public refusals to disavow candidacy, coupled with affirmative statements to their associates in response to private inquires. When nominated, they were expected to affect ignorance of the event until officially advised, some weeks after the convention, by a committee dispatched for the purpose.

Quiet anticipation is still the rule for potential candidates who await a draft or who hope for possible nomination as a compromise choice. Active candidates in recent years have usually adopted quite different styles of campaigning. In the states where primaries are contested it is possible to ap-peal directly to the voters. Candidates who openly enter the primaries are required by that fact to reject the earlier doctrine that the office should seek the man.

But by coming into the open, they have encountered the need for many difficult decisions in determining their personal campaign strategies. Should a willing candidate with substantial support announce early or late? Should he enter all of the primaries, some, or none? How should he behave toward the party organizations in strongly organized states, or the factional interests where organization is weak or divided? Under what conditions if any should he enter an open contest with a favorite son in the latter's own state? If he stays out of the primaries, or most of them, what other means are available for attracting national attention and approval? How much help can he anticipate from the mass media of communication? Which is more important, popular support or good relations with party leaders and strong state organizations? Should the candidate plan to be present at the convention city during the convention? What kind of a headquarters organization should he set up at the convention? What campaign should he plan for the final days? What campaign fund-raising commitments will be involved in the various strategic decisions? Where will the money come from?

Every one of these questions has undoubtedly been argued over by the inner circles of friends and supporters of major candidates of the last fifty years. The decisions in response to such questions have produced a wide variety in styles of campaigning. These different styles, in turn, have an effect on the extent to which popular mandates come into existence in support of the various candidacies.

Avowals of Candidacy

Formal avowals of candidacy now occur frequently in the fall and winter preceding the presidential year, but with notable differences in the practices of the various lasses of candidates, and little standardization of practice even within any one class. ncumbent Presidents have rarely considered it necessary to announce candidacy or a second term on their own initiative, ut have usually either admitted or denied heir availability at some point in a press onference. President Calvin Coolidge announced in 1927 that he did not choose to un in 1928. President Franklin D. Roosevelt permitted his name to stand in the primaries of 1940 and 1944, but in 1940 made no overt announcement until the convention met, and in 1944 delayed a statement up to a few days before the convention. President Harry S. Truman announced in March 1952 that he would not run again, after previously refusing to let his name be used in primaries where written consent was required. President Dwight D. Eisenhower announced his availability for 1956 at the end of February of that year.[3]

When an incumbent President is available, others of his party who announce assume the role of challenger automatically. Vice President John N. Garner's announcement in December 1939 that he would accept the presidential nomination if offered was a clear challenge of the incumbent champion. After an unproductive conference with President Truman in January 1952, Senator Estes Kefauver went ahead with an unconditional announcement of his own candidacy. Senate Minority Leader William F. Knowland announced in December 1955 that he planned to run if President Eisenhower did not do so; he withdrew after the eventual Eisenhower announcement.

Titular leaders have been treated with considerably less deference than Presidents, but Governor Franklin D. Roosevelt may have delayed his formal announcement in 1932 until late January partly because of the growing ambiguity in ex-Governor Alred E. Smith's position. Roosevelt was reportedly reluctant to announce early in any

event because of the hazards inherent in the front-runner position. Smith had stated in 1928 that he would not again be a candidate for public office, but he announced in February 1932.

Wendell Willkie maintained a posture of probable availability for a second nomination throughout his tenure as titular leader, breaking with Republican precedent in doing so. He began active campaigning in the fall of 1943; Harold E. Stassen also became a candidate in October of that year, and Governor John W. Bricker of Ohio announced in November. Governor Thomas E. Dewey of New York, on the other hand, was a reluctant candidate, at first taking the position that he would not run in 1944.

Dewey's prospective availability for 1948 did not deter other candidates and may have led some of them to announce unusually early. Stassen announced in January 1947, a year and a half before the convention. Senator Robert A. Taft announced in October 1947 and Governor Earl Warren in November. Dewey himself did not announce until January 1948. In 1955, Senator Kefauver waited until after Stevenson's announcement in November, then followed in December.

The only nominating campaign since 1940 that has involved neither an incumbent President nor an available titular leader was that of 1952 on the Republican side. Taft again announced in October of the previous year, as he had in 1947. He based his early decision in part on invitations to enter the primaries in Wisconsin and Ohio, where formal consent on his part was required. Warren followed in November and Stassen in December. In January 1952, Eisenhower, faced with entry of his name in the New Hampshire primary, stated from Paris: "Under no circumstances will I ask for relief from this assignment in order to seek nomination to political office and I shall not participate in the preconvention activities of others who may have such intention with respect to me." On this basis, he permitted his name to stand in

[3] See Chapter 4.

New Hampshire. He later returned from
Paris, retired from the army, and made his
opening campaign speech in Kansas on
June 4.

Reluctant candidates have continued to
follow the practice of announcing late or
not at all. General Douglas MacArthur
made no formal admission of availability
for 1952, although in the fall of 1951 he had
ranked second only to Eisenhower in a Gallup poll of voter preference, and second
only to Taft in a poll of the delegates who
had attended the Republican convention of
1948. Governor Stevenson repeatedly disclaimed candidacy up to the time of the
Democratic convention of 1952, although
never going so far as to say that he would
refuse the nomination if offered.

Aside from the Eisenhower case, in recent years important examples of announcements that were late but definite have occurred only in the Democratic party. The
Democratic contest of 1952 included Averell
Harriman's announcement in April, too
late to enter any primary except that of the
District of Columbia, which he won. Vice
President Alben W. Barkley announced in
late May, when it had begun to appear that
the Truman administration might have nowhere else to go in search of a candidate
that it could effectively support. In 1956,
Stevenson and Kefauver had the field
largely to themselves until the primaries
were over; Harriman announced almost immediately thereafter, in June.

Preconvention Campaign Patterns

Campaign styles that are related to particular types of candidacy and to the specific
opportunities of the various state systems
have already been commented on.[4] The development of these patterns over time, however, has been somewhat different in the
two major parties.

[4] See Chapters 10 and 11; also see Paul T. David,
Malcolm Moos, and Ralph M. Goodman, *Presidential
Nominating Politics in 1952* (1954), Vol. 1, pp. 186-
91.

The impact of the primaries on campaign
practices was at first felt mainly in the Re
publican party. This was conspicuously true
in 1912, but in some respects even more so
in 1920. Three leading candidates were in
volved in the Republican nominating cam
paigns of 1920: Governor Frank O. Low
den, General Leonard Wood, and Senator
Hiram Johnson. Wood and Johnson were
notably independent in their relationship
to established party leaders and organiza
tions. Both made substantial efforts to
mount campaigns in the states with pri
maries as well as to develop delegate
strength elsewhere. Lowden also ran in sev
eral primaries, but sought the cooperation
of the party organizations more actively and
avoided direct contests against favorite sons
In the end, large campaign expenditures
and hectic campaigning led to stalemate;
none of the front-runners could demon
strate that he was the predominant choice
of either the voters or the delegates. Since
each of the three was unwilling to com
promise or to support one of the others as a
second choice, the convention in effect was
returned to organization control, with the
result that it chose Senator Warren G. Har
ding as a dark horse.

In the Democratic party, most of the
leading candidates for the nominations
from 1912 to 1932 adopted essentially a defensive attitude toward the primaries.
Speaker Champ Clark and Governor
Woodrow Wilson were involved in the pri
maries of 1912, but not greatly on their
own initiative. In 1920 the Democratic situation was not conducive to extensive pre
convention campaigning. In 1924, William
G. McAdoo was more active in the pri
maries and in other ways than Governor
Alfred E. Smith, but his efforts obviously
did not swing the convention. In 1928,
Smith solidified his position with a minimum of preconvention campaigning and
with little opposition.

In 1932, Governor Franklin D. Roosevelt
pursued a long-prepared and most active
preconvention campaign through all of the

traditional channels. He was entered in several primaries, and suffered defeats in Massachusetts and California. He traveled little personally as a candidate and never let himself get into the position of seeming to stump the country before the convention. Three out-of-state candidates—Roosevelt, Smith, and Garner—were on the ballot of the California primary and the delegation was directly at stake, but not one of the three candidates entered the state for personal campaign activity. It is probable that Roosevelt was drawn by erroneous information into both the Massachusetts and California primaries, and that he might have declined both if he had anticipated an active contest.

Several features of the situation should be noted in interpreting Democratic party attitudes to the primaries during the period 1912-1948. Campaigning in the early primaries of 1912, 1920, and 1924 was not effective as a means of winning victory at the conventions of either party. Active primary campaigns, where they occurred, seemed to have the effect of hardening the differences among the leading candidates and of making each more unattractive to the supporters of the others. In general, any candidate who won a mere plurality became less available than before as a second choice of the other factions and could not push his strength as a first choice to the point required for victory. This kind of process could be seen to be especially dangerous in the Democratic party under the two thirds rule. The effect of the rule on the balloting in the Democratic conventions of 1912, 1920, and 1924 no doubt discouraged primary campaigns by Democratic candidates from then on while the rule lasted. After its repeal in 1936, the long period of the Roosevelt and Truman incumbencies led to a profound lack of interest in open preconvention campaigning by opposing candidates in the Democratic party.

Meanwhile, insurgency and open campaigning were largely out of fashion in the Republican party from 1928 to 1940. In 1940 the leading candidates who could be regarded as party regulars, Thomas E. Dewey and Robert A. Taft, were relatively new, unknown, and untried, and Senator Arthur Vandenberg was unwilling to campaign actively. Under the circumstances, Wendell Willkie was able to mount a remarkable campaign directed partly to the voters through the mass media and partly to influential local citizens through advertising, commercial, and banking channels. The combination brought him the nomination in a new type of convention stampede, which had the appearance in its final stages of being generated by gallery enthusiasm, but was probably influenced considerably more by a flood of telegrams and long-distance telephone messages to delegates from leading citizens at home. Major elements in the Willkie formula were used by several later campaigners for the Republican nominations—most notably by the leaders of the campaign to draft Eisenhower.

Republican party attitudes on preconvention campaigning probably changed substantially as the result of the 1940 and 1944 campaigns. Modern mass media and public relations techniques were seen as having possibilities for arousing the voters and so bringing pressure on the delegates. The primaries were not accepted as an effective means of winning a nomination, but after Willkie's defeat in 1944 they were increasingly feared as potentially fatal to a candidate's cause.

In 1948 the Republican titular leader and front-runner, Dewey, attempted at first to campaign mainly through organization contacts and traditional channels, but he entered a number of primaries by request and with assurances of strong support. Taft, the other organization favorite, entered fewer primaries, worked through his associates in appealing to the state party organizations, and relied for popular support upon his outstanding work in the Senate. Stassen, running mainly as an independent but with relatively ample campaign funds, entered as many primaries as possible, even challenging Taft in Ohio, and attempted to mount the broadest possible appeal to the voters. Stassen's tactics had some early success, with the result that Dewey found himself compelled to campaign actively in Oregon. There he not only accepted Stassen's challenge to a nationally broadcast radio debate but also campaigned throughout the state for several days by bus, making six to ten speeches a day—a performance the like of which no previous candidate of major stature had felt called upon to endure.[5]

The 1952 campaigns in the Republican party made the fullest use of the available techniques, but again with noteworthy differences in the style of the leading contestants. Stassen was again running as an independent, using the same strategy as in 1948 but with less adequate financing and markedly less success either in the primaries or elsewhere. Taft mounted a far more carefully organized campaign and gave it more personal attention. His strength again lay with the party organization regulars in the Middle West and South, but he tried hard to appeal to the public and to make a showing in a number of primaries.

In some respects the primaries may be said to have come into their own for the first time in the Republican campaign of 1952, although few of them yielded a clear decision between Taft and Eisenhower. In most cases after New Hampshire, moreover, the major demonstrations of popular support usually occurred despite the reluctance or nonconsent of one or both of the two leading candidates, as in Minnesota, Massachusetts, Nebraska, South Dakota, and Oregon. But the basic strength of the Eisenhower campaign lay in his evident ability to get votes. The record in the primaries was only one facet in demonstrating that ability, but it was clearly an important one.

The problems of preconvention campaigning were rediscovered in the Democratic party in 1952, with conspicuous signs of unpreparedness for an open nominating

situation. President Truman showed vast confidence in his ability to name his successor, but he evidently underestimated the danger, from his point of view, in letting Kefauver pile up a lead in the primaries while he and the other party leaders were failing to agree on any preferred candidate who was certainly available. Kefauver's showing in the primaries was clearly a surprise. He never came close to winning the nomination, but the brutal manner in which he was rejected left scars on the party and weakened its position in the general election.

In 1956 the campaigns in the Democratic party were notably similar to those of the Republican party in 1948. As a titular leader, Stevenson occupied a position analogous to Dewey's in 1948. Stevenson was equally reluctant to take on a heavy schedule of campaigning in the primaries, but found himself facing an opponent in Kefauver whose campaign style was similar to Stassen's. Stevenson, moreover, was under heavy pressure from state organizations and local factions to enter the primaries against Kefauver in several states where no strong favorite son was readily available. The result was four months of concentrated primary campaigning for both candidates, in which Kefauver won heavily in New Hampshire and Minnesota, the mid-campaign primaries were something of a draw, and Stevenson won in Oregon, Florida, and California. Harriman then announced and Kefauver withdrew; the conflict went on into the convention, and Stevenson won.

Candidate Activity at the Convention City

One of the most striking changes in styles of campaigning is in the customary behavior of the candidates while the conventions are in session. Before 1896 candidates seldom came to the convention; the few who were there were usually dark horses who were suddenly drafted—for example, Horatio Seymour, the Democratic candidate

[5] Cf. Malcolm Moos, *The Republicans* (1956), pp. 433-38.

of 1868, and James A. Garfield, the Republican candidate of 1880. In 1896, William Jennings Bryan and several of his major competitors were at the Democratic national convention, but all had parts to play as delegates and state party leaders.

For about forty years, from 1896 to 1936, the practice was mixed; the eventual nominees were rarely present at the convention city though other leading contenders were frequently there. In 1912, Wilson was at the governor's summer mansion in New Jersey when nominated in Baltimore; Clark was in Baltimore. In 1920, Harding was at Chicago when nominated there, but Cox was at home in Dayton, Ohio, when nominated in San Francisco. In 1928, Hoover was in Washington when nominated at Kansas City and Smith was in New York when nominated at Houston; in 1920, Smith, as a leading contender, had been in San Francisco. Throughout this period incumbent Presidents continued to remain aloof from the conventions and were never present for any purpose.

Until 1932 each party sent a committee to the nominee's home after the convention to inform him of the nomination—even if he had been present at the convention when he was nominated. The practice symbolized the nineteenth-century tradition that the possible candidate remained aloof while he awaited the call to duty. By 1932 this symbolism was clearly archaic, a fact dramatized by Governor Franklin D. Roosevelt when he flew from Albany to Chicago and appeared before the convention in person to accept the nomination.

In 1936 the Republican party still maintained the tradition by sending a committee to Topeka, Kansas, in late July to notify Landon of his nomination in early June, but Roosevelt again broke tradition by appearing at Franklin Field, Philadelphia, to accept his renomination. This may have been the first occasion on which an incumbent President addressed his political party in national convention assembled.

In 1940, Wendell Willkie "violated modern convention tradition by ambling around hotel lobbies buttonholing delegates and asking them to vote for him."[6] After the nominations he appeared briefly at the convention—with Mrs. Willkie—and promised to make the campaign a crusade. Nevertheless, the notification ceremony was maintained, and was turned to modern public relations uses by arrangements for an acceptance speech at Willkie's childhood home, Elwood, Indiana.

In 1944, at the height of the war, Roosevelt delivered his acceptance speech by radio and without coming to the convention. At the Republican convention that year, however, a committee of six was named to notify the nominee, to invite him to address the convention, and to escort him if he came, as Dewey promptly did. This completed the transition to a new usage in both parties, and in 1948, 1952, and 1956 each nominee appeared before his party's convention in its closing hours.

With this change, all pretense that the candidates for the nomination should stay away from the convention city vanished. After 1944 it was the custom for all admitted candidates, except an incumbent President, to come to the convention city early and set up campaign headquarters. An incumbent President awaiting renomination customarily arrived in time to appear in the hall soon after the vote.

In 1952, although not a candidate, President Truman established another new precedent by coming near the end of the proceedings to greet the convention and give his approval to the choice of a successor, who was also present. This is a precedent that may create interesting problems for the future. One can only speculate, for example, on what President Grover Cleveland would have done when Bryan was nominated in 1896 had the precedent existed at the time. The new practice clearly symbolizes a process of investiture for the incoming party leader.

[6] Moos, *op. cit.*, p. 411.

What can be said of the consequences of having the candidates at the convention city? First of all, it has meant more responsible attitudes in the private discussions that occur at the final time and place of decision, and a considerable curtailment of the wide latitude previously allowed to the candidate's managers. No longer can a candidate pretend that he did not know about what may have been said on his behalf by his managers at the convention.

Second, it has opened the way for face-to-face contacts between the candidate and the delegates whose support he is seeking. Delegations call on the candidates; candidates visit delegation meetings. Undecided delegates in strategic positions are often invited to question a candidate directly. Without claiming too much for this type of conference, one may feel confident that it can often have the effect of placing the delegate's duty and responsibility on a higher plane than might otherwise be the case.

Third, and sometimes most important, is the impact on the formation and expression of popular mandates in the final days of choice. Thanks in part to the intensive radio and television coverage of activities at the convention city in recent years, the whole country can reassess the candidates when seeing them come into action as the convention meets. If a true and massive popular mandate is to make its appearance in either party—a thing that happens rarely and that may not often be desirable—this is the final opportunity for such a mandate to crystallize and become manifest.

In any event, the party voters all across the country can reassess their previous positions at the time of the conventions if they see fit to do so. They are given information to consider that is nearly as extensive as that available to the delegates. They can then communicate with the delegates by mail, telegram, and telephone, and through the channels of the mass media. Although the results are not necessarily the same as those of a national referendum or plebiscite and are subject to all of the questions of differ-ential access and influence, they undoubtedly make themselves felt—and in a manner that shares both the virtues and the blemishes of processes that are long familiar in all types of American representative assemblies.

Campaign Styles as a
Product of Institutional Pressures

In the previous review of campaign styles, the rough outlines of a classification of candidates have also become apparent. A candidate may occupy the Presidency or the titular leadership, or some other political office, or no office; he may be willing or unwilling to be an active candidate; he may be an organization man or an independent; he may be a strongly factional leader or a well-known middle-of-the-roader; he may be aggressively ambitious or quietly so. All such factors tend to produce different kinds of candidates in one way or another. Some of the factors, moreover, tend to occur together and produce recurring types of candidates that are easily recognized when they appear. For each identifiable type, there is in turn a style of campaigning that tends to be regarded as normal, although the number of cases is too small to justify a highly formal classification.

Notwithstanding this variation, however, there has been an evolution of campaign styles that has affected almost all types of candidates. The tendency has been in the direction of campaigning that is more open, more competitive, and more deliberately designed to encourage the public to take a hand. The tendency is clearest in the case of the ambitious newcomers who court the populace with little backing or sponsorship from established leaders; but any admitted candidate is now expected to campaign in a manner that would have seemed remarkably aggressive a generation ago. Even the reluctant candidates find themselves engaged increasingly in a round of public appearances and other activities that are hard to fend off without seeming ungracious.

These changes are no doubt partly the reflection of general changes in the mass society of the world today, but also come back directly to the specific institutional factors and pressures that were mentioned at the beginning of the chapter. The presidential primaries, the public opinion polls, and the greater activity of press, radio, and television, all have the effect of creating opportunities for competitive self-display. These opportunities lead the public to expect a response from the candidates, and those expectations are in themselves pressures on the candidates. But the actual response still depends on what the candidate himself decides to do; he is not as helpless under these institutional pressures as it may seem.

It can be argued, for example, that the whole history of nominating campaigns in recent years would have been different but for the presence of two individuals, Harold E. Stassen and Estes Kefauver. Both had reason to think that they would never be seriously considered for a presidential nomination unless they could make a spectacular success in the primaries. Both were accustomed to slugging it out in state campaigns, and both could hope to make a showing in the presidential primaries by the same style of campaigning. Both were successful in finding groups of backers who would put up the necessary campaign funds.

In the absence of the primaries, Stassen and Kefauver probably would never have started or would have followed an entirely different style. The primaries thus seem to have made possible the appearance of candidates of this type, but did not make it inevitable that they would appear. It would be hard to name anyone else actually on the scene who could have campaigned in this style with similar effectiveness if these particular individuals had not been there to do it. Both Stassen and Kefauver seem to be genuine examples of personalities who created their role rather than the reverse.

Without Stassen and Kefauver, therefore, the nominating campaigns of recent years

might have been somewhat different. But what would they have been like? The supposition, for example, that Dewey and Stevenson would both have been allowed to coast into their second nominations seems a little too simple. Their opposition probably would have made less noise in the primaries, but opposition there would have been, and it might have broken loose in the primaries as well as in other ways.

Another possible suggestion is that Dewey and Stevenson were foolish to meet such challengers as Stassen and Kefauver with their own weapons. Why take part in party-splitting campaigns that weaken even the winner, it is argued; why not let candidates like Stassen and Kefauver wear themselves out in contests with favorite sons or, at worst, let them win a few delegates unopposed? This suggests that Dewey was wrong in getting entangled in selected primaries in 1948, and Stevenson equally so in 1956—and that both were again wrong in deciding to campaign actively in the later primaries after being beaten in the earlier ones.

Any such conclusion would require guessing at many relevant factors on which no adequate information is at hand. It would seem, however, that if the men who had to make the decisions had decided to disregard the challenges, they would have had to answer many difficult questions. Who were the favorite sons that could have saved the situation in various states if the front-runners had decided not to risk their own prestige there? Was it certain that Stassen or Kefauver could be stopped at the conventions if no serious effort had been made to stop them beforehand? If they were stopped by convention manipulation, how many millions of their ardent supporters would think the nomination had been stolen for a hand-picked choice? How much would this damage the party's prospects for winning the general election? Anyhow, how much reason did Dewey or Stevenson have to think that if they let the primaries go by default they would then be the convention choice? Might not Taft have been the Republican candidate in 1948 and Governor Averell Harriman or Senator Stuart Symington the Democratic choice in 1956?

At any rate, presumably after reviewing considerations of this kind, Dewey and Stevenson made their decisions. Since candidates and their managers have no safe standards for judging the effectiveness of different campaign styles and tactics, the tendency when in doubt is to be aggressive, to accept heavy burdens on the candidate's time and energy, and to use all the means of campaigning for which the money can be found. The publicly available evidence all indicates that when Dewey and Stevenson decided to enter the primaries they entered cautiously, reluctantly, and under some pressure from friendly state party organizations. Clearly the decisions were not made because either man had any desire to assume the campaign style he eventually accepted or was deliberately seeking to enhance the importance of the primaries.

So far as other leading actors in the recent nominating contests were concerned, Willkie picked the most difficult primary situation in the country for his comeback bid, believing that he had no satisfactory alternative. Eisenhowers supporters planned their early strategy around the New Hampshire primary because they needed a demonstration that Eisenhower's admitted popularity could be converted into actual votes. Taft, an organization man with a great name, preferred at all times to stay inside the organization, but his successive campaigns of 1940, 1948, and 1952 shifted steadily toward efforts to make a showing that would refute the oft-stated challenge, "Taft Can't Win."

The character of preconvention campaigning undoubtedly depends upon many factors, the most important of which is how far the nominating situation seems to be open or closed. The personalities of the leading candidates and their relationships to the state party organizations provide another complex set of factors. These may either foster open and highly active campaigning or damp it down.

The extent of chronic factionalism inside the national parties is still another factor and one that affects what kind of personalities will come into view as possible candidates. Insurgency within the parties may be taking over functions once performed by third-party movements. If this is true, factional interests may go to some lengths to find potential candidates with whom they can stir up the situation in the primaries.

With all this, however, it must be remembered that, when the major parties are closely matched, the basic drive in every national convention is to nominate a winner. Primaries, public opinion polls, and a style of campaigning that combines appeals to the national electorate through the mass media with active work at the grass roots—all seem to form an interlocking combination for the development and demonstration of vote-getting ability. In a really open nominating situation, the potential nominees who neglect any of these opportunities would seem to do so at their peril.

Campaign Styles and Campaign Finance

For active candidates and their supporters, the problem of money has been important from the first. With the coming of the primaries, and still more with the new campaigning styles since 1940, the availability of campaign funds is apparently becoming a serious limitation on running for the presidential nomination. It raises many questions for the candidates and also questions of public policy.

The available information for illuminating this problem is scanty. Few state laws on campaign finance are adapted to securing information on expenditures in the nominating campaigns. Federal law does not require any routine reporting of contributions or expenditures in such campaigns. Special investigations to uncover such information have been infrequent, the Kenyon Committee investigation of 1920 being the most noteworthy. Most of the research on campaign finance that has been attempted under private auspices has touched only the edges of the nominating process. This lack will be remedied to some extent when the research on which Alexander Heard of the University of North Carolina has been engaged for some years reaches publication, but he has confirmed the difficulties in securing comprehensive information in this field.[7]

*Financing Pre-
Announcement Activities*

The building up of a potential candidacy before any overt announcement is made can cost a good deal of money, although these activities seldom attract much attention. They involve mainly the potential candidate himself, his principal backers and managers, and often a formally organized committee or network of committees on his behalf.

The committees operate with varying degrees of independence and recognition from the candidate. When the objective is to persuade a reluctant candidate, or to draft him if necessary, voluntary committee operations take on a special importance. They may involve all types of campaign activities, with corresponding needs for money. The National Committee, Citizens for Eisenhower, reportedly spent $1,200,000 in its campaign to secure Eisenhower the 1952 nomination.[8] A considerable part of this sum was collected and spent before Eisenhower had returned from Paris and accepted his candidacy. Additional sums were undoubtedly collected and spent by state and local groups.

The National Committee, Stevenson for President, is reported to have collected only $20,300.91 during its entire existence in 1952, of which a balance of $507.13 was eventually contributed to the general election campaign.[9] Of the total, $12,859.64 was received during the ten days beginning on the Wednesday before the convention. The committee was said to have spent $2,993.79 for personal services; its other principal expenses were evidently for direct mailings, campaign buttons, telephone, and hotel space for its convention headquarters. The greater part of the committee's work was made possible by the contributed services of many talented volunteers. The Eisenhower committee, despite the far greater size of its expenditures, also made use of large amounts of unpaid, contributed services of all kinds.

The activities that went into the Eisenhower and Stevenson candidacies before the principals consented to run were in many respects unique. Something of the kind, however, happens in connection with many candidacies, and, when it does not happen spontaneously, there is usually an effort to stimulate it. Even a willing potential candidate hesitates to announce until he has had substantial assurances of support—such as commitments from those who can assist in building and financing a campaign organization and promises of help from other leaders whose eventual public statements favoring his candidacy will carry weight.

Potential candidates who seriously expect to run are therefore usually involved in a series of complex, delicate, and time-consuming activities toward that end. If the potential candidate is already in public life as a governor or senator, as is often the case, the activities blend into other phases of public and official activity so completely that they rarely become conspicuous. To the skilled observer, however, there are many telltale clues: statesmanlike utterances that have no apparent connection with the immediate constituency or official

[7] Letter, August 24, 1958.
[8] Testimony of Walter Williams, Hearings . . . Special Committee to Investigate Campaign Expenditures, 1952, U. S. House of Representatives, *Campaign Expenditures*, p. 111.

[9] These figures and the other material on the Stevenson committee in this paragraph are from Walter Johnson, *How We Drafted Adlai Stevenson* (1955), pp. 34, 38, 41, 44, 95, 117, 118, 122.

duties; a willingness to devote time and travel to carefully chosen speaking engagements from one end of the country to the other; most of all, the recruitment and utilization of a task force of associates who travel extensively and seem to be working hard at developing a candidacy, since there is no other visible explanation of what they are doing.[10]

[10] In 1957 and 1958, the three potential candidates on the Democratic side who seemed to show evidences of this type of activity more than any of the others were Senator John F. Kennedy, Governor G. Mennen Williams, and Governor Robert B. Meyner.

Any bibliography of the contemporary periodical literature on Senator Kennedy's activities during this period would be extensive, but the treatment in *Newsweek* of June 23, 1958, is an excellent example. His photograph, in color, was used on the cover against a Capitol dome background, with a cover caption reading "Jack Kennedy—Shadows of '60. Out in Front? Out on a Limb?" The feature story, pp. 29-34, included biographical details, family lore, legislative record, a quotation in which he disclaimed candidacy for the Presidency, and many details in support of the statement that "it is one of Washington's least-kept secrets that he is running as hard as good taste permits." It was stated that in 5½ months, he had received 2,568 invitations for speaking engagements and accepted 96. The story commented, "Significantly, he already maintains a revolving brain trust of professors at top Eastern universities who help with his major speeches." After comment on the political difficulties that face a wealthy candidate, the article turned to the Senator's religion and referred to "an analysis of polls and election returns which concluded that, while a Catholic may lose some Protestant votes because of his religion, he will more than make up for them by the Catholic votes he gets." A footnote pointed out that whereas "Catholics constituted about 10 per cent of the electorate in 1928 [when Al Smith was defeated] they now account for approximately 20 per cent."

Governor G. Mennen Williams received a similar treatment in a three-column story by Alan L. Otten in the *Wall Street Journal*, April 11, 1958. Noting that "the towering, youthful Soapy won't concede he's a candidate," the article stated that "Mr. Williams and a small group of devoted men around him have been dispassionately analyzing his apparent drawbacks as a national vote-getter. . . . They've decided which things they want to change and they're going about the task." After citing much evidence of precampaigning activity, the article returns to the problem of the public image and gives it intensive treatment. A Williams brain truster is quoted as saying, "If the mood of the party is moderation again, we couldn't get the nomination, no matter how we tried to change his image now. We can get the nomination only if the party's mood is an all-out New Deal one, so why should we become less New-Dealish?"

The financial requirements for activities of this kind are not necessarily large by comparison with what it costs to mount a campaign after becoming an announced candidate. But they can easily become large

---

Governor Robert B. Meyner was receiving extensive press coverage in 1957 and 1958 as a potential Democratic presidential nominee, but appeared to be pursuing a personal strategy that might permit him to emerge in the role of compromise candidate. He did not seem to be engaging as extensively as Kennedy and Williams in precampaign activities of the kind requiring large expenditures of energy, initiative, and money.

By midyear 1959, Williams and Meyner had become markedly less conspicuous as potential candidates, while three additional senators had moved into the limelight: Hubert Humphrey, Lyndon Johnson, and Stuart Symington. Humphrey was preparing actively for an open type of campaign in which he seemed likely to be Kennedy's principal opponent in several contested presidential primaries. His importance as a potential candidate seemed to derive in considerable part from the fact that Stevenson did not intend to conduct a preconvention campaign, with the result that many of the former Stevenson backers had moved into position to support Humphrey. Johnson and Symington seemed less likely to enter the primaries or to conduct open campaigns before the primaries were over, but seemed to be preparing for aggressive campaigning through organization channels, against the possibility that other candidates might encounter a stalemate.

Also by midyear 1959, Governor Edmund G. (Pat) Brown of California was attracting attention as potentially something more than a favorite son candidate for the Democratic nomination. His record as a governor was shaping up in a fashion that inevitably invited comparison with other governors who had won Democratic nominations in the past; and it seemed certain that this record would be brought effectively to the attention of the delegates, since the convention was scheduled to meet in California.

The possibility of a contest over the Republican nomination had also opened up as a result of the election of Nelson Rockefeller as governor of New York. Rockefeller was pursuing typical tactics of disclaimer for the time being, but open support for his nomination was becoming widespread, with many signs of organized activity. This in turn was inspiring a consolidation of support for Vice President Nixon much like what occurred in 1955 and 1956 when his second vice-presidential nomination seemed likely to come under challenge.

These notes should not be interpreted as an attempt to forecast the nature of the conflict in 1960. Rather, they are intended to illustrate the complexity of the pre-announcement struggle for position in the form that it has assumed as the result of the developments since 1940. If past experience is any guide, the relative standings of the potential candidates may change greatly during the months leading up to the conventions in 1960.

:nough to outgrow the personal and official
:esources of an officeholder who has no pri-
,ate fortune, especially when a task force
ncluding several full-time professional staff
nembers is put to work. Several of these
:ask forces in recent years have worked for
ɔotential candidates who were personally
wealthy or members of wealthy families. In
ɔther cases they have served potential candidates who presumably had developed
financial backing in previous campaigns for
ɔther offices. Little is known about these
matters in public or documented form, but
it can be surmised that pre-announcement
expenditures of $10,000 to $100,000 have
been common, and that at times the higher
figure has been exceeded substantially. By
midyear 1959, for example, the figure of
$1,000,000 was being mentioned as an esti-
mate of the pre-announcement campaign
costs in behalf of Senator John F. Kennedy,
but was also being vigorously denied by the
senator and his supporters.[11]

Financing Open
Nominating Campaigns

Open campaigns for a presidential nomination begin with some public act of announcement or acceptance of candidacy.
The formal announcement provides a legitimate basis for a broad fund-raising operation by a committee of supporters, and no
doubt the purpose of announcing in the fall
of the pre-election year has often been to
give time for raising money.

Committees that seek to draft a candidate
who has pointedly not announced usually
find fund raising extremely difficult so long
as there is any serious question about his
consent. When Eisenhower agreed, early in
January 1952, to let his name stand in the
New Hampshire primary, the basis was laid
for the further financial operations of the
Citizens for Eisenhower. But the Draft
Stevenson committee was almost forced to

disband in April 1952 when its candidate
convinced most of the possible contributors
that he would not be available.[12]

Home-state financial support is essential
for most candidates in the early stages of
their campaigns. Early financial support
from other quarters depends on how successful the candidate's promoters have been
in locating potential contributors before the
announcement. If the campaign develops
well, further financing becomes relatively
much easier, but if it drags, the sources of
money dry up. Failing campaigns usually
end with deficits. In a negotiated withdrawal from the race, the losing candidate's
deficit may be taken over or underwritten
by supporters of the winner. Or the deficit
may be met by some wealthy sponsor who
had underwritten the contingent risk. Or it
may remain as a personal obligation for the
unsuccessful candidate to work off over a
period of years.

The financial requirements of a completed nominating campaign are highly
variable and somewhat unpredictable.[13]

---

[12] Johnson, *op. cit.*, pp. 33-34.

[13] The main expenses in a high-cost nominating
campaign include the items below, although it
should not be assumed that all campaigns include
all of them. (Volunteers can be used for many types
of personal services if the campaign is successful
enough to enlist them. In a low-cost campaign some
of the other items listed can be curtailed or eliminated. Publicity expense, frequently the largest
single category, is less a problem if the candidate
is capable of making enough news to compel attention through news channels.)

National headquarters overhead: salaries of staff;
rental of space and equipment; telephone and telegraph; stationery and postage; travel expense.

Speakers' bureau: transportation of speakers; payments to speakers.

Publicity: radio and television broadcasts; direct
mail campaigns; printing of literature; campaign
buttons; billboard and newspaper advertising.

State and local headquarters overhead: potentially,
all of the above items on a state and local basis.

Special expenses in primary states: circulation of
petitions to get on the ballot; filing fees; payments
to watchers, runners, and other election day workers; transporting voters to the polls.

Special expenses in non-primary states: entertainment of delegates to state conventions; travel expense of delegates to state conventions.

Headquarters operations at national convention:
same as for other headquarters operations, but frequently on an extremely high-cost level for the time
involved.

---

[11] As noted by Marquis Childs in his syndicated
column. (*Washington Post and Times Herald*, July
7, 1959.)

The possibilities are indicated by Table 12.1, which shows the expenditures on behalf of the leading candidates of 1920—a time before either radio or television had become a part of the problem.

The campaigns of 1920 probably illustrated more fully than those of any previous year the effect of the primaries on expenses.

higher than ever before. As a part of hi study of all forms of political campaign fi nancing, Alexander Heard has estimatec that the total preconvention campaign out lays for 1952 were at least $7,000,000, witl goods and services contributed in kind run ning into additional millions. Most of the expenditures occurred in the Republicar

TABLE 12.1. REPORTED EXPENDITURES IN PRESIDENTIAL NOMINATING
CAMPAIGNS OF 1920[a]

Candidate	Total Reported Expenditures	Number of States Entered[b]	Average Expenditure per State[b]
	DEMOCRATIC		
A. Mitchell Palmer	$ 59,610	3	$19,800
James M. Cox	22,000	2	11,000
William G. McAdoo	None	—	—
Four Other Candidates	38,872	—	—
Subtotal	$120,482		
	REPUBLICAN		
Leonard Wood	$1,773,303	47	$25,000
Frank O. Lowden	414,984	12	35,000
Hiram W. Johnson	194,393	16	12,100
Herbert Hoover	173,542	—	—
Warren G. Harding	113,109	—	—
Calvin Coolidge	68,375	—	—
Four Other Candidates	121,845	—	—
Subtotal	$2,859,551		
Total, Both Parties	$2,980,033		

[a] Based on data from 66 Cong., 3d sess., S. Rept. 823, as printed at end of *Presidential Campaign Ex penses, Hearings* . . . Committee on Privileges and Elections, United States Senate (1921), Vol. 2, p. 2943 (Also known as the Kenyon Committee Hearings.)
[b] These columns are excerpted from tabulations by Louise Overacker, *The Presidential Primary* (1926) p.153.

The cost of the wide-open Republican race of that year has not often been matched in either party. Unfortunately, no comparable figures seem to be available for the Democratic nominating campaigns of 1932 and the Republican nominating campaigns of 1940 and 1948, in which relatively large sums may have been spent.

In 1952 expenditures on preconvention campaigning undoubtedly reached levels

party and were the product of the Taft Eisenhower struggle. Cash outlays for the Eisenhower preconvention campaign were estimated at $2,500,000 on the basis of incomplete but substantial evidence, including the previously noted $1,200,000 spent by the Citizens for Eisenhower committee, of which there is public record. No authoritative information is available for the Taft campaign, but in view of its scale of activity and longer duration, it seems probable that the Taft expenditures were at least as great as those for Eisenhower. No separate estimates are available for the Stassen, Mac-Arthur, and Warren campaigns. On the Democratic side in 1952 the Kefauver central headquarters reported cash outlays totaling $356,387. The Russell campaign probably involved something over $100,000, and the Kerr and Harriman campaigns considerably more.[14]

In 1956 the active contest was for the Democratic nomination, and may have involved preconvention cash outlays exceeding $2,500,000. Two national Stevenson committees reported expenditures of over $600,000; the total at all levels for the Stevenson campaign was probably at least $1,500,000. The Kefauver campaign, widely reported as ending in a deficit of more than $40,000, probably cost in total at least as much as his previous effort in 1952; and substantial expenditures were doubtless incurred in the Harriman campaign.

Once a decision is made to campaign in a primary state, a considerable expenditure must be faced. The extent to which funds can be raised locally is always a question. The impression seems to be general that most state campaigns require some outside money and that few state campaign organizations have any money to spare for the national campaign.

Campaigns in the non-primary states can involve costs as high as in primary states, but their nature and legitimacy are far from clear. In 1920, Wood and Lowden apparently spent about as much on the average in non-primary states as in primary states.[15] Much of this money no doubt was legitimately spent for campaign headquarters, local publicity, and representatives of the candidate at local and state conventions. But "in Missouri the Lowden forces freely passed around checks before the caucuses with no questions asked and in Georgia representatives of both Wood and Lowden were accused of influencing various negro factions by paying their expenses to the conventions, or by suggesting that postmasterships might be forthcoming."[16]

Ethical standards in these matters may have become somewhat higher in recent years, but if so the evidence is lacking. Elsewhere in this book an effort is made to bring together what is known about the financing of expenses for national convention delegates in 1952.[17] Much less is known about the "expense money" of state convention delegates in recent years. Provisions of state corrupt practices laws may restrict this practice in some states; in other states some provision is made from public funds. In 1956, Montana allowed state convention delegates seven cents a mile for necessary travel to the state convention, to be paid "out of the general funds of the county in the same manner as other election expenses."[18]

Political money in general, according to one political writer, comes from five principal sources: (1) wealthy "fat cats," (2) organized labor, (3) government employees, (4) the underworld, and (5) unorganized voluntary contributors.[19] The range of sources and their relative importance are probably somewhat different in nominating campaigns and in general election campaigns.

The contributors of great wealth—those affected by the limitation of $5,000 on contributions to a single political fund in the general election—undoubtedly have a

---

[14] This paragraph and the one following are based, with permission, on a portion of the manuscript of a forthcoming book, *The Costs of Democracy*, by Alexander Heard of the University of North Carolina

[15] Louise Overacker, *The Presidental Primary* (1926), pp. 153, 156.

[16] *Ibid.*, pp. 158-59, citing *Presidental Campaign Expenses* (1921), Kenyon Committee Hearings, Vol. 1, pp. 610 ff.; 945 ff.

[17] See Chapter 14, section on Expense as a Factor in Delegate Selection.

[18] Chapter 266 [Montana], Laws of 1955, as cited in *Manner of Selecting Delegates* . . . 1956, p. 76. (For compete citation of this publication, see Appendix E, footnote 2.)

[19] Duncan Norton-Taylor, "How to Give Money to Politicians," *Fortune*, May 1956, pp. 112-17, *et seq.*

special role in nominating campaigns, where there is no such limit. Colonel William C. Procter, for example, underwrote the Leonard Wood campaign in 1920 to the extent of $500,000, according to his own testimony.[20] This occurred before the existing limits on general election contributions were enacted. Those limits have probably had some influence on accepted notions of what is appropriate, even in areas where they are not legally applicable.

Organized labor's role in nominating campaigns remains obscure except as it secures direct representation among the delegates to the national conventions.[21] There is little reason to think that labor contributions are substantial factors at the national level in the nominating campaigns of either party. In state presidential primaries, if labor men are on the delegate slate of only one candidate, presumably labor may take an interest in the campaign financially as well as in other ways.

Government employees as sources of political money are probably much more important in state and local politics than in federal politics. Federal employees probably contribute even less to nominating campaigns than to general election campaigns, although federal political appointees can doubtless be tapped for the campaign of any heir apparent in the party in power. The employees of some state governments may have to contribute for a favorite son candidate.

Contributions from the underworld are never publicly welcomed by a candidate. One can suppose that such contributions are more important in sustaining certain county rings and city machines than in state politics generally, and more important in the politics of some states than for the federal government. But county rings and city machines also play a part in presidential nominations. Any candidate may wish to avoid tainted money and yet find it impossible to maintain the rigid discipline in his campaign organization that such avoidance would require.

The unorganized voluntary contributors, especially those who will contribute in amounts of $5 to $500 if invited to do so, may be the hope of the future in political finance; at least substantial efforts are being made in that direction. The national parties have been organizing special fund-raising efforts directed toward this group. The object is to drive home the idea that every citizen has a duty to contribute, according to his ability, to the party of his choice.[22]

These organized appeals to civic duty are still a long way from success in solving all the problems of party finance, but they may well be making it easier to raise money for nominating campaigns—provided the campaign managers can manage to locate and appeal to the potential contributors. As going concerns, the parties are able to maintain lists of past contributors and of finance committee volunteers with successful experience in money raising. Nominating campaigns are at a disadvantage unless their managers can get hold of the requisite lists and can recruit an effective group of solicitors. Sometimes the lists and the solicitors are inherited from previous nominating and general election campaigns. If they are not available, the problem of developing lists and recruiting solicitors may mean success or defeat for a candidate who is not personally wealthy or who has no wealthy backers.

---

[20] Overacker, op. cit., p. 160, citing Kenyon Committee Hearings, Vol. 1, pp. 188 and 198.

[21] See Chapter 5, section on Interest Groups and Their Leaders; Chapter 14, section on Representation of Organized Labor.

[22] One suggested scale of contributions begins at $25 annually for a $5,000 income, reaches the one per cent level at $18,000, and suggests 3½ per cent of income for those above $100,000. (Norton-Taylor, op. cit., p. 238.)

The public campaigns launched in 1958 by the American Heritage Foundation with the cooperation of the Advertising Council and the national committees of both parties seem important primarily as propaganda on the theme of civic duty in political giving. To the extent that such campaigns succeed, a long-range change in public attitudes may become their most important effect.

The Influence of Money on Mandates

With so much money in evidence in some nominating campaigns, inevitably the question arises of its influence on the outcome. The basis for forming an opinion is more available for the 1920 Republican campaign than for most others. In retrospect, it seems clear that the two strongest candidates, Wood and Lowden, might have done better with less money spent more wisely. Both became vulnerable to charges that were fully aired in a congressional investigation before the conventions even met. Harding became the winner with the smallest campaign expenditure of any of the five leading candidates. But the $100,000 spent on his behalf was a substantial sum; and one can question whether he would have come within range of the nomination even as a compromise candidate if much less had been spent.

Money cannot buy a nomination, but it can buy a candidate prominence if he is otherwise eligible. Potential candidates who are not able to finance themselves must therefore consult their prospective backers; and the response may settle whether they run or not. As one analyst has remarked in answering his own question on why so few candidates actually make the race, "the reason is that while many are available, few are processed."[23] This in turn raises questions about what kind of candidates are screened out before they start, and what types are preferred.

Wealthy candidates evidently start with a substantial advantage, yet in the end their wealth may be held against them unless they can project a particularly clear image of public-service motivations. On the other hand, with modern fund-raising techniques, a "popular" candidate who is not wealthy can almost make his need for funds an advantage, as contributors from one end of the country to the other become involved in a self-financing and self-inspiring type of campaign.

Candidates with a clear factional following in their party have a different basis for finding campaign funds. The standard-bearer of an important factional interest will find his faction rallying to organize his campaign and raise the necessary money. But, like the wealthy candidate who is in danger of being considered a front for the wealthy classes generally, the factional candidate may find that his sources of support rouse factional opposition that will defeat him.

A candidate who can symbolize his party's need for unity by maintaining a central position among the existing forces within the party will occupy still a different position. He is not likely to find substantial early support from any of the strongly factional interests within the party; on the other hand, he has a basis for a general appeal much like the appeal of the party itself in the general election campaign. A candidate in this position may be especially dependent on support fom state and local party organizations—in particular, those that care more for victory in November than for some acute factional interest. To the extent that the law restrains the activities of party organizations in nominating campaigns, it may tend to interfere with the development of such middle-of-the-road candidates.

The uses of money in nominating campaigns are so unregulated that many opportunities for questionable practices, or even for actual corruption, undoubtedly exist. Whether money is wrongly used to such an extent as to impair the quality of the choice is a question not easily answered. Undoubtedly it would be desirable to require reports from major contributors and all fund-raising committees in nominating campaigns. Yet the competition among candidates itself provides some built-in safeguards: under the acute pressures of competition there is always the risk that ques-

[23] Robert Bendiner, "How Presidents Are Made," *The Reporter*, Feb. 9, 1956, pp. 11-18. (This is an unusually good treatment of the problems involved in promoting a candidacy.)

tionable practices will be discovered and will boomerang. Congressional investigations are an ever-present threat, although they do not seem to have played a great part in any nominating campaign since 1920.

The need for corrective legislation may be less than the need for avoiding unwise meddling. Recently, for instance, there have been several bills under which, if they were enacted and proved constitutional, the voluntary committees for Eisenhower and Stevenson in 1952 could not have operated until these men were prepared to become announced candidates. It is, of course, possible to argue that no one should be permitted to raise money for a candidate who has not given his formal consent. But the tradition of the need for the office to seek the man is still strong enough in American politics to call for some recognition in any legislation that might be enacted, and especially in the case of the highest office in the land.

The Content of Nominating Campaigns

. . . . There's a lot more to winning an election than spending money, as all politicians know through sometimes they won't admit it.

The reason is that money may affect the *volume* of campaign communications and activities, but that has nothing to do with the more crucial matter, their *content*.[24]

A nominating campaign is a connected series of operations; it involves a great deal of talk, but it is made up of much more than talk. Like a military campaign, it involves movement, supply, attack, defense, and all requisite maneuvers. The candidates and their managers and supporters are continuously involved in decisions and expressive acts. The voters, on their part, are given an exposure to persons and events as well as to the words the candidates say.

[24] Alexander Heard, *Money and Politics* (Public Affairs Pamphlet No. 242, 1956), pp. 10-11. (Italics in original.)

In studies of what causes the voters to vote as they do in presidential elections, the main emphasis is being laid on three elements: the voter's relation to the party, his feeling about issues, and the personality of the candidate.[25] Something like three quarters of the voters call themselves either Democrats or Republicans. In general elections these voters will generally vote for their party unless they feel some special reason to vote the other way. But the candidate may have taken a stand on various issues that the voter does or does not approve, and that will affect his loyalty to the party. The voter may also be attracted or repelled by various aspects of the candidate's personality. The solid core of the party vote in a general election is thus made up of the voters who are already predisposed toward the party, who think the candidate agrees with them on the issues they think important, and who are attracted (or not repelled) by his personality.

The party vote weakens or splits when some of the party voters are repelled by the candidate's stand on the issues or by his personality, especially if the other party's

[25] Angus Campbell, Gerald Gurin, and Warren E. Miller, *The Voter Decides* (1954); Donald E. Stokes, Angus Campbell, and Warren E. Miller, "Components of Electoral Decision," *American Political Science Review*, Vol. 52 (June 1958), pp. 367-87. The research of this group is especially distinguished for its concentration of emphasis on work that seeks to determine the independence, interaction, and relative importance of the motivating factors of greatest interest to political scientists (and to candidates who are seeking voter support).

The approaches of sociology and social psychology to voting research are represented more fully in the works by Paul F. Lazarsfeld and his collaborators: Paul F. Lazarsfeld, Bernard Berelson, and Hazel Gaudet, *The People's Choice* (1944); Bernard Berelson, Paul F. Lazarsfeld, and William N. McPhee, *Voting: A Study of Opinion Formation in a Presidential Campaign* (1954).

A coordinated view of this entire field is supplied by Seymour M. Lipset, Paul F. Lazarsfeld, Allen H. Barton, and Juan Linz, "The Psychology of Voting: An Analysis of Political Behavior," in Gardner Lindzey (ed.), *Handbook of Social Psychology* (1954), Vol. 2, Chap. 30. See also the brief review of alternative research approaches in M. Brewster Smith, "Opinions, Personality, and Political Behavior," *American Political Science Review*, Vol. 52 (March 1958), pp. 1-17.

candidate is attractive. Party voters who thus find themselves with conflicting feelings are likely to stay home or, if they vote, may be tempted to vote for the candidate of the other party.

From one presidential election to another, there is always some change in the influences that move the voters. The opposing presidential candidates usually include at least one new personality, although this failed to occur in 1892, 1900, and 1956. The positions of the parties and the candidates even on the old issues may shift somewhat. More important, probably, are the new issues that come forward and the deflation of old ones by events. The party images in the public mind will change, though usually at only the slowest pace. Sometimes, however, when a party comes to power after a long time in the wilderness, the public image of it may change rapidly. Some of the voters in turn shift their party preference in response to the changes in party images, though generally with some time lag after they become aware of such changes. Party images that appeal to the young more than to the old also affect the electorate directly, through the constant accession of young voters and death of old ones. It is unusual for any large proportion of the voters to shift their long-term party allegiance in a single four-year period.

The psychological mechanisms by which the voter may reach a conclusion in a nominating campaign have been much less explored than those that operate in general elections. Moreover, although the party voters may or may not arrive at a mandate of one sort or another, it is the delegates who must reach a definite conclusion and make a nomination, whether their constituencies have reached a conclusion or not. Nominating campaigns thus seek to develop voter mandates, but also seek to develop favorable attitudes in the party organizations and among the delegates.[26]

[26] Delegates are subject to many influences in addition to voter mandates and their own perceptions of the merits of the candidates—most notably those of

For all three categories—party voters, organization members, and delegates—the factors that influence their choice for a nomination are presumably somewhat different from those that operate in a general election. In particular, loyalty to the party either has nothing to do with a nominating choice or has an effect quite different from that in an election. Usually the voter can assume that all the candidates for a party nomination are equally eligible in terms of party attachment and loyalty. Any doubt about this must usually be removed before a nominating campaign can begin—as the doubt of General Eisenhower's partisan loyalties was removed at the beginning of the 1952 nominating campaign. But the voter who has to choose among two or more of his party's candidates for the nomination cannot be guided simply by his party loyalties, as he may be in the general election in choosing between a Republican and a Democrat.

It is doubtless for this reason that so many voters take no part in the nominations. The choice cannot be made by some simple habit, as can many personal decisions, and without mental strain. In nominating decisions, the voter is asked to give close attention to many factors not easily appraised, and which he would not have to worry about in a general election. Not many voters care enough to take the trouble; those who do presumably serve as opinion leaders for many of their associates.

For the voters who do take part in the nominating process, the scheme of analysis developed in general election studies could probably be applied—with certain essential

the party cliques and organizations with which they are closely associated. Because of these differences, candidates often have to run two different campaigns simultaneously: one for a popular mandate and the other to win the consent or support of the party organizations and the delegates. One campaign may actually handicap the other, but the delegates as individuals and the organizations in their corporate capacity presumably respond in part to the same influences that move the voters; in any event they are much interested in whether the candidate can demonstrate voter appeal.

modifications—in analyzing how they decide upon their choice. Presumably, a party faction might play a role in the nominating choice comparable to that of the party in the election—if the voter recognizes one of the candidates as champion of his faction, and is willing to overlook the disfavor with which the whole idea of faction is regarded in the American culture. The voter may prefer a Taft to an Eisenhower or a Russell to a Kefauver primarily for factional reasons—but the issue is seldom presented as clearly as it was by the pairs just named. The hopeful candidate ordinarily seeks to avoid any clear identification with a faction and to cast himself instead in the role of the unifier who can appeal to all elements of the party as he leads it on to victory over the other party.

If the voter's loyalty to some faction is not ordinarily as potent in nominating choice as loyalty to party is in election choice—and it seems likely not to be—then one might assume provisionally that the candidate's stand on issues and his personality may carry correspondingly more weight. The relative influence of personality and issue positions has not been measured, but the campaign behavior of many candidates suggests that both are considered important.

The Display of Personality

Some public display of personality is inevitable for anyone seriously considered as a possible candidate, but the extent and manner of such display can vary over a considerable range, depending on the opportunities open to the candidate and the style of campaigning that he adopts. It can frequently occur best in the context of a discussion of issues or through involvement in some area of public policy.

Often these affairs seem to be arranged, not so much to put the candidate on record as advocating a particular course of action, but to convey an impression that he is highly familiar with the problems and com-petent to deal with them. Vice President Nixon's various visits abroad and Senator Hubert Humphrey's long conference in December 1958 with Soviet Premier Khrushchev not only helped to create for each man a public impression of competence to talk to the heads of other governments, but automatically put them in the main stream of page-one newspaper coverage. Candidates who are far removed from the main centers of communication and who have few occasions for dramatic or newsworthy action have much more difficulty in projecting a public image that gets through to the mass of the voters—and especially an image in which they are intimately associated with the salient concerns of the day.

Potential candidates who are not openly running but are obviously being considered become the object of a special type of scrutiny. In 1952, Eisenhower and Stevenson both came through such scrutiny with unusual success, not only because of their personal attitudes but because of the protection afforded by their respective situations. Eisenhower's position at the time made any overt seeking of the nomination seem inappropriate until called forth by a substantial popular demand. Stevenson's prior commitment as a candidate for governor of Illinois was a protection to him.

Before the invention of the primaries, a candidate who wished to avoid any appearance of preconvention campaigning could remain at home while his supporters came to him from afar. Governor Alfred M. Landon was the most recent candidate of some importance to carry on a preconvention "front porch campaign." He did as little as possible either to exhibit or to test his capacities before he was nominated. Only later was it discovered that his speaking was poor and that he was generally ineffective as a campaigner.[27] The Landon type of case is no longer common, but similar tactics are still pursued by candidates who look forward to the possibility of a compromise nomination. Active candidates for the nomi-

[27] Moos, *op. cit.* pp. 399-401.

nations are involved almost continuously in the display of personality, partly under controllable conditions but often too under conditions beyond their control.

The campaign strategy of a candidate and his way of carrying it out are highly revealing of whether he is reckless, bold, cautious, or timid; willingly candid or skillfully disingenuous; and democratic or authoritarian in his feeling about the problems of popular government. To the extent that he is on display, he needs to exhibit the virtues of statesmanship in terms that have wide appeal, while giving the impression of individuality as a person. To the extent that he campaigns in the primaries, he has the problems of adjusting to the political situation in the states concerned, each with its personalities, its memories, its particular problems, and its own feelings about the issues that are currently of national importance. Yet the candidate must maintain a stance throughout that will do no harm if reported in detail on the opposite side of the nation—as it probably will be by the press and other mass media if he says anything that will do him harm.

Some of the recent primaries have imposed the most grueling tests ever confronted by practicing politicians in search of office. The candidate has had to campaign at the state level much as he would if running for state office, but with untested associates in unfamiliar surroundings. He does this in state after state scattered across the nation and with primary dates ranging from March to June. He spends his energies to the point of utter exhaustion in meeting voters of every race, religion, and ethnic group at the local handshaking and food-eating level. Meanwhile he must talk almost continuously, partly on the great issues of public policy but also on every other subject.

Under such conditions it would not be strange if his public personality should wear thin. Taft left New Hampshire in 1952 with his reputation as a campaigner badly impaired. Stevenson had a similar ex-

perience in Minnsota in 1956. Both were widely reported as changing their styles of campaigning as the result. The conscious adaptation of the personality to the requirements of campaigning has become one of the most widely advertised aspects of public relations art. It may involve "a degree of deliberation ranging from the almost unconscious highlighting of an attractive quality to the deliberate promotion of a 'packaged' character."[28]

The nominating campaigns serve to rouse keen public interest in candidate personality, and in such questions as whether a change observed in the public personality of a well-known figure is "phony" or "real." A candidate who meets the voters also becomes accessible to observation and questioning by the press; this in turn feeds public discussion of his characteristics.

The Discussion of Issues

A candidate must express views on a wide range of subjects if he wishes to look like a stateman.[29] But the more definite his position and the more numerous the subjects he talks about, the more are voters likely to

[28] Bendiner, op. cit., p. 12.
[29] What may be a trend toward increasing commitment of candidates on public policy issues is indicated by the searching questions asked at press conferences and the degree of frankness with which the candidates feel impelled to respond. See, for example, the transcripts of the press conferences held respectively by Adlai E. Stevenson and Estes Kefauver after they announced in 1955 as candidates for the forthcoming Democratic presidential nomination. (New York Times, Nov. 17, 1955, p. 24; Dec. 17, 1955, p. 14.)
The modern usage in presidential press conferences is presumably the model for what is expected from candidates for the Presidency. The presidential press conference as it currently exists dates back only to the time of Woodrow Wilson, and owes its present form mainly to Presidents Franklin D. Roosevelt, Harry S. Truman, and Dwight D. Eisenhower, and their respective press relations advisers. See James E. Pollard, The Presidents and the Press (1947) and "Eisenhower and the Press: The First Two Years," Journalism Quarterly, Vol. 32 (Summer 1955), pp. 285-300; also Arthur Krock, "President and Press: Material for History," New York Times, April 14, 1957, p. E3; John Herling, "World's No. 1 Quiz Program," New York Times Magazine, June 9, 1957, pp. 11, 38, 40, 43.

disagree with him one way or another. Moreover, a position that may help to win the nomination may be a handicap when it comes to winning the election.[30]

Still other dilemmas arise in the discussion of issues in nomination campaigns. Should the candidate attack only the positions of the opposite party, or should he attack the views of a competing candidate? Should he direct his proposals to the entire electorate or only to his own party, which is about to decide whether to nominate him? If the candidates all stick to a "high-level" type of campaign—attacks directed only at the other party and addressed to the entire electorate—how are the voters within the party to choose? Should they be content to choose on points of attacking form, or entirely on personality?

These problems arise in nominating campaigns at all levels, from sheriff to President. In presidential nominating campaigns, candidates have often argued about major issues within one party or both more directly than in the general election campaigns that followed. There have been many variations, however, in the range of conflict and its relation to factionalism inside the parties.[31]

The conflict of 1912 between President Taft and Theodore Roosevelt represented most clearly a clash between progressive and conservative positions inside a party. In the Democratic party in 1924, McAdoo and Al Smith were regarded as in conflict on prohibition and on what to do about the Ku Klux Klan. But even more they were in sharp contrast to each other as personality types and as leaders of different sectional and interests groups within the party.

[30] This dilemma was illustrated by Vice President Nixon's campaign strategy in the 1958 mid-term campaign. Observers commented that a less partisan style of campaigning would have been more likely to be effective in increasing the Republican vote, but that Nixon was compelled to take a highly partisan line in order to hold the party together for the 1960 nomination.
[31] For one attempt to array a group of candidates along a spectrum from left to right, see "The Economics of Seven Democrats," *Fortune*, July 1956, pp. 74-77 *et seq.*

A sharp factional division was so persistent in the Republican party from 1940 to 1956 that few leading candidates for the party's nominations could escape involvement. Willkie, Dewey, and Eisenhower were in turn identified as leaders of an eastern internationalist wing. Taft was throughout a leader of the middle-western isolationist wing, although far from being as extreme as many of his followers. Stassen and Warren were never chosen as leaders by either faction, but they were unable to build strong central roles as party unifiers.

In the Democratic party, Kefauver developed a set of positions in 1952 that were somewhat distinctive, since in effect he was running against the leadership of his own party, but he apparently became far better known as a personality than as the symbol of any position on issues. In 1956, Kefauver and Stevenson both indicated in the early stages of their campaigns that they were more interested in attacks on the Republican party than on each other. Their respective positions on most subjects were never sharply distinguished, but in the heat of the campaign in Florida a point was reached where each was rather sharply attacking the behavior of the other.

From these few examples it can be suspected that factional alignments are indeed important in nominating decisions, but that most of the voters do not think of themselves as members of party factions. When candidates take stands on issues that are related to sleeping factional cleavage, however, old disputes may be awakened and many voters may be roused to take a hand. When this is done skillfully, the result may be that the tendencies of potential supporters are activated and reinforced, without attracting much attention from potential opponents.

Reshaping the Party Image

The attachment of the party voter to his party involves some mental picture of the party as a whole. At any one time, the collective party image in the minds of the party faithful is made up of such elements as its tradition, its memories, its leading men past and present, and its major acts when most recently in power.

Presidential election years may bring on a general reappraisal of the parties by the voters. In the party in power, however, the nominating campaigns are relatively incidental. Even if several candidates are competing for the nomination, the party image continues to be shaped mainly by the party's activities in office. To the extent that the existing party image appears to be unpopular, a would-be candidate may try to disassociate himself from the administration, but without seeming disloyal to the party's basic character.

Candidates for the nomination of a party out of power start with the fact that the party image as inherited from the time when it was thrown out of office is probably not attractive to a majority of the voters. The party must therefore either refurbish the inherited image somehow or run under a serious handicap. But the nomination must be obtained first, and to obtain it the candidate may have to win acceptance in quarters where the old party image still inspires intense loyalty. In bridging this dilemma, his main reliance may be the need of all concerned to be connected with a winner—even if they have to give up some of their old ideas about what the party stands for.

Probably most candidates hope to reshape the popular image of their party along lines that they think will make it more generally attractive, but this would seem to be an objective that generally cannot be openly pursued until after both nomination and election have been won.

* * * * * *

It seems clear that a candidate must appeal to a variety of motivations in seeking to obtain voter support for the nomination. In the first place, he needs to identify himself as a loyal party member, since the nomi-

nating decision will be made by other party members. Second, if the party is deeply split, he must develop a strategy for defining his own relationship to this conflict; for success, he must either identify himself with what turns out to be the winning faction or present himself successfully as the unifier who can bridge the factional division. Third, he must be prepared to discuss the issues, but his choice of issues and his manner of treating them will probably determine the kind of factional identification he acquires or avoids.

Fourth, and probably the most important, the candidate must convey an attractive image of personal qualities, including human warmth and cordiality, a prior record of accomplishment, apparent qualifications for high office, and recognition by his associates as a leader. In the end, such personal qualities would seem to be the principal basis for choice among the candidates whose factional and issue positions are all relatively compatible with the development of a majority mandate—of whom there are usually at least two or three in each party at any one time.

Functions and Effects

Candidates and party voters, interacting in the nominating contests of recent years, have established a series of precedents that add up to a new picture of what a nominating contest can mean. In years of contest, the standard nominating campaign of the future may be a composite of those that won for Willkie and Eisenhower their first nominations and for Dewey and Stevenson their second nominations.

On looking back, it is clear that the other two contested nominations since 1940 were different. Dewey won his first nomination in 1944 with a minimum of trouble and relatively little active campaigning after Willkie had defeated himself in the Wisconsin primary. Stevenson also received his first nomination in 1952 with practically no effort on his part.

The campaigns that won for Willkie and Eisenhower, and for Dewey and Stevenson on their second nominations, were not identical, but they demonstrated a series of elements tending to add up to the development of wide popular involvement and support. All four contests were notable for the extent to which the mass media became engaged in reporting, and seemingly also in seeking to influence the outcome of, a dramatic contest involving major personalities. They were noteworthy also for the extent to which channels of communication and activity were developed among those who do not ordinarily serve actively in party organizations but who do provide the sinews of war and who are in a position to exercise influence when they see fit to do so.

In the Willkie case, action in the primaries was not important; for twenty years primaries had been falling into disuse and Willkie began his 1940 campaign too late to use them. But in the other three cases, action in the primaries was an important feature, with each of the eventual winners proving that he could repel a challenge in primaries where the issue was clear and the outcome visible. In all four cases, when the primaries were over, a final push was mounted that reached its climax under the candidate's personal leadership at the convention, with a heavy mobilization of popular sentiment as the delegates reached the point of voting.

These changing patterns of nominating campaigns are increasingly under discussion. Much of the discussion focuses on the presidential primaries, with proposals to curtail their influence as well as to extend it. In the course of a television interview on June 1, 1958, for example, Adlai Stevenson commented that the presidential primary "is almost a useless institution." He went on to note the difficulties imposed on governors and other busy executives when required to campaign in the primaries. He commented on the small turnout in most primaries, and on the confusion and lack of uniformity in the rules, concluding:

Finally, it is terribly expensive; it's exhausting physically; you burn up yourself, you burn up your ammunition, you burn up your means. I think that it's a very, very questionable method of selecting Presidential candidates and actually it never does. All it does is destroy some candidates.[32]

Sober afterthoughts on the primaries of 1952 and 1956 have apparently been responsible for the repeal of the primary laws in Minnesota and Montana, and the near success of amending legislation in Florida. They also provided inspiration in 1958 for tentative plans credited to a number of the potential candidates for the 1960 Democratic nomination:

. . . the presidential aspirants, by mutual agreement, would cut up primary states among themselves according to geographical or ideological divisions. Only one candidate would enter in each of these states, with the net result that each would go to the national convention with fairly equal delegate strength.

As an alternative all candidates would stay out of a primary and the various states would elect "favorite son" slates which would be released at the convention.[33]

[32] *A Mike Wallace Interview with Adlai E. Stevenson* (pamphlet published by The Fund for the Republic, 1958), pp. 9-10.
[33] This plan, as reported in the *Milwaukee Journal* (and other newspapers), was unfolded at a meeting at the Wisconsin state Democratic convention in 1958 by Herbert J. Waters, administrative assistant to Senator Hubert H. Humphrey. Mr. Waters was reported as indicating that "none of the leading potential candidates for the Democratic presidential nomination looked forward to a grueling, expensive series of contests in presidential primaries. . . . Further, some of them, such as Humphrey or Senator Kefauver would find it difficult to enter primaries as active candidates because they must face re-election to the Senate in their home states, [in 1960] Waters said." The story went on to point out that "all it would take to upset the plan would be one major candidate who did not choose to abide by such an agreement as that proposed. . . . There are as many as 15 prominent Democrats who might be interested in the 1960 nomination. Getting all of these individuals to agree to anything would seem almost impossible. . . . There have been indications that Kennedy and Williams, at least, have been interested in the Wisconsin primary." See Edwin R. Bayley, "Plan to Avoid Contests Put to Democrats," *Milwaukee Journal*, June 17, 1958.
A year later Kennedy and Humphrey were both in Wisconsin on barnstorming trips, although neither had yet announced. Humphrey's principal objective was reportedly to make certain that he would have an opportunity to meet Kennedy in a

Under some conditions a boycott might reduce the number of states where active primary contests occur. The number of states with primaries conducive to such contests may also continue to dwindle. But nationwide campaigning to build up a popular mandate might go on without primaries, as long as the public opinion polls are available to record the results. Eventually, ways may be found to extend the effects of campaigning even in the states that have no primaries and in those where the delegates are elected unpledged.

The intensification of campaigning for popular support that has already occurred may rest on underlying changes in sentiments and conditions that are too powerful to resist. At any rate, public criticism of the primaries is noteworthy for the lack of any tendency to question the desirability of campaigning for popular support. It seems to be taken for granted that some appeal to the people is required to assure the legitimacy of the nominations, and that popular mandates, to the extent that they exist, must be given weight in the nominating choice as a condition for popular favor in the election campaign to follow.[34]

But a nomination is not an election, and it is not clear how much popular participation is genuinely necessary to assure the acceptance of a nomination as legitimate. No doubt a nomination will be regarded as illegitimate, and will be likely to attract punitive action in the election, when it goes contrary to a popular mandate that has attained the proportions of a visible majority. There is also much to be said for campaign procedures that are sufficiently open to permit a majority mandate to become visible if a contest is inevitable. The most difficult question may be whether the basic institutions of the system should be shaped to encourage contests or to discourage them. This aspect of the matter will receive further attention in Chapters 18 and 19.

Basically, the problem comes back to the utility of campaigning and the limits of rationality in nominating decisions, whether those decisions are to be made by the delegates, the party organizations, or the electorate. The chief presumable value of a campaign—as distinguished from the immediate purposes of the candidates—and the reason why time and other resources are devoted to campaigning would seem to be to improve the basis for rational choice. There has been a growing disillusionment over the extent to which general election campaigns fail to contribute to rational choice in elections. The presidential election of 1948 may have been the only one so far in this century in which a sufficient number of votes were changed from one party to the other, net, during the campaign to affect the outcome.[35] Nominating campaigns, however, may make a contribution of rationality to

---

primary contest in Wisconsin, this being considered a relatively favorable terrain on which to meet the front-runner. But the Democratic governor of Wisconsin, Gaylord Nelson, was reportedly trying hard to prevent a contest in the primary, urging Senator William Proxmire to run as a favorite son and considering the possibility of running himself if Proxmire declined, in order to avoid a party-splitting struggle in a year when the governorship would again be at stake. See the successive stories by Edward T. Folliard, *Washington Post and Times Herald,* June 13, 14, and 15, 1959.

By mid 1959 it seemed clear that there had been a noticeable turnaround of sentiment toward the primaries on the part of several of the most active prospective candidates for the Democratic nomination. Apparently these candidates were facing the prospect that, unless they could win primaries in which they had a genuine contest, they would find it difficult to make enough of a showing to win the nomination. Cf., for example, Jack Bell, "Vanishing Primaries Irk Kennedy," *Washington Post and Times Herald,* July 6, 1959. The sequence of past nominating cycles thus seemed to be repeating itself, with a possibility of active preconvention campaigns in the primaries of both parties in 1960.

[34] W. J. M. Mackenzie has commented on the lack of an adequate modern theory of the function of elections in western societies, but believes "that they

are essential to us as props of the sentiment of legitimacy and the sentiment of participation: and that these sentiments break easily and are hard to repair." See Mackenzie, "The Export of Electoral Systems," *Political Studies,* Vol. 5 (October 1957), p. 256. See also V. O. Key, *Politics, Parties, and Pressure Groups* (4th ed., 1958), pp. 589-90.

[35] The change that was brought about by President Truman's campaigning, as several studies agree, consisted, not of winning decisive numbers of Republicans over to vote for him, but of rallying Democrats who had for a time intended to stay home or to vote Republican.

nominating decisions greater than that made by election campaigns to election decisions.

Presidential election campaigns apparently have so little effect because most of the voters have made up their minds by the time the nominations are completed, if not at some considerably earlier period.[36] On most occasions the record of the party in power apparently contributes more to its victory or defeat at the next presidential election than anything further that the opposition party can do after it has made its choice of candidate. For some voters, the general election campaigns have no effect at all. For others—very likely the most numerous group in most elections—the campaigns merely reinforce existing predispositions. In other cases, the campaigns may have the effect of persuading some voters to come out and vote who otherwise would not bother to do so. Finally, the campaigns may convert some votes from one party to another; but the *net* change is likely to be very small indeed.[37]

Nominating campaigns may not have much more effect than general election campaigns when the interested voters are already well acquainted with the leading contenders. The Taft-Eisenhower contest of 1952 may have been such a case, since it involved two of the best-known public men of

the century. But the Eisenhower campaign made two major contributions that were probably vital. In its early stages in New Hampshire and Minnesota it showed that popular affection for a military hero could be converted into votes—as was never shown for General Douglas MacArthur. In its later stages it proved that Eisenhower himself was willing, however reluctantly, to take on the burdens of political leadership—to associate with working politicians, to accept the rules of the game, and to work for his own nomination and election. Without these two reassurances, it seems unlikely that Eisenhower could have gathered so much party organization support or that a majority of the delegates would have voted for him at the convention.

It is in the nature of presidential nominating contests, however, that new men are always under consideration and must sometimes be nominated. Occasionally all of the seriously available candidates for a party nomination are new to the national scene, as in the Republican party in 1940, when the choice lay mainly between three men whose fame had not yet matured: Dewey, a defeated first-time candidate for governor; Taft, a junior senator of two years' standing; and Willkie, a public utility magnate who had never held public office. More often, the leading availables include some well-known figures and others who are much less known. The limitations of the better-known men are likely to be about as well understood as their potentialities. But with the little-known personalities, it is necessary to guess about both their limitations and potentialities—unless the testing process before the convention is sufficient to bring out evidence of both.

It seems clear that without the kind of nominating campaigns that have recently occurred, popular judgment would be wholly inadequate for rational choice when new men must be considered. If the nomination were left entirely to the party organizations and the assembled delegates, a much more informed choice would be possible with a minimum of campaigning,

[36] Three items from the principal compilation of generalizations on voting behavior are pertinent (Berelson, Lazarsfeld, and McPhee, *op. cit.*, p. 345):

"(175) From one election to the next, over three-fourths of the voters in both do not change party position.

"(176) From two-thirds to three-fourths of the voters settle on their final vote by the time the political conventions are over.

"(177) Changes in party position during the campaign are fewer than changes between campaigns."

The first two of the three generalizations quoted were supported by findings in several different panel studies; the third was based on the Erie County, Ohio, study of the 1940 presidential election.

[37] The quotas of voters subject to the various effects were estimated as follows in a study of the 1940 election: no effect, one sixth; re-enforcement, one half; activation, one sixth; conversion, one sixth. (*Ibid.*, generalization 179, p. 345.) While these orders of magnitude have some inherent interest, there is no reason to suppose that the ratios remain unchanged from one election to another.

hough subject to the obvious limitations of the organization point of view. What is often overlooked, however, is that even the most knowledgeable party leaders cannot be sure how a potential new candidate will perform under conditions to which he has never been exposed.

No one can predict how a candidate will act under pressure until he has been placed under pressure. For a governor or senator of a major industrial state, the pressures and complexities of political life are great, but those of presidential campaigning and of the Presidency are so much greater that they are of a different order of magnitude. The Stevenson nomination of 1952 was at best a calculated risk for many of those who were most active in bringing it about. Stevenson was far better known as a personality and as a political leader than Landon had been in 1936, but he was completely untried in presidential campaigning or in meeting the voters for any purpose in any state other than his own.

Judged in terms of their contributions to the basis for rational choice, the recent patterns of nominating campaigns and the existing system of presidential primaries have much that can be said in their favor. The process extends over enough time to give candidates, voters, party organizations, and delegates an opportunity to reconsider and correct first impressions. The candidates are required to make a complex series of strategic decisions, each of which is vital enough to test the candidate's courage and intelligence, but few of which are likely to be fatal. The voters are given a chance to exert a substantial influence, without being given full control over decisions that must be made by the parties in their corporate capacities. The final decision is reserved to a meeting at which there is opportunity for negotiation, exchange of information, and the application of informed judgment.[38]

By comparison, the possibilities of rational choice would become much inferior if, on the one hand, there were a national primary in which the whole issue could be settled directly by the electorate on a single day; or, on the other, if the convention followed a campaign in which there had been no direct appeal to the voters and no testing of the candidates in elections outside their own states.

[38] The doctrine laid out in this paragraph was first expounded to the writers by Harold Stein of Princeton University, a student of decision-making who participated in the 1952 study in connection with the New York chapter.

13

Mass Media Effects and Voter Choice

IN EXPLORING the content of nominating campaigns, the previous chapter began a discussion of the problem of how voter attitudes evolve on prospective nominations. The subject is one that has been singularly neglected in the studies of voter psychology, yet the evolution of voter preferences in the selection of a first-time presidential nominee is undoubtedly a most complex business. This chapter undertakes initially to review the functioning and effects of the mass media, and then turns to the records of the public opinion polls for evidence of how voter choice has actually shaped up in the nominating campaigns of the period since 1936.

The Role of the Mass Media

The role of the mass media in nominating campaigns is one that would merit systematic data collection and analysis. All that is possible here is informed speculation on the basis of the experience as it has been historically observed. Some hypotheses can be suggested, however, that seem plausible enough for inclusion even in a beginning discussion.

The convention system originated some years before the telegraph came into use (the first line was authorized by Congress in 1843) and long before the first commercial telephone exchange was established (1878). Political communication was by word of mouth, discussion in meetings, correspondence by mail, printed flyers and leaflets, and the press as it then existed—a press that was limited in circulation and highly partisan in opinion and behavior.

The daily newspaper developed rapidly after the Civil War, along with the cities it served, and reached massive circulations at the penny price level in the latter part of the century. The Associated Press, formed in 1848 by six New York City newspapers, was reorganized in its modern form in 1893; wire service news was becoming steadily more important. The circulation of national magazines grew steadily throughout the nineteenth century—and has kept on growing in the twentieth; paid circulation increased from 139 to 185 million between 1946 and 1956.[1] The invention of motion pictures made possible the newsreel, which dates from 1909 and became important for a time for spreading visual and sound images of political candidates and events. Radio broadcasting came along in 1920, and leaped into political importance in the presidential campaign of 1924.

Television broadcasting, the newest of the mass media, had its modest beginnings just before World War II. In 1948 the television impact on presidential politics was small, but by 1952 the industry had expanded so far that revolutionary consequences were expected by some observers. Television receivers were available in 37 per cent of all homes; the average television set is said to have been used about 26 hours for watching the political conventions of 1952.[2]

[1] Leo Bogart, *The Age of Television* (2d ed., 1958), p. 7.
[2] *Ibid.*, pp. 15, 234. See also Charles A. H. Thom-

In 1954 advertisers and consumers together spent in all about $4 billion for television service, approximately the same amount they spent for space in newspapers and for their purchase in the same year.[3] By 1956 television receivers were available to at least three quarters of the total population; 93 per cent of the television homes saw something of the conventions on television, spending an estimated average of more than 16 hours.[4] Since then the availability of television has continued to move toward the saturation point, while public response to the medium has become increasingly routine.

The mass media are more ubiquitous in the United States than in any other country. This is especially true, moreover, in the field of politics. Many aspects of political life that the mass media here regularly treat as in the public domain are still considered privileged and private in other countries, including most of the democracies.

Functions of the Mass Media

The functions of the mass media in the nominating process include first of all their general activity as collectors and purveyors of news. The election process for the Presidency has been a mass media phenomenon in the United States for generations, but, until recent decades, in the nominating process the most vital flows of information were largely handled through other means. With the coming of the presidential primaries and more open patterns of campaigning, the news of the nominating process became much more accessible to the mass media and they assumed a corresponding importance. Further impetus was given to a long-standing tendency to make presidential politics a main focus of mass media attention.

As matters stand, the newspapers continue to hold their position as the principal source of detailed news for those who wish to follow the events of the nominating campaigns in depth. News magazines and other journals of national circulation have a special field as publishers of biographical articles detailing the qualifications and activities of prospective candidates for the nominations.[5] Radio is supreme as the hour-by-hour reporter of spot news as it occurs. Television is not far behind in spot news coverage, and often adds the further impact of the visual image of persons and events. Radio and television coverage of the national political conventions in recent years has been more continuous and complete than would be possible through any other medium, although the printed media continue to exploit their special advantages.

The mass media also perform several specialized functions that seem at times to be of critical importance in the nominating process. These may be listed as the pointing out of potential candidates, the clarification of the candidates' prospects, and the transmission of popular mandates as the time of final choice draws near.

In the making of decisions, recognition of the alternatives for choice is always a first and vital step. This is frequently overlooked in the study of elections, because in elections the alternatives have usually been determined already through the nominations

son, *Television and Presidential Politics* (1956); and Thomson, "Television, Politics, and Public Policy," in *Public Policy: A Yearbook of the Graduate School of Public Administration, Harvard University*, Vol. 8 (1958), pp. 368-406 (also issued as Brookings Institution Reprint No. 25).

[3] Bogart, *op. cit.*, p. 186. Consumer expenditure for television included the purchase, operation, and servicing of television receivers.

[4] *Ibid.*, p. 234.

[5] Cf. Chapter 12, footnote 10. Biographical articles on political figures (not limited to those who might conceivably become candidates for a presidential nomination) have been a staple part of the contents of popular magazines for a long time. One count found an average of sixteen such articles a year in *Saturday Evening Post* and *Collier's* combined, during the period 1901-1914; nineteen, 1922-1930; twenty-four, 1930-1934; thirty-one, 1940-1941. These figures constituted a declining portion of a total in which the relative share of attention given to persons in the entertainment field was rising, the point with which the analysis was mainly concerned. Nonetheless, the continuing major attention given political figures is evident. See Leo Lowenthal, "Biographies in Popular Magazines," in Paul Lazarsfeld and Frank Stanton (eds.), *Radio Research, 1942-1943* (1944). pp. 507-20; also reprinted in other collected volumes.

offered by the major parties. But the nominating process has to start at the beginning, although there is no single starting point where the potential candidates begin to become visible. It is in the nature of things that, when the identification becomes authoritative, the candidacy ceases to be potential and becomes actual.

The national magazines, the daily press and the other mass media have almost the entire responsibility, so far as the public at large is concerned, for pointing out the likely candidates during the early period when none of them has as yet formally announced and responsible party leaders are not yet willing to comment publicly. The field within which the potential candidates can be sought is established partly by the general structure of the political system, partly by the self-advancing activities of the rising personalities, and partly by the responses of the factional and party leaders who continuously hold the field under review. But the early movements of opinion are intangible and ambiguous; their adequate collection and interpretation require constant access to insiders who are willing to talk to their confidants in the press corps, but not for attribution. The result is a highly complex function in which a few top-flight political analysts excel, while other elements in the mass media provide supporting services and the apparatus of dissemination.

The clarification of the relative standing of alternative candidates is a further phase in the same type of activity, and one of the utmost importance during the period while a field of twenty or thirty potentials is being reduced to six or eight who will actually announce and three or four who will have some substantial chance of nomination. The mass media report the first evidences of public judgment, such as the presidential primaries and state party conventions. They interpret those events and report other interpretations by expert observers—in either case, offering useful guidance in the often foggy state of political opinion at this stage. They publish the public opinion polls and

act as their sponsors, since the major polls are commercial enterprises dependent upon the fees paid by the outlets through which they reach the public.

Finally, in deciding on their own allocations of news time and space, the mass media reflect their own judgments of the relative importance and newsworthiness of the respective candidates. Candidates that the media refuse to take seriously as news are likely to find their difficulties redoubled, while those who are given top news treatment take on the appearance of leaders. In making their judgments, the media are of course influenced by events, by whether a candidate already holds a public office, and by the ability of the candidates to create news; but wide discretion remains, along with wide opportunities for honest differences in perception and judgment. The cumulative effect of these judgments may well be the point at which the mass media have their greatest independent impact on the nominating process; certainly it is the point at which they are most directly compelled to take responsibility for decisions of important political consequence.

The further function of the mass media as the transmitters of the final popular mandates on presidential nominations is ill defined, largely unrecognized, and open to question in many ways. The fact remains that as long as most of the people cannot send a last message to the convention by any other route, whatever impressions of popular consensus are conveyed by the mass media are likely to carry weight. They also may supply the best estimates of party opinion in particular states, especially when other forms of evidence are lacking, conflicting, or unreliable—as they are apt to be in most states.

The mass media themselves, of course, have to struggle with incomplete evidence and the difficulty of reaching objectivity in the assessment of whatever evidence is available. But they are in a good position to collect all the available facts, and if some of them are biased in their interpretation they may be counterbalanced by others. Moreover, it is to their credit that they have backed the use of survey methods in the search for better evidence and better estimates, while also continuing to act as critics of survey results when they seemed deficient. When the mass media speak with something approaching a united voice in reporting the popular consensus, as they did in the Taft-Eisenhower struggle of 1952, the resulting impact on the convention delegates is obviously substantial.

Still another transmission function of the mass media is the selling of time on radio or television, by which means the candidates can speak directly to the audiences whose support they seek. In providing time, either paid or free, radio and television are subject to federal licensing and other forms of regulation that do not apply to the press. Under the Federal Communications Act, licensees have a general statutory obligation to serve the public interest. This includes an obligation to provide reasonable amounts of time for the broadcasting of information of public concern; when such programs are controversial, the treatment must be fair and balanced.

Furthermore, Section 315 of the Act provides that stations shall give equal access to all bona fide candidates for the same political office or nomination. This means that if free time is given to one candidate for a presidential nomination, time equal in amount and quality must be given to each of the other recognized candidates for the same nomination if they so request. Similarly, if time is sold to one candidate, equally good time must be sold to other candidates on demand.

These provisions have given rise to various issues of public policy and proposals for dealing with them.[6] Meanwhile, they have the effect of considerably reducing the free time for leading candidates that might otherwise have been given because of evident newsworthiness and public interest in their campaigns. Paid time obviously can be used only to the extent that campaign

funds permit; the increasing need for it has enhanced the importance of finance in nominating campaigns.

Much of the discussion of the political use of radio and television has been confined to the problems of avowed candidates in using free and paid time. But equally important effects may be achieved during the earlier phase, when the most important future candidates can still get on the air with no strings attached, merely because of their newsworthiness. Even after they have taken on the limitations of avowed candidates, the networks and the stations may continue to provide free news coverage of the candidates and campaign events, ending with the extensive coverage of the conventions. This contribution of radio and television as purveyors of news is on the whole probably more important than providing the candidates with a direct chance to be heard.[7]

Role Conflict in Function Performance

The news dissemination and related specialized functions of the mass media sometimes come in conflict. The traditional conflict is that between partisan and nonpartisan attitudes in reporting and commentary —between actively trying to influence the outcome and reporting as a neutral observer. Those who take an active part may

---

[6] See the two works by Charles A. H. Thomson, cited in footnote 2.

[7] The above was written before the full impact of the so-called Lar Daly decisions of the Federal Communications Commission in 1959 had become apparent. In August 1959, prompted by the FCC action, Congress amended Section 315 to provide that it shall not apply to the appearance of a legally qualified candidate on any bona fide newscast, news interview, news documentary (if the appearance is incidental to presentation of the subject covered); and that it shall also not apply to on-the-spot coverage of bona fide news events, including, but not limited to, political conventions or activities incidental to them. Language in the conference report made clear that the exemption also covers regularly scheduled panel shows. The new legislation reaffirmed the obligation of stations to act in the public interest and to afford reasonable opportunity for balanced discussion of conflicting views of issues of public importance. The amendment was signed by President Eisenhower on September 14, 1959, as Public Law No. 86-274.

range from the involved and highly factional partisan to the independent commentator. The latter seeks to maintain an Olympian stance of objectivity above the battle, but nevertheless will often state a definite opinion that he desires to have received with respect. His role overlaps that of the neutral reporters, who also range between merely presenting the unadorned factual situation on the one hand, and on the other providing considerable amounts of background and interpretation. These variations have long created problems in press coverage of complex political news, and became especially apparent as an issue in the television coverage of the political conventions of 1952.[8]

The issues of partisanship and of objectivity have been much debated in journalism, and have taken on added importance in recent years because of the shrinking number and growing size of the newspapers that survive. Most of the early newspapers in this country were violently partisan in both news treatment and editorial opinions; many, in fact, were openly avowed as party organs and supported by party funds. Gradually the ideal emerged of the independent newspaper, offering a balanced version of the news with a minimum of coloration in its news columns and also giving its opinions in nonpartisan but straightforward fashion in its editorial columns—an attempt to present news and opinion separately and both on a high level of objectivity. There has been considerable recent research on current deviations from this idea; but the amount of progress that has been made is probably more remarkable than the remaining lag.[9]

What has just been said applies directly to the handling of news and comment in presidential election campaigns. In nominating campaigns the problem takes a markedly different form. This is especially true when new political personalities are being built up in the earliest stages. Partisanship is largely irrelevant at this point, although not completely so. Ordinarily the problem is that of assessing newsworthiness, but sometimes it is evidently whether to engage in creating news where none exists.

Specifically, when someone previously little heard of is suddenly given wide attention in the mass media, what lies back of it? Is the man genuinely newsworthy, or is there a scarcity of news, or is this the effect of personal favoritism, or of the obscure workings of partisan, factional, and interest-group affiliations? On the other hand, when candidates who are displaying obvious strength are played down and disregarded, what are the reasons? The possible alternative motivations are so numerous and so unorganized, and probably often buried so deeply in the subconscious, that generalization is difficult and any clear assessment of the total situation is usually impossible. Accusations of bias in the press in candidate build-up and nominating campaigns have been relatively rare, but the presence of bias as a major factor has been neither proved nor disproved.[10]

[8] Thomson, op. cit., pp. 120-21; Bogart, op. cit., pp. 227-32.
[9] The "Canons of Journalism," as formulated by the American Society of Newspaper Editors, can be found in Frank L. Mott, American Journalism (1941), pp. 726-27; see also Mott's own comment on newspaper functions and the retreat from partisanship in his article "Newspapers in Presidential Campaigns," Public Opinion Quarterly, Vol. 8 (Fall 1944), pp. 348-67.

[10] Naturally enough, however, when the press does present something approaching a united front in behalf of one candidate and against others in a nominating campaign, those affected adversely inevitably tend to see bias in the behavior of the press. For example, Senator Taft after his defeat at the Republican convention in 1952 made no secret of his feeling that the press had been largely responsible. He spelled this out privately in a memorandum prepared at the time, purportedly written to prevent his followers from blaming each other for the debacle, in which he pointed to two underlying causes of his defeat, the first of which was "the power of the New York financial interests" and the second the press:
"Second, four-fifths of the influential newspapers in the country were opposed to me continuously and vociferously and many turned themselves into propaganda sheets for my opponent. Of course, this was not true of the McCormick papers, the Wall Street Journal, the Omaha World Herald, and the Los Angeles Times. The Philadelphia Inquirer, the Hearst papers, and the Knight papers remained neutral. But most other Republican papers were almost campaign sheets for Eisenhower and were

Radio and television as news purveyors have been involved in less acute conflict over their proper role than the press, for the obvious reason that the choice of roles is markedly more restricted. The statutory obligations of the broadcasting industry tend to rule out overtly partisan activities as between one candidate and another. A constitutional right to offer editorial opinions has been asserted on behalf of the industry, but has been little practiced in a way directly affecting candidate interests. On the occasions when the right has been exercised in some self-conscious fashion in commenting on public issues, equal time has usually been available on demand for appropriate spokesmen of opposing views. But even aside from the legal controls, the pressures of the market, especially the desire to retain audiences and sponsors of all shades of opinion, move the stations—if not the commentators—strongly in the direction of neutral objectivity. At times the nonpartisan role is doubtless a mask for preferences that are so strongly held that they influence the choice of unsponsored programs; but the role itself also influences attitudes. The whole broadcasting industry is undoubtedly much more neutral in actuality than it would be if it were not committed to a neutral role.[11]

Part of the reason for this neutrality arises out of the conflict between the drive to build massive audiences as an entertainment medium and the less powerful drive to perform a public service as a news medium. For the overwhelming bulk of their activity, radio and television alike must earn their living as entertainers. Newspapers also sell entertainment, but with much less effect on their news coverage. The news function still comes through in radio and television, but whether it comes through unimpaired, or as fully as it might, involves questions much too complex to pursue here.[12]

Mass Media Effects on Nominating Decisions

The previous discussion has made it evident that the mass media have many wide-ranging effects on the nominating process. Without them the vast growth of popular influence in recent years would have been impossible. This is not to say that the growth of the mass media is the whole explanation of this increased popular influence, although they played the most conspicuous part, for instance, in the build-up of Wendell Willkie in 1940. Rather, it might be argued that the mass media in their modern form, the presidential primaries, and the public opinion polls all have joined to bring about an increasing popular control of the nominating process, which no one of them alone would have been sufficient to produce.

Even if viewed merely as transmitters of news created by others, the mass media have had a far-reaching multiplier effect upon influences that might otherwise have remained inconsequential. Where time is of the essence, as it is under the fixed time tables of the nominating cycle, even a merely expediting effect may sometimes determine the outcome—as the Willkie case again attests.

Beyond their broad effects in bringing public influence to bear, the mass media have had a variety of more specific effects. They have changed the field of combat in ways that probably tend to favor certain personality types as candidates and to exclude others. They have paved the way for campaign strategies and tactics that would not otherwise be possible. They have made any potential candidate occupying the front-runner position with the voters much more conspicuous than he used to be, while also

___

supplemented by the violent support of every New Deal and so-called independent paper."
He returned to this theme and amplified it repeatedly in the memorandum. See Appendix F.

[11] For a further discussion of the issue, see Thomson, op. cit., pp. 121-24; for a discussion of the neutral character of broadcasting and the social and psychological reasons for it, Bogart, op. cit., Chap. 2, and especially pp. 37-38.

[12] Thomson, op. cit., especially pp. 119-20; Bogart, op. cit., Chaps. 3-6.

putting the other candidates under strong compulsions to develop counter-strategies emphasizing popular appeal. They have opened the national party conventions to popular inspection, and in so doing have brought changes in convention behavior and increased the pressure for other changes.

The media have furthered the tendency toward making a continuous process of the nominating and election campaigns, so that the conventions are increasingly treated as the kickoff of the election campaign rather than merely the climax of the nominating campaign. By the same token, the media have helped to increase the pressure for nominating decisions that are early in fact if not in form, so that the damage wrought by a hotly contested nominating campaign can be prevented or repaired before the party has to face the opposition in the heat of the election campaign. All of these effects, pressures, and tendencies are the result of the growing influence of public opinion, made possible by the mass media; but each has its own specific consequences that may take a long time to unfold in fullest effect.[13]

To the extent that the people take a greater interest and popular control increases, the basic effect is to shift the center of power in the nominating process and to increase the importance of popular mandates. When a popular choice does crystallize, however, what can be said about how the party voters reached their decision? What are the effects of communication through the mass media in this complex tangle of individual and group psychology? In Chapter 12's discussion of the content of nominating campaigns, it appeared that explanations that may account for voting decisions in elections may require extensive readjustment before they can be applied usefully to an understanding of the nominating process. Fortunately, such an understanding can be facilitated through use of Joseph T. Klapper's recently developed set

of general propositions on the audience effects of the mass media.[14]

The mass media, it would seem, can be

[14] The propositions are as follows:

"1. Mass communication ordinarily does not serve as a necessary and sufficient cause of audience effects, but rather functions among and through a nexus of mediating factors and influences.

"2. These mediating factors are such that they typically render mass communication a contributory agent, but not the sole cause, in a process of reinforcing the existing conditions. (Regardless of the condition in question—be it the level of public taste, the tendency of audience members toward or away from delinquent behavior, or their vote intention—and regardless of whether the effect in question be social or individual, the media are more likely to reinforce than to change.)

"3. On such occasions as mass communication does function in the service of change, one of two conditions is likely to obtain. Either:

"a. the mediating factors will be found to be inoperative, and the effect of the media direct; or

"b. the mediating factors, which normally favor reinforcement, will be found to be themselves impelling toward change.

"4. There are certain residual situations in which mass communication seems to wreak direct effects, or to directly and of itself serve certain psychophysical functions.

"5. The efficacy of mass communication, either as contributory agents or as agents of direct effect, is affected by various aspects of the media themselves or of the communication situation (including, for example, aspects of contextual organization, the availability of channels for overt action, etc.)."

See Joseph T. Klapper, "What We Know About the Effects of Mass Communication: The Brink of Hope," *Public Opinion Quarterly*, Vol. 21 (Winter 1957-58), pp. 453-74. The quoted passages above are from pp. 457-58. (All excerpts from the article quoted by permission *Public Opinion Quarterly*.)

In many nominating situations, there can be no reinforcement of "the existing conditions" because it is clear that a new nominee will have to be designated. The mediating factors that would tend toward a repetition of a previous choice then either become inoperative or become involved in the selection of the new choice. Among the relevant mediating factors for this purpose, as noted by Mr. Klapper, are the following:

—audience predisposition, which is absent in the specific sense when a new nominee must be chosen and can thus operate only in terms of predispositions toward the various factors of availability;

—selective exposure, by which the audience listens by preference to messages favoring the choice toward which it is already predisposed, a factor that becomes largely inoperative when a new choice must be made;

—primary group memberships, which operate to maintain the standards represented by the previous choice and when a new choice has to be made will enter into the search for a new application of such of the old standards as can be applied;

most influential in the formation of opinion on presidential nominations when the situation as a whole is most open and unsettled. Where a new choice must be made at the next national convention, which may still be four years in the future, the situation inevitably arouses wide-ranging speculation and some consideration of many different possibilities. Here the activities of the media in pointing out the potential candidates and making clear their relative prospects are of special importance.

There is ample room for the further development of theory in this field, but it seems clear that the party voter's decision in arriving at a nominating mandate involves an unusually complex interaction between psychological factors making for stability and those making for change. In making a new choice, voters, primary groups, and opinion leaders can all attempt to apply their previous standards of preference, but they may not find any potential candidate available who represents as good a fit as they would like. Some degree of adjustment to change thus becomes inevitable, and there will be much uncertainty over the outcome while adjustment is going on. The mass media supply an important part of the avenues of discussion through which the adjustment is sought.

At the same time, it is obvious that, while

—opinion leaders, who express the standards of the primary groups in the reinforcement of a previous choice, but must shift and rationalize their role when a new choice has to be made.

All of this helps to explain why it is "that although the media are relatively ineffectual in conversion, they are quite effective in forming opinions and attitudes in regard to *new issues*, particularly as these issues are the more unrelated to 'existing attitude clusters.' But it is precisely in reference to such issues that predispositions, selective exposure, and selective perception are least likely to exist, that group norms are least likely to pertain, that opinion leaders are least ready to lead—that the mediating forces of stasis, in short, are least likely to mediate. The intervening forces, in short, are likely to be inoperative, and the media are more likely to directly influence their audience." (*Ibid.*, p. 462. Italics in the original.) Klapper also cites Bernard Berelson, "Communications and Public Opinion," in Wilbur Schramm, *Communications in Modern Society* (1948), p. 176.

nominating choices are necessarily fluid in the early stages of a new preference, they can also be difficult to change if they once become firmly established. Three types of cases can be distinguished, of which only the third begins with the assumption that a new choice will be made.

In the first type, an incumbent President or Vice President is available for renomination to succeed himself. The party voters are usually offered no valid alternative to consider, and they tend to reject any alternatives when they do appear. Frequently it is impossible to find another candidate who will publicly admit that he would accept the nomination, or to find respectable backers for a contest against the incumbent. The situation becomes saturated with what the opinion analysts call "monopoly propaganda"—the kind of propaganda generally considered most successful.[15] The difficulties inherent in mounting an attack in such a situation were illustrated by the failure of the efforts to unseat President Truman at the Democratic convention of 1948 and to prevent Vice President Nixon's renomination in 1956.

In the second type of case, an out-party titular leader previously nominated and defeated is potentially available for another nomination. Renomination is no certainty and strong alternative candidates are usually available. The history of such cases suggests, however, that many party voters are reluctant to seek a new choice even when their previous choice has been defeated. Despite defeat, he may still look better than his competitors who had previously been considered and rejected; and for a considerable period he may look better than any of the new men who are just coming over the horizon. One can legitimately suspect that in 1948 the mass media and the popular verdict that they made possible were partly responsible for Dewey's second nomination, and in 1956 for Stevenson's second nomination—as well as for the fact that

---

[15] Klapper, *op. cit.*, p. 461, and sources cited by him.

Stevenson continued after 1956 to be a prominent possibility for 1960.[16]

In the third type of case, the previous choice is no longer available or else the prospect of his availability is so limited as to seem remote. If as many as three strong candidates are in the race, the popular preference may remain fluid until the convention has acted. But if there are only two candidates appealing to opposing factions, as in the Taft-Eisenhower struggle of 1952, popular attitudes can evidently become rigid before the convention. Still a different phenomenon occurs when the party following swings solidly for a single choice—illustrated in the two parties by the Hoover and Smith nominations of 1928, and in the Republican party by the Landon nomination of 1936 and the Dewey nomination of 1944.

The cases just cited all point to the "monopoly propaganda" advantages of the front-runner position if it develops prior to the convention with little opposition. In fact, the front-runner position seems to have become increasingly desirable even when it can be obtained and defended only through a hot struggle and at the risk of early defeat. On the Democratic side after 1956, the most actively potential candidates for 1960 showed every disposition to seek a commanding popular lead at the earliest possible date, and despite the reactions thereby engendered on the part of other candidates. This keen competition in the early stages probably marks a real change from the conditions of times past. If a continuing change has in fact occurred, the impact of the mass media and the growing involvement of the voters must be considered mainly responsible.

The Record of Voter Preferences

The public opinion polls in their present form have been a feature of presidential nominating and election campaigns since

1936. Previous types of "straw votes" by newspapers and magazines were largely abandoned after 1936 because of the failure of the postcard survey by the *Literary Digest,* which had predicted a sweeping victory for Governor Alfred M. Landon on the basis of several million returns from telephone subscribers and automobile owners. In the same year, the actual outcome was forecast with considerable accuracy by several polls using survey methods based on scientific sampling techniques. Of these, the most notable was that by George Gallup's American Institute of Public Opinion, founded in 1935.

Widely published in newspapers of mass circulation, the Gallup Poll has been a conspicuous feature of all subsequent presidential election campaigns. Competing polls, when available, have been useful mainly as a check on the Gallup findings. All were wrong together in the close election of 1948, which exposed various weaknesses in survey techniques, and also made it clear that any close election is likely to be genuinely unpredictable.[17]

The polls have had at least as much effect on nominating campaigns as on election campaigns—probably much more. The polls that are taken before the conventions have seldom been regarded as necessarily foretelling the convention action, but they are important in other ways. They indicate the development of public opinion at frequent intervals throughout the four-year period of the nominating cycle. They provide the only nationwide measures of voter preferences that become available before the convention. Thus they paint a background of specific information against which to interpret the activities of the candidates and the flow of events affecting their fortunes.

The polls also serve as guides in one way or another for the candidates themselves

[16] In this connection, consider Maurice Duverger's comment on the durability of party leaders who become established in parties with a massive popular base. *Political Parties* (1954), pp. 160-66.

[17] Committee on Analysis of Pre-Election Polls and Forecasts of the Social Science Research Council, "Report on the Analysis of Pre-Election Poll and Forecasts," *Public Opinion Quarterly,* Vol. 12 (Winter 1948-49), pp. 599-622; Frederick Mosteller, Herbert Hyman, Philip J. McCarthy, Eli S. Marks, David B. Truman, *The Pre-Election Polls of 1948* (1949).

CHART 13.1. VOTER POPULARITY OF FIRST-TIME NOMINEES
BEFORE THEY WERE CHOSEN, 1932-1952[a]

(Per Cent of Voters of Each Party Who Preferred Their
Eventual Candidate Before He Was First Nominated)

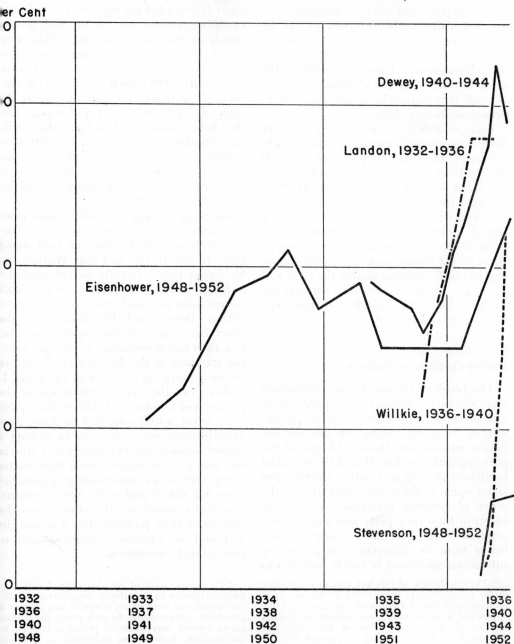

Dewey, 1940-1944

Landon, 1932-1936

Eisenhower, 1948-1952

Willkie, 1936-1940

Stevenson, 1948-1952

1932	1933	1934	1935	1936
1936	1937	1938	1939	1940
1940	1941	1942	1943	1944
1948	1949	1950	1951	1952

[a] Based on data from American Institute of Public Opinion.

and their supporters. Before the polls were available, would-be candidates and their sponsors did their utmost to test sentiment through correspondence and by sending out emissaries. These efforts were intended to build support and also to estimate how much of it they could count on, both at the conventions and in the election to follow. In the absence of tested polling methods, the estimates were frequently wide of the mark in forecasting the electoral outcomes. No sufficient factual basis was available to deflate conflicting claims.[18]

Each published poll is an event that may have consequences, especially when it upsets widely held preconceptions of how well the candidates are doing. The polls on the one hand act as a check on the mandates provided through primaries and party processes and on the other are claimed as a potential source of mandates in their own right. It has been suggested, for example, "that in the future such systematic soundings of public opinion among the rank and file of the nation's voters may perform the service which the presidential primaries were designed to do."[19]

Voter Polls
During the Phase of Latency

The phase of latency in the nominating cycle was earlier defined as the period from one presidential election until the beginning of the active contests for the next following nomination. During this period the polls regularly produce lists of the potential candidates in each party where the question seems open, ranking the candidates in the order of popular preference among the voters of their own party and among independent voters. The effect is to establish a list of those in each party for whom any substantial sentiment is visible and also to

record the changes of sentiment as they develop.

The polls begin after the election to record the immediate postelection situation. In the defeated party a preliminary judgment is recorded on whether the defeated candidate should run again, and if not which of the figures already within view might better do so. As time passes and events occur, these judgments tend to shift slowly up to the time of the mid-term elections. New names are then added to the preference lists, some names disappear, and the changes in order of rank are often striking. Another year of relative stability then usually ensues, followed by change in the fall and winter before the conventions as the eventual candidates announce and begin their campaigns.

Chart 13.1 shows the poll records, prior to various first-time nominations, of the men who actually became the next nominees. It records the fact that Willkie and Stevenson came virtually out of nowhere so far as rank-and-file preferences were concerned a few months before their first nomination. Dewey and Eisenhower, on the other hand, were leading figures long before their first nomination. Chart 13.2 shows the standing of the defeated candidate, in his own party, as recorded in the polls. It makes clear the striking difference in the positions of Landon and Willkie three years after defeat, a difference that no doubt gave Willkie some encouragement in seeking a second nomination. For Dewey and Stevenson, one pair of curves records their fluctuating success in maintaining popularity after one defeat and while moving toward a second nomination; the other shows the erosion of their position after a second defeat and an announced intention not to seek a third nomination.[20]

[18] The significance of this lack and its importance in the pre-polling era is suggested by the discussion of techniques for dealing with the claims of the opposition in a memorandum written by Senator Charles W. F. Dick of Ohio in May 1912. See Thomas E. Felt, "Organizing a National Convention: A Lesson from Senator Dick," *Ohio Historical Quarterly,* Vol. 67 (Jan. 1958), pp. 50-62.

[19] George Gallup and Saul F. Rae, *The Pulse of Democracy* (1940), p. 140.

[20] The cooperation of the American Institute of Public Opinion in assembling the material for the two charts and most of the tables of this chapter is gratefully acknowledged. In each chart, the various curves extend over whatever period is covered by the available information; Stevenson, for example, was not carried on the list of potential next Democratic nominees used in polling during 1957 and early 1958. In Chart 13.2 the Stevenson 1956-1960 curve shows poll data up to August 1, 1959.

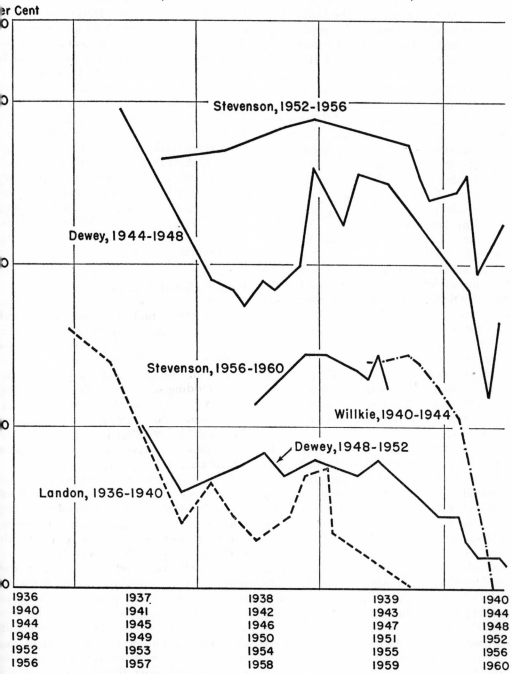

CHART 13.2. VOTER POPULARITY OF TITULAR LEADERS IN DEFEAT[a]

(Per Cent of Voters of Each Party Who Preferred Their Party's
Most Recently Defeated Candidate as Its Next Nominee)

er Cent

Stevenson, 1952-1956

Dewey, 1944-1948

Stevenson, 1956-1960

Willkie, 1940-1944

Dewey, 1948-1952

London, 1936-1940

1936	1937	1938	1939	1940
1940	1941	1942	1943	1944
1944	1945	1946	1947	1948
1948	1949	1950	1951	1952
1952	1953	1954	1955	1956
1956	1957	1958	1959	1960

[a] Based on data from American Institute of Public Opinion.

Who were the candidates preferred by the party voters during the intervals between the down-grading or disappearance of a previous nominee and the build-up of the next nominee? Landon was replaced by Senator Arthur Vandenberg between 1937 and the mid-term elections, and thereafter by Dewey, who had been defeated for governor of New York but had run a strong race. Between 1941 and 1944, Willkie, as soon as he slipped below top preference late in 1943, was replaced by Dewey. Between 1949 and 1952, Eisenhower replaced Dewey as top preference during most of the period, but Eisenhower was briefly topped by Senator Robert A. Taft in March 1952. On the Democratic side between 1949 and 1952, President Truman led the preference polls until he was replaced by Senator Estes Kefauver in April 1952.

The material reported by the polls is interesting as information; but does it have any actual effect on what happens during the phase of latency? It seems likely that it may have some effect upon the standing of the titular leaders and other well-known figures who were in the running at the time of the previous nomination. This effect is probably derived from the attention given the polls by political reporters and editors, party leaders, and the potential candidates themselves.

For the new men on the way up, the polls do not seem very useful in their present form as a means of identifying those who eventually will become important. In any poll earlier than January of the presidential year, the new men are generally running behind several relatively well-known figures, most of whom have disqualifications that will eventually prevent their serious consideration. It is when a previous unknown begins to move up from the 2 or 3 per cent level in the polls and rises steadily thereafter that politicians begin to pay attention; and the polls may have some effect at that time in pointing out possible future candidates.

It should always be remembered, however, that the time at which a preference poll is taken may have considerable effect upon the degree of seriousness with which the respondents answer. During the period of latency, respondents have little reason to think their answers are important, and, in any case, they often have not thought much about the question asked. Their answers, accordingly, may be quite offhand, as must have been the case with many individuals in the samples that in 1939 gave Charles Lindbergh 10 per cent of the vote for the next Democratic nomination and in 1949 gave Franklin D. Roosevelt, Jr., 22 per cent. As convention and election time nears, however, it can be expected that respondents consider their answers with an increasing sense of responsibility, culminating finally in the act of voting and the responsibility of an actual decision.

Voter Polls and Primaries

From March to June of the presidential year, preferences within the parties for the various candidates are being registered both in the public opinion polls and in the primaries. Do the polls and the primaries influence each other, and which way do the major influences run? Which has the greater effect upon the further development of voter sentiment? What are the effects so far as candidates, party leaders, and delegates are concerned?

Here again, adequate answers would require types of survey research that have rarely been attempted. A number of hypotheses are suggested, however, by the general pattern of the experience in the nominating campaigns of 1944 to 1956.

The primaries undoubtedly affect the polls; the polls probably have much less direct influence on the primaries. The news of the successive primaries affects the development of voter sentiment throughout the country. This is then reflected in the polls. Candidates, party leaders, and delegates probably react, like the voters, mainly to the successive primaries; but the poll re-

TABLE 13.1. REPUBLICAN VOTER PREFERENCES AMONG CANDIDATES FOR THE REPUBLICAN PRESIDENTIAL NOMINATION, FEBRUARY-JUNE 1948[a]

(by per cent)

Candidate	February	March	April	May	June
Dewey	38%	34%	29%	24%	33%
Stassen	15	15	31	37	26
MacArthur	14	19	16	12	11
Vandenberg	6	13	10	13	13
Taft	15	12	9	8	10
Warren	5	3	2	2	2
Martin	1	1	1	1	1
Others or No Opinion	6	3	2	3	4
	100	100	100	100	100

[a] Based on *Public Opinion Quarterly*. Vol. 12 (Fall 1948), p. 562.

TABLE 13.2. DEMOCRATIC VOTER PREFERENCES AMONG CANDIDATES FOR THE DEMOCRATIC PRESIDENTIAL NOMINATION, FEBRUARY-JUNE 1956[a]

(by per cent)

Candidate	February	March	April	May	June 15	June 29
Stevenson	49%	51%	39%	41%	42%	45%
Kefauver	17	18	33	29	26	16
Harriman	8	8	6	6	8	12
Johnson	3	2	3	4	4	—
Lausche	3	2	2	3	3	3
Russell	4	4	4	3	2	5
Symington	—	1	2	2	2	4
Rayburn	—	—	—	—	—	2
Others or No Opinion	16	14	11	12	13	13
	100	100	100	100	100	100

[a] Compiled from releases, American Institute of Public Opinion.

sults tend to repeat each impact and to clarify its importance for the candidates, the party leaders, and the delegates.

The candidates and party leaders may then revise their strategies, and delegates can think further about their eventual decisions at the conventions. Revisions in candidate strategy and behavior affect later primaries, which in turn affect general voter sentiment, which in turn is reflected in further opinion polls. When the later primary results differ markedly from the earlier ones, the polls may also show a sort of oscillation, with swings of sentiment in March and April tending toward equilibrium in May and June as the campaigning in the primaries comes to a close.

The oscillation pattern was demonstrated in the Republican nominating campaign of 1948 and the Democratic of 1956. The evolution of the Republican race in 1948 as reported by the Gallup Poll is shown in Table 13.1. Stassen came from behind to lead in April and May. Dewey again came into the lead in June after the effects of the Oregon primary had been felt, though his plurality was far short of a majority. MacArthur was at peak in March and declined thereafter. Taft, like Dewey, lost ground as Stassen gained, then began moving up again as Stassen declined, but he was running fifth in June, though he had been tied with Stassen for second place in February.

The oscillation pattern in the Democratic nominating campaign of 1956 is shown in Table 13.2. Kefauver's gains and Stevenson's losses after the New Hampshire and Minnesota primaries in March are apparent, along with the reversal that occurred after Stevenson's later victories in Oregon, Florida, and California. When Kefauver lost strength at the end of his campaign, however, Harriman gained more than Stevenson, and the no-opinion vote was almost as large at the end as at the beginning.

The polls reported effects in other years that were probably due mainly to the reports of the primaries, but did not show an oscillation pattern. In 1944, Willkie quickly dropped out of the polls after his primary

defeats and withdrawal, while Dewey assumed a commanding position, as indicated in Charts 13.1 and 13.2. In 1952 the build up in Kefauver's reputation as he won victories in the early primaries brought him from a score among Democratic voters 21 per cent in January to 45 per cent June and July.[21] On the Republican side 1952, Taft was briefly reported by the Gallup Poll in March as leading Eisenhower to 33 per cent among Republican voter but thereafter Eisenhower rose steadily a lead of 46 per cent to Taft's 35 on the e of the convention.[22]

Voter Polls and Final Decision

In the previous discussion, the publ opinion polls referred to were principal those indicating the standings of the candidates within their own parties. The "tri heat" type of poll, however, is in some spects more relevant to the final decision the convention.

"Trial heat" polls attempt to discov how a specific candidate of one party wou run against a specific candidate of the oth if the general election were held at the tin of the poll. Usually the candidate who lea the preference list within his own party also the one who at the same time runs be in trial heats against opposing party cand dates, but the two choices are not alwa the same, since the trial heats include vote of both parties and of none. Thus Eise hower was pre-eminent in the trial heats 1952 because of his great appeal to ind pendents and to many Democrats. Taft w never close to Eisenhower as a potenti winner against a Democratic candidat even though he was reported momentari as the leading preference of Republica voters.

The trial heat data frequently provide picture of the total situation quite diffe ent from that of the preference polls wit in each party, even when the ranking of th

[21] Releases from American Institute of Publ Opinion.
[22] *Washington Post*, July 2, 1952.

candidates remains in the same order. As of March and April 1940, for example, with the "phony war" dragging along in Europe and before the impact of the French collapse, several Republicans ran strongly against President Roosevelt in the trial heats: Dewey was polling 48 per cent of the total vote, Vandenberg 47, and Taft 42. But among the Republican voters who had a preference, Dewey was preferred by 43 per cent, Vandenberg by 22, and Taft by 17.[23]

The two sets of data in conjunction with each other sometimes throw light on the distribution and strength of second-choice support. In the case just cited, the trial heat data suggest that Dewey and Vandenberg each had strong second-choice support from voters who preferred the other as their first choice, while this was less true of Taft—although he too was evidently acceptable to millions of voters who did not consider him a first or even a second choice, since otherwise his showing in the trial heat would have been even poorer.

The distribution of second-choice support is of great importance in nominating contests when all the first-choice candidates fall short of a majority. If the Gallup Poll were to obtain and publish complete tabulations of second-choice data, in addition to the trial heat returns, it would often be possible to gain a clearer understanding of the relationships among the respective candidates and the factions providing their first-choice support. Which candidates might build up a majority if their second-choice support could be added to their first-choice support would be immediately apparent. The candidates who have little first-choice support but are important because of the strength and distribution of their second-choice support would also be identified in a way that does not occur at all at present.

The coalition possibilities would thus be greatly clarified by data showing both the amount of second-choice support for leading candidates and its location.[24]

The preference polls indicating the leading candidate in each party are the nearest approach to what might be considered a national popular mandate, at least when they report a majority preference in the party for a particular candidate. But a majority is seldom reported in the polls in a contest situation; and when all the leaders fall short of majority support the delegates are entitled to look elsewhere in their search for a mandate. The trial heat polls

[23] Hadley Cantril (ed.), *Public Opinion 1935-1946* (1951), pp. 616, 650-51. In each case the trial heat data were reported on a basis totaling 100 per cent for the two candidates, the undecided voters having been eliminated from the calculation. The risks involved in ignoring the undecided voters have become more apparent since 1940, and especially since 1948.

[24] The most useful type of poll for these purposes would be one somewhat akin to the scheme of majority preferential voting used in Australia, where the voter marks his order of choice among a full list of candidates; see Chapter 10. The object is to find where the votes supporting hopeless candidacies will go when their candidate is eliminated, in order to know which of the leading candidates has a chance to accumulate a majority. When only second choices are indicated, some votes will merely be transferred from one hopeless candidate to another equally hopeless. But in opinion polling it may not be practical to search the voter's preferences beyond a second or at most a third choice. Even these results would be valuable in indicating the structure of preferences. Knowing these facts about voter opinion within the parties will not necessarily predict a corresponding movement of delegate votes at the convention, but would assist candidates in planning their strategy while also providing additional data with which to analyze what happens in the conventions.

An alternative method of getting at the structure of voter preferences would involve the type of question in which the voter is asked, "If the choice for the .... nomination narrowed down to only two men, ... and ...., which would you prefer?" If this question were asked concerning a sufficient number of pairs of candidates, it would be possible to learn whether there is any single party choice who will be preferred to all the other possible candidates. It may also be discovered that there is no such choice, the situation being of the form in which candidate A is preferred to B by a majority, B is preferred to C (thus indicating that A would be preferred to C if the two majorities were the same and those composing them were consistent in the arrangement of their preferences), but C is in fact preferred to A by a majority, in which case there is no single majority choice on the basis of this method. It then becomes especially desirable to know more about the schedule of preferences on a basis permitting other calculations. For a further discussion of the problems in this area, see Duncan Black, *The Theory of Committees and Elections* (1958), Chaps. 9-11 and 18.

TABLE 13.3. REPUBLICAN PRECONVENTION PROSPECTS AGAINST ROOSEVELT, 1936, 1940, AND 1944: PER CENT OF THOSE HAVING PREFERENCES PREFERRING A POTENTIAL REPUBLICAN CANDIDATE TO ROOSEVELT[a]

Potential Candidate	1936	1940	1944
Borah	41%		
Vandenberg	40		
Landon	45		
Dewey		39%	49%[b]
Willkie		37	
Taft		36	
Hoover		30	
Bricker			44

[a] American Institute of Public Opinion polls as reported in Hadley Cantril (ed.), *Public Opinion 1935-1946* (1951), pp. 598, 626, 627, 635, 650, 651, 653. In most cases the data were reported on a basis already adjusted to 100 per cent for the two candidates, omitting the undecided voters; in the remaining cases this was done to make the figures in the table comparable. Where trial heat data were reported repeatedly for the same pairs of candidates, the last available figure before the convention is the one included here.
[b] April 1944; in March 1944, 45% if the war was still going on at the time of the election, and 58% if the war was over by the time of the election.

TABLE 13.4. REPUBLICAN PRECONVENTION PROSPECTS, JUNE 1948: PER CENT OF THE TOTAL ELECTORATE PREFERRING VARIOUS POTENTIAL CANDIDATES[a]

Potential Republican Candidate	Republican Candidate	Truman	Wallace	None or Undecided
Dewey	44%	32%	6%	18%
Vandenberg	42	32	6	20
Stassen	42	32	6	20
MacArthur	43	33	6	18
Warren	33	36	7	24
Taft	30	41	7	22

[a] From a *Fortune* poll by Elmo Roper, June 1948, as reported in *Public Opinion Quarterly*, Vol. 12 (Fall 1948), p. 563. The American Institute of Public Opinion apparently reported trial heat data only for Dewey against Truman and Wallace in June 1948, although reporting trial heat data for several other candidates in earlier months. (*Ibid.*, pp. 560-61.)

TABLE 13.5. DEMOCRATIC PRECONVENTION PROSPECTS AGAINST EISENHOWER, 1956: PER CENT OF THE TOTAL ELECTORATE PREFERRING VARIOUS POTENTIAL CANDIDATES[a]

Potential Democratic Candidate	Democratic Candidate	Eisenhower	None or Undecided
Stevenson	35%	62%	3%
Kefauver	34	60	6
Harriman	32	64	4

[a] American Institute of Public Opinion polls as reported in *Washington Post and Times-Herald*, July 13, 1956, for Stevenson and Harriman; April 15, 1956, Kefauver.

then become especially useful, because, among other reasons, the delegates presumably have a strong implied mandate to nominate a winner if possible. This is undoubtedly a major objective of most delegates, although subject to qualification when it conflicts seriously with other objectives.

The difficulties of the Republican party from 1936 to 1944 in searching for a candidate to run against President Roosevelt are indicated in Table 13.3. At no time did the trial heat data turn up a potential winner under the conditions prevailing at the time of the conventions, although they indicated differences in strength among the potential candidates.[25] Against President Truman in 1948 the opposite was largely true, as shown in Table 13.4, with four Republicans running strongly ahead of Truman and only Warren and Taft running behind. In 1956, as shown in Table 13.5, the position of the Democrats in seeking a candidate against

[25] The influence of the outbreak of war on Roosevelt's third-term prospects should be remembered. In May and June 1939, Dewey was leading Roosevelt 55 to 45 and 52 to 48 in trial heats; by December 1939, after the beginning of the war in Europe, Roosevelt was leading Dewey 54 to 46, according to the American Institute of Public Opinion.

President Eisenhower was much like that faced repeatedly by the Republicans in seeking someone to run against President Roosevelt.

When the 1952 conventions met, each party was in a state of great uncertainty on the choice of a nominee. This brought into play, as between the parties, one of the standard situations in the theory of games, that in which each of two opponents must weigh his strategy in the light of the alternative strategies available to the other. The situation in mid-June 1952, before either convention was held, can be represented by Table 13.6. This shows the trial heat data as reported by the Gallup Poll. The symbols "R," "D," and "X" indicate the apparent probable outcomes: Eisenhower could be expected to defeat either Stevenson or Kefauver, and Kefauver could be expected to defeat Taft. Between Taft and Stevenson, the statistical difference was much too small for any prediction, in a poll where the average margin of error is in the range of 2 to 6 per cent, and especially with 11 per cent of the voters still preferring neither or undecided.

The same kind of diagram could be con-

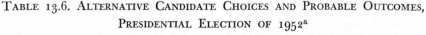

TABLE 13.6. ALTERNATIVE CANDIDATE CHOICES AND PROBABLE OUTCOMES, PRESIDENTIAL ELECTION OF 1952[a]

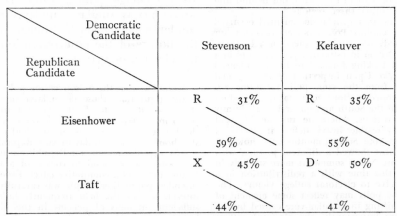

Republican Candidate \ Democratic Candidate	Stevenson	Kefauver
Eisenhower	R 31% / 59%	R 35% / 55%
Taft	X 45% / 44%	D 50% / 41%

[a] Numbers in the boxes are the estimated percentages of popular vote that would be obtained by each candidate against the other if the election were being held currently, as reported by American Institute of Public Opinion, release of June 17, 1952. The figures do not add to 100, since they do not include voters who were undecided or who insisted on preferring another candidate even when presented with a choice between two.

TABLE 13.7. PRECONVENTION TRIAL HEATS AND ELECTORAL OUTCOMES[a]

	Democratic Candidate, Per Cent of Popular Vote		Republican Candidate, Per Cent of Popular Vote	
Year	June Poll[b]	November Actual	June Poll[b]	November Actual
1936	56%	62%	44%	38%
1940	58[c]	55	42[c]	45
1944	51[d]	53	49[d]	47
1948	50	52	50	48
1952	34	44	66	56
1956	36	42	64	58

[a] All trial heat data from American Institute of Public Opinion; trial heat and voting data adjusted to 100 per cent two-party basis in each case to facilitate comparability.
[b] Preconvention trial heat data for the candidate actually nominated, against the other candidate actually nominated.
[c] No Roosevelt-Willkie trial heat was reported, presumably because of the suddenness of Willkie's rise to prominence as a leading candidate; the figures given here were based on responses to a question as to which party the respondent would vote for.
[d] From a release of April 25, 1944; no report for June.

structed with greater refinement by converting estimates of the popular vote into estimates of electoral college votes. In the example just given, this probably would have shown Taft as the winner over Stevenson.[26]

Table 13.7 indicates the extent to which

[26] The Gallup Poll (AIPO) sometimes reports trial heat data with a regional breakdown; in this case, the regional data were not reported and are not available, but it seems likely that Stevenson ran far ahead of Taft in the South, but behind him in each of the other three regions.

A similar case that can be documented occurred in 1957. The Gallup Poll reported that Senator John F. Kennedy was running ahead of Vice President Richard Nixon in estimated popular vote in a trial heat poll looking forward to the presidential elections of 1960. Upon inspection of the regional data reported from the same poll it became apparent that Kennedy's slim lead nationally rested on a heavy lead in the South and no lead at all in any of the other regions, where he ran well behind Nixon for a probable heavy defeat in terms of electoral college vote. Several months later, however, another trial heat showed a different picture, with Kennedy leading Nixon somewhat more strongly in popular vote, this time with a redistribution in a pattern conducive to electoral college victory. The second of these polls may reflect some element of band-wagon shifting in popular vote caused by the first poll. More importantly, the electoral college implications of the first poll may have led to some revision in Senator Kennedy's strategy as a potential candidate. For the poll data, see *Washington Post and Times-Herald*, Aug. 25, 1957, and Feb. 14, 1958.

the preconvention Gallup Polls have been in accord with the November outcome since 1936. They indicated the winner correctly in every instance except that of 1948, and in that year, the preconvention polls were more nearly right than others taken later in the campaign.[27] It should be noted, however, that, in every instance except 1940, Republican popular strength as it eventually materialized was overestimated by 2 to 10 percentage points, while Democratic strength was similarly underestimated; a similar phenomenon had much to do with the failure of the post-convention polls in the election of 1948.[28]

[27] The fact that the preconvention polls were more nearly right than those taken later suggests again the importance of the final stage of Truman's campaign in reactivating Democratic voters who, during the interval after the conventions, had intended to stay home on election day or vote Republican.
[28] In 1948 the reasons for Republican bias in polling results were found to consist of a number of factors that had a cumulative effect. Even when the intended population sample was carefully designed, interviewers in the field frequently failed to find sufficient numbers of persons in the highest and lowest income classes. To the extent that they were allowed discretion, the middle-class bias of many interviewers was probably reflected in their selection of respondents. Respondents in turn were influenced somewhat by the characteristics of the interviewers and by their assumptions about what would be a

Mandates vs. Results

Popular mandates always exert some influence, but they are not always obeyed. The circumstances in which a mandate is disregarded take on a special importance in the appraisal of nominating institutions.

Delegate Polls and Votes:
Criterion, Influence, and Result

The final vote on a nominating ballot is the point at which mandates are conclusively executed or disregarded. The outcome may remain in doubt until it occurs; more often, it is foreshadowed by earlier ballots on other issues and by the unofficial polls of the delegates before and during the convention. The Associated Press has long followed the practice of compiling a systematic run-down by states of known delegate preferences in connection with its reporting on the selection of delegates. In 1952 and 1956 the AP intensified its polling of the uncommitted delegates before the conventions. Other press services have made similar efforts.

The polls of the delegates serve as the best available criterion of delegate sentiment at any one time, just as the public opinion polls perform this function for the voters, and thus permit comparisons between the two bodies of sentiment when the information for the delegates is relatively complete. Usually, in the party out of power, the advance polls of delegates

have shown so many uncommitted that the result remained in doubt. In 1944, however, the AP poll made it clear in May that Dewey would probably be nominated on the first ballot in June, as he was. In 1952 it reported just before the Republican convention that the outcome between Taft and Eisenhower was still in doubt, even though most of the delegates were committed.

In 1956 both Associated Press and United Press began rechecking their polls of the Democratic delegates at intervals of a few hours just before the convention and during the opening days, maintaining a running tally that was continuously available. A week before the convention, Stevenson had a strong lead but much less than a majority. Truman's announcement of support for Governor Harriman complicated the situation as the convention opened, along with recurring argument about Stevenson's position on civil rights. Nevertheless, both press polls showed Stevenson steadily gaining during the first two days of the convention. The majority point was passed in the early hours of Wednesday morning. A bandwagon shift then occurred and he polled 66 per cent on the first nominating ballot on Thursday.

Advance polls of the delegates thus begin as mere reports of developing response to the popular and other mandates that are in process of formation, but, as the tension mounts, the delegate polls may themselves influence the outcome. When they reveal that sentiment is turning strongly toward a single outstanding candidate, they accelerate a development that would otherwise take place more slowly, with a plurality gaining momentum as it becomes a reported majority and a band-wagon movement ensues.

This is clearly another point at which noteworthy changes in the nominating process have been accumulating. When one candidate is showing strength in the delegate polls, other candidates are under pressure to make a similar showing by urging their

---

socially acceptable reply. When voters reported themselves undecided, it was necessary to make estimates of how they would probably vote; and these estimates proved somewhat erroneous. See the previously cited report (footnote 17), prepared under the auspices of the Social Science Research Council.

In one-party Democratic areas, many of these sources of bias work in the direction of inflated estimates of the prospective Democratic vote. The over-all bias in the Republican direction for the country as a whole is a reflection of the higher social and economic status of the Republican party following in areas outside the South; see Chapter 14.

supporters to become publicly committed. It becomes more difficult for any candidate to maintain reserves of hidden committed strength. For the delegates themselves, reticence about their commitments and intentions also becomes more difficult when other delegates, similarly situated, are making candid statements. Open contests thus tend to develop more openness of information;

brought together in Table 13.8 for several of the nominations since 1940. These data provide a kind of overview of recent convention action.

Dewey's nomination of 1944 was the only out-party case since 1940 for which a majority mandate could be found among the voters of the candidate's own party in advance of the event. Willkie in 1940, Eisen-

TABLE 13.8. PARTY VOTER ATTITUDES BEFORE AND AFTER NOMINATIONS FOR PRESIDENT, 1940-1956[a]

(in estimated per cent of all party voters)

Presidential Nominee, Party, and Year	Before the Convention			After the Convention		
	Preferred Eventual Nominee	Preferred Other Leading Candidates[b]	Undecided or Other	Pleased With Nomination	Not Pleased With Nomination	Attitude Undecided
Roosevelt (D, 1940)	92%	—%	8%	n.a.[c]	n.a.	n.a.
Willkie (R, 1940)	44	42 (2)	14	n.a.	n.a.	n.a.
Roosevelt (D, 1944)	90	—	10	n.a.	n.a.	n.a.
Dewey (R, 1944)	58	12 (1)	30	n.a.	n.a.	n.a.
Truman (D, 1948)	67	12 (1)	21	n.a.	n.a.	n.a.
Dewey (R, 1948)	33	60 (4)	7	61%	32%	7%
Stevenson (D, 1952)	12	73 (3)	15	54	26	20
Eisenhower (R, 1952)	46	35 (1)	19	77	19	4
Stevenson (D, 1956)	45	28 (2)	27	55	23	22
Eisenhower (R, 1956)	92[d]	—	8	71	11	18

[a] Releases of American Institute of Public Opinion, and other information supplied by the Institute.
[b] Per cent for those preferred by 10 per cent or more, and number (in parenthesis) of such candidates.
[c] Not available.
[d] In these cases the voter was not given a list of possible alternative candidates, but was asked: "Would you like to see Eisenhower run?"

and the stage is set for band-wagon movements even before the actual voting in the convention. Equally important, in a sharply focused contest between two strong candidates, the delegations containing most of the uncommitted delegates become clearly identified. These delegations are then under the spotlight of public attention until the action has been completed.

Voter Polls Before and After

Polls reporting voter opinion immediately before and after the conventions are

hower in 1952, and Stevenson in 1956 ranked about alike in the near majorities of out-party voters favoring their respective nominations. In each case there was also strong opposition.

Dewey's nomination in 1948 (the other out-party case) and Stevenson's in-party nomination in 1952 were not supported strongly by party voter mandates prior to the conventions. Both nominations were accepted favorably by most of the party voters after they had occurred, but the proportion of party voters who remained displeased or undecided was high, as it was again in Stevenson's case in 1956. The first Eisenhower nomination was received favorably by the voters of his party, despite the hard core of unhappy Taft supporters; in 1956 the opposition to another nomination had dwindled, but the number of Republican voters who were not certain of what they thought of the nomination after it had occurred was surprisingly high, and casts doubt on the preconvention finding of near unanimity.

For the four cases—other than Eisenhower in 1956—in which direct comparison can be made between the percentages of party voters who desired the nomination in advance (after considering alternatives) and the percentages of those who were pleased with the decision after the event, it is noteworthy that there was a substantial gain in preference for the nominee in every case. Presumably this is an illustration of a phenomenon that has been demonstrated repeatedly in various types of psychological research, where many respondents in experimental settings have been found to be quite willing to change their opinion when given an opportunity to agree with a different one that they consider authoritative for one reason or another.[29] The present cases are also in accord with other findings on the psychological tendency to accept a *fait accompli,* and on the importance of events, as compared with arguments, in changing opinion.[30] Against the background of this broader research, the proportions of party voters in each of the four cases who remained displeased or undecided may be the most striking aspect of those findings.

The Influence of Voter Choice

The materials assembled in this chapter and the previous one doubtless indicate a long-term increase in the influence of voter

[29] Joseph T. Klapper, *The Effects of Mass Media* (Bureau of Applied Social Research, mimeo., 1950), Memo. 4, pp. 43-44.
[30] Bernard Berelson, "Communications and Public Opinion," in Wilbur Schramm (ed.), *Communications in Modern Society* (1948), p. 175.

choice in nominating decisions. A fair appraisal of the extent to which voter influence is usually effective nonetheless remains difficult—not only because no tools of measurement are readily available, but also because simple observation would indicate that voter influence has been far more critical in some nominating decisions than others.

The attitudes that voters bring to the problem have obvious limitations. Charts 13.1 and 13.2 and Tables 13.1 and 13.2 demonstrated the extent to which preferences for one candidate rather than another can be highly unstable in many sets of nominating circumstances, with rapid changes in the standings of the candidates as the preconvention campaigns unfold. When attitudes change so rapidly, it can be assumed that they are not held with much firmness of conviction by the party voters whose preferences are being consulted. This may be a good thing for the party, in terms of ready acceptance of an authoritative decision when it has finally been made, but it does little to suggest that delegates to a party convention are always under strong compulsion to give the nomination to the leading popular preference within their party.

Even with the widespread availability of the Gallup Poll and similar reports, moreover, there are limitations on the extent to which popular preferences are understood by the officials within each party who might be considered experts. This can be illustrated, for example, by Table 13.9, which records the responses of Democratic county chairmen in the spring of 1952 when asked this question: "If the following were opposing candidates for President, which do you think would win?" Many of these chairmen later attended the convention as delegates, and they were probably about as well informed as the average delegate. No doubt they were somewhat biased in favor of the potential candidates of their own party, but those who responded had a much more favorable opinion of Stevenson's prospects than was justified by the objective situation.

Nearly half of them were of the opinion that he could defeat Eisenhower; considerable numbers believed that Kefauver, Barkley, or Russell could do so, although the respondents in these groups were greatly outnumbered by those who thought otherwise.

Popular preferences become doubtful—

Trial heat data reflect the views of independents and of voters who will cross party lines, but also the prospective party vote within each party. As indicators of sentiment, the trial heat results are far more stable than the preference polls, because, like an actual election, they reflect the large masses of party adherents who will even-

TABLE 13.9. EXPECTATIONS OF DEMOCRATIC COUNTY CHAIRMEN CONCERNING PROBABLE OUTCOMES WITH ALTERNATIVE CANDIDATE CHOICES, PRESIDENTIAL ELECTION OF 1952[a]

Republican Candidate \ Democratic Candidate	Stevenson	Kefauver	Barkley	Russell
Eisenhower	D 48% / 34%	R 33% / 48%	R 23% / 52%	R 20% / 56%
Taft	D 69% / 13%	D 62% / 18%	D 48% / 26%	D 43% / 32%

[a] The numbers in the boxes are the percentages of Democratic county chairmen who, responding in confidence to an inquiry by the American Institute of Public Opinion, estimated that the respective candidates would win if matched against the indicated candidate of the other party. (AIPO release of April 26, 1952.) The numbers do not add to 100 because from 18 to 26 per cent had no opinion on the various pairs.

and uncertainty concerning those preferences becomes legitimate—when several candidates are reported as almost equally strong in trial heat polling. Dewey, Willkie, and Taft were so closely bracketed in the spring of 1940 (as shown by Table 13.3) that the basis for convention choice remained doubtful, even if Willkie was in fact the leading preference of Republican voters when the convention met. In 1948, Dewey, Vandenberg, Stassen, and MacArthur were all reportedly leading Truman by about the same extent (as shown by Table 13.4); in 1956 the spread between Stevenson, Kefauver, and Harriman in trial heat polling (as shown by Table 13.5) was far more narrow than might have been supposed from other information.

tually vote for their party regardless of whom it nominates. Trial heats that reflect a clear difference between alternative candidates for the same nomination thus take on unusual importance, and especially when the candidates identified as running poorly in trial heats also run low on the preference scale in their own party. This is the position that Taft occupied in 1948 and 1952, and to some extent the position that Stevenson occupied in 1952.[31]

For many Republicans and most party neutrals, Eisenhower looked like a sure winner in 1952, whatever the Democrats did; while Taft looked like a probable loser.

[31] See Tables 13.1, 13.4, and 13.6; see also the concluding section of Chapter 15 on the situations of the two candidates in 1952.

The *New York Times,* which favored Eisenhower, published three editorials beginning July 1, 1952, entitled "Mr. Taft Can't Win." In the Democratic convention, which met after the Eisenhower nomination was an accomplished fact, Kefauver's better showing than Stevenson's in the primaries and polls was discounted for three major reasons. Kefauver looked like a certain loser against Eisenhower, since the polls were reporting a well-informed popular choice as between the two. As a new figure, Stevenson's relatively poor showing in the polls was assumed to underestimate his real vote-getting ability, and to be due to the limited national attention he had previously received. Finally, Kefauver was unacceptable to many party leaders, whatever his prospects, because of his bitter public response during the nominating campaign to their apparent disapproval.

Information on the second-choice preferences of the voters, if it were more extensively available, would probably serve both to indicate the extent to which one candidate is readily substitutable for another and to identify the less frequent instances in which voter majorities are solidly behind a leading choice or are definitely opposed to some well-known figure who remains the first choice of a minority. The first type of situation was illustrated in the spring of 1959 when the Gallup Poll published information on the second-choice preferences of the Democratic voters who still preferred Kefauver: 10 per cent for Kefauver, when redistributed, became Stevenson 3 per cent, Kennedy 2, Johnson 2, Symington 0, Humphrey 1, Others 1, and None, 1.[32] There was little in this pattern to suggest cohesion in the Kefauver following or any need for a clearly identified type of candidate to give it satisfaction. On the other hand, although the second-choice data do not exist to prove the point, all of the other information suggests that while there was a considerable popular mandate among Republican voters

[32] *Washington Post and Times-Herald,* May 17, 1959. Second-choice data were published on this occasion for Kefauver supporters on grounds that he had "virtually taken himself out of the race for 1960."

for the Eisenhower nomination in 1952, there was a much stronger negative mandate against the nomination of Senator Taft. Eisenhower was a possible second choice for many Taft supporters; for most Eisenhower supporters, Taft was not a possible second choice.

* * * * *

The net effect of all this seems to be mainly a clarification of the alternatives that face each party convention when it meets and an identification of the situations in which it is necessary to give close regard to voter sentiment, as distinguished from those in which it is not.

When a front-running candidate reaches the point where he is clearly the majority preference of the voters in his party, as in the Dewey case in 1944, majority support among the delegates comes rapidly and the contest is likely to be over before the convention meets. The idea of what constitutes a front-running candidate has changed, and the position of a strong front-runner has become both more legitimate and more frequently desirable. It is no longer possible without qualification to identify a candidate as the front-runner unless he is the leading preference of the voters in his party, as well as the leading choice of the delegates after information on delegate strength becomes available. A candidate who develops a strong lead in delegate strength without leading in voter preference becomes suspect, and has difficulty in maintaining a legitimate claim to the front-runner position.

Bipolarized situations in which the convention faces two strong candidates, and only two, are undoubtedly those that put the convention system under its greatest strain. These situations could always be clearly identified in terms of delegate strength when the voting began, and often long before. Now it is possible to trace the evolution of delegate strength for months before the convention and to compare that evolution, step by step, with the evolution of voter sentiment in preference polls and trial heats. The Taft-Eisenhower struggle may long be the classic case in which it was clearly evident that voter strength had accumulated predominantly behind one candidate and delegate strength behind the other. In the end, the convention was forced to decide whether it would go along with popular sentiment or disregard it. Popular sentiment proved controlling—and if it had not, it now seems entirely possible that the party would have lost the election.

The third type of situation is that in which the preconvention campaigns leave three or more candidates in the running, perhaps with an evident front-runner but with no demonstration of a majority mandate for any. In these cases discretion remains in the convention even more clearly than when it faces two strong candidates; and the extent to which the discretion of the convention either is or should be limited by the available indications of popular choice is a good question. The answer would seem to depend in part on the nature and strength of the plurality mandates obtained by the leading candidates. Probably it also depends in a rather vital way on the extent to which the situation has permitted the voters to examine all the valid alternatives. Underlying the whole problem, there is likely to be an implied negative mandate excluding many of the available compromise candidates and quite possibly some of the leading ones as well.

The plurality mandate registered for Senator Kefauver in 1952, for example, was weak not only because it was merely a plurality and one of very recent formation. It was weak also because many voters were looking for guidance from leaders whose views they wished to hear or because they were simply waiting for events to develop. Underlying this waiting attitude was a strong potential opposition to Kefauver, certain to become overt when the position of the leaders became clear. The situation was unusual, but not so unique that it may not happen again.

From all of this it can be concluded that the nominating process is indeed one where there is need for the services of a representative institution—one that can take the situation as it finds it, weigh up all the possibilities, and arrive at a decision in the name of the whole party. If the institution is indeed truly representative, there is little reason to think the party voters will be disregarded when they can speak with a clear voice. When they cannot, there still remains a need for a decision that will rally the party rather than divide it, if it is to enter the election contest with any hope of success.

14

Characteristics of Delegates and Delegations

THE NOMINATING process as a whole is often attacked in terms that question the motives of the delegates. There is, therefore, a need for information on whether the delegates in general are reputable people who could be expected to make their decisions on reputable grounds.

A second problem involves representation. To what extent are the delegates a representative group? More particularly, do the delegates and delegations properly represent their party constituencies? Do they represent the party electorates or merely the party organizations? And do they reflect accurately the differences between the Democratic and Republican party constituencies of their states?

Third, there is the problem of efficiency. To what extent are the delegates competent to perform the functions for which they are assembled? The nominating function? The platform-drafting function? The campaign-rally function? The governing-body function?

And fourth, the relevance of the above questions may be questioned. Just how important are the delegates in the nominating process? Does it matter whether they are reputable or representative or competent?

Questions of this type suggest a need for many different kinds of information. Some of that information is provided in other chapters, especially in the two on leadership centers (Chapters 4 and 5) and the two on selection systems (Chapters 10 and 11). Specific information on the characteristics of delegates and delegations, to the extent that it is available, can provide direct an-

swers to some of the questions, but most of it serves only as a basis for inferences that can be drawn with varying degrees of assurance.

The data of the present chapter have been taken from several different sources, principally the following: two questionnaire studies of delegates to the 1948 conventions; the 1952 David, Moos, and Goldman study for the American Political Science Association; more limited observation of the 1956 conventions by the writers of the present book; and, for a few specific kinds of facts, original compilations from the records of the conventions and historical sources of biographical information. Long-term trends can be shown for the last type of information, but not the others. For the chapter as a whole, many of the data are somewhat difficult to relate among themselves because of their variety and the limitations on their comparability.

The available information has been collected and presented, nonetheless, because it is difficult to form accurate impressions of the delegates through mere observation in the absence of concrete descriptive details. The conventions are such large affairs that the individual delegates tend to become faceless bodies in the mass. Yet most previous attempts to assess the conventions and their behavior have begun with assumptions about the delegates, assumptions that were not always stated and that were probably often erroneous. On the other hand, certain simple descriptive facts, once established as authentic, might so change current notions that many of the more damag-

CHART 14.1. AGE DISTRIBUTION OF THE DELEGATES,
NATIONAL PARTY CONVENTIONS OF 1948[a]

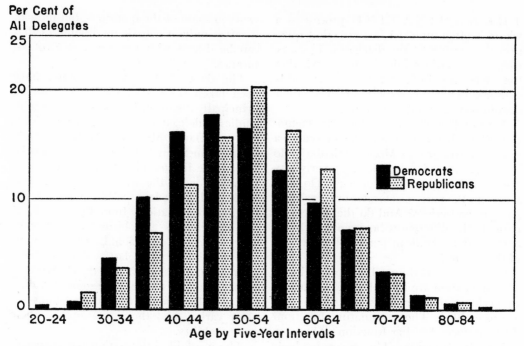

Per Cent of
All Delegates

Age by Five-Year Intervals

Democrats
Republicans

[a] See Appendix G.

ing questions would become irrelevant and would no longer be considered worth inquiry.

The chapter begins with characteristics that have their own interest for reasons that are apparent: age, sex, race, religion, educational status, income level. The problem of travel expense as a factor affecting selection is then taken up in the context of the previous discussion of income levels. The chapter then turns to the subject of occupations and membership and officeholding in economic interest groups. Next, attention is given to the available information bearing on the positions of the delegates in the party structure and their qualifications as indicated by rank and experience, with some comparative analysis of delegations in these respects. The chapter ends with a concluding discussion of the questions with which it opens.[1]

Ages of the Delegates

The age distributions of the delegates to the conventions of 1948, the only year for which such information has become available, are shown in Chart 14.1. The chart is based on two questionnaire studies conducted by mail, one by Charles L. Braucher, the other by Daniel W. Tuttle, Jr.[2]

All age groups from 30 to 75 were substantially represented, with a scattering of delegates below 30 and above 75. The average age of the Democratic delegates was 50, of the Republicans 52. In most age

[1] The rationale of the present chapter, its organization, and the treatment of its content all owe much to the work of the Interuniversity Summer Research Seminar on Presidential Nominating Politics, held at the Brookings Institution in the summer of 1955. Early drafts of material included in Chapters 14-18 were discussed by the seminar.

[2] Further details of the two studies are reported in Appendix G. The Tuttle study was the more elaborate, and is drawn on later in this chapter for a number of items for which it is the only source. The data from the two studies were combined in preparing the chart, although they are reported separately in Appendix G; despite minor variations between the two sets of data, the general patterns were closely similar.

groups below 50, there were proportionately more Democratic delegates than Republican, whereas from 50 to 70, there were proportionately more Republicans than Democrats. The general contours of the diagram suggest that in 1948 the Democrats were somewhat more successful than the Republicans in bringing in new blood.[3]

Women Delegates

A few states with advanced views sent women delegates to the national party conventions even before women's suffrage had been generally achieved. With the coming of the Nineteenth Amendment in 1920, the Democratic national committee was expanded to include as many women as men, one from each state; in 1924 the same step was taken by the Republicans. But no such rule was applied generally in making up the state delegations, despite a considerable increase in the number of women delegates in 1924, which was followed by some reduction in 1928. The historical record of numbers of women delegates and alternates, insofar as known, is given in Table 14.1.

The tabulation below of the per cent of women delegates in 1952, according to regions, shows noteworthy differences in the

| | Per Cent of Women Delegates, 1952 | |
Region	Democratic	Republican
Northeast	7.8%	10.9%
Middle West	12.8	8.6
South	10.3	7.4
West	21.6	16.5
Non-State Areas	17.6	9.5
National Average	12.5	10.5

regional averages in each party. (For the full tabulation of this 1952 data on number and per cent of women delegates by regions and states, see Appendix A, Tables 5 and 6.)

[3] For a discussion of the problem of aging in political organizations, see Maurice Duverger, *Political Parties* (1954), pp. 160-68.

In 1952 half of the members of the Florida Democratic delegation were women, as required by Florida state law for delegations elected in a primary, and in 1956 the provision applied to the delegations of both parties. Of all delegations at the 1952 conventions, there were six Democratic and

conservatism in the social structure of the various states. Party organizations that were loose, disorganized, or easily susceptible to insurgency were more likely to admit women to their delegations than those that were well knit and tightly controlled by male politicians of the older generation.

TABLE 14.1. WOMEN DELEGATES TO NATIONAL PARTY CONVENTIONS[a]

	Democratic		Republican	
Year	Delegates	Alternates	Delegates	Alternates
1892	—	—		2
1896	—	—	—	—
1900	1	—	1	—
1904	—	—	—	4
1908	2	3	2	—
1912	2	1	2	—
1916	11	11	5	9
1920	93	206	27	129
1924	199	310	121	285
1928	152	263	70	261
1932	208	270	87	307
1936	252	333	61	222
1940	208	347	78	231
1944	174	332	100	268
1948	192	320	112	254
1952	203	322	129	260
1956	287	391	208	355

[a] Figures for Republican delegates and alternates were obtained from the Women's Division, Republican National Committee. Figures for Democratic delegates and alternates through 1944, from M. J. Fisher and B. Whitehead, "Women and National Party Organization," *American Political Science Review*, Vol. 38 (Oct. 1944), p. 896, Table 1; for 1948, 1952, and 1956, from the Democratic National Committee.

The figures in the table are for actual delegates and alternates without regard to the extent of their voting rights, and could not be turned into percentages of convention strength without compiling totals of the numbers of persons attending the conventions in each category. In general, however, the voting strength of the conventions was relatively stable during most of the period, increasing from around 1,000 in 1908 to over 1,300 in each party in 1956. So far as actual attendance is concerned, in Democratic conventions some of the delegates were usually on a fractional vote basis, increasing the total number; this was true of most of them in 1956. In Republican conventions split-vote delegates were rarely seated. In both parties the number of authorized alternates was usually the same as the number of delegates, but in the Democratic convention of 1956 it was considerably smaller. See Chapters 8 and 9.

eight Republican in which the proportion of women was zero, despite provisions in the convention rules of each party for a platform committee composed of one man and one woman from each state delegation.

The extent to which women were able to secure places on the various state delegations in 1952 reflected a complex of many factors. One obviously was the degree of

Where the party leadership was modern in its point of view, places were found for women delegates even in tightly controlled slate-making.

On most matters, there was little evidence at either convention of any pronounced difference between the sexes in their voting. Where differences arose, they related mainly to the extent of the recognition that should be accorded women in politics, the one type of issue on which women are most likely to unite. This was shown in the discussion of the proposal to enlarge the Republican national committee by adding state chairmen from the states carried by the party. Women delegates made common cause in opposing this move, because it upset the existing balance between the sexes on the committee; it carried nonetheless.[4]

The proportion of women delegates may well be related to the consideration which the conventions may eventually give to women as candidates for the nominations. At the Democratic national convention of 1924, three women received one or more votes for the presidential nomination. One woman, Mrs. Leroy Springs, was formally proposed and seconded for Vice President, and received 38 votes. At the Republican convention of 1952 it was expected that Senator Margaret Chase Smith would be placed in nomination for the Vice Presidency—the first woman to be honored in that manner in the history of the Republican party—but Delegate Clare Boothe Luce explained that she was withholding the nomination at the request of Senator Smith. At the 1952 Democratic convention Judge Sarah T. Hughes and Mrs. India Edwards were both placed in nomination for the Vice Presidency and received demonstrations, but there was no objection when Delegate James Farley moved the Sparkman nomination by acclamation.[5]

In 1956 no women were placed in nomination by either party. At the Democratic convention, however, Mrs. Franklin D. Roosevelt was conspicuously active on behalf of the candidacy of Adlai E. Stevenson, although she was not herself a delegate.

Negro Delegates

Negro delegates have been conspicuous in southern delegations at Republican na-

tional conventions since the Civil War. In recent decades both parties have had a few Negro delegates from other parts of the country. It is extremely difficult, however, to obtain comprehensive and accurate information on Negro participation.

In 1952, Negro delegates seem to have held about 2.6 per cent of the voting strength in the Republican national convention, and about 1.5 per cent in the Democratic. At the Republican convention, at least thirty-two Negro delegates and fifty alternates were present; at the Democratic, an estimated twenty-four Negro delegates and nineteen alternates were present. Negroes did not appear in any southern Democratic delegation except that of Kentucky, but outside the South each party seems to have selected about the same number of Negro delegates and alternates. The Republican delegations from Georgia, Tennessee, Mississippi, Arkansas, Louisiana, and Oklahoma included eleven Negro delegates and thirteen alternates. In at least thirteen states both parties selected one or more Negroes: Massachusetts, New York, New Jersey, Pennsylvania, West Virginia, Kentucky, Ohio, Michigan, Indiana, Illinois, Missouri, Kansas, and California. Negroes also appeared in the Republican delegations of three other non-southern states, Delaware, Maryland, and Washington, and in the Democratic delegations of three other non-southern states, Wisconsin, Iowa, and Colorado.[6]

Most of the Negroes were district delegates from districts with large Negro popu-

[6] These data have been compiled mainly from the items on Negro representation that are indexed in *Presidential Nominating Politics in 1952*, but have been correlated with information on Negro participation in both national conventions of 1952 reported by Matthew Holden, Jr., for the Cooperative Research Project on Convention Delegates. Holden reported that lists of Negro delegates were being maintained by the staff of the Republican national committee and at Taft headquarters during the Republican convention, but he was unable to find any organized listing of Negro delegates at the Democratic convention. The Democratic delegations from Massachusetts, New York, and Pennsylvania each apparently included several Negroes, but the precise number was not available; in preparing the figures given in the present text estimates were made by the staff of the Brookings Institution.

[4] Paul T. David, Malcolm Moos, and Ralph M. Goldman, *Presidential Nominating Politics in 1952* (1954), Vol. 1, pp. 88-90.
[5] *Ibid.*, Vol. 1, pp. 99-100, 155-56.

lations; very few were delegates at large. The Kansas delegations of both parties, however, each included a Negro delegate at large from the city of Wichita.[7]

The patterns of Negro participation in 1952 suggested that both parties and several of the candidates were showing an increasing interest in the Negro vote. Valores J. Washington of Chicago's first congressional district was active as the director of the "Division of Minorities" of the Republican national committee and was himself a delegate from his home district. John O. Pegg, a Negro alternate delegate from Cincinnati, was at work at Taft headquarters with a substantial and active staff; every Negro Republican delegate was undoubtedly canvassed on behalf of the Taft cause. With some difficulty, it was possible to ascertain that the same function was being performed at Eisenhower headquarters by Prentice Townsend of Topeka, Kansas, a Negro vice chairman of the Kansas state central committee.

Most of the Negro delegates at the Republican convention were undoubtedly for Taft. Those who were for Eisenhower were more actively interested in civil rights legislation than those who supported Taft, but there was no conflict on the issue when the platform was brought before the convention for approval. The motion to approve the platform was seconded by Harold C. Burton, a Harlem delegate who had switched to Taft at the beginning of the convention, but switched back again to Eisenhower on the following day in a delegation meeting presided over by Dewey.[8]

Both of the Negro members of the Eighty-second Congress were present as delegates at the Democratic national convention of 1952. William L. Dawson represented the Chicago first district, while Adam Clayton Powell, Jr., of the New York twenty-second (Harlem) district was a delegate at large. Dawson had an office at convention headquarters as vice chairman of the Democratic national committee, but took the position that it was unnecessary to provide for any caucusing or coordination on the part of Negro delegates.[9] Dawson himself served on the platform committee, where he was one of the moderates favoring compromise in the drafting of a civil rights plank. Powell was in charge of the Negro section of the Harriman headquarters, the only well-staffed unit of its kind at the Democratic convention.

Most of the Negro delegates at the Democratic convention were well integrated into their respective delegations and the liberal and labor organizations with which they were associated. A racial bloc as such did not emerge. Apparently no Negro caucus was ever held, and the nearest thing to it was a purely social gathering on Sunday, July 20, to which the leading southern candidate, Senator Richard Russell, sent a representative bearing a ham and a turkey.[10]

Inner strains within the parties were revealed by oddities of convention behavior. At the Republican convention, the blessings of Heaven were invoked by no less than two Negro ministers and seconding speeches by Negro delegates were arranged for both the Taft and Eisenhower nominations. At the Democratic convention, no Negro minister officiated and no seconding speeches were made by Negroes. Yet the effort to draft a civil rights plank that would retain the Negro vote or at least avoid affronting it was a major objective at the Democratic convention, one that the party managers pursued with some success under great difficulties.

Negro voters were underrepresented at the party conventions of both parties in 1952, insofar as the arithmetic of propor-

---

[7] A policy decision to include a Negro delegate was taken at a Kansas state Republican meeting on Kansas Day, January 30, 1952. Those responsible for slate-making in the Democratic party presumably decided that they could do no less in a state with so much early history involving race relations. See David, Moos, and Goldman, *op. cit.*, Vol. 4, pp. 310-11, 314, 317, 323, 326.

[8] *Ibid.*, Vol. 2, p. 164; RNC, *Proceedings*, 1952, p. 324.

[9] Holden ms. reports, previously cited.

[10] *Ibid.*

tionate representation is relevant. In most northern industrial states, however, they were probably closer to full representation at the conventions than they were in the state legislatures or in Congress. But even token representation can have an importance all its own. Little research would be needed to support the conclusion that the addition of even one Negro to a previously all-white delegation may profoundly change its behavior on civil rights.

Religious and Ethnic Group Representation

The Tuttle study of the 1948 delegates was successful in obtaining a considerable amount of information about the religious affiliations of the delegates.[11] Protestants made up the largest percentage for both conventions. The Democratic convention had the greater number of Catholics and Jews; this accorded with their most usual party affiliations in 1948 and earlier years. It can be inferred from the figures that Irish,

[11] See Appendix G.

Italian, Polish, and other ethnic groups predominantly of the Catholic faith were represented mainly at the Democratic convention. The major divisions, in percentages of total delegates, were as follows:

Religious Affiliation	Democratic Delegates	Republican Delegates
Catholic	27.5%	6.1%
Jewish	2.1	0.7
Protestant	63.8	87.1
Other	2.0	2.6
No Formal Affiliation	4.6	3.5
	100.0	100.0

Among the Protestant delegates there was a difference between the parties in proportionate denominational affiliations, as indicated in Table 14.2.[12] Among the larger denominations, as the third column of Table 14.2 indicates, those that are usually

[12] Among the denominations ordinarily referred to as Protestant, there are a number in which some of the members occasionally object to the usage. In the context of the present discussion, it is believed that using the designation "Protestant" for such denominations will not be seriously misleading.

TABLE 14.2. DENOMINATIONAL AFFILIATIONS OF PROTESTANT DELEGATES, 1948[a]

Denomination	Democratic Delegates, Per Cent	Republican Delegates, Per Cent	Ratio, (R) to (D)
Christian Science	0.4%	1.7%	4.3
Congregational	3.2	8.7	2.7
Protestant[b]	3.7	8.5	2.1
Presbyterian	9.2	17.0	1.8
Christian	2.5	4.4	1.8
Episcopal	11.2	17.2	1.5
Unitarian	0.9	1.3	1.4
Methodist	18.1	16.8	0.9
Lutheran	3.4	3.0	0.9
Baptist	9.1	7.0	0.8
Mormon	2.1	1.5	0.7
Total Protestant	63.8	87.1	1.4

[a] See Appendix G.
[b] Not elsewhere classified.

associated with relatively higher social and economic status had a higher proportion of delegates at the Republican convention. This was in accord with known differences in the social and economic compositions of the party followings at the time.

Most religious and ethnic groups are represented to some degree in both party conventions, but there is much variation in practice from state to state, as the 1952 study of delegate selection discovered. In competitive two-party states where these minorities are conspicuous in all forms of political activity, such as Massachusetts, the delegations of both parties are likely to show the effects of the tradition of the balanced ticket. In states where one party is dominant, the delegations of the dominant party rarely include much representation of minority groups. In states with presidential primaries, some types of primary foster balanced tickets while others militate against them. Ticket balancing is difficult where unpledged district delegates run separately in their own districts. Where delegation slates are made up on a state-wide basis, there is more incentive and more opportunity to provide representation for all politically important groups.

Educational Status

The educational status of the delegates of 1948 is indicated by the tabulation in the next column, in percentages based on an average of results obtained in the Braucher and Tuttle studies.[13]

These figures suggest that delegates are an exceptionally well-educated group, even if some allowance is made for possible upward bias in the data because of the greater tendency of educated persons to respond to questionnaires. Over half of the delegates of 1948 were college graduates and over one third had received one or more years of postgraduate education—in most cases probably in law schools, in view of the high proportion who were lawyers. The differences be-

[13] See Appendix G.

Education Reported	Democratic Delegates	Republican Delegates
College and Postgraduate Training	34.3%	34.0%
Completed College Only	21.9	24.5
Attended College Without Finishing	21.8	23.1
	78.0	81.6
Completed High School Only	11.4	11.3
Attended High School Without Finishing	5.3	3.9
	16.7	15.2
Elementary Schooling Only	5.3	3.2
	100.0	100.0

tween the parties were remarkably small, considering the generally higher social and economic status of the Republican party.[14]

The age distribution of the delegates of 1948 should be borne in mind in appraising their educational attainments. The years following World War I were a time of great change in the educational opportunities available to young people in the United States. Delegates who were 55 years old or older in 1948 were over 23 in 1916, and most of them by that time had finished their formal education. These made up about 41 per cent of the Republican delegates and 35 per cent of the Democratic. The delegates who were under 50 years of age in 1948 would have been much more influenced by the great expansion in high school and college education that occurred in the 1920's.

By 1948 the conventions were beginning to reflect rather fully this democratization of higher education in the United States.

[14] The educational status of the delegates of 1948 was apparently a little higher than that of the state governors in office between 1930 and 1940, 23 per cent of whom had not gone farther than high school, and not much below that of United States Representatives in office in 1941-1943, 12 per cent of whom had not gone beyond high school. See Donald R. Matthews, *The Social Background of Political Decision-Makers* (1954), pp. 29, 63.

This was doubtless even more true in 1952 and 1956. A significant change has occurred since as recently as the conventions of 1940 and 1944.

Income Levels

Information concerning the income levels of the delegates to the 1948 conventions is available from the Tuttle study.[15] The reported percentage distributions by income levels are shown in the tabulation below.

Reported Annual Income	Democratic Delegates	Republican Delegates
$50,000 or more	4.0%	9.4%
25,000–49,999	8.1	11.3
10,000–24,999	37.7	31.3
5,000– 9,999	29.0	31.7
3,500– 4,999	11.9	10.0
Under 3,500	9.3	6.3
	100.0	100.0

The 1948 conventions of both parties were drawn much more from the upper-income levels of the population than from the lower. In both conventions there was a heavy concentration around the $10,000 level. The Democratic median income was $10,150; the Republican, $10,900.[16] It is

impressive to discover that nearly 10 per cent of the Republican delegates who responded had incomes of $50,000 a year or more, and it is surprising to learn that the proportion of such delegates among the Democrats was as high as 4 per cent. The differences between the two parties in their conventions, moreover, while in accord with the greater average incomes of Republican voters, were not sufficiently great to give expression in any clear fashion to the average differences in income levels between the parties in the electorate. Survey data for 1948 indicated that voters in the income groups under $3,000 were voting Democratic two to one, while those above $5,000 voted Republican two to one. The break-even point between the parties was apparently around $4,000.[17]

The income data for the delegates to the 1948 conventions can also be compared by regions.

	Median Income of Delegates	
Region	Democratic	Republican
Northeast	$12,700	$17,750
Middle West	8,350	11,350
South	12,100	8,750
West	10,600	9,750
Forty-eight States	10,150	10,900

In one-party states and areas, it can be supposed that prosperous individuals tend to congregate in the dominant party; and this may account for the higher Democratic

---

[15] See Appendix G.

[16] In appraising these figures, the levels of prices and incomes prevailing in 1948 should be recalled. Ten years later an income level around $15,000 a year would have been required to maintain the social and economic status attached in general to incomes between $10,000 and $11,000 in 1948. Between 1946 and 1956, for example, the lower-income limit of the upper 5 per cent of all consumer units went up from $9,180 to $13,490, an increase of 47 per cent. Average family incomes for all families rose from $4,130 in 1947 to $6,130 in 1957, again a rise of nearly 50 per cent in a ten-year period during which there was little change in the shape of the income curve. In 1947, 2 million families and unattached individuals were receiving incomes of $10,000 or more; in 1957, 2.2 million were receiving incomes of $15,000 or more. See U. S. Department of Commerce, *Income Distribution in the United States* (1953), p. 81; Selma F. Goldsmith, "Size Distribution of Family Income," *Survey*

of Current Business, Vol. 38 (April 1958), pp. 10-19, Tables 1, 2, and 10.

The occupational data presented later in the chapter indicate that relatively few convention delegates are dependent upon fixed-salary arrangements beyond their own control. Most of them are members of the independent professional and entrepreneurial classes that are least subject to the retarding effects of fixed-salary arrangements in a time of inflation and of growth in total national production. Hence it can be expected that the median income of delegates to the conventions of 1960 will be above $15,000.

[17] Angus Campbell, Gerald Gurin, and Warren E. Miller, *The Voter Decides* (1954), pp. 72-73.

income figure for the South. The income data for 1948 delegates support this hypothesis when regrouped in terms of the apparent party alignments of the respective states in presidential politics, as indicated by the tabulation below.[18]

	Median Income of Delegates	
State Alignment	Democratic	Republican
Democratic	$10,106	$ 9,835
Competitive	10,040	11,365
Republican	8,000	11,950

Precise information has not become available about the income levels of the delegates of 1952 and 1956, but most of the clues for 1952 suggest that there may have been some widening in the difference of average income between Republican and Democratic delegations outside the South. In New Jersey, for example, the impression was gained that most of the Democratic delegates were in the $5,000 to $10,000 income brackets, while at least three fourths of the Republican delegates were in the over-$10,000 income group.[19] In the southern states it is probable that average incomes continued to be higher in the Democratic delegations than in the Republican, but persons of ample means were found on most of the southern delegations of both parties. The Kentucky Republican delegation, for example, was reputed to include at least four millionaires, while the Arkansas Democratic delegation was referred to as including "only two."[20] Delegations of both parties from Texas, Oklahoma, and

Louisiana were studded with names of wealthy individuals.

Expense as a Factor in Delegate Selection

The privilege of taking part in a national convention is an expensive one for most delegates. The normal supposition is that the delegate will pay any personal expenses that may be involved in his selection, will pay his transportation and living expenses, and will contribute if necessary to a fund for maintaining a delegation headquarters at the convention. In 1952 many delegates were accompanied by their wives or other members of their family, further increasing the expense involved.

In most parts of the country in 1952 it no longer seemed to be the custom to require specific large contributions to party treasuries as a condition for being a delegate.[21] When $100-a-plate fund-raising dinners were held in a state during the preconvention campaigns, however, it seemed to be generally assumed that delegates would attend. Similar contributions may have been made by most delegates as a matter of the party loyalty that is considered routine for prominent party members. Delegates elected in primaries were occasionally required

---

[18] The classification of states by party alignment is the same as that used elsewhere in this book; in general, states that voted for the same party no more than five times in the presidential elections of each period (1896-1924 and 1928-1956) are classified as competitive; those voting one way six times or more are classified as aligned with the party for which they voted predominantly. See Chapter 16, Table 16.6, and Appendix A, Table 4.

[19] David, Moos, and Goldman, op. cit., Vol. 2, pp. 199, 207.

[20] Ibid., Vol. 3, pp. 151, 257.

[21] In New Jersey Republican circles, for example, "a former unwritten rule" that delegates at large make a political contribution of $1,000 was no longer in effect. (Ibid., Vol. 2, p. 199.) But in Indiana would-be Republican delegates in 1952 were required to pay a $500 assessment in advance of their selection; complaints were made that this was a change in the rules, and that in former years it had not been necessary to pay the assessment in advance. (Ibid., Vol. 4, pp. 82-83.) This was the largest mandatory assessment of which evidence was found in surveying delegation selection in 1952. Democratic party rules in Indiana did not provide for as large an assessment as the Republican, but delegates were assessed $200 for the state central committee and alternates $100. (Ibid., Vol. 4, p. 90.) Another relatively high assessment was found in Iowa, where Democratic delegates were assessed $150 and alternates $75 for "headquarters expense" at Chicago. It was thought that a desire to secure funds for the party treasury was a factor in that state in sending an oversize Democratic delegation. (Ibid., Vol. 4, p. 209.)

o pay filing fees.[22] They also usually met heir own campaign expenses, if any; and hose selected by party processes usually had comparable expenses for attendance at state party conventions and other meetings.

The average personal expense involved in serving as a delegate in 1952 was probably between $200 and $500 for most of the delegates. Transportation expense to Chicago was of course heavy from the western states and greatest of all from Alaska, Hawaii, and Puerto Rico. Living expenses for the week at the convention city probably ranged between $50 and $100 for most delegates unaccompanied by members of their families.[23]

Various arrangements were made in some states to assist delegates in meeting their travel expenses. North Dakota provided by law for reimbursing such expenses from public funds up to a flat rate of $200, with the result that personal ability to pay was not as important in delegate selection there as elsewhere.[24] In Wisconsin the Republican party headquarters for the state continued a custom of offering each delegate $100 to help defray his expenses.[25] In the California Kefauver delegation the chairman and his alternate were "provided funds by the treasurer of the northern California Kefauver campaign committee," and the vice chairman was a paid employee of the

delegation.[26] A few other state or local party organizations were reported as providing financial assistance.[27] It was reported from New Mexico that the convention expenses of the Democratic state chairman have usually been paid in the past from party funds, but in 1952 the chairman refused this assistance.[28]

Some of the labor union officials who served on delegations were probably able to obtain assistance from their unions or from union members; indications to this effect were reported for the New Jersey, Michigan, and California Democratic delegations.[29] The practice of taking up a collection to help finance the travel of a representative to a national meeting is a long-standing custom in some local unions; something of this sort seems to have occurred in Michigan.[30] Some of the government officials, businessmen, and labor leaders who served on delegations may have had other business to transact in Chicago, in which case presumably at least a part of their travel expense could have been charged to public, corporate, or union funds without infringing the regulations of the Internal Revenue Bureau or any statute. A few delegates were newspaper proprietors or editors

---

[22] In West Virginia filing fees were $20 for delegate at large, $10 for district delegates and alternate delegates at large, and $5 for alternate district delegate. (*Ibid.*, Vol. 2, p. 295.) In Alabama, where the amounts went into the party treasury, the filing fees ranged from $50 to $5. (*Ibid.*, Vol. 3, p. 198.)

[23] These were contemporary estimates. With the progress of inflation in hotel and restaurant charges, the lower items will doubtless seem outdated to any experienced traveler. The expense estimate for serving as a delegate from Hawaii in 1952 was placed at a minimum of $700, seemingly a low estimate. (*Ibid.*, Vol. 5, pp. 274, 280.) Estimates of around $500 came from several western states. (*Ibid.*, Vol. 5, pp. 16, 21, 49, 241.) For Democrats from New York the figure was placed at "$300 to $500." (*Ibid.*, Vol. 2, p. 163.) Would-be Democratic delegates in Idaho were required to post a $1,500 performance bond before being considered. (*Ibid.*, Vol. 5, p. 37.)

[24] *Ibid.*, Vol. 4, pp. 245, 247.

[25] *Ibid.*, Vol. 4, p. 140. Most of the delegates accepted the money in 1952, but one or two Warren delegates did not.

[26] *Ibid.*, Vol. 5, p. 241.

[27] *Ibid.*, Vol. 2, pp. 110, 171-72, 199; Vol. 3, p. 110.

[28] *Ibid.*, Vol. 5, p. 134.

[29] *Ibid.*, Vol. 2, p. 208; Vol. 4, p. 61; Vol. 5, p. 241.

[30] The extent to which a labor union, local or national, can legally use its regular funds to finance the travel expenses of a delegate to a national political convention is a subject on which legal authorities can sharply disagree. According to a publication by the Republican National Committee, "It is unlawful for any . . . corporation, or any labor organization, to make a contribution or expenditure in connection with any election to any convention or caucus held to select candidates for such office." (Quoted in Paul P. Van Riper, *Handbook of Practical Politics*, 1952, p. 81.) But when labor unions have deliberately violated the statutes in question in an effort to secure court rulings on the constitutionality of the provisions and the extent of their effectiveness, the courts have usually refused to take punitive action. See Joseph Tanenhaus, "Organized Labor's Political Spending: The Law and Its Consequences," *Journal of Politics*, Vol. 16 (Aug. 1954), pp. 441-71, notably at pp. 459-61. See also "Labor Political Activity Challenged," *Congressional Quarterly Weekly Report*, June 27, 1958, pp. 824-825.

and filed dispatches from the conventions; presumably their expenses were paid.

Whether delegate expenses could properly be paid out of candidate campaign funds was a sensitive issue throughout the preconvention campaigns of 1952.[31] The greatest furor arose about the end of May when it was announced that Republican delegates from all parts of the country were being invited to visit General Eisenhower at New York, Abilene, or Denver before the convention, presumably with their expenses paid. David S. Ingalls of the Taft campaign organization was quoted as saying that the plan "comes pretty close to . . . bribery and is only one example of the money poured by Wall Street into the Eisenhower campaign." Wesley Roberts of the Eisenhower campaign organization called the Ingalls statement a "false and vicious charge," and went to to say:

The Eisenhower national headquarters is not paying any delegates' expenses. Many delegates have expressed a desire to meet with Gen. Eisenhower and they have been invited to meet with him. In accordance with usual custom, their expenses will be paid either by themselves or by local committees, clubs or individuals.[32]

Another allegation, given wide publicity in the syndicated column of Drew Pearson, was that several members of the California Kefauver delegation had been offered free tickets to Chicago if they would switch their votes to Senator Robert S. Kerr after the first ballot. The charges were made with varying degrees of circumstantiality by Pearson and by Kefauver managers in California and Chicago, and were instantly denied by Senator Kerr.[33] A day or two later Kerr issued a similar denial of having paid the travel expenses of a Wyoming delegate.[34] The money problem was undoubtedly acute for several of the Kefauver delegates from California. The slate had been put together with some difficulty, for under California law it was presumed to be necessary to have a complete slate of seventy-six would-be delegates in order to get on the ballot at all. Eleven or twelve members of the delegation, after being elected, failed to make the trip to Chicago and were replaced by alternates.[35]

Project reporters for the American Political Science Association found it difficult to obtain information on the extent to which delegates received financial assistance. One, who resides in a Mountain state, commented as follows:

This is an important point. I am convinced it is an area where delegates can be picked up—not in [state name] alone. Some delegates would refuse any help on their expenses—others do not find the obligation galling. But I could not say who receives and who doesn't. When I check politicians on the point they give a knowing look and proceed to the next question. If I were a candidate or his manager and had the money and few scruples, I should certainly investigate this area very thoroughly before accepting the thesis that all delegates want to pay their own way and remain independent.

Nevertheless, in many instances project reporters did obtain positive statements from reliable sources that all members of a specific delegation were paying their own expenses. They frequently commented on the number of delegates who appeared well able to bear the burden without undue hardship. Even a cynic may conclude that, under the suspicious scrutiny with which delegates and candidates were confronting

---

[31] In 1956 there was little occasion for the issue to arise on the Republican side. On the Democratic, the Harriman campaign was suspected of extending financial assistance to some of the delegates. Rumors to this effect were denied at the convention. (*Newsweek,* Aug. 26, 1956, p. 11.)

[32] The quotations are from an Associated Press story in the *Washington Post,* May 31, 1952, a pro-Eisenhower newspaper.

Ingalls had also asked whether former Governor George T. Mickelson of South Dakota had paid his own way to Paris, France, to see General Eisenhower. Mickelson was reported as saying, when asked, that the bill had been paid by the National Eisenhower Committee, but that he had also spent $300 of his own money. Mickelson headed the defeated slate of Eisenhower delegates in South Dakota.

[33] Signed story by James A. Hagerty, *New York Times,* July 16, 1952; Drew Pearson column, *Washington Post,* July 16, 1952; United Press story from Los Angeles, *Washington Post,* July 17, 1952.

[34] *Washington Post,* July 19, 1952.

[35] David, Moos, and Goldman, *op. cit.,* Vol. 5, pp. 237, 238, 241.

each other in 1952, the delegates who compromised themselves by accepting assistance cannot have been very numerous.

A more important point is the obvious influence of the cost in favoring the selection of well-to-do delegates. Only persons with substantial means could serve as delegates from Hawaii or Puerto Rico; this was openly recognized in the selection process by both parties in those areas.[36] Elsewhere it was frequently referred to as limiting selection. It seemed to be important for both political parties in most of the western states. It was a problem in making up Democratic delegations even in states as close to the convention city as Michigan and Wisconsin, in view of the unusually strong desire in those states to include working-class representatives on the delegations.[37]

Occupations and Connections with Interest Groups

The occupations of the delegates are of interest both for what they reveal directly and for what they suggest concerning relations with economic-interest groups of political importance.

Occupations of the Delegates

The occupations of the delegates of 1948, according to the Tuttle study (see Appendix G), were reported as shown in Table 14.3. The most noteworthy features revealed by the table are the concentrations of lawyers and businessmen, the large number in other middle-class occupations, and the generally close similarity of the occupational distributions in the two parties. The Republicans had more bankers and manufacturers, the Democrats more contractors and merchants, as might have been expected. But the main categories suggesting important interparty differences were those for public officials and labor union representatives. Both differences are confirmed by data from other sources and for other years.

Democrats holding high public office in federal, state, and local government seem to appear as convention delegates much more frequently than their Republican counterparts, even when allowance is made for being in office or out of office.[38] Labor union officials have served only rarely as delegates to Republican conventions in recent years, but have made up a substantial percentage of the Democratic delegates.

The miscellany of occupations found among the delegates is a striking feature of any report on the subject, but also is confusing in terms of the representation of economic-interest groups. The representation problem for agriculture, business and industry, and organized labor is discussed in later subsections; here it may be noted, however, that the occupational connections of the delegates need also to be interpreted against the background of their party activities and offices.

Four fifths of the respondents to the Tuttle study of the 1948 delegates indicated that

[36] *Ibid.,* Vol. 2, pp. 346, 351; Vol. 5, p. 274.

[37] The selection of Los Angeles as the Democratic convention city for 1960 immediately created problems for party leaders who wished to guard against scandal in the financing of delegate travel expense, as well as for the would-be delegates facing the prospect of an expensive trip. Solutions were sought through some form of party policing of the situation, with apparently no consideration for the possibility that the problem could be brought under federal legislative control. See William S. White, "Democratic Convention Warning: Party to Guard Against Tainted Money Aiding Delegates on Long Trip." (Washington, D.C.) *Evening Star,* March 4, 1959.

Appropriate amendments of the Federal Corrupt Practices Act and some federal government contribution to the travel expenses of the delegates were suggested by the present writers in concluding a previous study. (David, Moos, and Goldman, *op. cit.,* Vol. 1, p. 245.)

[38] Specific tabulations based on convention records appear later in this chapter for governors, senators, and representatives in Congress, with some additional information for other categories of officials. For governors, see also Chapter 5, Table 5.2. An independent tabulation made by *U. S. News & World Report* of data from the 1952 study for the American Political Science Association found 123 federal officials at the Democratic convention, 46 at the Republican; 215 state officials at the Democratic convention, 130 at the Republican; and 273 local government officials at the Democratic convention, 111 at the Republican. (*U. S. News & World Report,* Feb. 3, 1956, p. 31.)

they regularly attended state and county party organization meetings. At least three fifths either were or had been county organization officers; nearly one half were or had been state party officers. Most delegates, in other words, are active party workers

devotes much of his time and energy to politics as an engrossing side line, but looks to some other occupation for his principal sources of income, and frequently contributes his own money while doing party work. Individuals of this type in the upper levels

TABLE 14.3. OCCUPATIONAL DISTRIBUTION OF 1948 NATIONAL CONVENTION DELEGATES[a]

(in per cent)

Occupations	Democratic Delegates	Republican Delegates
Public Officials	5.3%	2.8%
Lawyers and Judges	35.4	36.0
Publishers and Editors	3.8	3.6
	44.5	42.4
Other Professional Occupations		
Physicians	2.3	1.7
Engineers	1.2	0.6
Educators	3.1	2.1
Others Not Classified	5.0	7.9
	11.6	12.3
Business Occupations		
Bankers	1.9	2.8
Contractors	1.6	0.2
Manufacturers-Owners	6.6	10.2
Merchants and Dealers	6.2	3.8
Real Estate and Insurance	7.1	8.8
	23.4	25.8
Farmers and Ranchers	6.6	7.5
Labor Union Representatives	2.1	0.2
Homemakers	5.3	4.1
Retired Persons	0.5	1.1
All Others	6.0	6.6
	100.0	100.0

[a] See Appendix G.

who frequently hold party office at about the rank of county chairman or state committee member. Few of these party offices pay salaries. The key to the occupations from which the delegates come is that in the main they are occupations that do not prevent party activity and officeholding.

In 1952, as in 1948, the typical delegate appeared to be the kind of individual who

of state and local politics, even when considered party professionals, are drawn predominantly from among the proprietary, self-employed, and non-employed classes in the population. Occupations in which an interest in politics may be occupationally helpful are liberally represented; but it would be even more true to say that other occupations in which an active interest in partisan politics is frowned upon are underrepresented.[39]

Lawyers have their own special affinity for politics, and there should be no surprise in the fact that probably one third or more of the delegates of recent years were lawyers.[40] But lawyers, doctors, dentists, morticians, real estate agents, insurance agents, automobile dealers, merchants generally, owner-managers of small manufacturing enterprises, and the wives of all such persons have special opportunities for political participation—opportunities that are not as readily open to those who are employed for wages or salaries in the middle ranks of business, industry, education, and the public service.[41] The men and women who arrive at the conventions as delegates undoubtedly act to some extent as representatives of their own occupational interests, but those who are active party workers are also used to thinking in terms of constituencies that include many specialized groups as well as the entire mass of party voters.

Representation of Agriculture

In 1948, according to the Tuttle study, about one delegate in six claimed membership in the "Farm Bureau" although only about one delegate in fifteen was a farmer or rancher—apparently a sign of the joining proclivities of political activists in regions where agriculture was important.[42]

The 1952 study of delegate selection found a scattering of farmer delegates that may have aggregated 4 or 5 per cent of the convention membership of that year. Approximately twenty-six of the Democratic delegations and twenty-three of the Republican included one or more delegates who called themselves farmers. Relatively few who were reported as "farmers" were dependent on agriculture as their primary source of livelihood; often they derived much or most of their income from other sources.

The reports of 1952 included only a few references to farmer delegates who had filled posts of leadership in the national farm organizations.[43] No evidence was

[39] For party officeholders, the question of when politics ceases to be an avocation and becomes a vocation is not easily answered. In any situation where competition between the parties is keen, a party chairmanship is likely to become a strenuous full-time activity during any campaign period, while also involving considerable amounts of work the year around. Incumbents of such posts come to be considered party professionals, even when they draw no direct pay. The sources of indirect remuneration are highly variable from one situation to another. The most common types of benefit probably consist of access to information that may be useful, a generalized improvement in career prospects and money-making opportunities, and various immediate rewards in the form of political power and prestige.

The extent to which the tangibles and intangibles provide an economic balance for the time and energy of party workers is a subject on which much more work would be needed to support generalizations. What is most clear is that the tangible outlays of active party service can be identified much more easily than any system of financially comparable tangible rewards. Gossip in knowledgeable quarters frequently holds, for example, that an active national committee member will have to spend at least $5,000 a year of his or her own money. State chairmen, and county chairmen in urban counties, are more likely to be provided with paid staff and other facilities, but most of the 3,000 county chairmen in each party probably provide their own facilities. An increasing number of state and county party chairmen have been placed on a salaried basis in recent years—the salaries being paid from funds raised for party activities—but there is no indication that this has happened for the other members of state and national party committees.

[40] One study of state legislatures in thirteen regionally distributed states found that 28 per cent of the members were lawyers. In a recent Congress, the percentages were 57 per cent in the Senate and 56 per cent in the House of Representatives. Among the high-prestige occupations, the law seems to provide the greatest opportunities for a political career and the lowest occupational risk in entering it. See Donald R. Matthews, *op. cit.*, pp. 30-32; Joseph A. Schlesinger, "Lawyers and American Politics: A Clarified View," *Midwest Journal of Political Science*, Vol. 1 (May 1957), pp. 26-39.

[41] The general problem is discussed by Andrew Hacker in *Politics and the Corporation* ("Occasional Paper" published in 1958 by The Fund for the Republic).

[42] "Farm Bureau" was the only agricultural item in a check list of diverse types of organization as carried in the questionnaire. Those claiming membership in the "Farm Bureau" included many officeholders, party officials, lawyers, homemakers, retired persons, and persons reporting dual occupations.

[43] The Iowa Republican delegation included four well-to-do farmers, one of whom, Harold McKinley, was chairman of the Republican Farm Council. The South Dakota Republican delegation included two persons who were said to be prominent in the Farmers Union. The New Hampshire Republican

found of any concerted attempt by any leading farm organization to secure the election of its state and local leaders as delegates to either national convention in 1952.

There seem to be two reasons for this passive attitude toward the delegate selection process. In the first place, the farm organizations were interested more in programs than in candidates, and therefore tended to rely on the same lobbying techniques to which they were accustomed in dealing with legislatures, state and federal. The major farm organizations in 1952 showed little interest in the nominations, but they all were actively presenting views to the platform committees of both national conventions. In the second place, nonpartisanship has been the traditional policy of the farm organizations; and they apparently have not developed any special technique for dealing with nominating problems.[44]

Representation of Business and Industry

The Tuttle study found that in 1948 the business occupations supplied the largest occupational group other than lawyers, with little difference between the parties. It also found that 47 per cent of the Democratic delegates and 57 per cent of the Republican were members of chambers of commerce—figures showing some party difference but even more similarity.

The Republican party has been suspected so often of closer connections than the Democratic with the upper levels of the business community that it has seemed worth while

to search further for relevant quantitative evidence. The delegate lists of both party conventions of 1952 were therefore checked against the contemporary volumes of *Who's Who in Commerce and Industry* (about 32,500 listings) and *Poor's Register of Directors and Executives* (about 80,000 listings). Over 250 delegates were found who appeared in one of these volumes or the other, usually in both. Those delegates were distributed as follows:

| | 1952 Delegates in Major Business Directories | | | |
| | Democratic | | Republican | |
Region	Number	Per Cent	Number	Per Cent
Northeast	51	12%	60	16%
Middle West	22	5	46	12
South	30	7	11	5
West	14	5	20	9
Non-State Areas	4	12	2	10
Total	121	7	139	12

The pattern shown by the tabulation for 1952 is similar to that revealed in the regional tabulations of 1948 delegate income levels, except for the western region. For the Northeast and Middle West the proportion of outstanding businessmen was markedly higher among the Republican delegations than the Democratic delegations. In the South the relationship was reversed, as might be expected in an area where the Democratic party is dominant. In the West in 1952 the difference between the parties paralleled that in the Northeast and Middle West, unlike the income data for 1948.[45]

Important business interests have been involved in the nominating processes of both political parties for a long time. The delegate data are in accord with the com-

---

delegation included one delegate who was a "recognized leader in farm groups." The New Mexico Democratic delegation included five farm owners, of whom one was an official in a New Mexico agricultural organization. The Georgia Democratic delegation included seven farmers, of whom four were members of agricultural organizations. (David, Moos, and Goldman, *op. cit.*, Vol. 2, p. 38; Vol. 3, p. 110; Vol. 4, pp. 205, 268; and Vol. 5, p. 133.)

[44] See Chapters 4 and 5. See also Wesley McCune, "Farmers in Politics," *Annals of the American Academy of Political and Social Science*, Vol. 319 (Sept. 1958), pp. 41-51.

[45] Tabulations of the kind just displayed could be made for 1956 and for years prior to 1952, and might throw some light on long-term trends in party realignment. In view of the cost and labor factors involved, this has not so far been done.

mon belief that the involvement has been greater in the Republican party in recent years, but the degree of influence within the Democratic party seems still to be considerable.[46]

Representation of Organized Labor

The Tuttle study of the 1948 delegates carried a special question on labor union membership.[47] The returns obtained are tabulated below, in percentages.

Labor Union Membership	Democratic Delegates	Republican Delegates
Yes	9.7%	2.7%
No	90.3	97.3
CIO Affiliate	2.8	0.6
AFL Affiliate	5.3	1.5

As noted previously, 2.1 per cent of the Democratic delegates in 1948 reported their occupation as labor union representative, presumably occupied full time as such, whereas only 0.2 per cent of the Republican delegates so reported. (Table 14.3) In 1952 the Democratic convention again showed substantial direct representation of organized labor, for on the basis of incomplete data it appears that more than 100 of the 1,642 delegates, or 6.3 per cent, were elected union officials or professional union representatives. There may have been as many among the alternate delegates, but no systematic effort was made to collect information about the alternates in the 1952 survey.

It is possible to classify the Democratic delegations of 1952 in four categories on the kind and amount of labor representation. (For the full tabulation of the classifications and sources of the information, see Appendix A, Table 7.)

(1) The delegations from sixteen states and Puerto Rico apparently contained no labor union members or representatives.

(2) Those from six states and Hawaii each included at least one delegate who was known or presumed to be a union member. Apparently these delegates were serving as individuals and their labor connection may have had little or nothing to do with their selection.

(3) The delegations from fifteen states included labor representation through the special allotment of one to three seats for the purpose.[48]

(4) Delegations from eleven states, the District of Columbia, and Alaska had notably substantial labor representation, in plain recognition of labor's importance in the politics of the state; outstanding were Michigan, Wisconsin, and Minnesota. Some of the labor officials who served as delegates, an unknown proportion, were presumably local union elective officers who continued to work at their primary occupations while also engaging in political and union activities. In states of this fourth category, and to some degree in the third as well, organized labor was apparently felt to be an integral part of the Democratic party for delegation

[46] See Chapters 4 and 5. For a recent discussion of the role of businessmen in politics, see Robert F. Lenhart and Karl Schriftgiesser, "Management in Politics," *Annals of the American Academy of Political and Social Science*, Vol. 319 (Sept. 1958), pp. 32-40.
The thesis that businessmen who wish to influence legislation must become active in nominating and electing politics, abandoning any policy of party neutrality, is argued effectively by Horace E. Sheldon in "Businessmen Must Get Into Politics," *Harvard Business Review*, Vol. 37 (March-April 1959), pp. 37-47. For a contrary view, see Charles P. Taft, "Should Business Go in for Politics?" *New York Times Magazine*, Aug. 30, 1959, pp. 10ff.
[47] See Appendix G.

[48] In Maine, for example, the Congress of Industrial Organizations was given one delegate seat, as it had been in 1944 and 1948; it was reported from Maine that "the unions may possibly spend more money helping Democratic candidates in Maine than the party raises itself." The Connecticut Democratic delegation included one delegate each for the American Federation of Labor and the Congress of Industrial Organizations, as well as labor people among the alternate delegates. The Kentucky Democrats provided a third delegate seat for the United Mine Workers, in addition to recognizing the AFL and CIO. In Arkansas, Governor Sid McMath allotted a third seat to one of the railway brotherhoods. (David, Moos, and Goldman, *op. cit.*, Vol. 2, pp. 9, 22, 143, 145; Vol. 3, p. 157, 257.)

slate-making purposes, rather than an outside force with which to negotiate.

The Republican delegates of 1952 included few representatives of organized
labor. Among them were the late William
Hutcheson of Indiana, emeritus president
of the AFL Carpenters union, and Basil D.
French, a prominent AFL leader in New
Hampshire, and several labor leaders in the
California Warren delegation. No other indications of significant labor representation
in Republican delegations were found in
the 1952 survey.

The interval between the 1952 and 1956
conventions was marked by the amalgama-
tion in December 1955 of the American
Federation of Labor and the Congress of
Industrial Organizations. Their political action committees were replaced by the AFL-
CIO Committee on Political Education
(COPE). The entire labor movement was
in a state of reorganization during most of
1956. Relatively few strong initiatives were
taken on political matters, the principal objective being the retention of previous gains.

Quiet efforts were apparently made to increase the number of labor delegates at the
Democratic convention of 1956. This may
have succeeded in maintaining labor's proportionate strength in a convention in
which the total number of delegates was increased from 1,642 to 2,477. But there was
little evidence of labor caucusing at the
1956 convention; estimates of the total
number of labor delegates were not readily
available, and the top labor leaders stayed
behind the scenes except for their public
appearances on platform matters. A solid
core of labor voting strength seems, however, to have become established at Democratic national conventions as a supporting
base for intervention by the labor leaders
in open nominating situations.[49]

[49] See Chapters 4 and 5. On leadership tactics in
1956, see the Periscope item in *Newsweek*, Aug. 26,
1956, p. 11. Two years later, *Newsweek* referred to
Walter Reuther's power as a kingmaker at the Democratic convention of 1956, "where he shattered the
Harriman boomlet not only by swinging the more
than 40 UAW member delegates to Adlai Stevenson
but also by persuading about 150 other CIO mem-

Public and Party Officials Serving as Delegates

The party conventions bring together a
cross section of officialdom from the executive and legislative branches of all levels of
government, and also from all parts of the
party hierarchy. Elective executives from
mayor to governor and President; high appointive officials of state and federal government; city councilmen, state legislators,
representatives in Congress, senators; party
officials from county committeemen to national committee chairmen—all may serve
as delegates if they can get themselves
elected.

The extent to which current and past
public and party officials of the highest rank
and distinction served as delegates in 1956
is indicated by Table 14.4. The number of
such delegates increased from 492 in 1952
to 628 in 1956.[50] In percentage terms, at the
Democratic conventions the proportion
dropped from 18.3 per cent in 1952 to 15.9

ber delegates and Gov. G. Mennen Williams to come
out for Stevenson, too." (March 31, 1958, p. 25.)

For statements of relevant doctrine by labor leaders, see James B. Carey, "Organized Labor in Politics," *Annals of the American Academy of Political
and Social Science*, Vol. 319 (Sept. 1958), pp. 52-62;
also see Gus Tyler, *A New Philosophy for Labor*
("Occasional Paper" published in 1959 by the Fund
for the Republic). Tyler says (p. 7) that "the almost
unanimous policy of American labor today is to
practice non-partisan endorsement: the Gompers
methodology grafted onto the program of the social reformers."

It will apparently be some time before the doc-
trinal statements of the leaders of either business or
labor catch up with their actual practice, but there
are undoubtedly major differences of opinion among
the labor leaders on the practical issues. George
Meany was recently said to "prefer continuing but
not extending organized labor's involvement in
party conventions," whereas Walter Reuther was
said, not only to favor such extension, but to be
willing "to have labor's weight be thrown into the
always dangerous primaries." (Warner Bloomberg,
Jr., Joel Seidman, Victor Hoffman, "Labor's Political
Power," *New Republic*, July 13, 1959, pp. 11-15.)
It should be noted that the position attributed to
Meany would involve no retreat from past practice.

[50] The figures are based on a comparison of the
delegate lists with the relevant directories of public
and party officials and the contemporary volumes of
Who's Who in America.

TABLE 14.4. DELEGATES TO THE NATIONAL CONVENTIONS OF 1956 WHO HAD ATTAINED DISTINCTION AS PUBLIC OR PARTY OFFICIALS

Category	Numbers of Delegates		
	Democratic	Republican	Total
Public Officials Currently in Office			
Governors of States	19[a]	15	34
United States Senators	34	25	59
Representatives in Congress	65	24	89
Distinguished Federal Executives[b]	—	6[c]	6
Other Distinguished Public Officials[d]	59[e]	20[f]	79
	177	90	267
Party Officials of High Rank			
State Committee Chairmen[g]	39[h]	33	72
State Committee Vice Chairmen[i]	25	17	42
National Committee Members[j]	56[k]	38[l]	94
Other Distinguished Party Officials[m]	4	7	11
	124	95	219
Distinguished Past Holders of Public and Party Office[n]	94	48	142
Total in Above Categories	395	233	628
Total Number of Delegates	2,477	1,323	3,800

[a] Does not include Governor LeRoy Collins of Florida, who was an alternate; he is, however, included in Chapter 5, Table 5.2.

[b] Federal executives present as delegates whose biographies were included in the contemporary volume of *Who's Who in America*. The President, the Vice President, and appointive officials of sub-Cabinet rank or higher are usually so included.

[c] Includes Governor Samuel Wilder King of Hawaii.

[d] Mayors of cities of 500,000 or more; state lieutenant governors, speakers of lower houses of state legislatures, state attorney generals, state secretaries of state; together with other public officials not elsewhere classified—sixteen Democrats and two Republicans—whose biographies appeared in the contemporary volume of *Who's Who in America*.

[e] Includes E. L. Bartlett, Delegate to Congress from Alaska.

[f] Includes Mrs. Elizabeth P. Farrington, Delegate to Congress from Hawaii.

[g] Does not include chairmen of non-state area party committees.

[h] Does not include State Chairman Robert Humphreys of Kentucky, who is classified among the Senators.

[i] Includes vice chairmen of non-state area party committees.

[j] Includes national committee members from non-state areas.

[k] Does not include the following who were national committee members: Thomas D'Alesandro, Jr., of Maryland, Leo Graybill of Montana, Carmine DeSapio of New York, David Lawrence of Pennsylvania, and Ben Ramsey of Texas, who are classified among Other Distinguished Public Officials because of other positions; Theodore Francis Green of Rhode Island, who is classified among the Senators; and Mrs. Iris F. Blitch of Georgia, who is classified among the Representatives.

[l] Does not include the following who were national committee members: Theodore R. McKeldin of Maryland, who is classified among the Governors; Mrs. Cecil M. Harden of Indiana, Dean P. Taylor of New York, Clarence J. Brown of Ohio, Carroll Reece of Tennessee, who are classified among the Representatives. Also does not include twenty-four Republican state chairmen who also served as national committee members and delegates in 1956, and are included in State Committee Chairmen.

[m] Party officials serving as delegates whose biographies were included in the contemporary volume of *Who's Who in America*.

[n] Delegates listed in the contemporary volume of *Who's Who in America* whose biographies reported past incumbency in public or party office.

in 1956, mainly because of the 50 per cent increase in the total number of delegates. At the Republican conventions, however, the proportion rose from 15.8 per cent in 1952 to 17.6 in 1956. The small group of Republican federal executives who served as delegates in 1956 was responsible for only a minor part of this increase, which occurred generally throughout the various categories of public and party officeholders.[51]

Each category of public and party officials who serve as delegates can be further studied in terms of historical trends. Information of this kind is summarized here to the extent that it has been possible to collect it for governors, senators, and representatives in Congress.

The data indicate that the highest-ranking public and party officials have become increasingly willing to serve as delegates and increasingly successful in obtaining the opportunity. Their number fluctuates from convention to convention and varies between the parties and among the categories of offices and situations. But the tendency of the number to increase suggests that the conventions are achieving a higher status in the American political system and that their value to the parties and to the delegates is increasing.

[51] It may also be reported, for whatever it is worth in the appraisal of reputability, representativeness, and competence, that 238 of the Democratic and 159 of the Republican delegates of 1952 were currently the subjects of biographies in *Who's Who in America*. The numbers in 1956 were 329 and 237 respectively, a total of 566. For the most part, these were the same delegates in 1956 that are the subjects of Table 14.4, which is pitched in general at the *Who's Who* level of ex officio distinction. But the table includes state party chairmen and vice chairmen, who do not ordinarily appear in *Who's Who in America*; and not all of the governors, senators, representatives in Congress, and national committee members who served at the conventions were listed currently there, although all persons in these categories are normally subject to such listing if they cooperate in providing biographical material. On the other hand, there were a few delegates of the *Who's Who* level of distinction whose biographies showed no evidence of public or party office, past or present. The numbers of such delegates were as follows: 25 Democratic and 37 Republican in 1952; 31 and 50 respectively in 1956.

Governors

Over two thirds of the governors in each party were members of delegations in 1956, and in most of these delegations they held the chairmanship. For a century the tendency of governors to serve as delegates has been slowly rising. During most of the period, Democratic governors were more frequently present than Republican, but the Republican proportion exceeded the Democratic at least in 1872 and 1928.[52]

Service as a delegate is far from equally convenient for all the state governors. Presumably those who are safely in office for a further period are in the best position to serve, while those engaged in difficult reelection campaigns are in the poorest—unless they are able to use service at the convention as a means for helping their campaigns at home.

In 1952 the forty-eight state governors included eighteen whose terms did not expire for another year or more, and fourteen of these were convention delegates. Five governors were nearing the end of their terms but were ineligible to succeed themselves; four of these were delegates. Three were retiring voluntarily from the governorship, two of them to run for the Senate; only the third was a delegate. Of the twenty-two governors running actively for re-election, thirteen were delegates nonetheless.

In general, the governors running for re-election in the safest Republican states were apparently the least likely in 1952 to be delegates. Most of the thirteen governors who were delegates while running for re-election were Democrats, some of whom had already won their nominating contests in the primaries, others had not. Four of the thirteen were defeated either in the primaries or in the general election, while one, Adlai E. Stevenson, withdrew from his

[52] See Chapter 5, Table 5.2. The table includes only selected convention years prior to 1928. In the rare instances where governors have served as alternate delegates, they were included in Table 5.2 and in the percentage computations.

gubernatorial race when nominated for the Presidency.[53]

Senators

Of the ninety-six United States senators in 1956, not quite two thirds were delegates or alternate delegates. Ten were chairmen, one of whom was chairman of a dele-

mainly on delegations chaired by national committeemen or state chairmen.

The historical record of service by senators on delegations, insofar as it has been collected, appears in Table 14.5.

The century-long tendency toward greater participation is as apparent for senators as it is for governors, but the senators started sooner. The Republican senators,

TABLE 14.5. SENATORS SERVING ON DELEGATIONS TO NATIONAL PARTY CONVENTIONS, 1928-1956, AND SELECTED PRIOR YEARS

| | Number of Senators[a] | | Number on Delegations | | | | Per Cent on Delegations | |
| | | | Democratic | | Republican | | | |
Year	Dem.	Rep.	Delegates	Alternates	Delegates	Alternates	Dem.	Rep.
1848	33	22[b]	9	—	1[b]	—	27.3%	4.5%
1860	36	26	4	—	2	—	11.1	7.7
1872	17	52	5	—	3	1	29.4	7.7
1884	36	40	5	—	8	—	13.9	20.0
1896	39	43	21	—	14	—	53.8	32.6
1908	31	61	16	—	25	—	51.6	41.0
1920	47	49	20	1	16	1	44.7	34.7
1928	46	49	24	1	21	—	54.3	42.9
1932	47	48	26	1	22	—	57.5	45.8
1936	69	25	56	2	3	2	84.1	20.0
1940	69	23	42	1	6	—	62.3	26.1
1944	58	37	36	—	15	—	62.1	40.5
1948	45	51	26	2	21	—	62.2	41.2
1952	50	45	38	4	18	—	84.0	40.0
1956	49	47	34	2	25	—	73.5	53.2

[a] The number of senators of the two major parties was frequently less than the authorized strength of the Senate because of vacancies and the occasional election of third-party senators.
[b] Whig.

gation including an incumbent governor. Three junior senators served on delegations chaired by their senior senators; some thirty-two served on delegations chaired by governors. The other fourteen senators served

[53] Governor Allan Shivers of Texas was facing a contest in a primary election on Saturday of the week of the Democratic national convention, the day on which the convention actually adjourned. This coincidence may not have been entirely unrelated to his much-televised behavior and tactics at Chicago. He won renomination.

however, have lagged not only behind the Democratic senators but also behind the Republican governors. Until 1956 there had been no visible evidence of increasing attendance by Republican senators since the turn of the century. The proportion was especially low in 1936 and 1940, when the Senate contained few Republicans except from the strongly Republican states.

The senators from the competitive two-party states have long been the ones most likely to be present as delegates in their party conventions. The tendency was so conspicuous that it became apparent by inspection as the historical figures were being collected, most notably in the case of states that had one senator of each party. That the tendency still persists can be seen in Table 14.6. It can be supposed that sena-

Different forces have been at work in the one-party Democratic states. Increasingly the southern state delegations have been in a minority position on critical issues at the Democratic conventions. Southern senators have been needed at the conventions to help defend sectional interests. Presumably for this reason, and perhaps because of

TABLE 14.6. PARTICIPATION OF SENATORS IN NATIONAL PARTY CONVENTIONS, BY PARTY ALIGNMENT OF THE STATES, 1948-1956

Category of States by Party Alignment[a]	Number of Senators Serving as Delegates, and Total Number[b]			Per Cent of Senators Serving as Delegates		
	1948	1952	1956	1948	1952	1956
DEMOCRATIC SENATORS FROM:						
Democratic States	12/18	18/21	16/23	67%	86%	70%
Competitive States	16/27[c]	23/29[d]	20/26[c]	59[c]	79[d]	77[c]
Republican States	0/0	0/0	0/0	—	—	—
	28/45	41/50	36/49	62	82	73
REPUBLICAN SENATORS FROM:						
Republican States	2/14	2/13[c]	4/11	14	15	29
Competitive States	14/31	14/29	20/32	45	48	63
Democratic States	5/6	2/3	1/1	83	67	100
	21/51	18/45[c]	25/47	41	40	53
BOTH PARTIES						
Total	49/96	59/95[c]	61/96	51	62	64

[a] Based on the same classification of states by party alignment used elsewhere in the book; see Chapter 16, Table 16.9, and Appendix A, Table 4.
[b] In each cell of these columns, the denominator is the total number of senators of the party from the category of states, and the numerator is the number who were serving as delegates in the year concerned.
[c] Includes two senators serving as alternate delegates.
[d] Includes four senators serving as alternate delegates.
[e] One vacancy in Nebraska.

torial and presidential prospects have always been most closely related in the competitive states; that there is in these states the closest connection between state and national politics; and that for these reasons their senators find it desirable to take an active part in the national conventions. The growing number of competitive states is thus probably one reason for the long-term uptrend in senatorial participation.

their own zest for all forms of national politics, most of the southern senators have usually been delegates in recent years.

The tendency of the Republican senators from the one-party Republican states not to serve as convention delegates has existed from the first and still persists. The reasons for this tendency are not readily apparent, except possibly the absence of the forces that impel the participation of Democratic senators from the southern states. On the other hand, the occasional Republican senator from a Democratic state almost invariably attends his national convention as a delegate. The counterpart category did not exist on the Democratic side in the years covered by Table 14.6, but came into existence in 1958 with the election of Senator Edmund S. Muskie of Maine and Senator Vance Hartke of Indiana.

are shown in Table 14.7 for the three most recent convention years, and also for 1848 and 1884 as samplings of the earlier years.

The greater participation of Democrats and the strong uptrend of the last three convention years in both parties are the most conspicuous features of the table. A total of 119 members of the House, or 27.4

TABLE 14.7. REPRESENTATIVES IN CONGRESS SERVING ON DELEGATIONS TO NATIONAL PARTY CONVENTIONS, SELECTED YEARS

| Year | Number of Representatives[a] | | Number on Delegations | | | | Per Cent on Delegations | |
| | | | Democratic | | Republican | | | |
	Dem.	Rep.	Delegates	Alternates	Delegates	Alternates	Dem.	Rep.
1848	131	117[b]	17	—	9[b]	—	13.0%	7.7%
1884	198	121	9	0	19	1	4.5	16.5
1948	185	244	28	3	13	7	16.8	8.2
1952	232	201	42	14	15	3	24.1	9.0
1956	231	201	65	15	24	15	34.6	19.4

[a] The number as reflected in the *Congressional Directory* current at the time of the party conventions. For the three most recent years, the total number of seats has been 435, but a few seats are usually vacant at any one time because of death, and occasionally there are one or two members who disclaim allegiance to either major party.
[b] Whig.

Senators can attend the conventions without serving as delegates or alternate delegates, and usually receive many privileges as distinguished guests when they do so. In times past, many senators have probably preferred to come as guests rather than as delegates when divisive issues were certain to come to a vote. But the pressures now seem to run in the direction of a need for delegate status even when senators might prefer otherwise.[54]

Representatives in Congress

The numbers of members of the House of Representatives serving on delegations

[54] See Chapter 9.

per cent, were delegates or alternates in 1956. The historical figures confirm the impression that since the beginnings of the system a few representatives have taken part in the conventions, but they do not show whether there has been a long-term trend. (The figures for a larger number of years have not been collected because of the cost and labor factors involved.)

The top leaders of both parties in the House have served as delegates in recent years: Sam Rayburn of Texas, Joseph W. Martin, Jr., of Massachusetts, John W. McCormack of the same state, Charles A. Halleck of Indiana. Rayburn and Halleck were prevented from serving as delegates in 1952 by factional fights at home, but all four of the leaders served as delegates in 1948 and 1956.

A few states have been responsible for much of the attendance by members of the House in recent years, as the tabulation below indicates.[55] In most other states the

States	Year	Dem.	Rep.
New York	1948	4	5
	1952	8	3
	1956	7	8
California	1948	4	4
	1952	4	4
	1956	9	8
Georgia	1948	0	0
	1952	10	0
	1956	1	0
Mississippi	1948	7	0
	1952	2	0
	1956	6	0

sending of House members as delegates or alternates has been too intermittent to indicate any established custom. There has, however, been a clear shift upward in the number of state delegations in the House of each party that have been represented by at least one member serving as a delegate or alternate at the respective party convention. The numbers and percentages of such delegations are shown below.

Party Delegations in the House of Representatives

Year	Total Number	Represented at Convention	
		Number	Per Cent
DEMOCRATIC			
1948	33	15	45.5%
1952	36	24	66.7
1956	37	29	78.4
REPUBLICAN			
1948	35	9	25.7%
1952	32	10	31.2
1956	38	14	36.8

Members of the House who belong to a minority of one kind or another have apparently served as delegates more often than other House members. The senior Negro congressman, William Dawson, has served

[55] In 1948 and 1956, Mississippi's entire Democratic delegation in the House of Representatives (seven and six respectively) were members of its convention delegation; in 1952, Georgia's convention delegation included its entire ten-man Democratic House delegation.

repeatedly as a delegate. Among the women members of the House, three were delegates in 1952 and seven in 1956. In state delegations where one party was dominant but the other had one or two seats in the House, the minority party was likely to send its representatives as delegates while the majority party usually did not.

In the early days of the convention system, congressmen who served as delegates attracted criticism on the ground that the conventions had been established in order to remove the nominating function from Congress and restore it to the people. There seems to be little criticism of this sort today, and favoring arguments now find expression more often—among them that members of Congress are especially well qualified, and that working relationships between the executive and legislative branches would be improved if members of the House had more responsibility in the nominating process. Under present apportionment rules, moreover, even if all the members of the House were delegates, they would rarely hold as much as one quarter of the voting strength in either national convention.

The present-day objections to putting members of the House on delegations appear to stem mainly from considerations of local politics. From New Jersey, for example, it was reported in 1952 that the "general lack of serious consideration for congressmen seems to reflect a conviction that a candidate's name should appear only once on the ballot, that party honors should be spread over as wide a field as possible, and that valuable prestige patronage should not be wasted." The further comment was made that "congressmen are not likely to be chosen as delegates unless they are coincidentally real grass-roots leaders and centers of power in their party."[56] Apparently the members of the House who are "centers of power" were considered exceptional even in their home districts.

The increase in congressional representation from 1948 to 1956 coincided with the

[56] David, Moos, and Goldman, op. cit., Vol. 2, pp. 213-14.

joint service of Martin and Rayburn as permanent chairmen in the conventions of their parties.[57] Perhaps the thought has occurred to an increasing number of state party leaders since 1948 that it is helpful to have at least one member of the House on the state's delegation as long as the party leader in the House is to be the convention chairman. The members themselves may have helped to plant this thought. Perhaps the leaders in the House have also quietly passed the word to their colleagues that it would be helpful if more of them were on the floor at the conventions. In any event, the function of the congressional elements of each party as a communications network in the nominating process undoubtedly can be enhanced if more of the members take part in the conventions.[58]

Experience of the Delegates in Prior Conventions

About 40 per cent of the delegates in each convention of 1952 had served on an earlier delegation at least once, as the tabulation below indicates.[59]

Known Years of Service	Democratic Delegates	Republican Delegates
1952 and 1948	28.7%	30.5%
1952 and 1944, not 1948	6.3	7.1
1952 and 1940, not 1944–1948	4.0	1.7
	39.0	39.3

The proportion of continuous service records ranging back through several conventions were practically identical in the two parties at the conventions of 1952 and 1956,

as shown in Table 14.8. In 1952 the record for consecutive convention service was held by Samuel E. Koenig, a Republican delegate of New York City, who had attended twelve conventions, beginning in 1908. In 1956 a similar record was achieved by Senator Theodore Francis Green of Rhode Island, who had served in Democratic conventions since 1912.

The close similarity of the inverted seniority pyramids of Table 14.8 is remarkable, particularly in view of the fact that the total number of Democratic delegates in 1956 was about 50 per cent larger than their 1952 total. These relationships attest to the institutional stability of the party system and to the considerable similarity of the delegate selection practices of the two parties.

As might be expected, the long-service delegates included many of the more distinguished members of delegations. Among the delegates of 1956 who were listed in *Who's Who in America*, over half had served in 1952. As Table 14.9 indicates, continuous service in three conventions or more was several times as frequent among the *Who's Who* group as among other delegates.

An institution as complicated as the modern national party convention would hardly be able to function, much less complete its work in four or five days, if it did not have an enormous accumulation of convention experience within its own ranks. For the newcomer, the environment is one of the utmost confusion. Yet an immense amount of effective activity is being conducted with great rapidity and amidst many pressures. The fact that all of this activity is possible and that the results fall rapidly into place is largely due to the skill and experience with which the old hands go about their business.

The data on experience tend to support and give further meaning to a three-part classification of the delegates that is impressionistic but useful in understanding the operation of the conventions. First are those who occupy bottleneck positions of one sort or another and who usually work to the point of exhaustion during the convention.

[57] See Chapter 4.
[58] See Chapter 5.
[59] In view of the configuration of this tabulation and that of Table 14.8, it can be estimated that another 1 or 2 per cent of the delegates of 1952 had served prior to 1940 without serving in the meantime. Complete data were compiled for 1948; see Table 14.8, footnote a. The figures for 1940 and 1944 were based on a 20 per cent sample.

TABLE 14.8. CONTINUOUS SERVICE RECORDS, DELEGATES OF 1952 AND 1956[a]

(in per cent)

Consecutive Conventions Attended[b]	Democratic Conventions		Republican Conventions	
	Delegates of 1952	Delegates of 1956	Delegates of 1952	Delegates of 1956
2	28.7%	28.1%	30.5%	28.6%
3	12.6	10.7	12.4	12.7
4	6.3	4.7	5.5	6.6
5	3.4	2.3	3.1	3.2
6	1.4	1.1	1.2	1.6
7	0.8	0.4	0.8	0.8
8	0.6	0.2	0.3	0.5
9	0.2	0.1	0.2	0.2
10	0.1	—[c]	0.1	0.1
11	0.1	—[c]	0.1	—
12	—	—[c]	0.1	—

[a] The data pertain to persons who had full delegate status in 1952 and 1956, as the case may be, but service in prior years as either a delegate or alternate was recognized for the purpose of compiling the record of continuous service. All names on the 1952 permanent roll as delegates were checked against the listings for the same states in 1948. Having identified the group that had served twice consecutively, that group in turn was checked against the listings for 1944, and so on as far back as continuous service was found. The same procedure was repeated for the 1956 delegates.

[b] Including the convention of 1952 or 1956, as the case may be.

[c] Less than .1 per cent.

TABLE 14.9. CONTINUOUS SERVICE RECORDS IN PRIOR CONVENTIONS BY DISTINGUISHED DELEGATES AND OTHER DELEGATES OF 1956[a]

(per cent serving on delegations, 1932–1952)

Year	Democratic		Republican	
	Distinguished Delegates	Other Delegates	Distinguished Delegates	Other Delegates
1952	54.7%	23.9%	48.2%	24.0%
1948	30.5	7.5	26.7	9.4
1944	14.5	3.1	14.3	4.8
1940	7.0	1.5	8.4	2.0
1936	4.4	0.6	3.6	1.1
1932	2.6	0.05	1.6	0.6

[a] The "Distinguished Delegates" include 566 whose biographies were carried in the then current edition of *Who's Who in America*, plus 29 who were governors, members of Congress, or national committee members, for all of whom biographies would normally be carried in *Who's Who in America*.

They are the key figures in the convention organization as a whole, in the organizations supporting each candidate, and in the leadership of each major delegation. They may number as many as a hundred in each party's convention. With rare exceptions, they are persons with much previous experience.

The second category includes the delegates who have definite assignments without occupying critical positions, or who are able to take an active but independent part in the proceedings. This category is much more indeterminate in size, fluctuating with the nature of the situation, the position of the major delegations, and the inclinations of individual delegates. Under some circumstances it may range up to a third or more of the delegates. Most of those in this category have had some previous experience.

The third category consists of all the rest of the delegates—those whose largely passive role is to attend, listen, and vote, although they may have some opportunity to speak in delegation meetings. This is the only role for which most delegates are qualified unless they have attended at least one previous national convention.[60]

Leadership Resources in Delegations

The 628 delegates of 1956 who had attained a relatively high level of political distinction (Table 14.4) and the 1,075 who had served in 1952 as well as 1956 (Table 14.8) were not equally distributed among the 107 delegations.[61] For each category, the

[60] Other kinds of relevant experience can of course help. One member of the Kefauver campaign organization of 1952 has commented that many of the Kefauver delegates were especially ineffective because of their general lack of state party convention experience. Most of them had been elected in primaries.

[61] The 107 consisted of delegations at each convention from the 48 states, Alaska, Hawaii, District of Columbia, Puerto Rico, and Virgin Islands; and one at the Democratic from the Canal Zone.

proportions within delegations ranged from zero to half the delegation or more. Most of this variation among delegations seemed to follow no significant pattern, except that the larger delegations usually contained larger numbers, and often larger percentages, of distinguished and experienced delegates than the smaller ones did.

Some variation among the regions was apparent, although probably less marked in 1956 than in previous years.[62] The tabulation below shows the regional averages in percentages. The high percentage of experienced delegates from the Northeast, and the interparty differences in the South are apparent in these figures.

	1956 Delegates	
Region	Politically Distinguished	Served in 1952
DEMOCRATIC		
Northeast	16.9%	39.0%
Middle West	12.6	32.9
South	16.8	16.0
West	16.0	26.4
Non-State Areas	31.4	39.2
National Average	15.9	28.1
REPUBLICAN		
Northeast	21.0%	41.9%
Middle West	18.8	27.5
South	10.8	20.6
West	18.8	19.6
Non-State Areas	29.2	29.2
National Average	17.6	28.6

In any event, when a state delegation contains several high public and party officials presumably it will be relatively more effective in convention sources of leadership. When incumbent officeholders are

[62] Some experimental tabulations for 1952, not included here, revealed a wider range of variation and a considerably larger number of delegations with few or no delegates of political distinction and experience. This may have been the result of the number of insurgent delegations elected in each party in 1952.

lacking, former officials may be almost equally important in contributing to delegation effectiveness.

The Evolution and Recent Status of Delegate Characteristics

Information on the age, sex, race, religion, education, income levels, occupations, public and party officeholding, and prior convention experience of the delegates has been set forth in the present chapter. Such information is not directly conclusive on any of the questions of reputability, representativeness, and competence with which the chapter began. For the delegates in the mass, however, the statistics form a striking pattern that tends to refute much derogatory comment on the conventions.

The facts suggest that the great majority of the delegates were well qualified to deal with the problems of their political parties, and that they were about as reputable a group of individuals as could reasonably be expected in any large political assembly in this imperfect world.

If this was true in 1948, 1952, and 1956, was it always true? Has there been a sharp break with the past at some point, or a gradual improvement, or not even that?

Looking back over the sequence of American political history for the factors most directly affecting the selection of national convention delegates, it cannot be said that there was any one sharp break with the past that decisively changed the character of the delegates. Probably the four most striking developments, all of which have come during the last half century, were the presidential primaries for the election of delegates in some states, first important in 1912; the reform of Republican apportionment rules after the fiasco of 1912, which reduced the representation of the rotten-borough districts of the South; the ratification of the woman suffrage amendment in August 1920, followed by greatly increased inclusion of women in the conventions; and the Hatch Acts of 1939 and 1940, prohibiting many state and federal executives below the sub-Cabinet level from serving as delegates.

Both conventions now include several hundred delegates elected in public primaries, including the district delegates who comprise the bulk of the delegations from the five largest states. Election in a primary usually brings into effect the state election laws; and whatever the other consequences may be, these delegates have run the gantlet of many provisions that restrain corruption and subject elected officials to a public scrutiny of their qualification for positions of trust. Both national conventions also now include several hundred women among the delegates and alternates; and many of the men delegates are accompanied by their wives, a noteworthy change from the situation as it once existed. The party in power no longer sends to its convention large numbers of federal officeholders, including the mass of patronage appointees from the South who were so offensive an element in the Republican conventions of 1900 to 1912 and in some earlier years.

The specific changes just cited, however, are probably not as important as the more intangible factors that have been affecting the long-term development of the political parties in the United States. These include the coming of age of the immigrant groups and the changing nature of the big-city political machines; the virtual disappearance of the state-wide bosses of the Boss Platt type; civil service reform and more frequent enforcement of standards of honesty in the awarding of government contracts; the growing importance of organized labor and its interest in direct political action; the increasingly active interest in the party organizations of both parties taken by middle- and upper-class people with a public-service orientation; a noteworthy shift of political power from the party officials, whether bosses or not, to elected officials with a direct responsibility to the public, such as the governors and senators; and finally, the rising standards of education and social responsibility throughout the country. Changes of this kind are probably mainly responsible for the fact that while the conventions of recent years have had many superficial resemblances to those of 1900, the delegates from many states were of a measurably different type.

Not all of the elements of this conclusion are capable of proof with the evidence currently available, but of the broad outlines of the change there is no doubt. The delegates of recent years were better educated, less boss-ridden, better adjusted to the requirements of an open political system, and generally more trustworthy in all respects than those of half a century earlier. The United States political system still leaves much to be desired, but it is in a much more reputable condition than formerly; and to a large extent the change has been mirrored in the composition of the delegate groups that cast the deciding votes at the national political conventions.

As for representativeness, the historical evidence does not supply a basis for many specific deductions—except perhaps where reputability and representativeness tend to overlap. Delegates who were boss-ridden, ill educated, and preoccupied with the hope of political spoils were not, by our modern standards, proper representatives of any normal constituency. To the extent that the delegates have become more reputable, they may be said to have also become more representative.

Taking the situation as it has appeared in recent years, however, the representative character of the delegate groups has been good in some respects, deficient in others. It has been often pointed out that the delegates are not typical of their constituents, because so high a percentage of them are white, male persons of mature age, usually with a college education, a business or professional occupation, and a higher-than-average income. But there is every reason to believe that this is the kind of representative that most constituents would wish to have; certainly it is the kind they usually elect whenever any opportunity for choice is presented. As Harold F. Gosnell and John A. Fairlie point out, the idea of

agency, of being qualified to be present in place of another and on his behalf, has implications for the characteristics of the representative as well as for his acts on behalf of his constituents.[63] Frequently, the constituent wants a representative who can take care of his interests better than the constituent himself could hope to do.

No statistical measures are available on the total extent to which the delegates of recent years have had the characteristics desired by their constituents. Such information as there is suggests a situation that was mixed but generally favorable. Observers at the conventions, foreign and domestic alike, have frequently commented favorably on the extent to which the conventions present a cross section of American types in speech, dress, and behavior generally, implying that it was a cross section of reputable types. Project reporters for the American Political Science Association in 1952 usually closed their reports with comment to the effect that the delegations they had studied were generally representative of the party organizations and party constituencies in the states concerned.

In probing for weak spots, however, three further questions could be asked on the matter of delegate characteristics at recent conventions. Was there adequate representation of minorities? Was the representation of the majority groups provided too often by professional politicians who were not representative of their constituencies? And were the differences between the party electorates mirrored at the conventions?

The available information on minority group representation has been presented earlier. It can be inferred that minorities who recognize themselves as such are intent upon being represented by delegates from their own ranks; certainly they often claim to be underrepresented if they fail to achieve a quota proportionate to their num-

[63] Gosnell, *Democracy—The Threshold of Freedom* (1948), pp. 131-32, citing Fairlie, "The Nature of Political Representation," *American Political Science Review*, Vol. 34 (April and June 1940), pp. 236, 456.

bers. If this is the test, most of the identifiable minorities have been underrepresented in the recent conventions of both parties.

The question on whether too many of the delegates were professional politicians goes to the heart of one of the major problems of any party system. Those who make politics either a vocation or a major avocation usually develop characteristics and attitudes that are not shared fully by the electorate. Yet someone must do the party work; and it is those who do the work who are most likely to turn up as national convention delegates. The organization regulars who constituted so large a portion of the delegations from many states in 1952 were probably not entirely the kind of delegates that the party electorates would have preferred, even when they said and did what their constituencies desired.

Partly because so many of the delegates in recent years were party professionals, but also for many other reasons, it was abundantly clear that the differences between the conventions in their social and economic composition did not adequately reflect the differences between the parties in the electorate. Traces of these party constituency differences—but only traces—were visible in the divergent religious and ethnic affiliations of the delegates, in slightly differing average income levels, and in the greater direct representation of business at the Republican convention and of organized labor at the Democratic. Presumably these differences, even though minor, were helpful to the respective conventions in keeping clear the fundamental differences between the parties while writing platform provisions and choosing candidates.

Questions of competence are not easily answered beyond what has already been said, no matter how much information is collected. Undoubtedly, however, the delegates had greater competence for the performance of some of their functions than for others. On the whole, they appeared well qualified to deal with the nominating function. For the platform function, the essential problem is the manning of the resolutions committee; and there the Democrats appeared to be better situated than the Republicans in view of their much larger corps of senators and representatives in Congress who were serving as delegates and were thus available for assignment to the committee.[64]

On the campaign-rally function, the conventions have usually done a reasonably good job when they were able to deal effectively with their other functions. With so many candidates for offices at all levels taking part, the conventions extend their campaign-rally function to the congressional and state campaigns as well as the presidential. They signify the unity of their respective parties, when such unity actually exists; and because they are so broadly representative, they are especially well qualified to rally party sentiment for all of the concurrent campaigns that occur in the presidential years.

Finally, there is the governing-body function, for which most of the delegates seemed ill prepared, needing to be briefed by some much more extended preparation in advance of the conventions than has usually occurred. But in that area the failures of leadership have typically been much more of a problem than the actual voting of the delegates on issues laid before them—perhaps because of the problems in organizing the leadership of the parties, as noted in Chapters 4 and 5 and as further discussed in the final chapter of this book.

[64] The Republican situation on manning the resolutions (platform) committee was better in 1956 than in 1952, as indicated by the following statistics of members of the two houses of Congress who actually served on the respective committees.

	Democrats		Republicans	
	Senate	House	Senate	House
1952	9	4	2	1
1956	5	11	10	3

15

Delegation Organization, Decision-Making, and Voting Behavior

FOR MANY PURPOSES, the working unit at a national convention is the state delegation rather than the individual delegate. The ordinary delegate seldom takes an individual part in the deliberations except in the meetings of the state delegations. Any clear understanding of the convention must therefore involve some systematic consideration of the state delegations: their position and make-up as organized groups; their methods of reaching decisions; their voting behavior and other activities.

By the time a delegation is selected, it is likely to have a whole series of commitments, express or implied, in regard to its choice of candidates, its positions on issues, and its relation to state and national party organizations. The manner in which a delegation organizes, reaches internal decisions, and eventually votes is inevitably affected by its previous commitments.[1]

Delegation Organization

The members of each delegation are seated together in the convention hall and are required to have a delegation chairman who can act as spokesman. In other respects the delegations may decide for themselves on their organization and activities.

When, Where, and How to Organize

When members of a delegation are selected by a state party convention, an organizing meeting may be held immediately after the convention. In any event, it is usually clear where the responsibility will rest for further action. In a state where delegates are elected in primaries, an organizing meeting is usually convened by the state party chairman, the national committeeman, or the highest ranking member of the delegation—the governor, for instance, if he is a delegate.[2]

[1] The present chapter leans heavily on the five-volume study *Presidential Nominating Politics in 1952*, which includes a narrative account of the origins and behavior of each of 104 delegations to the 1952 conventions—all except the one- and two-man delegations from the Virgin Islands and the Canal Zone. No similar body of information is available for any other convention; and while the narrative form of the data makes quantitative summary difficult, it does permit the exploratory identification of behavioral patterns much more easily than might have been possible with a more highly structured inquiry.

As in the case of the previous chapter on delegates, the present chapter owes much to the discussions of the Interuniversity Summer Research Seminar on Presidential Nominating Politics at the Brookings Institution in the summer of 1955; Warren E. Miller was especially helpful in the seminar

in identifying the importance of the factor of commitment in the analysis of delegate voting behavior.

After the analysis had been revised in the light of the seminar discussions and further research, comments on the social psychology of the chapter were received from Samuel J. Eldersveld, Harold Guetzkow, and F. P. Kilpatrick, which were of great assistance in a final revision.

[2] Where delegate selection is highly atomized, there may be doubt concerning who can successfully convene an organizing meeting, as was the case for both Oregon delegations in 1952. See Paul T. David, Malcolm Moos, and Ralph M. Goldman, *Presidential Nominating Politics in 1952* (1954), Vol. 5, Chap. 11.

The Florida presidential primary law of 1955 met this problem by providing that each slate of candidates for delegate should designate an organizing

Traditionally, it seems to have been assumed that each delegation would hold its organizing meeting in its hotel after arrival in the convention city.[3] But in 1952 most of the delegations met and organized before leaving their home state, and this seems to be the modern tendency.[4] The advance committee work of the conventions is impeded when delegations fail to organize and to designate their committee members well ahead of time. Republican national rules have long required each state delegation to select its members for the credentials and resolutions committees "immediately" after the delegation itself is selected. For 1960 the Democratic party provided that delegations should select their members for major committees at least fourteen days before the convention.[5]

Wherever the organizing meeting of a delegation is held, the business usually includes the election of a chairman, vice chairman, and secretary; designation of members to serve on the convention committees; some understanding about the financing of a delegation headquarters at the convention; arrangements about the distribution of guest tickets for the convention hall, which may have a controlling effect on the selection of the visitors from the state who accompany the delegation; and a decision about when and where to meet again—a decision that is usually contingent on the amount and kind of discussion that the delegation sees in prospect.

---

chairman, to be identified on the ballot, who would have the duty, if elected, of convening the organizing meeting at an appropriate time and place. (Chapter 29947, Sen. Bill No. 1120, Approved by the Governor June 18, 1955.)

[3] The assumption is apparent in Clarence Cannon, *Democratic Manual* (1956), p. 22.

[4] No information on first meeting was available for fifteen Republican and thirteen Democratic delegations of 1952. For the others it was reported that thirty-four Republican and twenty-seven Democratic delegations organized in their home state, three Republican and thirteen Democratic delegations at the convention city, and one of each on the train. California delegations were required by state law to hold an organizing meeting before leaving the state.

[5] *Democratic Digest*, Oct. 1959, p. 11.

Frequency and Nature of Meetings

Delegations usually arrive at the convention city on the Sunday before the convention opens, hold delegation meetings on Sunday afternoon or evening, and frequently meet thereafter at their hotels in the morning of each day the convention continues, since the daily convention sessions do not usually begin before noon. Delegations also caucus at the convention, at their seats or in rooms provided for the purpose, either before or during the sessions of the convention.

Some situations obviously call for much more discussion in delegation meetings than others. In 1952, at both conventions, the first meetings after arrival were important affairs for almost every delegation. Both conventions faced the unusual possibility that roll call votes might occur even before the conventions were fully organized.

At these early meetings national committee members and other advance representatives reported on the business of the preceding days, on the procedural issues that had come to light, and on the apparent standing of the candidates. At the Democratic convention, with a dozen candidates in the running, favorite son candidates met with their home state delegations. Adlai Stevenson met with the Illinois delegation to ask their help in keeping him out of the race, and other candidates moved about seeking to hold support in committed delegations and to attract support elsewhere. The Republican convention, with fewer candidates and a more sharply focused race, still had many similarities to the Democratic situation. In both parties the delegates were coming to grips, sometimes for the first time, with the immediate issues on which they might be required to take a stand soon after the convention opened. Debate was earnest and prolonged in many delegations.

The procedure of delegations in holding further caucuses was affected by the traditions of the state party, the unfolding business of the convention in question, and particularly by size.[6] Delegations of average size —twenty-four to sixty, including alternates— usually met daily or oftener to keep abreast of events and develop their strategy accordingly. Small delegations often found formal meetings unnecessary after the organization business was settled. Large delegations, such as those of New York, Pennsylvania, Ohio, and Illinois, tended more than the delegations of average or smaller size to leave matters to the inner group of leaders after the conventions were once under way. The California delegations in both conventions were exceptions, holding frequent caucuses.

In the meetings in 1952 that were open to observation, or for which adequate reports could be obtained, parliamentary rules on the whole were used. Any delegate could have his say, even though the leaders were usually allowed to suggest the decisions in the end. Rank-and-file delegates were obviously in a position of heavy dependence upon the leaders for information bearing on tactical decisions, and this tended to limit the character of the debate.

Many delegation meetings were closed to strangers, whether held at the delegation's headquarters or at the convention hall, but even at closed meetings a few favored guests were likely to be present. These frequently included influential citizens and officials from the state, trusted editors or political reporters from the state's leading newspapers, and liaison representatives of any candidate whom the delegation currently favored.

Chairmen:
Selection and Functions

About 80 per cent of the delegation chairmen of 1952 and 1956 were currently holding some other public or party office, with public officials outnumbering the party officials in the Democratic party but not in the Republican. The principal classes of official status are shown in Table 15.1. In states

[6] See the discussion of the consequences of massive size, Chapter 9.

where the party in question held one or more high public offices the highest-ranking public official serving on the delegation was generally selected as chairman. Governors, when present as delegates, served as chairmen over 80 per cent of the time in the four conventions studied. In the absence of a governor, when one or more senators were present as delegates the ranking senator served as chairman in more than half of such cases. The frequent use of state party chairmen as delegation chairmen was noteworthy at the Republican conventions, but mainly in the case of states where the party held no top-ranking public offices. The comparatively few national committeemen who served as delegation chairmen were almost all individuals of considerable power in their respective state parties.

A small group of 1952 delegation chairmen are identified in the table as campaigners for candidates, not elsewhere classified. These were all men who seemingly had never held any important public or party office, but who arrived at the conventions as delegation chairmen presumably because of their work in the states in support of some particular candidate. The three chairmen of this type at the Democratic convention were all Kefauver supporters; of the seven at the Republican convention, three were for Eisenhower, four for Taft.

A delegation chairman occupies a strategic position. He is frequently approached by emissaries of all kinds on the assumption, which may or may not be correct, that he is in a position to negotiate for his delegation. In the convention, it is the chairman who reports the vote of the delegation. He may have some measure of discretion about the vote he reports, subject to the possibility of challenge through a demand that the delegation be polled.[7] In delegations that

[7] In New York Democratic delegations, it is said to be traditional for the chairman to estimate the vote in consultation with the leaders of conflicting groups in the delegation, whereupon the chairman then decides what voting division to report for the record. See David, Moos, and Goldman, op. cit., Vol. 2, p. 174.

The roll call vote in the Republican national con-are cohesive and disciplined the chairman's powers, during the short period while the convention is in session, may approach those of the traditional political boss. In splintered delegations where cohesion is at a minimum the chairman is an important communication center. The *ad hoc* nature

Yet the chairmen are in some respects the unknown men of the conventions.[8] Interviewers working at the conventions have sometimes found it hard to learn just who is chairman of a delegation. Neither party recorded the list of chairmen in its official proceedings until 1956, when the practice

TABLE 15.1. PRINCIPAL POLITICAL IDENTIFICATIONS OF DELEGATION CHAIRMEN, 1952 AND 1956[a]

	Democratic		Republican	
Status	1952	1956	1952	1956
Public Officials				
Governors of States	14	16	11[b]	13
Senators	6	6	6[c]	4
Representatives	2	1	1	1
Other	9[d]	8	1	3[d]
	31	31	19	21
Party Officials Not Holding Public Office				
State Committee Chairmen	3	7	11	14
National Committeemen	5	5	4	8
Other	2	1	4	1
	10	13	19	23
Former Public and Party Officials	4	3	6	4
Campaigners for Candidates[e]	3	—	7	—
Other and Unidentified	4	5	2	4
Total	52	52	53[b,c]	52

[a] The tabulations do not include chairmen for the one- and two-man delegations from the Virgin Islands and Canal Zone, but do include chairmen for delegations from the District of Columbia, Alaska, Hawaii, and Puerto Rico. For 1952, compiled from relevant state chapters in Paul T. David, Malcolm Moos, and Ralph M. Goldman, *Presidential Nominating Politics in 1952* (1954); for 1956, compiled from the official proceedings of the two conventions with assistance from the staffs of the respective national committees.
[b] Includes one governor who was a co-chairman.
[c] Includes one senator who was a co-chairman.
[d] Includes governor of Hawaii.
[e] Not elsewhere classified.

of most convention arrangements, the short time span, and the characteristic confusion, all tend to place responsibility on the delegation chairman. Presumably they also give him a considerable measure of power.

vention of 1952 on adding certain state chairmen to the national committee showed indications of being an "administered" vote in many delegations, but was probably quite unusual in the extent to which this seemed to be the case. See *ibid.*, Vol. 1, p. 89.

was adopted at the suggestion of the American Political Science Association. Chairmen have seldom undertaken to meet as an organized group, although an executive

[8] Professor Samuel J. Eldersveld of the University of Michigan led interview teams of graduate students who sought with considerable success to interview each delegation chairman at each party convention in 1952 and 1956. The results of this research are being prepared for publication.

committee of heads of delegations might be a useful innovation.[9]

Leadership and Group Organization Within Delegations

Within a delegation there may be an informal leadership that is more important than the chairman and other officers. Effective leadership may also shift in accordance with the demands of the moment. In rare instances the leadership situation may be so uncertain that the delegation gives the appearance of a mere collection of individuals going their several ways. More often, when delegations lack cohesion, they are split into two or more factions, each with its own leadership. Even when a delegation is unified, the persons of greatest influence may not be delegates themselves; they may not even be physically present at the scene of the convention.[10]

Most of the delegations in 1952, however, contained some sort of an inner circle that usually took the initiative in mobilizing the delegation when necessary. Presumably the chairman was a member of such a group in almost every instance, though not always the most important member. This inner circle was sometimes identical with a similar

long-established group in the state organization. In other cases no such identity existed, particularly when the delegation was the result of successful insurgency, or of factional conflict on a winner-take-all basis in which the party regulars had been defeated. Despite these variations, a few generalizations can be tentatively offered.

(1) When a delegation contains a strong group of ranking public and party officials, they will almost automatically select the chairman and constitute themselves an inner circle around him. The presence or absence of such a dominant group is thus a matter for special observation and consideration.

(2) National committee members are convention officers with special privileges as such; hence they are in a strategic position to provide delegation leadership in dealing with the convention management and with other political leaders and delegations. They form an important part of the communications network even when they are not themselves delegates. Their positions are stronger when they are also accredited as delegates, and still more so when elected to delegation chairmanships.

(3 When a delegation is strongly supporting a favorite son for the nomination, this generally overrides other considerations, and the inner circle is apt to be made up of the favorite son's principal supporters in the delegation.[11]

(4) Delegations that lack ex officio leadership groups often come out of state party situations where there is disorganization, instability, or successful insurgency. A delegation that has won as an insurgent faction in a winner-take-all contest is likely to have a strong leadership of its own, with its key man as delegation chairman.

(5) In larger delegations the leaders are usually found among the delegates at large

[9] In international conference practice it has long been customary to form an executive committee of heads of delegations, which usually maintains a firm control over matters of arrangements and procedure throughout the conference. It has not been customary to form such a body at national party conventions; presumably this lacuna in institutional arrangements is the result of the presence of the national committee members and the recognition accorded them. But it would be difficult for the national committee to function as such after the convention has once come into session, and it does not attempt to do so. The result is that the functions that might otherwise be performed by an executive committee of heads of delegations devolve informally on the convention officers, on the cliques by which they are surrounded, and occasionally on specially called meetings at which there is an attempt to secure representation of all convention factions. For accounts of how the acute opening questions of procedure were dealt with in 1952, see David, Moos, and Goldman, op. cit., Vol. 1, pp. 73-76, 121-27.

[10] Such a case was the Arkansas Democratic delegation of 1952, awaiting word from the governor back home, who in turn was in communication with President Truman's entourage at Chicago. See ibid., Vol. 3, p. 260.

[11] This was the situation in 1952 in the Republican delegations of Ohio, California, and Minnesota, and in the Democratic delegations of Tennessee, Kentucky, and Oklahoma. Favorite son aspects of the situation were less controlling of leadership structures in the 1952 Democratic delegations of New York, Illinois, and Georgia, although all three had favorite son candidates.

rather than among the district delegates. But this distinction of the delegates at large is rarely important when they make up a third or more of the delegation, as often happens in small states under fractional vote and bonus vote rules.[12]

(6) Some delegations contain a large number of outstanding personages, while in others the recognizable leaders who stand out from the rank and file may be few or none.[13]

(7) Large delegations are likely to subdivide into several smaller groups along lines of territorial or factional cleavage, each of which smaller groups may have an identifiable leadership of its own.[14]

(8) Opposing voting commitments may operate to divide a delegation into rigidly structured separate groups; the extent to which such groups are able to work together on more general concerns of the delegation and the state party varies widely.[15]

Tightly constructed delegations lifted intact from the larger political organization of the state party come at one end of the scale of internal delegation organization. In such

delegations, nearly everyone knows in advance his position in the scheme of things, including where he should turn for advice and who is likely to turn to him for it. Other delegations, especially when they have been elected in a state where the party is badly disorganized, must find their internal leadership, if any, after they have been formed.

Despite these differences, much of the research and theory in the field of group psychology might be applicable in the study of the state delegations if sufficient access could be obtained. The subject invites a kind of research attention it has never had. Meanwhile, the range of variation is so great that even relatively crude types of observation may yield valuable information for some of the types of variation that occur.[16]

Decision-Making Within Delegations

The major subjects for delegation decision consist essentially of the positions to be taken on the candidates, on platform issues, and on seating and rules problems, often involving the relationship between state and national party organizations. There may also be collateral questions of delegation role and tactics. These in turn lead frequently to consideration of whether the delegation will seek to act as a unit or not.

Candidate Support

At the time delegations are selected, some are completely committed to a single candidate, others completely uncommitted. The range of commitment among the fifty-four Democratic delegations in 1952 is indicated in Table 15.2. Stevenson had few delegates, since he had refused to enter any of the primaries or to campaign. Five delegations had commitments to home-state favorite sons, three to President Truman, and one

[12] See Chapter 9.

[13] Both Delaware delegations of 1952, for example, seemed to be composed almost entirely of "leaders." The contrasting extreme was provided by the two Arizona delegations.

[14] Within a New York state delegation, for example, the delegates from each of the five counties of New York City may form a subgroup under its own leadership. For comment on the factors that militated for and against unity within New York delegations, see David, Moos, and Goldman, *op. cit.*, Vol. 2, pp. 164-65, 174-76, 180-82.

[15] The Wisconsin primary in 1952 produced a Republican delegation that contained twenty-four Taft delegates and six Warren delegates. The two groups reflected a long-standing division in the state party and went their ways separately even though seated together at the convention. (*Ibid.*, Vol. 4, p. 139.) Occasionally the splinter groups consist of only one, two, or three individuals who avoid association with others in the delegation wherever possible. For illustrations from the Connecticut and New York Republican delegations, see Chapter 11 of the present book; and David, Moos, and Goldman, *op. cit.*, Vol. 2, pp. 137, 165.

On the other hand, the Minnesota primary produced a Republican delegation of twenty-four Stassen delegates and four Eisenhower delegates, but the delegation functioned as an organized group throughout the convention. *Ibid.*, Vol. 4, pp. 174-78.

[16] See Appendix H for a discussion of the applicability of small group research to delegate study.

TABLE 15.2. Commitment and Candidate Agreement of Democratic Delegations of 1952 When Selected[a]

Status of Delegations by Majority Commitment	Number of Delegations	Average Index of Candidate Agreement[b]	Apparent Distribution of Voting Strength When Selected, Number				
			Stevenson	Kefauver	Russell	Others	Undecided or Unknown
Majority Firmly Bound to a Leading Candidate	7	100.0	—	162	16	—	—
Majority Preferring a Leading Candidate	6	79.2	12	40	75	27	—
Majority Committed to a Non-Leading Candidate	9	100.0	—	—	—	156	—
Majority Preferences Undecided or Unknown	32	0.4	3½	—	—	3	735½
Total (1,230 delegate votes)	54	38.2	15½	202	91	186	735½

[a] For sources, details by states, and explanatory comments, see Appendix A, Table 8.
[b] Computed by summing for each group of delegations the largest blocs of committed or preferring votes in each delegation and determining the percentage they constituted of the total number of delegate votes in the group. The authors are indebted to Professor Harold Guetzkow for suggesting "the index of candidate agreement" as the designation for this statistical measure.

to Averell Harriman. More than half of the delegates found themselves in the thirty-two delegations where there was no substantial evidence of commitment or firm preference at the time of selection.

By the time the convention opened Harriman had announced as a candidate and had acquired the nearly solid support of the previously uncommitted New York delegation; he also had the solid support of the District of Columbia delegation, and scattered votes elsewhere. Other candidates had gained strength and the number of favorite sons had increased. The tally two days before the convention was as follows, according to the Associated Press:

Stevenson	41½
Kefauver	257½
Russell	161½
Harriman	112½
Others	277
Uncommitted, in Dispute or Unknown	380
	1,230

With this distribution of voting strength, most of the delegations found themselves debating the choice of candidate at length throughout the early days of the convention. Sentiment for Adlai Stevenson gathered rapidly in the previously uncommitted delegations; he polled 273 votes on the first ballot. Russell polled 268 votes on the first ballot and was still polling 261½ on the third. Kefauver reached a maximum of 362½ votes on the second ballot and was holding 279½ at the end of the third ballot after losing the others to Stevenson. Most of the strength previously committed to Harriman and the other lesser candidates switched to Stevenson on the third ballot, giving him a near majority which was then made overt.

How did the delegations that voted for Stevenson reach their decision? A considerable amount of descriptive information is available in the 1952 study.[17] The probability seems to be that, aside from the hard-core support for Kefauver and Russell, Stevenson was an acceptable second or third choice for almost all the other delegations,

[17] David, Moos, and Goldman, op. cit., Vol. 1, Chap. 4, and the state chapters in the other four volumes.

whatever their preliminary commitments. Many of the middle-of-the-road delegations were willing to take Stevenson as their first choice at any time if assured that he was in fact available and would make an active campaign.

President Truman's influence was a factor after Vice President Alben W. Barkley withdrew, but the swing to Stevenson was well along before Truman made his final position clear. The leadership of the liberal-labor bloc, although previously inclined to support Kefauver, reached the conclusion along the way that he could not be nominated and that neither could Harriman; whereupon Stevenson became the only satisfactory remaining choice from their point of view. Harriman became aware before the balloting that he might find it desirable to concede after one or two ballots; New York leaders were already having difficulty in holding the delegation for him. Delegation leaders in the uncommitted delegations assessed top-leadership attitudes, rank-and-file

sentiment, and their own perceptions of the candidates—and drifted steadily toward Stevenson as they expressed their views in delegation meetings. Individual delegates by the hundreds made their own assessments. The result was a gathering consensus that showed little evidence of dictation or overwhelming influence from any single power center.

The Republican pattern of delegation commitment at the time of selection in 1952, as shown in Table 15.3, was remarkably different from the Democratic. Among the fifty-three delegations, thirty-eight had commitments to one or the other of the two leading candidates. In thirteen of these cases the commitment extended uniformly to the entire delegation. In most of the other cases the committed majorities were lopsided, as reflected in the high average indices of candidate agreement. Three delegations were committed to favorite sons: Governor Earl Warren of California, former Governor Harold E. Stassen of Minnesota,

TABLE 15.3. COMMITMENT AND CANDIDATE AGREEMENT OF REPUBLICAN DELEGATIONS OF 1952 WHEN SELECTED[a]

Status of Delegations by Majority Commitment	Number of Delegations	Average Index of Candidate Agreement[b]	Apparent Distribution of Voting Strength When Selected, Number			
			Eisenhower	Taft	Others	Undecided or Unknown
Majority Firmly Bound to a Leading Candidate	7	93.4	33	98	6	—
Majority Preferring a Leading Candidate	31	85.3	338	295	2	44
Majority Committed to a Non-Leading Candidate	3	96.7	4	—	118	—
Majority Divided Between Leading Candidates	2	38.0	10	16	4	12
Majority Preferences Undecided or Unknown	10	9.3	16	20	2	188
Total (1,206 delegates)	53	71.5	401	429	132	244

[a] For sources, details by states, and explanatory comments, see Appendix A, Table 9.
[b] Computed by summing the largest blocs of committed or preferring votes in each delegation and determining the percentage they constituted of the total number of delegates in the group.

and Governor Theodore Roosevelt Mc-Keldin of Maryland.

By the time the convention met, nearly a hundred of the delegates were involved in seating contests.[18] After the convention had acted on these contests, the changes in the distribution of apparent voting strength were as tabulated below.[19]

The balance of power in the Taft-Eisenhower conflict thus rested mainly with the uncommitted and favorite son delegations, although the small groups of uncommitted delegates in other delegations were also the object of an intense struggle. Pennsylvania and Michigan were the largest of the uncommitted delegations. Their chairmen—Gover-

	Total	Eisenhower	Taft	Other	Undecided or Unknown
Uncontested	1,110	406	458	131	115
Contested					
As Temporarily Seated	96	21	72	0	3
As Finally Seated	96	64	27	1	4
Totals					
As Temporarily Seated	1,206	427	530	131	118
As Finally Seated	1,206	470	485	132	119
Commitments When Selected of Those Finally Seated (Table 15.3)	1,206	401	429	132	244

The New Jersey delegation (38 votes) moved from an undecided position to one strongly favoring Eisenhower between the time of selection and the opening of the convention; Eisenhower's other gains during the period consisted of a few votes each in scattered delegations. The seating contests were settled favorably to Eisenhower with the help of the delegations supporting the minor candidates and a majority of the undecided delegates. This outcome was obviously a major blow to the Taft candidacy, though he was still leading in committed delegate strength when the seating contests had been settled.[20]

nor John S. Fine and National Committeeman Arthur Summerfield—withheld commitment until final delegation caucuses before the balloting and urged their delegates to do likewise. Both delegations had meetings with the candidates and both deliberated at length.

Among the three favorite son delegations, the Maryland delegates were released by Governor McKeldin on the first day of the convention, when he was invited to place General Eisenhower's name in nomination. Most of the Minnesota delegates who were committed to Stassen were long-time personal supporters, but several developed an early preference for Eisenhower; the entire delegation became increasingly anxious to join the Eisenhower band wagon as the convention days went by. On the morning of the balloting Stassen released several delegates who wished to move at once and authorized the others to shift at the end of the first ballot if Eisenhower should receive as many as 580 votes. The California delegation, pursuing a strategy that depended on a convention stalemate, stayed solidly with

[18] In most cases it was apparent when the contesting delegates were selected that these seating contests would be taken to the convention. The data of Table 15.3 relate in all cases to the delegations as finally seated.

[19] All figures relating to commitment on the eve of the convention are based on the Associated Press tally of that time, recapitulated by delegations on the basis of action on the contests. See David, Moos, and Goldman, *op. cit.*, Vol. 1, p. 54.

[20] For a comment by Senator Taft on the contests, see Appendix F; for the general outlines of the development, see David, Moos, and Goldman, *op. cit.*, Vol. 1, Chap. 3.

Warren until the end. Tabulated below is the vote in the four critical delegations at the end of the first ballot and before the rest of the Minnesota delegation shifted to complete the Eisenhower majority.[21]

Delegations	Eisen-hower	Taft	Stassen	Mac-Arthur
Pennsylvania	53	15	—	2
Michigan	35	11	—	—
Maryland	16	8	—	—
Minnesota	9	—	19	—
	113	34	19	2

In both conventions of 1952, the delegates were frequently polled in delegation caucuses during the early days of the conventions to ascertain their current intentions. Such polls were taken on the initiative of members of the delegations and were in no way binding. Delegates wished to know where their fellow delegates stood, and sometimes moved to find out before the leaders were ready for even a preliminary crystallization of sentiment. Every such poll, once taken, necessarily influenced the delegates who were still undecided.

For delegates who arrive at the convention with no definite mandate, the process of reaching a decision has long been in question. How many are in a position to act independently and in good faith as representatives of their constituencies? And how many are subject to undue influence?

There were various known instances in 1952 where the possibilities existed for what might be considered undue influence. The Arkansas and Georgia Democratic delegations were almost completely controlled by their respective governors, but there were also indications that the governors might be acting mainly as channels for the conveyance of popular mandates. Governor Fine of Pennsylvania was credited with controlling from fifteen to thirty delegates in a delegation that included a number of state government patronage appointees. Governor Thomas E. Dewey of New York was reported on several occasions as engaging in tactics that some delegates found oppressive. County leaders from metropolitan areas seemed highly influential in a number of delegations.

The impression remains, however, that while all the delegates were subject to many influences, for the most part the pressures from one direction were offset by those from another. Most of the uncommitted delegates apparently in the end had to make their own decisions in terms of their own perceptions of the candidates and of the situation, often influenced by majority sentiment in their delegations.

There were no reported deals involving whole delegations at either convention in 1952—a fact that can be variously attributed to the high-mindedness of the candidates, to a possibly rising level of political ethics in both parties, and, in the Democratic party, to the disappearance of the two thirds rule. Twenty years earlier, the two thirds rule was a basic element in generating the "deal" by which the California and Texas delegations were transferred to Governor Franklin D. Roosevelt and in return Speaker John N. Garner was nominated for Vice President. Even in that historic instance, however, the deal was almost stopped by opposition within the Texas delegation, which reportedly went along by the narrow vote of 54 to 51.[22]

The unit rule was in effect for twenty delegations at the Democratic convention of 1952. Many of these delegations would have been solid even without the rule, but in other cases the rule affected the vote. The net effect was apparently a minor increase in the Stevenson vote, but at a time when his nomination was already assured. In 1956

---

[21] For fuller accounts of what went on in the four delegations, see *ibid.*, Vol. 2, pp. 243-45, 272-75; Vol. 4, pp. 49-54, 175-79.

[22] Many delegates were reportedly absent when the vote was taken, and the vote itself indicates that many fractional-vote delegates were counted in the meeting as having a full vote, since the delegation held only 46 votes in the convention. The reported vote of 54 to 51 appears in most of the standard sources.

the unit rule apparently favored the nomination of Senator John F. Kennedy in the vice-presidential contest; he was defeated nonetheless.[23]

Platform Provisions

Platform provisions are frequently hard fought in the resolutions committee of the convention, but only rarely come to a roll call vote on the convention floor. Republican conventions have had no floor fight on a platform issue since 1932. The debate on civil rights proposals and the two roll calls on that subject were a major feature of the Democratic convention of 1948, but no platform issues were debated or separately voted on in 1952 or 1956.[24]

In the absence of prospective floor action, most individual delegates are not compelled to take a stand on platform provisions except to the minor extent involved in a perfunctory approval of a platform already agreed elsewhere. Platform issues may sometimes be discussed in delegation caucuses in connection with the original selection of members to serve on the resolutions committee, at other times when those members report, and particularly if there is a possibility of bringing a minority report to the convention floor for action. As a rule, when a delegation has a position that will be at issue in the platform decisions, its strategy and tactics are fully discussed prior to the convention—often at the state convention of the party.

In recent years the Democrats seem to have had more discussions of platform questions than the Republicans, since the Democrats have had more delegates with controversial proposals to urge upon the convention. The situation in the Republican party was undoubtedly somewhat different during the period when the La Follette Progressives were repeatedly raising platform issues in Republican conventions.

Relationships of State and National Party Organizations

On a few occasions delegations have come to the conventions with specific instructions for dealing with issues of relationship between the state and national parties. Instances would include the reapportionment changes at the Republican convention of 1916, the revocation of the two thirds rule at the Democratic convention of 1936, and the approval of the Mitchell Committee report on state party obligations to the national party at the Democratic convention of 1956.[25]

On some other occasions a delegation has arrived with a proposal that led to change in internal party relationships, although there had been no widespread preparation among the other delegations. The restricted credentials under which the Mississippi delegation came prepared to take part in the 1948 Democratic convention, while serving notice that it might not support either the party's platform or nominees, formed one such example. The delegation was seated nonetheless, although it later bolted, and thus was established a precedent of considerable importance in southern preparations for the 1952 convention.[26] Another example was the proposal by the Wisconsin Republican delegation of 1952 that led to the expansion of the national committee to include the state party chairmen in Republican states.[27]

In both 1952 conventions, however, a series of issues involving relationships between state and national party organizations arose somewhat spontaneously from the nature of the situation, for which most of the delegations were unprepared. In the Republican convention these issues began with the so-called Fair Play proposal to limit the voting rights of contested delegations seated on the temporary roll. The televised hearings of contests before the credentials com-

---

[23] See Chapter 9.
[24] In 1952 the Georgia and Mississippi delegations requested that their votes be recorded "No" when the platform was adopted.

[25] See Chapters 8, 9, 11.
[26] David, Moos, and Goldman, *op. cit.*, Vol. 1, pp. 101-06.
[27] *Ibid.*, Vol. 1, 88-90.

mittee of the convention followed, greatly sharpening the issues in the seating contests. Finally, the permanent rules were amended in order to reduce the hazards to the national party arising from the weakness of its affiliates in the South.[28] The delegations supporting Taft or Eisenhower tended to judge these issues mainly in terms of their candidates' interests. The other delegations devoted considerable time to reviewing the arguments, and in the end their votes were decisive. Their conclusions seem to have been based to a large extent on an independent assessment of the issues as they appeared at the time.

In the Democratic convention the restricted credentials of several southern delegations and the prospect of another party bolt like that of 1948 led to what was known as the "loyalty oath" resolution, followed by questions on the extent to which the Virginia, South Carolina, and Louisiana delegations would be permitted to take further part in the convention. These issues led to prolonged and sometimes angry debate. The internal deliberations of most delegations were frequently confused and often referred more to expediency than to principle, but nonetheless led to important voting decisions.[29] In the end the southern delegations remained in the convention. The extent to which any disciplinary effect was actually achieved remains a question, but the party nominees were accepted as such in every state, unlike the situation in 1948. There was little overt bolting by dissident state party organizations, although many of the southern leaders individually supported Eisenhower in the campaign, and he carried several southern states.

The crises over the relationships between state and national party organizations that arose in both conventions of 1952 were not unrelated. They arose in one way or another from the disjointed relationships be-

tween the organizations in the southern states and their respective national party organizations, and the issues were sharpened by the intensely competitive position of the parties in that year.

Variations in Delegation Behavior

Delegations obviously differ in their voting behavior, as shown by a century and a quarter of roll call voting records, but they also differ in many other types of behavior. Some of these peculiarities are the planned result of conscious decisions; others are evidently the unplanned product of factors that may never reach the level of conscious perception. Any attempt at analysis can only be exploratory in the present state of knowledge, but it may be worthwhile to review some of the factors and to illustrate the kinds of activity that seem to result.[30]

Commitment has been treated so far as an absolute, meaning that a delegate has a binding mandate or a firm intention to vote for a specific candidate. This usage is relevant and adequate so far as much voting analysis is concerned, and will be retained, but it does not cover all delegate behavior prior to the voting nor the changes that occur if the first ballot fails to settle the outcome. Commitment to candidates actually varies over a considerable range of intensity and emotional involvement.[31]

[30] The factors that seem most worthy of attention can be identified as commitment, candidate agreement, factional division, cohesiveness, internal leadership, and ideology. The activities that result, aside from voting, involve collective, segmented, and atomized patterns of behavior; activity vs. passivity in giving support and taking initiative; the use or non-use of accredited representatives; and no doubt other dimensions of variant activity in the formulation and pursuit of delegation goals.
[31] Readers who are familiar with the state chapters of the 1952 study will be aware of the wide differences in the reliability of the data on commitment at the time of selection. In some instances commitment was clear as a matter of public record through the operations of a primary election or a resolution in a state party convention. In other cases it had to be inferred from information reported in the press or from the structure of the situation as a whole. The data assembled in Appendix A, Tables 8 and 9, may therefore involve some

[28] Ibid., Vol. 1, Chap. 3.
[29] Ibid., Vol. 1, Chap. 4; see also state chapters, particularly for the southern states most involved and for Michigan, Minnesota, Illinois, Pennsylvania, and New York.

Candidate agreement has likewise been treated as a definite arithmetical ratio; namely the proportion of the members of a delegation who are "committed" to the delegation's leading choice. This usage permits the easy computation of an index of candidate agreement, which is in turn useful in making gross comparisons between delegations, categories of delegations, and even whole conventions. In effect, the index is a measure of the amount of agreement on a candidate within delegations at a given point in the development, which is in turn relevant to the amount of agreement that can be expected in the voting. But where the personal commitment of the delegates varies widely in intensity, or rests upon differing bases of factional connection, leadership, or ideology, a lack of agreement may be apparent in other forms of behavior even when there is an appearance of agreement in first-ballot voting.

Factional divisions are found in most delegations unless they have been elected in a state-wide contest on a winner-take-all basis, or unless the state party organization has attained such unity and internal discipline as have rarely been seen in recent years.[32] Divergent factions frequently support the same candidates or other objectives, but still maintain separate identities that obviously affect the possibilities for a common strategy. On the other hand, groups otherwise agreed may divide on candidates and thus develop internal factional cleavages for the time being.

Cohesiveness is used here as meaning the attraction of members to their delegations as organized groups. For some purposes, cohesiveness is the converse of factional division within delegations, but it is also related to intensity of shared commitment and to degrees of uniformity in agreement

on a candidate. Cohesiveness may be the temporary product of these other factors. It may also exist independently and have a prior origin in the long-term associations of high status individuals in the state party organization. In this case, the uniformities of commitment and candidate agreement and the absence of factional division may be the result of cohesiveness rather than the other way around.

The effectiveness of delegation leadership depends closely on the factional patterns, on how firmly the state party leaders are established in the delegation, and in fact on whether the state party itself is cohesive and effectively led. One of the most important findings of the 1952 study was that a disintegration of state party leadership had occurred rather widely throughout the country in both parties. New sources of leadership were coming forward in many states, but had not yet solidified their positions nor achieved much recognition.

Differences of ideology have always been important in comparative state politics, and become apparent in the study of delegations. The civil rights issues result in differing positions on an important scale of ideological differences. Delegations with strong organized labor representation presumably have some ideological characteristics not common to other delegations, while an opposite type may be found in those representing conservative business interests. The delegations that come out of regular party organizations probably reflect a rather specialized ideology—that is, their attitudes toward the necessities of political activity are quite different from those of the average citizen. Insurgent delegations usually represent some divergent type of special ideology.

All of these differences are undoubtedly reflected in the patterns of delegation decisions. A close reading of any detailed account of delegation activity will reveal signs of their influence. For the present, however, it may suffice to offer a few illustrations from the experience of 1952 showing how various special influences affected the activities of delegations.

erroneous attributions of commitment. On the other hand, among the delegates whose preferences were recorded as undecided or unknown, undoubtedly there were some whose probable preferences were rather clearly understood by other individuals who occupied strategic positions in the selection process.
[32] See Chapter 9.

The Ohio Republican delegation of 1952 would have been noteworthy in any political convention. Made up of high-status and active Ohio Republicans, all devoted to Senator Taft, it had been put together with meticulous care in preparation for a supreme effort. Factional divergences had been suppressed and a Stassen challenge thrown back in selecting and electing the delegation. It was completely committed, internally cohesive, strongly led, highly experienced, and energetically active. Every delegate had an assignment, and it was reported that every delegate carried through his assignment on a day-and-night schedule up to the final nominating vote.[33] Ohio has a well-developed tradition on how to operate in a political convention, and the lore of the conventions was apparent in delegation operations.[34]

The New Hampshire and Vermont Republican delegations were completely committed and internally cohesive, but not very active. Both delegations, one elected in a primary, the other in a state convention, were solidly for Eisenhower. The members who were assigned to the convention committees worked hard, and Governor Sherman Adams of New Hampshire became an Eisenhower floor manager. But most members of the two delegations were given no specific assignments, and, because they were so completely committed, were not subject to the heavy pressures that were applied to uncommitted groups.[35]

The California Democratic delegation, committed to Senator Kefauver in a winner-take-all conflict, showed agreement in its voting but not in its other behavior, was

ineffectively led, and was somewhat divergent in ideology from most of the convention. The individual delegates had enthusiasm and energy, but the delegation lacked cohesiveness. It was not a team when organized and the party dissidents of which it was largely composed did not have time to become one.

The delegation held frequent caucuses, but there was much confusion, misinformation, and lack of information. . . . Decisions were made largely in terms of what Kefauver would presumably desire rather than the delegation's own judgment. . . . Political inexperience and lack of convention "know how" marked the delegation as amateurish. But in terms of its mandate from the Democratic voters of California, the delegation made every effort to carry out that mandate.[36]

The Oregon Democratic delegation was a group that was firmly committed, but factionally divided and inactive. There had been no organized slate-making; the "organization faction" won six places, the "ADA faction" also won six, with all twelve pledged by state law to Senator Kefauver because he had won the preference poll feature of the primary. Some individual delegates were busy and worked hard.

But the most prominent feature of the Oregon delegation was the lack of unity and cooperation among its members. The delegation as a group had no central purpose, and as a group it was not effective.[37]

The Michigan Republican delegation in 1952 was the outstanding example of one that successfully maintained an uncommitted position until a late stage in a close race, was highly cohesive in organizing for delegation activity even though somewhat divided in its voting, was led with great skill, and was continuously active as a delegation on its own initiative. Prior to the convention Chairman Arthur Summerfield went to unusual lengths to maintain equally cordial relations with Senator Taft, General Eisenhower, and General Douglas MacArthur. At the convention the delega-

---

[33] David, Moos, and Goldman, op. cit., Vol. 4, Chap. 2.
[34] As an example of Ohio traditional wisdom, see the secret memorandum by Senator Charles W. F. Dick of Ohio in preparation for the Republican convention of 1912 (published with the permission of the Senator's heirs by Thomas E. Felt), "Organizing a National Convention: A Lesson from Senator Dick," Ohio Historical Quarterly, Vol. 67 (Jan. 1958) pp. 50-62.
[35] J. Duane Squires, "A Delegate's View of the Republican Convention of 1952," New England Social Studies Bulletin, Vol. 10 (March 1953), pp. 4-10; David, Moos, and Goldman, op. cit., Vol. 2, p. 61.

[36] David, Moos, and Goldman, op. cit., Vol. 5, p. 243.
[37] Ibid., Vol. 5, p. 210.

tion caucused frequently, debated its way through the issues, and carried out its decisions effectively. It was especially notable for its "Delegate Contact Operation," a systematic plan for collecting and compiling information twice daily on the activities and plans of other delegations, in order to provide guidance for its own decisions. Alternate delegates and Michigan visitors provided the manpower for this operation.[38]

The New Jersey Democratic delegation was uncommitted but cohesive as a group. It was relatively well led, but generally inactive in its behavior at the 1952 convention. The delegation

entrained for Chicago unpledged, uninstructed, and unbossed for the first time in over twenty years; and its ultimate choice among the presidential candidates was almost as uncertain actually as it was legally.[39]

Some of the most effective Stevenson supporters were among the delegates, and the group became one of the first large undecided delegations to give the bulk of its strength to Stevenson, while favoring Kefauver for Vice President. Cohesion and a definite point of view were indicated by its unanimous vote against the seating of Virginia. But even after deciding for Stevenson, it did little to provide organized support on his behalf in dealing with other delegations.

There were many delegations at the 1952 Democratic convention that were uncommitted, relatively uncohesive, and somewhat passive in their attitudes. The Washington state delegation was one example. It was produced in a state convention, yet seemed to have none of the supposedly typical features of a machine-made product. An absence of strong leadership and almost no liaison with the national convention management were its conspicuous characteristics. The result was

a voting pattern in which each individual voted as his "best judgment" directed, and the delegation possessed too little "cohesion" to exert much effect upon the course of the nominating process at Chicago.[40]

When delegations are uncommitted to a particular candidate, they may still be deeply interested in finding one who can win and whose objectives for the party will be similar to their own. This was the basic attitude of most of the Democratic delegations from pivotal states in 1952. Southern Democratic delegations, on the other hand, were in some cases much less concerned with finding a candidate who could win than one who would accept their point of view on states rights and civil rights. A few other delegations had specialized concerns that took priority over nominating goals. Delegations from the western states, for example, in most cases had a special interest in public land and public power questions; the Alaska and Hawaii delegations were mainly interested in statehood.

The delegates pledged to Senator Kefauver, a fighting candidate who was outspoken critical of party officials and party procedures, were undoubtedly the ones who brought the most hostile attitudes to the convention as an institution. Believing that they represented the "voice of the people" and that the nomination was in danger of being "stolen" by the "party bosses," the Kefauver delegations from several states developed something akin to a persecution complex.[41] Their minds were unprepared to take part effectively in a convention that regarded itself as having an entirely free field of choice and full responsibility for naming the candidates.

Candidate Agreement in Delegation Voting

Even when the presidential nomination is sharply contested and many ballots are required, some delegations vote as solid units throughout. Others, even when divided, usually show lopsided majorities for one candidate or another. Since these phenomena are reflected in the roll call voting records of the conventions, they lend them-

[38] *Ibid.*, Vol. 4, p. 51.
[39] *Ibid.*, Vol. 2, p. 208.
[40] *Ibid.*, Vol. 5, p. 180.

[41] *Ibid.*, Vol. 3, pp. 180-81 (Tennessee delegation); Vol. 4, p. 275 (South Dakota Delegation); Vol. 5, p. 243 (California delegation).

selves to statistical analysis and interpretation for both parties over long periods of time. The present section brings together the salient data on candidate agreement in delegation voting since 1896, and then suggests some of the possible interpretations of the long-term fluctuations.

The Long-Term Record

Indications of delegation candidate agreement in voting on presidential nominations in each of the contested conventions since 1896 are given for the Democratic and Republican parties in Table 15.4. These data reflect enough variation to be confusing at first sight, but some noteworthy regularities can be found on careful inspection.

It is apparent throughout the table that, in a divided convention, the division is usually more *between* delegations than *within* them. Candidate agreement within the convention is measured, as shown in the table, by the average of the leading votes in all roll calls divided by total convention vote.[42] The tendencies of each delegation to take on identity as an organized group, to respond to the same mandates and pressures from home, and to provide a protective environment for uncommitted delegates who decide to go along with the delegation majority, are all reflected in the substantial differences between average indexes of candidate agreement within delegations and

the counterpart averages for whole conventions.[43]

Despite the tendencies toward candidate agreement in delegation voting, when the average vote for the leading candidate in the convention as a whole is below the 50 per cent mark on repeated balloting, some division is usually apparent in a majority of the delegations. The data for the Republican conventions in Table 15.4 show this relationship without exception; the data for Democratic conventions do so except for 1896 and 1912.

On the other hand, there is a clear tendency for the average index of delegation candidate agreement to be higher when the convention is giving the leader a larger vote —i.e., where one candidate looks like a winner, the delegations tend to show less internal division.[44]

The statements just made apply in varying degrees to both parties, but the substantial differences between the parties are the most obvious features of the tables. Solid delegation voting has been much more prevalent in Democratic conventions than Republican, along with somewhat higher average indexes of delegation candidate agreement.

At least three different contributing rea-

---

[42] It is mathematically impossible for the average index of candidate agreement in delegations to fall below the counterpart average for the convention as a whole. When the spread between the two averages constitutes more than half the distance between the convention average and 100 per cent, it can be said that the division in the convention is more between delegations than within them. This condition occurred in all of the conventions reported in Table 15.4 except the following: Democratic, 1908, 1940; Republican, 1916, 1940. In the contested Republican conventions of 1928-1956, however, the average index of delegation candidate agreement was only slightly above the mid point between the average per cent of leader vote and 100 per cent: 78.1 vs. 76.0 In multi-ballot conventions the average per cent for the leader is an average of the leader percentages of each ballot; and the figure is thus comparable with the average index of candidate agreement within delegations throughout the same balloting.

[43] Similar forces apparently operate in the state delegations of each party in Congress, despite the greater apparent independence of the individual member. See David B. Truman, "The State Delegations and the Structure of Party Voting in the United States House of Representatives," *American Political Science Review*, Vol. 50 (Dec. 1956), pp. 1023-45.

[44] The amplitude of fluctuation is not the same and in rare instances there is even difference in the direction of movement; nevertheless, the correlation between delegation candidate agreement and convention vote for the leader has been computed as .69 for the Democratic conventions in Table 15.4, and .91 for the Republican conventions. When the data for both parties are combined, the correlation coefficient is computed as .76 with a standard error of .13, which means that the coefficient is well within the range of statistical significance. The coefficients for the parties separately are also statistically significant, despite the smaller numbers of cases on which they are individually based. Thus all three figures tend to substantiate the positive relationship: delegations tend to be more internally agreed on a single candidate as the percentage of the leader's vote increases.

TABLE 15.4. INDICATIONS OF DELEGATION CANDIDATE AGREEMENT, CONTESTED
CONVENTIONS, 1896-1956, EXCLUDING NON-STATE DELEGATIONS[a]

Convention Year and Nominee	Proportion of 48 Delegations Voting Solidly		Average Index of Candidate Agreement[b]	Average Per Cent of Convention Vote for Leading Candidate[c]
	Number	Per Cent		
DEMOCRATIC				
1896 (Bryan)	26	54.2%	88.4	37.4%
1904 (Parker)	37	77.1	89.1	65.8
1908 (Bryan)	34	70.8	91.4	88.7
1912 (Wilson)	24	50.0	89.0	46.1
1920 (Cox)	14	29.2	77.6	40.3
1924 (Davis)	16	33.3	84.9	39.8
1928 (Smith)	39	81.2	95.7	66.8
1932 (Roosevelt)	39	81.2	95.2	58.5
1940 (Roosevelt)	35	72.9	93.0	86.0
1948 (Truman)	41	85.4	97.5	75.1
1952 (Stevenson)	18	37.5	81.4	35.7
1956 (Stevenson)	26	54.2	89.9	66.0
Average per Convention				
1896–1924	25.2	52.5%	86.7	53.0%
1928–1956	33.0	68.7	92.1	64.7
REPUBLICAN				
1896 (McKinley)	28	58.3%	91.0	69.0%
1908 (Taft)	36	75.0	95.8	71.6
1912 (Taft)	20	41.7	88.1	52.1
1916 (Hughes)	12	25.0	64.1	29.4
1920 (Harding)	11	22.9	76.7	32.4
1928 (Hoover)	30	62.5	90.3	76.9
1940 (Willkie)	4	8.3	69.1	38.9
1948 (Dewey)	10	20.8	72.3	43.4
1952 (Eisenhower)	10	20.8	80.5	48.9
Average per Convention				
1896–1924	21.4	44.6%	83.1	50.9%
1928–1956	13.5	28.1	78.1	52.0

[a] Contested conventions are defined as those in which the winner received less than 90 per cent of the vote at the end of the roll call on the first ballot; see Chapter 16. Non-state delegations are those of the "non-state areas" of 1956 as defined throughout this book; the table includes the delegations of Oklahoma, Arizona, and New Mexico for the early years when these states were still territories.

[b] *The average index of candidate agreement* is calculated as follows: In a one-ballot convention, the index of candidate agreement for a delegation represents the proportion of total delegation strength given to the candidate most favored by that delegation. For example, in 1948, North Carolina gave 19 votes to Russell and 13 to Truman. The Russell vote, being the larger, was divided by the total delegation strength of 32, to give the resulting index of 59.4. In all one-ballot conventions, the vote used was that of the roll call before vote switching.

In multi-ballot conventions, the largest blocs of votes for each roll call are summed and an average obtained, which average is then divided by the total delegation vote. In the case of the conventions with many ballots, a sampling procedure was used to select the ballots for study, on the assumption that the sample would sufficiently reflect the patterns of delegation voting behavior. Convention and regional averages in Tables 15.4 and 15.6 were obtained by averaging the percentages for individual state delegations, treating each delegation as a unit and disregarding the factor of size.

[c] *The average per cent of convention vote for the leading candidate* is provided as an indicator of the amount of division in the convention as a whole during the course of the voting. The averages were computed for one-ballot conventions as follows: total vote received by the winner on the roll call before vote shifting, divided by total convention voting strength.

For multi-ballot conventions, the averages were computed as follows: average of the total votes received by the leader on each roll call, divided by total convention voting strength. For example, in the Democratic convention of 1952, Kefauver led on the first ballot with 340 votes and on the second with 362½. Stevenson led on the third ballot with 613 votes (before Utah shifted 4½ votes). The three totals— 340, 362½, and 613—produce an average total of 438.5, which, when divided by the convention total of 1,230, resulted in the average percentage vote of 35.7 for leading candidate. Except for sampling procedure in the case of long-ballot conventions, all statistics are based upon all votes cast during roll calls, but not including band-wagon vote shifts after last ballot. In some cases the last ballot is excluded from all computations on grounds that it occurred after a clear band-wagon shift.

sons can be noted for the differences between the parties in the candidate agreement and solidity of delegations. First is the two thirds rule, applicable in Democratic conventions until 1936. Usually it contributed to a higher average vote for the leader in the convention as a whole, although during the periods of stalemate in some long-balloting conventions the opposite may have been the case. The deals and other negotiations required for accumulating a two thirds vote, moreover, presumably made for delegation unity even where the unit rule was not in effect. The unit rule itself was a second factor; it applied to as many as fourteen state Democratic delegations in 1956, seventeen in 1952, and probably more in earlier years—quite possibly to all of the twenty-six state delegations that voted solidly in 1896.[45] The third reason for the difference is the greater Republican emphasis upon the right of individual congressional districts to select and instruct their own delegates, features of Republican practice that frequently encourage splinter voting within delegations.[46]

[45] See Chapter 9. The rule also applied to several non-state delegations in 1952 and probably other years.

[46] See Chapter 9. These three factors—two thirds rule, unit rule, and congressional district autonomy—are presumably related to the finding that the correlation between average delegation candidate agreement and convention vote for leader was only .69 in Democratic conventions, .91 in Republican. Although these correlations themselves are statistically significant, their difference would not usually be considered so, since the possibility that it might occur by chance is nearly 1 in 5. But in this case, the technical test for statistical significance serves mainly to remind the student of the small number of cases involved and the complexity of the other factors that were also at work to hold down the precision with which any correlation could become completely evident. For example, the chronic sectional split in the Republican party between Northeast and Middle West probably tended to increase candidate agreement within delegations from each section, as the split within the Democratic party between North and South has done in some instances in recent years. On the other hand, long multi-ballot conventions probably encourage delegation splitting as new coalitions are formed, tested, and reformed. The greater incidence of such conventions in the Democratic party would thus tend to reduce its average index of candidate agreement in delegations relative to the Republican.

The Democratic party has provided only four

The differences between the parties are further apparent in Table 15.5, which shows the relative numbers of state delegations that have voted solidly for one candidate from beginning to end of a convention. Among the Democrats, no state delegation has failed to vote solidly in at least three of the twelve contested conventions since 1896, Florida being the state at the low end of the scale in this respect, with Maine, Vermont, and Pennsylvania ranking next as the most frequently split delegations. At the other end of the scale, the Democratic delegations that voted solidly throughout ten or more of the twelve conventions were Mississippi and Texas, twelve, Kansas, eleven, and Delaware, Georgia, Kentucky, Louisiana, Idaho, and Utah, ten. All of these except Utah were unit-rule states in recent conventions and presumably throughout the period, as Utah may have been earlier. It should be remembered, however, that even a unit-rule delegation can report a split vote when sufficiently divided—the rule does not operate when there is less than a majority for any single candidate.

cases of contested presidential nominations since the repeal of the two thirds rule. This is not a sufficient number of cases to permit computation of a correlation coefficient that would ordinarily be considered significant, but it is nonetheless interesting to find that when the correlation is computed for these conventions, it proves to be .91—exactly the same as that for the total Republican experience. This seems to suggest that the two thirds rule may have been the most important factor producing interparty differences in delegation candidate agreement.

It also happens that there were five cases in each party where the average percentage of vote for the leader was under 50 per cent, four of which occurred in the Democratic party while the two thirds rule was in effect. For these cases, the correlation between convention vote for the leader and the average index of delegation candidate agreement is .60 for the Democratic cases, .69 for the Republican. This finding also suggests that despite the unit rule there is little difference between the parties in delegation candidate agreement once the effect of the two thirds rule has been minimized.

The higher incidence of completely solid delegation votes in the Democratic party is obvious, but many Republican delegations failed to be solid by only one or two votes. The unit rule is probably much more important in raising the number of apparently solid delegations than in causing any great increase in voting agreement, which may already be very high for other reasons.

TABLE 15.5. FREQUENCY OF STATE DELEGATIONS VOTING SOLIDLY THROUGHOUT
PRESIDENTIAL NOMINATING BALLOTING IN ONE OR MORE
CONTESTED CONVENTIONS, 1896-1956

Number of Conventions in Which Voted Solidly	Number of State Delegations Voting Solidly as Indicated	
	Democratic[a]	Republican[b]
0	0	1
1	0	6
2	0	8
3	1	11 (median)
4	3	8
5	8	10
6	6	4
7	10 (median)	0
8	7	0
9	4	0
10	6	—
11	1	—
12	2	—
	48	48

[a] Twelve conventions.
[b] Nine conventions.

TABLE 15.6. DELEGATION SOLIDITY AND CANDIDATE AGREEMENT IN
CONTESTED CONVENTIONS, BY REGIONS, 1896-1956

Area	Democratic				Republican			
	Solid Delegations, Per Cent[a]		Average Index of Candidate Agreement		Solid Delegations, Per Cent[a]		Average Index of Candidate Agreement	
	1896–1924	1928–1956	1896–1924	1928–1956	1896–1924	1928–1956	1896–1924	1928–1956
Northeast	35%	63%	81.8	90.1	43%	29%	83.4	81.6
Middle West	53	61	85.7	91.9	50	21	88.1	77.4
South	67	74	90.4	94.0	28	27	77.1	76.7
West	55	76	89.0	94.6	60	36	85.1	76.6
48 States	52	68	86.7	92.6	45	28	83.1	78.1

[a] This means the per cent of all delegations that voted solidly for the same candidate throughout a ngle national convention, regardless of the number of roll call votes involved at that convention.

On the Republican side of Table 15.5 one delegation, Illinois, was split in its voting at all of the nine contested conventions. Six were split in all but one: New York, New Jersey, Pennsylvania, Virginia, North Carolina, and Georgia. In many of these cases the split consisted of no more than three or four deviant delegates in a delegation otherwise united. This is a hazard to which the largest delegations seem more subject than those of smaller size. District voting in primaries was also a factor in all of the non-southern states of the group. At the other end of the scale the four states whose Republican delegations were most frequently solid were Vermont, Arizona, Oregon, and California. The first two are small and the other two have long been subject to primary laws producing delegations instructed on a state-wide basis.

The data have been reorganized in Table 15.6 to reflect such regional differences as may exist. Among the Democrats the tendency to solid voting and candidate agreement has increased in all areas, while among the Republicans it has decreased. The table shows clearly the Democratic disunity in the Northeast before 1924.

Interpretations of Long-Term Fluctuations

The data on candidate agreement have been presented both for what they show directly and for whatever light they throw on long-term tendencies within the parties. Some conclusions can be drawn from the data with much more assurance than others; all the possible conclusions concerning long-term tendencies seem distinctly speculative. They involve an assessment of factors that cannot be measured and that seem to work at times in opposite directions.

The data in the tables previously presented have been arranged wherever possible to permit the easy comparison of the period 1896-1924 with that of 1928-1956. These periods not only are of equal length, but also coincide with turning points of some importance in the evolution of the party system. In the present case, howeve[r] the comparisons are hampered by tw[o] major difficulties.

One difficulty is the variable timing an[d] effect among the states of such changes [as] the installation of the various types of pr[i]maries, the fluctuating use of the primari[es] by the candidates, the disappearance of th[e] two thirds rule in the Democratic party i[n] 1936, and the more gradual erosion of th[e] unit rule. These factors collectively a[re] probably responsible in part for the fa[ct] that split conventions do not lead to sp[lit] delegations as often in the Democratic par[ty] as in the Republican.

The other difficulty in making perio[dic] comparisons within the parties results fro[m] the fact that average convention split in th[e] Republican party was about the same i[n] both periods, while in the Democratic par[ty] it has been much less since 1924. As Tab[le] 15.4 shows, leading candidates averaged 5[0] per cent of the vote in the contested Dem[o]cratic conventions of 1896-1924, 65 per cen[t] in those of 1928-1956. The first period in[-] cluded the long-balloting conventions [of] 1912, 1920, and 1924, whereas the secon[d] included the short balloting and heavy m[a]jorities of 1928, 1940, and 1948. Presumab[ly] the lopsided convention majorities of th[e] later period were the principal cause of th[e] increase in the proportion of solid deleg[a]tions and the higher average index of cand[i]date agreement.

These difficulties can be avoided (whi[le] incurring others) by looking to the Dem[o]cratic conventions of 1896 and 1952 as po[s]sibly more representative of their respecti[ve] periods than any set of averages, since i[n] this way the effect of abnormally lopsid[e] majorities is eliminated. Each of these wa[s] a relatively short multi-ballot conventio[n] that ended by choosing a first-time nomine[e,] William Jennings Bryan in one case, Adl[ai] E. Stevenson in the other. The average p[er] cent of convention vote for the leading ca[n]didate was about the same in the two case[s.] The number of solid delegations decline[d] from 26 to 18, while the average index [of] delegation candidate agreement declin[ed] from 88.4 to 81.4—differences that have at least a family resemblance to the Republican figures in Table 15.4, in which the period averages shifted down from 21.4 to 13.5 in the number of solid delegations and from 83.1 to 78.1 in the average index of delegation candidate agreement.

The data just cited are the basis for the conclusion, such as it is, that there has been a long-term decline in average candidate agreement in Republican delegations, and possibly also in Democratic, coupled with a decline in the proportion of delegations that vote solidly under any given set of circumstances. The conclusion is of little value in developing expectations for the future, however, unless the forces producing such a long-term change can be better understood.

A long-term decline in agreement within delegations and a corresponding increase in split voting might be interpreted as an indication of a long-term decline in state-wide boss control. Split voting does not conclusively establish the absence of boss control, but it points in that direction, unless other evidence suggests a different conclusion in specific instances. In fact, the amount of split voting that has gone on for sixty years suggests the possibility that state-wide boss control was never as widespread as many people have thought, although there may have been plenty of bossism at city and county levels and many working agreements among the local bosses on how to operate at the state-wide level.

Another theory equally compatible with the data might start with the premise that cohesiveness within a state party organization is usually voluntary and depends to some extent on the intensity with which the state party is pursuing its various goals. This kind of voluntary cohesiveness might show itself in two ways, so far as voting on the choice of a presidential candidate is concerned: united voting when the issue is seen as involving a substantial threat to state party goals; divided voting when no threat is apparent and the alternatives are almost equally acceptable.

State parties that are coming up from a minority position to one of potential majority strength are usually highly tolerant of certain kinds of dissent within their own ranks; they have to be in order to grow. It is the party organizations in such situations that have been progressively abandoning the unit rule in the Democratic party. More generally, they seem to have been responsible for much of the increase in split voting within Democratic delegations in recent years.

Factional infighting on a winner-take-all basis, on the other hand, with its consequences for unity in delegation voting, seems to be a characteristic of parties that have become accustomed to a position of dominance in their states, where the major political decisions are made within the dominant party rather than through a two-party contest. This type of factional conflict has existed in the Democratic party in several southern states over long periods of time. In the northern states where the Republican party was dominant for a generation or more, a winner-take-all type of factionalism seems to have been rather common. In some of these states, through a form of cultural lag, it has continued to be characteristic of Republican party organizations that are gravely threatened or already outnumbered by a growing Democratic party.

Factors of the kind just described can be traced most easily in the experience of particular states, though they become apparent at times in considerable numbers of states. A more pervasive type of influence, however, can be identified as the decline of sectionalism in politics and the rising importance of nationalizing forces that cut across all states. When convention voting divides along sectional lines, most of the delegations from each section vote with high agreement. Conversely, nationalizing forces might be expected to cause divisions within many delegations similar to the division in the convention as a whole.

In both parties the convention contests from 1896 to 1912 were closely tied to regional economic problems, such as free silver and the protective tariff. In the Democratic party sectionalism has persisted in convention voting whenever the problems of civil rights have been at issue. The vote by which President Truman was renominated in 1948 was one of the most sectional votes ever observed—the convention as a whole was split three to one along sectional lines, and the average index of delegation candidate agreement was 97.5, with forty-one delegations voting solidly pro or con—both the highest figures in the record.

Recent Republican contests have been relatively much more free of sectional issues and much more dominated by overriding national concerns, such as the conduct of international relations and the fundamental relations between the federal government and its component parts. Divisions within the Republican party have become nationwide. Even in areas where one political philosophy has been dominant within the party, the minority has often been sufficiently strong and vociferous to achieve some recognition. The results were apparent in the divided delegation voting of the Republican conventions of 1940, 1948, and 1952. Only four delegations stayed solid throughout the voting that nominated Wendell Willkie, and only ten during Dewey's second nomination and Eisenhower's first.

Similar tendencies were probably present in the split voting of most of the non-southern delegations at the Democratic conventions of 1952 and 1956. For the long-term future, they may be among the most important factors affecting the general patterns of convention voting.

Voting Behavior as End Product

Delegates act as members of delegations in all the ways that have been previously indicated, but when they vote they have an inescapable personal responsibility. This is true even under the unit rule, since the vote must be counted in the delegation before the rule can be applied.

Viewed as an end product, the voting behavior of the conventions is a summation of the voting decisions of the individual delegates. The votes that come before the nominating votes are in some respects those in which the delegates have the greatest freedom of personal judgment, but they are also a part of the process of conflict and maneuver by which the alternatives have been limited before the time comes to vote on the nominations. If the nomination is at all in doubt, the vote on it is the final act of fulfillment in which each individual delegate justifies his existence as a member of the convention.

Convention voting behavior has not been previously subjected to the kind of research and analysis that has been attempted for certain other types of voting. In studies of presidential and congressional elections, for example, quantities of empirical data have been collected through interview methods, as well as by the use of election returns, and a considerable body of explanatory theory has grown up.[47] Similar techniques have not been applied to delegate voting in conventions, and no similar body of theory can be said to exist.

Many of the materials from which a theory might be constructed, however, have been assembled in the previous discussions of mandating, nominating campaigns, characteristics of delegates, and decision-making within delegations. Throughout those discussions there has been frequent reference to the importance of commitment when selected as a factor. The first step in a systematic approach to the analysis of delegate voting behavior would therefore seem to be a clarification of the relationships between commitment when selected and the composition of the final nominating vote.

Prior Commitment and Voting Behavior

The data previously used in Tables 15.2 and 15.3, can be reassembled against the final nominating votes of 1952 at the point where the outcome became visible and assured:

[47] See Chapter 12.

he critical moment when the transfer of a ew votes would complete a majority. The results of this retabulation of the data are shown in Tables 15.7 and 15.8.[48]

The sources from which the major Democratic candidates of 1952 derived their final votes from delegates who were orginally committed to favorite sons and minor candidates. Kefauver gained and held only 88 votes from sources other than those originally committed. The major portion of Russell's vote came from delegates who

TABLE 15.7. SOURCES OF THE FINAL VOTE BEFORE VOTE SHIFTING,
DEMOCRATIC NATIONAL CONVENTION, 1952[a]

Categories of Delegates in Terms of Commitment When Selected and Voting Behavior on Final Ballot Before Shifting	Number of Delegations with Majority of Delegates in Category	Final Vote for Leading Candidates			
		Stevenson	Kefauver	Russell	Others
. Stayed with Original Commitment:					
a. Firmly Bound to Final Choice	7	—	$151\frac{1}{2}$	16	26[b]
b. Known to Prefer Final Choice	6	$15\frac{1}{2}$	40	75	—
. Changed from Original Commitment:					
a. Changed from a Non-Leading Candidate	8	115	20	1	24[c]
b. Changed from Kefauver	1	7[d]	—	$2\frac{1}{2}$[d]	1[d]
. Uncommitted When Selected:					
a. Undecided or Preference Unknown	32	$475\frac{1}{2}$	68	167	25
Total (1,230 delegate votes)	54	613	$279\frac{1}{2}$	$261\frac{1}{2}$	76[e]

[a] Based on Appendix A, Table 8, and David, Moos, and Goldman, *Presidential Nominating Politics in 952* (1954), Vol. 1, pp. 152-53, Table 6, except that in the present retabulation the Utah vote is included s given on the third ballot before the remainder of the delegation was switched to complete Stevenson's 1ajority. (*Ibid.*, p. 153, footnote c.)
Any reader who seeks to reconcile the present table with Table 15.2 will probably need to refer to the ources in detail for a full tracing of the movement of votes, but in some cases the reconciliation will ecome evident by taking cross totals of the lines in Table 15.7, adjusting as indicated for relevant nformation in the footnotes that follow, and comparing with the appropriate column totals in Table 5.2. For example, the total of the votes in line 2a of the present table is 160, to which should be added he 26 votes for "Others" in line 1a to obtain the 186 votes at the bottom of the "Others" column in Table 15.2. (Tables 8 and 9 of Appendix A and Tables 15.2, 15.3, 15.7, and 15.8 were primarily the work f Paul T. David.)
[b] Entire Kentucky delegation for Alben W. Barkley as originally committed.
[c] Entire Oklahoma delegation switched to Barkley after being released by Senator Robert S. Kerr.
[d] One Oregon vote from Kefauver to Stevenson, the others from Maryland.
[e] In addition to the 50 votes for Barkley accounted for in footnotes b and c, includes $17\frac{1}{2}$ other arkley votes, 3 votes for Senator Paul H. Douglas, 3 for Oscar Ewing, $\frac{1}{2}$ for Governor Paul A. Dever, nd 2 reported as "not voting."

onvention votes are shown in Table 15.7. tevenson's vote came predominantly from he delegates who were undecided at the ime of their selection, with another 115

[48] Although the information as to commitment is nreliable in border-line cases, it is considered adeuate for the purpose of the comparisons shown in 1ese tables, which have been constructed primarily ● illustrate a system of analysis that is helpful in arifying what happened in 1952, and that may be ven more useful on future occasions.

were not specifically committed when selected, but who undoubtedly preferred a candidate who would champion the factional interests of the South.

Most of the favorite son delegates were released along the way or departed on their own initiative. Kentucky stayed with Barkley until the end; the Kerr delegates from Oklahoma eventually moved to Barkley.

Delegates with votes numbering $308\frac{1}{2}$

had been selected with some sort of original commitment to Stevenson, Kefauver, or Russell.[49] Of these delegates, all but those with 10½ votes, as shown in item 2b, stayed with their original commitment on the final ballot. At the critical point in the voting, Stevenson derived only 7 of his 613 votes from changers who had originally been committed to Kefauver.

favorite son delegates previously committe to McKeldin and some of those committe to Stassen, as previously noted. All the at tempts to pressure or persuade the delegate originally committed to one or the other o the leaders produced only 14 delegates wh can be identified as changers: 6 who lef Eisenhower and 8 who left Taft. These wer located in 7 uninstructed delegations; non

TABLE 15.8. SOURCES OF THE FINAL VOTE BEFORE VOTE SHIFTING, REPUBLICAN NATIONAL CONVENTION, 1952[a]

Categories of Delegates in Terms of Commitment When Selected and Voting Behavior on Final Ballot Before Shifting	Number of Dele- gations with Ma- jority of Delegates in Category	Final Vote for Leading Candidates		
		Eisenhower	Taft	Others
1. Stayed With Original Commitment:				
a. Firmly Bound to Final Choice	9	37	98	95[b]
b. Known to Prefer Final Choice	31	358	323	8
2. Changed from Original Commitment:				
a. Changed from a Non-Leading Candidate	1	21	8	—
b. Changed from Eisenhower	—	—	4[c]	2[d]
c. Changed from Taft	—	6[e]	—	2[f]
3. Uncommitted When Selected:				
a. Undecided or Preference Unknown	10	173	67	4
Total (1,206 delegates)	51[g]	595	500	111[h]

[a] Based on Appendix A, Table 9, and David, Moos, and Goldman, op. cit., Vol. 1, pp. 95-97, Table which records the final vote before vote shifting.
[b] Includes 70 California Warren delegates, 19 Minnesota Stassen delegates, 6 Wisconsin Warren dele gates.
[c] 1 Rhode Island, 3 Missouri.
[d] 1 Rhode Island to Warren, 1 Oklahoma to MacArthur.
[e] 2 South Carolina, 3 Arkansas, 1 Alaska.
[f] 1 West Virginia to MacArthur, 1 Arkansas to MacArthur.
[g] Two other delegations originally contained majorities divided between leading candidates, as noted i Table 15.3.
[h] In addition to the delegates accounted for in footnote b, includes 5 other Warren delegates, 1 Stasse delegate, and 10 MacArthur delegates.

At the Republican convention of 1952 the issue was mainly determined, as shown in Table 15.8, by the 244 delegates whose preferences were apparently undecided or unknown at the time of their selection. Of these, 173 voted for Eisenhower. He also gained over 40 votes in the settlement of seating contests, together with most of the

[49] The figure is the sum of the first three columns of votes in Table 15.2.

had been formally pledged, although thei preferences were believed to be known a the time of selection.

Voting Motivations and Their Analysis

Similar analyses must be made for othe conventions, probably using data that wi not exist unless collected for the purpos on future occasions, before the generalizations that seem most obvious can be adequately tested. The present tabulations for 1952 suggest, however, that the motivations of the changers who depart from a leading candidate, contrary to their original commitment, will not be very important in any comprehensive analysis. The small number of such changers is the most striking feature of the data reviewed here. Commitments to major candidates that existed when the delegates were selected were usually honored; the decisive votes were found among the delegates whose commitments were to a minor candidate and even more among those who were uncommitted.

Among the delegates committed to leading candidates, however, those who stayed to the end with the losers—Kefauver, Russell, and Taft—take on special interest. Here there are questions about the bases of the original commitment, ranging from the statutory to the psychological, as discussed in earlier chapters. But assuming an original commitment to a candidate who runs strongly enough to place among the leading contestants, why did these delegates stay with him as long as they did after the probability of defeat had become all too apparent?

In most cases, the delegates in these die-hard groups were evidently much more interested in defending a cause to which they had become attached than they were in finding a place on the winning side. The calculations of self-interest in a hoped-for victory may have influenced their original decision, but the months of conflict that had followed had the effect in most cases of hardening their commitment into a matter of principle. They had assimilated a set of dogmas and had acquired the characteristics of the "true believer."

The favorite son delegations offer another opportunity for analysis, but their motivations (where the favorite son was only that and nothing more) do not appear to have differed very much from those of the delegates who were originally uncommitted—members of these delegations split in about the same ratios. The available data from the 1952 study suggest that in most of these cases the influence of the favorite son himself was not much stronger nor greatly different from that of other types of leaders in an uncommitted delegation. Where there was an observable difference, it was mainly in the timing of the switch. Delegates in a favorite son delegation were usually reluctant to depart from their instructions until released, but were also prepared to apply pressure to secure a release when necessary.

The die-hard delegations that stayed with their favorite sons even after their cause seemed hopeless were decidedly different in their behavior. At the Republican convention the California Warren delegation was pursuing a strategy that apparently had the effect of holding the Warren delegates from Wisconsin and attracting a Rhode Island delegate. Whether this strategy was fully rational is a good question, especially if it is assumed that the leaders of the delegation were accurately informed in advance of the first ballot of the prospective outcome. But the delegation had little to lose by waiting through one ballot, and it had a certain pride in maintaining the dignity and status of its candidate. In the quite different case of the Kentucky delegation at the Democratic convention, state pride and loyalty to their candidate after a public rebuff were doubtless of major importance.

In strong contrast in both conventions were the delegates and delegations who had successfully avoided commitment at the time of selection and who were thereafter in a position to maintain their freedom of action. Such delegates were much more willing to discuss their possible candidate preferences after they had been chosen than before. This was a characteristic type of behavior in those states where it is traditional that a delegate should be selected on his own merits or on the basis of party loyalty rather than because of his association with some national candidate.

Delegates selected under such circumstances sometimes made known their intentions soon after they were chosen. Others consulted and deliberated, sometimes announcing a conclusion before leaving home for the convention, but often not, especially where entire delegations had decided to maintain an uncommitted posture until after they arrived at the convention. From the points of view of emotional involvement and rational choice, these delegates were in a better position to judge the merits of the candidates and their electoral prospects than were those who had been committed at the time of their selection, but they were also more exposed to a variety of band-wagon considerations and to the pressures and irrationalities of a confusing environment.

Presumably these delegates may have responded to some extent to the same complex of factors by which the rank-and-file party voter is moved when he is forced to contemplate a choice in a primary election. As noted in Chapters 12 and 13 these factors need much further clarification in terms of the psychology of the individual voter's decision. But uncommitted delegates occupy a far more complex position. They are subjected to an intensive cross fire of pressures from the time of selection to the time of final decision. In some cases, as noted earlier, these pressures are so heavy and so much from one direction that they take on aspects of coercion. Even where this is not the case and where the countervailing pressures merely serve to increase the delegate's store of information, he remains subject to his basic relationships with his constituency and his delegation. Many delegates are also officeholders with obligations of public leadership—and, by the same token, publics of their own to which to respond.

The uncommitted delegates face a choice that involves the clarification of their own personal preferences. It equally involves their estimates of constituency reaction and the interpretations placed on the situation by other members of their delegations.[50] A delegate who must face other members of his delegation day after day, who must vote

on the record publicly if required, and who must return home to face constituents who are familiar with his record, is obviously in a position far different from that of the ordinary voter with a secret ballot in a closed polling booth. This is so much the case that the mechanisms of choice for an involved member of a delegation may indeed differ widely from those of the ordinary uninvolved voter.

Voting as the Final Test of Representativeness

Concepts of representation and of representativeness were examined in Chapter 10 for their applications in the mandating of delegates. The concept of representation, however, involves much more than the issues of mandating. Representation is a complex condition that can be said to exist when the characteristics and acts of the presumed representative are in accord with the desires, expressed and unexpressed, of his constituency.[51]

The "acts" of the delegate may be "expressive acts," as when making a speech to his delegation or to the convention, or "acts of power," as when voting. What the party constituent presumably wants is a delegate with satisfactory characteristics who expresses satisfactory views and votes in a satisfactory way. The delegate becomes fully representative of his party constituents to the extent that he meets all three tests. Representative institutions are usually thought to have reached a high level of effectiveness when it can be surmised that the members of an assembly are thus representative of a majority of their constituents most of the time.

The characteristics of the delegates were examined in Chapter 14. Some conclusions were reached at the end of that chapter on the extent to which the characteristics of the delegates have recently been in accord

[50] See also the discussion of the processes of alliance in Chapter 17.

[51] This statement is somewhat paraphrased from the formulation in Harold F. Gosnell, *Democracy—The Threshold of Freedom* (1948), p. 130.

with the desires of their party constituents. For the second test of representativeness, the expressive acts of the delegates, it is necessary to look mainly at what goes on in delegation meetings, for which any form of public record is seldom available. Where important debate occurs directly on the floor of the conventions, however, a few delegates become conspicuous for their "expressive acts," sometimes with important consequences in terms of their standing with their constituencies.

Few delegates were able to take part directly in the emotion-laden debates of the 1952 conventions without affecting their own political futures.[52] The probability is that most of the delegates who took a direct part in the open meetings did manage to express views and take positions that met with the approval of most of their party constituents. The Tennessee Democratic delegation, however, was probably unrepresentative of a majority of its constituents in aligning itself so clearly with the northern liberal wing of the Democratic party, where their candidate, Senator Estes Kefauver, had found most of his support.

In the roll call votes of the conventions, unlike debate, all delegates participate.

Every delegation records its vote, with the possibility that the delegation may be polled to put individual delegate votes on record. Voting is the final test of the representativeness of the delegates; and for the 1952 conventions, at least, a considerable amount of information is available that bears on this point.

Important preliminary votes at the Republican convention of 1952 came on the so-called Fair Play resolution and on the seating of the Georgia delegation; at the Democratic on the so-called "loyalty pledge" and, later, on the seating of the Virginia delegation. All of these votes were on matters where public opinion was unformed and the delegates largely uninformed when the conventions met. Public and delegates alike learned something from the informal discussions, credentials hearings, and formal debate that preceded the votes. Were the delegates representing their party constituencies accurately when they voted?

Militant supporters of Taft and Eisenhower had no trouble in deciding how to vote. They followed a clear line of candidate interests. The delegates who were undecided as between Taft and Eisenhower almost all voted for the Fair Play amendment. In doing so, many of them undoubtedly believed that they were making a long-overdue reform. Four days later a similar change was made in the permanent rules without discussion and with no opposition. The vote on the Georgia seating was closer and less influenced by public opinion. The Georgia case was highly confused in terms of law, evidence, and applicable party principles, but the story as reported from the state seemed on the whole to favor the decision reached by the convention.

The Moody resolution and Virginia seating votes in the Democratic convention of 1952 involved issues that were a by-product of acute factional conflict within the party. Here again the militants on each side had no trouble in deciding how to vote, and in their voting they may have been representative of constituencies of the same stripe. The moderates had more difficulty, and so did their constituencies, in following the

[52] Examples could be multiplied, but a few may suffice. (For further details of the episodes mentioned below, see David, Moos, and Goldman, op. cit., Vol. 1, and relevant state chapters in the other four volumes.) Washington State Senator Donald W. Eastvold made his political reputation in the debate on the seating of the Georgia delegation at the Republican convention. He was later rewarded by the voters of his state in the race for the state attorney generalship. Governor John S. Battle received a hero's welcome when he returned to Richmond after his impassioned and successful defense of the Virginia delegation at the Democratic national convention. Governor Gordon Browning of Tennessee did much to bring on his primary election defeat in the Tennessee gubernatorial contest when he supported the Moody resolution at Chicago and later cast the entire vote of the Tennessee delegation against the seating of Virginia. Orville L. Freeman of Minnesota, then a gubernatorial candidate in Minnesota but young and politically unknown outside of his own state, became conspicuous at the Democratic convention for the courage with which he repeatedly challenged the rulings of Chairman Sam Rayburn at a time when better-known leaders were unprepared to act. Freeman was defeated in the gubernatorial race of 1952 but was successful in the elections of 1954, 1956, and 1958.

argument. The same caution and desire for party harmony that eventually led a majority of the delegates—including 132 who changed their votes—to vote for the Virginia seating were doubtless factors with interested members of the party electorate.

On the nominating votes, evidence is available both from the public opinion polls and from the presidential primaries for the appraisal of representativeness. Eisenhower was leading Taft by an average of 44 to 35 per cent in popularity among Republican voters on the last three Gallup Polls before the convention. Among independent voters, his lead over Taft was estimated at 50 to 18 per cent on July 1, 1952.[53] These voters had no direct claim to representation at the Republican convention, but their views were part of the evidence to be considered by delegates who had a mandate to seek a winner.

The returns in the presidential primaries were more difficult to interpret but reflected a special kind of reality not to be found in public opinion polls: the votes of registered voters who were prepared to go to the polls and vote a Republican primary ballot. To some extent, also, the primaries reflected differences in constituency opinion from district to district and state to state.

Eisenhower had won substantial victories over Taft in New Hampshire and Massachusetts, where the issue was clearly drawn and hard fought; in New Jersey, where Taft declined to campaign after Governor Alfred E. Driscoll had declared for Eisenhower; and in Oregon, where Taft strategists had succeeded in keeping Taft's name off the ballot but where delegates committed to him were decisively defeated. Eisenhower also made a remarkable showing through a write-in vote in Minnesota; and this early "moral victory" led to a rash of write-in campaigns elsewhere in states that permitted them.

Taft was a clear victor in an organized write-in contest with Eisenhower in Nebraska. He also won a straightforward contest with Eisenhower in South Dakota by a

[53] *Washington Post*, July 2, 1952.

very narrow margin, and was a plurality winner in Wisconsin, where Eisenhower declined to run. Overwhelming votes for Taft in Ohio, Illinois, and West Virginia, where Eisenhower was not on the ballot, were offset by the equally lopsided vote for Eisenhower in Pennsylvania, where Taft was not on the ballot.

The general pattern suggests that Eisenhower was the preferred choice of a majority of the voters who normally vote Republican in most eastern, western, and southern states, while Taft was the preference of the Republican voters in several middle-western states. If this is correct, the vote by which Eisenhower was eventually nominated—614, to 500 for Taft—was remarkably representative, although low by comparison with the number of states and districts where Eisenhower was the probable majority preference.

The contest for the Democratic nomination was eventually conducted mainly among Kefauver, Russell, and Stevenson, but others were prominent before the convention. In Gallup Polls of Democratic voters prior to the Democratic national convention of 1952, comparative percentage standings were reported as follows:

June 8, Kefauver, 45 per cent; Barkley, 17; Stevenson, 10; Russell, 10; Harriman, 5; Others and Undecided, 13.

July 13, Kefauver, 45 per cent; Barkley, 18; Stevenson, 12; Russell, 10; Harriman, 5; Others and Undecided, 10.[54]

Kefauver had entered almost all of the available presidential primaries, and won all of those where he had no active opponent of presidential candidate stature. He was pitted directly against such an opponent in four cases: Truman in New Hamp-

[54] No statistical information is available on the structure of second-choice preferences, but in terms of the factional alignments of the candidates it can be supposed that Stevenson was a highly acceptable second choice to most of the Barkley and Harriman voters. For most of the Russell voters he was clearly more acceptable than Kefauver, and for most of the Kefauver voters he was probably much more acceptable than Russell. The case well illustrates the need for specific information about the distribution of second-choice preferences when no candidate is preferred as a first choice by a majority.

shire (March), Kerr in Nebraska (April), Russell in Florida (May), and Harriman in the District of Columbia (June). Kefauver defeated Truman and Kerr, but was himself defeated by Russell and Harriman.

Stevenson withheld consent for any entering of his name in presidential primaries, and his preconvention fame was largely due to indications that he would be the choice of the party leaders if he consented to run. He was a close second to Kefauver in the "trial heat" public opinion polls where they were pitted individually against Taft or Eisenhower, even though he was much less well known as a public figure at the time.[55] Stevenson's speech at the opening of the convention, widely seen and heard on television, made a strong impression on Democrats throughout the country as well as on the delegates, and as the convention proceeded he came into increasing prominence as the most likely nominee.

Stevenson was undoubtedly regarded favorably as a second-choice candidate by many voters who were opposed to each other in their first-choice preferences. He may have replaced Kefauver as the plurality preference in the national party electorate by the time the voting came at the convention. The evidence to prove the case either way is lacking, but soon after the convention it was reported that 54 per cent of the voters who considered themselves Democrats were pleased by the nomination.[56] Stevenson was clearly weaker than Eisenhower in terms of rank-and-file support within his own party, as the election proved; but it seems probable that he was the strongest candidate available to the Democrats when the nominating decision was made.[57]

Successful representation is not merely a matter of carrying out decisions that have already been reached by a constituency. It also involves sensitivity by the representatives in giving effect to the unexpressed desires of the constituents in a way that they will later approve. In some ways the Stevenson nomination was a triumph for the convention as a representative institution, since it seemingly found the one choice who was most generally acceptable throughout the party's national constituency—and did so in a situation where a national primary would probably have found the same choice unavailable. Unlike a primary election, the nominating convention can enlarge the field of choice to include new alternatives when necessary; the 1952 experience was a striking illustration of its capability in this regard.

In both parties the conventions of 1952 were operating in situations of strain much greater than usual. In each case, fears were widely expressed in advance that an unrepresentative choice would be reached—yet in the end the over-all performance of the conventions was excellent. Undoubtedly both parties were on their good behavior because of the prospects for a close race. Whatever the reasons, there seems to be no reliable basis for attacking any major vote in either convention as unrepresentative. This was an achievement of some significance, particularly by contrast with conditions that were typical as recently as the period from 1896 to 1924.

[55] Chapter 13, Tables 13.6 and 13.9.
[56] Chapter 13, Table 13.8.
[57] A dissenting view has been argued by Alfred de Grazia in *The Western Public—1952 and Beyond* (1954), pp. 33-36, on the basis of interviews with Democrats who were dissatisfied with the Stevenson candidacy and who would have preferred Kefauver. But this evidence seems to have been weighed with little or no effort to estimate the number, location, and effectiveness of the Democrats who would have been dissatisfied if Kefauver had been nominated:

the Dixiecrats, who might thereby have carried South Carolina, Mississippi, Louisiana, and Kentucky for Eisenhower; the personal following of President Harry S. Truman, who had little reason to develop enthusiasm for a Kefauver candidacy; and the regular organization Democrats of the big-city machines, who likewise had little enthusiasm for a Kefauver candidacy, in view of his repeated attacks on them while seeking the nomination. A Kefauver nomination might have forestalled some of the defections from the Democratic party that occurred in 1952, but undoubtedly would have provoked alternative defections in other quarters.
The same body of interview data is analyzed with somewhat different conclusions by Angus Campbell, Gerald Gurin, and Warren E. Miller, *The Voter Decides* (1954), pp. 52-64.

16

Power and Effectiveness in Convention Voting

THE PRESENT CHAPTER is concerned primarily with power and effectiveness as displayed in the records of convention voting, particularly in the final votes on presidential nominations in conventions since 1896. When votes are applied in support of the winner at the end of a period of conflict, there is a concrete display of effectiveness in the use of power. In Chapter 17 a broader type of analysis is concerned with the patterns of events that preceded the nominating ballots and the strategies that went into them. Chapter 18 deals with the electoral consequences of convention action. First of all, however, it is necessary to take some note of the voting procedures that are used, and the frequency with which voting occurs. All three chapters rely heavily on the voting records as contained in the official proceedings, but the present chapter is most directly based on undisputed factual materials. As in other fields of voting study, it seems desirable to become rather fully acquainted with the actual voting returns before attempting the more speculative types of analysis and interpretation.

Voting Procedures of the Conventions

Two methods of voting are used predominantly by the conventions: voice votes —taking the "Ayes" and the "Noes" at the call of the chairman—and roll call votes. A standing vote was formerly taken occasionally as a substitute for a voice vote, and

in the Democratic party was used until 1952 in determining whether a roll call vote was required.

Voice and Standing Votes

In both parties the rules have provided almost from the beginning that nominations shall be made by roll call vote, but any other business may be settled by voice vote unless there is objection. Ease and speed of action make voice votes the generally preferred method, as attested by the statistics of Table 16.1.

Most voice votes are unanimous or nearly so—an obvious consequence of the fact that most of the motions so put to a vote are either routine or else present formal actions on which the interested parties have already agreed. Such motions include the usually routine business in the approval of convention officers, appointment of committees, election of a new national committee composed of nominees provided by state party action, and the courtesy resolutions of appreciation with which every convention closes.

Business that is not only important but highly controversial is sometimes decided by a voice vote with no apparent objection. After a century of conflict, the two thirds rule was rescinded in the Democratic convention of 1936 by a mere voice vote; the supporters of the two thirds rule had sought a system of bonus votes as a substitute with some success, but in any event were already sufficiently informed on how much they were outnumbered.[1] In 1952 the Taft forces recognized defeat and moved to settle the Texas contest by a voice vote—after a debate that occupies eighteen pages in the printed record.[2] The previous roll call vote on the Georgia contest was accepted as conclusive.

The opposite also occurs: demands, sometimes successful, for a roll call vote, when those demanding the vote are well aware that it will go against them. Eight roll call votes were held on credential mat-

sheer animosity among the factions present. Rules have been developed to limit roll call voting, partly to expedite the work of the conventions in general, but mainly because of such obstructionist tactics as the above. These rules also undoubtedly increase the operative authority of the convention officers.

Voice votes may be taken even when the division in the convention is close and the outcome uncertain; it is then that they become most questionable as a method of

TABLE 16.1. FREQUENCY OF TYPE OF VOTE, NATIONAL PARTY CONVENTIONS, 1864-1956[a]

(excluding nominating votes)

Time Period	Number of Conventions	Voice Votes[b]		Roll Call Votes	
		Total Number	Average per Convention	Total Number	Average per Convention
DEMOCRATIC CONVENTIONS					
1864–1892	8	364	45.5	28	3.5
1896–1924	8	331	41.4	32	4.0
1928–1956	8	306	38.3	9	1.1
REPUBLICAN CONVENTIONS					
1864–1892	8	331	41.4	29	3.6
1896–1924	8	260	32.5	18	2.3
1928–1956	8	255	31.9	7	0.9

[a] Similar statistics for the period prior to 1864 have been omitted in view of the limitations of convention records during that period.
[b] Includes all standing votes, except those that were taken merely to determine whether the roll should be called.

ters alone during the Republican convention of 1880, despite the fact, which became steadily more obvious, that all would be decided in the same direction by approximately the same margin. An even more extreme case occurred in the unfinished Democratic convention of 1860 at Charleston, in which nearly every vote was taken by roll call, even though some were unanimous. Usually, a losing side that demands a roll call is seeking to put the vote on record for future reference; but, as the instances just cited illustrate, the demand may reflect

reaching a just decision. Several sources of error intrude. Even in a meeting much smaller than a national convention, voice votes are likely to leave an honest chairman in doubt when the division is closer than three to two. In the nominating conventions, spectator interference in the voting has frequently been indicated; chairmen have often threatened to clear the galleries and at times motions to that effect have been made from the floor, but instances in which this sanction was actually applied have been extremely rare.[3]

[1] See Chapters 8 and 9.
[2] RNC Proceedings, 1952, pp. 196-215.

[3] The Democratic convention of 1892 referred a resolution to the national committee to exclude provision for seating in the galleries from all future

Fractional votes and the presence of alternate delegates introduce further complications. In 1896 a Republican convention chairman permitted a standing vote in the face of strong protest that it would give undue weight to certain oversize delegations that had been seated on a split vote basis.[4] Similar difficulties can arise when using voice votes if a number of oversize delegations are present. The situation has occurred frequently in Democratic conventions, as noted in Chapter 9, yet voice votes are much used. Alternate delegates, usually seated in the back of the hall, are not supposed to join in voice votes, but they cannot easily be prevented from doing so, with results that may distort the vote.

The discretion of the chairman is a final and perhaps the principal source of error in the calling of close votes, although the appropriate exercise of the chairman's discretion in such matters may occasionally contribute to good order in the work of the convention. If the issue is minor and the vote divided, getting the issue settled is frequently more important than belaboring the point through a more tedious procedure. If the chair feels that a more precise form of voting is required, it is within his prerogative to ascertain whether there is demand for a roll call.[5] Usually, the chair rules without hesitation even when the voice vote is close, and calls for a further vote only on demand, if then.[6]

The rules for obtaining a roll call vote on issues other than nominating are intended to guard against the abuse of the chairman's authority; presumably they usually have that effect because of the precautionary restraint that they impose, even though they are not frequently used. In Republican conventions, after the original stabilization of procedures and until 1920, a roll call could be obtained if demanded by majorities of only two delegations—a provision that permitted the La Follette insurgents to obtain many roll calls during the period of their activity. In 1924 the rule was changed to require majorities in six delegations. A roll call was denied in 1928 because only five delegations requested it.

Democratic conventions until 1956 followed the rule of the House of Representatives and required a standing vote of 20 per cent of the delegates present to obtain a roll call vote. The rule was difficult to apply when the proportion desiring a vote was not much over 20 per cent, and, after some apparent abuse in 1952, it was amended in 1956 to require majorities in eight delegations. Even this provision leaves much to the discretion of the chairman, as became apparent in 1956 when delegations desiring a roll call on the civil rights issues of the platform were unable to obtain recognition.[7]

---

conventions; no action was taken by the committee. See DNC *Proceedings*, 1892, pp. 180-81.

At the Whig convention of 1848 the delegates are said to have gathered for the balloting behind closed doors and with spectators, including reporters, refused admittance. See Holman Hamilton, *Zachary Taylor*, Vol. 2: *Soldier in the White House* (1951) p. 91.

[4] RNC *Proceedings*, 1896, p. 43.

[5] On one occasion at the 1952 Democratic convention Chairman Sam Rayburn was able to discover that a roll call vote was demanded on an appeal from his earlier ruling in regard to the status of Virginia, whereupon the vote was taken, his ruling was reversed, and Virginia was seated. See Paul T. David, Malcolm Moos, and Ralph M. Goldman, *Presidential Nominating Politics in 1952* (1954), Vol. 1, pp. 141-47.

[6] At the Republican convention of 1904 an issue pertaining to the voting rights of the Hawaiian delegation came to a vote. The chairman, whose hearing was evidently unusually good, called the

vote as carried and was subsequently upheld on roll call by a vote of 495 to 490. See RNC *Proceedings*, 1904, pp. 129-32.

[7] It was apparent to observers who were present, including one of the present writers, that a considerable number of delegation standards were waving to signal their request for recognition. Members of some of these delegations, interviewed at the time, were under the impression that an agreement had been obtained among at least eight delegations to seek a roll call on a proposed amendment of the platform. But some of the leaders of these same delegations were in conference with the chairman at the rostrum, with results not made public. The chairman went ahead with the voice vote without making any statement on the parliamentary situation, leaving a residue of dissatisfaction on this and other rulings that led to the suggestion from some quarters that a different presiding officer should be chosen in 1960. In September and October 1959, Speaker Sam Rayburn himself indicated reluctance to serve again as convention chairman, and promised a statement before Congress met again.

Table 16.1 indicates that the number of roll call votes on non-nominating issues has declined sharply in recent years. As the conventions became larger and more cumbersome, the delays of roll call voting became more irksome; yet there has been no recent experimentation with any of the alternatives to the voice vote as a means of getting a more accurate vote without going all the way to a roll call.

Standing votes with an estimate or a count by appointed tellers are a frequent procedure in other large gatherings when faced with division on important issues. They could again be used effectively in the conventions if all delegates held the same voting rights and if the specific area occupied by the delegates were policed sufficiently to keep others out. However, the kind of teller vote used in the House of Representatives, in which the members on each side of the issue file rapidly between a pair of tellers for the count, does not seem likely to be practical in the conventions.

Written or printed ballots have apparently never been used and might require more preparation than is usually feasible when non-nominating issues come to decision. They might be practical when platform and other questions come out of committee with both majority and minority reports to formalize the alternatives in advance. Voting machines have been successfully used in state party conventions in Indiana, with 1,800 or more delegates present, and presumably could be used in the national conventions, at the cost of some major changes in convention procedure.[8] In 1956 the parties began to experiment for the first time with electrical scoreboards, by which a cumulative record of the vote could be displayed in the hall while a roll call vote was in process.

Pending some decisive improvement in their other voting procedures, the conventions will continue to find it necessary to use the roll call procedure even on undramatic questions whenever an accurate vote is essential in a divided situation. Meanwhile, the absence of a roll call cannot be accepted as assuring the validity of a voice vote in the conventions as recently conducted. The current procedures do not adequately protect the institutional integrity of the conventions.

Roll Call Votes

A roll call vote in the conventions of either party is taken by calling the roll of the states and the non-state areas that are represented, in response to which each chairman reports the vote of his delegation. The vote is on the record and appears in full in the verbatim record of the official proceedings. In the early conventions the states were called in a stipulated order, based partly on geographical location and partly on the order in which they had entered the Union. At the Republican convention of 1868, however, there was a controversy over whether Kansas should be called before West Virginia. Later Republican conventions changed to an alphabetical order of the states, and Democrats followed suit. Until recently the territories and other non-state areas were called last; in 1956 the Democrats included them in the general alphabetical order.

States that come early in the voting order are faced with the risk of commiting themselves before much evidence has appeared on how the vote will go. If they wish, they can pass and be called again at the end of the roll. Any delegation also may change its vote at the end of the roll up to the time when the final tally is announced.

In Republican conventions it has been established that the vote must reflect the votes of individual delegates as accurately as possible; Democratic conventions still permit the use of the unit rule when imposed by state party action on delegations elected in party meetings. In both parties a simple majority of those present and voting has always been deemed sufficient for a decision, except that a two thirds vote was required for nominations in Democratic conventions until 1936.[9]

[8] See description of Indiana system in Appendix E.

[9] See Chapter 9.

If any delegate rises to challenge the vote as reported by the delegation chairman, the delegation may be polled by calling the roll of the individual members. This has occurred frequently in the conventions of both parties, with attendant delays. In 1956 the Democratic convention adopted new rules under which the convention chairman may send a representative to the delegation to conduct the poll while the roll call proceeds with other states, unless an open poll in the hearing of the entire convention is demanded by one third of the members of the delegation.[10]

Voting by roll call is the most accurate procedure available to the conventions. Presumably it is reasonably accurate most of the time—at least sufficiently so to avoid error in the decision—since interested delegates and other observers can maintain their own tallies if they wish. The published proceedings attest, however, that the totals as tallied are frequently out of accord with the details of the vote as stenographically recorded.[11]

Committee Votes

Much of the preparatory work for the conventions is carried on in the national committees. Later, while the conventions are in session, much of the actual business is transacted in the committees on credentials, rules, and resolutions (platform). Voting in the national committees occurs by voice vote and by roll call, the latter procedure usually being used on any controversial issue of importance. Similar procedures are used in the convention committees, plus a frequent use of voting by show of hands; when committee action results in both majority and minority reports, members approving each report are usually recorded.

Voting by proxy occurs in the national committees, and on some occasions it has been indicated that considerable numbers of proxies were in the hands of the chairman. Little is known about what effect this practice has had on the committee decisions in recent years, but apparently it has not been a source of complaint.

A more serious difficulty in using committees to expedite convention action is that, in most of them, all the states have equal representation. Each state has two members in the national committee (but recently the state party chairmen of states voting Republican have been added to the Republican national committee), and the resolutions committee. In each other committee, representation is also equal, whether by one or two members. Under this system states with a majority of the votes in the convention can be outvoted in committee. It is true that the result can be overturned when it reaches the convention—but only at the cost of much trouble and delay. At the Republican convention of 1952, for instance, a committee vote of 30 to 21 on the Georgia seating question was reversed by the convention. The voting division by states was approximately the same in both instances, but the votes of the large delegations became fully effective only in the full convention.[12]

[10] Clarence Cannon, *Democratic Manual* (1956) p. 49.
According to the recollection of teller clerks present in 1956, the new rule was called into play on only two occasions. In one instance the delegation receded from its demand for a poll while the chairman's representative was on his way. In the other, the delegation agreed to let its previous report stand after a poll had been taken by the chairman's representative.
These recollections, and those of other eyewitnesses, suggest that the new rules had the effect for which they were intended—that of greatly reducing the number of frivolous demands for delegation polling in order to give each delegate his moment of publicity. (Information supplied by Democratic National Committee, Feb. 24, 1959.)
[11] Some of the difficulties in obtaining an accurate vote were noted in Chapter 9. Discrepancies in the votes as recorded are noted in the forthcoming book by Richard C. Bain, *Decisions and Voting Records of the National Party Conventions* (Brookings Institution).

[12] David, Moos, and Goldman, *op. cit.*, Vol. 1, pp. 77-84.
The decision to hold the Democratic convention of 1960 in Los Angeles was taken by a vote in the Democratic national committee; the losers contended that their states provided 65 per cent of the party's delegate and electoral college strength, although they

The Republican party has provided since 1928 for weighted voting by states in the national committee on one important matter: the infrequent occasions when it is necessary to fill a vacancy on the national party ticket occurring between the adjournment of the convention and the action of the electoral college after the election. (Such a contingency had last occurred in 1912, when James S. Sherman, the Republican vice-presidential nominee, died on October 30.) Each Republican convention, before adjourning, now adopts a resolution authorizing the national committee members from each state, in any such emergency, to cast the full vote to which the state was entitled at the convention.

In 1956 the Democratic convention adopted essentially the same provision.[13] (The Democratic party last faced the situation when Benjamin Fitzpatrick of Alabama declined the vice-presidential nomination in 1860, on which occasion the national committee nominated Herschel V. Johnson of Georgia unanimously by acclamation.[14])

No form of weighted voting has so far been adopted for any of the convention committees, but some action is clearly needed so that the conventions can more safely leave major portions of their work to the committees. The present tendency is to increase the work of the committees and to transact more of their work before the convention meets, thus shortening the convention sessions, reducing dullness, and making it easier for them to operate as a

campaign rally in facing the television cameras.

A simple alternative to weighted voting that seems readily feasible would be an increase of the representation of the larger state delegations on the committees. One specific proposal that has had some discussion would give each larger state a committee member in each committee for every 12 votes that it has in the full convention, while leaving to every state a minimum of one or two members, as the case may be. Under this plan the platform committees would be increased to about 140 members and the other committees to about 120— groups of substantial size but not much larger than the existing platform committees, which already have more than 100 members. The committees would then be substantially more representative, and the large states could assign seats to their major regions, many of which have distinctive political identities.[15]

Nominating Votes as Measures of Power and Effectiveness

The preliminary votes in national committee, convention committees, and full convention involve power and effectiveness in the use of power, but they must be assessed largely in terms of their relationship

---

[15] This proposal was mentioned in Charles A. H. Thomson's *Television and Presidential Politics* (1956), p. 90. At the request of staff members of both national committees, it was worked out in full detail in letters from Paul T. David to the two national committee chairmen, Feb. 6, 1956, but was not acted upon at the 1956 conventions. The letters presenting the proposal noted that the manpower requirements of the expanded committees could be somewhat offset by curtailing the number of major committees. The committees on permanent organization have in recent years merely reported arrangements already developed in the national committees. Credentials and rules committees have both been important, but they overlap so much that they could be combined. Most of the smaller states would probably have little objection to a reduction in the number of committees, since they seldom provide full representation on all of them at present. Even when they do designate members for all the committee positions to which they are entitled, their members are often absent.

---

were defeated by a vote of 68 to 37 against Philadelphia and a vote of 71 to 35 for Los Angeles. The choice of Los Angeles was opposed by Massachusetts, New York, New Jersey, Pennsylvania, Ohio, Illinois, and most of the southern states. (W. H. Lawrence, "Democrats Confirm Los Angeles for '60," *New York Times*, Feb. 28, 1959.) In this instance, obviously there will be no practical opportunity for the convention to reverse the committee.

[13] Democratic National Committee, *Interim Report of Special Advisory Committee on Rules,* June 10, 1955, pp. 10, 39; Clarence Cannon, *op. cit.* (1956), p. 8; DNC *Proceedings,* 1956 (unpublished transcript).

[14] DNC *Proceedings,* 1860, p. 185.

to the grand climax of the nominating ballots (as will be discussed in Chapter 17). Most of these earlier votes are difficult to study with accuracy, because few of them are taken by roll call and even those do not always involve the basic power alignments of the convention. The nominating votes, on the other hand, inevitably involve questions of power whenever the outcome is in doubt; and considerations of power and its exercise frequently lead to divided votes on nominations even when the outcome is not in doubt.

The behavior of the conventions in the making of presidential nominations is in strong contrast to their behavior on almost every other subject, and is a clear indication of the primacy of this function.[16] The formal action by which a candidate is nominated for President of the United States is the most impressive, deliberate, and carefully safeguarded act of each convention. The Republican party has never dispensed with the calling of the roll on a presidential nomination in its entire history. The Democratic party, since 1840, has done so only rarely—the cases being those of 1888, 1916, and 1936, in each of which an incumbent first-term President was being renominated by acclamation. The roll call vote has become an important symbol of legitimacy even when it is unanimous, in some instances especially so.

The nomination for Vice President has usually been given less attention by the conventions and the formalities have been more often dispensed with. Vice-presidential nominations have nonetheless involved serious conflict on a number of occasions,

including the Democratic convention of 1956. When sharp divisions occur in vice-presidential voting, the roll call votes that result have considerable interest.

The basic statistical data that are available for the study of power and effectiveness in the nominating votes consist essentially of the voting strength that is apportioned to the delegations and the records of how that strength was used at the critical point on the nominating vote. To aid in the study and understanding of these data, three measures have here been developed:

1. The percentage of total convention voting strength held by each delegation.

2. The percentage of the total critical vote for the winner contributed by each delegation.

3. A winner-support ratio, consisting of the ratio of the percentage of contribution to the percentage of voting strength.[17]

The three measures are so much used in the remainder of this chapter that they must be clearly understood in order to follow the analysis. They can be readily illustrated; the largest state, New York, will serve the purpose. In the Democratic convention of 1952, New York held 94 of the 1,230 convention votes. On the third and critical ballot, it gave 86½ votes to Adlai E. Stevenson, who received a total of 613 votes before vote shifting began. From these figures, by simple arithmetic, New York had 7.6 per cent of the convention voting strength; it contributed 14.1 per cent of the winning critical vote; and its winner-support ratio was 1.85, or 14.1 divided by 7.6.

---

[16] According to one scholar, "many students of party find in the nominating process the most unique and exclusive function performed by parties. It is regarded as their dominant mode of functioning and all else either follows or is of subordinate importance." See Neil A. McDonald, *The Study of Political Parties* (1955), p. 25.

Occasionally a doubt is expressed whether a national party system can be said even to exist in the United States. That doubt does not impress the present writers; but they do accept the party system in its national aspects as based centrally and predominantly on the presidential nominating function in the party conventions.

[17] In one-ballot decisions, the vote as it stands at the end of the calling of the roll before any vote shifting has usually been taken as the critical vote in Brookings studies. In multi-ballot conventions, it is usually the similar point at the end of the roll call on the final ballot. In some multi-ballot cases, however, the final ballot appears to reflect so much vote shifting brought on by a previously manifest outcome that the semifinal ballot is adjudged the better measure of the critical vote. The concept of the critical vote as developed in the Brookings studies is thus essentially that of the vote at the point where the outcome becomes manifest and vote shifting begins that is clearly band wagon in character. The problem of assessing the data will be fully presented in the forthcoming Brookings book by Bain, *op. cit.*

A delegation that divides its vote precisely the same way as the whole convention has a winner-support ratio of 1.00; one that is unanimously backing a loser at the time of the critical vote has a ratio of 0.00. In 1956 all but a small fraction of the New York delegation stayed with Governor Harriman and went down to defeat, with a winner-support ratio on that occasion of only 0.08.

In the six contested Democratic conventions of the period 1928-1956, New York's average percentage of voting strength was 7.9 per cent. Its average contribution to the winning vote was 7.5 per cent. Its average winner-support ratio for the period therefore was 0.95.

The period from 1928 to 1956 included eight Democratic conventions. Six have just been referred to as "contested." The two omitted are 1936, in which Roosevelt was renominated by acclamation, and 1944, in which he received 92.3 per cent of a one-ballot vote. A protest vote was visible in 1944, but it seems reasonably clear that the issue was not seriously contested. On the other hand, the six conventions regarded as "contested" include that of 1940, in which, to be sure, Roosevelt received 86.0 per cent of the vote on a single ballot, and that of 1948, in which Truman received 76.8 per cent of the vote, again on a single ballot. In both instances, however, there had been a record of preconvention attempts to run serious opposing candidates, and the votes finally cast in opposition were a die-hard residue.[18]

[18] Most statistical work involves the selection of numerical criteria that are partly arbitrary. In the present study a convention has been taken as contested if the winner had received less than 90 per cent at the end of the roll call on the first nominating ballot. This is a convenient figure in terms of handling the data and the number of cases that it retains for the averages; but it has also been examined against a wide variety of historical evidence of the kind indicated in the cases of 1940 and 1948, and appears defensible from any point of view.

One further point of statistical technique merits notice. This is the use of the "winner-support ratio" instead of a simple percentage of delegation strength applied in support of the winner. In the previous instance, for example, when New York gave Stevenson 86½ of its 94 votes in 1952, it was giving him

The winner-support ratio has been used for the present analysis because it provides a simple index of the voting records of delegations or groups of delegations as compared to the conventions as a whole, showing relative success in supporting winners, which can be seen at a glance without having to adjust for convention split. Even the fact that upper limits vary considerably from convention to convention, between periods, and between parties has its own rationale: a delegation voting 100 per cent for the winner in a convention in which the winner receives 89 per cent of the vote does not accomplish so remarkable a feat as

92.0 per cent of its available strength. This figure reflects a simpler concept and is closer to the underlying figures. But the winner-support ratio seems preferable for the present study because it indicates the relative degree to which a particular state was ahead of or behind the developing sentiment of the convention as it moved toward the moment of decision. This feature is of interest in assessing the effective use of such power as each state may possess.

Regardless of how the convention as a whole splits for and against the winner, any delegation that splits its vote in the same proportions will have a winner-support ratio of 1.00. Those giving a lower percentage to the convention winner than the convention average will fall below 1.00, while those giving a higher percentage will rise above 1.00. The lower end of the scale cannot fall below zero votes for the winner, or a winner-support ratio of 0.00, but the upper range is determined by the average convention split for the winner before the final shifting, and varies inversely with the winner's share of the total convention vote.

The mathematician will note, and the nonmathematical reader should be warned, that winner-support ratios should not be added or subtracted. When conventions are combined for an entire period, or when delegations are combined into groups, resulting winner-support ratios must be calculated directly from combinations of the raw voting data. Such combinations, however, have the effect of pulling down the unusually high state winner-support ratios. The highest actual average winner-support ratios for single states during the periods used in this chapter were: 1896-1924—Democratic, 1.52, Republican, 1.90; 1928-1956—Democratic, 1.50, Republican, 1.83. Period averages for all of the states appear in Appendix A, Table 10.

Although this is the first full published explanation of the winner-support ratio and its technical uses as a statistical tool, some preliminary findings resulting from its use were published in Stephen K. Bailey, et al., Research Frontiers in Politics and Government (Brookings Lectures, 1955), p. 188; and in Paul T. David, "The Changing Party Pattern," Antioch Review, Vol. 16 (Fall 1956), pp. 333-50 (also published as Brookings Institution Reprint No. 15).

one voting 100 per cent for the winner when the convention average is only 33 per cent.

Regional Patterns of Power and Effectiveness

The basic tools previously noted—measures of strength, contribution, and winner support—can be flexibly applied for a wide variety of analytical purposes. The comparative record of individual states has interest, especially for people who live in those states.[19] The record of the big states individually takes on national interest, in view of their apparent power and strategic position. Various aggregates are even more important. Those selected for principal attention in the remainder of this chapter include the comparative records of the major regions, the records of groups of states that diverge from each other in party alignment, and finally the records of the big states as a group by contrast with the states of average size and those that are smaller.

Regional Divisions of Voting Strength

The distribution of convention voting strength among the major regions and the non-state areas in the contested conventions of the period 1896-1956 is shown in Table 16.2.[20]

[19] State averages are shown in Appendix A, Table 10.

[20] The use of the regions for this kind of analysis is a point requiring comment, since there is little agreement on the precise boundaries that can be used in defining the regions. West Virginia has been treated here as a northeastern state, although it is often assigned to the South in other classifications, as are Maryland and Delaware occasionally. Kentucky and Oklahoma are treated here as southern states, Missouri as a middle-western state, although all have border state characteristics.

Each of the four great regions has nonetheless a distinctive historical identity that gives it meaning for students of American history and geography. The other groupings by which the data can be aggregated in summary form also have their limitations; and the regions are by no means a purely statistical abstraction as viewed by most of those who attempt to follow the course of American political events.

As the table indicates, almost every convention shows some minor shifting in voting strength. These shifts result from changes in apportionment after each decennial census, from changes in the convention rules on apportionment, and from the variable voting records of the states, reflected in recent years in bonus votes at following conventions.[21] The West has steadily increased its proportionate voting strength at the expense of the other regions, but especially at the expense of the Middle West, because of a much more rapid growth in population. The West has also benefited disproportionately from the bonus voting systems of both parties, as the South has also done in the Democratic party. The non-state areas, however, have increased in voting strength mainly because of more generous treatment in the apportionment rules of recent years. In the Republican party the voting strength of the South was reduced in the reforms of 1916, and southern voting strength is still somewhat smaller in Republican conventions than in Democratic.

A further increase in western voting strength will presumably occur when the 1960 census is given effect in the convention apportionments of both parties in 1964, in view of the rapidity with which the population of California and other western states has increased since 1950.

Variations in Regional Contributions to Winning Votes

The percentage contributions of the various regions to the winning votes in the contested conventions of 1896-1956 are shown in Table 16.3.

The regional fluctuations in contribution to the winner show various noteworthy

It may be that the distinctions between the regions are losing their importance. As long as these distinctions persist, however, the regions will remain useful as a means of grasping the relationships of descriptive materials that become too confusing when presented separately for all the states.

[21] See Chapter 8.

features. Some votes were much more sectional than others, and especially so in the Democratic conventions. The South and the Northeast often disagreed, as might be expected. Bryan and Davis were supported in the South and opposed in the Northeast; Smith, Truman, and (in 1952) Stevenson were opposed in the South and supported in the Northeast. On the other hand, Parker in 1904 found strong support in

both the South and the Northeast and was opposed in the West. These alignments register the principal sectional disputes of the time, such as the earlier East-West dispute

TABLE 16.2. REGIONAL STRENGTH IN CONVENTION VOTING, CONTESTED
NATIONAL CONVENTIONS, 1896-1956[a]

(in per cent)

Convention Year and Candidate	Northeast	Middle West	South	West	Non-State Areas
DEMOCRATIC					
1896 (Bryan)	28.8%	32.7%	28.2%	9.0%	1.3%
1904 (Parker)	28.8	32.0	27.8	9.0	2.4
1908 (Bryan)	28.7	32.0	27.9	9.0	2.4
1912 (Wilson)	29.3	30.4	27.2	10.2	2.7
1920 (Cox)	29.3	30.5	27.2	10.1	2.9
1924 (Davis)	29.2	30.4	27.1	10.0	3.3
1928 (Smith)	29.1	30.4	27.1	10.0	3.4
1932 (Roosevelt)	28.6	30.0	26.9	11.2	3.3
1940 (Roosevelt)	28.9	29.3	26.5	11.8	3.5
1948 (Truman)	28.7	26.4	28.2	14.4	2.3
1952 (Stevenson)	26.7	27.3	27.6	16.1	2.3
1956 (Stevenson)	26.5	25.9	28.6	16.8	2.2
REPUBLICAN					
1896 (McKinley)	28.9%	32.8%	28.3%	9.3%	0.6%
1908 (Taft)	29.4	32.6	28.6	8.4	1.0
1912 (Taft)	29.7	31.1	27.5	10.4	1.3
1916 (Hughes)	32.1	33.9	22.3	11.1	0.6
1920 (Harding)	32.2	34.0	21.6	11.2	1.0
1928 (Hoover)	32.4	33.8	19.8	13.1	0.9
1940 (Willkie)	32.2	32.2	21.3	13.0	1.3
1948 (Dewey)	30.9	31.3	21.4	15.2	1.2
1952 (Eisenhower)	30.4	30.8	19.0	18.1	1.7
1956[b] (Eisenhower)	28.1	28.6	24.6	16.9	1.8

[a] Computed from the votes assigned to each state as recorded in the official proceedings; states grouped by regions as indicated in Appendix A, Table 10.
[b] Although there was no contest at the 1956 Republican convention, it is included here in order to show the full 60-year shift in voting strength on a basis comparable to the Democratic figures. The South gained greatly in 1956 by virtue of its high Republican vote in 1952. Its similar voting record in 1956 will prolong this effect at least into the 1960 convention.

over free silver and in recent years the North-South dispute over civil rights.

Five nominations received more than 40 per cent of their support from a single region—Bryan in 1896, Parker in 1904, Wilson in 1912, Smith in 1928, and Stevenson in

(in per cent)

Convention Year and Candidate	Northeast	Middle West	South	West	Non-State Areas
DEMOCRATIC					
1896 Convention Strength[b]	28.8%	32.7%	28.2%	9.0%	1.3%
1896 (Bryan)	4.8**	30.6	47.2**	14.8*	2.6
1904 (Parker)	35.7**	18.3**	40.9**	3.0*	2.1
1908 (Bryan)	24.6*	33.6	29.0	10.1	2.7
1912 (Wilson)	26.4	40.9**	22.4*	8.0	2.3
1920 (Cox)	36.2**	29.9	22.2*	7.8	3.9
1924 (Davis)	17.4**	30.5	38.7**	9.4	4.0
1928 (Smith)	42.6**	25.2**	11.7**	15.2	5.3
1932 (Roosevelt)	18.6**	32.1	32.0**	12.6	4.7
1940 (Roosevelt)	27.9	32.7	23.9	13.1	2.4
1948 (Truman)	35.9**	35.1**	6.8**	19.2*	3.0
1952 (Stevenson)	44.2**	36.2**	4.7**	11.5*	3.4
1956 (Stevenson)	27.6	29.6*	17.6**	21.9*	3.3
1956 Convention Strength	26.5	25.9	28.6	16.8	2.2
REPUBLICAN					
1896 Convention Strength	28.9%	32.8%	28.3%	9.3%	0.6%
1896 (McKinley)	14.2**	43.2**	32.9*	9.1	0.6
1908 (Taft)	20.1**	29.8	37.1**	11.7	1.3
1912 (Taft)	26.7	16.0**	42.3**	12.5	2.5
1916 (Hughes)[c]	37.7**	22.3**	23.9	15.5*	0.6
1920 (Harding)	25.1**	28.6**	38.9**	5.5**	1.9
1928 (Hoover)	39.9**	19.7**	22.7	16.5	1.2
1940 (Willkie)	49.0**	24.5**	14.4**	11.2	0.9
1948 (Dewey)[d]	45.0**	18.4**	20.9	13.8	1.9
1952 (Eisenhower)	50.5**	18.8**	17.3	12.6*	0.8
1952 Convention Strength[e]	30.4	30.8	19.0	18.1	1.7

[a] Regional percentages of the total critical vote, as compiled in the forthcoming book by Richard C. Bain, *Decisions and Voting Records of the National Party Conventions*. For explanations of the concepts, see the previous section of this chapter.

The single asterisk (*) indicates that the difference between the percentage of vote contributed to the winner (present table) and the percentage of strength held by the region (Table 16.2) is statistically significant; the double asterisk (**) indicates that the difference is highly significant. In this table and the tables to follow, unless otherwise indicated, relationships are considered statistically significant if they test at the .05 level, and highly significant if they test at the .01 level or higher, using the standard formula for the significance of the difference between two proportions.

[b] Convention strength percentages from Table 16.2 are included at the beginning and end of each section of the table as a convenience in interpreting the percentages of contribution.

[c] Based on second ballot. Convention adjourned after second ballot, and most candidates other than Hughes withdrew before and during roll call on third ballot.

[d] Based on second ballot. Convention adjourned after second ballot, and third ballot was 100 per cent for Dewey after withdrawal of other candidates.

[e] No contest at the 1956 Republican convention.

1952. There were some Democratic nominations that met with relatively little regional opposition, such as Bryan on his third try in 1908, Cox in 1920, and Stevenson in 1956.

In the contested Republican conventions, regional differences were less strongly marked but there were some clear cases of strong regional support. McKinley was pushed by the Middle West as a favorite son. In 1912 the rotten borough delegates from the South supported Taft, the incumbent President. Hughes, Hoover, Willkie, Dewey, and Eisenhower in their times were the favorites of the Northeast. Eisenhower in 1952 was the only candidate shown in the table to draw more than 50 per cent of his support from a single region.

Regional Winner-Support Ratios

The percentage of the winning vote given by a particular region does not satisfactorily indicate the sentiments of the delegations from that region unless it is judged in proportion to the region's relative voting strength. The winner-support ratios by regions are given for the contested conventions of 1896-1956 in Table 16.4. Changing patterns of regional effectiveness in supporting winners at the conventions are evident in the figures for both parties.

In the Democratic case, the Northeast has fluctuated widely, with low scores in 1896, 1924, and 1932—being especially affected in 1932 by the sharp contest between Smith and Roosevelt from New York.

The Middle West has had the most consistent record as a region, seldom dropping to a winner-support ratio below 1.00 and never very far below.

The South was more successful in supporting winners in earlier years than later. It led the way to John W. Davis in 1924 and supported Franklin D. Roosevelt in 1932, but has ranked low in every convention since that year.

The West, on the other hand, swung erratically in the earlier years and has backed winners most of the time since 1928. California's choice of Kefauver in the 1952 primary, however, pulled down the western record for that year.

The non-state areas generally have thrown their limited strength to the winners, except in 1904, 1912, and 1940. Their behavior in 1940 was all the more surprising, since they were opposing the renomination of an incumbent President, Franklin D. Roosevelt.

In the Republican conventions of 1896-1952, the Northeast moved from low-average success in winner-support to a position of relative dominance. Only in 1916 of the earlier years, when Charles Evans Hughes of New York was nominated, was the winner-support ratio above 1.00. On the last three occasions, however, the Northeast was not only very high but the only one of the four major regions above 1.00. It is notable that in 1952, when the Northeast was giving Eisenhower more than 50 per cent of his winning vote in the Republican convention, it was also giving Stevenson 44 per cent in the Democratic convention; because of the smaller regional strength in the Democratic convention the winner-support ratio for Stevenson in the Northeast, at 1.66, was identical with that for Eisenhower.

The Middle West has failed to back a winner strongly in the Republican convention since McKinley in 1896. In most cases, particularly in the more recent conventions, it has been notably low.

For the South, high winner-support ratios have usually occurred when a Republican has occupied the White House, with the addition of 1896, when Mark Hanna's well-executed preconvention campaign proved fruitful, and 1920, when the South was especially high for Harding.

The West, with the exception of 1920 when Hiram Johnson, a loser, held the California delegation, was relatively high through 1928, but has since been below average. The western pattern in recent years has been heavily weighted by the big California delegation, which has frequently been tied to an unsuccessful favorite son.

TABLE 16.4. REGIONAL WINNER-SUPPORT RATIOS, CONTESTED PRESIDENTIAL NOMINATIONS, 1896-1956

Convention Year and Candidate	Critical Vote, Per Cent[a]	Winner-Support Ratios[b]				
		Northeast	Middle West	South	West	Non-State Areas
		DEMOCRATIC				
1896 (Bryan)	49.3%	0.17**	0.94	1.67**	1.64*	2.03
1904 (Parker)	65.8	1.24**	0.57**	1.47**	0.34*	0.88
1908 (Bryan)	88.7	0.86*	1.05	1.04	1.13	1.13
1912 (Wilson)	57.9	0.90	1.34**	0.82*	0.78	0.84
1920 (Cox)	63.9	1.24**	0.98	0.82*	0.77	1.32
1924 (Davis)	52.4	0.60**	1.00	1.43**	0.94	1.22
1928 (Smith)	65.9	1.47**	0.83**	0.43**	1.52	1.52
1932 (Roosevelt)	59.1	0.65**	1.07	1.19**	1.12	1.43
1940 (Roosevelt)	86.0	0.96	1.12	0.90	1.11	0.70
1948 (Truman)	75.0	1.25**	1.33**	0.24**	1.33*	1.33
1952 (Stevenson)	49.8	1.66**	1.33**	0.17**	0.71*	1.50
1956 (Stevenson)	66.0	1.04	1.14*	0.61**	1.31*	1.52
		REPUBLICAN				
1896 (McKinley)	69.1%	0.49**	1.31**	1.16*	0.98	0.97
1908 (Taft)	71.6	0.68**	0.91	1.30**	1.40	1.26
1912 (Taft)	52.1	0.90	0.52**	1.54**	1.20	1.92
1916 (Hughes)	33.3	1.18**	0.66**	1.07	1.39*	1.00
1920 (Harding)	38.1	0.78**	0.84**	1.80**	0.49**	1.84
1928 (Hoover)	76.9	1.23**	0.58**	1.14	1.26	1.30
1940 (Willkie)	45.7	1.52**	0.76**	0.68**	0.86	0.67
1948 (Dewey)	47.1	1.46**	0.59**	0.97	0.91	1.63
1952 (Eisenhower)	49.3	1.66**	0.61**	0.91	0.70*	0.48

[a] The winner's percentage on the critical vote is included to facilitate interpretation of the winner-support ratios in the different conventions. In 1908, for example, with a critical vote of 88.7 per cent, it was not possible for any winner-support ratio to be as high as some of the winner-support ratios in 1896, when the critical vote was 49.3 per cent. See text for earlier explanation of the winner-support ratio and its derivation.

[b] The single asterisk (*) indicates that the winner-support ratio so identified is based upon a difference between percentages of strength and of contribution that is significant, on the basis of a standard statistical test; the double asterisk (**) indicates that the difference is highly significant.

The non-state areas have followed somewhat the same pattern as the South, which in some ways they resemble in the Republican party. In recent years, however, they have behaved more erratically.

Summary Review
of Regional Patterns

The data of the three preceding tables, taken together, demonstrate that there have been noteworthy differences in regional voting behavior in the conventions of both parties. In most cases, there seems to be enough of a central tendency in regional voting behavior to justify the use of regional averages for the periods 1896-1924 and 1928-1956, although it is obvious that the dispersion around the averages is much greater for some regions and periods than for others. The regional averages by periods are brought together in Table 16.5; similar data for the individual states and non-state

TABLE 16.5. REGIONAL VOTING STRENGTH, CONTRIBUTION TO WINNER, AND WINNER-SUPPORT RATIOS IN CONTESTED CONVENTIONS BY PERIODS, 1896-1924 AND 1928-1956

Party and Region	1896–1924			1928–1956		
	Voting Strength, Average Per Cent (a)	Contribution to Winner, Average Per Cent[a] (b)	Winner-Support Ratio, Average (b/a)	Voting Strength, Average Per Cent (c)	Contribution to Winner, Average Per Cent[a] (d)	Winner-Support Ratio, Average (d/c)
			DEMOCRATIC			
Northeast	29.0%	25.5%**	0.88	28.0%	32.4%**	1.16
Middle West	31.3	30.7	0.98	28.1	31.8**	1.13
South	27.6	32.3**	1.17	27.5	16.2**	0.59
West	9.6	8.6	0.90	13.6	16.0	1.18
Non-State Areas	2.5	2.9	1.15	2.8	3.6	1.29
All Delegations	100.0	100.0	1.00	100.0	100.0	1.00
			REPUBLICAN			
Northeast	30.5%	23.0%**	0.76	31.4%	45.3%**	1.44
Middle West	32.8	29.0*	0.88	32.0	20.1**	0.63
South	25.7	35.8**	1.40	20.3	19.5	0.95
West	10.1	10.8	1.07	15.0	13.9	0.93
Non-State Areas	0.9	1.4	1.48	1.3	1.2	0.93
All Delegations	100.0	100.0	1.00	100.0	100.0	1.00

[a] The single asterisk (*) indicates that the difference between percentage of contribution so identified and the counterpart percentage of regional strength is significant, on the basis of a standard statistical test; the double asterisk (**) indicates that the difference is highly significant. The winner-support ratios based upon these indicated percentages of contribution and strength are similarly significant.

When the scores for one region are compared with those of other regions, highly significant differences are found for all the combinations in the Democratic party during the period 1896-1924 except between the Middle West and the West, which is significant, and the Northeast and the West, which is not significant. In the latter period, differences between the Northeast and the Middle West, the Northeast and the West, the Middle West and the West are not significant; the others are highly significant. For the Republican party, all differences are highly significant except between the Middle West and the West in the first period and the South and the West in the second, neither of which is significant.

areas can be found in Appendix A, Table 10.[22]

The figures of Table 16.5 confirm in summary fashion the high points of what has previously been reviewed. For the Democratic party, the South was the leading source of support for the winners in the conventions of 1896-1924, but fell to a low estate in that regard after 1928. The other regions all gave uniformly high support to the winners during the period 1928-1956; no single region appeared to be dominant in the making of Democratic nominations during that period.

For the Republican party, the South led as a source of votes for the winners during the earlier period, although it supplied none of the candidates. They were mostly from the Middle West, which ranked second during that period as a source of votes for the winners, although the West was higher in average winner-support ratio. During the more recent period the Northeast was strikingly dominant, with an average winner-support ratio of 1.44; all of the other regions were below average in winner support, the Middle West especially so. This statistical contrast obviously reflects the vic-

[22] The items in Table 16.5, particularly the regional winner-support ratios, are in the nature of a score card reflecting a summary of past success and failure in a competitive struggle. The interpretation of these relationships, however, involves centrally the problem of statistical significance. To what extent are the observed differences in winner-support ratio between regions, parties, and time periods the result of random chance? Or, what comes to almost the same thing for purposes of analysis, to what extent are they the reflection of the impact of a complexity of factors and events so innumerable and so incapable of disentanglement from each other that explanatory theory becomes impossible?

On the first question, the extent to which the differences may be due to chance, the usual tests for statistical significance are available. The results of applying these tests are reported in a footnote to the table.

If it is assumed that the larger differences and the over-all pattern of the table as a whole reflect identifiable general patterns of relationship, the development of explanatory theory will still remain difficult. Partial approaches to the problem appear elsewhere in the present chapter and in other chapters. But, explainable or not, the record of a major region in so important a field of human action remains in itself a datum of considerable interest and one with its own consequences for the future.

tories of New York over Ohio in recent Republican contests.

State Party Alignment as a Factor in Winner Support

Tables 16.6 and 16.7 present the data on winner support in three categories of states by party alignment. To complete the accounting, the delegations from non-state areas are also included; in the tables they have been placed after the delegations from the minority party states, at the end of each list, since delegations from the non-state areas often behave like those from states where the party concerned is weak.

During the earlier period twenty-four states were classified as predominantly Republican. They held nearly 60 per cent of the total voting strength in the Republican conventions. Had they agreed among themselves, they could easily have nominated the Republican party candidates; but, as the tables show, the disagreement of the Republican delegations from these states was wide. The actual decisions on Republican nominations mainly reflected a coalition of the delegations from about half of the Republican states with most of the delegations from the competitive and Democratic states. During the more recent period, on the other hand, the competitive states held about two thirds of the strength in each party convention. No nomination could be made in either party without substantial participation by the delegations from competitive states. They did participate in the nominations of both parties about in proportion to their strength, i.e., with average support ratios close to 1.00.

The conditions for electoral victory differed markedly between the two periods, presumably with some influence on the considerations taken into account by each party in nominating candidates. During the earlier period no Democratic candidate could seriously hope to win the election unless he could carry not only all the Democratic and competitive states, but also many of those

TABLE 16.6. VOTING STRENGTH, WINNER CONTRIBUTION, AND WINNER-SUPPORT RATIOS IN RELATION TO STATE PARTY ALIGNMENT, 1896-1924 AND 1928-1956[a]

Category and Numbers of Convention Delegations	1896–1924			1928–1956		
	Voting Strength, Average Per Cent	Contribution to Winner, Average Per Cent[b]	Winner-Support Ratio, Average	Voting Strength, Average Per Cent	Contribution to Winner, Average Per Cent[b]	Winner-Support Ratio, Average
DEMOCRATIC DELEGATIONS						
Democratic States (14, 12)[c]	28.6%	33.4%**	1.17	24.1%	20.4%**	0.85
Competitive States (10, 29)	12.2	10.9**	0.90	65.3	66.6	1.02
Republican States (24, 7)	56.7	52.7*	0.93	7.9	9.4**	1.19
Non-State Areas (7, 7)	2.5	2.9	1.15	2.8	3.6	1.33
All Delegations	100.0	100.0	1.00	100.0	100.0	1.00
REPUBLICAN DELEGATIONS						
Republican States (24, 7)	59.7%	46.3%**	0.76	10.5%	9.7%	0.92
Competitive States (10, 29)	12.6	15.5**	1.23	68.7	67.4	0.98
Democratic States (14, 12)	26.8	36.8**	1.37	19.5	21.7**	1.11
Non-State Areas (6, 6)	0.9	1.4	1.49	1.3	1.2	0.99
All Delegations	100.0	100.0	1.00	100.0	100.0	1.00

[a] In each period, states were classified as Democratic or Republican if they voted for the corresponding candidate in at least six of the eight presidential elections, and competitive if they voted for each party no more than five times of the eight. All Progressive votes in 1912 and 1924 were classified as Republican for this purpose, and all Dixiecrat votes in 1948 were classified as Democratic. States that provided one or two splinter votes in the electoral college count were assigned in accordance with the predominant portion of their vote. Oklahoma was assigned to the Democratic group for the first period on the basis of going Democratic four times and Republican once in the five elections after admission to statehood. Arizona and New Mexico split their vote evenly in the four elections after their admission to statehood and were assigned to the competitive group in the first period.

The listing of states by categories for each period, with a further grouping by regions within each category, appears in Appendix A, Table 4.

[b] The single asterisk (*) indicates that the difference between the percentage of contribution so identified and the counterpart percentage of voting strength is significant, on the basis of a standard statistical test; the double asterisk (**) indicates that the difference is highly significant. The winner-support ratios based upon these indicated percentages of contribution and strength are similarly significant.

When the scores for one group of delegations are compared with those of another within the same party and time period, the differences are found to be highly significant or not significant (n.s.) as indicated in the following tabulation:

	1896–1924	1928–1956
Democratic:		
Democratic/competitive	**	**
Democratic/Republican	**	**
Republican/competitive	n.s.	**
Republican:		
Republican/competitive	**	n.s.
Republican/Democratic	**	**
Democratic/competitive	**	**

[c] Numbers in parentheses mean: 14 Democratic states in 1896-1924, 12 in 1928-1956, etc.

normally voting Republican.[23] Conversely a Republican candidate could win merely by holding intact the entire group of Republican states. In the more recent period neither party could hope to win without carrying half or more of the competitive states.

These considerations, however, do not seem to be reflected in the tables in any self-

from where the party was strongest had the lowest average ratios.

On the other hand, during the earlier period the distribution of winner-support ratios was U-shaped in the Democratic party—that is, the delegates from strongly Democratic states were usually supporting the nominee. This was a period of Demo-

TABLE 16.7. WINNER SUPPORT AT THE CONVENTIONS IN RELATION TO
STATE PARTY ALIGNMENT, 1896-1924 AND 1928-1956[a]

	1896–1924				1928–1956			
		Percentage of Times in Categories of Winner Support[b]				Percentage of Times in Categories of Winner Support[b]		
Category of Convention Delegations	Winner-Support Ratio, Average	Below 0.90	0.90 to 1.10	Above 1.10	Winner-Support Ratio, Average	Below 0.90	0.90 to 1.10	Above 1.10
	DEMOCRATIC DELEGATIONS							
Democratic States	1.17	26.2%	3.6%	70.2%	0.85	36.1%	8.3%	55.6%
Competitive States	0.90	45.0	1.7	53.3	1.02	27.6	6.9	65.5
Republican States	0.93	45.8	6.3	47.9	1.19	9.5	7.2	83.3
Non-State Areas	1.15	22.2	3.7	74.1	1.33	12.8	0.0	87.2
All Delegations	1.00	38.4	4.4	57.1	1.00	25.4	6.4	68.2
	REPUBLICAN DELEGATIONS							
Republican States	0.76	45.9%	4.1%	50.0%	0.92	36.8%	18.8%	52.1%
Competitive States	1.23	32.0	2.0	66.0	0.98	38.8	7.8	53.4
Democratic States	1.37	17.1	12.9	70.0	1.11	50.0	3.6	46.4
Non-State Areas	1.49	23.8	0.0	76.2	0.99	36.8	0.0	63.2
All Delegations	1.00	33.7	5.7	60.6	1.00	38.4	9.0	52.6

[a] See Table 16.6 for note on classification of the states and numbers of delegations by categories.
[b] Delegations were assigned to the columns in accordance with their winner-support ratios in individual conventions.

evident way. Rather, to the extent that the tables show any clear pattern, they mainly show it for the dominant party—the Republican in the period 1896-1924 and the Democratic in 1928-1956. In each of these cases, the delegations from the states and the areas where the party was weakest recorded the highest winner-support ratios, while those

[23] The distributions of voting strength in the electoral college by groups of states were similar to those in the conventions, especially during the earlier period. See Chapters 3 and 8.

cratic weakness, when the party lost six of the eight presidential elections and won the other two with less than a popular majority in one case and the closest of majorities in the other.

For the Republican party in its period of weakness since 1928, however, the distribution is not U-shaped; the progressions are on the whole similar to those of the earlier period but not as steep. The Republican party, however, was not as weak during the recent period as the Democratic party was during the earlier one.

With these various evidences in mind, what can be said about the reasons for the different behavior of delegations from the states where their party is strong or weak? And why is it that regular types of behavior have appeared in each party when it was strong, but much less so or not at all when it was weak?

The outline of an explanatory theory that attempts to answer these questions is as follows:

1. Delegates of the nationally dominant party coming from competitive states have a strong motive for wanting a winning candidate because of the coattail effect of a presidential winner, who may help to carry many of the state candidates to victory.[24] This motive, however, has little force during a period of party weakness. Accordingly it is not surprising that Table 16.7 shows the Democrats from competitive states reaching a winner-support ratio above 1.10 only 53 per cent of the time in the earlier period and 66 per cent of the time since 1928, and exactly the reverse in the Republican conventions.

The delegates often disagree as to which candidate is the most likely winner, and, when their party is strong, they often have a choice between several candidates who could win; otherwise the scores during periods of party strength would probably be much higher.

2. Delegates from states where their party is in the minority are strongly motivated to seek a winning candidate in the national election, for several reasons. There is federal patronage if their party is in the White House. Even if they do not personally get jobs, their local prestige is enhanced by a

national victory, and in some states they may hope for enough coattail effect eventually to pull them out of their minority position in the state. Sometimes, too, the minority party members have been so ground down that they have developed a deep sentimental attachment to their national party, which will make its success appear worth any sacrifice of personal preferences.

These peculiarities of the minority position would seem likely to cause the delegates from such states to give eager and early support to the candidate who seems to them to have the best chance to run a strong race. This band-wagon tendency is shown in the statistics both for periods of general party strength and for periods of general party weakness. The same peculiarities attach to the position of both parties in a non-state area where the appointive positions in government depend even more completely on Washington. Accordingly, the highest winner-support ratios are found for the non-state delegations more frequently than for any other group.

3. Delegations from states where the party is strongest often are the least interested in finding a nominee who can carry the states that will be critical for national party victory. Their local position may be so secure that they would rather see their party lose the presidential election than have it win with a candidate who is, from their point of view, unsatisfactory. Other things being equal, they would undoubtedly prefer to see their party win nationally, but their desires in this respect may be overshadowed, rather than reinforced, by state and local considerations.

4. Motivations related to the hope of general-election success all tend to break down when there is little reason to anticipate victory, whoever the candidate might be. In such a situation, reason might dictate the choice of a strong candidate to build up the strength of the party vote in the competitive states against some more favorable occasion. But short-range and parochial considerations of a different sort can become

[24] Recent research on the coattail effect has made it clear that it is most crucial in competitive states and congressional districts; and that the presidential candidate runs ahead of his party most strongly, as a rule, in those areas where the party is traditionally weak. See Malcolm Moos, *Politics, Presidents, and Coattails* (1952), pp. 82-118; Charles Press, "Voting Statistics and Presidential Coattails," *American Political Science Review*, Vol. 52 (Dec. 1958), pp. 1041-50.

much more powerful when national victory is unlikely, even if strong candidates are available. Party traditionalists may tend to revert to dreams of an ideal candidate better suited to an earlier era than to the current struggle in the competitive states, or the political leaders may prefer a weak candidate who will not disturb their normal operations. In any event, the delegations from the competitive states probably tend to become less influential in a losing year. They can hope to become more influential, compared with the one-party states of their own party, when victory seems probable with the right candidate.

5. A correct judgment as to what kind of candidate would be most likely to win is an essential element in the operation of all the various motivations previously noted. Delegates from states in which their own party is dominant have relatively little knowledge of how a close election is won in other states, and are apt to be especially vulnerable to errors of judgment. Wide differences in perceptions of the situation and of the candidates were probably somewhat more prevalent in the era before scientific polling techniques became as well established as they are today.[25]

Big States vs. Small in Winner Support

The mathematical equations of power indicate that a presidential nomination is unlikely to be seriously contested unless some of the big state delegations are opposed to each other on the issue.[26] A group of small delegations might provide a substitute for one or two large ones in putting

up a candidate when sectional or oth[er] bonds of cohesion are unusually strong, b[ut] this does not seem to have happened ofte[n] Each of the major candidates is usually su[p]ported by several delegations of large a[nd] average size, and the smaller delegatio[ns] adhere to one of these groups. But wh[en] this occurs, do the small delegations le[ap] into the struggle like the large ones? Or [do] they quickly find the band wagon and su[p]port the winning candidate?

Delegation voting behavior is related [to] size in the summary figures of Table 16.[ ] In each period and each party the deleg[a]tions of the large states held about o[ne] third of the total convention voti[ng] strength, as did the delegations from t[he] middle-sized states; the delegations from t[he] small states and the non-state areas togeth[er] held about one third of the strength.

The figures in the table make it cle[ar] that, when the delegations are grouped [by] size, no group has a monopoly of winn[ing] support. Some curious differences appea[r], however, when comparisons are made b[e]tween the two parties and the two time p[e]riods included in the table.

Table 16.8 parallels Tables 16.6 and 16[.7] in the extent to which it brings out regula[r]ities in the data and in the quadrants i[n] which those regularities appear. The reg[u]larities are again clearest for the Repub[li]can party during the earlier period when [it] was strongly dominant, next for the Dem[o]cratic party during the more recent perio[d] when it was moderately dominant and f[or] the Republican party during the recent p[e]riod of moderate weakness, and least of a[ll] for the Democratic party during the earli[er] and weaker period.[27]

All of this tends to suggest the gravit[a]tional influence of the effective centers [of] power that are at work during the nomina[ting]

[25] Although, for the purposes of the previous statistical analysis, the states were assigned to categories of party alignment in terms of their voting in presidential elections, this may differ widely from the balance of party dominance in the state government. A classification of states by some more complicated system of criteria would produce somewhat different results. There is little reason, however, to think the major patterns of relationship would be greatly changed; in some cases they might be clarified and strengthened.

[26] See Chapter 8.

[27] This parallelism in the relationships appears i[n] spite of the fact that there was much rearrangeme[nt] of states in moving from one set of categories to t[he] other. The party alignment categories involved wi[de] swings from one period to the other in the size [of] the respective groups of states, and both sets of cat[e]gories involve considerable shifts in the compos[i]tion of the groups from one period to the other.

ng process. Power for this purpose evidently becomes more effective and more highly organized during those periods when a party frequently wins possession of the White House—that is, when there is a band wagon that is likely to go somewhere, the weaker units of the system are usually the quickest to climb aboard. In both sets of categories this means first of all the party organizations in the non-state areas. In one set of categories it also means the party organizations in the small states; in the other, those in the states where the party is weak because the other party is dominant. Conversely, the stronger units of the system include the centers of resistance to the even-

TABLE 16.8. WINNER SUPPORT AT THE CONVENTIONS IN RELATION TO DELEGATION SIZE, 1896-1924 AND 1928-1956[a]

Category and Numbers of Delegations	1896-1924				1928-1956			
	Winner-Support Ratio, Average[b]	Percentage of Times in Categories of Winner Support			Winner-Support Ratio, Average[b]	Percentage of Times in Categories of Winner Support		
		Below 0.90	0.90 to 1.10	Above 1.10		Below 0.90	0.90 to 1.10	Above 1.10
		DEMOCRATIC DELEGATIONS						
Large States (6, 6)[c]	0.96**	41.6%	2.8%	55.6%	0.94**	38.9%	5.6%	55.5%
Middle States (13, 14)	1.02	35.9	1.3	62.8	0.95**	35.7	9.5	54.8
Small States (29, 28)	1.01	41.4	6.3	52.3	1.09**	20.2	6.5	73.3
Non-State Areas	1.15	22.2	3.7	74.1	1.33	12.8	0.0	87.2
All Delegations	1.00	38.4	4.4	57.2	1.00	25.4	6.4	68.2
		REPUBLICAN DELEGATIONS						
Large States (6, 6)	0.74**	53.3%	6.7%	40.0%	0.93**	50.0%	8.3%	41.7%
Middle States (13, 14)	1.05**	33.8	6.2	60.0	0.97*	42.9	7.1	50.0
Small States (29, 28)	1.19**	31.0	6.2	62.8	1.11**	33.9	11.6	54.5
Non-State Areas	1.49	23.8	0.0	76.2	0.99	36.8	0.0	63.2
All Delegations	1.00	33.7	5.7	60.6	1.00	38.4	9.0	52.6

[a] For each period the delegations were classified by arraying them in rank order by size, with the non-state delegations at the bottom. The array was then divided into three groups, each of which held as nearly one third of the voting power as possible, counting down from the top. The top one third included six states for each period, but not the same six for the two periods or the two parties.
See Appendix A, Tables 11 and 12, for additional data by states and delegations for the period 1928-1956. The computations for the period 1896-1924 were similar.
[b] The single asterisk (*) indicates that the winner-support ratio so identified is based upon a difference between percentages of strength and contribution that is significant, on the basis of a standard statistical test; the double asterisk (**) indicates that the difference is highly significant.
Since all of the groups except those for the non-state areas involve approximately the same numbers of delegate votes, levels of statistical significance can be specified that are broadly applicable in making comparisons between groups. In general, the difference between the winner-support ratio of one group and that of another is significant or highly significant if it exceeds the amount specified in the following tabulation. (Non-state groups are excepted in all cases because of the small numbers involved.)

	Significant	Highly Significant
Any Democratic group when compared with any other Democratic group	.04	.06
Any Republican group when compared with any other Republican group	.05	.07
Any group in one party when compared with any group in the other party	.05	.07

[c] Numbers in parentheses mean: 6 large states in 1896-1924, 6 in 1928-1956, etc.

tual nominee as well as the centers where power is being organized effectively in his support. In one set of categories the stronger units are the big states; in the other, the states where the party is dominant or strongly competitive.

The mechanisms through which these influences work can be further identified to some extent. In the party in power, small-state and non-state delegations are probably more amenable to pressure from the incumbent administration when it is seeking to influence the forthcoming nomination. The party organizations (and the party voters) in small states may be more susceptible to intensive cultivation during active preconvention campaigns when victory is in the air. Federal patronage may be relatively more important in small states than in large states, thus intensifying the small states' desire to make the band wagon before the critical vote if the party has a hope of winning the election. Whatever the party prospects, small states are seldom committed to a favorite son and are thus spared the defeats often suffered by the large states that regularly offer favorite sons.

Most of these factors had little or no force in the Democratic party during the period 1896-1924. The only contested Democratic convention that was followed by electoral victory was that of 1912. In 1896 and 1920 the party held the White House, but the incumbent administration had almost no control of the convention or the nomination. Conversely, such factors were conspicuously operative in the Republican party before 1924 and in the Democratic party after 1928; and they were more operative in the Republican party during the second period than they had been in the Democratic during the first, obviously because the Republican party was in a less hopeless position at the beginning of the period and after 1944.

The Idiosyncrasies of the States

The percentage distributions of Tables 16.7 and 16.8 demonstrate that delegations are usually either high or low in winner

support, and seldom provide merely average support on any given occasion. This is the natural consequence of the tendencies toward delegation agreement on candidates, as noticed in Chapter 15: an agreed delegation that votes for a winner has a high winner-support ratio, while one that votes for a loser has a low ratio.

A more complex phenomenon, but one that can be amply documented, is a frequent tendency for delegations of the same state and party to support either winners or losers at successive conventions. This may continue for as long as a generation, as indicated in the previous tables and the related appendix materials. In fact, most of the states in each group and party had an average winner-support record either below 0.90 or above 1.10 in each period.

The states with a close-to-average record in one party or the other for an extended period were exceptional. New York was an illustration on the Democratic side; in six contested conventions it gave its support mainly to winners on three occasions and mainly to losers on the other three, for an average winner-support ratio of 0.95. But between 1928 and 1956 there were only nine such states on the Democratic side and five on the Republican—states, that is, with average winner-support ratios between 0.90 and 1.10 for the period and party, as shown in Appendix A, Tables 11 and 12.

Presumably a continuing tendency to support losers at several consecutive conventions could not easily occur except in association with a persistent tendency toward some form of dissident factionalism in relation to the national party. The states that have ranged near the bottom since 1928 in winner support give support to this thesis. Processes of factionalism of this scale and duration, moreover, have involved deeply entrenched sectional or economic forces and a durable leadership that could provide and develop definite though unsuccessful candidates for the presidential nominations. The forces and the leadership may both be powerful for periods of ten to thirty years, but do undoubtedly tend to change with the succession of the generations.

The large and the middle states with the highest winner-support scores and those with the lowest, for the period 1928-1956, were as follows.[28]

Democratic		Republican	
Michigan	1.47	New York	1.72
Pennsylvania	1.35	New Jersey	1.53
Iowa	1.27	Massachusetts	1.51
Minnesota	1.26	Missouri	1.25
Illinois	1.24	Pennsylvania	1.20
New Jersey	1.22		
		California	0.43
Georgia	0.46	Illinois	0.42
Virginia	0.11	Ohio	0.32
Texas	0.00	Wisconsin	0.19

The extent to which the position of the major states can change in the course of a generation is illustrated with special clarity by the record of the states that now rank as the top seven in population.

New York and Ohio have special interest as the principal sources of presidential candidates; of the twenty individuals who have received one or more nominations since 1896, eight were from New York, four from Ohio, and one each from eight other states.[29] Pennsylvania, until recently second in size, has seldom had a favorite son in either party and has supplied no actual nominee since General Winfield S. Hancock in 1880. When it was most extreme in its Republicanism, during the period 1896-1924, Pennsylvania was relatively successful in following the winner at Democratic conventions but highly unsuccessful in promoting a winner at Republican conventions. Since 1928, after again becoming competitive in presidential politics, it has been suc-

cessful in backing winners for the nominations of both parties.

Illinois and California, like Pennsylvania, have improved their records at Democratic conventions; unlike Pennsylvania, they have insisted on backing losers at Republican conventions. Illinois is especially remarkable for its two-generation record of dissidence in Republican presidential politics; it rejected the leadership of Ohio during one period and that of New York during the other. Texas and Michigan have had oddly similar records at Republican conventions, while poles apart in recent years at Democratic.

The winner-support ratios of the seven states for the two periods were as follows:[30]

State	Democratic		Republican	
	1896–1924	1928–1956	1896–1924	1928–1956
New York	0.73	0.95	0.97	1.72
Ohio	1.15	0.88	1.14	0.32
Pennsylvania	1.11	1.35	0.13	1.20
Illinois	1.08	1.24	0.35	0.42
California	0.62	0.93	0.84	0.43
Texas	1.09	0.00	1.35	0.91
Michigan	1.29	1.47	1.35	0.78

The changing positions reflected in these figures should provide their own warnings about prediction for the future. It cannot safely be assumed that the states that have been most effective in presidential nominating politics during the last thirty years will be equally so in the next thirty. New York has seemingly benefited in recent years from the increasing nationalization of politics, communication, and economic life. The position of New York may also be especially strong because of its central location as a state in the eastern metropolitan complex— the geographic area from Boston to Washington, D.C., in which a population of more than 25 million is now aggregated. But there have been times when New York di-

[28] These figures are all drawn from Appendix A, Tables 11 and 12, which also show the number of conventions during the period in which each of the states was high, average, or low for the winner. The 0.00 score for the Texas Democratic delegation is based on the critical vote at the several conventions, including the Texas vote for Garner in 1932 before the switch to Roosevelt.

[29] See Chapter 7.

[30] From Appendix A, Table 10.

vided its strength between two favorites of
its own in the same party, and the same phenomenon may occur for the wider metropolitan area of the Northeast as Massachusetts, New Jersey, and Pennsylvania challenge New York in the production of strong
candidates for the nominations.

The alternative power centers in Ohio,
Illinois, Texas, and California have fared
poorly in each party when they attempted
to stand alone. If they could unite in either
party against the leadership of the Northeast, especially at a time when the Northeast was itself divided, they might succeed
in dominating one party or the other for a
time. But in any such contest the outcome
will remain in doubt, and, in any of these
states individually, it is difficult to see what
either party would have to gain by continuing a policy of dissidence for another
generation.

High winner-support ratios may signify
either skill in finding the band wagon or
successful leadership in directing where the
band wagon is to go, just as the converse
may signify either bad guessing or stubborn
adherence to a losing cause. The big state
delegations are clearly more likely to be influenced by the presence or absence of a
favorite son, but, even aside from this factor, they seem more compelled than the
smaller delegations to exercise the prerogatives either of leadership or of responsible
choice.

Because of their size and their corresponding involvements in national politics,
the big states probably tend to become committed somewhat earlier than the others.
Once committed, they often stay with their
choice, even when the result is defeat.
Smaller states can probably avoid commitment to a loser with less difficulty, and
therefore find it easier to shift to the winner
on or before the critical ballot. But even
among the small states there are some that
have backed losers for all or most of a
generation.

Every analysis that brings up data for in-

dividual states makes clear the wide variation in the behavior of individual state
delegations, even when conditions appear
to be similar. This is especially apparent in
Tables 10, 11, and 12 of Appendix A,
wherein convention voting results are included for each of the forty-eight states. In
each analysis enough evidence of meaningful pattern can be found to intrigue the
student and to suggest interpretive comment on the reasons for the striking differences that appear between groups of states.
But every state is to some extent unique
and has its own unique patterns of behavior
within each of the national parties. Where
those patterns are both persistent and important for the effectiveness of state action,
they merit examination on a state-by-state
basis; such examination, however, would go
far beyond the possibilities of the present
chapter or the present book.

The analyses in the present chapter suggest that the effectiveness with which the
various states and non-state areas utilize
whatever voting power they have depends
on a number of conditions, some of which
can be identified and connected with their
apparent effects.

Voting effectiveness has been related to
regional identifications, to differences of
size among the states, and to the differences
caused by one-party dominance in a state
or by an active competitive situation. Outside these characteristics, there are marked
idiosyncrasies of certain states, some of
which flow from peculiarities in the state
primary election systems, as discussed elsewhere. When all the general factors that
can be distinguished and analyzed are taken
into account, they may add considerably to
an understanding of why the various states
use their convention votes with greater or
less effectiveness. The ultimate result of
such understanding might be an increase in
the efficiency of the conventions as instruments for producing nominations that
would most nearly represent the desires of
each party.

17

Voting Strategies and the Road to Consensus

THE VOTING PROCEDURE of the conventions provides many of the opportunities for strategy that are available to contending factions. Voting can be used as the means of developing and dramatizing issues, especially when the voting is by roll call and in public. Generally a roll call vote produces some new information even for those previously well-informed, and it pushes the undecided delegates into positions in which they tend to become committed in one direction or another.

Votes early in the conventions can be used to test sentiment, to measure the strength of opposing groups, to limit the alternatives, and to demonstrate in practical fashion that the alternatives are indeed limited, all in preparation for the final choice of a candidate. This is true even for the votes that deal ostensibly with matters other than the nominations. These early votes have their own distinctive character and purposes, but they also require careful examination on their relation to any contest that may be going on over the nomination.

Frequency and Type of Voting by Non-Nominating Functions

In addition to nominating the candidates, the convention has three other functions that have become increasingly manifest: it writes the platform, it serves as a campaign rally, it acts as the governing body of the national party. Each of these functions involves voting; the respective

numbers of votes by functions since 1864, other than on nominations, are shown in Table 17.1.

The Platform

In modern times, every national convention has prepared and adopted a party platform. The ostensible object is to show in detail the program on which the party will contest the presidential election. Platforms have varied widely in the extent to which they achieved this object, and there is an extensive literature discussing how far they should seek to do so. Both parties make it a point, however, to recapitulate the record of their opponents in failing to live up to their platform commitments, and the results are actively used in the campaign.

The platform involves a considerable amount of work prior to and during every national convention. Most of the organized interest groups come before the platform committee and make specific proposals. The actual drafting is performed by a relatively small group of leaders and specialists —in the case of the party in power usually with active White House participation— and reaches final form in a committee composed of two representatives of each state delegation.[1]

Struggles over party policies reach a high

[1] It can be asked how much Woodrow Wilson had to do with the Democratic platform of 1920, or Calvin Coolidge with the Republican platform of 1928; but there has probably been no in-party case since 1928 in which there was not active White House participation.

level of intensity in the platform committee. Divided votes seem to occur frequently; even more, however, the process is one of negotiation, with the objective of composing a document that the committee can recommend unanimously.

Platform adoption by the full convention requires only a single voice vote in the absence of attempts to amend. Amending attempts are usually prepared by a minority report from the platform committee; such

seems to have occurred between 1896 and 1924. This was a period, as noted in Chapter 3, in which the parties were more highly sectional than they had been previously or have been since. Each party found its main base of support in large areas of the country where it had almost complete control of state and local government. Factionalism was rife in the one-party areas, where it often provided the only effective means for registering political opposition. The fac-

TABLE 17.1. NUMBERS OF NON-NOMINATING VOTES BY FUNCTION,
NATIONAL PARTY CONVENTIONS, 1864-1956

Time Period and Number of Conventions	Platform		Campaign Rally		Governing Body	
	Voice Votes	Roll Call Votes	Voice Votes	Roll Call Votes	Voice Votes	Roll Call Votes
DEMOCRATIC CONVENTIONS						
1864–1892 (8)	17	6	68	0	279	22
1896–1924 (8)	14	10	88	0	229	22
1928–1956 (8)	22	3	133	0	151	6
Total	53	19	289	0	659	50
REPUBLICAN CONVENTIONS						
1864–1892 (8)	14	1	42	0	275	28
1896–1924 (8)	10	7	21	0	229	11
1928–1956 (8)	8	2	40	0	207	5
Total	32	10	103	0	711	44

reports have at times involved a fair amount of voting activity, as indicated by the tabulation below of numbers of votes on minority reports.

Period	Democratic		Republican	
	Voice	Roll Call	Voice	Roll Call
1864–1892	10	4	6	1
1896–1924	7	7	3	5
1928–1956	14	3	0	2

The greatest amount of serious platform controversy, as indicated by roll call voting,

tional differences found expression in the platform controversies; inability to reach agreement was sometimes followed by overt party bolting.[2]

In the period from 1928 to 1956 the platform committee gained increasing control of platform drafting in both parties. There were few serious minority reports or noteworthy attempts to amend. In the Republi-

[2] Adoption was by roll call vote in the Democratic conventions of 1872, 1876, and 1896, with, in 1876, a further voice vote to make it unanimous. The Republican convention of 1896 took a roll call vote on the financial plank and adopted the remainder by voice vote; in 1912 the platform was adopted by roll call vote. Adoption has been uniformly by voice vote in both parties since 1912.

can convention of 1928 an attempt to amend the agricultural plank was defeated on roll call vote. In both party conventions of 1932 attempts to secure more vigorous language favoring the repeal of prohibition were defeated by roll calls. A variety of other proposals were defeated by voice votes at the Democratic convention of 1932; one, an innocuous proposal for governmental interest in human welfare, was approved. In 1948 the Democratic convention was the scene of two hard-fought roll call votes on amendments to the platform language—agreed on in committee—concerning civil rights. A southern amending proposal was defeated 925 to 309. A northern substitute was then approved 651½ to 582½, whereupon all of the Mississippi delegation and half of the Alabama bolted the convention. The same issues brought attempts at floor action in 1956, but no amending vote was obtained and the platform was declared adopted by voice vote. The extraordinary character of the action in 1948 becomes especially apparent in retrospect.

The differences between the national parties, for public policy as well as other matters, are probably symbolized more clearly by their presidential candidates than by their platforms. This increases the importance of the nominations.[3]

The Campaign Rally

The campaign-rally function may occasionally take precedence over both the nominating and platform functions when a President is being renominated, as it did when Jackson's renomination was confirmed at Baltimore in 1832.[4] The same could be said of the more recent occasion when Dwight D. Eisenhower was renominated at San Francisco in 1956. Political managers have always been aware of the campaign-rally aspect and have treated it in accord with its true importance, even when unwilling to admit that it is one of the manifest purposes of the convention.

Everything that the convention does or fails to do is involved in its success as a campaign rally—the hard core of platform and nominating action most of all. But there are many aspects of convention behavior that arise almost entirely from the campaign-rally purpose, including voting on resolutions to applaud party figures and the party record, to register condolences on behalf of the deceased, to thank the hosts, the press, convention servants, and others who contribute to the convention operation, and

---

[3] Cf. Paul T. David in Stephen K. Bailey et al., *Research Frontiers in Politics and Government* (Brookings Lectures, 1955), pp. 190, 194.

The differences of program implied in candidate choice are of some importance because of the frequency with which it is argued that the American political parties have no significant differences in their programmatic objectives. The primacy of the nominating function seems to be one of the main bases for this contention, presumably because of an implied assumption that nominating choices are made without regard to their policy implications.

Throughout convention history there have been occasions on which the choice of nominee had high policy consequences. Van Buren's defeat and Polk's nomination in the Democratic convention of 1844 had exactly such consequences in regard to the annexation of Texas and relations with Mexico. In most conventions, when there is a real contest, there are substantial divergences between the ideological positions of the several contenders. The extremists do not often win, but it is out of the conflict between them that the choice emerges, and the choice is in part the resultant of the previous conflict on policy. A compromise choice, when made, has its

own consequences that will clearly be different from a choice at one end of the spectrum or the other. What is called a compromise choice, moreover, frequently means a candidate who has avoided identification with extreme positions but who nonetheless has a definite orientation that is both compatible with majority interests in his own party and capable of being distinguished from the positions likely to be taken by the other party.

To be competitive, the parties need to be different but not so different that each cannot seek majority support. Whatever clarity of differences is achieved in the choice of candidates is often considerably obscured by the behavior of each party's representatives in Congress, which in turn is often more dependent on whether or not the party is in power in the Executive Branch than on any long-term party identification with a set of program issues. Neither the Democratic nor the Republican party is likely to be very successful in presenting a single clear image of its over-all party position until some means has been found for achieving a greater integration between the views of the presidential and congressional wings of each party than has so far been customary.

[4] As noted by David B. Truman in Arthur W. Macmahon (ed.), *Federalism Mature and Emergent* (1955), p. 119.

so on. Resolutions of this kind seldom require roll call votes, but are a prolific source of voice votes in both parties.[5]

From the earliest times the Democratic party has been much more profuse than the Republican with voting actions of this kind. The difference, as shown in Table 17.1, is too great to be accidental, and is in accord with the greater air of informality in Democratic proceedings and the more frequent development of opportunities for individual delegates to receive momentary recognition. Most of these actions occur when the convention is marking time, but presumably it is believed that they make some contribution to party morale.

Even in such affairs the amount of good feeling or ill in the convention is reflected. During the period 1928-1956 the Democratic conventions with the fewest courtesy resolutions were those that nominated Al Smith in 1928 and Harry S. Truman in 1948. In each case, the front-runner was nominated on the first ballot but an adamant opposition refused to make the nomination unanimous. At the other extreme, the highest number of courtesy resolutions occurred in the Democratic convention of 1936, in which there were also fifty-six seconding speeches for Roosevelt and seventeen for Garner.

The Governing Body

The convention acts as the principal party governing body, to the extent that any governing is done in the American national parties. In a sense, everything the convention does governs the party; certainly the nomination of a candidate for President of the United States is the most important action the party can take. But the governing-body function can be used conveniently to refer to a series of activities that are some-

[5] At the Democratic convention of 1896 an attempt to amend the platform to commend the incumbent Cleveland administration was defeated on a roll call vote. This was essentially a campaign-rally type of action, although treated in the previous tables as a vote on platform.

what distinct from the nomination of candidates and the adoption of platforms, that have a separate logic of their own, and that make their own contributions to party survival, stability, and adaptation. These include all decisions on credentials and seating, convention organization, committee appointments, rules and order of business, parliamentary proceedings, recess and adjournment, national committee appointments, and all housekeeping business directed to the continuity and effectiveness of national party activity during the four-year intervals between national conventions. To the extent that the governing-body function is performed between conventions, it is vested in the party national committees, which are in turn subordinate to the national conventions.

These organizational details have been a prolific source of voting activity. Most of this has been completely routine and has been handled by voice votes, as shown in Table 17.1, but roll call votes taken on governing-body matters have been much more numerous than those on platform matters, and often more numerous than those directly required for the nominations. The specific subjects of roll call action are indicated in Table 17.2.

Since 1928 both parties have completed their convention business with fewer votes, both by voice and by roll call, than in former periods, as the tables indicate. The reduction in the number of roll call votes has been especially striking. Accumulated experience undoubtedly accounts for much of the change. Even a cursory reading of the proceedings of the earlier conventions reveals much uncertainty about routine procedure, and many of these questions made a vital difference in the control of the convention as long as the issue seemed in doubt. In Democratic conventions the two thirds rule and the order of business were recurring points of contention. In Republican conventions the voting strength and recognition of southern delegations were for several decades ever-present problems.

In both parties difficult votes on recess or

adjournment were common for a long time. Usually associated with protracted periods of balloting on nominations, they persisted longer in the Democratic conventions because of the balloting difficulties encountered in 1912, 1920, 1924, and 1932. In long-balloting conventions, votes on recess or adjournment can become critical in the tactics of one faction or another. When several ballots have been taken and one candidate appears to be gaining strength, factions supporting other candidates may seek to force adjournment in order to cool off the developing enthusiasm. On other occa-

factions turned back the national committee candidate for temporary chairman by a vote of 424 to 384; nevertheless, Blaine was later nominated. At the Democratic convention of 1896 the silver faction, although anything but a cohesive group, upset the nominee of the national committee for temporary chairman and took control of the convention.

The temporary chairmanship was contested in both parties in 1912. At the Republican convention Taft forces elected their candidate for chairman by a vote of 558 to 501, with many delegates voting whose cre-

TABLE 17.2. ROLL CALL VOTES REQUIRED FOR CONVENTION OPERATIONS, NATIONAL PARTY CONVENTIONS, 1864-1956[a]

Subject of Voting	Democratic Conventions			Republican Conventions		
	1864–1892	1896–1924	1928–1956	1864–1892	1896–1924	1928–1956
Credentials and Seating	2	4	3	15	4	3
Convention Chairmanship	0	2	1	1	1	0
Rules and Procedure	10	7	0	5	4	2
Recess or Adjournment	10	9	2	7	2	0
Total	22	22	6	28	11	5

[a] Excluding actions on platform and nominations. The roll call vote at the Democratic convention of 1904 on a proposed reply to the candidate, Alton B. Parker, is classified as a platform vote. Parker had stated his support for the gold standard and disagreement with the platform in a telegram; his nomination was allowed to stand.

sions, a recess may be sought to permit negotiations in an attempt to break a stalemate. In either case the adjournment may be bitterly fought by the supporters of the front-runner, who may fear some new coalition stronger than his previously apparent opposition.

Struggles over the convention chairmanship that reach a roll call vote have been extremely rare in either party, with a total of only five cases since the Civil War. All involved bitter factional struggle, usually in the form of an insurgent attack upon an "old guard" leadership. The first of the five cases occurred in the Republican convention of 1884, when a coalition of anti-Blaine

dentials were dubious at best. This early Taft victory practically determined the defeat of Theodore Roosevelt's effort to take the nomination. At the Democratic convention Bryan opposed the temporary chairman nominated by the conservative wing, Alton B. Parker, the party's presidential candidate of 1904. Although the effort was unsuccessful, its effect was to unsettle the forces backing Champ Clark, and Wilson was eventually nominated with Bryan's support.

Only one of the five contests involved the post of permanent chairman. At the Democratic convention of 1932, Franklin D. Roosevelt scored an initial victory when his candidate for permanent chairman, Senator David I. Walsh, was elected by a 54 per cent majority, instead of the pro-Smith candidate whom the national committee had chosen. The vote was a sign that Roosevelt was the front-runner, while also indicating his prospective difficulties in accumulating a two thirds majority for the nomination.

Consequences for Strategy of the Rules and Order of Business

The rules and order of business have important consequences for the strategy of action in the conventions.[6] The conse-

[6] So also does the question of which party's convention meets first. For a time there was apparently a theory that the party in power should hold its convention first. See for example, Theodore W. Cousens, *Politics and Political Organization in America* (1942), pp. 366-367. But this theory has no basis in the experience of the Whig-Democratic two-party system of 1840-1852, and seems to have arisen during the long period when the Republican party was in power, during which it did meet first. The Democrats met first during the first Cleveland administration, but not during the second nor during the Roosevelt and Truman administrations.

In 1956 both parties experimented with shifting their conventions to August. The Democrats met in Chicago, beginning on August 13, and the Republicans in San Francisco on August 20. The Democratic decision to open on August 13 seems to have been made without much regard to whether the Republicans met earlier or later, and in terms largely of pinning down the necessary facilities at a time when they were available.

In preparation for 1960 the Democrats again moved somewhat more rapidly than the Republicans in reaching a final decision and announced that the convention would open in Los Angeles on Monday, July 11, 1960. Somewhat later the Republicans announced that their convention would open in Chicago on Monday, July 25. The return to July as the month for both conventions was apparently dictated by a feeling of need for additional time to organize the campaign. The decision to meet in different cities was taken despite the most intense pressure from press, radio, and television for successive meetings in the same city to facilitate the problems of coverage.

The party that holds its convention last has the advantage of knowing what the other party has decided, but the disadvantage of a shorter time in which to organize its campaign and the further disadvantage of staging its convention for a national audience already somewhat jaded by the proceedings of the previous convention. The strategic advantages of meeting second have apparently been discounted heavily by Democratic party officials in recent years.

quences of the two thirds rule in this regard (as noted in Chapter 9) during its century of existence are relevant to the present chapter in connection with the number of votes required to nominate and the alliances that have been involved in building up the required majorities. The unit rule has had lesser consequences, but it was directly involved in the unsuccessful strategy of the Grant supporters in 1880 (as also noted in Chapter 9).

The rules under which contested delegates could be temporarily seated and could vote while still under challenge were central to the strategy by which the Taft administration controlled the Republican convention of 1912. These traditional rules also provided the opportunity to capitalize on the issue of the so-called Texas steal at the Republican convention of 1952. The first test vote, as engineered by the Eisenhower managers, came on an amendment of the rules to restrict the voting rights of contested delegates who were temporarily seated. The vote, 658 to 548, was a clear signal of the probable defeat of Senator Robert A. Taft, but this vote was not all for Eisenhower. It could not have been won without the 70 votes of the California delegation, which on the nominating ballot went to Governor Earl Warren.[7]

The new Republican rules of 1952 provided that only those delegates seated by a two thirds vote in the national committee could vote while under contest. This provision seemingly would have produced more legitimate outcomes in a number of earlier conventions, but it is also capable of offering new strategic opportunities for the future. Any faction holding more than one third of the national committee will be in a position to prejudice the initial voting rights of delegates from any state in which it has taken the trouble to set up a contest.[8]

[7] See Chapter 11 for further details on the 1912 and 1952 seating contests. Taft himself attributed the California vote in 1952 to a desire to stalemate the convention; see Appendix F.

[8] The potential hazards to the legitimacy of future convention action under the new rule have been developed more fully in an informal memorandum by Richard C. Bain of Brookings Institution.

When a close decision on the nomination is in prospect, even a limited use of these opportunities in states where contests can readily be arranged might be decisive. Presumably the main safeguard against this kind of behavior must be found in the pressure of public opinion for legitimacy and good order in the conduct of party affairs—a pressure that has often been relatively effective in states where the parties are competitive, and that may carry increasing influence at the national level for similar reasons.[9]

The order of business under which the conventions conduct their activities has its own effects for timing and therefore for strategy. The conventions are called to order by the national committee chairman. He presides during the first formal action—on acceptance of the temporary roll of authorized delegates supplied by the national committee. Any questions on the temporary seating or the provisional rules must be dealt with at that time, offering the first available opportunity for challenge by any group that has been dissatisfied with previous action in the national committee. The election of the temporary convention chairman comes next and offers another opportunity for challenge, as previously noted. The convention committees on credentials, permanent organization, rules and order of business, and resolutions (platform) are then appointed. These actions are almost invariably routine.

The committees usually report in the order in which they are appointed, subject to some variation when a committee needs additional time to complete its report. Usually it is deemed unwise to proceed with other business until the report of the credentials committee has been disposed of, thus ordinarily settling questions on contested seating for the duration of the convention. The committee on permanent organization recommends the final slate of convention officers, including the permanent chairman; its report may be acted on next. The timing of the rules committee report has rarely

been controversial and has sometimes preceded, sometimes followed, the election of the permanent chairman, but he is invariably installed before any action is taken on the platform or on nominations.

Early in convention history, the conventions came to the practice of adopting party platforms before turning to the nominations. In 1872, however, the Republican convention had renominated Ulysses S. Grant and chosen his new running mate before the platform committee was ready to report. At the Democratic conventions of 1880, 1912, and 1916 one candidate or both had been nominated before the platform was taken up for action. Occasionally the suggestion has been made that it would be better in principle to act on the platform only after completing the nominations, in order to permit the chosen candidate to have his say on platform provisions before they become final. So far, the conventions have not found this argument convincing, but on the occasions when platform action came after the nomination, the debate and the voting were perfunctory, as the suggestion doubtless contemplates.[10]

The nominating procedures come next after platform action. First, the roll of the states is called to permit delegations to place names "in nomination" or to give notice that they will do so, with nominating and seconding speeches and demonstrations and then the actual balloting. When the level of tension is high, procedural issues may be raised even after the convention has begun the actual balloting.

[10] The convention records have been searched for instances in which opposing candidates seemed to become highly involved in controversy over platform provisions. Very few such cases have been found, and, except in the well-known case of Bryan in 1896, they have mostly involved minor or losing candidates. Winning candidates have generally stayed clear of involvement in platform fights; such conflict has generally been resolved with enough success to satisfy all except dissident minorities with strong views. Public votes on platform issues have usually been lopsided, and seldom as close as two to one. On the other hand, procedural issues and other matters involving convention control have frequently been of great interest to factions contending over the nomination, and have been very close, as the tables later in this chapter will demonstrate.

[9] Cf. Chapter 11.

Such occasions are rare, however, and usually involve some unanticipated conjuncture of events, as in the Virginia seating vote while the roll was being called for nominations at the Democratic convention of 1952. Recent convention chairmen have rarely permitted the kind of tactics in which William Jennings Bryan indulged during the proceedings of 1912.[11]

The vice-presidential nomination has invariably come after the presidential. The procedure is substantially the same but names are more often placed in nomination purely for courtesy, after which the proposed candidate expresses appreciation and withdraws. Frequently the nomination is uncontested, and sometimes it is perfunctory indeed. At the Republican convention of 1952, for example, the chairman received a motion, duly seconded, to nominate Richard M. Nixon for Vice President by acclamation and, hearing no objection, declared the motion carried. This may be the only case on record in which a candidate was nominated by acclamation through the silence of the participants.

The strategic possibilities would be greatly changed if the candidates for both offices were nominated together as a ticket or if the vice-presidential nomination were made first. Both proposals have been made and have received some consideration in recent years.[12] During the period when Stephen A. Mitchell was chairman of the Democratic national committee, and during his later chairmanship of the Mitchell committee, he discussed these proposals informally with a number of party leaders, but found little support for any change, even though the undesirable aspects of existing practices were generally admitted.[13] Any change in procedure would probably have the effect of establishing a visible group of separate candidates for the vice-presidential nomination, who might then ally themselves in one way or another with the various presidential candidates.[14] A vote on the vice-presidential nomination, if taken first, would have the close attention of the delegates and the country, and, when there is a contest over the presidential nomination, might provide the most important test vote leading up to the final balloting.

Ratification vs. Decision-Making

A first-term incumbent can usually expect renomination without difficulty, but this was not the experience of Franklin Pierce in 1856, Benjamin Harrison in 1892, or William Howard Taft in 1912. In a wide-open out-party nominating situation, on the other hand, a contest usually seems inevitable, but the contest for Landon's nomination in 1936 was over before the conven-

[11] At the point when nominating speeches were about to begin, Bryan requested and received "unanimous approval" to address the convention, and then requested that the rules be suspended for action on a resolution reading in part that "we hereby declare ourselves opposed to the nomination of any candidate for president who is the representative of or under obligation to J. Pierpont Morgan, Thomas F. Ryan, August Belmont, or any other member of the privilege-hunting and favor-seeking class." (DNC *Proceedings, 1912,* p. 129.) The resolution was eventually adopted after dropping an additional clause that demanded withdrawal from the convention of any delegates connected with those interests. All three men named had provided major financial support for the campaigns of Democratic candidates.

During the fourteenth ballot, when Nebraska was called, Bryan asked unanimous consent to "explain" his vote. This was first declined and then granted after a magnanimous motion by the chairman of the Clark delegation from Missouri. Bryan then made a lengthy speech in which he stated that he and his friends would not vote for Clark as long as the latter was receiving the vote of the Tammany delegation from New York City (which had switched to Clark on the previous ballot).

On both occasions, Bryan threw the convention into an uproar. As the party's titular leader and three-time nominee, most recently in 1908, he was taking advantage of a unique position.

[12] The first proposal originated with Judge Thomas N. Fasso of New York; the second in the book by Paul T. David, Malcolm Moos, and Ralph M. Goldman, *Presidential Nominating Politics in 1952* (1954), Vol. 1, pp. 229-31.
[13] Letter, February 20, 1959.
[14] This in turn might tend to foreclose the possibility of the vice-presidential nomination being given to a really serious candidate for the Presidency—which has seldom actually happened, despite the case of Senator Estes Kefauver in 1956. See Chapter 7.

TABLE 17.3. FIRST-BALLOT DIVISIONS OF THE PRESIDENTIAL NOMINATING VOTE, DEMOCRATIC CONVENTIONS UNDER THE TWO THIRDS RULE, 1832-1932

		Situation on First Ballot					
		Front-Runner		Number of Candidates Polling Stated Percentages			Number of Prenominating Roll Call Votes
Year	Per Cent on First Ballot		Nominated or Not	3%–10%	10%–20%	20%–100%	
Over 90%							
1832	100.0%	Andrew Jackson	Yes			1	0
1836	100.0	Martin Van Buren	Yes			1	0
1840	100.0	Martin Van Buren	Yes			1	0
1888	100.0	Grover Cleveland	Yes			1	0
1900	100.0	William Jennings Bryan	Yes			1	0
1916	99.9	Woodrow Wilson	Yes			1	0
1872	93.7	Horace Greeley	Yes			1	2
Between 75% and 90%							
1908	88.7%	William Jennings Bryan	Yes	2		1	1
1928	77.2	Alfred E. Smith	Yes	5		1	0
1864	75.3	George B. McClellan	Yes	1	1	1	0
Over 66 2/3%, under 75%							
1904	67.9%	Alton B. Parker	Yes	2		2	1
1892	67.8	Grover Cleveland	Yes	1	2	1	1
Under 66 2/3%, over 50%							
1932	57.7%	Franklin D. Roosevelt	Yes	3	1	1	4
1876	56.6	Samuel J. Tilden	Yes	2	2	1	2
1844	54.9	Martin Van Buren	No[a]	1		2	1
Under 50%, over 40%							
1860	48.0%[b]	Stephen A. Douglas	Yes	1	2	1	25
1884	47.8	Grover Cleveland	Yes	3	2	1	6
1856	45.8	James Buchanan	Yes		1	2	14
1848	43.1[c]	Lewis Cass	Yes	1	2	1	7
1912	40.5	Champ Clark	No		2	2	3
Under 40%							
1924	39.3%	William G. McAdoo	No	5		2	3
1852	39.2	Lewis Cass	No[a]	3		2	3
1868	33.1	George H. Pendleton	No[a]	4	2	2	5
1896	25.3[d]	Richard P. Bland	No	4	2	1	5
1920	24.3	William G. McAdoo	No	4	1	2	3
1880	23.2	Winfield S. Hancock	Yes	5	1	2	3

[a] The actual nominee received no votes on first ballot.
[b] 16.7 per cent of delegates did not vote. Based on first ballot of Charleston Convention.
[c] 12.4 per cent of delegates did not vote.
[d] 19.1 per cent of delegates did not vote.

tion began, as was also the case for Dewey's in 1944.

For some purposes the level of conflict is more basic to the analysis of convention behavior than the apparent pattern of leadership confirmation or succession within which conflict occurs. The number and relative strength of the candidates is usually the best indicator of the amount and kind of conflict that will occur.

The range of distribution in number and strength of candidates at the opening of balloting in Democratic conventions under the two thirds rule is indicated in Table 17.3. The conventions are listed in order of rank on the basis of the front-runner's first-ballot vote, and are arranged in six groups, according to the categories indicated in the table. In the top group there was no contest of importance over the nomination. In the next group there was a hard core of opposition, but not enough to threaten an effective veto. In the third group, those with the required two thirds but just barely so, the outcome was in doubt until it occurred, with some risk of an effective veto up to the conclusion of the ballot. In all the cases in the first three groups, the nomination was of course completed on the first ballot.

The fourth group, those where the front-runner polled less than the required two thirds but more than an absolute majority, included only three cases in a century. Roosevelt and Tilden were victorious in the end; Van Buren, out of office and seeking his third nomination for President, was not. The possibility of a veto under the two thirds rule was thus demonstrated in the case of a candidate who came into the balloting with more than 50 per cent of the votes.

In the fifth group the front-runner came into the balloting with less than a 50 per cent majority but within 10 per cent of it. Four of the five in this group were eventually first-time nominees; Champ Clark was turned back by Woodrow Wilson, despite the fact that he received more than 50 per cent at one point in the balloting.

The sixth group includes six cases where the front-runner polled less than 40 per cent on the first ballot. Only one was nominated—Hancock, who entered the balloting with only 23 per cent of the vote but nonetheless proved strongest in a field of weak candidates.

Similar data for the first ballots in the conventions of the Republican party and its predecessors are shown in Table 17.4. In all of these conventions, nominations were settled by majority vote; the cases have been arranged in five groups. In the top group, there was again virtually no contest. The second group includes four cases where there was opposition but not enough to pose a serious threat, although these were all first-time nominations. The third group includes three cases where a majority was polled but with less than 10 per cent to spare; two of these were incumbent Presidents, Benjamin Harrison and William Howard Taft, who won renomination but not election.

The fourth group, those below a majority but over 40 per cent, includes four cases with a very mixed record. General Eisenhower was so near a majority that he went over the line on the switch of a few votes. President Fillmore was seeking nomination to succeed himself but did not make it, despite his high front-runner vote. Blaine was front-runner against an incumbent President, Chester A. Arthur, and defeated him. Grant was seeking a third-term nomination after two terms in the White House and one out of office.

The fifth group includes the cases in which the front-runner polled less than 40 per cent, eight in all. Two at the top of this group won their nominations, as did Hughes at the bottom; all of the others were discarded before the issue was settled.

To complete the series, the experience of the Democratic party since it adopted majority rule in 1936 is presented in Table 17.5. The party's experience under the ma-

TABLE 17.4. FIRST-BALLOT DIVISIONS OF THE PRESIDENTIAL NOMINATING VOTE, NATIONAL REPUBLICAN, WHIG, AND REPUBLICAN CONVENTIONS, 1832-1956

	Situation on First Ballot						
	Front-Runner			Number of Candidates Polling Stated Percentages			Number of Prenominating Roll Call Votes
Year	Per Cent on First Ballot		Nominated or Not	3%–10%	10%–20%	20%–100%	
	Over 90%						
1832	100.0%	Henry Clay	Yes			1	0
1844	100.0	Henry Clay	Yes			1	0
1868	100.0	Ulysses S. Grant	Yes			1	0
1872	100.0	Ulysses S. Grant	Yes			1	0
1900	100.0	William B. McKinley	Yes			1	0
1904	100.0	Theodore Roosevelt	Yes			1	1
1944	100.0	Thomas E. Dewey	Yes			1	0
1956	100.0	Dwight D. Eisenhower	Yes			1	0
1936	98.4	Alfred M. Landon	Yes			1	0
1932	97.6	Herbert Hoover	Yes			1	1
1924	96.0	Calvin Coolidge	Yes			1	0
1864	93.3	Abraham Lincoln	Yes			1	3
	Between 60% and 90%						
1928	76.9%	Herbert Hoover	Yes	3		1	2
1896	73.4	William B. McKinley	Yes	4		1	1
1908	71.6	William Howard Taft	Yes	4		1	5
1856	64.3	John C. Frémont	Yes			2	0
	Over 50%, under 60%						
1892	59.2%	Benjamin Harrison	Yes			3	3
1840	58.3	William H. Harrison	Yes	1		2	(?)
1912	52.1[a]	William Howard Taft	Yes	2		1	7
	Under 50%, over 40%						
1952	49.3%	Dwight D. Eisenhower	Yes	1		2	3
1852	44.9	Millard Fillmore	No	1		2	4
1884	40.8	James G. Blaine	Yes	2	1	2	1
1880	40.2	Ulysses S. Grant	No[b]	2	1	2	11
	Under 40%						
1948	39.7%	Thomas E. Dewey	Yes	4	1	2	0
1848	39.4	Zachary Taylor	Yes	1	1	2	1
1876	37.7	James G. Blaine	No	3	2	1	2
1860	37.3	William H. Seward	No	1	3	2	0
1940	36.0	Thomas E. Dewey	No	5	2	1	0
1920	29.2	Leonard Wood	No	4	1	2	0
1888	27.5	John Sherman	No	5	4	1	1
1916	25.3	Charles Evans Hughes	Yes	7	2	1	0

[a] 32.3 per cent of delegates did not vote.
[b] The actual nominee received no votes on first ballot.

jority rule is too brief to merit much discussion, but seems in general to conform to the patterns displayed in Table 17.4. Roosevelt in 1940, Truman in 1948, and Stevenson in 1956 might all have faced a potentially different outcome under the two thirds rule. As a modest front-runner in a field of several candidates, Kefauver joined a goodly number of other similar front-

never entirely complete or accurate. On the other hand, it can be surmised that the candidate managers of the past usually had a rather good notion in advance of their candidate's prospective first-ballot strength. In a situation of some complexity, later ballots were much more likely to be affected by events during the convention than the opening nominating ballot, which

TABLE 17.5. FIRST-BALLOT DIVISIONS OF THE PRESIDENTIAL NOMINATING VOTE, DEMOCRATIC CONVENTIONS UNDER MAJORITY RULE, 1936-1956

		Situation on First Ballot					
	Front-Runner			Number of Candidates Polling Stated Percentages			Number of Prenominating
Year	Per Cent on First Ballot		Nominated or Not	$3\%-$ 10%	$10\%-$ 20%	$20\%-$ 100%	Roll Call Votes
	Over 90%						
1936	100.0%	Franklin D. Roosevelt	Yes			1	0
1944	92.3	Franklin D. Roosevelt	Yes	1		1	0
	Between 60% and 90%						
1940	86.1%	Franklin D. Roosevelt	Yes	2		1	0
1948	76.8	Harry S. Truman	Yes			2	2
1956	66.0	Adlai E. Stevenson	Yes	2	1	1	0
	Under 40%						
1952	27.6%	Estes Kefauver	No	3	1	3	2

runners who failed to achieve their party's nomination.

The data on which Tables 17.3, 17.4, and 17.5 are based show what actually happened rather than what was expected in advance of the conventions. Presumably the votes were affected somewhat by the strategies that were pursued after the convention opened and before the first nominating ballot. Under modern conditions, it is possible to look at advance polls of how the delegates are expected to vote; these polls are in some respects a better indication of the early strategic situations than anything formerly available, even though they are

always involved many advance commitments—*pro forma* and otherwise—not necessarily expected to hold good if the nomination required several ballots.

Strategy of Non-Nominating Roll Call Votes

The most obvious reason for taking a roll call vote is to reach a decision that will be in accord with the will of the majority where views are closely divided. However, if this were the most frequent actual reason, it could be expected that most non-nominating roll call votes would be settled by rather close margins. A voice vote should suffice when the division is heavily in one direction; but many roll call votes have been taken which resulted in heavy majorities, as indicated by Table 17.6. More than one third of the votes in the two parties, as shown in the table, were settled by majorities of 65 per cent or more.

often sought votes that they knew they could not win, if the issue seemed calculated to split the majority or otherwise embarrass it. Frequently the purpose has been to advertise an issue for propaganda purposes and to make plain the position of the contesting groups. Occasionally a roll call is merely a tactic for delay, since it is always time-consuming.

TABLE 17.6. FREQUENCY OF NON-NOMINATING ROLL CALL VOTES BY PERCENTAGE LEVELS OF THE WINNING VOTE, NATIONAL CONVENTIONS, 1864-1956

Percentage Level of Winning Vote	Democratic		Republican		Both Parties	
	Number	Per Cent	Number	Per Cent	Number	Per Cent
50–55%	20	29.0%	22	40.7%	42	34.2%
55–60	11	15.9	9	16.7	20	16.3
60–65	11	15.9	8	14.8	19	15.4
65–75	12	17.5	6	11.1	18	14.6
75–85	9	13.0	0	0.0	9	7.3
85–100	6	8.7	9	16.7	15	12.2
Total	69	100.0	54	100.0	123	100.0

The two thirds rule was long held responsible for the fact that roll call votes were more numerous in Democratic conventions than in Republican. Its influence is probably reflected in Table 17.6, since only four of the cases in the Democratic figures have occurred since 1936. Party strategists theorized that in view of the difficulties in aggregating any coalition reaching two thirds, a strong candidate should demonstrate his strength by seeking a victory on some preliminary issue that could be settled by majority vote. Conversely, hardcore centers of opposition may have sought to demonstrate in advance that they held enough voting power to impose a veto; for this purpose, any vote of even 25 or 30 per cent could be impressive.

Other reasons for obtaining a roll call vote have doubtless been important at times. Majorities already assured of their strength have sometimes obtained roll call votes to smoke out the minority, possibly for later punitive action. Minorities have

Tables 17.3, 17.4, and 17.5 show that prenominating roll call votes were rare in the conventions that moved easily toward a first-ballot choice, were most common in the conventions that involved close contests, and were less common in the conventions that began with no single outstanding candidate. In these less common cases, especially in Republican conventions, roll call votes may have been avoided at times by tacit consent, because no candidate was in a position to demonstrate strength.

The critical vote on the nomination was nevertheless significantly related to at least one earlier roll call vote on some subject in about three quarters of the contested conventions from 1832 to 1956. The principal instances of this kind that are apparent from the voting records of the conventions are brought together in another way in Tables 17.7 and 17.8.

During the course of the analysis of this data, it was discovered that the early voting behavior of the delegations that were

TABLE 17.7. RELATIONSHIPS BETWEEN SELECTED ROLL CALL VOTES AND THE CRITICAL BALLOT FOR THE WINNER, CONTESTED DEMOCRATIC CONVENTIONS, 1832-1956[a]

Per Cent for Winner, First Ballot	Year, Candidate, and Subject of Selected Roll Call Vote	Total Convention			High for Winner[b]			Low for Winner[c]		
		Per Cent for Winner, Critical Ballot	Majority on Roll Call Vote, Per Cent[d]	Index of Relationship[e]	Per Cent for Winner, Critical Ballot	Majority on Roll Call Vote, Per Cent[f]	Index of Relationship[g]	Per Cent Against Winner, Critical Ballot	Majority on Roll Call Vote, Per Cent[h]	Index of Relationship[g]
	CONVENTIONS WITH A FIRST-BALLOT WINNER									
88.7%	1908 Bryan: Credentials	88.7%	62.0% (N)	0.45	100.0%	69.9% (N)	0.40	53.5%	72.7% (A)	0.62
76.8	1948 Truman: Moody Resolution	75.0	74.9 (N)	0.96	97.5	98.7 (N)	0.98	95.6	100.0 (A)	0.91
67.9	1904 Parker: Credentials	65.8	68.4 (N)	0.85	99.3	96.3 (N)	0.94	87.6	73.4 (A)	0.72
67.8	1892 Cleveland: Tariff Plank	67.7	62.4 (A)	0.39	95.0	51.9 (N)	0.14	72.9	83.9 (A)	0.78
	Average			0.66			0.62			0.76
	CONVENTIONS WITH A STRONG FRONT-RUNNER WHO WON									
57.7%	1932 Roosevelt: Louisiana Credentials	57.7%	55.4% (N)	0.95	94.4%	89.4% (N)	0.92	86.8%	85.8% (A)	0.98
56.6	1876 Tilden: Platform	54.8	69.0 (N)	0.70	89.5	88.7 (N)	0.98	83.9	53.2 (A)	0.39
48.0	1860 Douglas: Recommit Platform	50.0	50.2 (A)	0.99	89.7	89.0 (N)	0.99	86.9	86.9 (A)	1.00
47.8	1884 Cleveland: Unit Rule	57.9	58.2 (N)	0.87	84.4	78.6 (N)	0.88	73.0	65.8 (A)	0.86
45.8	1856 Buchanan: Adjourn After 13th Ballot	56.8	55.4 (N)	0.85	92.9	84.6 (N)	0.83	83.6	77.1 (A)	0.87
43.1	1848 Cass: Table Motion on Two Thirds Rule	53.8	52.4 (N)	0.72	93.5	71.4 (N)	0.56	91.2	89.0 (A)	0.96
	Average			0.85			0.86			0.84
	CONVENTIONS IN WHICH THE WINNER WAS WEAK ON FIRST BALLOT									
29.8%	1912 Wilson: Temporary Chairman, Parker	58.1%	53.2% (A)	0.55	94.2%	63.0% (N)	0.38	85.5%	72.8% (A)	0.75
23.2	1880 Hancock: Previous Question, Credentials	43.2	54.1 (A)	0.57	76.5	54.7 (N)	0.57	84.9	63.2 (A)	0.57
22.2	1952 Stevenson: Virginia Seating	49.8	55.7 (A)	0.54	88.2	58.0 (N)	0.39	85.3	69.2 (A)	0.68
14.7	1896 Bryan: Temporary Chairman, Daniel	49.2	61.4 (A)	0.45	96.2	81.4 (A)	0.70	95.2	56.3 (N)	0.22
12.2	1920 Cox: Minority Platform, Prohibition	63.9	67.8 (N)	0.38	90.1	52.3 (N)	0.15	80.0	92.4 (N)	0.75
2.2	1924 Davis: Ku Klux Klan	52.4	50.1 (N)	0.65	92.1	70.7 (N)	0.57	82.3	67.7 (A)	0.71
	Average			0.52			0.46			0.61

(Continued on page 422)

a Although this table and Table 17,8 between them cover the entire convention experience from the beginnings of the system to 1956, they do not happen to include either the earliest conventions or those of 1956. All conventions are included in which:

1. The winner received less than 90 per cent of the vote on the first ballot. All unanimous or near unanimous first-ballot nominations are excluded by this criterion.
2. The winner received more than 25 per cent of the vote but less than 90 per cent at the end of a roll call prior to the vote shift resulting in unanimous or near-unanimous nomination. Such cases as the nominations of Polk in 1844, Pierce in 1852, and Seymour in 1868 are excluded by this qualification. In these cases, no critical vote can be established because the nomination resulted from a quick shift from substantially zero support for the winner to substantially 100 per cent support.
3. A non-nominating roll call vote was taken prior to the critical nominating ballot.
4. On the non-nominating roll call, the delegations high for the winner voted in substantially different proportions than the delegations low for the winner.

Of the conventions that met the first three criteria, only one failed to meet the fourth. In the 1920 Republican convention, a roll call was taken to adjourn after the third ballot. The delegations high for Harding on the subsequent critical ballot voted in substantially the same proportions on the same side of the adjournment questions as the delegations low for Harding. The index of relationship for the convention as a whole was 0.25, and for the high for Harding group (see note g) results in a negative index. On this basis, about half of all the conventions are included, and about three quarters of those that were contested.

When more than one roll call vote on another subject occurred before the final nominating ballot, the one selected is generally the first one. In a few instances, where several such votes occurred, the one that seems most representative of the struggle within the convention is selected. Further details concerning the votes and the voting sequence will appear in Richard C. Bain, *Decisions and Voting Records of the National Party Conventions* (Brookings Institution, forthcoming). The methods of analysis that underlie Tables 17.7 and 17.8 were developed by Mr. Bain, in consultation particularly with F. P. Kilpatrick of the Brookings staff.

b All delegations casting a higher percentage of their vote for the nominee than the convention average on the critical ballot; for example, in the first line of the table, all delegations giving more than 88.7 per cent of their vote to Bryan on the critical ballot in 1908. In this instance, the delegations high for the winner gave him their entire vote, 100.0 per cent, while the converse group of delegations low for the winner voted 53.5 per cent against him.

c All delegations casting a lower percentage of their vote for the nominee than the convention average on the critical ballot. For convenience, the reciprocal is shown in the table as their vote against the nominee.

d Winning side of the question; whether "Aye" or "No" indicated by (A) or (N). In case of votes for temporary chairman, a vote for the name indicated is treated as an affirmative vote.

e The index of relationship is a measure of the degree to which delegations tended to cast their votes on one side or the other of a roll call issue in the same proportions as they subsequently did for or against the convention winner on the critical ballot. The index for the total convention is computed from the data used separately in computing the indexes for the high-for-winner and low-for-winner groups described in note g below. Details of calculation are also included in note g.

f Side of the question receiving a majority of the votes of the high-for-winner group of delegations; usually but not invariably the winning side. Whether "Aye" or "No" indicated by (A) or (N).

g A measure of the tendency for high-for-winner or low-for-winner delegations to cast their vote on one side or the other on the selected roll call in the same proportion as they subsequently did for or against the convention winner on the critical ballot. The index ordinarily corresponds directly to $1 - 2d$, where d is the difference between the two percentages of vote being compared. Thus, in 1908 the high-for-winner group for Bryan gave him 100.0 per cent of its vote, and voted 69.9 per cent on the negative side of the credentials question. The difference between the two percentages is 30.1, which becomes 0.30 when converted to a decimal fraction and rounded. $1 - 2d$ thus produces an index of 0.40. Exceptions occur when a substantial number of votes are not cast, as in the case of a bolt, or a contested delegation did not vote on its own case.

The index of relationship is based on the assumption that the high- and low-for-winner groups vote on opposite sides of the question. However, in a few instances, a majority of votes for both groups were cast on the same side, although in different proportions. Thus, in 1920 high-for-winner delegations voted 52.3 per cent and low-for-winner delegations 92.4 on the negative side of the question. Since it is obvious that most of the affirmative vote came from the high-for-winner group, some relationship exists between the vote on the issue and the vote for the nomination, even though a majority of both groups do vote on the same side of the question. In such cases the index of relationship is calculated as usual for the group voting most solidly on the question (the low-for-winner group in the example above), but for the group deeply split, the vote on the opposite (or minority) side of the question is used in the calculation.

Table 17.7. Relationships Between Selected Roll Call Votes and the Critical Ballot for the Winner, Contested Democratic Conventions, 1832-1956[a]

(Continued from page 421)

For those interested in the technical details, it should be noted that the actual calculations were made in all cases from the votes rather than percentages. The procedure is as follows:

1. Obtain the difference between the majority vote of the high-for-winner group on the roll call vote and the vote for the winner on the critical ballot.
2. Multiply the difference in number of votes by 2 (disregarding signs).
3. Divide the result by the total number of votes held by the high-for-winner group.
4. Subtract the proportion thus obtained from 1.00.

Follow the same procedure to obtain the index for the low-for-winner group. To obtain the index for the total convention, add the results obtained in step 2 for the high- and low-for-winner groups, divide by the total number of votes in the convention, and subtract from 1.00. As an illustration, of the 1,234 votes in the 1948 Democratic convention, 936 were held by the delegations voting higher than the convention average for Truman, of which 913 votes actually were cast for him. These delegations voted 924 votes on the negative side of the Moody resolution. The calculations therefore are:

$$924 - 913 = 11; \ 11 \times 2 = 22; \ \frac{22}{936} = .024; \ 1.00 - .02 = 0.98$$

The low-for-winner group consisted of 298 votes, 285 of which were cast against Truman, and all of which were cast on the affirmative side of the Moody resolution. The difference of 13 multiplied by 2, divided by 298, equals .087, which subtracted from 1.00 after rounding results in an index of 0.91.

For the index of relationship for the total convention, double the differences for the high and low groups is $2(11 + 13) = 48$, which divided by the total number of votes in the convention (1,234) is .039. Subtracted from 1.00 (again after rounding), the resulting index is 0.96.

[a] Side of the question receiving a majority of the votes of the low-for-winner group of delegations; usually but not invariably the winning side. Whether "Aye" or "No" indicated by (A) or (N).

TABLE 17.8. RELATIONSHIPS BETWEEN SELECTED ROLL CALL VOTES AND THE CRITICAL BALLOT FOR THE WINNER, CONTESTED WHIG AND REPUBLICAN CONVENTIONS, 1832–1956[a]

Per Cent for Winner, First Ballot	Year, Candidate, and Subject of Selected Roll Call Vote	Total Convention			High for Winner[b]			Low for Winner[e]		
		Per Cent for Winner, Critical Ballot	Majority on Roll Call Vote, Per Cent[d]	Index of Relationship[c]	Per Cent for Winner, Critical Ballot	Majority on Roll Call Vote, Per Cent[f]	Index of Relationship[g]	Per Cent Against Winner, Critical Ballot	Majority on Roll Call Vote, Per Cent[h]	Index of Relationship[g]
	CONVENTIONS WITH A FIRST-BALLOT WINNER									
76.9%	1928 Hoover: Credentials	76.6%	62.1% (N)	0.72	98.3%	81.2% (N)	0.66	64.3%	73.5% (A)	0.81
73.4	1896 McKinley: Previous Question, Credentials	69.1	60.5 (A)	0.78	95.4	80.8 (A)	0.71	83.7	79.8 (N)	0.92
71.6	1908 Taft: Reapportionment	71.6	51.6 (N)	0.54	97.7	72.3 (N)	0.49	83.4	91.4 (A)	0.84
59.1	1892 Harrison: Credentials	59.1	52.1 (N)	0.86	81.3	69.1 (N)	0.76	71.1	70.4 (A)	0.98
51.5	1912 Taft: Temporary Chairman, Root	51.5	52.6 (A)	0.92	85.6	82.7 (A)	0.94	89.3	84.4 (N)	0.90
49.3	1952 Eisenhower: Brown Amendment	49.3	54.6 (N)	0.81	83.4	79.4 (N)	0.92	85.9	71.2 (A)	0.71
Average				0.77			0.75			0.86
	CONVENTIONS WITH A STRONG FRONT-RUNNER WHO WON									
44.6%	1852 Scott: Rules, Delegation Voting	44.6%	50.9% (A)	0.88	89.8%	95.6% (A)	0.88	94.3%	88.3% (N)	0.88
40.8	1884 Blaine: Temporary Chairman, Lynch	45.7	52.5 (A)	0.83	76.0	69.0 (N)	0.86	82.0	72.2 (A)	0.81
39.4	1848 Taylor: Rules, Delegation Voting	47.2	55.2 (N)	0.95	77.4	72.3 (A)	0.90	81.4	81.3 (N)	1.00
Average				0.89			0.88			0.90
	CONVENTIONS IN WHICH THE WINNER WAS WEAK ON FIRST BALLOT									
25.7%	1916 Hughes: Adjourn After 2d Ballot	33.3%	70.8% (A)	0.87	53.4%	56.1% (A)	0.81	93.4%	90.3% (A)	0.94
21.9	1860 Lincoln: Credentials	49.7	61.6 (A)	0.82	79.9	88.1 (A)	0.84	90.5	79.9 (N)	0.79
10.2	1888 Harrison: Credentials	33.5	67.3 (N)	0.44	81.0	82.9 (N)	0.96	89.8	59.1 (N)	0.02
8.7	1876 Hayes: Credentials	50.8	50.6 (N)	0.19	91.3	54.6 (A)	0.27	97.9	54.6 (N)	0.13
0.0	1880 Garfield: Order of Business	52.8	56.1 (N)	0.83	90.5	83.9 (N)	0.87	79.4	68.6 (A)	0.79
Average				0.63			0.75			0.53

a For explanatory footnotes, see Table 17.7.

eventually high for the winner was frequently quite different from that of the delegations that eventually proved to be low for winner. The votes were therefore analyzed separately for each of these groups as well as for the convention as a whole. In the usual case, but with interesting exceptions, the delegations that opposed each other on the nomination were opposed in about the same degree on the related earlier vote.

The 1948 Democratic convention provided a clear example of relationship in the vote on the resolution to amend the platform on civil rights, moved by ex-Governor Dan Moody of Texas. The delegations high for Truman voted 97.5 per cent for him on the nomination and 98.7 per cent against the Moody resolution. The delegations low for Truman voted 95.6 per cent against him on the nomination and 100.0 per cent for the Moody resolution. The anti-Truman delegations thus were solid on the platform issue and only slightly less so against his nomination.[15]

The Brown amendment vote at the Republican convention of 1952 was highly related to the nominating ballot, but more so on the side of the delegations that were high for Eisenhower than those that were low. Among the Eisenhower supporters the index of relationship was 0.92; among his opponents only 0.71.[16] The Republican convention of 1888, the first at which Benjamin Harrison was nominated, provided an example of a different kind of extreme relationship: the index for the delegations high for the winner was 0.96, for the others 0.02. The delegations that eventually supported the winner were nearly solid on an early test vote on credentials, while the other delegations were deeply divided in their own ranks on that issue.

For each of the three groups of conventions in the tables—those with a first-ballot winner, those with a front-runner who went on to win the nomination, and those in which the eventual winner was weak on the first ballot—average indexes of relationship have been computed. They are given here in Table 17.9.

In each party the highest average indexes of relationship are found for the conventions that began with a strong front-runner who required more than one ballot to win; the next highest for the conventions with first-ballot winners; and the lowest for those in which the eventual winner was weak on the first ballot. Not all of these differences are statistically significant, since the averages for each party rest at most on the data from six conventions, but they are all in accord with the differences in strategical situations that characterize each group of conventions.[17]

In the contested conventions that move to a first-ballot winner, the leading candidate is usually so near to nomination when the convention opens that the result seems inevitable. The candidate has little need to seek a test vote to prove his strength, but opposition groups may insist on an early record vote—for home consumption, for publicity purposes, to demonstrate that their strength though limited is real, or just because they are angry. In such cases the opposition to the winner is often more nearly solid than his supporters, many of whom may be simply riding the band wagon. Thus in such conventions it comes about that the average index of relationship is higher for the opposition delegations than for those supporting the winner.

In the conventions with a strong front-runner whose victory is not yet assured, control of the convention always has the possibility of becoming critical. An early vote on an issue of convention control is therefore likely to be sought either by the

---

[15] See Table 17.7, line for 1948.
[16] See Table 17.8, line for 1952. The "index of relationship" is not a correlation coefficient, although it resembles it in appearance, varies between 0.00 and 1.00, and does in fact indicate the general level of relationship between the variables. For a number of technical reasons, the most commonly used measures of correlation do not serve well in the analysis of the convention voting records. See the footnotes to Table 17.7 for the method of computing the index of relationship.

[17] See footnote b of Table 17.9.

front-runner or by a coalition of the forces that are trying to stop him. Voting relationships become very tight in these cases because they are so clearly tests of strength. The high indexes of relationship are the result, along with patterns of voting that are

nominating balloting, but, as the tables show, the relationships are typically less close in these confused situations.

Tables 17.7 and 17.8 can be used as indexes to the convention history of the two parties on the strategic use of prenominat-

TABLE 17.9. RELATIONSHIPS BETWEEN SELECTED ROLL CALL VOTES AND THE CRITICAL BALLOT FOR THE WINNER IN CONVENTIONS WHERE SUCH RELATIONSHIPS WERE FOUND, 1832-1956[a]

(in average indexes)

Categories[b]	Total Convention	High-for-Winner Delegations	Low-For-Winner Delegations
DEMOCRATIC CONVENTIONS			
First-Ballot Winner	0.66	0.62	0.76
Strong Front-Runner Who Won	0.85	0.86	0.84
Winner Weak on First Ballot	0.52	0.46	0.61
REPUBLICAN CONVENTIONS			
First-Ballot Winner	0.77	0.75	0.86
Strong Front-Runner Who Won	0.89	0.88	0.90
Winner Weak on First Ballot	0.63	0.75	0.53
CONVENTIONS OF BOTH PARTIES			
First-Ballot Winner	0.72	0.69	0.82
Strong Front-Runner Who Won	0.86	0.87	0.86
Winner Weak on First Ballot	0.57	0.59	0.58

[a] See Tables 17.7 and 17.8 for individual conventions and explanatory footnotes.
[b] Using the combined data for the two parties, the differences between categories are found to be significant (*), highly significant (**), or not significant (n.s.) as follows, on the basis of a standard statistical test:

	Total Convention	High-for-Winner	Low-for-Winner
First-Ballot Winner/Strong Front-Runner	n.s.	n.s.	n.s.
First-Ballot Winner/Winner Weak on First Ballot	*	n.s.	**
Strong Front-Runner/Winner Weak on First Ballot	**	**	**

In similar comparisons for the parties separately, the addition of a very few cases that maintained the pattern would produce relationships that would test high for statistical significance.

relatively much more consistent than those found in other types of convention.

In the conventions that begin with much fragmentation of strength and great uncertainty concerning the eventual winner, there is less tendency to force issues for the purpose of providing test votes. Roll call voting may nonetheless occur with some frequency because of the amount of confusion and internal conflict that is characteristic of such conventions. The results usually prove to have some relationship to the eventual

ing votes. Many of the specific instances will be recalled by students of American history; a considerable amount of lore has grown up about some of them.[18]

Convention strategists have been prepared to take credit for test votes that advanced the fortunes of their candidates, but the interpretation of these events has often

[18] Brief summaries of these events will appear in the forthcoming book by Richard C. Bain, *Decisions and Voting Records of the National Party Conventions* (Brookings Institution).

been obscure or actively controversial. In most cases, the easiest supposition is probably the correct one: that an early vote, regardless of its subject, was known at the time to be important to one or more of the candidates, and accordingly brought out a voting pattern in which most of the delegates were expressing their candidate preferences. But it should not be assumed too easily or completely that the early votes merely reflect existing preferences on candidates. The highest art, apparently, is to arrange a strategic vote on which the uncommitted delegates, or even delegates committed to another candidate, will be compelled to vote their consciences in a direction favorable to a particular candidate. They are then at least somewhat committed to the fortunes of the candidate with whom they have become associated.[19]

Different theories apply in the case of the early votes that correlate with the final votes when a different candidate is nominated after the rejection of the front-runner, the runner-up, and sometimes others of prominence. Here the prenominating vote or votes have often served to identify the elements of the majority that will eventually coalesce around the winner, while also serving to identify the minority elements in the conventions that will probably be defeated in the end.

Prenominating divisions with an observable relationship to the final outcome have not always occurred in the conventions that ended by nominating a compromise candidate. In the Democratic conventions of 1844, 1852, and 1868, Polk, Pierce, and Seymour were nominated respectively by a sudden swing of the entire convention after lengthy balloting had severely damaged the prospects of all the leading candidates. The nominee received a majority that consisted of the entire convention after a previous

---

[19] The early votes in the Republican convention of 1952 seem to have served this purpose perfectly from the point of view of the Eisenhower strategists. The delegates who were uncommitted as between Taft and Eisenhower on the nomination mostly voted for the proposals put forward by the Eisenhower managers.

At the Democratic convention of 1912 the heart of Bryan's strategy was a series of actions that had the effect of splitting the support of Champ Clark. Wilson's support was mainly from the progressive wing of the party, whereas Clark entered the convention with considerable blocs of support from both progressives and conservatives. By forcing issues that involved the cleavage, Bryan compelled the Clark progressives to vote against the interest of their own candidate. Eventually they left him in the nominating balloting. In this instance Bryan also developed a rationale for bringing his own vote to the Wilson side, since he had entered the convention as a member of the Nebraska delegation, elected in a primary won by Clark. There is also the possibility, for which no verification seems to exist, that he was preparing the way for a fourth nomination for himself in a situation where he might have won if nominated.

The technique used for testing relationship by dividing the convention along lines of high or low for the eventual nominating winner can also be applied in terms of the vote for any candidate for the nomination. When this is done for the Democratic convention of 1912, the mathematical relationships underlying Bryan's strategy become apparent, as indicated in the following tabulation of the first-ballot vote of the delegations high for the candidates noted and the index of relationship with their vote for Bryan as temporary chairman.

	Wilson	Clark	Harmon	Underwood
For Candidate, First Ballot	78.2%	94.5%	69.7%	67.3%
Bryan for Chairman				
For	76.9%			
Against		54.2%	76.9%	82.7%
Index of Relationship	0.99	0.20	0.86	0.69

The total convention vote split 46.7 per cent for Bryan and 53.3 per cent for Parker on the temporary chairmanship. Delegations high for Wilson on the first nominating ballot gave Bryan very nearly the same percentage of vote for temporary chairman, with an index of relationship of 0.99. The high-for-Clark delegations, on the other hand, gave Clark 94.5 per cent of their vote but split almost exactly the same as the total convention on the chairmanship vote for a low index of relationship of 0.20. Harmon and Underwood delegations were as solidly against Bryan for chairman as Wilson's were for him, and were in fact more anti-Bryan than they were pro-Harmon or Underwood. On the assumption that a vote for Bryan indicated sympathy for the liberal side of the basic convention split, obviously the largest reservoir of liberal votes outside the initial Wilson support lay in the Clark delegations.

Before the convention opened Bryan had sent identical telegrams to the major candidates urging opposition to the selection of Parker as temporary chairman on the grounds that he was "most conspicuously identified with the reactionary element of the party." He received a favorable reply only from Wilson.

record of voting in which no support for him had become apparent.

At the Republican convention of 1920 no division preceded the balloting. During the balloting a roll call occurred on a motion to adjourn, but the results had no significant correlation with later action, and the motion itself seems to have been a spontaneous response to a situation in which the delegates were sufficiently hot, tired, hungry, and frustrated. At the Republican convention of 1940 no test vote preceded the balloting; Willkie started low on the first ballot, then rose strongly on each successive ballot.

In all the other cases in which the conventions nominated a candidate who ran third or lower at the start, some kind of a division occurred before the nominating balloting (or on another subject during the balloting) that eventually proved to have a significant correlation with the final outcome.

The Number of Ballots Required to Reach Consensus

The number of ballots required to complete a presidential nomination is related to the amount of division with which a convention opens; but this in turn seems likely to be related to the basic nominating categories of leadership confirmation and succession that were identified in Chapter 6. It could be expected that each of these categories might have its own special pattern of convention voting, influenced by the extent to which consensus has been achieved before the convention meets, by the amount of factional conflict, and by the type of decision that is made in resolving the conflict where it exists. Tables 17.10 and 17.11 provide the materials for testing these expectations. In the tables the nominations have been arrayed within each category in accordance with the number of convention ballots that each required. Where the number of ballots was the same, other factors have been used to array the nominations in

an order reflecting the apparent amount of conflict; where no difference in conflict is apparent, the listing is chronological.

Confirming Existing Leadership

In seventeen of the sixty-three major-party nominations since the beginnings of the convention system, the party conventions confirmed an existing leadership by renominating an incumbent President; eight of the cases were Democratic, and nine Republican. In addition, titular leaders have been renominated by the Democrats four times and by the Republicans once, producing a total of twenty-two cases of leadership confirmation, as shown in the tables.

All of these nominations were made by a single convention ballot, with the sole exception of the Republican renomination of Thomas E. Dewey in 1948, which required three ballots. Usually there was no other candidate who polled as much as 10 per cent of the vote, although five of the twenty-two cases provided exceptions to this rule. In twelve of the twenty-two conventions, no roll call vote was taken on any subject prior to the presidential nomination. Where such votes did occur, they were as a rule related only slightly, if at all, to the nomination, since in most cases no nomination contest was going on. The main exception was the Republican convention of 1912.

The nominations that have confirmed an existing leadership provide most of the cases in which a high degree of nominating consensus has been achieved before the conventions even meet. No doubt this could have been expected for incumbent Presidents, but not so much so for titular leaders.

Recognizing Inheritance of Leadership

Twice in the Democratic party, twice in the Republican, and twice in the latter's predecessor parties—six cases in all—the

TABLE 17.10. PATTERNS OF VOTING ON PRESIDENTIAL NOMINATIONS, DEMOCRATIC CONVENTIONS, 1832-1956

| Year | Nominee | Number of Candidates Polling Stated Per Cent at Any Time | | Number of Roll Call Votes | | Smallest Majority, Prenominating Roll Call Vote | Voting Majorities and Pluralities, Per Cent | | | |
| | | | | | | | First Ballot | | Critical Ballot[a] | |
		10% to 20%	Over 20%	Prenominating	On Nomination		Original Front-Runner	Eventual Nominee	Original Front-Runner	Eventual Nominee
					CONVENTIONS CONFIRMING AN EXISTING LEADER					
1832	Andrew Jackson		1	0	1	—	100.0%	100.0%	100.0%	100.0%
1840	Martin Van Buren		1	0	1	—	100.0	100.0	100.0	100.0
1900	William Jennings Bryan		1	0	1	—	100.0	100.0	100.0	100.0
1916	Woodrow Wilson		1	1	1	81.4%	100.0	100.0	100.0	100.0
1936	Franklin D. Roosevelt		1	0	1	—	100.0	100.0	100.0	100.0
1888	Grover Cleveland		1	3	1	52.3	100.0	100.0	100.0	100.0
1944	Franklin D. Roosevelt		1	0	1	—	92.3	92.3	92.3	92.3
1908	William Jennings Bryan		1	1	1	60.3	88.7	88.7	88.7	88.7
1940	Franklin D. Roosevelt		1	0	1	—	86.0	86.0	86.0	86.0
1892	Grover Cleveland	2	1	1	1	62.0	67.6	67.6	67.6	67.6
1956	Adlai E. Stevenson	1	1	0	1	—	66.0	66.0	66.0	66.0
1948	Harry S. Truman		2	2	1	52.8	76.8	76.8	75.0	75.0
					CONVENTIONS RECOGNIZING INHERITANCE OF LEADERSHIP					
1836	Martin Van Buren		1	1	1	52.4%	100.0%	100.0%	100.0%	100.0%
1928	Alfred E. Smith		1	0	1	—	77.2	77.2	77.2	77.2

Year	Candidate								
CONVENTIONS ACCEPTING INNER GROUP SELECTION									
1872	Horace Greeley	1	2	1	78.4%	93.7%	93.7%	93.7%	93.7%
1864	George B. McClellan	1	0	1	—	75.3	75.3	75.3	75.3
1904	Alton B. Parker	2	2	1	64.7	67.9	67.9	67.9	67.9
1880	Winfield S. Hancock	2	3	2	53.5	23.2	23.2	43.2	43.2
1884	Grover Cleveland	2	8	2	50.2	47.8	47.8	57.9	57.9
1848	Lewis Cass	3	8	4	50.2	43.1	43.1	53.7	53.7
CONVENTIONS FINDING A COMPROMISE CHOICE									
1844	James K. Polk	3	1	9	55.6%	54.9%	0.0%	0.0%	100.0%
1868	Horatio Seymour	5	8	22	54.8	33.1	0.0	0.0	100.0
1852	Franklin Pierce	4	5	49	55.8	39.2	0.0	0.0	95.3
1924	John W. Davis	3	9	103	50.0	39.3	2.8	1.3	52.4
CONVENTIONS DECIDING A FACTIONAL STRUGGLE									
1876	Samuel J. Tilden	2	3	2	70.2%	56.6%	56.6%	56.6%	56.6%
1952	Adlai E. Stevenson	1	2	3	53.8	29.5	22.2	21.2	49.8
1932	Franklin D. Roosevelt	1	5	4	54.2	57.7	57.7	59.1	59.1
1896	William Jennings Bryan	1	2	5	60.3	25.3	14.7	25.9	49.2
1856	James Buchanan	3	21	17	51.9	45.8	45.8	56.8	56.8
1860	Stephen A. Douglas	2	36	26	50.2	48.0	48.0	50.0	50.0
1920	James M. Cox	3	7	44	57.6	24.3	12.2	24.6	63.9
1912	Woodrow Wilson	2	6	46	50.6	40.5	29.8	30.9	58.1

ᵃ By definition, the critical ballot is the total vote for the winning candidate before band-wagon vote shifting. Accordingly, in some one-ballot conventions the critical-ballot percentage is smaller than the first-ballot percentage, since the latter includes the vote shifts.

TABLE 17.11. PATTERNS OF VOTING ON PRESIDENTIAL NOMINATIONS, NATIONAL REPUBLICAN, WHIG, AND REPUBLICAN CONVENTIONS, 1832-1956

Year	Nominee	Number of Candidates Polling Stated Per Cent at Any Time		Number of Roll Call Votes		Smallest Majority, Prenominating Roll Call Vote	Voting Majorities and Pluralities, Per Cent			
							First Ballot		Critical Ballot[a]	
		10% to 20%	Over 20%	Prenominating	On Nomination		Original Front-Runner	Eventual Nominee	Original Front-Runner	Eventual Nominee
				CONVENTIONS CONFIRMING AN EXISTING LEADER						
1872	Ulysses S. Grant		1	0	1	—	100.0%	100.0%	100.0%	100.0%
1900	William McKinley		1	0	1	—	100.0	100.0	100.0	100.0
1956	Dwight D. Eisenhower		1	0	1	—	100.0	100.0	100.0	100.0
1904	Theodore Roosevelt		1	1	1	50.3%	100.0	100.0	100.0	100.0
1932	Herbert Hoover		1	1	1	59.9	97.6	97.6	97.6	97.6
1924	Calvin Coolidge		1	0	1		96.0	96.0	96.0	96.0
1864	Abraham Lincoln		1	3	1	64.8	95.7	95.7	95.7	95.7
1892	Benjamin Harrison		3	3	1	51.2	59.1	59.1	59.1	59.1
1912	William Howard Taft		1[b]	7	1	50.3	52.0	52.0	52.0	52.0
1948	Thomas E. Dewey	1	2	0	3	—	39.7	39.7	47.0	47.0
				CONVENTIONS RECOGNIZING INHERITANCE OF LEADERSHIP						
1832	Henry Clay		1	0	1	—	100.0%	100.0%	100.0%	100.0%
1844	Henry Clay		1	0	1	—	100.0	100.0	100.0	100.0
1928	Herbert Hoover		1	3	1	60.6%	76.6	76.6	76.6	76.6
1908	William Howard Taft		1	5	1	51.6	71.6	71.6	71.6	71.6

Year	Candidate			Critical ballot					
CONVENTIONS ACCEPTING INNER GROUP SELECTION									
1868	Ulysses S. Grant	1	0	1	100.0%	100.0%	100.0%	100.0%	—
1936	Alfred M. Landon	1	0	1	98.4%	98.4	98.4	98.4	—
1856	John C. Frémont	2	0	2	63.5%	63.5	63.5	63.5	—
1916	Charles Evans Hughes	2	1	3	33.3	33.3	25.7	25.7	70.4%[b]
CONVENTIONS FINDING A COMPROMISE CHOICE									
1876	Rutherford B. Hayes	3	2	7	50.8%	46.4%	8.1%	37.7%	51.4%
1920	Warren G. Harding	1	3	10	38.0	25.3	6.6	29.2	71.8
1880	James A. Garfield	1	3	36	52.8	41.4	0.0	40.2	51.9
CONVENTIONS DECIDING A FACTIONAL STRUGGLE									
1944	Thomas E. Dewey	1	0	1	100.0%	100.0%	100.0%	100.0%	—
1896	William McKinley	1	3	1	69.9	69.9	69.9	69.9	60.5%
1952	Dwight D. Eisenhower	2	3	1	49.3	49.3	70.1	70.1	53.3
1840	William Henry Harrison	2	0	n.a.[c]	58.3	58.3	58.3	58.3	—
1860	Abraham Lincoln	2	3	3	49.7	38.6	21.9	37.3	61.5
1848	Zachary Taylor	3	2	4	47.2	47.2	39.4	39.4	56.5
1884	James G. Blaine	2	4	4	45.7	45.7	40.8	40.8	50.0
1940	Wendell L. Willkie	3	0	6	42.9	5.7	10.5	36.0	—
1888	Benjamin Harrison	2	4	8	33.5	27.6	10.2	27.5	60.6
1852	Winfield Scott	2	6	53	44.6	44.9	44.6	44.9	50.3

[a] By definition, the critical ballot is the total vote for the winning candidate before band-wagon vote shifting. Accordingly, in some one-ballot conventions the critical-ballot percentage is smaller than the first-ballot percentage, since the latter includes the vote shifts.

[b] No other candidate received above 10 per cent, although Theodore Roosevelt was just under that figure. Nearly 33 per cent of the delegates withheld their votes, most of them in compliance with Roosevelt's request.

[c] The nomination was made by a nominating committee, and the only published reports available are from the report of the committee. Since the committee was in session continuously for many hours many previous votes undoubtedly were taken, and several candidates may have figured in the voting besides those included in the committee report.

nomination has seemed to recognize and confirm an inheritance of leadership by an understudy, or has recognized a party leader already so outstanding that the nomination seemed to be his as a matter of course. Few in number as these cases are, it still seems worth noting that the voting pattern has been identical with that typical of nominations confirming an existing leadership. All were one-ballot nominations. In no case was there a competitor who polled as much as 10 per cent of the convention vote. In three of the six conventions there was no pre-nomination roll call vote on any subject.

Accepting Inner Group Selection

Six Democratic nominations and four Republican have been classified as instances of inner group selection. Five of these ten nominations required only a single ballot, but in most of the ten cases one or two minority candidates each polled at least 10 per cent of the convention vote.

In five of the six Democratic conventions roll call votes were taken prior to the nominations, usually several such votes and rather sharply divided. Of the four Republican conventions of this group, only one, that of 1916, had a roll call vote on any subject before the nomination balloting.

The voting pattern in most of the conventions in this group suggests that some degree of consensus had been worked out before the convention met, but that the decision was usually one requiring negotiation, opportunity for dissent, and final adjustment at the convention itself.

Finding a Compromise Choice

Four Democratic and three Republican nominations have been classified as representing compromise at the end of a factional struggle, with long balloting the rule rather than the exception. The number of candidates polling at least 10 per cent at

one point or another was four, five, or six. Without exception, divided votes on other issues preceded the final ballot on the nominations and some of these votes were closely contested.

The most recent cases in this category are those of Harding and Davis in 1920 and 1924, respectively; all the other five cases are distant by at least three quarters of a century. Most of the conditions that were conducive to dark horse compromise candidacies have disappeared. The two thirds rule was one of the most important of those conditions, possibly by itself responsible for all four of the cases in the Democratic party. The persistent strong bifactionalism of the Republican party was a basic conditioning factor. This has not yet disappeared, but seems unlikely to develop very often as close a balance as it had from 1876 to 1892 and again in 1952. In any event, the tactic of awaiting or even promoting a deadlock was formerly encouraged by the absence of reliable information about attitudes and intentions, which was characteristic of most of the conventions of the past when they first assembled. Under modern conditions, so much information is systematically collected and published concerning the attitudes of voters, party officials, and convention delegates that the range of opportunity for the tactics of deadlock has been reduced.

Deciding a Factional Struggle

Eight Democratic nominations and ten Whig and Republican were classified as factional victories in situations of insurgent or coordinate factionalism. In only two of the eighteen cases, concerning Dewey in 1944 and McKinley in 1896, was the probable outcome so clear in advance of the contion that it could be said to be generally anticipated. Tilden and Franklin D. Roosevelt were front-runners so far as evidence of popular support was concerned, but they faced stiff opposition and there was at least a possibility that they could be blocked under the two thirds rule. In all the other cases a hard fight was anticipated. In a number of them a candidate who placed second, third, or fourth in the early balloting came from behind to win—notably, Bryan, Wilson, and Cox among the Democrats, and Lincoln, Benjamin Harrison, and Willkie among the Republicans.

Four of the eight Democratic nominations required extremely lengthy balloting, all under the two thirds rule; among the ten Whig and Republican nominations, this was true only for Winfield Scott, the last of the Whig nominees. There were always several roll call divisions before the long-drawn-out nominating balloting began in the Democratic conventions, and usually in the Republican. On many of the roll calls the conventions were sharply divided into nearly equal groups, with the victors winning by majorities barely over the 50 per cent mark.

Dates recent and distant appear in each part of the list for each party, but the long-balloting conventions seem to be mostly of the past, the short-balloting conventions mostly somewhat more recent. The probability is that the outcome of most nominating contests will be generally anticipated in the future before the conventions meet. And, if the lines are closely drawn between opposing candidates of nearly equal strength, the issue is still likely to be settled with a minimum number of ballots.

This conclusion seems to be borne out both by the long-term trends in the convention balloting and by action in recent conventions. Notwithstanding the heat of the Taft-Eisenhower contest in 1952 and the closeness of the division among the convention delegates, the issue was decided in a single nominating ballot. In the Democratic convention of 1952 a reluctant candidate was brought to the point of nomination in three ballots all held during one day. In both parties the preconvention campaigns, ably abetted by the party leaders and the mass media, had settled much of the convention business before the convention even met.

Consensus in Making Nominations for the Vice Presidency

The amount of difficulty involved in agreeing on a vice-presidential nominee is somewhat indicated by the numbers of ballots required for a decision, the numbers of competing candidates, and the size of the opposing vote, if any. Experience in these matters is summarized by periods in Table 17.12.

In the pre-Civil War period one-ballot nominations were a rarity in either party. Usually there was a contest in which two to five candidates were able to poll at least 10 per cent of the convention vote. Leadership influence on the choice was evidently weak, disunited, and somewhat random in its effects, as the accounts of the times suggest.

From the Civil War onward, one-ballot nominations were the rule, with four exceptions in the Democratic party and two in the Republican. The Republican convention of 1868 nominated Grant for President with happy unanimity, but the Radical Republicans in control of the convention required five ballots to make a vice-presidential choice among eleven starters, four of whom polled over 10 per cent in the early balloting. In somewhat similar fashion, abetted by the two thirds rule, the Democratic convention of 1896 also required five ballots, with sixteen starters, four of whom polled over 10 per cent. Bryan had just been nominated for President and was present at the convention, but refused to take any position on the choice of a vice-presidential candidate. His Nebraska delegation refrained, at his request, from voting on the issue.

At the Democratic convention of 1912, in Baltimore, the delegates were exhausted by the time Woodrow Wilson was nominated on the forty-sixth ballot. Wilson himself was at Sea Girt, New Jersey, at the end of a rather inadequate long-distance telephone connection. Eleven candidates were entered in the race for the vice-presidential nomination, three polled over 10 per cent, and two ballots were required. Wilson apparently concurred in the selection of Thomas R. Marshall, though with little enthusiasm.

At the Republican convention of 1924, President Coolidge seemingly had little control of the vice-presidential nomination. Frank O. Lowden, whose record on agricul-

The vice-presidential nominating conte[s] was the main event of interest at the Dem[o] cratic convention of 1944. It was a demo[n] stration of the power of strong leadership i[n] a situation of factional conflict. At the d[e] sire of President Roosevelt and with the a[c] tive concurrence of a group of norther[n]

TABLE 17.12. VICE-PRESIDENTIAL NOMINATING PATTERNS, 1832-1956

Pattern Categories	Democratic Party				Republican Party[a]			
	1832–1860	1864–1892	1896–1924	1928–1956	1832–1860	1864–1892	1896–1924	1928–1956
Number of Nominations	7[b]	8	8	8	7[c]	8	8	8
Number of Nominations by Extent of Balloting:								
One Ballot	3	8	6	6	2	7	7	8
Two Ballots	3	0	1	2	4	0	0	0
Three to Five Ballots	1	0	1	0	1	1	1	0
Number of Conventions in Which Various Vice-Presidential Candidates Polled 10% or More of the Vote:								
One Candidate	1	5	3	5	2	2	4	6
Two Candidates	3	2	1	2	1	2	3	1
Three Candidates	1	0	2	0	2	3	0	1
Four Candidates	0	1	2	1	2	1	0	0
Five Candidates	2	0	0	0	0	0	1	0
Number of Conventions in Which the Vote Against the Eventual Nominee on the Critical Ballot Was:								
Less Than 10%	0	4	3	4	2	2	2	6
More Than 10%, Less Than 25%	2	2	0	0	0	0	2	1
More Than 25%	5	2	5	4	5	6	4	1

[a] Includes National Republican and Whig.

[b] At the Democratic convention of 1840 no vice-presidential nomination was made.

[c] The Whigs held no national convention in preparation for the elections of 1836, and accordingly n[o] vice-presidential nomination was made.

tural matters was definitely in opposition to Coolidge's position, was nominated on the second ballot and promptly refused the nomination. The wishes of both the Coolidge forces and the senatorial "old guard" were then disregarded in the third-ballot nomination of Charles G. Dawes. Herbert Hoover received 234½ votes on the same ballot, although he had not been mentioned in the previous balloting.

party leaders, Harry S. Truman was nom[i] nated for Vice President in the face of fa[c] tional opposition from the supporters of th[e] incumbent Vice President, Henry Wallac[e] and from the supporters of the souther[n] preference, James S. Byrnes. The operatio[n] required two ballots, even though the tw[o] thirds rule was no longer a factor.

Two ballots were also required for th[e] vice-presidential nomination of Senat[or]

Estes Kefauver at the Democratic convention of 1956. The presidential nominee, Adlai Stevenson, like Bryan in 1896, went to some pains to maintain a hands-off attitude. The result was open conflict in the convention.

The six instances just reviewed illustrate a variety of situations in which conflict can arise that can be settled only by a convention vote. There have been other contested vice-presidential nominations in which the outcome was nonetheless settled in a single ballot, as shown in Table 17.12. In all, thirty-nine of the sixty-two major-party nominations for Vice President have been contested to the extent of an opposition vote of 10 per cent or more on the critical ballot. In thirty-two of the sixty-two cases, fourteen of which have occurred since 1896, the opposition has exceeded 25 per cent of the vote.

Every contested vice-presidential nomination tends to suggest limitations of the consensus achieved in the prior presidential nomination, but it is only when both nominations are contested that the voting records can be readily compared. The cases of this kind are brought together in Table 17.13, in which for each party the cases are arrayed in accordance with the extent to which the vice-presidential nominee received support from the same delegations that had been high in their support for the presidential nominee. Over one third of all vice-presidential nominations appear in this table.

When the nominations for both offices are contested, it is apparent that a wide range of variation can occur in the relationships between the winning combinations. In four Democratic cases and two Republican, the vice-presidential nominee found his support predominantly (ratio above .10) among the delegations that had been high for the winner of the presidential nomination. These cases included the choice of Bryan's running mate in 1896, the choice of Senator Kefauver in 1956, and the renomination of President Taft's running mate in 1912.

The opposite situation appears in four of the Democratic cases and three Republican. Wilson's running mate in 1912 was more the choice of other delegations than of those that had supported the presidential nominee, as was Cleveland's running mate of 1892, Adlai E. Stevenson the elder. The same situation applied to two of the Republican vice-presidential nominees who later succeeded to the Presidency, Coolidge and Arthur. On the other hand, in most of the Republican cases delegation voting behavior on the vice-presidential nomination seemingly had almost no relationship of any kind to the previous voting for a presidential nominee—delegations that had been high for the winner split on the vice-presidential nomination in substantially the same proportions as those that had been low. The frequent lack of interest in the vice-presidential choice is probably indicated by the apparently random nature of these variations.

In eleven instances from 1832 to 1956, the vice-presidential nomination was contested even though the presidential nomination was not.[20] The cases, arrayed in chronological order, are shown in Table 17.14.

The historic evidences of conflict shown in the table do not directly indicate the degree to which the presidential nominee was taking a personal interest in promoting a vice-presidential nomination to suit his own preferences, as was the case, for instance, with Jackson in 1832, Lincoln in 1864, and Roosevelt in 1944. It is to be expected, moreover, that the increasing importance of the Vice Presidency may increase the tendency for the presidential nominee to take a strong hand in the vice-presidential nomination, and for his adherents to follow his lead. If this is the case, should future additions be made to Table 17.13 in its depiction of conflict over both nominations, they would tend to fall in the top category, with a high ratio of support

[20] Here, as elsewhere in this book, a nomination is considered uncontested if the opposition vote was less than 10 per cent at the end of the roll call on the first ballot.

TABLE 17.13. RELATIONSHIPS BETWEEN CRITICAL BALLOTS FOR PRESIDENTIAL
AND VICE-PRESIDENTIAL NOMINATIONS WHEN BOTH
NOMINATIONS WERE CONTESTED, 1832-1956

| Year | Presidential and Vice-Presidential Nominees | Critical vote for Vice-Presidential Nominee, Per Cent | Ratio of Support to Convention Average[a] | |
			High-for-Presidential-Nominee Delegations[b]	Low-for-Presidential-Nominee Delegations[c]
	DEMOCRATIC CONVENTIONS			
1896	William J. Bryan—Arthur Sewall	28.1%	1.47	0.56
1856	James Buchanan—John C. Breckinridge	16.9	1.36	0.59
1956	Adlai E. Stevenson—Estes Kefauver	40.2	1.29	0.38
1904	Alton B. Parker—Henry G. Davis	65.4	1.26	0.59
1940	Franklin D. Roosevelt—Henry A. Wallace	56.9	1.09	0.72
1928	Alfred E. Smith—Joseph T. Robinson	67.4	1.08	0.84
1848	Lewis Cass—William O. Butler	44.9	0.88	1.18
1912	Woodrow Wilson—Thomas R. Marshall	36.0	0.83	1.20
1892	Grover Cleveland—Adlai E. Stevenson	44.2	0.72	1.40
1924	John W. Davis—Charles W. Bryan	21.7	0.65	1.10
	REPUBLICAN CONVENTIONS			
1912	William Howard Taft—James S. Sherman	54.2%	1.62	0.29
1876	Rutherford B. Hayes—William A. Wheeler	48.4	1.24	0.82
1888	Benjamin Harrison—Levi P. Morton	71.2	1.10	0.95
1860	Abraham Lincoln—Hannibal Hamlin	41.6	1.07	0.91
1916	Charles E. Hughes—Charles W. Fairbanks	87.4	1.07	0.90
1884	James G. Blaine—John A. Logan	94.3	1.05	0.95
1908	William Howard Taft—James S. Sherman	83.3	1.01	0.97
1896	William B. McKinley—Garret A. Hobart	59.7	0.97	1.07
1940	Wendell Willkie—Charles L. McNary	89.0	0.95	1.04
1920	Warren G. Harding—Calvin Coolidge	68.5	0.87	1.15
1880	James A. Garfield—Chester A. Arthur	61.9	0.70	1.26
1856	John C. Frémont—William L. Dayton	62.3	0.53	1.44

[a] For each group of delegations, defined below, this means the ratio of its percentage of support for the vice-presidential nominee to his average vote in the convention on the critical ballot. For example, when Arthur Sewall was nominated in 1896, the high group was giving him 41.3 per cent of its vote, 1.47 times his convention average, while the low group was giving him 15.7 per cent of its vote, 0.56 times his convention average.

[b] Delegations voting higher than the convention average for the presidential nominee.

[c] Delegations voting lower than the convention average for the presidential nominee.

among the supporters of the head of the ticket, and fewer evidences of indifference.

Split Conventions and the Processes of Alliance

Any convention is split when it has two or more actively competing candidates, but the basic split may be primarily concerned either with the candidates as personalities or with something deeper that merely finds

for that party's nominations had been previously identified as factional leaders, but Republicans, like the Whigs before them, have been more willing than Democrats to resolve factional conflict by taking someone from outside regular politics as a candidate. Factional patterns in the Democratic party have been more complex and less clearly linked to candidate interests. There has been a long-term strain between the party's urban and rural adherents, a persistent sectionalism involving the South, and occasion-

TABLE 17.14. CONTESTED VICE-PRESIDENTIAL NOMINATIONS OCCURRING WHEN THE PRESIDENTIAL NOMINATION WAS NOT CONTESTED, 1832-1956

Year and Party	Presidential and Vice-Presidential Nominees	Vice-Presidential Nominee's Per Cent on Critical Ballot	Maximum Strength of Nearest Competitor
1832-D	Andrew Jackson—Martin Van Buren	73.2%	17.3%
1836-D	Martin Van Buren—Richard Johnson	67.2	32.8
1844-W	Henry Clay—Theodore Freylinghuysen	56.4	30.2
1864-R	Abraham Lincoln—Andrew Johnson	39.5	21.3
1868-R	Ulysses S. Grant—Schuyler Colfax	34.8	31.8
1872-R	Ulysses S. Grant—Henry Wilson	48.5	42.8
1888-D	Grover Cleveland—Allen G. Thurman	83.2	12.3
1900-D	William J. Bryan—Adlai E. Stevenson	59.7	31.6
1924-R	Calvin Coolidge—Charles G. Dawes	61.5	21.1[a]
1932-R	Herbert Hoover—Charles Curtis	55.0	15.8
1944-D	Franklin D. Roosevelt—Harry S. Truman	27.1	36.5

[a] Maximum strength of nearest competitor on third ballot taken after Frank Lowden refused the nomination. Lowden was nominated on the second ballot following a band-wagon vote switch when his critical vote at the end of the roll call reached 37.2 per cent. Maximum strength of Lowden's nearest competitor was 15.5 per cent.

expression through them. The nature and orientation of any basic split is highly relevant to the kind of conflict that will occur, as well as the amount of conflict. The same factors control the processes of alliance that will be available for the development of the required convention majorities.

Orientation of Basic Convention Split

Some kind of bifactional pattern has persisted in the Republican party throughout most of its history. Many of the candidates

ally a struggle about some temporary issue of immediate importance.

In the conventions where one candidate is strong enough at the start to be assured of the nomination, any opposition that insists on putting up a fight is more likely to represent a continuing factionalism than the momentary interests of a minority contender. Such opposition may have difficulty in finding any single, relatively strong personality behind whom to center its interests. This was true in 1928 of the opposition to both Al Smith's nomination and Herbert Hoover's.

Conversely, in the conventions where the

nominating situation is so splintered that three or four contenders seem almost equally strong at the beginning, the problem frequently is to find a cleavage line that will identify a majority, after which the majority may be able to reach its own consensus on a preferred candidate. In the Democratic convention of 1896 the silver issue served the purpose. An early vote on the convention chairmanship made clear the division between the gold and silver Democrats, and also showed the strength of the silverite majority. Thereafter, the silver group dominated the convention and the only question was which of their number would be nominated.

At the Republican convention of 1920 there was no pronounced ideological split of any kind and less bifactionalism than usual. The three strongest candidates, however—Leonard Wood, Frank Lowden, and Hiram Johnson—had all disqualified themselves in one way or another during their preconvention campaigns. Each of the three was almost completely unacceptable to a majority of the delegates other than his own supporters. The convention majority presumably wanted a regular Republican who was popular and broadly unobjectionable. It found him in Warren G. Harding.

The most difficult conventions are those in which two strong candidates are each in a position to veto the nomination of the other. This kind of situation reached its most overt form in the Democratic party under the two thirds rule, where a candidate or a faction with 35 per cent of the vote could veto the nomination of a candidate with more than 50 per cent. When cases of this type also involved commitments of high intensity in each camp, the contest was inevitably of long duration and uncertain outcome, whether the basis of commitment was personal, ideological, or sectional —or all three, as in the struggle over the nomination of Stephen A. Douglas in 1860.

In conventions operating under majority rule the mathematical possibilities for stalemate are less apparent, yet stalemate has repeatedly seemed possible when two strong

candidates have faced each other. In such cases the heat of the battle for the nomination will often bring the candidates to adopt extremist positions. Each candidate is likely to develop in his partisans a strong distrust for his opponent, with the result that neither one can become the second choice of the supporters of the other. This seems to have occurred rather often, even in cases where the ideological differences between the contending groups were unimportant.

This is why the choice in a bipolarized situation must be made in the end by the center groups who are uncommitted; yet, by that time, the center groups may distrust both candidates, or may conclude that, regardless of their merits, a choice of either would endanger party prospects because of the divisive effect of their previous campaigns. This is the classic situation for the choice of a compromise candidate such as Rutherford B. Hayes (in 1876) or James A. Garfield (in 1880). It was avoided at the Republican convention of 1952 mainly because only one of the two leading candidates was a genuine factional leader. Eisenhower had done relatively little to arouse factional hostilities, had made no personal attack on Taft, had demonstrated his popular appeal, and could thus receive the votes of the uncommitted delegates.

The Processes of Alliance

Alliances in the conventions are made under circumstances that have many different variations. One set of variations is suggested by the motives that can be drawn upon for alliance and support. These might be classified as follows:

1. Presence and absence of shared goals
   a. Issues
   b. Group affinities
   c. Party regularity
2. Attractions and repulsions of candidate personality
3. Bargaining considerations
4. Sanctions
   a. Prospects for reward
   b. Dangers of reprisal

In every contested convention these factors were presumably operative in the preconvention campaigns, but without settling the choice. The same factors carry on into the convention and underlie the processes of alliance that are available for the development of a conclusive majority. Further events, new issues, and new information may also arise to move the process along in the convention, within the limits which had been built up by the time the convention opened.

Issues may form a clear basis for alliances when the issues themselves are clear. There has been, for example, a persistent set of issues, changing only in their outward form, between the rich and the poor. In earlier years of pioneering and land settlement these economic issues chiefly took the form of debtor-creditor differences on monetary and other policies, differences that in turn became rather clearly sectional. After the turn of the century the so-called progressive-conservative axis came into operation in each party, with differences on such matters as the regulation of the trusts, railroad and public utility rate control, and conservation. During the last generation principal issues of this kind have included tax policies, public services, and welfare legislation.

Sometimes the economic issues have been only vaguely apparent. Moreover, they have seldom had the effect of arraying the candidates and the delegates along a single scale of differences except when some specific economic question was dominant, as in the silver-gold struggle of 1896. Questions of race, religion, and civil rights have had a profoundly crosscutting effect. So also have the increasingly important questions of foreign policy, particularly in view of their complex relationships to the ethnic origins, present occupations, and geographic locations of the population. In this complex network, contenders can always hope to find groups with positions near enough their own to open up the possibility of an alliance.

Group affinities have probably been more important to the creation of alliances than issues that were clearly recognized as such. The factors of geography, sectionalism, and a willingness to support friends and neighbors have often had some apparent influence; other things being equal, delegates evidently prefer to support a candidate from their own section or near by. Religious and ethnic groups have been important in the Democratic party, especially when non-Protestant candidates have been in the running. Conflict between party regulars and insurgents has been recurrent in both parties and at times has provided a distinctive basis for group alliances.

A candidate himself may exert a positive gravitational pull or a negative kind of repulsion. The positive force is at work when a strong candidate progressively increases his following among the previously uncommitted delegates, without strongly repelling any. The opposite phenomenon occurs when the uncommitted delegates find themselves increasingly repelled by a candidate who may look relatively strong, but who is also arousing hostility in many quarters, often for divergent reasons.

Factors of the kind just indicated determine the larger framework, within which candidates must usually settle their immediate tactical questions in terms of their current levels of strength. Front-runners who are running strongly usually seek means to demonstrate their strength by getting the votes of new adherents placed on the record. When one candidate is well ahead, other candidates almost invariably seek to develop coalition strategies that have at least the limited objective of stopping the front-runner. After the balloting actually starts, a front-runner who begins to lose ground from one vote to another rarely recovers, whatever his original strength may have been.

In situations where three or more candidates are all fairly strong, the distribution of second-choice support becomes critical, for reasons that are mathematically inherent. In such a case the strategies of the lesser candidates may be devoted mainly to the development of second-choice support for themselves. They can then wait hopefully, while the candidates who are strong on a first-choice basis, but who have also awakened hostility in other quarters, have their run in the early balloting. After it has been proved that none of the two or three leaders can win, second-choice preferences come into play and the eventual winner begins to become apparent.

Throughout the negotiations that attend the processes of alliance, bargaining considerations of one sort or another are usually present. Bribery and other forms of corrupt bargaining have often been charged but seldom proved; usually they have involved relatively small blocs of votes that were not critical. "Deals" presumably take place more often in a form that occurs informally in politics at all levels in the search for combinations that can be supported as a ticket— "You support my man for this, and I will back yours for that." Exchanges of support may also involve special arrangements in connection with transfers of campaign funds and the assumption of campaign deficits; there is a shadowland in this area that needs to be opened up to public inspection. Whether or not the bargaining is overt or in terms of specific rewards, it proceeds on the assumption that it is impossible to accept benefits without incurring obligations. Probably what is most often sought is a general but explicit understanding that, in the event of victory, obligations will be recognized in connection with access to the new administration, appointments, and other governmental decisions involving wide discretion.

All of this has long been known in the abstract and in terms of the lore of the conventions as they existed during the nineteenth century and well into the twentieth. But some aspects of the situation have undoubtedly changed, for reasons noted in the discussion of nominating campaigns in Chapter 12. Popular mandates have become more definite in recent years and information concerning mandates has become much more widely available. This clearly affects both the extent to which the choice of nominee is left to the conventions and the kinds of alliance that can be made. Opposition to a front-runner, unless based on clearly legitimate grounds, has become more dangerous as a convention tactic. The mechanisms of reward and penalty are much more clearly operative. When a delegate can identify the candidate most favored by his own party's electorate, he can reappraise what attitude his constituency is likely to take if he decides not to go along. When he can identify a prospective general-election winner on what seems to be sound information, he can form a correspondingly clear idea of the prospective rewards of victory and the penalties of defeat.

This does not mean that the classic situations will not recur. They may, however, occur less frequently and in some categories not at all. But if it should happen that two front-runners are closely matched or if the situation somehow spreads out into a contest between three or four candidates of nearly equal strength, the outcome will certainly remain in doubt until it has occurred, and the processes of alliance within the convention will be important.

The Limits of Convention Action

Since this chapter has been so largely concerned with matters of strategy and maneuver, it is well to recall that the opportunities open, in practice, to any party convention are limited by the situation within which it meets. Sometimes there is no apparent opportunity to change what has already become preordained. In other instances, major decisions remain to be made by the convention itself.

Even in these latter cases, however, the convention is free to act only in a relative sense. Issues have already been drawn. Candidates and their supporters have waged their campaigns openly or covertly. The stage has been set for certain possible coalitions, and other coalitions have been made improbable if not impossible. The emotional pitch has been established. The pieces for the game are all there—what remains is to see how skillfully the players will use them. For each convention the number and relative values of the pieces differ, but, as in the end game in chess, the available strategies are restricted by the pieces, their value, and their position when the players take their seats.

Many of those who participate in the conventions see them mainly as recurring bouts in the internal struggles of the parties. They tend to use the conventions as opportunities for factional display; in doing so, they give more prominence to a secondary activity than it deserves and place added limits on major activities. But the tendencies revealed in the tables on roll call votes early in this chapter suggest that the decision processes once most useful for factional display are beginning to atrophy, and that the conventions may find further ways to restrict them. In any event, a party convention can engage in only a very limited number of activities; predominantly, it is a strategic crossroad in the more comprehensive nominating and party processes.

To the extent that the conventions do have power, their capabilities for damaging their respective parties may be greater than for repairing and rebuilding them. Any convention has the power to degrade the image of its party even in victory, or to lessen its popular appeal and make victory impossible for the time being. On the other hand, when the party has already been severely damaged by the preconvention campaigns, the convention has only limited capacity to heal the breach. But hope springs eternal, and the conventions, like other aggregations of humanity, can always hope to transcend their own usual limitations. Sometimes they even seem to succeed.

18

Convention Action and Election Results

EACH OF THE ACTIVE partici-
pants in making a presidential nomination
presumably holds some view of the future
—a view that he attempts to have taken into
account in choosing the nominee. Inevitably
the choice between candidates is also a
choice between strategies for the pursuit of
various goals, goals that in turn depend on
alternative views of the future. Such goals
include winning the election if possible;
winning in a way that will commit the
party in one direction rather than another;
holding together the coalition that the party
represents if it looks like a winning coalition, and sometimes even if it does not; enlarging the party's total following in the
electorate, especially when this is essential
to win.

The calculations underlying these various strategies involve the size of the party's
apparent hold on the electorate and the
composition of its holding; the other party's
hold on the electorate and the composition
of *its* holding; and the size and composition
of the uncommitted portion of the electorate. Working politicians usually begin
their more important labors by confronting
the voting statistics of the last previous election; and in doing so they are concerned
not only with the national totals but also
with the distribution of the vote by states
and in terms of the broadly defined interest
groups that can take a hand in the outcome.
A serious discussion of alternative candidates involves many factors, but the candidates' prospective effect upon the party vote
as last recorded is one factor not likely to be
overlooked.

The prospective relationships between
what the convention does and what will
happen in the election are thus clearly central to the problem of decision, but the
basis for anticipating those relationships is
frequently cloudy indeed. Expectations inevitably must be formed on the basis of
experience; but the experience that is relevant is so infinitely complex that few can
undertake to understand more than some
small portion of it. Insofar as research can
assist, it must seek out those portions of the
historical experience that seem most helpful
as background, and especially those that
lend themselves somehow to analysis looking toward the clarification of expectations.

Obviously this has been a problem underlying the selection of materials and their
presentation throughout the present book.
This chapter, however, seeks to go somewhat farther in the clarification of the relationships between convention action and
election results. In doing so, it deals first
with the long-term growth in the party
vote of each party as expressed in the national election returns. Here there are some
clues to the effects of one type of candidate
rather than another on the voting totals,
but the long-term record as a whole seems
more useful as orienting background than
as the basis for any highly conclusive type
of analysis.

The chapter then turns to the relationships between convention action and voter
turnout in the individual states. Here there
does seem to be an opportunity for theory
construction and relatively elaborate forms
of statistical analysis. The approach that is

presented is new in the study of voting behavior. It is the result of repeated efforts and much labor, but will require examination by many other scholars before it will be possible to know how close the present results may come to being definitive within the scope of what they attempt.[1]

The third major section of the chapter turns to a still different subject, the extent to which the occurrence of one nominating pattern rather than another is related to victory in the election that follows. The patterns used in this analysis are those identified in Chapter 6—leadership confirmation, inheritance, inner group selection, compromise in stalemate, and factional victory—in each case treating the in-party experience separately from that of the out-party.

The three subjects just noted do not exhaust the possibilities for studying the relationships between convention action and election results. They do, however, all have a bearing on victory in the election immediately in prospect when each convention is held; they also are all closely related to the problems and mechanisms of long-term change in the composition and alignment of the parties. The chapter concludes with some further observations on these problems.

Fluctuations in Growth in the Party Vote

During the period from 1832 to 1892 the popular vote in presidential elections increased by an average of 16.5 per cent from one presidential election to another. From

1896 to 1956 the average was 11.3 per cent.[2] But the growth in the popular vote has not occurred evenly from one year to another, either in total or in the vote of each party. Rather, as shown in Table 18.1, it has come in spurts, sometimes as the result of factors extraneous to the party system, but also frequently in circumstances in which the nominees chosen by the conventions may have been critical to the result that occurred.

On three occasions since 1832 the popular vote has increased by more than 40 per cent from one presidential election to the next. The largest of these increases, 60 per cent, occurred in 1840; it was the product of intensified popular campaigning after a period of rapid extension of the franchise. The next largest, 44 per cent, occurred in 1920, the year of the introduction of women's suffrage in all of the states where it had not previously been provided. The other large increase, 43 per cent, occurred in 1868 and was attributable primarily to the cessation of the Civil War.

On three other occasions since 1832 the popular vote actually declined from its level of four years earlier. Two of these were war years—1864 and 1944. The one peace-time year was 1904, when many voters, faced with the choice between Alton B. Parker and Theodore Roosevelt, simply stayed home.

Party bolting and third-party movements have had a mixed effect on turnout and the major-party vote. In 1856 and 1860 they were associated with a considerable upsurge in the total popular vote. In 1912 they clearly had a depressing effect, with many voters staying home when they found themselves cross-pressured between tradi-

[1] First attempts at analysis in this field were discussed with members of the Interuniversity Summer Research Seminar on Presidential Nominating Politics, held at the Brookings Institution in the summer of 1955. A revised approach was discussed with a number of scholars in the spring of 1959, including V. O. Key, Jr., of Harvard University, Richard M. Scammon of the Governmental Affairs Institute, and Yvette Gurley, F. P. Kilpatrick, Walter S. Salant, and Beatrice Vaccara of Brookings Institution. The various comments received were helpful in maturing the analysis, but none of those mentioned should be held responsible for what is included here.

[2] For the entire period 1832-1956 the average was 13.5 per cent. In each case the rates given are based on geometric averages of the ratios shown in Table 18.1. The geometric average is a type of average that is especially appropriate for use in computing an average of ratios; it gives emphasis to relative rather than absolute differences in the items entering into the average. For a discussion of the geometric mean, see, for example, Robert E. Chaddock, *Principles and Methods of Statistics* (1925), pp. 125-27.

TABLE 18.1. LONG-TERM GROWTH IN THE POPULAR AND PARTY VOTE FOR PRESIDENT, 1832-1956[a]

Year	Ratio of Popular Vote to That Cast in Last Previous Election[b]			Percentage of Popular Vote Polled		
	Total	Democratic	Republican[c]	Democratic	Republican[c]	Other Parties[d]
1832	1.05	1.06*	1.04	54.8%	25.5%	19.7%
1836	1.24	1.11*	1.40	50.9	49.1	—
1840	1.60	1.47	1.72*	46.8	52.9	0.3
1844	1.12	1.19*	1.02	49.6	48.1	2.3
1848	1.07	0.91	1.04*	42.5	47.3	10.2
1852	1.10	1.31*	1.02	50.7	43.9	5.4
1856	1.28	1.14*	0.97[e]	45.2	33.3	21.5
1860	1.16	0.75	1.39*	29.5	39.8	30.7
1864	0.86	1.33	1.18*	45.0	55.0	—
1868	1.43	1.50	1.37*	47.3	52.7	—
1872	1.13	1.05	1.19*	44.0	55.7	0.3
1876	1.30	1.51	1.12*	51.0	48.0	1.0
1880	1.10	1.03	1.10*	47.9	48.3	3.8
1884	1.09	1.11*	1.09	48.9	48.3	2.8
1888	1.13	1.13	1.12*	48.7	47.9	3.4
1892	1.06	1.00*	0.95	46.1	43.0	10.9
1896	1.15	1.15	1.37*	45.9	51.1	3.0
1900	1.00	1.00	1.02*	45.5	51.7	2.8
1904	0.97	0.80	1.06*	37.6	56.4	6.0
1908	1.10	1.26	1.01*	43.1	51.6	5.3
1912	1.01	0.98*	0.45	41.9	23.2	34.9
1916	1.23	1.45*	2.45	49.3	46.1	4.6
1920	1.44	1.00	1.89*	34.1	60.3	5.6
1924	1.09	0.92	0.97*	28.8	54.0	17.2
1928	1.27	1.79	1.36*	40.8	58.1	1.1
1932	1.08	1.52*	0.74	57.4	39.7	2.9
1936	1.15	1.20*	1.06	60.2	36.5	3.3
1940	1.09	0.98*	1.34	53.9	44.7	1.4
1944	0.96	0.92*	0.99	51.7	45.9	2.4
1948	1.02	0.97*	1.00	49.4	45.0	5.6
1952	1.26	1.13	1.54*	44.4	55.0	0.6
1956	1.01	0.94	1.05*	41.5	57.4	1.1

[a] Sources: Election returns for 1832 from Charles O. Paullin, *Atlas of the Historical Geography of the United States* (1932); 1836-1892, inclusive, from W. Dean Burnham, *Presidential Ballots, 1836-1892* (1955); 1896-1932, inclusive, from Edgar E. Robinson, *The Presidential Vote, 1896-1932* (1934); 1936-1956, inclusive, from Bureau of the Census, *Statistical Abstracts, 1936-1956.*
[b] Winner indicated by asterisk (*).
[c] Includes predecessor parties.
[d] In years for which no percentage is shown, polled less than .1 of 1 per cent.
[e] Whig vote in 1852 used as the base in calculating ratio.

444

tional loyalties and a new popular movement. In 1924 there was a noteworthy increase in total vote and a decline in the vote of each major party.

Repeat engagements by the same pairs of opponents seem to retard growth in the vote. In 1892, which was also an important third-party year, Cleveland and Harrison were running against each other for the second time, and the total vote increased only 6 per cent. The second engagement between Bryan and McKinley in 1900 and that between Stevenson and Eisenhower in 1956 each led to virtually no increase in the total vote. Aside from these instances, when the same candidate has run more than once he has run against a different opponent.

The records of the Presidents who ran more than once were widely variable; from Van Buren on, the ratios of the party vote of their own party in the election of the year of their first nomination and in successive elections were as follows:[3]

Martin Van Buren (1836): 1.11*–1.47
Abraham Lincoln (1860): 1.39*–1.18*
Ulysses S. Grant (1868): 1.37*–1.19*
Grover Cleveland (1884): 1.11*–1.13–1.00*
Benjamin Harrison (1888): 1.12*–0.95
William McKinley (1896): 1.37*–1.02*
William Howard Taft (1908): 1.01*–0.45
Woodrow Wilson (1912): 0.98*–1.45*
Herbert Hoover (1928): 1.36*–0.74
F. D. Roosevelt (1932): 1.52*–1.20*–0.98*–0.92*
Dwight D. Eisenhower (1952): 1.54*–1.05*

Success and failure in the presidential office is reflected rather directly in these statistics. The Presidents who won a second term usually increased the party vote substantially in their second election, but at a lesser rate than in their first. Wilson's record was outstanding for his large increase in the party vote in his second race, after achieving no increase in his first.[4] Van

Buren, who did even better than Wilson in his second race, was defeated nonetheless in the popular upsurge of 1840. Cleveland did relatively well in his second race but was defeated; did less well in his third and won. Spectacular fall-offs in the party vote were associated with the failures of Taft and Hoover to win a second term.

Renominated titular leaders have tended to repeat their previous vote but not to increase it. Cleveland's ratio in 1892, running as a titular leader, was 1.00. Bryan, in his first race in 1896, pulled up the previous Democratic vote with a ratio of 1.15, held steady with a ratio of 1.00 in 1900, and almost precisely recovered the losses of the Parker campaign with a ratio of 1.26 in 1908. Dewey's ratio of 0.99 in the war year 1944 failed to better the previous Willkie vote; in 1948 Dewey failed to better his own previous vote, with a ratio of 1.00. In 1952, Stevenson pulled up the previous Democratic vote, with a ratio of 1.13, but failed to hold the same level in 1956, with a ratio of 0.94.

Usually the winning party increased its vote at a higher rate than the losing party, as might be expected; the average difference in vote gain between winning and losing parties, 1832-1956, was 10 per cent.[5] But the losing party increased its vote at a higher rate (or fell back less) than the winning party in eleven of the thirty-two elections. In most of these cases the losing party, even though it lost, was achieving a recovery from disaster in either the most recent election or the one preceding. The most noteworthy cases of this kind include the Republican ratio in 1916 of 2.45 and the Democratic ratios in 1864 of 1.33; 1868, 1.50; 1876, 1.51; 1908, 1.26; 1928, 1.79.

The cases just noted help to explain why the candidates who achieved the largest gains in party vote were not always the

---

[3] As in Table 18.1, an asterisk indicates victory in the election. Year of first nomination in parenthesis.

[4] The total vote increased sharply in 1916, with only two major-party candidates and with women's suffrage newly effective in several states. The choice between the candidates was relatively clear and many voters were acutely concerned about the international situation.

[5] For the period 1832-1892, the average difference was 6.8 per cent; for 1896-1956, 12.6 per cent. If we are now moving into an era of closer party balance, as suggested in Chapter 3, the difference may revert to something like that prevailing before 1896.

winners. Among the six Democratic candidates who increased the party vote by more than 40 per cent, four lost—Van Buren (1840), Seymour (1868), Tilden (1876), and Smith (1928); Wilson (1916) and Roosevelt (1932) won. On the Republican side, Hughes (1916) lost; William Henry Harrison, the Whig candidate of 1840, Harding (1920), and Eisenhower (1952) won. The candidates who had the misfortune to incur the greatest losses of party vote, with a falloff of 20 per cent or more, were all defeated. They included two Democrats, Douglas (1860) and Parker (1904), and two Republicans, Taft (1912) and Hoover (1932). Douglas and Taft were victims of party splits. Parker was probably the most conspicuous example of a candidate who was nominated by the wrong political party, while Hoover was a victim of the Depression.

Many factors influence the growth of the party vote of each party, but one of the clearest aspects of the total experience is the rarity of the occasions on which either party has been able to grow by taking votes, net, directly from the other. Presumably there are always a few floating voters who move from one party to the other, but large net transfers seem unlikely to occur very often except when there is an actual decline in the vote of one party. Table 18.1 shows only six cases in which actual declines in the party vote of one party were associated with increases of 1 per cent or more in the vote of the other: 1848, 1860, 1904, 1932, 1940, and 1956.[6]

The decline in the Democratic vote of 1848 was largely due to third-party movements, while that of 1860 was the result of the party split. In the election of 1904 some

Republicans doubtless voted for Parker and even larger numbers of Democrats probably voted for Roosevelt, with many members of both parties staying home.

The election of 1932 was the outstanding case in modern times in which large blocs of voters transferred directly from one political party to the other. There was a decline of 26 per cent in the Republican vote and an increase of 52 per cent in the Democratic, with little increase in third-party voting.[7] In 1940 there was apparently a small net movement back to the Republican party, as there may also have been in 1944. The wartime decline of 1 per cent in the Republican vote in 1944 might otherwise have been greater; the Democratic vote declined 8 per cent. In 1956, there may have been a net transfer of Democratic votes from Stevenson to Eisenhower of 5 per cent or more. The same effect on the figures could have been produced by equivalent numbers of Democrats staying home, coupled with a slight increase in turnout for Eisenhower by non-Democrats.[8]

---

[6] While the table seems to indicate that 1856 was such a case, it was actually the first presidential election of the new Republican party, which nearly came up to the 1852 vote of the Whig party. The reconstruction of the parties, however, doubtless involved much churning around of voter alignments in 1856 as well as 1860. There was probably some loss of Democratic voters to the Republican party in 1856, offset by even larger temporary accessions of southern Whigs.

[7] Something similar probably occurred in 1920, even though it is not revealed in the figures of Table 18.1. The failure of the Democratic vote to grow with the advent of women's suffrage in 1920, with the Republican vote nearly doubling, was equivalent to a substantial transfer of Democratic votes to the Republican party.

[8] The year 1952 was not included in the above discussion because Table 18.1 gives no reason to suspect any substantial net transfer of Democratic votes to the Republican column; Stevenson's vote was 13 per cent larger than Truman's. Survey data are available, however, that purport to show that 24 per cent of the Eisenhower vote of 1952 came from Truman voters of 1948, while only 74 per cent of the Stevenson vote came from Truman voters, the balance being made up of 3 per cent who voted for Dewey in 1948, 16 per cent who did not vote, 5 per cent who were too young to vote, and 2 per cent who voted third party or whose vote was not ascertained. But the same survey data make it clear that memories of 1948 voting had "slightly inflated" the Truman vote; and it seems more than possible that most of this inflation occurred among the Eisenhower voters who said that they had voted for Truman. If the percentages noted above were applied to the 1952 figures to compute the Truman vote of 1948, he would be credited with some 4 million votes more than he actually received, without allowing for four years of mortality in the voting population. Hence the case for a large net transfer of Democratic votes to Republican in 1952 does not seem to have been proved, although perhaps a

Since the average growth in popular vote from one election to another was around 11 per cent for the period 1896-1956, as noted earlier, either party can grow by a corresponding amount without being dependent on taking votes from the other party, assuming no change in turnout rates. But the whole look of the figures suggests that when substantial upswings occur in the total popular vote, they generally reflect an induction of new voters into the system and a change in turnout rates that is much more favorable to one party than the other. This can occur, moreover, without involving any reduction in the vote of the other party. When the prospective winning party seems likely to achieve a great increase in turnout, even the losing party may achieve some increase as it struggles to compete—as the Democrats demonstrated with their 13 per cent increase in 1952.

Convention Action and State Voter Turnout

The action of a party convention in choosing one candidate rather than another could be expected to have the effect of improving the party's position relatively in some states and impairing it in others. Where there are genuine differences in sentiment among the states and where these differences are reflected in the convention voting, it could be expected that corresponding differences would occur in the response of the party voters in the following election. *If no other factors intervened and a perfect correlation existed in the directions of movement, the party vote would swing up most strongly in the states whose delegations won their choice at the convention, while it would swing up less strongly or not at all in the states whose delegations were defeated at the convention.*

In the previous section, it was noted that

the growth of the national vote throughout the years has been highly irregular, sometimes taking great jumps, at other times actually falling from a previous peak. This irregularity is even more noticeable when the records of individual states are examined: for the period 1896-1956 the total popular vote dropped from one presidential election to the next in an average of nearly one state in four on each occasion. And irregularity is also conspicuous for the party vote of each party in the individual states: the Democratic vote registered declines in 42 per cent of the cases, the Republican in 36.[9]

A question for exploration is the extent to which this fluctuation is related to the choice of candidate and the voting records of the state delegations at the national conventions. Perfect correlation obviously should not be anticipated, since many other factors intervene. These factors do not easily lend themselves to measurement, and they are too numerous and their interrelations too complex for precise forms of analysis. A close study of the data suggests, nonetheless, that some of the factors operate with enough frequency and are sufficiently important to merit listing them as elements in a tentative outline of relationships between voting at the conventions and the subsequent swings in party vote in the respective states.

Factors Affecting Vote-Swing Relationships

The factors affecting vote-swing relationships operate in different ways and with dif-

---

transfer occurred of around one third or one half of that indicated by the survey data. For the data, see Angus Campbell, Gerald Gurin, and Warren E. Miller, *The Voter Decides* (1954), pp. 6, 16-17.

[9] These averages are based on a widely fluctuating experience. From 1896 to 1956 there were three years in which the popular vote increased in every state—1916, 1928, and 1952; as for declines, in 1944 the popular vote declined in nearly three quarters of the states, and in 1912 in almost exactly half. The Democratic vote increased in every state in two elections, 1916 and 1932; the Republican in 1916, 1920, and 1952. On declines, there were five years in which the Democratic vote declined in 60 per cent or more of the states—1900, 1904, 1924, 1944, and 1948; three years in which the Republican vote declined in 60 per cent or more—1912, 1924, and 1932.

ferent weights under different conditions, but they generally can be classified under one of three types: those tending toward positive relationships; those that obscure or flatten the relationship by the randomness of their effects; and those that actually tend to reverse the relationship. The factors leading toward positive relationship may do so in two ways: action of delegates at the convention *in support of* a winning candidate may be followed by high voter support at the polls; or action of the delegates *in unsuccessful opposition to* a candidate may be followed by low voter turnout for the convention choice.

Random factors, as the term implies, are unpredictable in the way they affect the relationship. However, when these factors can be identified in a situation, they may serve as a basis for prediction that the action of the delegates in the convention may not be relied upon as an index of what the voter reaction will be—a highly useful bit of intelligence for the practicing politician. Negative factors are those which tend to encourage high voter response to convention choices rejected by delegates representing the constituencies (or low voter response to the choices supported by these delegates).

FACTORS LEADING TO POSITIVE RELATIONSHIP. The principal hypothesis can be stated as follows: a positive relationship between convention voting and vote swing in the states is most likely to occur when there is clarity of issues and personalities as perceived by the delegates and the voters. When issues are sharply drawn and candidates are well known both as individuals and in terms of their identification with important issues, the mandates to convention delegates become more definite and the actions of the delegates can be clearly appraised by their constituents. The delegate who transgresses a genuine mandate from a majority of his constituents can expect an adverse reaction at the polls. The following kinds of situations can be defined as among those likely to result in clear mandates, sharp decisions, and strong voter response.

A high level of public awareness on a major national issue.

A high level of geographic orientation on an issue.

A widely known candidate, whose reputation is based upon his political activity and whose stand on public issues is clear.

A sharply fought preconvention campaign, in the course of which loyalties have been intensified and enmities sharpened.

Clear identification of a candidate with political, social, or economic groups that can become apparent in the geography of voter alignment.

FACTORS LEADING TO RANDOM EFFECTS. Just as clarity of the situation encourages positive relationship, ambiguity tends to reduce it. When there is no major issue dividing the nation, either generally or sectionally, or when a candidate is selected who has little identification with the issues that are currently most divisive, delegates have no way of knowing how their constituents will respond and, in general, have some reason to expect a response of apathy. When a candidate is selected who is not well known to the general public, public opinion concerning him must be formed by his actions after nomination. When a candidate is selected from outside the political world, he is usually chosen on the basis of vote-getting qualities that he is presumed to have—but those qualities have had little previous testing at the polls and can only be estimated. Even if the estimate proves correct so far as the party's national vote is concerned, an advance estimate of the differential effects from state to state could have little basis. The following kinds of situations can thus be defined as among those likely to produce random effects and an absence of relationship, either positive or negative.

Low level of conflict over issues and between prospective candidates *or* compromise selection after deadlock of leading candidates.

Lack of a clear *political* image of the nominee.

Preconvention campaigns in which delegates are selected by organizational methods without much publicity or commitment.

A band-wagon effect, when one candidate is so far out in front that his nomination seems inevitable, thus encouraging delegates to join the coalition early and without regard to whether their constituents are favorable.

A heavy cross-over vote in which the voters of one party vote for the candidate of the other primarily as a protest against the candidate selected by their own party.

FACTORS LEADING TO NEGATIVE RELATIONSHIP. The factors that lead to negative relationship, as distinguished from merely random effects, seem to occur only infrequently, but at least three kinds of situation can be distinguished in which there is a basis for anticipating a negative—or reversed—relationship between convention voting and the swings in party vote.

The first of these occurs when there is a profound change in the political situation between convention and election—one, moreover, with which the candidate becomes identified in a way that tends to reverse his field of support in the electorate. The latter qualification is important; in its absence, change between convention and election would have merely random effects.

The second occurs when the candidate's position on issues, as revealed during the campaign, proves to be quite different from what was assumed when he was nominated. Here again, the effect must extend to the point of an actual reversal—a discovery that the candidate is definitely in opposition to major goals of the nominating coalition—if a negative relationship is to result rather than something merely random.

The third occurs when party leaders from areas where the party is relatively strong deliberately unite to select a candidate best suited, in their judgment, to appeal most where the party is weak—whether to repair a bolt of the previous year or in an attempt to bring out large segments of the previously nonvoting public. The assumption generally is that the candidate will do well enough in the party leaders' own areas to make victory possible if he is sufficiently attractive in other areas. In extreme cases this may be a strategy of desperation in a party situation of great weakness. But when it is successful in lifting the party's national vote substantially it can be viewed as a response to a national mandate in which many delegates are disregarding the immediate views of their own constituents.

*   *   *   *   *   *

This outline of tentative hypotheses on the probable existence of positive, random, and negative relationships between convention voting and later vote swing can be tested against the actual experience, but valid testing requires the construction of an array of tables that resist easy consideration. In each convention-election situation, the several factors appear in different combinations and with different levels of importance for individual factors in relation to each other. Furthermore, the complex of factors involved for one state or area delegation-voter relationship may differ widely from others in the same election year. Accordingly, it is no easy task to estimate even approximately the full effect of any one factor or group of factors in a specific election situation. However, even a cursory examination of the statistical record of elections in the past reveals a wide range from high positive to equally high negative reaction of the voters to the actions of their delegates in the conventions. The following sections attempt to provide measures of the direction and degree of the total relationship—the resultant of the pressure of the many factors involved in each convention-electoral situation. Against the information thus provided, historical knowledge of the personalities and forces involved in each convention year can then be examined in a search for clues to a better understanding of the total process.

Many readers may find it preferable, especially on a first reading, to merely scan or entirely omit the following section on the statistical record, going directly to the successive sections in which the experience of the parties is interpreted in the light of the statistical record. Those who find the interpretive material of enough interest to merit close study of how it was derived can then return to the paragraphs and tables that follow here, and to the technical footnotes that provide further explanation.

The Statistical Record

Tools of measurement are required if the hypotheses just outlined are to be tested. For voting at the conventions, the winner-support ratio developed in Chapter 16 is available. For vote swing in the states, the simplest measure is the ratio between the party's vote in one presidential election and the vote polled by the party in the last preceding presidential election. After experimenting at length with other and more complicated devices, the present authors concluded that this simple ratio is by far the most useful tool in comparisons with convention voting.[10]

By using the winner-support and vote-swing ratios, it is possible to arrive at a four-way classification in which all states participating in a national convention can be assigned to groups identified as follows:

HH, High for winner at convention, high upswing in party vote.
HL, High for winner at convention, low upswing in party vote.
LH, Low for winner at convention, high upswing in party vote.
LL, Low for winner at convention, low upswing in party vote.

In this classification the HH and LL categories both provide examples of positive relationship, since there is consistency in the two kinds of movement, while the HL and LH categories both provide examples of negative relationship, using the terms "positive" and "negative" in the usual statistical sense. The classification is basic to the tables that follow, and a brief comment is therefore necessary on how the states are classified as high or low in each case.

The winner-support ratio has the effect of indicating automatically the states that were above or below average in their support for the winner at the convention: states with ratios above 1.00 can be classified as high, those below 1.00 as low. This tendency was discussed in Chapter 16 and is illustrated most clearly in Appendix A, Tables 11 and 12. It will be recalled, moreover, that in convention voting few states are "average" on any given occasion. Winner-support ratios are usually well above or well below 1.00, thus dividing the states into clearly defined high and low groups.

On vote swing in the states, the problem of dividing between high and low is not so easy.[11] There is no clear division between one group that can be called high in vote swing and another that can be called low; states tend to cluster in the middle of the range. The arithmetic average or the median can be used as the cut point, and the resulting groups of high and low can be used in making the four-way classification. But difficulties result when a cut point is used for vote swing that produces groups different in size from those produced in the convention division.[12] An arbitrary cut point has therefore been used in classifying states as high or low in vote swing: for each year

---

[10] Comparisons of the state party vote for a given year with a computed long-term trend often produced skewed results, for in a year when the election swings sharply in the direction of one party, most states swing above their own trend lines. Use of percentages of the major-party vote introduces a different set of difficulties; on many occasions, the actual party vote in a state increases sharply, indicating some satisfaction with the party candidate, while the party's percentage of total popular vote may even fall because of an even greater increase in the vote for the other party. State percentages of the total national party vote for a given year proved inadequate because of wide variations in voting habits in the several states and differences in state size.

[11] High or low vote-swing classifications are necessarily relative terms. In some years most if not all states drop from their previous party vote, in which case those states that drop the least are classified as "high" in vote swing. In other years most if not all states swing upward in party vote, and states in which the increase is the least are classified as "low" in vote swing.

[12] Assume, for example, a case with forty-eight states in which the rank order of the states on the winner-support ratio is identical with their rank order on the vote-swing ratio, and in which the use of the averages produces thirty states classified as high in winner support and twenty in vote swing. On this basis there will be twenty states in the HH category, ten in HL, and eighteen in LL. Ten states have thus been assigned to a nonrelated category, although the example begins by assuming perfect relationship in rank order.

TABLE 18.2. RELATIONSHIPS BETWEEN VOTING FOR THE WINNER AT CONTESTED CONVENTIONS AND SWINGS IN THE PARTY VOTE IN THE SUBSEQUENT PRESIDENTIAL ELECTIONS, 1896-1956, BY STATES IN TERMS OF THEIR NUMBERS OF ELECTORAL COLLEGE VOTES[a]

Year	Presidential Candidate	HH	HL	LH	LL	Total Number of Electoral College Votes
		DEMOCRATIC CONVENTIONS AND VOTES				
1896	Bryan	114	94	94	142	444
1904	Parker	228	73	73	102	476
1906	Bryan	292	78	78	28	476
1912	Wilson	125	166	175	59	525
1920	Cox	214	113	114	90	531
1924	Davis	110	128	129	164	531
1928	Smith	299	40	38	154	531
1932	F. D. Roosevelt	192	88	85	166	531
1940	F. D. Roosevelt	298	112	117	4	531
1948	Truman	349	55	44	83	531
1952	Stevenson	96	171	171	93	531
1956	Stevenson	260	102	108	61	531
	Total	2,577	1,220	1,226	1,146	6,169
		REPUBLICAN CONVENTIONS AND VOTES				
1896	McKinley	197	106	106	35	444
1908	Taft	225	94	95	62	476
1912	Taft	210	73	82	160	525
1916	Hughes	137	173	169	52	531
1920	Harding	102	133	135	161	531
1928	Hoover	256	105	103	67	531
1940	Willkie	52	175	177	127	531
1948	Dewey	161	121	127	122	531
1952	Eisenhower	89	177	178	87	531
	Total	1,429	1,157	1,172	873	4,631
	Totals, Both Parties	4,006	2,377	2,398	2,019	10,800

[a] For explanation of the categories and the method of classification, see text.

in which the party vote is studied, the states are placed in rank order on the basis of the vote-swing ratio, and the same number is called high (measured in electoral college votes) that was found to be high at the convention on the basis of the winner-support ratio. For example, in 1940 the Democratic vote swing varied by states from 1.44 to 0.76. Delegations from states with 410 electoral votes had voted *for* Roosevelt at the convention (voted high); delegations from states with 121 electoral votes had voted *against* Roosevelt at the convention (voted low). When the states were arrayed from high to low in order of vote swing in the election, the cut point was determined by counting electoral votes down from the top to the point nearest 410 votes. Through Iowa, with a vote-swing ratio of 0.93, this total was 401. Indiana, also with a vote-swing ratio rounding off to 0.93, was next in order with 14 electoral votes, running the total to 415. The latter sum, being closer to 410 than the total excluding Indiana, 401, was adopted as the cut-off point. Thus all states with vote-swing ratios of 0.93 or greater were classified as high, and states with ratios of 0.92 or lower were classified as low in vote swing.[13]

Table 18.2 shows the results, counting the states in terms of their numbers of electoral college votes, of applying this classification system to the contested conventions of 1896–1956 and the elections that followed. The table indicates some of the wide variation of pattern that has occurred in relationships between convention voting and vote swing in the states: for example, the high positive relationship after the nomination of Al Smith in 1928, the random results of the Davis nomination in 1924, the striking negative impact of the

Willkie nomination in 1940. However, Table 18.2 should be taken primarily as an illustration of the method and as an intermediate step to the tables that follow. It is weak as a direct indication of relationship because, in a few instances, a part of the indicated relationship is spurious.[14]

In Table 18.3 the states are again given their electoral college weight, the years of contested conventions in each party have been listed in the order of the degree of relationship that is found between convention voting and vote swing in the states, and measures of the degree of relationship are supplied—for the states high at the convention taken as a group, for those that were low, and for the total group. Readers who are interested only in the general conclusion for each convention year can concentrate their attention on the index of relationship provided in the last column of the table. This index is comparable to a coefficient of correlation and provides a measure ranging between 0 and 1.00, plus or minus, thus indicating degrees of positive or negative relationship.[15]

---

[13] In counting down from the top of the vote-swing rank order in terms of the numbers of electoral college votes, the cut point fell *within* states in some cases, as in the example cited. Such minor variances were disregarded, and in such instances states were assigned to the category in which they were predominantly located. In four cases, however, the cut point fell near the middle of a large state; in these cases the electoral vote of the state was prorated accordingly between the categories.

[14] The decision on cut point between states high and low in vote swing, made for the reasons that were indicated in footnote 12, has the effect of permitting a perfect relationship to become apparent where it exists, but can also indicate relationship in some types of situation where it does not exist. Assume, for example (treating the states as equal units for simplicity), that thirty-six states vote high at the convention and twelve states vote low; and further that all of the twelve states that are low at the convention are high in vote swing. There will then be twelve states classed as LH, which will in turn mean that twelve states will be HL (since by definition at least twelve states must be low in vote swing and they must be found among the group high at the convention). The remaining twenty-four states will be classed as HH—indicating a considerable amount of positive relationship in a situation where all of the relationship at the low end of the scale, at least, is negative. This kind of case can occur only where there is imbalance in the size of the high and low groups and where also the relationship is strongly negative in the smaller of the two groups. It is illustrated in Table 18.2 mainly by the Roosevelt nomination in 1940, in which the superficial appearances indicate a positive relationship, on the high side, although this was not actually the case, as will be indicated by Table 18.3.

[15] For statisticians, the index can be identified as the phi coefficient (Φ), for which further explanations can be found in standard statistical textbooks.

As Table 18.3 indicates, the Al Smith nomination of 1928 produced what were statistically the most highly significant positive relationships between convention voting and vote swing in the states in the entire body of experience reviewed here. There was a high order of positive relationship both for the states voting high at the convention and for those voting low; most of the states that voted for Smith at the convention also had a high turnout of Democratic vote in the election that followed, while in most of the states that voted against Smith at the convention, the party turnout was indeed low. In four other Democratic cases—Truman in 1948, Roosevelt in 1932, Parker in 1904, Bryan in 1896 —highly significant positive relationships were found; a significant positive relationship was found for Cox in 1920. Relationships were random in three cases, while in another three, Roosevelt in 1940, Stevenson in 1952, and Wilson in 1912, highly significant negative relationships were found. The Republican experience shows a narrower range between extremes and a higher proportion of cases in which the relationship was negative. Highly significant or significant positive relationship was found for Taft in 1912 and 1908, and for Hoover in 1928. The relationship could be classed as random in three cases, and as highly significant negative in another three: Hughes in 1916, Eisenhower in 1952, and Willkie in 1940.[16]

So far the discussion of relationship between convention voting and vote swing in the election has been concerned with the direction of movement: whether high winner support was followed by high vote swing, and vice versa. But where there is significant relationship in direction of movement, the relationships are largely dependent for their importance on the size of the vote swing in the respective groups of states. The basis for studying this is provided by Tables 18.4 and 18.5.

Table 18.4 reports the average vote-swing ratio in each of the four categories of states

---

[16] For readers who desire to look further for meaning in the other columns of the table (especially for the differences in voting behavior between states high and low at the conventions), and for those technically interested, the following explanations are offered. Taking the first line of the table as an example, the states voting high for Al Smith at the convention (HH plus HL) held a total of 339 electoral college votes, or 63.8 per cent of the total electoral college strength of 531. If there were no relation between convention winner support and election vote swing, it could be expected that the same proportion of the high convention voting group, 63.8 per cent of 339 electoral votes, or 216, would be held by states ranking high in election vote swing. But the actual electoral college strength of those both high for Smith at the convention and high in vote swing (HH) was 299. The ratio of actual to expected was 1.38, indicating a high positive re-

lationship for the states high at the convention in this case. The term "expected" in the column heads of this table thus means what would be expected in the absence of relationship either positive or negative; in other words, this is testing against the null hypothesis.

The same process applied to the states voting low for Smith at the convention indicates more than twice the electoral vote in the low vote-swing group that could be expected in the absence of relationship —a ratio of 2.20, indicating high positive relationship on the low voting side. For highs and lows together as the total convention, the ratio is 1.58, and the phi coefficient is .63.

The detail of the table has been presented here mainly for what it shows of differences in subsequent voting behavior between the states high and low at the conventions. The highest ratios of actual to expected (positive relationship) are all found in the case of groups voting low at the convention: the hard-core oppositions to the nomination of Truman in 1948, Smith in 1928, and Parker in 1904. The lowest ratios of actual to expected (negative relationship) are also mostly found in the case of the groups voting low at the conventions, meaning that an apparently strong opposition at the convention was followed by a favorable response to the candidate in the states concerned. Instances of this phenomenon include the favorable vote for Roosevelt in the states that voted against him at the convention in 1940, and the similar occurrences in states that had voted, at the conventions, against Wilson in 1912 and Hughes in 1916. On the other hand, the Willkie showing in 1940 was relatively low in the states that had voted for him at the convention (while high in the states that had voted against him), this being the leading example of a low ratio of actual to expected (negative relationship) in the case of states voting high at the convention.

As a final point, it would be noted that the methodology of this table was utilized in part to avoid the problems of spurious relationship noted in footnote 14. There is every reason to think that the relationships that are found and that test for statistical significance are indeed genuine, even though in many cases the degree of relationship that they indicate is relatively low.

TABLE 18.3. RELATIONSHIPS BETWEEN CONVENTION WINNER SUPPORT AND VOTE SWING IN SUBSEQUENT ELECTION, WEIGHTED BY ELECTORAL COLLEGE STRENGTH; BY YEAR, IN ORDER OF DEGREE OF RELATIONSHIP[a]

Year	High for Winner at Convention				Low for Winner at Convention				Total Convention			
	Total HH+HL	Actual HH	Expected HH	Ratio, Actual to Expected	Total LL+LH	Actual LL	Expected LL	Ratio, Actual to Expected	Actual HH+LL	Expected HH+LL	Ratio, Actual to Expected	Index of Relationship[b]
					DEMOCRATIC CONVENTIONS AND VOTES							
Cases of Positive Relationship												
1928	339	299	216	1.38	192	154	70	2.20	453	286	1.58	.63**
1948	404	349	307	1.14	127	83	30	2.77	432	337	1.28	.37**
1932	280	192	146	1.32	251	166	120	1.38	358	266	1.35	.35**
1904	300	228	188	1.21	176	102	65	1.57	330	253	1.30	.33**
1896	208	114	97	1.18	236	142	126	1.13	256	223	1.15	.15**
1920	327	214	201	1.06	204	90	78	1.15	304	279	1.09	.10*
Cases of Random Relationship												
1956	362	260	247	1.05	169	61	54	1.13	321	301	1.07	.08
1908	370	292	287	1.02	106	28	24	1.17	320	311	1.03	.04
1924	238	110	107	1.03	293	164	161	1.02	274	268	1.02	.02
Cases of Negative Relationship												
1940	410	298	321	0.93	121	4	26	0.15	302	347	0.87	−.18**
1952	267	96	134	0.72	264	93	131	0.71	189	265	0.71	−.29**
1912	291	125	161	0.78	234	59	149	0.40	184	310	0.59	−.49**
Total	3,796	2,577	2,411	1.07	2,373	1,146	1,034	1.11	3,723	3,445	1.08	.09**

	High for Winner at Convention				Low for Winner at Convention				Total Convention			
Year	Total HH+HL	Actual HH	Expected HH	Ratio, Actual to Expected	Total LL+LH	Actual LL	Expected LL	Ratio, Actual to Expected	Actual HH+LL	Expected HH+LL	Ratio, Actual to Expected	Index of Relationship[b]
Cases of Positive Relationship												
1912	283	210	153	1.37	242	160	112	1.43	370	265	1.40	.40**
1908	319	225	214	1.05	157	62	51	1.22	287	265	1.08	.09*
1928	361	256	245	1.04	170	67	54	1.24	323	299	1.08	.09*
Cases of Random Relationship												
1948	282	161	150	1.07	249	122	117	1.04	283	267	1.06	.06
1920	235	102	105	0.97	296	161	164	0.98	263	269	0.98	−.02
1896	303	197	207	0.95	141	35	45	0.78	232	252	0.92	−.09
Cases of Negative Relationship												
1916	310	137	179	0.77	221	52	94	0.55	189	273	0.69	−.32**
1952	266	89	134	0.66	265	87	132	0.66	176	266	0.66	−.34**
1940	227	52	97	0.54	304	127	174	0.73	179	271	0.66	−.35**
Total	2,586	1,429	1,484	0.96	2,045	873	943	0.93	2,302	2,427	0.95	−.05**

REPUBLICAN CONVENTIONS AND VOTES

[a] For explanations of terms and methods, see text, especially footnotes 15 and 16. The term "expected," as used in the column heads of this table, means what would be expected in the absence of any relationship between convention and election voting. The figures for what could be "expected," computed from those in the "total" columns as explained in text footnote 16, can thus be used to test the extent to which the actual result in each case is above or below such an expectancy, indicating a positive relationship when the actual result is more than "expected," and a negative relationship when it is less than "expected."

[b] The single asterisk (*) indicates that the difference between the actual and the expected frequencies for the total convention is significant on the basis of a standard statistical test; the double asterisk (**) that it is highly significant.

TABLE 18.4. RELATIONSHIPS BETWEEN CONVENTION WINNER SUPPORT AND DEGREE OF VOTE SWING IN SUBSEQUENT ELECTION, WITH PERCENTAGE OF ELECTORAL COLLEGE IN EACH CATEGORY, CONTESTED CONVENTION YEARS, 1896-1956

Year	Total Party Vote Swing Ratio[a]	HH Vote Swing Ratio	HH Per Cent Electoral College	HL Vote Swing Ratio	HL Per Cent Electoral College	LH Vote Swing Ratio	LH Per Cent Electoral College	LL Vote Swing Ratio	LL Per Cent Electoral College
DEMOCRATIC CONVENTIONS AND VOTES									
Cases of Positive Relationship									
1928	1.79	2.53	56%	1.09	8%	1.72	7%	1.03	29%
1948	0.97*	0.99	66	0.84	10	0.93	8	0.65	16
1932	1.52*	1.80	36	1.34	17	1.87	16	1.29	31
1904	0.80	0.92	48	0.68	15	0.88	15	0.62	22
1896	1.15	1.90	26	0.98	21	1.22	21	0.84	32
1920	1.00	1.23	40	0.64	21.5	1.40	21.5	0.66	17
Cases of Random Relationship									
1956	0.94	1.01	49	0.85	19	0.96	20	0.79	12
1908	1.26	1.34	62	0.97	16	1.27	16	0.92	6
1924	0.92	1.15	21	0.74	24	1.13	24	0.70	31
Cases of Negative Relationship									
1940	0.98*	1.01	56	0.88	21	1.02	22	0.82	1
1952	1.13	1.15	18	0.87	32	1.43	32	1.02	18
1912	0.98*	1.04	24	0.88	32	1.12	33	0.87	11
REPUBLICAN CONVENTIONS AND VOTES									
Cases of Positive Relationship									
1912	0.45	0.51	40%	0.35	14%	0.55	16%	0.34	30%
1908	1.01*	1.09	47	0.93	20	1.02	20	0.90	13
1928	1.36*	1.58	48	1.16	20	1.43	19	1.18	13
Cases of Random Relationship									
1948	1.00	1.05	30	0.93	23	1.14	24	0.99	23
1920	1.89*	2.25	19	1.97	25	2.41	26	1.53	30
1896	1.37*	1.48	44	1.17	24	1.37	24	1.08	8
Cases of Negative Relationship									
1916	2.45	3.44	25	1.77	33	3.06	32	1.68	10
1952	1.54*	2.06	17	1.40	33	1.76	34	1.36	16
1940	1.34	1.45	10	1.25	33	1.55	33	1.20	24

[a] Winner in election indicated by asterisk (*). In these vote-swing ratios, as in Table 18.1, the ratio is that of the party vote in the election concerned to the party vote in the last previous election. A ratio of 1.00 thus reflects a vote identical with the one previously cast, while a ratio of 1.79, for example, reflects a vote in which there was a 79 per cent increase.

TABLE 18.5. DIFFERENCES IN AVERAGE VOTE-SWING RATIOS BETWEEN STATES BY CONVENTION CATEGORIES AND BY VOTE-SWING CATEGORIES[a]

Year	States by Convention Categories			States by Vote-Swing Categories		
	High for Winner HH+HL	Low for Winner LH+LL	Difference High vs. Low	High Vote Swing HH+LH	Low Vote Swing HL+LL	Difference High vs. Low
DEMOCRATIC CONVENTIONS AND VOTES						
Cases of Positive Relationship						
1928	2.27	1.16	1.11	2.41	1.04	1.37
1948	0.97	0.75	0.22	0.99	0.77	0.22
1932	1.62	1.45	0.17	1.82	1.32	0.50
1904	0.85	0.72	0.13	0.91	0.65	0.26
1896	1.37	1.00	0.37	1.47	0.89	0.58
1920	1.00	0.99	0.01	1.28	0.65	0.63
Cases of Random Relationship						
1956	0.96	0.89	0.07	1.00	0.83	0.17
1908	1.25	1.19	0.06	1.33	0.96	0.37
1924	0.92	0.91	0.01	1.14	0.72	0.42
Cases of Negative Relationship						
1940	0.97	1.01	−0.04	1.01	0.88	0.13
1952	1.06	1.23	−0.17	1.25	0.94	0.31
1912	0.93	1.03	−0.10	1.09	0.88	0.21
REPUBLICAN CONVENTIONS AND VOTES						
Cases of Positive Relationship						
1912	0.50	0.41	0.09	0.53	0.34	0.19
1908	1.01	0.97	0.04	1.06	0.92	0.14
1928	1.39	1.31	0.08	1.52	1.17	0.35
Cases of Random Relationship						
1948	0.99	1.01	−0.02	1.09	0.92	0.17
1920	2.12	1.82	0.30	2.33	1.65	0.68
1896	1.38	1.33	0.05	1.43	1.15	0.28
Cases of Negative Relationship						
1916	2.29	2.65	−0.36	3.20	1.75	1.45
1952	1.51	1.56	−0.05	1.85	1.38	0.47
1940	1.29	1.37	−0.08	1.52	1.23	0.29

[a] See footnote to Table 18.4 on the conversion of vote-swing ratios to rates of increase or decrease in the vote concerned.

as defined in Table 18.2 (HH, HL, LH, and LL), listing the convention years in the same order from positive to negative relationship as in Table 18.3. For convenience in reference, the national average of party vote swing is repeated from Table 18.1.

For most convention years, Table 18.4 shows wide differences in vote swing between the states relating positively on the high voting side (HH) and those relating positively on the low voting side (LL). On the other hand, the differences between the two categories of negative relationship (HL and LH) are smaller than those in the categories of positive relationship (HH and LL) in sixteen of the twenty-one conventions listed. Since the statistical probability against such a distribution appearing by chance is highly significant, the experience of these twenty-one cases would appear to support the hypothesis that there is a tendency toward a positive relationship between convention action by individual delegations and subsequent voting by their constituents.

Table 18.5, however, provides a better basis for examining the differences in vote swing, even though it may be found useful to go back to Table 18.4 for additional detail when examining any year under close study. In Table 18.5 averages are provided for the states when regrouped on the basis of each set of major categories. Here it becomes apparent that the average difference in upward vote swing between the states voting high at the convention and those voting low was substantial indeed in five of the six Democratic cases where positive relationship was found, while the opposite differences were also substantial in two of the three cases of negative relationship. Similar but mostly smaller differences were found in the Republican cases of positive relationship.

The Hughes case in 1916 shows the largest negative difference in either series, while the Harding case in 1920 shows a large positive difference in vote swing in a case previously classed in Table 18.3 as one of random relationship. In this instance, the positive difference in vote swing

seems to have been due mainly to the oddities of the variable impact of national women's suffrage in 1920.[17]

Table 18.5 also reports the difference in average vote swing between the total groups of states classed as high in vote swing and those classed as low. This difference is reported to provide a guide for the appraisal of the difference in vote swing between the convention categories. Where there is a high degree of positive relationship, it could be expected that the difference in vote swing between the convention categories would be comparable to that between the vote swing categories. The table shows one case, in fact, where it was identical: the Truman nomination in 1948, where the positive relationship was nearly perfect so far as degrees of vote swing are concerned. Relatively high relationships of the same kind were noteworthy in the cases of Smith in 1928 and Bryan in 1896.

The Democratic Experience

The Democratic experience as a whole conforms much more than the Republican to an anticipation of positive relationships between winner support at the conventions

[17] Women began voting in presidential elections in Wyoming, Colorado, Idaho, and Utah in 1900 or earlier; Washington and California in 1912; Arizona, Kansas, and Oregon in 1912 or 1916 (the state constitutions were amended in 1912 in those cases); and Illinois, Nevada, and Montana in 1916. Several other states, including New York, provided through state action for women's suffrage in all elections between 1916 and 1920, but their action was overtaken by the amendment of the federal Constitution before the election of 1920. See Howard R. Penniman, Sait's American Parties and Elections (5th ed., 1952), pp. 57-58.
In the states that already had women's suffrage in 1916, which means most of the western states plus Illinois, the vote swing from 1916 to 1920 would tend to be less than average, while it would tend to be more than average in all of the other states where women's suffrage was effective for the first time. New York, which voted for Harding at the convention, was the most outstanding case of high swing resulting largely from the coming of women's suffrage. Pennsylvania voted against Harding at the convention and managed to remain low in vote swing despite the arrival of women's suffrage.
The western states were in fact all low in Republican vote swing in 1920; all but one were also low in Democratic vote swing.

and vote swing in the states. Averages for the entire Democratic experience since 1896, as shown in Table 18.3, show a small over-all positive relationship, whereas the similar over-all averages for the Republican experience indicate a low order of negative relationship. This analysis probably would not have been pursued to its present conclusions if early indications of positive relationships on the Democratic side had not been found.[18]

[18] In an early phase of the research for this book, a considerable amount of labor was expended upon an analysis in which it was assumed that positive relationships between convention voting and party vote swing might be found in either party, but probably with clarity only in those years and states in which the delegation of one party had supported a winner at the convention while the delegation of the other party had supported a loser. The states meeting these specifications were identified for the years 1928, 1940, 1948, and 1952, in which contested conventions occurred in both parties, and a much more elaborate process of measuring vote swing against the state's own averages was applied than that used in the present analysis. Results were then compared in each party for the state groups.

This early attempt failed to find any significant general relationship on the Republican side, but did find that support vs. non-support for the Democratic candidate at the convention seemed to be related to about a 6 per cent difference in Democratic vote in the non-southern states, and about a 16 per cent difference in the southern states, without regard to what happened on the Republican side. It was in the light of this experience that it was concluded that the party vote of each party could be treated independently for the purpose of this type of analysis. This in turn made it possible to use the years of contested conventions in one party without regard to whether a contest had occurred at the convention of the other party, thus broadening the base of the analysis.

The earlier analysis was based upon the vote swing around the state's own averages, measured as percentages of the two-party vote. All of the figures were thus affected by developments in the vote of both parties rather than merely one, but the basic weakness of the technique seemed to result mainly from an excessive reflection of the national vote swing rather than the relative popularity of the candidate in the several states. Thus, most states had high Republican indexes in 1928 and again in 1952 and 1956, moderately high in 1948, and low in the other years. Democratic indexes were approximately the reverse. The present technique, using only swing from the previous election year and using the actual votes for each party separately, gives a better indication of the relative success of a candidate in holding or improving the vote base that he inherited from his predecessor in each state.

In intermittent attempts over a five-year period, several months of computation time were devoted

The amount of variation from convention to convention in the direction and degree of relationship between convention voting and party vote swing, however, is a much more important finding than the contrasting averages for the total experience of the parties since 1896—especially when it becomes possible to account for that variation in terms of the kinds of factors previously outlined. Undoubtedly considerable portions of the variation were both accidental and unanticipated, but some of the more remarkable cases were also, for some of the participants, the intended results of rational foresight and deliberate choice.

The most extraordinary showing in the tables, from many points of view, is the record of the results of Al Smith's nomination in 1928. Often considered one of the most badly defeated candidates of modern times, Smith has occasionally been given some grudging recognition for his achievement in pulling up the party's percentage of the total popular vote from the 29 per cent at which Davis left it to 41 per cent in 1928 (Table 18.1). Students of voting behavior have also noted Smith's powerful effect on the party vote in some states.[19] But Smith's 79 per cent increase in the national Democratic party vote from the previous election was an all-time high, still unbroken, for a Democratic convention nominee.[20] In

to analyses that have since been discarded but which made their contribution to the development of the present analysis. This analysis is primarily the work of Richard C. Bain.

[19] Most notably Samuel Lubell in The Future of American Politics (1952), Chap. 3, partly on the basis of research by S. J. Eldersveld; and V. O. Key, Jr., as cited in Chapter 3, footnote 1, of this present book.

[20] Higher ratios were recorded in the Republican party, but were less meaningful of genuine increases in the party vote. Hughes' ratio of 2.45 in 1916 must be read against the ratio of 0.45 in 1912. The ratio of the 1916 to 1908 Republican votes is 1.11, or an 11 per cent increase; and most of this can be traced to the states granting women's suffrage during the interval. Hughes' ratio for 1916 to 1908 in the remaining states averaged 0.98—no net increase at all—although the increase in total popular vote in those states averaged around 10 per cent. Harding's ratio of 1.89 in 1920 was similarly inflated, but to a much greater extent, by the arrival nationally of women's suffrage.

the states that were high for Smith at the convention the average increase was 127 per cent, while in those that were low at the convention it was 16 per cent, a difference of 111 percentage points (Table 18.5). In the states that were high for Smith at the convention and also high in vote swing—56 per cent of the electoral college—his increase in the party vote was 2½ times (HH ratio 2.53); while in the states that correlated low (LL), with 29 per cent of the electoral college, the party vote stayed level with a vote swing ratio of 1.03 (Table 18.4). The Hoover nomination of the same year also produced a dramatic increase in the Republican vote, largely as a response to Smith's nomination; in combination, the two nominations produced the highest rate of increase in popular vote between 1876 and 1956, with the sole exception of 1920, the year when national women's suffrage arrived.

The Smith case thus emerges as the leading example of what a sharply defined nominating decision can do to the party vote. When nominated, Al Smith was one of the best known political figures in the country. His whole reputation, moreover, was based on his record in politics, with issue positions of high visibility on the Ku Klux Klan, prohibition, and the rights of a citizen of the Catholic faith to run for office. He was a symbol of the desire of the urban masses for political recognition. His contribution to the later development of the Democratic party by enlarging its working class following in such states as Massachusetts, New York, New Jersey, Pennsylvania, and Michigan has been often noted. Much less has been said about the effects of his nomination on the Democratic vote in the states where the Progressives had been strongest in 1924: he more than doubled the Democratic vote in ten of those states. In Wisconsin, Minnesota, and North Dakota, the increase was sevenfold.

The Smith nomination illustrates almost all of the factors previously identified as leading to positive relationship between convention voting and vote swing. In 1928 there was no sharply fought preconvention campaign, but the party struggles of 1920 and 1924 had already served the purpose so far as his candidacy was concerned. The relationship was not perfect, however; three states in which the vote swing was high voted *against* Smith at the convention: Ohio, Florida, and Nebraska. In six other states that had voted *for* Smith at the convention, the vote swing was rated low: New Mexico, Kentucky, Delaware, West Virginia, Arkansas, and New Hampshire. The last two nevertheless increased their Democratic popular vote over 40 per cent.

Opinions can differ on whether or not the Smith nomination was a good thing for the Democratic party, but it would be difficult to argue that any other possible candidate could have increased the party vote so much in 1928, and especially in states where the party was so much in need of an increase if it was again to become competitive. The contrast is especially striking against the record of Smith's two immediate predecessors, Cox and Davis.[21]

Four other Democratic nominations were clearly followed by positive relationship and noteworthy effects in vote swing. The Truman case in 1948 was the clearest of all in displaying the resistance of a minority at the convention, with that minority in turn backed strongly by their constituents in the election. There was relatively much less positive relationship on the high side at the convention, where Truman derived organizational and band-wagon support from many states that did little for him in the election.

In 1932, Franklin D. Roosevelt had avoided strong commitments on divisive issues and had conducted his campaign mainly through organizational channels,

[21] Tables giving winner-support and vote-swing ratios for individual states for each contested convention and following election since 1896, and a further discussion of what they show, will appear in the forthcoming book by Richard C. Bain, *Decisions and Voting Records of the National Party Conventions* (Brookings Institution).

factors adverse to a positive relationship. But the major opposition to the Roosevelt nomination was centered in the Smith camp, and had all of the characteristics displayed in Smith's previous campaigns. Aside from the Garner strength in California, Texas, and Oklahoma—states in which the Roosevelt-Garner ticket doubled the Democratic vote of 1928—the balance of Roosevelt's critical ballot opposition was almost entirely located in the northeastern states where Smith was strong. Roosevelt eventually carried these states in the election, but in most of them the vote swing from 1928 to 1932 was far below the national average.

The Parker nomination in 1904 and the Bryan case in 1896 were similar to each other in positive correlation for reasons related to the opposite characteristics and followings of the two candidates. In the Bryan case, strong positive relationship could be expected from the candidate's own characteristics, and there was indeed a high vote upswing in the middle-western and western states that supported his nomination. But the soft-money states, mainly midwestern, that voted against Bryan because they stayed to the end with Bland were perfectly willing to vote for Bryan in the election, while some of the southern states that supported his nomination were low in vote swing. Bryan's northeastern opposition at the convention, however, was clearly reflected in the adverse vote at the polls in that region. The Parker nomination came largely as a retreat from Bryanism, and was supported by eastern industrial and conservative southern states. In these states the Democratic vote was largely maintained, rather than dropping off sharply, as it did in many of the soft-money states that opposed the Parker nomination.

The Cox nomination in 1920 was classed in Table 18.3 as one of positive relationship, but the actual difference in average vote swing between states high and low at the convention, as shown in Table 18.5, was almost imperceptible. The issue may have been somewhat confused by the differential impact of national women's suffrage, but as a candidate Cox had many of the characteristics that might have been expected to lead to random effects. He was not a first choice for most of those voting for him at the convention, was selected only after lengthy balloting, and did not convey a clear political image.

The three Democratic cases in which there was no significant correlation all displayed in various ways the factors leading to random effects. Davis in 1924 was a compromise choice after one of the most extreme instances of convention deadlock. Bryan in 1908 was a third-time nominee, a first-ballot winner on a lopsided vote, a beneficiary of organizational type preconvention campaigns and band-wagon movements, and opposed mainly by factional adversaries whose voter support was limited.

The Stevenson nomination in 1956 was the remaining instance of the three. His first nomination in 1952 had been followed by a negative relationship; by 1956 he was far better known for his stands on political issues, and there were noticeable traces of positive relationship between convention voting and voter response throughout the country. In the three states—Oregon, Florida, and California—where he had won primaries after hard battles with his later teammate, there were substantial increases in the party vote, illustrating the tendency of strong preconvention campaigns to produce a positive relationship. But Stevenson's chief opponent had conceded before the convention met, in most states the preconvention campaign was conducted primarily through organizational channels, and there were large elements of band-wagon vote in his first-ballot victory.

Highly significant negative relationships were found in three Democratic cases, most noticeably in the Wilson case of 1912. Wilson's final nominating coalition was achieved with great difficulty and was in some respects a strange mixture. In the election Wilson ran somewhat better in the states that had voted against him at the convention than in those that had voted for him (Table 18.5), further evidence of the negative relationship reported in Table 18.3. Clues to the reasons for the relationship can be found in the experience of individual states, but a sufficient general explanation is the fact that, as a candidate, Wilson was bracketed in the public mind somewhere between the progressive Roosevelt and the conservative Taft. This provided the opportunity for his victory in a three-way contest, but his differential effect upon the Democratic vote in individual states was largely unpredictable in advance of the event.

In 1952, Stevenson ran 16 per cent better in the states that voted against him at the convention than in those that voted for him (Table 18.5).[22] The case is one of the clearest examples of negative relationship between convention voting and party vote swing. It can also be viewed as one of the classic examples of candidate selection by the party leaders without reference to established popularity with the general public, and with a view to securing a candidate who could run reasonably well in areas opposed to his nomination and in which the party had suffered a previous bolt. The case takes on additional oddity, however, from the fact that the public leadership of the movement to draft Stevenson, and much of his actual convention support, came from liberal and labor leaders who were looking for a candidate who could run well in their own states, but who would also be sufficiently acceptable to the party leaders to have some chance of nomination.[23]

The relationships by regions between convention voting and later vote swing in the Stevenson case are indicated by the tab-

[22] The 17-point spread between 1.06 and 1.23 is 16 per cent of the smaller figure; this arithmetical distinction is relatively unimportant here but more important in studying the Republican cases of negative relationship in Table 18.5.
[23] On the complexities of how Stevenson came to be nominated the first time, see Chapter 4; also see Paul T. David, Malcolm Moos, and Ralph M. Goldman, *Presidential Nominating Politics in 1952* (1954), Vol. 1, p. 17.

ulation below, in which the numbers (other than the vote-swing ratio) represent the electoral college strength of the groups of states.

Region	Category of Relationship			
	HH	HL	LH	LL
Northeast	68	64	9	12
Middle West	20	82	—	51
South	8	—	120	18
West	—	25	42	12
Total	96	171	171	93
Vote Swing	1.15	0.87	1.43	1.02

Stevenson ran fairly well in the northeastern areas where much of his convention support had centered; he ran even better in California and in the southern states, all of which except Arkansas had voted against his nomination. In the Middle West he fell below his national average in most of the states that had supported his nomination at the convention, with random results in those that had opposed it. He proved rather consistently not to be an attractive candidate in rural areas, despite the band-wagon support he had received from a number of rural states at the convention.

From the point of view of those who were trying to bridge the gap between the party's urban and industrial elements, on the one hand, and its southern strength, on the other, while holding the party vote elsewhere, the results of the Stevenson nomination provided confirmation for the wisdom of the choice. In view of the sharp cleavages to be bridged in the aftermath of the 1948 bolt, the maneuver probably would not have been possible except with a candidate whose issue positions were both moderate and little known at the time.

The other Democratic case of negative relationship was that of Roosevelt in 1940. Here the situation was in some respects the opposite of the Truman nomination in 1948; the hard core of opposition to Roosevelt's third nomination at the convention, mainly centered in the Northeast, found almost no voter support in its constituencies. This extreme case of negative relationship in states low in convention support was probably due in large part to the wartime developments abroad and Roosevelt's response to them, reviving his popularity in some areas and depressing it in others.

The Republican Experience

The Republican experience offers fewer cases of contested nominations for study than the Democratic, and still fewer in which relatively high degrees of positive relationship are found between convention voting and vote swing. The leading case was the William Howard Taft nomination of 1912, in which the convention was sharply divided. In the party split that followed, Taft brought out 50 per cent of the previous party vote of 1908 in the states that had supported him at the convention, 41 per cent in those that had not (Table 18.5)—a clear case of positive relationship. But the results were mixed; several states that voted against him at the convention were relatively high in vote swing; while in the southern states, all of which except newly admitted Oklahoma were for him at the convention, the vote swung low.

The Taft case of 1908, managed by the incumbent Roosevelt administration, provided another instance of significant positive relationship. Efforts to get out the vote were evidently effective in most of the states that voted high at the convention. The southern states, joined by Nevada, were uniformly at the top of the list in Republican vote swing. In this year when the administration-guided steamroller was in full operation and victory was in prospect, the patronage-hungry apparently went all out. With the low vote base involved in the South, not many votes were required to produce impressive results in percentage terms.

The Hoover nomination of 1928 was made in a party in power after an organizational type preconvention campaign and

with some band-wagon shifting as the result of Lowden's unexpected withdrawal from the race. Nevertheless, there were significant evidences of positive relationship in the later voting. In many of the middle western states that had opposed the nomination, the vote swing was low. In the states that related high (HH), nearly half of the electoral college, the increase in party vote was 58 per cent (Table 18.4). The southern and western states were almost all found in this category, but presumably for different reasons. The size of the southern vote for Hoover was largely a protest against the Smith nomination, whereas the western was probably in part a tribute to Hoover's western origins; Smith also ran well in the West.

The Dewey nomination in 1948 showed traces of positive relationship, like Stevenson's in 1956, but can also be classed as one of random results. There had been a hot preconvention campaign during the period when Stassen looked like a front-runner, and Dewey had addressed himself to a number of major issues while campaigning. But the greater part of Dewey's preconvention campaign was conducted through organizational channels, and his critical vote on the second ballot at the convention included a considerable amount of band-wagon support. More important, probably, was the kind of campaign he chose to wage after the convention, which developed no clear political image of his intentions if elected and inspired few strong reactions on the part of the voters.

The Harding nomination in 1920 produced random effects, on the basis of the proportions of electoral college strength held by the states in the various categories (Table 18.3). Nevertheless, Harding's nomination was followed by a more than doubling of the party vote in the states that supported him at the convention, against an 82 per cent increase in the others (Table 18.5)—a positive relationship. But this was the year in which women's suffrage became effective in all states, after having previously arrived in most of the western states and

Illinois.[24] The comparisons based on percentages of vote swing were heavily affected by a few states and thus are difficult to interpret, but for most states an impression of random or even negative relationship, rather than positive, seems to be justified. The Progressives had returned to the fold in the 1916 campaign, but were still touchy. A compromise candidate was needed who could satisfy the majority coalition without again repelling the erstwhile bolters. The Harding choice met the tests, and, despite his somewhat colorless appeal, he produced one of the party's greatest victories.

The McKinley nomination of 1896, made by a party out of power, was seemingly akin to the kind of contested nomination usually followed by positive relationship in the voting, but the actual results were random and even somewhat negative. The opposition to McKinley in the convention was led by Pennsylvania, Massachusetts, and other eastern states, but in the election most of the Northeast swung high for McKinley. In the states that related high (HH)—nearly half of the electoral college—McKinley pulled up the vote by 48 per cent (Table 18.4); but in the nonrelated LH group, mainly northeastern states, the upswing was 37 per cent—in large part no doubt as a protest against the Bryan nomination in the Democratic party, an example of a cross-over protest vote leading to random or negative relationship.

Three of the Republican nominations were followed by vote swings showing a highly significant negative relationship with the convention voting. In the first of these, Hughes ran 16 per cent better in the states that had opposed his nomination at the convention in 1916 than in those that had favored it (Table 18.5).[25] The nomination was largely managed by the group that had insisted on nominating Taft in 1912, and the case was a prime example of motivations that can be powerful in a year follow-

ing a disastrous party bolt. The leading figures of both camps in 1912 were eliminated from consideration in the search for a candidate who would be at least acceptable to the bolters—even if he was not the first choice of anybody. Hughes was a distinguished former governor who had been aloof from the struggle as a Supreme Court justice. He was not popular with the Progressives who had returned to the convention, but he ran well in the erstwhile bolting states and elsewhere, and came near defeating the incumbent Wilson, thus suggesting that the strategy was well justified even if not wholly successful.

The Eisenhower case of 1952 has been classed as one of highly significant negative relationship on the basis of the proportions in the various categories of states (Table 18.3). The tabulation below of electoral college strength by categories and by regions may help to give a clearer picture of a complex set of relationships.

Region	Category of Relationship			
	HH	HL	LH	LL
Northeast	18	127	—	8
Middle West	10	41	37	65
South	46	—	90	10
West	15	9	51	4
Total	89	177	178	87
Vote Swing	2.06	1.40	1.76	1.36

Eisenhower had the almost solid support of the Northeast at the convention yet pulled up the Republican vote in that area less than elsewhere. In the Middle West, where much of the convention opposition had centered, there was a mixture of random results and positive relationship on the low side, with many states in the LL category. In the West, where convention opposition was equally strong, the relationship was almost entirely negative. In the South, Eisenhower pulled up the Republican vote from under 2 million to nearly 5 million, and the effect was felt without much regard

[24] See footnote 17, above.
[25] The spread of .36 between 2.29 and 2.65 is 16 per cent of the lower figure.

o how the southern delegations had voted: most of them had opposed his nomination. For the country as a whole, the Republican vote nearly doubled in the states where vote swing was classed as high, 50 per cent of the electoral college; in areas where vote swing was classed as low, it still averaged nearly 10 per cent increase (Tables 18.4 and 18.5).

Taking the country as a whole, Eisenhower ran better by about 3 per cent in the states that voted against him at the convention than in those that voted for him (Table 8.5).[26] This difference is so small that it would be easier to consider it an indication of random effects than of significant negative relationships. Random effects could be expected, moreover, from the fact that the candidate came out of a nonpolitical career and had no clear political image when he was nominated, even though he obviously had great popular appeal. The negative relationship, however, has something in common with other leading cases of nominations followed by negative relationship: the desire of the leaders supporting the winner to find a candidate whose characteristics were such that he could heal breaches in the party and also pull out masses of new voters. If Senator Taft had been nominated, a positive relationship between convention voting and vote swing probably would have resulted, at least outside his areas of southern support. Eisenhower was a success in part because in many of the areas of Taft organization strength he was able to run even better than in areas where his own convention support had been mobilized.

The Willkie nomination of 1940 was the other case of highly significant negative relationship, on the basis of the measures applied in Table 18.3. He ran better by about 8 per cent in the states that voted against him on the critical ballot at the convention than in those voted for him (Table 18.5).[27]

[26] The .05 difference between 1.51 and 1.56 is 3 per cent of the smaller figure.
[27] The .08 difference between 1.29 and 1.37 is 6 per cent of the smaller figure.

The tabulation below shows the distributions of electoral college strength by categories and regions.

Region	Category of Relationships			
	HH	HL	LH	LL
Northeast	27	88	—	44
Middle West	4	38	79	40
South	7	43	53	43
West	14	6	45	—
Total	52	175	177	127
Vote Swing	1.45	1.25	1.55	1.20

Willkie was a candidate who came out of a nonpolitical career. He was the product of a last-minute campaign that involved no record in the primaries, a sixth-ballot choice after Taft and Dewey had been rejected on their first bids for the nomination. Few delegates had any direct mandate for Willkie or any firm basis for predicting in what way their constituents would react to his nomination.

All of these factors could have been expected to lead to random effects, of which many were apparent. The more difficult question is why the relationships were also significantly negative. As in the Roosevelt case in 1940, the major explanation probably involves the influence of developments between conventions and election, which had the effect of strengthening voter support for Roosevelt in the Northeast and weakening it in parts of the Middle West. Many of the internationally-minded voters of the Northeast might otherwise have voted for Willkie, and his pulling power with isolationist voters in the Middle West as the alternative to Roosevelt might have been less.

It is probable also that there was something of the kind previously noted in the Eisenhower case: a candidate with great appeal for party neutrals and previous non-voters may have his greatest effect in swelling the party vote in precisely those areas where many of the party regulars are most opposed to his nomination. Where this occurs, a negative relationship between convention voting and later vote swing is the natural result.

General Observations

The experience reviewed in the previous pages is much too complex for easy summary, but it does seem to bear out the kind of approach suggested in the listing of factors affecting turnout with which this discussion began. There are, moreover, a few other general aspects of the experience that may well attract attention despite their somewhat elusive quality.

One can wonder, for example, to what extent the personality differences between the Democratic and Republican parties are reflected in the differing extent to which they have thrown up cases of positive relationship between convention action and voter response since 1896. The Democratic party has undoubtedly been somewhat more inclined than the Republican to choose candidates whose political personalities were clearly defined, who had definite attractions for some voters and repulsions for others on the basis of their known political positions.

The total experience can also be looked at in terms of the differing problems of a party that has a majority following in the electorate, and one that does not. The party with a majority following, especially when it is currently holding the White House, usually assumes that its basic problem is to hold together the coalition it already possesses, unless definite opportunities are available for the recruitment of new voters to replace those who are most dissident. The party with a minority following, and especially when it is the party out of power, cannot hope to win by nominating a candidate who will meet with favor only among its previous following.

The minority major party has sometimes been accused of trying to commit political suicide by insisting on the choice of a candidate in its own image.[28] This is one of the hazards of binding primaries and tight mandates in the minority major party. But in any political party with the will to live, some leaders are usually present who have their eye on where additional voter support can be found without losing what the party already has. These are the leaders who take a national view of their party's problems and prospects and are most inclined to search out candidates who can broaden the party's popular appeal in states and regions where it has lost ground.

Tendencies of this kind are undoubtedly pushed along by the public opinion polls in their present form, which have done much to strengthen the hands of the kinds of leadership just described. One can only speculate on what the polls would have indicated in regard to the first-time candidacies of Wilson and Hughes. Each was a response to a highly special kind of situation. But the polls undoubtedly had a powerful role in the respective first-time choices of Willkie, Eisenhower, and Stevenson. Even in the difficult minority situation in which the Republican party found itself, there is obvious room for doubt that either Willkie or Eisenhower could have been nominated without the indications provided by the polls that each could broaden the party's popular base. They were the party's only candidates since Harding and Hoover to do so. Stevenson was not the choice of the polls in 1952, but his selection was facilitated by the extent to which it had been demonstrated that the alternative candidates of what appeared to

[28] Writing on the tendencies toward a downward spiral in an American political party when long out of power, Julius Turner commented, "There is a tendency for party leaders to 'put principle above politics' and to insist upon their own economic or social dogmas regardless of the popularity of such dogmas with the electorate. This tendency increases as the party's popularity decreases, because a decline in the party's membership reflects the withdrawal of dissident leaders who had previously moderated the policies formed by the ruling group. This trend, unless interrupted, would lead to the suicide of the minority party." See Turner, "Responsible Parties: A Dissent from the Floor," *American Political Science Review*, Vol. 45 (March 1951) pp. 143-52; quotation from pp. 151-52. See also Ivan Hinderaker, *Party Politics* (1956), pp. 634-36.

be a majority party were unlikely either to defeat Eisenhower or to hold together the party's following.

The polls increase the leverage of the independent voters in the entire nominating process by providing indications of independent voter sentiment that would not otherwise be available. They also tend to concentrate the attention of the delegates, as well as party leaders, on national tendencies, as distinguished from the trends of individual states. Few delegates are in any position to measure precisely the sentiments of their own constituents. When presented instead with relatively authoritative measures of sentiment for the entire national electorate, delegates can more easily disregard divergent sentiment at home even when it is known to exist.

All of this is compatible with a decline in sectionalism that has been going on for other reasons; in turn it probably helps along that decline. The present research has had no opportunity to investigate the extent to which convention voting between 1832 and 1892 was followed by positive relationship in the vote swing of individual states, but in that era of sectional politics one could suppose that such relationship may have occurred more often than it has since 1896. If this is true, the considerable number of cases of negative relationship found in the present inquiry may in fact deserve to be regarded as one of the evidences of nationalizing tendencies in American politics.

Nominating Conflict and Election Victories

The sixty-three major-party presidential nominations since 1831 were all classified in Chapter 6 in terms of a series of nominating patterns. It became apparent that some of the patterns were much more frequently associated with electoral success than others. From this experience, the following propositions can be derived:

1. When harmony attends the nominating process for the in-party, its chances of winning the election are good.

2. When conflict leading to factional victory attends the nominating process for the in-party, its chances of winning the election are poor.

3. When harmony attends the nominating process for the out-party, its chances of winning the election are poor.

4. When conflict leading to factional victory attends the nominating process for the out-party, its chances of winning the election are good.

These propositions are purely empirical. They are based on more than a century of experience with the convention system of presidential nominations, but rest on only sixty-three nominations, which in turn provide thirty-one pairs of cases for study.[29] The statistical basis for inferences is accordingly limited, but is nonetheless important enough to merit close study. With sufficient research, substantially the same propositions could be tested against the experience in nominating governors in states and in time periods where there has been relatively about as much competitive balance between the parties as in the federal system. Larger numbers of cases would be available and the problems of statistical significance would become minor. The qualification in regard to competitive balance, however, is highly important, for reasons that will become apparent in the discussion that follows the presentation of the available statistical material.

The data of Chapter 6 on nominating patterns have been supplemented in Table 18.6 by adding the pertinent figures on electoral success. For example, of the six in-party nominations between 1832 and 1892 that confirmed an incumbent President in the party leadership, three led to victory at the polls. The proportion of these cases resulting in electoral success was thus 3/6. The similar proportion for the more recent sixty-year period is 9/11. It thus becomes

---

[29] It will be recalled that the Whigs held no national convention and made no single nomination in 1836; hence there was no pair for that year.

apparent that the renomination of an incumbent President has been not only more frequent than formerly but more frequently successful. On the other hand, renomination of out-party titular leaders has become more frequent without so far becoming more successful; Grover Cleveland's third nomination remains the only successful instance of its kind.

Nominations reflecting inheritance were more successful for the in-party than the

tion, with the proportion of victory about the same in the two time periods.

Each of the relationships expressed by a fraction in Table 18.6 has meaning in its historical context, but, from a statistician's point of view, the numbers are too small in most of the cells to be significant.[30] Further results can be obtained, however, by collapsing the table into a smaller number of cells. Types A, B, and C—confirmation, inheritance, and inner group selection—have

TABLE 18.6. PROPORTION OF PRESIDENTIAL NOMINATIONS RESULTING IN ELECTORAL SUCCESS, BY TYPE OF NOMINATION AND IN-POWER AND OUT-POWER STATUS OF THE PARTIES, 1832-1892 AND 1896-1956[a]

Type of Nomination	Party in Power		Party Out of Power	
	1832–1892	1896–1956	1832–1892	1896–1956
A. Confirmation	3/6	9/11	1/1	0/4
B. Inheritance	1/2	2/2	0/1	0/1
C. Inner Group Selection	1/2	0/0	1/5	0/3
D. Compromise in Stalemate	2/2	0/0	2/3	1/2
E. Factional Victory	1/4	0/3	4/5	4/6
Total	8/16	11/16	8/15	5/16

[a] In each cell of the table, the denominator is the total number of nominations and the numerator is the number of nominees who won in the ensuing general election. See Chapter 6 for the classification on which this table is based.

out-party, while nominations producing inner group selections and compromise nominees had a mixed record. Such nominations served the in-party reasonably well before 1892, but none were made thereafter by an in-party between 1896 and 1956. Inner group selections did poorly for the out-party in both periods, with three losers in three tries in the more recent period.

Nominations reflecting factional victory provide another category in which the differing records of in-party and out-party are conspicuous. Victory for a factional candidate in the party in power has rarely led to success in the following election. In the out-party, factional victory has led to election victory in most of the instances in which conflict occurred over the nomina-

[30] In such a table, numbers of at least 5 in a cell are required before statistical significance begins to become possible for the individual items; and, if the number is only 5, all items must be uniformly in the same direction for statistical significance on the basis of standards commonly applied. When an event can happen in only one of two ways, the probability that 4 events will all happen in the same way on a purely random basis is approximately 6 in 100; for 5 cases, about 3 in 100, or less than 5 per cent. When 1 item of the series deviates, 8 items are necessary for significance; when 2 items deviate, 11 items are necessary for significance; and so on. Cell values of 0/5, 1/8, 2/11, 3/14, 4/16, 5/19, and 6/21, and the converse values (5/5, 7/8, 9/11, etc.) all meet minimum tests of statistical significance, but just barely so.

The significance of the differences between cells is another matter. In this particular case, if the results of confirming an existing leadership in the in-party are compared with the results of confirming an existing leadership in the out-party for the period 1896-1956—9/11 vs. 0/4—the difference is highly significant from a statistical point of view.

enough in common as low-conflict patterns to justify combining them. They show similar configurations in the respective cells, have a self-evident similarity in assuring a considerable continuity of leadership within the party concerned, and involve types of decision in which conflict levels typically are low and similar, as demonstrated in Chapter 17. In view of the limited evidences of time trend in most categories, moreover, there is obvious merit in considering the entire collection of items without regard to when they occurred. Table 18.6 can thus be brought down to six cells with the following proportions of wins as the result.

Type of Nomination	In-Party	Out-Party
ABC. Low-Conflict Patterns	16/23	2/15
D. Compromise in Stalemate	2/2	3/5
E. Factional Victory	1/7	8/11

The propositions stated at the beginning of this section are based primarily on this tabulation. The Type D cases of compromise in stalemate were omitted from the formulation because of their ambiguity; they begin in vigorous conflict but end in harmony, whereas the Type E high-conflict cases of factional victory are in sharp contrast with the low-conflict patterns of Types A, B, and C. The statistical outcome in the winning and losing situations as identified in the propositions can thus be reassembled as follows:

Winning situations
Low conflict in the in-party (ABC)	16/23	70%
High conflict in the out-party (E)	8/11	73%
Total	24/34	71%

Losing situations
High conflict in the in-party (E)	1/7	14%
Low conflict in the out-party (ABC)	2/15	13%
Total	3/22	14%

The difference between the winning and losing situations in terms of the proportions of wins is highly significant from a statistical point of view. The propositions thus seem to be supported by the data.

Results When
Nominating Patterns Are Paired

As noted, each major-party nomination, with the exception of that made by the Democrats in 1836, was one of a pair of nominations. If the nominating patterns of the parties are considered in the combinations provided by these pairs, a second set of propositions can be derived as follows:

1. When harmony attends the nominating process in both major parties, the in-party nominee almost invariably defeats the out-party nominee.

2. When vigorous conflict attends the nominating process in both parties, the out-party nominee usually defeats the in-party nominee.

3. When the in-party nominating process is harmonious but the out-party nomination involves vigorous conflict, the out-party nominee has more than an even chance to win.

4. When the in-party nominating process involves conflict but the out-party nominating process is harmonious, a conjuncture that is extremely rare, no generalization can be made concerning the probable outcome.

The opposing pairs of 1832 and 1840-1956 can be taken as a set of thirty-one, in which the combinations that produced the eighteen in-party wins can be displayed as shown in Table 18.7. (For the complete listing of the pair combinations, arrayed by categories, see Appendix A, Table 13.)

The contrasting in-party and out-party positions are again strikingly apparent. In twelve pairings of low-conflict type nominees, the in-party lost only once—President Benjamin Harrison to ex-President Cleveland in 1892. The in-party won only once in seven times with a Type E nominee, and this victory was achieved against an out-party Type C nominee—Buchanan against Frémont, the first nominee of the new Republican party in 1856 and classed in Chapter 6 as a case of inner group selection.

In-Party Type \ Out-Party Type	ABC Low-Conflict Patterns	D Compromise in Stalemate	E Factional Victory	Total In-Party Wins
ABC Low-Conflict Patterns	11/12	2/3	2/7	15/22
D Compromise in Stalemate	1/1	0/0	1/1	2/2
E Factional Victory	1/2	0/2	0/3	1/7
Total In-Party Wins	13/15	2/5	3/11	18/31

[a] The cell values 11/12 and 13/15 attain statistical significance when considered in isolation; the cell values 15/22, 1/7, and 3/11 come close to statistical significance.

Out-party winning combinations can be seen more clearly in Table 18.8, which presents the mirror image of Table 18.7.

The out-party won only twice in fifteen tries with a low-conflict type nominee: Cleveland against Harrison, as already noted, and once against an in-party Type E nominee, when Cleveland (classed as a case of inner group selection) defeated Blaine in 1884. But the out-party's record of success with nominations won in factional victories was spectacular: eight wins in eleven tries, of which five in seven were against an in-party nominee of the low-conflict type. Willkie in 1940 and Dewey in 1944 were the two defeated out-party Type E candidates, running against an in-party Type A, Franklin D. Roosevelt; the public opinion polls reported in Chapter 13 suggests that either Willkie or Dewey might have won in the absence of the war conditions that brought on Roosevelt's third and fourth nominations. The other Type E (factional victory) candidate shown as defeated was Governor Samuel J. Tilden, running in 1876 against an in-party Type D (compromise in stalemate) candidate, Governor Rutherford B. Hayes, in an election that left ample room for doubt concerning whether the party in power had actually won.

The cases just reviewed seem to reflect

Out-Party Type \ In-Party Type	ABC Low-Conflict Patterns	D Compromise in Stalemate	E Factional Victory	Total Out-Party Wins
ABC Low-Conflict Patterns	1/12	0/1	1/2	2/15
D Compromise in Stalemate	1/3	0/0	2/2	3/5
E Factional Victory	5/7	0/1	3/3	8/11
Total Out-Party Wins	7/22	0/2	6/7	13/31

[a] The cell values attaining statistical significance are the converse of those noted for Table 18.7.

the effects of widely divergent levels of conflict so consistently that a retabulation of the data on a single measure of conflict would be desirable. Unfortunately, there is no single best measure of conflict levels, and the different numerical indicators of nominating conflict are not easily combined. For the total historical experience, however, the difference between a single-ballot nomination and a multi-ballot nomination usually makes the distinction between low and high levels of nominating conflict. Among the thirty-eight Type ABC nominations, only six required more than a single nominating ballot; among the twenty-five Types D and E nominations, only three were made without requiring more than one ballot, as shown in Chapter 17, Tables 17.8 and 17.9.

Using the distinction between single- and multi-ballot nominees (S and M), the in-party nominees can be arrayed against the out-party nominees with the proportions of wins as diagramed below. This diagram in-

In-Party	Out-Party		Total Wins
	S	M	
S	10/11	5/10	15/21
M	0/2	3/8	3/10
Total Wins	10/13	8/18	18/31

dicates that when single-ballot nominees faced each other, the in-party nominee won ten times in eleven; when multi-ballot nom-

471

inees faced each other, the out-party won five times in eight.

A similar diagram, produced from Table 18.7 by collapsing Types D and E into a single category, indicates a similar but nonetheless somewhat different set of pro-

In-Party	Out-Party ABC	Out-Party DE	Total Wins
ABC	11/12	4/10	15/22
DE	2/3	1/6	3/9
Total Wins	13/15	5/16	18/31

portions. The principal relationship given new emphasis by this diagram is indicated by the DE/DE cell, in which the one in-party winner was Governor Hayes, the compromise candidate in the previously noted case of 1876.[31]

The four propositions that were stated on page 469 would thus seem to find support generally in the experience summarized in the tables. These propositions would seem to have some predictive value during periods when the national party system is operating in what has been considered normal fashion and as long as relevant factors in the system itself remain unchanged. The rare exceptions to the first two propositions have occurred mainly under conditions that were quite exceptional in the history of the party system. The system itself may eventually change in ways that would invalidate the propositions; the kinds of change that would be involved may become somewhat more apparent after a further examination of the meaning of the relationships.[32]

[31] Types D and E were collapsed together in this diagram to match the split between single- and multi-ballot conventions; all candidates who reflected compromise in stalemate were selected after long balloting, and their nominations certainly occurred in conventions marked by conflict. But the conflict was settled by compromise rather than victory when these nominations were made, and it could therefore be argued almost as easily that the Type D cases should be consolidated for analysis with the ABC group in both in-party and out-party.

[32] The drafting of the four propositions was weighed with the problems of statistical significance in mind. In the last two four-cell diagrams, the

Do the Relationships Indicate Causation?

The two sets of propositions discussed involve a situation that is all too familiar, one in which the statistical evidences of relationship are relatively clear but all of the problems of causation remain obscure.[33]

Does the in-party win because of harmony? Lose because of conflict? If either answer seems obviously yes, why does harmony in the out-party indicate defeat and conflict lead (sometimes) to victory? Is conflict over the out-party nomination actually a cause of victory? Or is it merely a response, not necessarily helpful, to a situation in which victory is possible?

The in-party and the out-party occupy situations inherently so different that the sources of harmony and of conflict in the two cases are also distinctly different. Harmony over the succession in the in-party is essentially the product of organizational activity in a situation of strength. It does not arise from a lack of potentially strong candidates or from a lack of desire for the nomination on their part. But the potential competitors are deterred by the strong position of the party's leader when seeking renomination for himself or when actively in-

cross-relationships on the diagonal between the cells representing harmony in both parties vs. conflict in both are clearly the stronger. The differences on this diagonal are significant in both diagrams, highly so in one. The differences between the top cells (S/S vs. S/M, ABC/ABC vs. ABC/DE) are nearly significant in one case, definitely so in the other. The vertical relationships in the right-hand column are not significant, and no relationships involving the lower left-hand cell are significant. All references are to the four inner cells, disregarding totals along the bottom and right-hand side.

[33] The term causation is used here in the ordinary or common-sense meaning of cause and effect, and with full regard for the fact that the terminology of causation has become unfashionable in much current discussion of scientific methodology. As Herbert A. Simon points out, notions of causality continue to find common use in scientific writing, when the scientists are writing about specific research problems, as distinguished from the methodology of science. It would seem almost impossible to write the discussion that follows in any other fashion that would be intelligible; and, if any defense is necessary, it will have to be found in considerations of the kind that Simon notes; see his *Models of Man* (1957), pp. 10-12, 34-35.

volving himself in the choice of a successor. They are also deterred by the difficulties in securing political and financial backing for a bid that takes on the color of insurgency.

Out-party harmony—meaning, for this purpose, a lack of active competition for the nomination on the part of several strong contenders—is typically the product of disinterest in a situation of weakness in which victory seems impossible or unlikely. In such a case there may not be many strong candidates from whom to choose, especially if the party has been long out of power and has lost most of the gubernatorial and senatorial elections in pivotal states. Among such potentially strong candidates as the party does have available, moreover, several may prefer to wait until a more promising occasion, leaving to someone else the task of maintaining the party vote in the interval. In such a case several weak candidates are usually available, but only the strongest is likely to secure enough political and financial backing to make a showing at the convention.

Conflict situations are the converse of the types of situation just described. Conflict over the in-party nomination is typically the product of disorganization in a situation of relative weakness, one in which the incumbent leader is unwilling or unable to achieve a united choice of a successor. Usually the situation is also one in which the prospects of victory are limited, with the result that the disciplinary sanctions available to the leadership are weak. At the same time, however, victory seldom seems impossible to the strategic figures in a party in power; defeat, if it is to occur, is usually anticipated as a temporary condition during which party control will remain important for the future. Either way, the in-party nomination remains valuable and will be actively contested if the situation is open enough to permit a contest.

Conflict over the out-party nomination is associated with the expectation of victory in a situation where organizational discipline is weak and open factional contests are normal. The anticipation of presidential vic-

tory is brought on usually by a series of party successes in gubernatorial and senatorial elections. These produce their own crop of rising and potentially strong candidates for the presidential nomination. There is no central leadership strong enough to outrank the rising candidates or to prevent them from competing with each other in the forums of national attention. Glamour accumulates on behalf of those who excel in this type of competition; and they have eventually provided the winners in the classic cases of party overturn.

In-party harmony probably does have a causal relationship to party victory, even if it is also the product of a situation in which victory is likely. If a causal relationship does exist, however, it must be because conflict over the succession is more discreditable in the in-party than the out-party. Organizational discipline is more likely to be considered a necessity in the in-party, since high effectiveness in the conduct of the government is impossible without it. Conflict over the in-party nomination can rarely occur without seeming inherently to discredit the party's governmental record. In a broadly intuitive way, therefore, public attitudes seem to accept harmony as legitimate in the choice of an in-party successor; by the same token, conflict tends to become illegitimate in the in-party, although this tendency is less clearly defined.

Out-party conflict probably also has a causal relationship to party victory, but only within limits and under conditions in which it is possible to have too much of a good thing. Conflict as such does not seem discreditable in the out-party, since no structure of leadership has been created in which any single leader is acknowledged as entitled to supremacy. Conflict therefore starts from a premise of legitimacy, unlike the in-party situation; and open conflict is one of the best means of attracting public attention, displaying the qualities of the opposing candidates and eventually conferring upon one of them the aura of victory in the nominating contest.

Conflict can thus be helpful in the out-party—as long as the contestants refrain from discrediting each other and the adherents of the several contestants are prepared to accept the ultimate choice. The two conditions are associated with each other, and both are frequently absent. When they are absent, a compromise choice may provide the only means to victory.

Harmony and conflict alike probably have differential effects in which the consequences for voter attitudes should be distinguished from the consequences for party activity and leadership support. For the ordinary voter, a sharp nominating contest may serve more to awaken interest than to stir any intense degree of emotional involvement, whereas the party professionals and political leaders become highly involved. The winner in a nominating contest may thus find that the allegiance of the party voters who had favored another candidate is easier to secure than that of the party activists and leaders who had supported his opponents. Yet, without the help of those activists and leaders, the mobilization of the full party vote may be difficult, and if they have been sufficiently outraged they may even become leaders in bolting movements.

In the light of this discussion, what kinds of system change might occur that would invalidate the sets of propositions stated above? For the in-party, conflict over the succession—short of a complete party split—would be compatible with victory if the in-party were to become so dominant that the out-party could not ordinarily hope to win. In the one-party states, conflict over the nominations of the dominant party for governor has occurred often without seeming to endanger the party's continuation in office. It is a tribute to the strength of the two-party system nationally that this kind of situation has been reached so rarely and to so limited an extent at the national level. Should it come to prevail, however, conflict over the nominations of the in-party would probably be accompanied most of the time by harmony in the nominations of the out-party and would be followed by victory for

the nominations of the in-party in most such cases. The fourth proposition of the second series would thus be completed, while the second and third propositions might require some adjustment.[34]

There is more reason for wondering whether system changes can be identified that would lead to greater conflict over the in-party nominations in situations of close party balance—and if so, with what effects on the in-party's prospects for victory. The Twenty-second Amendment may be such a system change. It seems likely to encourage conflict over the in-party succession, but whether the conflict so engendered will reach levels incompatible with electoral success is not clear. In conjunction with the public opinion polls and, possibly, a spreading disposition to insist on greater popular control even in the party in power, the amendment may be bringing new forms of legitimacy to conflict over the in-party succession. Even if this should be true—and it will be many years before enough experience accumulates to know—those participating in contests over the next nomination of the party in power will be required to exercise great skill if they are to avoid discrediting each other and the party's governmental record.

In the out-party, a major question is whether system changes could occur that would achieve a reduction in conflict over the nominations while improving the party's prospects for victory, or at least not impairing them. There is food for thought in the fact that the out-party was able to win eight of the fifteen elections between 1832 and 1892 in which it had a candidate, but only five of the sixteen elections between 1896 and 1956, as shown in Table 18.6. The

---

[34] The cases most relevant to the fourth proposition, listing the in-party nominee first, were those of Buchanan vs. Frémont, 1856; Garfield vs. Hancock, 1880; and Blaine vs. Cleveland, 1884. These nominations were all made under conditions of out-party weakness; the Cleveland nomination involved the most conflict of the three out-party cases and was the only one that won. The three cases all happened within a period of thirty years, and none has occurred since 1884.

earlier period was one in which the in-party frequently rejected its own leadership or confirmed it only after conflict, and also one in which the in-party frequently found itself in conflict over its new nominations. Lessening conflict over in-party nominations has been associated with the high proportion of in-party wins since 1896. If the newly effective Twenty-second Amendment does increase the amount of conflict over in-party nominations, it may tend to reduce the proportion of in-party wins in the future; but some reduction in out-party conflict might also be a factor in improving the out-party record if it could be interpreted as a sign of strength rather than weakness.

The out-party probably does little to help its own position when many candidates enter the field whose prospects are minimal, or when several of the most able out-party leaders devote themselves to coalition efforts intended primarily to stop a front-runner by discrediting him. The out-party may also be pursuing a self-defeating policy when it requires so vigorous a contest before any titular leader can secure renomination. Many observers were convinced that the sharp conflicts in which Dewey and Stevenson were required to engage in order to secure their renominations in 1948 and 1956 were not helpful to the prospects of their respective political parties.

In the Democratic Advisory Council, the Democratic party has been experimenting with a new device for strengthening the collective leadership of the presidential wing of the party when it is out of power. Whether devices of this kind may ultimately reduce the frequency or the intensity of conflict over out-party nominations remains to be seen. They can be regarded, however, as part of a general change—brought on by the increasing pressures of party competition—in which a more circumspect attitude toward all of the more undesirable forms of conflict may be developing in both parties, whether in power or not. If this is true, it seems likely that there may be some decline in the frequency of conflict over the out-party nomination that becomes excessively bitter, coupled with some general improvement in the out-party's electoral prospects; in which case, the propositions previously stated would indeed become subject to modification.

Mechanisms of Long-Term Change

This chapter has been mainly concerned with the relationships between convention action and the outcome in the election that followed. The party nominations would also seem to merit attention, however, as a central mechanism through which the parties influence their own longer-term futures. This influence is of course the most apparent when the immediate effect of a convention decision is to split the party concerned so completely that its defeat is catastrophic. But the convention actions that produce a landslide movement of the voters from one party to the other have also had a decisive effect upon national history, and every convention nomination, with its differential effects among the states, has some influence on the long-term drift in party composition.

The reorganization of the party system in the elections of 1852, 1856, and 1860 was a direct consequence of the nominating decisions of a twenty-year period. In the view of one historian, the Whigs exhibited almost incredible folly in their rejection of President Fillmore in 1852.[35] The action was largely responsible for the breakup of the Whig party—without which the early arrival of the Republicans as a major party probably would have been impossible and the Democrats would have been much less likely to split. The Democrats in turn might have saved the situation if they had been able, without dividing, to nominate Douglas in 1852 or 1856 instead of waiting until 1860, when the issue was probably beyond repair.

[35] Wilfred E. Binkley, *American Political Parties, Their Natural History* (3d ed., 1958), pp. 179-80.

In later years, party bolting has been happily free of the threat of civil war, but it has remained as the most potentially dramatic consequence of a nominating decision. Each of the major bolting episodes since the Civil War has been relatively short lived, but each has left its mark on the parties. Eventually the party bolters are reabsorbed into one major party or the other, but not always into the one they had left. Many of the bolting Republicans of 1912 and 1924 moved into the Democratic party of 1932 and later years. In 1952, many of the bolting Dixiecrats of 1948 evidently voted for Eisenhower; in 1956 they either stayed home, voted third-party, or voted Republican. Their future remains uncertain as the most dissident element in either national party.

Landslide shifts such as those of 1896 and 1920 represent still a different kind of formation. In 1896 both parties were ready for reorganization, in terms of their own internal majorities and the issues of the day, but the majorities in either party have seldom been able to work their will in the choice of nominees as clearly as they did in that year. In 1920 the brief revival of the Democratic party that had occurred under Wilson was ended by a postwar revulsion and an immense outpouring of the voters, as the Harding nomination provided the chosen vehicle for a "return to normalcy."

The elections of 1928, 1932, and 1936 were unique as a progression of events that changed the party system. In 1928 the Democratic party was restored to competitive status by a great enlargement of its following in critical areas. In 1932, by virtue of the economic adversity that had overtaken the Republican party and the country, the Democratic portion of the electorate was enlarged by another 50 per cent. In 1936 these gains were consolidated by another 20 per cent increase—the response of the electorate to the first term of the Roosevelt administration. The Smith nomination was critical to the outcome in the first election in the series of three, while the Roosevelt performance in office was critical to the outcome in the third. Their impact in three successive elections rebuilt the Democratic party.

In the longer perspectives of a century or more, these three elections can be seen as the basic shift that brought the American party system into accord with the requirements of a modern economic order. National economic issues that cut across all sections of the population were recognized as controlling in a time of general economic adversity. The Democratic party became truly national in its orientation, as it had not been for most of a century. The Republican party was placed on notice that it would probably have to become truly national in order to become again effectively competitive.

In successive pairs of candidates, the parties have continued to offer the voters a meaningful choice: Roosevelt and Willkie; Roosevelt and Dewey; Truman and Dewey; Stevenson and Eisenhower. The clarity of the choice has varied from election to election, but at no time has it returned to the ambiguity of a decision between Calvin Coolidge and John W. Davis. Meanwhile, other aspects of party realignment have had time to come into operation, so that reinforcing steps have been taken that tend to solidify the whole result.

In each of the large industrial states except Texas, the realignment in the national party electorates has been accompanied by a party realignment along parallel lines within the electorate of the state. Even in Texas there has been a clarification of factional lines within the dominant party that has had many of the same effects. Similar developments have occurred in most of the other northern and western industrial states, even those that are relatively small in population. Changing party patterns have also occurred in all of the southern states that are being subjected to industrialization and the movement into metropolitan areas. During a few recent years the process has been obscured in the South by the sharp effects of the desegregation decisions of the Supreme Court; but this too is beginning to pass into history.

Within the state party systems of each of the major states, party realignment has heavily involved the state party leaderships in unavoidable internal conflict. These involvements become visible mainly in connection with the participation of the state in the politics of presidential nominations and elections, when the state party is compelled most clearly to participate in national party action and to respond to political forces generated elsewhere. But the process has gone on to involve the selection of the candidates for governor and members of both houses of Congress. There has been a time lag in the response of the party systems in these cases, while older party leaderships lived out their time; nevertheless, enough time has elapsed to produce a considerable change in all of these cases.

The results are apparent in the composition of the delegations at the national party conventions. The conventions of both parties are made up predominantly of delegates and delegations whose orientations are to the great American middle class and to the central concerns of the whole national electorate. But in each case the delegates are aware that they represent a political party that has its own distinctive identity—one that must be preserved, renewed, and further developed, if it is to be politically successful. Their search is for the candidate, in each case, who can best express that identity while mounting the broadest possible appeal to the voters who will come out only if they like the candidate.

This is a formula that has much to recommend it. In terms of the practicalities of the moment, the preservation, renewal, and further development of the identity of the Democratic party may involve some shrinkage in its total party following, particularly in the South, if it is to become sufficiently homogeneous to be able to live with itself. The Republican party's problem is equally, or even more, difficult. Somehow it must recover from the divided personality of the days when it was a dominant party, and learn to live with a situation in which it must be sufficiently united to be competitive. This in turn seems to involve the problem of how to become a modern political party that is both conservative and vital—a problem not necessarily beyond solution.

19

The Nominating Process
and the Future of the Party System

THE NOMINATING contests at the conventions and the elections that follow provide regular opportunities for decisive change in the ordering of political affairs. Frequently it has been observed that the decisions at the conventions may be more critical than those left to the general election. If a systematic general theory of political change in the United States is ever constructed, it will undoubtedly give a central place to the presidential nominating process.

The conventions are important, moreover, not only for their immediate consequences. The collateral decisions that are necessary to operate the nominating machinery tend to set the structure of the party system as a whole. They help to form and reform the broad lines of the coalitions of which each party is composed. They shape the future evolution of the party institutions. They affect the extent to which the party can bring cohesion and clear purpose to the work of government—or the extent to which it will retreat from this task, leaving a governmental vacuum to be filled by other mechanisms of some more obscure and less definable sort.

For each of their decisions the party conventions have an inescapable responsibility. They were created to cope with the specific problems of nominations and to give more recognition to party leaders outside of Congress. But once available, they have unavoidably met other problems and had other effects. For the future, questions concerning what can and should be done about either the nominating process or the party system become largely questions concerning what can be done by the parties when in convention assembled.

The Central Position of the Nominating Process

The nominating process occupies a central position in the party system by virtue of both its manifest function and its latent functions. The manifest function is to identify in each party the candidate for President who is entitled to the party designation—with all this entails in the conferring of legitimacy, securing a place on the ballot, and assuring the loyalty and the votes of the party faithful. The most important latent function—one that is seemingly in process of becoming manifest—is the designation of a candidate who will also be recognized as the chief party leader.

The ambiguity of this second function is inherent in the dependence of the leadership on victory in the election. A century ago, in either major party, the nominating act was merely the designation of a candidate for the ensuing campaign, to be discarded if he lost and to be disregarded as much as possible in party matters even if he won. The one-term doctrine for the Presidency that flourished in both parties for several decades was an aspect of these attitudes.

In the decades that have since elapsed, it has become settled custom that if the party candidate becomes President he is indeed entitled to recognition as the chief leader of his party for all purposes—in the government, in the party organization, and in the electorate. But in the party that loses, the defeated candidate has no secure entitlements. He is now generally known as the titular leader of his party, but the extent to which this designation has meaning remains obscure.

Whatever the eventual fate of the candidate, a nomination for President is still a sufficient glory in either major party to exercise a profound effect upon all political arrangements. The nomination is the last hurdle but one on the course that leads to the highest position open to an American citizen. The nominating process occupies a central position, like all processes controlling advancement, because it exerts a substantial influence on the behavior of actors throughout the system, an influence much greater than they are able to exercise on it. The relationship is not exclusively one-way, but it is primarily so.

The nominating process exerts both a gravitational pull and a screening effect. Both are felt from the earliest phases onward in the development of candidates. The pull becomes apparent in the potential candidates' actions to acquire suitable types of experience, to develop their abilities selectively, and to take on the attributes of availability. The screening effect is apparent in the early stages in the rejection of individuals with unwanted characteristics, and in the way the standards of choice become progressively more stringent at higher levels of candidate advancement.

The screening effect is much more obvious in its presence and its consequences than the gravitational pull: as an election nears, the number of those who can be seriously regarded as available is reduced from possibly a few hundred in the entire adult population to a number that is usually smaller than a dozen in either political party. The gravitational pull nevertheless has a pervasive effect, not only in developing the supply of candidates but in many other ways. It must necessarily also affect the behavior of all persons connected with the potential candidates and with the channels through which they might advance. This is most obvious for their immediate associates, but party managers, interest-group leaders, and other would-be king-makers are also among those clearly affected.

Consequences also arise for the structural relationships between large segments of the political system: most specifically for the relationships between party groups in the legislature and the executive, for the role of the governors, and for the status of major power centers external to the government of the day. Whatever the angle of view, the nominating process is a vital factor in the channels of leadership advancement that give political structure to the social system.

Relationships to Candidate Competence

The most basic questions concerning the nominating process are those that examine its manifest function in the choice of candidates. Is the process capable of selecting the most able candidates available in the two parties for a final choice by the electorate? Or, if not the most able, candidates who would be fully competent, if elected, to meet the responsibilities of the office?

This is a question that comes close to the issues of national and world survival. It is no more capable of a conclusive answer than most such questions. But it does suggest the importance of elements that move the process toward the selection of competent candidates or alternatively push it away from that desirable goal.

One such group of elements consists of the short-run and long-run considerations that compete for recognition. The difference is posed most vividly by the contrast between ability to win the election as the sole basis for candidate selection and on the other hand ability to lead and operate the government. Obviously some thought has always been given to both sets of considerations and to others as well; but there have been times in American history when the contrast has been starkly put. The Whig party seems to have committed suicide by its penchant for selecting vice-presidential candidates solely to balance the ticket and without regard to whether they could provide party or governmental leadership if called upon to do so.

When James Bryce was writing his classic work, *The American Commonwealth,* he repeatedly emphasized the extent to which the party managers of the day, in their advancement of candidates, were concerned with capacities for winning rather than for governing. But when Theodore Roosevelt selected William Howard Taft instead of Elihu Root as his successor, he is said to have given the problem balanced consideration. He thought Root would make the better President, but could not be elected. In any event, he had no doubt at the time that Taft, who could be elected, would make a competent and highly desirable President.

A system that would chronically reject governmental ability in its selection of top leaders while emphasizing skills limited to the pursuit of electoral majorities would seem to be one headed for disaster. Conversely, a system that seeks a balanced pattern of electoral and governmental success in its choice of top leaders would seem to have achieved a degree of maturity compatible with survival.

If the balance of short-run and long-run considerations has changed for the better, three factors may perhaps be given most of the credit. One is the increasing influence throughout the nominating process of responsible elective officials of high rank, as distinguished from party bosses who could hold power without becoming directly accountable for the conduct of the government. Presidents concerned with the choice of a successor, governors who deal with the manifold responsibilities of a state, senators who have repeatedly faced a statewide elec-

torate—all can be expected to bring different attitudes to the nominating process from those attributed to the party bosses of yore. The bosses have become less conspicuous while the elective officials have moved in strongly.

A second factor, if it really exists, may represent a maturing of the American culture. There appears to be a growing disposition on the part of the electorate to judge the candidates by the qualities that will be required after they enter office, rather than merely by those that are conducive to proficiency in campaigning. This tendency is probably furthered by the active participation of elective officials in the nominating process. It may also be furthered by a greater tendency for public-spirited citizens to join actively in the party process through the club movements and the regular party organizations of a number of states. Both types of individuals can bring to bear a sophisticated knowledge of what is required in a candidate and an ability to be publicly critical when they find it lacking. Under modern conditions of large-scale government, there is a special need to judge the candidates in terms of their ability to recruit able associates, their capacity for political leadership, and their emotional stability under the pressures of office. The presumed divergence between the ability to win and the ability to govern would cease to exist if the electorate could reach the point of being adept at estimating capacity for success in office as a basis for electoral choice.

A third factor, also speculative but one for which it is somewhat easier to find evidence, is an apparent tendency for elective office to become more attractive and more accessible to the members of each oncoming generation who are marked for success and have the widest field of choice in deciding on their careers. This has been illustrated by the number of able younger candidates for the elective offices of intermediate rank who have come over the horizon in recent years. A public-service type of motivation may be spreading. If it is, it would be one of the most hopeful signs for the future.

Relationships to Popular Control

Characteristics of the nominating process have also a most vital relationship to a central question of American political life—the extent to which the political system can be or should be subjected to popular control.

The convention system was established in part as a revolt against the undemocratic aspects of nominations by the congressional caucuses. From the first, the conventions were more representative of the party electorates than the caucuses. If the convention nominations were defective for a considerable period, it was not from any lack of desire to put up candidates who would be broadly representative; rather, there was frequently an excess of catering to a presumed popular demand for candidates who had no commitments and no enemies, who were available precisely because they had done nothing to help solve the problems of the day. But popular control was indirect, to say the least. To the extent that it existed, it was based on opinion largely unformed by any adequate confrontation of the candidates before their nomination—the aspect of the situation that has changed most within the last fifty years.

Clearly there has been a great increase in popular participation. The increase has been brought about by the spreading influence of the mass media, the presidential primaries in certain states, the use of public opinion polls to measure the standing of the candidates for the nominations, and the changing responses of the candidates themselves to these and other factors. The candidates have developed new attitudes on the extent to which it is appropriate and essential to appeal to the popular will, along with new attitudes on the kind and amount of campaigning that is legitimate in doing so.

Much of the struggle that used to occur in the conventions has been shifted to the preconvention period. With the more open and more frequent commitment of delegates to the leading candidates and with the Associated Press and other news services counting the vote in advance, most of the losers in recent times probably know that they are beaten before the convention opens. Generally they are too deeply committed to withdraw in advance of the formal voting, but their power to bargain before admitting defeat has been greatly reduced by the fact that so much is known about delegate commitments and intentions.

Popular control thus seems almost complete within either political party when opinion is clearly developed in support of a majority choice. The popular mandate is in doubt when several strong candidates for the nomination remain in the running until the end. In such a situation it would be hard to deny the prerogative of the convention without destroying it—without turning over the choice to a national primary election, to be settled either by a mere plurality of the party or else through some form of runoff or transferable vote. Either course would present many hazards that seem unnecessary and that would be difficult to assess in advance.

Despite the frequent lack of a clear popular mandate, in practice there has been a considerable long-term shift away from situations of stalemate in which a compromise candidate can or must be selected. Instead, contests have been brought to resolution in recent years through a clearly defined victory in voting at the conventions. The development and reporting of widespread public sentiment within the party concerned had much to do with these results.

The values associated with popular control of the political system are deeply imbedded in the democratic ethic, but other values have also been coming to the fore during the last half century. By itself, popular control provides no complete answer to the problems of the national consensus and of an adequate leadership in developing it. Yet those problems have become increasingly pressing. The dangers of the times impose heavy requirements for the kind of consensus that is not only broadly based, but also adapted to the objective requirements of national and world survival.

Political leaders are clearly needed who will do more than follow their followers, who will assume the burdens of political education, who will grasp the nettle firmly when moral leadership is the country's greatest need. Men of these capacities are prone to recognize their own limitations and to hesitate before volunteering for the rough-and-tumble of political life. They are unlikely to enter the race for high elective office in any considerable numbers unless they have already been brought into political office at lower levels. When they do not volunteer, they may have to be drafted; and if the system fails to bring such men into positions where they can be recognized, the system itself may need to be changed.

Relationships to Clarification of Party Roles

Candidate choice involves a search for many abilities, but in choosing a candidate a political party is doing much more than selecting a man. It is also deciding its future, insofar as that future can be influenced or controlled by the collective decisions of the presidential wing of the party.[1]

The future of a political party depends mainly on its continuing success in developing the position it proposes to occupy in relationship to the needs of the times. This is a far more complicated problem than the writing of formal platform statements. Essentially it involves the clarification and adaptation of the party role.

By comparison with other types of organizations, political parties are relatively plastic, owing to their open membership, the limited authority of their formal officeholders, and a tradition of freedom of action for many centers of initiative. The capacity of the parties to adapt themselves to new requirements, however, is by no means unlimited. Each party is limited at any one time by its inherited character—the groups of which it is composed, the memories they preserve, and the specific characteristics that remain from past adaptive efforts, successful and unsuccessful.

External events and pressures beat against the complex of inherited character, and it is the task of party leadership to find a road to success through the prejudices of the past, the expediencies of the moment, and the demands of the future. For any organization, this is a task beset by many perils during the interval between the decline of a former top leadership and the coming to full authority of a new top leadership. It is a special characteristic of American political parties that considerable portions of their total life history are devoted to passing through such intervals.

During the interregnums that are so characteristic of an American party when it is out of power, and that occasionally occur even in a party supposedly in power, many voices speak on the problems of the future party role. They speak with unequal authority, and no one voice is likely to be decisive. The process goes on until there is at least some vague crystallization of alternative concepts of the future party role, and an alignment of candidates for the nomination who seem to be associated with one concept or another.

The roster of available candidates thus takes form as a spectrum of alteratives for the future of the party. Some observers will discuss that spectrum mainly in terms of victory or defeat in the ensuing election. Inevitably, the participants most involved will also examine closely its potential consequences for the position of every affiliated group interest now within the party or that might be attracted to it. The prospects for

---

[1] The concepts of top leadership and its functions that were propounded by Philip Selznick in *Leadership in Administration* (1957) were especially helpful in the development of the following paragraphs.

victory or defeat can be weighed—collectively, publicly, and with a degree of rationality. The prospective effects on group affiliations are also weighed—separately, privately, and with a heavy loading of emotional feeling. The submerged position of these effects among the party motivations does not lessen their importance. It probably increases it.

The act of choosing a candidate generally produces a considerable immediate clarification of the party's future role. By virtue of the alternatives that have been considered, the candidate stands before the public for the time being as the most concrete expression of the direction in which the party is moving. As he campaigns, in his effort to muster the faithful and recruit the undecided, the candidate continues to clarify the party position, mainly by expounding the party conception of the national position. In either party, this is his most important function in the period between convention and election.

After the election the defeated candidate is committed, at best, to a holding operation in which he seeks to maintain the party role as he has defined it, to the extent that that role can be exercised in the party of the opposition. The national committee chairman who was chosen or approved by the candidate continues in office as a national party spokesman, and the defeated candidate usually retains a degree of control over the party machinery as titular leader and as a party spokesman in his own right. Other party leaders resume their accustomed activities, and the party awaits another opportunity for decisive action.

To the candidate who wins comes the great opportunity to consolidate the concept of the party role that he represents. This is the reward for which the choice was made at the convention. It is only in the event of victory that the wisdom of the party choice can be fully tested. As President of the United States, the winning candidate will have an unmatched opportunity to organize and direct his party as a basis for governmental power. When this operation is performed with skill, the party learns how to make its greatest contribution to the national consensus. It also revitalizes itself for the long-term future.

This whole cycle has been traced through at some length in order to underline not merely the importance of the choice at the convention, but some of its essential characteristics. The aspirants for a nomination differ not only in the alternative concepts of party role that they represent, but in their capacity to bring any concept to success. The greatest hazard in going outside the normal channels of recruitment to find a candidate lies here. No doubt there are times when only the inspired amateur will do; but it would be strange indeed if competence for the highest public and party leadership could ordinarily be developed without the extensive training that only a previous political career can provide.

Problems of Preparation and the Channels of Advancement

The importance of the channels of advancement in any political system would seem to be obvious. Yet in most political systems those channels evolve with little overt concern for the types of personality that they select, the character of the preparation that they provide, and the effect they produce on the political order.

Certainly no part of the American political system has been more unplanned than those portions that control career advancement in the direction of the Presidency. Most proposals to reform the presidential nominating process have started by assuming that there will always be an ample supply of well-qualified candidates, and that the only issues of public policy are those relating to the final machinery of choice. Even the machinery is often discussed without regard to its potential effects upon the kind of candidates who will be in available supply.

The problem of supply starts with the question of who is willing to enter politics and why. Despite the possibility that the gifted amateur may be called into politics at some higher level as a candidate for senator, governor, or President, the question of recruitment mainly arises at the lower levels of political office. Most of the candidates for high elective office have previously held office at some lower level and have several times been through the testing experiences of a political campaign. But at the lower levels the problems presented in most states by the existing systems of primary elections become acute.

The Problems of the Primaries

The problems of primary elections were summarized as follows in 1951 by a committee of the most respected civic reform organization in the country:

The present direct primary systems have often produced disorderly scrambles for office by self-seekers and have not, as a rule, resulted in the nomination of qualified and civic-minded citizens who should be attracted to public life. They have not provided voters with effective choices between suitable candidates, which is essential if the democratic process is to have its true meaning. Unless good candidates are nominated, good candidates cannot be elected to public office. Reform of the primary system is needed to bring about healthy, vigorous party life, to provide more effective party leadership, to attract abler candidates to run for public office and to enable the rank and file of voters to hold the party leadership to an effective responsibility.[2]

The principal reform advocated by the committee was the rejection of the frequently held belief that party organizations should not interfere in the selection of candidates. Rather, the committee urged, the organizations have a positive duty to seek out and recruit suitable candidates; and they should be helped in this task by giving their candidates a preferred place on the

[2] National Municipal League, Committee on Direct Primary, Joseph P. Harris, Chairman, *A Model Direct Primary Election System* (1951), p. 7.

primary ballot. Popular control would be maintained, along with opportunities for insurgency, by continuing to allow relatively easy access to the primary ballot for other candidates who are in fact genuine members of the party whose nomination they seek.

The influence of the primaries runs through the whole American political system. The presidential primaries have been deeply influenced by the precedents of primaries developed for other purposes. The idea that there should be no provision for a draft and that candidates should be chosen only from among those who are openly seeking the nomination is a product of the thinking fostered by the primaries. So many of the most active members of both political parties have made their way up through a regime of wide-open primaries and the resultant party irresponsibility, that it would be strange if they came naturally to other habits of thought.

Fortunately, despite many legal obstacles, the party organizations have been taking more responsibility for their candidates in recent years. There is a growing recognition that the minority party must see to it that every important elective office is contested if it is to maintain itself as a functioning unit in a two-party system. Where there is active competition between the parties, many ways have been found, both formal and informal, to consolidate party strength behind strong candidates in the primaries in the interests of a stronger general election campaign.

In several states new forms of local party clubs, joined together in state assemblies, have injected new life into the parties. Based on an explicit, dues-paying membership, the club organizations have provided channels through which widely scattered bands of activists with a concern for public policy can play a continuous role in the affairs of the party. These groups can encourage able young people to run for offices on the lower rungs of the political ladder, and help them climb to higher levels of political leadership as rapidly as they are ready. With a strong membership base, moreover, such groups can also contribute to popular control by their influence on the party's leadership.

The issues of the primaries and of their relationships to the party organizations are far from generally resolved, but the once-strong tendencies to curtail party responsibility for candidate selection seem to be undergoing reversal.

The Training of
Senators and Governors

The candidates for the party nominations for President and Vice President are drawn typically from among those who have been holding office as senators or governors during the previous ten years. The talent available at any one time reflects mainly the political practices and the career inflow of the previous thirty years. The earlier stages in the careers of those men are important for the preparatory experience that they have provided. Several issues are worth noting, beginning with that hardy perennial, the relative availability of governors and senators.

The total historical experience indicates a considerable preference for governors in the choice of presidential candidates. As of 1959, the Democratic party had not nominated an incumbent senator since Stephen A. Douglas in 1860; the Republican party had nominated only one incumbent senator in its entire history, Warren Gamaliel Harding in 1920. But senators have been chosen for the vice-presidential nominations with growing frequency in recent decades. Moreover, senators have recently seemed to show greater strength in the pursuit of presidential nominations. They have received an increasing share of mass media attention, and have ranked high in the public opinion polls in advance of the conventions.

If senators and governors are to continue highly available, as seems likely, the more important problem is not how to decide which should be most available, but rather how to improve the potentialities of each. Each office has its own characteristic limitations as a preparation for the Presidency.

Senators suffer from the lack of executive experience, from specialization in legislative work, from a habit of mind in which time is rarely of the essence, and from an over-identification with the rights of the legislative branch of the government. Substantive specialization in the work of particular committees, the legislative habit of mind, and a tendency to over-identify with the legislative branch are all products of long years of habituation in Congress—both houses of which believe in the advantages of specialization for their members and in the vigilant maintenance of their own constitutional prerogatives. But these limitations do not affect all senators equally. Many of them have had extensive executive experience before entering the Senate. Those who are chosen for posts of party leadership in the Senate are also given a type of such experience.

The collective effect of these various factors seems to be that members of the Senate who seek presidential nominations must win the prize during their early years in the Senate or not at all. The spreading influence of a competitive, two-party state politics, with an increasing number of states with one senator of each party, has increased the importance of party lines within the Senate and, to some extent, seems to have expedited Senate careers. It has produced enough competitive pressure on committee assignments to bring reforms in the assignments available to junior senators. It has permitted the election of relatively young senators to the leadership posts, where they have had special advantages in the development of availability and, equally important, in acquiring a highly relevant kind of preparatory experience for possible service in the Presidency.

The senators who have ranked high on the scale of availability in recent years have been relatively junior men, generally in their first or second terms. They have displayed many of the personality characteristics that are so attractive in the glamorous and rising young governors of the hard-fought, competitive, two-party states. If the Senate goes on developing its opportunities for its most able younger men, it will continue to hold a strong position in the development of candidates for President and Vice President.

The governors suffer from limitations that are characteristically the opposite of those affecting senators. They suffer most of all from a lack of association with the issues of national policy, especially issues in the areas of defense and foreign relations. In the press of executive duties, moreover, they have little time available for deliberation and study, particularly for issues other than those that are currently acute in their own states. They are restricted by the tradition that a governor should stay close to the job in his own state, and by their own loyalties to the job. They have only limited access to the forums of national debate and to the centers of national and international news attention. In many states, they are hampered by peculiarities of their term of office.

As in the case of the senators and their limitations, not all governors are affected alike by the factors just listed. Governors of New York have been conspicuously available for the presidential nomination partly because their state has given them the means of overcoming most of these limitations. New York has a form of state government in which the governor is master in his own house, can organize his executive duties effectively, and can control his own schedule sufficiently to find time for policy issues and for extended absences from the state when necessary. His term of office, four years staggered against the presidential term without limitation on number of terms, is ideally adapted to the requirements of campaigning for the Presidency—the somewhat ironical result of a state con-stitutional reform that was ostensibly adopted to promote a greater separation of state and national politics. New York has its own built-in potentialities for access to the mass media, and the state is of sufficient size and complexity to justify the governor in taking an active interest in practically every national issue. It offers unrivaled preparation for the Presidency, and unrivaled opportunities for the development of availability.

Other states will continue to find it difficult to match the opportunities of New York, but the other large states could do more than they have done. Pennsylvania could safely remove its four-year limitation on the tenure of governors, since there is now an effective two-party competition in the state. Ohio recently changed to a four-year term, instead of the two-year term of office by which its governors were formerly harassed; Michigan and Texas could do the same. Illinois could revise its existing four-year term to stagger it against the presidential term, thereby removing future governors from the difficult situation in which Governor Stevenson found himself in the winter and spring of 1952. California, which is much like New York in its formal arrangements, may need to make a variety of informal adjustments if its governors are to take a more important role in national partisan leadership. In particular, there may be need for a more tolerant attitude toward the governor's absences from the state, and a greater willingness to encourage his active participation in the development of not only national but also international policy.

The seven largest states all have their unique opportunities, but the same could be said of another dozen states that are sufficiently large and complex to develop the abilities of any executive. Individually and collectively, the governors of these states could do much to improve the forums of national attention to which they already have access, and to develop others. They have more to gain than anyone else from an improved organization of the national party conventions, and from the reform of the voting structure of the convention committees and the national committee.

Their own annual governors' conference is deserving of more attention and further development. The party caucuses that inevitably occur at the conferences could be recognized more openly as legitimate additions to the institutional apparatus of the national parties. For example, the party national committees might be invited to provide appropriate staffing to assist the caucuses of each party. Perhaps, if the realities of the two-party system are to be fully recognized in the governors' conference, the time has even come to abandon the amiable pretense that the sessions when all governors of both parties are present are "nonpolitical."

The Democratic governors have a special interest in the Advisory Council that was formed after the 1956 elections (see Chapter 5), in which a number of governors are among the most active participants. The Council exists primarily as the collective spokesman for the presidential wing of the party when it is out of power in the White House.[3] It takes on some of the characteristics of a combined shadow Cabinet and shadow White House staff. As a center of leadership in the formation of party and national opinion, it cannot easily compete with the Presidency, but it does seem to be

more effective than any previously developed mechanism in filling the vacuum that otherwise is so likely to exist in the out-party.

The Advisory Council in its first years was effective in considerable part because of the forum it provided for the only living ex-President of the party and for its titular leader. But its members also included several of the leading contenders for the nominations of the future. It could be further developed as a forum in which the party's leading governors could participate. It can provide a bridge between the party's executive leadership when last in the White House and the executive leadership that it may find when it next gains office.

The Republican party, when out of power, has experimented with a number of policy conferences and other devices that are sometimes referred to as similar to the present Democratic Advisory Council. They had an essential difference, however, in that they were not adequately representative of the previous or future leadership in the presidential wing of the Republican party. They performed few of the functions of a shadow White House and contributed little to continuity in the executive leadership of the party. If some more effective instrument is to be formed when the Republican party is next out of power, leadership from the party's titular leader and national committee chairman, together with the support and active participation of its incumbent governors in competitive states, will undoubtedly be needed.[4]

[3] The reference to "the presidential wing of the party," here as elsewhere in the chapter, means simply those elements of either party, whether in power or not, that have their roots in the coalition that currently holds the White House, or last held it, and that are primarily preoccupied with winning it the next time, as distinguished from the congressional establishment of each party and the associated elements that are preoccupied with congressional politics.

There is of course obvious overlap between the presidential and congressional wings of each party, but each has a distinct leadership and a somewhat different constituency. In each party the presidential wing has several million voting constituents at any one time who are not represented in Congress by members of their own party, many of whom have little hope of securing such representation but all of whom can hope for victory in the next presidential election.

[4] Although in power, the Republican party has recently been considering problems akin to those of a party out of power as the result of its defeats in the mid-term elections of 1958 and President Eisenhower's inability, under the Twenty-second Amendment, to succeed himself. In January 1959 an extensive plan for party reforms was reportedly prepared. It contemplated more systematic efforts "to provide sustaining funds on a regular monthly basis," a much larger field force on the national party payroll, an advisory committee to meet frequently with the national chairman, emphasis on the recruitment of better candidates for Congress, and a variety of efforts to remake the party image and bury factionalism. See Albert Clark and Lester

Other Sources of Nominees

The Vice Presidency, the Cabinet, and, in the out-party, the titular leadership are other sources of aspirants for presidential office. The Vice Presidency has evolved in recent years into a useful collection of preparatory duties and roles. It seems likely to go on developing favorably if the parties continue to nominate vice-presidential candidates who are reasonably compatible with their ticket leader and who have similar qualities of availability.

The Cabinet could be a natural source of well-prepared candidates for the presidential nominations of the party in power. It supplied William Howard Taft in 1908 and Herbert Hoover in 1928.[5] In recent decades, there has been a tendency to emphasize the administrative duties of Cabinet members, but the President clearly needs political lieutenants as well as administrative subordinates. This need might be met more fully, with other desirable consequences, if there should be a greater disposition to appoint former governors to Cabinet office. Meanwhile, the functions of Cabinet members as political leaders need further development for many reasons. To the extent that this occurs, the Cabinet may again become more available as a potential source of presidential timber.

The out-party titular leadership also has further possibilities as a road to the White House, but involves many special problems that can be left for discussion later in this chapter.

* * * * * *

Toward the end of the last century James Bryce summed up his view of the channels of advancement to the American Presidency in an essay that has often been quoted.[6] Since then the system has become much more successful in producing Bryce's ideal type: statemen who are "men of education, of administrative experience, of a certain largeness of view and dignity of character." The system tends to find these men through procedures that are compatible with a federal government and a pluralistic society. The system is still uniquely American in its characteristic refusal to look mainly to those who have had preparatory training in the national government in the highest administrative posts short of the Presidency. Rather, it has looked mainly to those who have held the office that is the counterpart of the Presidency in the most important states of the federal union, without closing the door to any other source of talent.

There is much about this system that is altogether desirable. In any event, the essential characteristics that have just been noticed are not likely to change soon. They provide a broad field for choice, and it is for this very reason that it would be well to improve the quality of preparatory opportunities across a broad front. Fortunately, most of the changes that are needed for this reason would also be generally beneficial and could be advocated for many other reasons as well.

Problems of Popular Control

For more than a century the values associated with popular control have been among the main factors of change in the

Tanzer, "GOP Strategy: Secret Memo Blueprints Plan to Rebuild Party, Win Election in 1960," *Wall Street Journal*, Jan. 14, 1959. These proposals apparently were received favorably at the following meeting of the party's national committee at Des Moines. See *Washington Post and Times Herald*, Jan. 24, 1959.

A Republican Committee on Program and Progress, under the chairmanship of Charles H. Percy, was appointed. The committee prepared a series of Task Force Reports and a brief general statement. These were released in October 1959; the committee was then disbanded.

[5] As noted in Chapter 7, Arthur Holcombe has emphasized the tendency of a party in power to pick its candidates from among those closely associated with the administration, unless for one reason or another the administration had become discredited. See Holcombe, *Our More Perfect Union* (1950), pp. 82-87.

[6] *The American Commonwealth* (3d ed., 1895), Vol. 1, Chap. 8: "Why Great Men Are Not Chosen Presidents."

American political system. They have deeply affected the presidential nominating process, but in this area popular control has developed slowly and incompletely. Constitutional restrictions on federal authority have been a limiting factor; so also have been the problems that direct popular control creates.

Many of the most acute students of American political institutions have been reluctant to see any further extension of popular intervention in the nominating process, because so many of the existing measures for that purpose seem gravely defective. If the influence of these measures were to be extended, their more serious deficiencies would need to be cured and other goals would need to be kept in balance. Popular control is a useful virtue in a political system, but so also are such other factors as stability, competence, foresight, and a gifted leadership.

*Proposals for a
National Presidential Primary*

Proposals for a national presidential primary have been before Congress almost continuously for about half a century. The form of these proposals has varied, but most of them have had as their objective a national primary election, held throughout the country on the same day, at which the presidential candidates of the two major parties would be selected through the action of the voters attached to the respective parties. According to the Gallup Poll, this kind of proposal has had majority support among the voters for a long time; at times it has also had substantial support in Congress.

Such a system would necessitate an amendment of the federal Constitution, and some form of the proposal has often been introduced in Congress as part of a larger proposal that would also include reform of the electoral college. In these cases the electoral college provisions have generally received most of the attention and

discussion, despite the fact that the nominating provisions involve issues of equal or greater difficulty.

The basic vice of all the proposals for a national primary, in the opinion of the present authors, is their general failure to recognize the essential characteristics of the nominating process. The nomination differs in many important respects from a general-election choice between major-party nominees. As was said at the beginning of this book, the most critical aspects of the nominating process arise from the fact that the alternatives of choice must be discovered as a part of the process. The choices must somehow be reduced to a manageable number; and in open nominating situations, even after a considerable amount of clarification has occurred, the number of genuine availables is seldom as few as two. Usually there are several actual and potential candidates of varying and often noncommensurable statuses remaining for final consideration, with an extremely complex structure of second- and third-choice preferences in the minds of those most vitally concerned.[7]

This means that if a choice among all of

[7] For about two centuries elections theorists with mathematical training have discussed the problem of what candidate could be adjudged best if information were available on the entire scale of preferences as held by each person entitled to vote. The problem is not necessarily determinate even in mathematical terms and with full information. One recent author believes that, in general, that candidate should be selected who could defeat each of his opponents when paired against only one opponent at a time, but points out that there may be no such candidate, which would in turn mean that there was no single genuine majority choice. With repeated voting, as in the conventions, there is opportunity for those voting to reconsider their respective scales of preferences in the light of the information provided by the voting; and it is because of this fact that a majority choice eventually becomes possible under the convention system. See Duncan Black, *The Theory of Committees and Elections* (1958), especially Chaps. 9 and 10, and A. D. Roy's review of the book in *The Economic Journal*, Vol. 69 (June 1959), pp. 367-69. For a discussion of an attempt to adjust polling to the type of situation in which convention delegates are placed, see Chapter 13, subsection on Voter Polls and Final Decision, and especially footnote 24.

the noteworthy alternatives were somehow to be submitted to a primary election in which all party voters might take part, the winner in a first election, more likely than not, would still be only a minority choice—unless a pre-primary convention had been held to narrow the field by convincing some of the candidates that their prospects were hopeless, while rallying party support for the candidate or candidates most favored by the convention.[8] But any combination of convention and primary would be cumbersome. If the convention were continued as an essential step, the primary would tend to become a costly and distracting addition to a process already sufficiently long and elaborate. Moreover, the increasingly important campaign-rally aspect of the national convention, while continuing in full force in the party with an uncontested candidate, would be rendered impossible in the party with an open nomination still to be decided by the primary. It is hard to imagine professional political leaders submitting to such a suicidal condition as the penalty for a contested nomination.

At the national level and with all of the complexities of federal politics, if a primary were to be held without benefit of prior convention action, some form of runoff election or transferable vote would be a minimum safeguard. Even in state elections, where the situation is much more likely to restrict the number of potential candidates, a one-shot primary for the selection of candidates for governor is hazardous.

Whatever might be done, however, any national primary would remain subject to the danger that the most attractive candidate or candidates would not be on the ballot, and to the further danger that there would not be a sufficient turnout of the voters to insure representation of actual party sentiment, even about the candidates who might happen to be on the ballot. These are risks that would be inherent in almost any conceivable form of primary, though they are usually glossed over when a primary is being advocated. They are hazards to which the conventions are much less subject because of their wide discretionary authority to deal with the actual situation as they find it.

It thus seems unlikely that any form of national primary could be trusted to do as good a job as the conventions in finding and installing the popular choice of each party. In addition, there are many other weighty reasons for opposing a national primary. In an active contest the campaign fund requirements would be prodigious, and would automatically restrict the choice of candidates to those who could find the necessary financial backing. Every serious candidate would be required to develop a strong national organization to fight his campaign from one end of the country to the other. This in turn would sharpen the lines of factional division within each party; organized factions and their candidates would be likely to continue in action from one election to another, especially in the party out of power. The disruptive effect would be serious in either party when facing an open nominating situation, would weaken its position in the general election, and would leave it in a poor position for the tasks of government if it should happen to win.[9]

Other Proposals for Federal Action

A new type of proposal to stimulate state action has been pending in recent years. First introduced in 1952, the proposed "Presidential Primaries Act" would au-

[8] The possibilities for combining convention and primary action are explored in Paul T. David, Malcolm Moos, and Ralph M. Goldman, *Presidential Nominating Politics in 1952* (1954), Vol. 1, pp. 211-13.

[9] For a fuller discussion of the arguments pro and con a national primary, see David, Moos, and Goldman, *op. cit.*, Vol. 1, Chap. 6. For testimony in opposition to the several constitutional amendment proposals to create a national primary, as pending in 1955, see statement of Paul T. David in Hearings . . . Committee on the Judiciary, U.S. Senate (1955), *Nomination and Election of President and Vice President*, pp. 207-17.

thorize federal payments to states holding presidential primaries conforming to the terms of the act. The act would also provide for a federal Presidential Primaries Commission of five members, to compile a uniform ballot for each party in all the conforming states, containing only the names of candidates qualified by petitions from 1,000 or more persons in each of three quarters of those states. Proposed candidates could decline the use of their names. The delegates elected in the primaries would be pledged to the candidates winning pluralities in their respective constituencies.

If legislation of this kind were to be enacted and accepted by most of the states, many of the most undesirable consequences of a national presidential primary would ensue. No one could become an active candidate without substantial campaign funds and a nationwide campaign organization. The pledging provisions might also produce deadlocked conventions rather often. In such a deadlock, there might be some possibility of turning eventually to a candidate who had remained aloof from the preconvention campaigns; but the whole spirit of the proposal seems intended to rule out the possibility of a draft and to restrict the choice to those who have mounted open, nationwide campaigns involving elaborate preparatory efforts for many months before the convention.[10]

Somewhat similar disturbing effects might also come from federal legislation that has been proposed for an entirely different purpose, the reform of the corrupt practices laws in order to bring campaign expenditures under more effective control, chiefly in presidential election campaigns and in campaigns for the Senate and House of Representatives. In several of these proposals, however, primary elec-

tions are included, and the definitions of an election are even written in a fashion that includes national convention action on presidential and vice-presidential nominations.

In most of the bills embodying these proposals the drafting is so poorly designed from the point of view of its effect upon campaigns for a presidential nomination that the probable consequences in that area were evidently not fully considered. But in one version of the Gore bill (S. 440, 86 Cong.), where a considerable attempt was made to write provisions specifically concerned with campaigns for a presidential nomination, no voluntary committee seeking to draft a candidate would be permitted to spend more than $1,000 in any one year without the candidate's consent. This kind of provision, if seriously enforced, would make impossible even such modest efforts as those represented by the "Draft Stevenson" committee in the spring of 1952, not to mention the far larger financial and organizational effort that was placed behind the Eisenhower candidacy before he agreed to become an open candidate for the nomination.

Action by the States

The existing presidential primaries are the most obvious current form of popular control of the presidential nominating process. The disorder of the existing system of primaries is the result of the diversity of action in the states. Additional states could act to provide primaries, but at the moment there is more need for the amendment of existing statutes to clarify objectives and to adopt more effective means for attaining them.

Without repeating all that was said in Chapter 10, the following points can again be emphasized. All presidential preference polls that are merely advisory or that are separated from the election of delegates should be eliminated because of the gratuitous confusion that they introduce into the

---

[10] For a further discussion, see David, Moos, and Goldman, *op. cit.*, Vol. 1, pp. 217-24. Versions of the proposal introduced by Senator Paul H. Douglas and Representative Charles E. Bennett in 1955 and 1957 provided less stringent pledging provisions than those contained in their original versions. The proposal was introduced in the Eighty-sixth Congress by Mrs. Elizabeth Kee of West Virginia as H. R. 112.

system. All systems requiring would-be delegates both to name a preferred candidate on the ballot and to obtain his consent before doing so should be repealed. They restrict the voters to an inadequate set of alternatives for choice, foster favorite son and dummy candidates, and lead frequently to the formalization of invalid mandates. If generally extended, moreover, such primaries could make it impossible to choose any candidate who had been still refusing to campaign openly at the time of filing for the primaries.

If primaries giving popular control are desired, while avoiding the technical deficiencies that have been so widely prevalent, the Florida model is available. It facilitates contests between organized slates of delegates who are permitted to indicate their candidate preference on the ballot without securing consent; "no-preference" slates may also secure access to the ballot when the situation is such that they see some chance for election. The Florida system can ordinarily be expected to put before the voters the most attractive available candidates, is compatible with the operation of a draft, will probably cut down any favorite son who is not a genuine favorite, and seems unlikely to produce a seriously invalid mandate.[11]

The Florida model is good enough in its technical aspects to make possible a high degree of direct popular control. It would require a minimum of change in customary election procedures while protecting and extending the characteristics of the national conventions as representative institutions. If the Florida type of presidential primary were installed in as many as six or eight widely distributed states, the nominating system as a whole would be moved a considerable distance farther in the direction of a relatively sound form of popular control.

[11] The Florida system referred to is the one adopted in 1955, used in 1956, and which apparently will be used again in 1960. See Chapter 10 and Appendix C.

This is a possibility that puts the more difficult problems in their most acute form. Is it desirable to move farther in the direction of preconvention nominating campaigns that will require a campaign fund of at least a million dollars as the entrance fee for every willing candidate? Is it desirable to force candidates into still more extensive campaigning at the grass-roots, with attendant strain and physical exhaustion? In the states where the parties are competitive and are beginning to develop a more effective two-party system of government, is it desirable to take the risk of splitting the state party organization by a focused contest in a presidential primary? At the national party level, is it desirable to provide further opportunities for a sharply divisive factionalism, led by opposing champions who every four years may return to contest the party nominations in grass-roots campaigns from one end of the country to the other?

These questions may help to explain why the present authors have only a moderate enthusiasm for the Florida primary as it operated in 1956, despite the fact that they had a good deal to do with designing the statute that provided it. They still believe that it was a constructive development under the conditions prevailing in that state, as it might be in other states where the local party system is badly out of balance.

The New York primary, on the other hand, may be an attractive model for states where there is an effective two-party system but also some reluctance to leave delegate selection entirely to the party organizations. Under the New York system the selection of delegates at large is left to the parties; the district delegates are chosen in primary elections in which all registered party members may vote.

The number of contests has been restricted in New York by difficult filing requirements, but this is not a necessary feature of the system. Contests for district delegate are frequent in the primaries of other states with similar systems. The delegates do not give their presidential preferences on the ballot, but can become identified informally with a candidate through other media whenever they think best. The voter's choice is relatively simple, since he is concerned only with the delegates to be elected from his own district.

The New York type of system has the merit of providing many opportunities for the voters to take a hand without inviting the kind of preconvention campaigning that tends to split the state party organizations. Adopted more widely, it would eliminate many procedural irregularities and would result in conventions in which most of the members had accepted the obligations of a public election. Even if adopted nationally, it would leave the conditions of preconvention campaigning relatively fluid. The opportunities for a draft would remain open whenever necessary. Candidates running openly would not have to campaign to the point of exhaustion in individual states, or spend unconscionable sums of money. The New York system does not go all the way in the direction of popular control, but it does give the voter the same kind of opportunity that he enjoys in the election of the members of a legislature.

Other Solutions

Much of what was implied in the questions about the Florida primary is already here—and for reasons not easily reversed, whatever is done about the presidential primary laws. The mass media will continue to operate, public opinion polls will continue to provide readings on the candidates, candidates who are eager and willing to campaign openly will continue to appear, and factional interests will continue to exploit the situation in any way they can. There is thus an acute need to find solutions for problems that will continue to exist, regardless of the form of the primaries.

Something could be done about some of

the specific problems raised by the primaries for preconvention campaigning. The primaries would not necessarily increase the burdens of campaign expense and of pressures on the candidates if other kinds of offsetting action were taken. One line of action would consist of moving the primaries closer in date to the conventions, simplifying the filing requirements, and holding open the opportunities for filing as late as possible before the primaries. Some form of national leadership through the conventions or the governors' conferences may be necessary to secure such action on a wide front.

Another desirable change would consist of more self-restraint on the part of the candidates. This may seem a hopeless counsel, but it is conceivable as a course of action whenever the candidates in either party are closely bound together in a web of intra-party relationships and are clearly aware that continued friendly relations will be necessary for party success in the election.

Self-restraint on the part of the candidates would have the virtue of solving many of the problems of factional divisiveness and excessively bitter conflict in nominating campaigns. If self-restraint is achieved, however, it will be the result of the social, organizational, and competitive situations within which the candidates and their parties find themselves. These in turn have their own causes and do not have to be taken for granted as incapable of improvement. The social relationships among the candidates are at least in part the result of the channels of advancement by which they have come within striking distance of a nomination. The organizational structure within the parties has much to do with those channels and with the overt control of relationships among the potential candidates. But most of all, the competition between the parties tends to control the behavior of the leading actors within each party.

Under existing conditions, popular control may be indirect, but it appears to be highly effective whenever the national parties are closely competitive. This is true despite the clutter of the primaries, the lack of effective popular control in most state convention systems, and the immense welter of confusion that surrounds the whole process. Rectification and clarification are needed in a hundred different ways, many of which would increase popular control or make it more effective. But the more essential point would seem to be the competitive health of the two-party system.

The most compelling restraint that can be placed upon the behavior of a majority party is not as a rule the possible insurgency of its own members, but rather an increase in the votes of the other party. In state politics the history of the last twenty years displays case after case on the Democratic party side, and some on the Republican, in which minority party situations have been retrieved by effort, intelligence, and the holding out of a set of specific political goals. If the Republican party could mount a vigorous effort during the next twenty years in states where it has typically been in the minority, many of the more acute problems of popular control in both political parties would disappear from view. It seems likely that this would be true for long-standing problems of the presidential nominating process, as well as for many other aspects of the party system.

Problems in Bringing the Conventions Up to Their Potentialities

If the conventions need reforming—and many people believe they do—there is also need for a more general recognition that the way to reform lies in improvement rather than in abolition. Some fifty years of propaganda on behalf of presidential primaries have tended to highlight the failings of the conventions, since the primary proposals have in general emphasized the desirability of replacing the convention system with another instrumentality rather than remedying its failings. Yet the continuing contributions made by the conventions to the survival and stability of the American political order are unique, indispensable, and, granted our form of Constitution, probably irreplaceable.

The durability of the two-party system is not something to be taken for granted. An effectively competitive two-party system is an artificial creation that is dependent for its maintenance upon suitable mechanisms, among which a regularly meeting national convention in each party would seem to be one of the most essential. The services of the convention as a general conclave for the selection and recognition of top leadership in each party, and for its replacement when necessary, could be abandoned only at serious national peril.

In the performance of the nominating function, the conventions are pre-eminent. Their record in making the party nominations has been good, and it has also been an improving record, especially in recent decades. With majority rule firmly installed in both parties, fiascos such as the Democratic convention of 1924 seem unlikely to occur again. If titular leaders continue willing to accept greater responsibilities and if there is some further clarification of relationships among all the out-party leaders, divisive preconvention campaigns of the sort that led to Harding as the compromise Republican choice in 1920 may also be somewhat ameliorated in the future.

Further improvement in nominating performance will depend partly on the party leadership, as just indicated, and partly on how delegates are selected and instructed in the states, about which enough has been said earlier in the book. The more important problems in bringing the conventions up to their potentialities arise chiefly in connection with their operation as campaign rallies, their work in drafting the platforms, and their duties as the governing body of each party.

The Rally Function as a Problem

The convention is clearly taking on increasing importance in each party as the campaign rally that starts the national political campaign. This is suggested not only by many recent aspects of convention organization and behavior but also by the political stature of those who attend, including the incumbent President, former Presidents, titular leaders, and congressional leaders who take a growing part in convention leadership. It is also attested by the coverage given the conventions through every medium of communication, by the intensity of the attention they attract from the electorate and the public at large, and by the pressures throughout the party organizations to bring more delegates, alternates, and visitors to the conventions.

Recent studies of voting have found that many voters review their party preferences most actively at the time of the conventions, with the object of deciding for whom they will vote in the forthcoming election. The conventions have the effect of projecting an image of the parties in their collective, corporate identity. They provide a setting within which the major-party leaders and the eventual candidates can be subjected to an intense form of public scrutiny. All these aspects have been amplified by television broadcasting. In 1952, for example, the conventions repeatedly attracted television audiences larger than most of those that would view the speeches and rallies in the later campaign.[12]

Political strategists of both parties have thus been compelled to recognize that the campaign begins at the convention, not afterwards, and that it should therefore be conducted as a major segment of the campaign. Pressures mount for broad participation by local political leaders from all over the country who can be energized and sent home to work enthusiastically in the campaign. Pressures also mount to show the

convention in the guise of a happy family gathering, keeping the less attractive forms of conflict off stage, in the relative privacy of the committees.

In view of these pressures, and the importance of the convention's legitimate role as a campaign rally, it seems clear that the problems created by this aspect must be dealt with by suitable changes in the rally operations rather than by a futile attempt to abolish them. A desire to abolish the rally function seems to be implicit in many of the proposals, not only for extending the primaries, but also for drastically reducing the size of the conventions, restricting the time given to showmanship, and making their agenda more businesslike. Some reforms of this kind might improve the effectiveness of the conventions even as campaign rallies—evidences of gross incompetence in putting on a production inspire no public enthusiasm—but for the most part the problems of massive size must be accepted. A convention as big as the Democrats planned for 1960 may not be necessary, but something comparable to the Republican convention of 1956 and the conventions of each party in 1952 has probably become a minimum in a country as big as the United States.

Granting this, a specific four-point program for dealing with some of the problems might consist of the following steps.

1. *More effective scheduling and execution of preparatory work in advance of the conventions.* In recent years, the national committees have gradually moved toward earlier scheduling of their preparations and convention committees have begun to meet more regularly during the week before the convention. Changes of this kind should be pressed further with the objective of having all of the committees ready to report no later than the second day of the session.

2. *Changing the structure of the national committee and convention committees to make them more representative.* One proposal, developed in Chapter 16, would give every state 1 vote in committee for every 12

[12] Charles A. H. Thomson, *Television and Presidential Politics* (1956), pp. 44-45, 58.

votes on the convention floor. If this kind of change were placed in effect, more business could be entrusted to the national committee and other committees meeting in advance of the conventions, with less danger that recommendations would only have to be reversed by the convention as a whole.

3. *Providing an executive committee of heads of delegations, modeled somewhat on the standard operating procedures of large international conferences, to secure a more effective control of convention time and operations.* A representative agency is needed that can privately take measures on behalf of the whole body, including an advance review of the slate of convention officers recommended by the outgoing national committee and a daily review during the convention of the agenda proposed for action, the motions that will be made from the floor, the division of time in any prospective debate, and the floor managers who will be responsible for the use of time on each side. In such an executive committee each chairman of a state delegation might be accompanied by one adviser if so desired, and authorized to vote the delegation's strength in settling agenda questions. The committee should be convened by the national chairman on the day before the convention opens, and it might continue him as its chairman or elect a new one, as it sees fit.

On the face of it, an executive committee to secure a tighter control over what happens on the floor may seem undemocratic. But, in a meeting as large as a party convention, unrestrained freedom of the members to offer motions and speak from the floor is physically impossible. Some control is necessary to allow any business to be transacted, and in present practice the control, by the time the convention is doing business, is in the hands of one man—the permanent chairman, customarily the party leader in the House of Representatives. In view of the frequent differences in point of view between the congressional and the presidential wings of the party, it seems fair to suggest that a system of control by a committee clearly representing the whole presidential constituency would often be likely to satisfy the desires of the majority more closely than the control exercised in recent years by the party leader in Congress and the associates with whom such a leader inevitably surrounds himself.[13]

4. *More frequent meetings of the conventions, with biennial meetings as a first step.* Conventions in the mid-term years would provide a means for focusing national attention upon the parties and their current status at the beginning of each contest for control of Congress.

The party in power could hold a mid-term convention along lines very similar to the convention at which an incumbent President is renominated. In view of the President's vital interest in having a Congress controlled by his party, he would be received at the convention as the head of the party, responsible in conjunction with the congressional leaders for leading its mid-term campaign for control of Congress. A new platform would be adopted, expressing the consensus of the party in the Executive Branch, in Congress, and in the electorate. A new national committee could be elected, reflecting, where necessary, the internal party changes of the previous two years. Most of all, the convention would dramatize the effort to rally the party for the kind of campaign that might prevent the weakening of congressional strength which has typically affected the party in power in its off-year elections.

For the party out of power, the organization of a successful mid-term convention would be more difficult, because of the ambiguities that surround the problem of leadership in the out-party. But leadership problems are not solved by refusing to take any action for their solution, and it is the out-party that needs a mid-term convention most of all, in order to discover how agree-

---

[13] On the distinction between congressional and presidential wings, see footnote 3.

ment can be reached on its various problems in the name of the whole party—especially on the problems involved in reversing the verdict of the previous election. Platform issues could reach their greatest importance in the mid-term convention, with a genuine clarification of the extent to which the out-party's various leaders have been really speaking for it. A new national committee could be elected, at the point in time when changes in national committee structure are usually most critical in an out-party.

The party, if it saw fit, could take special action to designate a campaign leader who would serve explicitly as the principal party spokesman for the period of the mid-term campaign.[14] The Democratic party in 1954, for example, might have designated Adlai Stevenson as its campaign leader, who would then have had the explicit backing of the whole party in the mid-term campaigning that he actually undertook. Under the somewhat different conditions of 1958, the Democrats might have chosen Stevenson again, or they might have looked elsewhere —perhaps calling former President Truman back to a temporary task of leadership—or Senate leader Lyndon Johnson might have been tapped for the role. All three men were active nationally in the mid-term campaign, but no one of them was able to lay claim effectively to the title of official spokesman for the whole party. Yet, with the President and Vice President moving increasingly into leadership roles for the party in power in mid-term campaigning, the party out of power finds itself equally in need of a voice that will be correspondingly entitled to national attention.

Action problems of this kind are material

to the holding of a mid-term convention as a campaign rally, because no group of political leaders is likely to undertake the hazards involving in convening an assembly that has authority to act, unless there is business in prospect on which action would be profitable. Once assembled, with legitimate business to transact, a mid-term out-party convention could do much to refurbish the party image, put into perspective the relationships between the leaders of the presidential and congressional wings of the party, and tighten up the party organization for the mid-term battle.

In either party, of course, the organization of a mid-term convention would immediately place a claim on a large block of prime network time on television and radio —valuable free advertising that would help to offset the cost and trouble of the meeting.

The Ambiguities of the Platform Function

The platform drafting at the conventions presumably makes some contribution to their over-all importance, but the assessment of the contribution is not easy. Only on the rarest occasions has some great issue of public policy so dominated convention proceedings that the nominating act became secondary, as occurred in the origins of the Republican party and in the Democratic conventions of 1860, 1896, and 1924— occasions that foreshadowed a basic reconstruction of the party system. It would be difficult to argue that such occasions will become more frequent in the future.

But there is no doubt that the platform struggles at each successive convention seem to involve a vast amount of work, time, and activity by leaders of national opinion who seldom give time to efforts that they feel to be inconsequential. The platform hearings at the conventions provide opportunities for participation by all the great organized interest groups, and tend to establish mutual relationships of commitment when their platform proposals are accepted. Such

---

[14] This is an alternative proposal to a comprehensive plan, previously proposed by one of the present authors, for increasing the status of the titular leader. As a more limited proposal, it probably has greater feasibility, partly because a wider range of candidates could be considered for the mid-term campaign leadership than for a continuing titular leadership. For the earlier proposal, see Paul T. David, "A New Role for the Opposition Party Leader," *New York Times Magazine*, Sept. 18, 1955, pp. 15, 30, 32.

groups, when they are more successful in obtaining their desired planks in one party than the other, have a definite incentive to abandon neutrality for active participation in the election campaign that follows.

Members of Congress, with their concern for public policy, are also becoming increasingly involved. A tradition is developing in each party by which the congressmen who are delegates are considered especially eligible for service on the platform committees. As these factors converge, and with the growing importance of all public policies, there may be an increasing tendency to hold the parties responsible for the promises made in their platforms.

The platform function nonetheless remains highly ambiguous, largely because it is mainly a pronouncement of the presidential wing of the party. There is only a loose connection between platform adoption and the conduct of the congressional campaigns—and the further behavior of the members who are elected to represent the party in Congress. Platforms are written for use in *presidential* campaigns, yet they consist largely of proposals for legislation that will be meaningless unless there is *congressional* action. Thus the function performed by any party platform seems likely to remain ambiguous until the national parties find some means for giving greater coherence to the congressional campaigns that trade on the party name and are conducted under the party banner. Mid-term conventions, with their inevitably greater emphasis on platform action for a purely congressional campaign, might be a substantial step in that direction.

The Governing of the Parties

The work of the conventions in governing the parties is the least understood of all convention functions and the most difficult to appraise. As a function it originated in the activities incidental to the nominating, platform-drafting, fund-raising, and cam-

paigning activities of the parties.[15] In recent years the governing function has begun to be recognized as capable of making its own contribution to party survival, stability, and adaptation to new conditions. It is the aspect that offers the greatest opportunity for further development, precisely because it is the one that has so far been least developed. Yet it has taken shape sufficiently to demonstrate the variety, scope, and latent power of its potentialities—and some of the problems that will arise if those potentialities are exploited.

The work of the convention as a governing body includes first of all the decisions that are necessary to constitute the assembly. When a convention decides which delegates or delegations are entitled to seats, it is making the most elemental of all constituting decisions. These decisions can also have far-reaching consequences for the state parties concerned as well as for the total structure of the national party. The national party has here its own instruments for the development of greater consistency and cohesion within its own ranks—instruments of such potency that they can be used only infrequently and with the greatest caution.

A state party organization whose delegation is refused seating automatically loses legitimacy so far as its immediate future relationships to the national party are concerned. It may secure a prompt and easy return to national party recognition if its accepts the convention decisions, cooperates in campaigning for the national ticket, and pays its share for the support of the national headquarters. Conversely, if it proceeds to bolt the party in the presidential campaign, sanctions of varying degrees of severity may be imposed, depending upon the situation

[15] Fund raising is included in this list because one of the main reasons for the establishment of each party's national committee, elected at the convention, was to provide a mechanism through which to raise funds. This continues to be one of the main purposes of the committee and, therefore, indirectly, of the convention.

and the unity and energy of the national party leadership.[16]

The convention also acts as a party governing body when it adopts rules for its own composition and procedure. Most of this work reached stability in the early decades of the convention system, so much so that it was possible to overlook the far-reaching possibilities inherent in any major change in convention rules. But the Republicans' action in 1916 to reform their convention apportionment did much to re-emphasize the importance of the rules, as well as to restore confidence in the party's basic procedures. When the Democratic convention of 1936 revoked the two thirds rule, in effect for more than a century, it made a profound change in the constitu-

tional structure of the national Democratic party—and in the unwritten constitution of the United States.

Majority rule on nominations has made other changes possible at Democratic national conventions that might otherwise not have occurred, including the relatively firm handling of civil rights issues in 1948 and of party loyalty issues in 1952, and the adoption of the Mitchell committee recommendations in 1956 on the relations between state and national parties.[17] So far as the voting structure of the convention is concerned, in both parties the way appears to be open for other changes that would further rationalize the basis for convention representation and reform the voting structure of the convention committees. Elements of the system that provide equal voting for all states become increasingly unrealistic as the national committee and the convention committees of each party take on a larger burden of preparatory work in advance of the conventions.

The convention acts most conspicuously in governing the party when it acts to ensure the continuity and effectiveness of national party activity between the conventions. Each convention regularly designates the members of the party national committee for the term continuing until the next convention, and may also instruct the committee or define its duties.

Republican party rules, as readopted at each convention, have provided in some detail for the organization and functioning of the Republican national committee. Democratic party precedents and practice for the national committee have been codified in Clarence Cannon's *Democratic Manual,* issued every four years since 1928 for Democratic national convention delegates.[18]

[16] A national party that has lost the election is in a poor position to discipline bolting elements. It may have to receive them back into the fold, so as to build a coalition that can effectively seek a majority in the electorate, as in the Republican party after the split of 1912.

If the national party wins despite overt bolting by disaffected elements, it is in a better position to administer sanctions. Such elements may have already lost representation on the national committee through failure to secure delegation seating, with consequences in federal patronage that are almost automatic in a winning party, and they are not likely to receive favorable treatment in the staffing of executive agencies except on the basis of specific understandings about future behavior. They may be denied social recognition at national party gatherings, and are likely to end the four-year cycle by again facing a seating challenge at the convention. Committee assignments in Congress may also be withheld or removed, as happened to the bolting Progressives of 1924 in the following Congress, and to Senator Wayne Morse after he bolted the Republican ticket in 1952.

A winning party, however, has few sanctions that can be rationally imposed if the probable result is a destruction of its majority. The bolting Democrats of 1948 received relatively gentle treatment, presumably because the national party's electoral majorities were thin and the presidential majority rested on a somewhat different base from that in Congress. Under the leadership of President Truman, the presidential wing of the party was nonetheless able to pursue a line of policy that involved disciplinary consequences for the elements that had bolted his election. This was presumably deemed necessary, among other reasons, to maintain the party's presidential majority in the northern states. Even a losing party may rationally impose sanctions if the readmittance of bolting elements seems certain to drive away even larger elements of support.

[17] One of the little-noticed but important recommendations of the Mitchell committee as adopted was a specific provision for the ouster of any national committee member who failed to cooperate in the election campaign for the convention's nominees.

[18] According to Congressman Cannon, the manual was first prepared for the 1920 convention and was used also in 1924; it was issued in printed form for the first time in 1928.

In two successive meetings after the election of 1956 the Democratic national committee debated, and in 1957 adopted, formal rules to govern its structure and activities. Presumably these rules will be reported to the convention in 1960.

The national committees are clearly subordinate to the conventions by which they are created and, in theory at least, may be limited to activities approved by the conventions. In practice, between conventions the national committee is largely on its own in the determination of its functions and activities, since, when the convention adjourns, it adjourns *sine die*. Essentially the committee tends to approve whatever is laid before it by the chairman, although not always with complete agreement. Party headquarters organizations of some strength have grown up under the leadership of the national committee chairmen in recent decades. These organizations are more and more a source of initiative in focusing the internal relationships of the party on which each successive convention will have to act, either directly or by default.

The suggestion noted earlier in this chapter, that the conventions should meet at least biennially, has been offered repeatedly, from various sources, in recent years.[19] The fact that the conventions have been meeting only every four years has undoubtedly been a major limitation on their capacity to act as governing bodies in the general sense. Any decision to meet biennially would have the effect almost automatically of increasing the importance of the conventions as party governing bodies.

In both parties the financial support of the national party activities needs to be rationalized if headquarters staffs are to be strengthened and funds provided for campaigns in states where the party is weak. Many state party organizations have always been casual about meeting their quotas for the support of the national party. Their attitudes are the natural result of the fact that the financial relationships that are considered essential in any other national voluntary organization—farm, business, labor, women's, veterans', or whatever—have never been built into the structure of the parties.

What is needed is recognition of what might be called the principle of no representation without taxation. When a state organization has failed or refused to meet its financial responsibilities to the national party, there would seem to be ample reason, in the absence of extenuating circumstances, for withholding the voting rights of its delegation at the next convention. Voting rights might also be withheld in the national committee during the interim. The methods by which state financial quotas have been determined have been surrounded by obscurity in both parties, although the Democratic national committee established a state quota appeals board in 1959. More vigorous action to enforce the quotas would inevitably involve putting them on some publicly defensible basis, and probably adopting them in the full national convention.[20]

[19] American Political Science Association, Committee on Political Parties, *Toward a More Responsible Two-Party System* (1950), pp. 5, 38; Estes Kefauver "Indictment of the Political Convention," *New York Times Magazine*, March 16, 1952, pp. 9, 59-61, 63; Norton E. Long, "Patriotism for Partisans: A Responsible Opposition," *Antioch Review*, Vol. 12 (Dec. 1952), pp. 448-56; David, *op. cit., New York Times Magazine*, Sept. 18, 1955; address by former Senator Herbert H. Lehman at the Lexington Democratic Club, New York City, as reported in *New York Times*, Jan. 19, 1957.

[20] Although the above proposal has been presented in its briefest form, with no attempt to spell out the difficulties that are inherent and the means that might be found for dealing with them, it should not be supposed that the authors are unaware of the difficulties. Some of these are technical and arise out of the disjointedness of existing arrangements of the parties and of public law. The important difficulties are political, arising out of the reluctance of some state party leaders to accept the kind of financial arrangements that are needed if the national parties are to be effective as organizations. The problem may soon become even more acute than in the past if the Advertising Council-American Heritage Foundation campaign for mass financial support of the parties should be increasingly successful. In 1958 the campaign reportedly did little to benefit the national parties because the local organizations that had made collections on the basis of the national campaign retained almost all of the funds. See Stephen K. Bailey, *The Condition of Our National Parties*, pp. 12-13. (This paper of Professor Bailey's was commissioned and published by the Fund for the Republic in 1959.)

As currently organized, the conventions are more representative of the whole party following than any other party body, but reforms are still needed in the basic convention apportionment system. The parties did not give fair representation or serve their own needs in 1956 when, in the eight mountain states, there was one Democratic convention vote for each 7,000 party voters and one Republican convention vote for each 12,000, but in New York, Pennsylvania, Ohio, Illinois, and California, only one Democratic vote for each 29,000 party voters, and only one Republican vote for every 39,000 voters. Some plan of reapportionment should be adopted that would move the conventions closer to fair representation, not so much of the state populations as of the voters who constitute the parties. The authors of this study would favor the plan previously referred to as equal representation of states and voters,

under which the representation of the states where the party is strong would be increased and that of those where it is weak in votes would be curtailed, even though wide discrepancies would still remain.[21]

For the achievement of any of the reforms previously suggested, leaders will be needed in strategic positions who are convinced of the need to strengthen the national parties, and who are prepared to act firmly to that end. If the situation has been correctly assessed, it can be expected that such leaders will begin to appear with increasing frequency as the product of the competition between the parties in the states where they are competitive. But any innovating change on matters of importance will need the approval of the convention, express or implied, if the change is to become solidified as a permanent feature of the party institutions. The conventions have great opportunities to strengthen the foundations of the American system of government.

Attempts by national party leaders to secure more positive arrangements for national party finance may doubtless antagonize some state party leaders whose cooperation is needed; and they in turn may find support in the local constituencies. But all of the alternative courses of action (or, more accurately, inaction) also have their disadvantages.

The proposal is one that, if taken seriously, may lead to a kind of political process long familiar to those concerned with the financing of public international assemblies, a form of political organization in which membership is voluntary. In the early days, the typical procedure was the assessment, by formal action of the international assembly, of what were called "contributions." The formal action was always preceded by long argument over the principles of assessment and much haggling behind the scenes. It then developed that various national governments somehow failed to pay. Sanctions were then considered, but the whole situation was so embarrassing that nothing was done until delinquencies became conspicuous over a period of years. Finally, after more argument, the assembly would muster its strength and conclude that voting rights must be denied, after long notice, to the members who failed to pay. The delinquents then paid.

This sequence had already occurred so many times that it could be clearly foreseen when the United Nations charter was prepared, and a provision for the denial of voting rights after two years of delinquency was therefore included. The provision is substantially self-operating, since a delinquent member probably could be challenged on a point of order if it attempted to vote, and the provision thus seems to have served the purpose for which it was intended.

Dilemmas in Out-Party Leadership

The structure of national party leadership—or, as some critics would see it, the lack of structure—presents several dilemmas in connection with every problem of party effectiveness, including those just canvassed. Some of the dilemmas exist whether the party is in power or out of power in the Executive Branch of the government, but in recent years they have usually been more acute in the party out of power.

Coordinate Factionalism

First and most characteristic are the dilemmas of coordinate factionalism: the situation where no faction is in clear control of the major posts of party leadership, and

[21] See Chapter 8 and Tables 8.4 and 8.6. Under the suggested apportionment each state would receive first an equal number of convention votes corresponding to its Senate seats, but the bulk of the apportionment would be divided among the states in proportion to their popular vote for the party's candidate for President in the last previous election.

several factions are struggling to obtain that control. This is the situation that existed within both parties during most of the nineteenth century, whether they were ostensibly in power or not. It often produced a candidate who had been a victorious leader in the factional struggles but was unable to win the election because of the bitterness that had attended his nomination. It sometimes produced a compromise candidate who could win the election but could not provide adequate leadership in the Presidency.

The system as a whole made it difficult to determine who was responsible for party performance, or to clarify the popular images of the parties as alternative vehicles for public action. Whatever clarification emerged in a single election campaign was likely to be confused or reversed by the choice of candidates four years or eight years later. But the system did have certain advantages that presumably contributed to its ability to survive.

During this period, no sectional leadership was beyond challenge and the practice of negotiation and coalition among sectional leaders was fostered. It was equally true that no machine-type of national party organization could become genuinely effective. The lesser types of manipulation represented by control of the national committee were always challenged, often successfully. The parties were free to choose the man of the hour, if he had become visible under the conditions of career advancement that prevailed within the parties. It was possible to nominate and elect, though as a minority choice, a President who could win the Civil War, but only after twenty years of failure to find, install, and support the kind of President who might have prevented it.

Factionalism is defended by those who prefer open conflict within the parties to any clarificaton of competitive roles that might involve greater cohesion within the parties. But is impossible to disregard the changes that have been brought by the rising strength of the Presidency, by the disciplinary effect of the responsibilities of government, and by the resulting tendencies toward cohesion under the leadership of the President in the party in power—particularly when that party holds, not only the White House, but also majorities in both houses of Congress and in more than half the state governments.

When the out-party displays all of the characteristics of factional disruption while attempting to compete with an incumbent party that has taken on qualities of unity, the contest can become highly one-sided. Typically, under these conditions the out-party cannot win unless the in-party defeats itself—or is defeated by circumstances beyond its control and for which the out-party is equally lacking in responsibility.

Congressional Leadership

One frequently advocated solution for the dilemmas of out-party factionalism is to let the out-party leaders in Congress take control. They hold positions of recognized legitimacy within the government, even when their party is in the minority in Congress and out of power in the Executive Branch. Frequently they represent the dominant faction of the party in the areas where it is most entrenched. They have influence with members of the national committee because of their access to the powers of government and for other reasons. At times they have been able to dictate the choice of a new national committee chairman and to make him a member of their own inner group. At the convention, when they have mobilized behind a particular candidate for the nomination, they have almost invariably been able to assemble a substantial block of votes in his favor.

But other dilemmas result when the leaders in Congress dominate their party nationally while it is out of power in the Executive Branch. Typically, they are more responsive to their own special constituencies than to the entire national party constituency. To be sure, those who have been most successful as congressional leaders are apt to be men who have had regard for all the interests of the national party, but inevitably they tend to see those interests from the perspective of the congressional wing. To the extent that they hold the limelight while the party is out of power, they frequently convey an essentially negative image of their party. Their leadership responsibilities tend to make them more concerned with congressional prerogatives than with the attainment of presidential victory. In seeking a presidential nominee, they usually prefer a candidate who can be expected to defer to Congress when issues arise between the branches of the government.

There is nothing unethical about any of these attitudes. They are the natural product of the structure of government under the separation of powers. But they do tend to unfit the leaders of Congress for the leadership of their national party, and particularly in the choice of a presidential candidate who will maintain and utilize the powers of the presidential office and of the Executive Branch.

The problem has been stated in the abstract and in terms that apply to either party when out of power. There are, however, distinct differences between the parties, which have existed throughout most of their history. The Republican party has long permitted its congressional leaders to play a larger role in the selection of its presidential candidates than has the Democratic party. Nineteenth-century Republican congressional leaders were leaders of dominant party factions, and highly influential at every Republican national convention during that period, even when unable to control the choice. In the present century they have been credited with Harding's nomination in 1920; in 1940, 1948, and 1952 they offered a principal candidate in the person of Senator Robert A. Taft, although defeated on each of those occasions. Congressional leaders of the Democrats,

drawn mainly from the southern and border states, were lacking in presidential availability for decades after the Civil War. They had influence in the search for acceptable candidates but were rarely able to dominate the choice. They were somewhat involved in the first nomination of William Jennings Bryan, who led major elements of the Democratic party for sixteen years thereafter and in 1912 was instrumental in the defeat of Champ Clark for the nomination. When the congressional leaders were given their choice for the nomination in 1904, the party suffered one of its most disastrous defeats. They have been noteworthy figures in the conventions of recent decades, but their influence has not been conspicuously powerful in the actual choice of nominees.

The Role of the Titular Leader

The above review of experience suggests another alternative to the dilemmas of factionalism in the out-party—an active role for the party's titular leader, including renomination at the next convention, when this is appropriate, and influence on the choice of a successor, when a new choice must be made. This course also has its dilemmas, both those that have been illustrated by the experience so far and those that might arise if a more powerful structure of leadership were to be developed around the titular leader.

The outstanding characteristic of the experience so far is that no renominated titular leader has yet won the Presidency—except Cleveland, who had previously been President. This leads to dilemmas of interpretation as well as action. Were the titular leaders renominated only in losing situations? Are the titular leaders useful in stabilizing the leadership in the presidential wing of the out-party *only* during long periods when victory is hopeless? It is possible for a previously defeated candidate to win if given the chance when prospects are favorable?

Various opinions could be offered in response to these questions. The opinions of the present authors are as follows. Bryan's renominations in 1900 and 1908 occurred in losing situations, but he probably did more to maintain the strength of the party vote in those years than any other available candidate could have done. Stevenson's renomination in 1956 also occurred in a losing situation. Dewey's renomination in 1948, however, was not in what was considered a losing situation. He ran well, and many observers believe that if the Republicans had not fallen prey to overconfidence he might well have won. He also suffered from the reluctance of congressional and certain other party leaders to accept him in fact as the titular leader of his party during the interval between his first and second nominations. Winner-take-all tactics in both Republican factions had left a divided party for the general-election campaign of 1948.

All the titular leaders who have been active as such have done much to maintain party strength during periods when severe attrition could otherwise have been anticipated. Their usefulness continued, moreover, even after the tide had turned and the prospects for victory were improving. Bryan's usefulness continued between 1908 and 1912, reaching its climax in Wilson's nomination. Al Smith was useful to his party between 1928 and 1932, despite the division that he eventually brought on by his belated decision to seek a second nomination. Landon was useful between 1936 and 1940, in part because he had removed himself from consideration for the next nomination. Party prospects were expected to be excellent when the second Roosevelt term was over; Landon helped to improve them by his organizational activities. Dewey's usefulness between 1948 and 1952 was limited by the circumstances of his defeat; yet he was largely responsible for the choice of the successor who brought victory to the party in 1952.

As to whether it is possible for a defeated candidate to win on some later occasion, there is no doubt that previous defeat has consequences for future electoral success. A defeated candidate is the victim of an unfair psychological phenomenon: his inevitable human frailties will be fully appraised and probably magnified in the search for the causes of his defeat; whereas a candidate who has reached the top through an unbroken series of resounding electoral successes takes on luminous qualities of charisma that make him seem larger than life.

In the political systems of other democratic countries a party that suffers defeat while in power is likely to re-examine its leadership and may change it. But if defeat comes again to a party already out of power, the responsibility is likely to be widely shared within the party, with little tendency to make the leader the scapegoat unless he has proved conspicuously deficient. The leadership may then stay in place until the party eventually wins power and for a considerable period thereafter. Loyal service during years of defeat is the leader's best claim to his position when victory again becomes possible.

American attitudes toward defeated candidates for high elective office seem to be the product of special circumstances. The diminution in charisma that follows defeat is of special electoral importance in a system where it is possible, in effect, to elect the man without electing the party and to defeat the man without defeating the party—as seems to have occurred in 1956. The effect on a defeated candidate is redoubled when he holds no public office, or holds one in which the term is expiring. Unlike the normal situation of the leader in a defeated party under most parliamentary systems, he may then find himself with no appropriate public or official position through which to maintain his prestige and his claim to public attention after defeat.[22]

[22] This aspect of the situation may be changing in a way that will make it less frequent in the future, so far as defeated presidential candidates are concerned. Senators no longer feel called upon to resign their seats while running for President. Governors

Whatever the reason, a more mature attitude toward the future potentialities of defeated candidates seems to be coming into vogue. If they run well even in defeat, they have important assets in the form of a reputation, a name that is known, and a popular following. In recent years defeated candidates for governor and senator who have kept on running have eventually marked up some impressive victories. The same phenomenon could have occurred at the presidential level forty years ago if Charles Evans Hughes had been willing to run in 1920.

Collective Leadership of the Presidential Out-Party

The titular leaders of a defeated national party will continue to occupy a somewhat parlous position until one of them finally succeeds in leading his party to victory in a subsequent election. Meanwhile, they have already achieved enough recognition to suggest that it will not be easy in the future for the congressional leaders of either party to seize control when the party loses its hold on the White House. The experience of the Democratic Advisory Council since 1956 further suggests that it is possible for the presidential wing of a party out of power, as represented in the party's national committee, to build and maintain its own continuing structure of leadership, not only without the consent of the party's congressional leaders, but also in the face of their opposition.

In this particular instance, success undoubtedly has been due in large measure to the fact that three of the party's principal leaders were agreed on the need for uniting its executive leadership in the new Council. Former President Harry S. Truman, titular leader Adlai E. Stevenson, and national

chairman Paul M. Butler all stood solidly together on this point. All have served actively on the Council under Butler's chairmanship. Their joint service has had much to do with the relative ease with which the work of the Council has been financed through special fund-raising activities, and also the ease with which the party's leading candidates for its next presidential nomination have been recruited for membership on the Council, where they will share responsibility for its work in the months leading up to the convention of 1960.

This recent experience of the Democratic party leads to a final dilemma for consideration, one that may be more serious in the future but that is already being illustrated by the current experience. If the presidential and congressional wings of the same national party build strong but separate leadership structures to meet the demands of their overlapping but different constituencies, what will happen? Will the result be open warfare, carrying over into the next national convention? Or will conflict be held within bounds, with the congressional leaders retaining their ascendancy in Congress and the executive leaders retaining theirs in the national party and in the electorate, and with both groups joining to pass the torch to whatever candidate is finally nominated?

It might seem that this dilemma could be avoided by merging the congressional and executive leadership of the out-party in the same party council, but such a merger would risk doing violence to the inherent logic of the American scheme of government. It is not attempted even in the party in power. The President and his aides meet with the congressional leaders of his party at weekly intervals when Congress is in session, but neither group is in a position to bind the other; joint statements are never issued; nothing is settled by a vote; and the relationship goes forward essentially as a negotiation between representatives of differing constituencies.

of New York, Ohio, and California occupy an even more advantageous position, since they are at midpoint of their terms in every presidential year, unlike the situation of one third of the senators and most of the other governors.

This seems a more appropriate model for the out-party than the kind of composition that was originally proposed for the Democratic Advisory Council when it was formed after the election of 1956. The refusal of the congressional leaders to serve can be seen, in retrospect, as having permitted the emergence of the Council as the focus of the presidential wing of the party—an organization that might in time be able to achieve a fairly equal negotiating balance with the congressional leaders. This was a relationship that was not gained easily even by the Presidency, but it is one that could be fostered for the future, whether in victory or defeat, if the forthcoming Democratic convention of 1960 should take action to clarify the status of the Council and to assure its continuation in that party in an appropriate form.[23]

Meanwhile, the Democratic Advisory Council is too recent a prototype to bear much weight in planning the internal structure of either party for the future. Success or failure in any new institution of this kind is so much at the mercy of the accidents of personality and circumstance that even a sound model may fail, while a seemingly unsound model might succeed, thereby producing in time its own mutations in the system.

What is important is the fact that there is increasing recognition of the need for some form of stability and continuity in the leadership of the presidential wing of the party out of power. So far, historically, it has been almost impossible to provide such continuity, because the executive group is out of office when it is out of power. The national party conventions, meeting only once in four years, have taken no responsibility

for assuring leadership continuity in the presidential wing of the party. Without such continuity, the out-party is never really ready to assume the tasks of government even if it does happen to win.

Goals for the Party System

Any attempt to formulate goals for the American party system is a hazardous undertaking. Yet there is probably no other area of American life in which agreement on a set of workable goals is so greatly needed. The party system underlies the government and links it to the body politic. Without a party system in adequate health and functioning, the survival of the nation itself may be endangered, along with the world-wide interests with which the nation is associated.

One attempt to state a set of minimum goals for the party system was as follows:[24]

1. A party system in which each of the major parties is sufficiently in accord with the underlying national consensus to be safely entrusted with power.

2. A party system in which each of the parties is sufficiently strong and internally cohesive to develop and carry out a governmental program of at least minimum adequacy if it succeeds in gaining power.

3. A party system in which the two major parties are sufficiently competitive to be able to replace each other in power at intervals of reasonable frequency.

The first of these three goals is so basic that even to state it ought not to be necessary. Nevertheless, many of the political scientists who have evidenced concern over the effectiveness of the party system have been suspected of attempting to disrupt the national consensus, or have been accused of making proposals that would have that effect. Hence it is desirable to give prominence to the goal of preserving the national

[23] In the paper commissioned by the Fund for the Republic (*op. cit.*, pp. 12, 14), Stephen K. Bailey has recommended that the parties "create by formal action of the two national conventions, permanent advisory councils and staffs to both national committees." He further comments, in discussing this proposal, "Although the advisory councils should explicitly represent the executive wing of their parties, they should include in their membership, at least as non-voting observers, the congressional party leaders or their designates."

[24] This formulation first appeared in a paper by Paul T. David, "Intensity of Inter-Party Competition and the Problem of Party Realignment," presented at the annual meeting of the American Political Science Association, September 1957.

consensus, and to use it as a test for all instrumental proposals.

The importance of the second goal—internal strength and cohesion—becomes apparent whenever there are conspicuous evidences of weakness and disorder in either party. The goal itself seems to have wide acceptance. Disagreement begins when measures are discussed for the actual attainment of greater cohesion within the parties, especially when the measures involve anything other than voluntary consent on the part of all concerned.

The third goal—parties sufficiently competitive to alternate in power at intervals of reasonable frequency—is inherently appealing in its overt demonstration that the electorate does in fact have more than one alternative that will be compatible with survival as a free country. But the third goal might not win wide acceptance if it did not seem essential for the other two.

Alternation in power, which means alternation primarily in the holding of executive authority, seems to be the only means of demonstrating on a current basis that each of the parties can be safely entrusted with power and that each can pull itself together sufficiently when in office to operate a government. When one party is too long in executive authority, in the nation or in a state, the party out of power may become merely a dissident minority in the electorate, so far out of accord with the national consensus that it is not even a useful opposition party. Or it may disintegrate to the point where, if it does gain power, years of rebuilding will be necessary before it can become adequately effective—or, as happened in the 1820's, it may even die, leaving the two-party system then dependent for rebirth on a split of the dominant party.

In considering what frequency of party overturn would be desirable, however, it needs to be remembered that there can be an alternation of weakness as well as of strength. When both parties are alternately voted out of office on every consecutive opportunity, as occurred in every presidential election from 1840 to 1852 and again from 1884 to 1896, there is little reason to think that either party is achieving much success in resolving its own inner conflicts or in solving the problems of government.

All the concerns of this book are relevant in one way or another to the attainment of the three goals specified above. The topics that have been emphasized in this final chapter seem especially relevant. To recapitulate, the following changes are needed:

• • • wider acceptance of the principle that the party organizations have a positive responsibility to recruit able candidates into the channels of political career advancement at all levels of elective office;

• • • a broader and sounder base of recruitment for governor and senator, with a wider distribution of opportunities through which the most able governors and senators may secure timely preparation for further political advancement;

• • • further development of the office of governor in the pivotal states, of the posts of party leadership in the Senate, of the Vice Presidency, and of the titular leadership of the out-party to give preparation for those who may later become President;

• • • adequate provision for popular influence in the nominating process, but with recognition also of the requirements for party cohesion and stable leadership;

• • • renewed efforts to protect and enhance the institutional integrity of the national conventions and to utilize their powers effectively;

• • • more effective organization of the leaders of the executive wing of each national party, especially for the periods when it is out of power in the White House, as an essential means to the legitimate achievement of the previous objectives.

Each of the three goals to which these changes are related was deliberately stated in relative terms. Each goal needs to be attained sufficiently for the requirements of the body politic under the circumstances prevailing. From one point of view, for example, the party system would be assessed as grossly out of accord with all three goals from 1896 to 1952, in view of the infrequency of party overturn, the difficult situation of whichever party was out of power at any given time during that whole period, and the recurring crises of war and depression that could all be attributed in considerable part to previous periods of political ineptitude. Yet the nation fought two world wars successfully, had long periods of prosperity, and from almost any point of view enjoyed a rising level of well-being.

The present and the future, however, are already bringing greater demands than the past. No one knows what it will take to meet those demands in the future or whether we are meeting them now—sufficiently for national or world survival, or economic stability, or any other phase of economic and political well-being. What we do know is that we live in a different world from that of 1896, one that will severely test all political and governmental institutions.

For the future, we shall need a party system that does a better job in the achievement of all three goals than has been the case so far. Furthermore, it would seem that before we can have it we shall need much clarification of many aspects of the party system, including some changes in statute law, other changes in the organization of political bodies, and, most of all, changes in the customs, and practices of the national political parties, with appropriate action by the national conventions to indicate consent or give active approval.

All of this implies a considerable development in the American political culture if the specific institutional modifications are to be achieved and assimilated. Culture change seldom comes rapidly, but it does come in response to events, environmental pressures, and those qualities of vision without which the people perish. The events and the environmental pressures are here. It remains to be seen whether the necessary qualities of vision will be provided, and soon enough, by some inspired national leadership.

APPENDIXES

A

Tables

TABLE 1. PRESIDENTIAL AND VICE-PRESIDENTIAL NOMINEES
OF THE MAJOR PARTIES, 1832-1956[a]

	Democratic		National Republican, Whig, Republican	
Year	Presidential Candidate	Vice-Presidential Candidate	Presidential Candidate	Vice-Presidential Candidate
1832	Andrew Jackson*	Martin Van Buren	Henry Clay	John Sergeant
1836	Martin Van Buren*	Richard M. Johnson	(no convention)	
1840	Martin Van Buren	(no nominee)	William Henry Harrison*	John Tyler
1844	James K. Polk*	Silas Wright[b] George M. Dallas[c]	Henry Clay	Theodore Frelinghuysen
1848	Lewis Cass	William O. Butler	Zachary Taylor*	Millard Fillmore
1852	Franklin Pierce*	William R. King	Winfield Scott	William A. Graham
1856	James Buchanan*	John C. Breckinridge	John C. Frémont	William L. Dayton
1860	Stephen A. Douglas	Benjamin Fitzpatrick[b] Herschel V. Johnson[d]	Abraham Lincoln*	Hannibal Hamlin
1864	George B. McClellan	George H. Pendleton	Abraham Lincoln*	Andrew Johnson
1868	Horatio Seymour	Francis P. Blair, Jr.	Ulysses S. Grant*	Schuyler Colfax
1872	Horace Greeley	B. Gratz Brown	Ulysses S. Grant*	Henry Wilson
1876	Samuel J. Tilden	Thomas A. Hendricks	Rutherford B. Hayes*	William A. Wheeler
1880	Winfield Scott Hancock	William H. English	James A. Garfield*	Chester A. Arthur
1884	Grover Cleveland*	Thomas A. Hendricks	James G. Blaine	John A. Logan
1888	Grover Cleveland	Allen G. Thurman	Benjamin Harrison*	Levi P. Morton
1892	Grover Cleveland*	Adlai E. Stevenson	Benjamin Harrison	Whitelaw Reid
1896	William Jennings Bryan	Arthur Sewall	William McKinley*	Garret A. Hobart
1900	William Jennings Bryan	Adlai E. Stevenson	William McKinley*	Theodore Roosevelt
1904	Alton B. Parker	Henry G. Davis	Theodore Roosevelt*	Charles W. Fairbanks
1908	William Jennings Bryan	John W. Kern	William Howard Taft*	James S. Sherman
1912	Woodrow Wilson*	Thomas R. Marshall	William Howard Taft	James S. Sherman[e] Nicholas Murray Butler[f]
1916	Woodrow Wilson*	Thomas R. Marshall	Charles Evans Hughes	Charles W. Fairbanks
1920	James M. Cox	Franklin D. Roosevelt	Warren G. Harding*	Calvin Coolidge
1924	John W. Davis	Charles W. Bryan	Calvin Coolidge*	Frank O. Lowden[b] Charles G. Dawes[c]
1928	Alfred E. Smith	Joseph T. Robinson	Herbert Hoover*	Charles Curtis
1932	Franklin D. Roosevelt*	John N. Garner	Herbert Hoover	Charles Curtis
1936	Franklin D. Roosevelt*	John N. Garner	Alfred M. Landon	Frank Knox
1940	Franklin D. Roosevelt*	Henry A. Wallace	Wendell L. Willkie	Charles L. McNary
1944	Franklin D. Roosevelt*	Harry S. Truman	Thomas E. Dewey	John W. Bricker
1948	Harry S. Truman*	Alben W. Barkley	Thomas E. Dewey	Earl Warren
1952	Adlai E. Stevenson	John J. Sparkman	Dwight D. Eisenhower*	Richard M. Nixon
1956	Adlai E. Stevenson	Estes Kefauver	Dwight D. Eisenhower*	Richard M. Nixon

[a] Winning party candidate is indicated by asterisk (*). William Henry Harrison and Zachary Taylor were Whig winners; the first nominee of the new Republican party was John C. Frémont.
[b] Nominated but refused.   [c] Named by convention.   [d] Named by Democratic national committee.
[e] Died October 30, 1912.   [f] Named by Republican national committee.

TABLE 2. PARTY COMPOSITION OF THE HOUSE OF REPRESENTATIVES BY REGIONS, 1897-1959[a]

Year	Number of Democratic Members from Each Region					Number of Republican Members from Each Region				
	NE	MW	S	W	Total	NE	MW	S	W	Total
1897	10	25	82	5	122	99	87	12	5	203
1899	35	31	94	3	163	74	93	7	11	185
1901	21	35	95	2	153	89	91	6	13	199
1903	32	36	105	5	178	88	99	4	15	206
1905	21	12	103	1	137	99	124	6	20	249
1907	28	31	106	1	166	92	104	7	20	223
1909	25	41	101	4	171	95	95	12	17	219
1911	55	61	107	4	227	64	73	7	17	161
1913	81	83	115	11	290	50	55	7	15	127
1915	41	61	115	10	227	94	80	7	17	198
1917	37	48	115	12	212	93	94	7	19	213
1919	40	27	114	10	191	95	113	7	22	237
1921	15	5	107	4	131	119	137	15	29	300
1923	48	34	115	9	206	88	106	7	24	225
1925	33	28	115	7	183	102	111	8	26	247
1927	39	33	116	7	195	97	107	7	26	237
Average, 1897–1927	35	37	107	6	185	90	98	8	18	214
1929	34	21	103	5	163	101	120	18	28	267
1931	46	50	117	7	220	90	92	6	26	214
1933	69	95	116	31	311	66	37	2	11	116
1935	84	87	117	34	322	51	39	3	9	102
1937	90	90	116	37	333	45	35	3	5	88
1939	60	54	116	30	260	73	80	3	13	169
1941	73	49	115	28	265	60	84	4	15	163
1943	53	25	118	26	222	79	102	4	23	208
1945	60	36	117	29	242	72	94	5	19	190
1947	36	20	115	17	188	96	110	7	32	245
1949	66	55	118	24	263	66	76	4	25	171
1951	60	36	116	22	234	73	93	6	27	199
1953	49	33	109	19	210	80	94	9	38	221
1955	58	44	110	20	232	71	85	10	37	203
1957	52	46	110	25	233	76	83	10	31	200
1959	72	67	111	32	282	56	61	9	26	152
Average, 1929–1959	60	51	114	24	249	72	80	6	23	181

[a] For each year in the table, the figures relate to the members of the House of Representatives elected in the previous year, with numbers and party affiliations as reported in the first issue of the *Congressional Directory* for each incoming Congress. Members unaffiliated with a major party and seats vacated through death after the election are omitted. The symbols NE, MW, S, and W refer to the four major regions as defined throughout the present book; see Table 10 of this appendix, for example, for a listing of states by regions.

See Chapter 3 for discussion of the data.

TABLE 3. NUMBERS OF STATES BY REGIONS IN WHICH THE THREE MAJOR STATE-WIDE ELECTIVE OFFICES (GOVERNOR AND U. S. SENATOR) WERE HELD BY MEMBERS OF THE SAME POLITICAL PARTY OR WERE DIVIDED BETWEEN THE PARTIES, 1897-1959[a]

(selected years)

Year	Democratic				Divided				Republican			
	NE	MW	S	W	NE	MW	S	W	NE	MW	S	W
1897	1	1	10	—	4	6[b]	2[b]	7[b]	7	5	—	2
1905	1	—	12	—	1	2	—	5	10	10	—	4
1913	1	1	11	4	8	6	2	4	3	5	—	3
1921	—	—	10	—	5	3	3	6	7	9	—	5
1929	1	—	11	1	2	4	2	7	9	8	—	3
1937[c]	4	5	13	8	6	5	—	3	2	1	—	—
1945	2	—	11	5	6	5	2	5	4	7	—	1
1953	2	1	12	—	3	5	1	8	7	6	—	3
1959	—	4	12	5	8	7	1	8	4	1	—	—
Average, 1897–1921	1	0[d]	11	1	4[e]	4	2	6[f]	7	7	0	3
Average, 1929–1953	2	2[f]	12	3[e]	4	5	1	6	6[f]	5[e]	0	2

[a] Sources: *Congressional Directory* for senators and, after 1905, the governors of the states and territories. Governors for 1897 and 1905 from *World Almanac* for those years. In the case of Colorado, where the governorship was a subject of contest in 1905, the Republican lieutenant governor who eventually became governor was counted in the tabulation. The 1959 figures include the new states, Alaska and Hawaii. See Chapter 3 for discussion of the data.

[b] In three states of the Midwest, one state of the South, and four states of the West, at least one Populist governor or senator was involved in the party division.

[c] All three offices were held by the Farmer-Labor party in Minnesota in 1937, which state was therefore omitted from the figures.

[d] Actually 0.5, rounded down to conform to total.

[e] Rounded down 0.5 to conform to total.

[f] Rounded up 0.5 to conform to total.

TABLE 4. A CLASSIFICATION OF STATES BY PARTY ALIGNMENT IN PRESIDENTIAL POLITICS[a]

1896–1924			1928–1956		
Democratic	Competitive	Republican	Democratic	Competitive	Republican
Virginia	Maryland	Maine	Massachusetts	New Hampshire	Maine
North Carolina		New Hampshire	Rhode Island	Connecticut	Vermont
South Carolina	Missouri	Vermont	West Virginia	New York	
Georgia	Nebraska	Massachusetts		New Jersey	Indiana
Florida	Kansas	Rhode Island	Missouri	Delaware	North Dakota
Kentucky		Connecticut		Maryland	South Dakota
Tennessee	Montana	New York	North Carolina	Pennsylvania	Nebraska
Alabama	Idaho	New Jersey	South Carolina		Kansas
Mississippi	Wyoming	Delaware	Georgia	Ohio	
Arkansas	Nevada	Pennsylvania	Kentucky	Michigan	
Louisiana	New Mexico	West Virginia	Alabama	Illinois	
Oklahoma	Arizona		Mississippi	Wisconsin	
Texas		Ohio	Arkansas	Minnesota	
		Michigan	Louisiana	Iowa	
Colorado		Indiana			
		Illinois		Virginia	
		Wisconsin		Florida	
		Minnesota		Tennessee	
		Iowa		Oklahoma	
		North Dakota		Texas	
		South Dakota			
				Montana	
		Utah		Idaho	
		Washington		Wyoming	
		Oregon		Colorado	
		California		Utah	
				Nevada	
				New Mexico	
				Arizona	
				Washington	
				Oregon	
				California	

[a] See Chapter 16 for discussion of the data and Table 16.6 for a note on the classification system. In each category the states are arranged in accordance with a standard geographic system of listing, with regional divisions indicated by space separations.

TABLE 5. NUMBER AND PER CENT OF WOMEN IN 1952 DEMOCRATIC CONVENTION DELEGATIONS; STATES IN PERCENTAGE RANK WITHIN REGIONS[a]

Region and State	Number	Per Cent[b]	Region and State	Number	Per Cent[b]
Middle West	57	12.8%	*Northeast*	34	7.8%
Missouri	12	29	Vermont	3	30
North Dakota	4	25	Maine	4	29
Iowa	9	20	New Hampshire	3	25
Kansas	3	15	Rhode Island	3	15
Minnesota	5	15	West Virginia	3	11
Wisconsin	5	14	Maryland	3	8
Michigan	8	11	Massachusetts	4	6
Indiana	3	10	New Jersey	2	6
Illinois	5	7	Connecticut	1	5
Ohio	3	5	Pennsylvania	4	5
Nebraska	0	0	New York	4	4
South Dakota	0	0	Delaware	0	0
West	63	21.6%	*South*	45	10.3%
California	27	36	Florida	12	50
Washington	10	31	Kentucky	8	22
Montana	5	25	Georgia	4	11
Arizona	4	20	Tennessee	4	11
Utah	4	20	Arkansas	3	9
Idaho	4	17	North Carolina	4	9
Nevada	3	15	Oklahoma	3	8
Wyoming	3	15	Virginia	3	8
Colorado	2	8	South Carolina	1	5
New Mexico	1	4	Louisiana	1	4
Oregon	0	0	Texas	2	3
			Alabama	0	0
			Mississippi	0	0
			Non-State Areas	5	17.6%
			Alaska	2	33
			District of Columbia	2	17
			Puerto Rico	1	17
			Hawaii	0	0

[a] Compiled from official delegate lists by the staff of the Brookings Institution on the basis of the apparent sex of delegates as indicated by their names; the staff of the Democratic national committee was consulted in connection with a few cases where the name did not clearly appear to indicate the sex of the delegate.

See Chapter 14 for discussion of the data.

[b] The percentages for the states have been rounded; those for the regions have not.

Region and State	Number	Per Cent[b]	Region and State	Number	Per Cent[b]
Middle West	32	8.6%	*Northeast*	40	10.9%
Minnesota	8	29	Vermont	3	25
Wisconsin	5	17	Connecticut	5	23
Iowa	3	12	Maine	3	19
Missouri	3	12	Maryland	4	17
Kansas	2	9	Massachusetts	5	13
Ohio	5	9	Rhode Island	1	13
North Dakota	1	7	New York	10	10
South Dakota	1	7	New Jersey	3	8
Indiana	2	6	Pennsylvania	5	7
Illinois	1	2	West Virginia	1	6
Michigan	1	2	Delaware	0	0
Nebraska	0	0	New Hampshire	0	0
West	36	16.5%	*South*	17	7.4%
Montana	3	38	Florida	5	28
Idaho	5	36	South Carolina	1	17
Utah	3	21	Louisiana	2	13
Washington	5	21	Texas	5	13
Nevada	2	17	Arkansas	1	9
California	11	16	Alabama	1	7
New Mexico	2	14	Oklahoma	1	6
Colorado	2	11	North Carolina	1	4
Wyoming	1	8	Georgia	0	0
Arizona	1	7	Kentucky	0	0
Oregon	1	6	Mississippi	0	0
			Tennessee	0	0
			Virginia	0	0
			Non-State Areas	2	9.5%
			District of Columbia	2	33
			Alaska	0	0
			Hawaii	0	0
			Puerto Rico	0	0

[a] Compiled from official delegate lists by the staff of the Brookings Institution on the basis of the apparent sex of delegates as indicated by their names; the staff of the Republican national committee was consulted in connection with a few cases where the name did not clearly appear to indicate the sex of the delegate.
See Chapter 14 for discussion of the data.
[b] The percentages for the states have been rounded; those for the regions have not.

TABLE 7. ORGANIZED LABOR AT THE DEMOCRATIC NATIONAL CONVENTION, 1952[a]

(A Classification of Fifty-Two Delegations in Categories on the Basis of the Number of Labor Union Members in Each Delegation, Where Specific Information Was Available)

Category 1: Apparently No Union Officials or Representatives Among Delegates	Category 2: Presence by Chance of One or More Union Members as Delegates	Category 3: Representation by Special Allotment of One to Three Seats for Labor Delegates or Alternates	Category 4: Substantial Number of Labor Delegates in Relation to Size of Delegation
NORTHEAST			
New Hampshire	1: Maryland	1: Maine	6: Massachusetts[b]
New York	1: West Virginia	2: Vermont[c]	4: New Jersey
Delaware		2: Rhode Island	8: Pennsylvania
		2: Connecticut	
MIDDLE WEST			
South Dakota	1: Nebraska	1: Indiana	4: Ohio
		2: Iowa	17: Michigan
		1: Missouri	6: Illinois
		1: North Dakota	9: Wisconsin
		1: Kansas	12: Minnesota
SOUTH			
Virginia	1: North Carolina	2: Georgia	
South Carolina			
Florida		3: Kentucky	
Tennessee	1: Oklahoma	3: Arkansas	
Alabama		1: Texas	
Mississippi			
Louisiana			
WEST			
Idaho	1: Montana	1: Utah[c]	4: Colorado
Wyoming		2: Washington	2: Nevada
New Mexico			5: California[d]
Arizona			
Oregon			
NON-STATE AREAS			
Puerto Rico	1: Hawaii		3: District of Columbia
			2: Alaska
Total	7	22[e]	82

[a] Based on information compiled from David, Moos, and Goldman, *Presidential Nominating Politics in 1952* (1954) supplemented by additional information obtained through interviews and correspondence. Clarence A. Berdahl supplied information for the Illinois delegation and G. Edward Janosik supplied information for the Pennsylvania delegation.

See Chapter 14 for discussion of the data.

[b] The Massachusetts delegation was said to have included twelve labor union officials among the delegates and alternates; the figure of six delegates used here is an estimate.

[c] Alternate delegates.

[d] "About ten labor officials" were also included among the California alternates and sub-alternates.

[e] Does not include the alternate delegates of Vermont and Utah.

TABLE 8. COMMITMENT AND CANDIDATE AGREEMENT OF DEMOCRATIC DELEGATIONS OF 1952 WHEN SELECTED[a]

Status of Delegations by Majority Commitment[b]	Index of Candidate Agreement, Per Cent[c]	Apparent Distribution of Voting Strength When Selected, Number					Elected in Public Primaries, Number	Selected by Party Processes, Number
		Steven-son	Kefau-ver	Rus-sell	Others	Unde-cided or Unknown		
Firmly Bound to a Leading Candidate[d]								
New Hampshire	100.0%	8					8	
Wisconsin	100.0	28					28	
Oregon	100.0	12					12	
California	100.0	68					68	
Maryland	100.0	18						18
South Carolina*	100.0			16				16
Tennessee*	100.0	28						28
Subtotal	100.0	162		16			116	62
Preferring a Leading Candidate[e]								
Ohio	50.0%		27		27		54	
South Dakota	100.0		8				8	
Florida	79.1		5	19			24	
Rhode Island*	100.0	12						12
Virginia*	100.0			28				28
Georgia*	100.0			28				28
Subtotal	79.2	12	40	75	27		86	68
Committed to a Non-Leading Candidate[d]								
Minnesota	100.0%				26		20½	5½
Connecticut*	100.0				16			16
Michigan*	100.0				40			40
Kentucky*	100.0				26			26
Oklahoma*	100.0				24			24
District of Columbia*	100.0				6			6
Puerto Rico*	100.0				6			6
Alaska*	100.0				6			6
Hawaii	100.0				6			6
Subtotal	100.0				156		20½	135½

[a] For discussion of data, see Chapter 15. The table is compiled from David, Moos, and Goldman, *Presidential Nominating Politics in 1952* (1954).

[b] Delegations operating under the unit rule are indicated by an asterisk (*); see Chapter 9.

[c] The largest bloc of committed or preferring votes as a percentage of total delegation strength.

[d] In these cases commitment took the form of a statutory pledge imposed through a primary or a resolution of instruction imposed by state party authority.

[e] In these cases preference was expressed or implied by recording the name of a preferred candidate on the ballot, or by winning election in a contest on a basis of apparent known candidate preferences, or by winning election uncontested because of an assumed candidate preference, or by holding a known candidate preference at a time of selection in a party body.

Delegations in which precisely half preferred a leading candidate are also included in this category, since, in all such cases observed in 1952, the remainder of the delegation was either divided or had a merely formal preference for a favorite son candidate.

TABLE 8 *(continued)*

Status of Delegations by Majority Commitment[b]	Index of Candidate Agreement, Per Cent[c]	Apparent Distribution of Voting Strength When Selected, Number					Elected in Public Primaries, Number	Selected by Party Processes, Number
		Steven-son	Kefau-ver	Rus-sell	Others	Unde-cided or Unknown		
Preference Undecided or Unknown								
Massachusetts						36	36	
New York						94	90	4
New Jersey						32	32	
Pennsylvania						70	60	10
West Virginia						20	20	
Illinois						60	50	10
Nebraska						12	12	
Alabama						22	22	
Maine						10		10
Vermont						6		6
Delaware*						6		6
Indiana						26		26
Iowa						24		24
Missouri						34		34
North Dakota*						8		8
Kansas*	21.0%	3½		3		9½	16	
North Carolina						32		32
Mississippi*						18		18
Arkansas						22		22
Louisiana*						20		20
Texas*						52		52
Montana*						12		12
Idaho*						12		12
Wyoming						10		10
Colorado						16		16
Utah						12		12
Nevada						10		10
New Mexico						12		12
Arizona*						12		12
Washington						22		22
Virgin Islands						2		2
Canal Zone						2		2
Subtotal	0.4	3½		3		735½	322	420
Total (1,230 votes)	38.2%	15½	202	91	186	735½	544½	685½

Status of Delegations by Majority Commitment	Index of Candidate Agreement, Per Cent[b]	Apparent Distribution of Voting Strength When Selected, Number				Elected in Public Primaries, Number	Selected by Party Processes, Number
		Eisen-hower	Taft	Others	Unde-cided or Unknown		
Firmly Bound to a Leading Candidate[c]							
Wisconsin	80.0%		24	6		30	
Oregon	100.0	18				18	
Vermont	100.0	12					12
Indiana	93.7	2[d]	30				32
Kentucky	95.0	1[e]	19				20
Tennessee	100.0		20				20
Mississippi	100.0		5				5
Subtotal	93.4	33	98	6		48	89
Preferring a Leading Candidate[f]							
New Hampshire	100.0%	14				14	
Massachusetts	73.7	28	3		7	38	
New York		6					6
New York	90.6	81	1		8	90	
West Virginia	37.5	1	15			16	
Ohio	100.0		56			56	
Illinois			10				10
Illinois	98.0	1	49			50	
South Dakota	100.0		14			14	
Maine	68.8	11	5				16
Rhode Island	100.0	8					8
Connecticut	90.9	20			2		22
Iowa	57.7	15	9		2		26
Missouri	92.3	24	2				26
North Dakota	57.1	1	8		5		14
Kansas	90.9	20	2				22
Virginia	60.9	1	14		8		23
South Carolina	100.0		6				6
Georgia	76.5	13	2	1	1		17
Alabama	64.3	4	9		1		14
Arkansas	90.9	1	10				11
Louisiana	86.7	13	2				15
Texas	86.8	33	5				38
Montana	87.5	1	7				8
Idaho[g]	100.0		14				14
Wyoming	50.0	2	6		4		12
Colorado	83.3	15	2	1			18
Utah	100.0		14				14
New Mexico	50.0	3	7		4		14
Arizona	71.4	2	10		2		14
Washington	83.3	20	4				24
Alaska	100.0		3				3
District of Columbia	100.0		6				6
Subtotal	85.3	338	295	2	44	278	401

TABLE 9 *(continued)*

Status of Delegations by Majority Commitment	Index of Candidate Agreement, Per Cent[b]	Apparent Distribution of Voting Strength When Selected, Number				Elected in Public Primaries, Number	Selected by Party Processes, Number
		Eisenhower	Taft	Others	Undecided or Unknown		
Committed to a Non-Leading Candidate[c]							
California	100.0%			70		70	
Minnesota		4		3			7
Minnesota	85.7			21		21	
Maryland	100.0			24			24
Subtotal	96.7	4		118		91	31
Divided Between Leading Candidates							
North Carolina	34.6%	5	9		12		26
Oklahoma	43.8	5	7	4			16
Subtotal	38.0	10	16	4	12		42
Preference Undecided or Unknown							
New Jersey	5.3%		2		36	38	
Pennsylvania		2	3	2	3		10
Pennsylvania	17.1	7	9		44	60	
Nebraska					18	18	
Michigan	15.2	7	6		33		46
Delaware					12		12
Florida					18		18
Nevada					12		12
Hawaii					8		8
Puerto Rico					3		3
Virgin Islands					1		1
Subtotal	9.3	16	20	2	188	116	110
Total (1,206 votes)	71.5%	401	429	132	244	533	673

[a] See footnote a, Table 8.
[b] See footnote c, Table 8.
[c] See footnote d, Table 8.
[d] District delegates who preferred Eisenhower without being formally committed and who refused to accept the action of the state convention in instructing the entire delegation for Taft.
[e] One delegate who preferred Eisenhower without being formally committed was specifically exempted from convention action instructing the other delegates for Taft.
[f] See footnote e, Table 8.
[g] Idaho was "uninstructed" but "honor bound" to support Taft, with a unit rule to facilitate enforcement of majority preference in the delegation.

TABLE 10. STATE VOTING STRENGTH, CONTRIBUTION TO WINNER, AND WINNER-SUPPORT RATIOS IN CONTESTED CONVENTIONS BY PERIODS[a]

(Column A: Voting Strength, Average Per Cent; B: Contribution to Winner, Average Per Cent; C: Winner-Support Ratio, B/A[b])

Region and State	Democratic 1896-1924			Democratic 1928-1956			Republican 1896-1924			Republican 1928-1956		
	A	B	C	A	B	C	A	B	C	A	B	C
Northeast												
Maine	1.16%	1.00%	0.86	0.95%	1.28%	1.35	1.21%	0.77%	0.64	1.30%	1.83%	1.41
New Hampshire	0.77	0.65	0.84	0.72	0.84	1.17	0.81	0.61	0.75	0.93	1.54	1.66
Vermont	0.77	1.10	1.43	0.56	0.80	1.43	0.81	1.15	1.42	0.93	1.50	1.60
Massachusetts	3.25	2.15	0.66	3.03	3.14	1.03	3.41	2.53	0.74	3.33	5.03	1.51
Rhode Island	0.87	0.66	0.76	0.95	1.21	1.27	0.93	1.07	1.15	0.84	1.08	1.29
Connecticut	1.32	1.02	0.77	1.42	1.79	1.26	1.37	2.03	1.48	1.69	2.25	1.33
New York	8.01	5.88	0.73	7.89	7.51	0.95	8.38	8.15	0.97	8.54	14.69	1.72
New Jersey	2.44	1.97	0.81	2.73	3.34	1.22	2.58	2.07	0.80	3.10	4.74	1.53
Delaware	0.58	0.26	0.45	0.61	0.92	1.51	0.61	0.81	1.33	0.82	1.16	1.41
Maryland	1.54	1.65	1.07	1.45	1.41	0.97	1.62	1.50	0.93	1.71	2.62	1.53
Pennsylvania	6.88	7.64	1.11	6.14	8.32	1.35	7.27	0.92	0.13	6.70	8.03	1.20
West Virginia	1.42	1.48	1.04	1.56	1.80	1.15	1.49	1.42	0.95	1.53	0.87	0.57
Total	29.01	25.46	0.88	28.01	32.36	1.16	30.49	23.03	0.76	31.42	45.34	1.44
Middle West												
Ohio	4.54%	5.22%	1.15	4.37%	3.82%	0.88	4.76%	5.42%	1.14	4.83%	1.54%	0.32
Michigan	2.80	3.62	1.29	3.23	4.73	1.47	2.95	3.99	1.35	3.60	2.83	0.78
Indiana	2.89	3.71	1.28	2.31	2.37	1.02	3.03	2.34	0.77	2.78	2.24	0.81
Illinois	5.30	5.70	1.08	4.99	6.17	1.24	5.58	1.96	0.35	5.35	2.24	0.42
Wisconsin	2.48	2.07	0.83	2.17	2.47	1.14	2.58	1.38	0.53	2.44	0.46	0.19
Minnesota	2.16	1.41	0.65	2.11	2.67	1.26	2.26	1.54	0.68	2.32	1.21	0.52
Iowa	2.51	1.76	0.70	1.97	2.51	1.27	2.62	1.61	0.61	2.28	1.79	0.78
Missouri	3.44	2.30	0.67	2.89	2.15	0.74	3.59	5.53	1.54	2.92	3.66	1.25
North Dakota	0.84	0.61	0.73	0.72	1.06	1.47	0.89	0.54	0.61	1.05	0.50	0.48
South Dakota	0.87	0.79	0.91	0.72	0.81	1.13	0.93	0.61	0.66	1.05	0.42	0.39
Nebraska	1.54	1.30	0.84	1.14	1.27	1.11	1.62	1.30	0.80	1.50	1.08	0.72
Kansas	1.93	2.22	1.15	1.47	1.79	1.22	2.02	2.76	1.37	1.87	2.16	1.16
Total	31.30	30.71	0.98	28.09	31.82	1.13	32.83	28.98	0.88	31.99	20.13	0.63

South

Virginia	2.32%	3.23%	1.39	2.17%	0.25%	0.12	2.06%	2.44%	1.18	1.75%	2.00%	1.14
North Carolina	2.28	2.82	1.24	2.45	2.34	0.96	2.28	2.63	1.15	2.16	2.41	1.12
South Carolina	1.74	2.30	1.32	1.50	0.75	0.50	1.53	2.38	1.56	0.75	0.92	1.23
Georgia	2.61	2.85	1.09	2.34	1.08	0.46	2.30	2.84	1.23	1.44	2.00	1.38
Florida	1.03	1.15	1.12	1.56	1.07	0.69	0.93	1.65	1.77	1.28	1.29	1.00
Kentucky	2.51	3.23	1.29	2.17	2.09	0.96	2.62	4.26	1.63	2.19	1.71	0.78
Tennessee	2.32	2.58	1.11	2.20	1.63	0.74	2.28	3.53	1.55	1.80	1.37	0.76
Alabama	2.22	2.02	0.91	2.00	1.27	0.64	1.94	2.92	1.51	1.28	1.46	1.13
Mississippi	1.90	2.50	1.32	1.67	0.79	0.47	1.66	2.40	1.45	0.82	0.50	0.61
Arkansas	1.70	1.38	0.81	1.72	2.07	1.20	1.62	2.00	1.23	1.09	0.83	0.76
Louisiana	1.80	2.73	1.52	1.78	1.75	0.98	1.57	2.57	1.64	1.18	1.24	1.05
Oklahoma	1.58	1.61	1.02	1.95	1.17	0.60	1.74	1.96	1.13	1.78	1.12	0.63
Texas	3.56	3.89	1.09	4.03	0.00	0.00	3.13	4.23	1.35	2.80	2.53	0.91
Total	27.57	32.29	1.17	27.54	16.26	0.59	25.66	35.81	1.40	20.32	19.38	0.95

West

Montana	0.68%	0.64%	0.94	0.89%	1.21%	1.36	0.73%	0.58%	0.79	0.87%	0.87%	1.00
Idaho	0.68	0.68	1.00	0.83	1.25	1.51	0.73	0.46	0.63	1.00	1.00	1.00
Wyoming	0.58	0.69	1.19	0.67	1.00	1.49	0.61	1.15	1.90	0.82	1.00	1.22
Colorado	1.03	1.12	1.09	1.17	1.46	1.25	1.13	1.04	0.92	1.37	1.58	1.15
Utah	0.68	0.74	1.09	0.83	1.16	1.39	0.73	1.00	1.37	1.00	0.83	0.84
Nevada	0.58	0.61	1.05	0.72	0.66	0.92	0.61	0.86	1.41	0.82	1.00	1.22
New Mexico	0.61	0.36	0.59	0.81	1.02	1.26	0.57	0.61	1.07	0.84	0.83	0.99
Arizona	0.58	0.47	0.81	0.81	0.96	1.19	0.52	0.69	1.33	0.84	0.96	1.13
Washington	1.12	1.05	0.94	1.59	1.98	1.25	1.20	1.42	1.18	1.73	2.12	1.22
Oregon	0.87	0.89	1.02	1.03	1.31	1.27	0.93	1.04	1.12	1.21	1.83	1.50
California	2.18	1.35	0.62	4.22	3.97	0.93	2.33	1.95	0.84	4.47	1.92	0.43
Total	9.59	8.61	0.90	13.57	15.98	1.18	10.09	10.80	1.07	14.97	13.94	0.93

Non-State Areas

Alaska	0.58%	0.87%	1.50	0.50%	0.50%	1.00	0.24%	0.39%	1.63	0.25%	0.25%	1.00
Canal Zone	0.13	0.15	1.15	0.35	0.40	1.14	—	—	—	—	—	—
District of Columbia	0.58	0.61	1.05	0.50	0.75	1.50	0.16	0.19	1.19	0.32	0.30	0.94
Hawaii	0.48	0.51	1.06	0.50	0.73	1.46	0.24	0.42	1.75	0.41	0.38	0.93
Philippine Islands	0.29	0.20	0.69	0.25	0.25	1.00	0.16	0.15	0.94	0.09	0.12	1.33
Puerto Rico	0.48	0.58	1.21	0.50	0.69	1.38	0.13	0.23	1.77	0.21	0.12	0.57
Virgin Islands	—	—	—	0.18	0.27	1.50	—	—	—	0.02	0.04	1.83
Total	2.54	2.93	1.15	2.78	3.59	1.29	0.93	1.38	1.48	1.30	1.21	0.93

[a] See Chapter 16, Table 16.5, and related text.

[b] Winner-support ratios are calculated directly from the actual voting records, and due to rounding may deviate slightly from the B/A ratios based upon the percentages in the table. See the following page for a brief discussion of levels of statistical significance in this table.

A Note on Levels of Statistical Significance in Table 10

Some guidelines can be offered even though no effort has been made to compute significance levels for all of the states under all of the various conditions presented. In general, any winner-support ratio in the table can be considered either significant or highly significant, as the case may be, if it departs from an average ratio of 1.00 by the amounts indicated below, plus or minus, for a state of approximately the same size in the party and time period in question.

	Democratic		Republican	
	1896–1924	1928–1956	1896–1924	1928–1956
Significant Departures from 1.00:				
Smallest States	.16	.15	.16	.16
Medium States	.09	.08	.10	.11
Largest State	.05	.04	.05	.05
Highly Significant Departures from 1.00:				
Smallest States	.24	.23	.24	.24
Medium States	.15	.12	.15	.17
Largest State	.07	.06	.08	.08

On the basis of these criteria, for example, it can be said that Maine, one of the smallest states, showed a highly significant tendency to oppose winners in Republican conventions during the period 1896-1924 and to support them during the period 1928-1956 (ratios 0.64, 1.41).

For comparisons between individual states, the general level of significance of the difference can be estimated by using the larger figure for the size of states being compared. For example, in comparing Delaware with New York for the Democratic period 1896-1924, the difference between the ratios would have to be at least .16 to be considered significant, and .24 to be highly significant. The difference was, in fact, more than either of these amounts.

States are defined as "smallest," "medium," or "largest" for the purposes of the above tabulation in accordance with their rank in average convention voting strength as shown in Table 10. The smallest states are in general those holding less than 1.5 per cent of the convention voting strength; medium states, those holding more than 1.5 but less than 3.0 per cent; and the largest states, those holding more than 3.0 per cent.

Delegations by Size	Average Winner-Support Ratio[b]	Number of Times in Winner-Support Category[c]			Delegations by Size	Average Winner-Support Ratio[b]	Number of Times in Winner-Support Category[c]		
		Below 0.90	0.90 to 1.10	Above 1.10			Below 0.90	0.90 to 1.10	Above 1.10
Large States					Montana	1.36	0	1	5
Pennsylvania	1.35	0	1	5	Maine	1.35	0	0	6
Illinois	1.24	1	0	5	Oregon	1.27	1	0	5
New York	0.95	3	0	3	Rhode Island	1.27	1	0	5
California	0.93	2	0	4	Connecticut	1.26	1	0	5
Ohio	0.88	2	1	3	New Mexico	1.26	0	0	6
Texas	0.00	6	0	0	Colorado	1.25	0	2	4
					Washington	1.25	0	2	4
Total	0.94	14	2	20	Kansas	1.22	1	0	5
					Arkansas	1.20	1	0	5
Middle States					Arizona	1.19	1	0	5
Michigan	1.47	0	0	6	New Hampshire	1.17	1	1	4
Iowa	1.27	1	1	4	West Virginia	1.15	1	3	2
Minnesota	1.26	0	2	4	South Dakota	1.13	2	0	4
New Jersey	1.22	1	0	5	Nebraska	1.11	1	1	4
Wisconsin	1.14	1	1	4	Louisiana	0.98	2	0	4
Massachusetts	1.03	2	0	4	Maryland	0.97	3	0	3
Indiana	1.02	2	0	4	Nevada	0.92	3	0	3
Kentucky	0.96	2	0	4	Florida	0.69	3	1	2
North Carolina	0.96	3	0	3	Oklahoma	0.60	4	0	2
Tennessee	0.74	3	0	3	South Carolina	0.50	4	0	2
Missouri	0.74	2	2	2	Mississippi	0.47	4	0	2
Alabama	0.64	3	2	1					
Georgia	0.46	4	0	2	Total	1.09	34	11	123
Virginia	0.12	6	0	0					
					Non-State Areas				
Total	0.95	30	8	46	District of Col.	1.50	0	0	6
					Virgin Islands	1.50	0	0	6
Small States					Hawaii	1.46	0	0	6
Idaho	1.51	0	0	6	Puerto Rico	1.38	1	0	5
Delaware	1.51	0	0	6	Canal Zone	1.14	1	0	5
Wyoming	1.49	0	0	6	Philippine Is.[d]	1.00	1	0	2
North Dakota	1.47	0	0	6	Alaska	1.00	2	0	4
Vermont	1.43	0	0	6					
Utah	1.39	0	0	6	Total	1.33	5	0	34

[a] Each group of state delegations approximated one third of the total convention voting strength. Large delegations were those ranging between 7.89 and 4.02 per cent in convention voting strength; middle delegations, those between 3.22 and 2.17 per cent; small state delegations, those between 1.95 and 0.56 per cent; and non-state delegations ranged between 0.50 and 0.18 per cent.
  See Chapter 16 for discussion of the data.
[b] Average for six contested conventions.
[c] Delegations were assigned to categories represented by the columns in accordance with their winner-support ratios in individual conventions.
[d] Conventions of 1940 and before only.

Delegations by Size	Average Winner-Support Ratio[b]	Number of Times in Winner-Support Category[c]			Delegations by Size	Average Winner-Support Ratio[b]	Number of Times in Winner-Support Category[c]		
		Below 0.90	0.90 to 1.10	Above 1.10			Below 0.90	0.90 to 1.10	Above 1.10
Large States					Georgia	1.38	0	1	3
New York	1.72	0	0	4	Connecticut	1.33	1	0	3
Pennsylvania	1.20	1	0	3	Rhode Island	1.29	0	2	2
Michigan	0.78	2	0	2	South Carolina	1.23	2	0	2
California	0.43	3	0	1	Wyoming	1.22	0	2	2
Illinois	0.42	3	1	0	Nevada	1.22	1	0	3
Ohio	0.32	3	1	0	Washington	1.22	1	0	3
					Colorado	1.15	1	1	2
Total	0.93	12	2	10	Alabama	1.13	1	1	2
Middle States					Arizona	1.13	1	1	2
New Jersey	1.53	0	0	4	Louisiana	1.05	1	1	2
Massachusetts	1.51	0	1	3	Montana	1.00	1	1	2
Missouri	1.25	0	1	3	Florida	1.00	2	0	2
Kansas	1.16	1	0	3	Idaho	1.00	2	0	2
Virginia	1.14	1	0	3	New Mexico	0.99	2	1	1
North Carolina	1.12	0	1	3	Utah	0.84	1	1	2
Texas	0.91	2	0	2	Arkansas	0.76	3	0	1
Indiana	0.81	2	0	2	Nebraska	0.72	4	0	0
Iowa	0.78	2	0	2	Mississippi	0.61	3	0	1
Kentucky	0.78	2	1	1	West Virginia	0.57	3	0	1
Tennessee	0.76	3	0	1	North Dakota	0.48	3	1	0
Oklahoma	0.63	3	0	1	South Dakota	0.39	3	0	1
Minnesota	0.52	4	0	0					
Wisconsin	0.19	4	0	0	Total	1.11	38	13	61
					Non-State Areas				
Total	0.97	24	4	28	Virgin Islands[d]	1.82	0	0	1
Small States					Philippine Is.[d]	1.37	0	0	2
New Hampshire	1.66	0	0	4	Hawaii	1.02	2	0	2
Vermont	1.60	0	0	4	District of Col.	0.91	1	0	3
Maryland	1.53	0	0	4	Alaska	0.83	2	0	2
Oregon	1.50	1	0	3	Puerto Rico	0.61	2	0	2
Delaware	1.41	0	0	4					
Maine	1.41	1	0	3	Total	0.99	7	0	12

[a] Each group of state delegations approximated one third of the total convention voting strength. Large delegations were those ranging between 8.54 and 3.60 per cent in convention voting strength; middle delegations, those between 3.33 and 1.75 per cent; small state delegations, those between 1.73 and 0.75 per cent; and non-state delegations ranged between 0.41 and 0.02 per cent. For discussion of the data, see Chapter 16.

[b] Average for four contested conventions.

[c] Delegations were assigned to categories represented by the columns in accordance with their winner-support ratios in individual conventions.

[d] Part of the period only.

TABLE 13. NOMINATING PATTERNS AND ELECTORAL SUCCESS[a]

Year	Party in Power, Party and Nominee	Party Out of Power, Party and Nominee	Opposed Nominating Types[b]		Ratio of In-Party Vote to Out-Party Vote[c]
1936	(D) F. D. Roosevelt	(R) Landon	A/C	S/S	1.65
1904	(R) T. Roosevelt	(D) Parker	A/C	S/S	1.50
1928	(R) Hoover	(D) Smith	B/B	S/S	1.42
1956	(R) Eisenhower	(D) Stevenson	A/A	S/S	1.38
1832	(D) Jackson	(NR) Clay	A/B	S/S	1.30
1872	(R) Grant	(D) Greeley	A/C	S/S	1.27
1864	(R) Lincoln	(D) McClellan	A/C	S/S	1.22
1908	(R) Taft	(D) Bryan	B/A	S/S	1.20
1900	(R) McKinley	(D) Bryan	A/A	S/S	1.14
1948	(D) Truman	(R) Dewey	A/A	S/M	1.10
1916	(D) Wilson	(R) Hughes	A/C	S/M	1.07
1892	(R) B. Harrison	(D) Cleveland	A/A	S/S	0.93*
1924	(R) Coolidge	(D) Davis	A/D	S/M	1.87
1868	(R) Grant	(D) Seymour	C/D	S/M	1.11
1844	(W) Clay	(D) Polk	B/D	S/M	0.97*
1940	(D) F. D. Roosevelt	(R) Willkie	A/E	S/M	1.20
1944	(D) F. D. Roosevelt	(R) Dewey	A/E	S/S	1.13
1888	(D) Cleveland	(R) B. Harrison	A/E	S/M	1.02*
1848	(D) Cass	(W) Taylor	C/E	M/M	0.90*
1840	(D) Van Buren	(W) W. H. Harrison	A/E	S/M	0.88*
1932	(R) Hoover	(D) F. D. Roosevelt	A/E	S/M	0.69*
1912	(R) Taft	(D) Wilson	A/E	S/M	0.55*
1880	(R) Garfield	(D) Hancock	D/C	M/M	1.01
1876	(R) Hayes	(D) Tilden	D/E	M/M	0.94[d]
1856	(D) Buchanan	(R) Frémont	E/C	M/M	1.37
1884	(R) Blaine	(D) Cleveland	E/C	M/M	0.99*
1852	(W) Scott	(D) Pierce	E/D	M/M	0.87*
1920	(D) Cox	(R) Harding	E/D	M/M	0.57*
1896	(D) Bryan	(R) McKinley	E/E	M/S	0.90*
1952	(D) Stevenson	(R) Eisenhower	E/E	M/S	0.81*
1860	(D) Douglas	(R) Lincoln	E/E	M/M	0.74*

[a] For the years 1832 and 1840-1956; includes all cases in which both major parties nominated their candidates in national conventions.
See Chapter 18 for discussion of the data.
[b] The first pair of symbols indicates the categories of the respective nominees on the basis of the classification developed in Chapter 6, and used in Table 18.6 of Chapter 18; the second pair of symbols indicates whether each nominee was a single- or multi-ballot choice of his convention. In each pair the in-party nominee appears first.
[c] Out-party win is indicated by asterisk (*).
[d] The vote was contested in several states, and Hayes won by an electoral majority of one when all contests were decided in his favor.

B

States with Presidential Primary Laws

THE FOLLOWING SIX states that had authorized presidential primaries by 1916 used them only in the years indicated before repealing them, or letting them fall into disuse:[1]

Iowa	1916
Vermont	1916-1920
North Carolina	1920 (Rep. only)
Michigan	1916-1928
North Dakota	1912-1932
Georgia	1912, 1920-24, 1932 (Dem. only)

Fifteen states have had some form of presidential primary legislation continuously in effect in presidential years since 1916. In most of these, delegates have been elected in primaries in both political parties in each presidential year. Maryland, however, has only a preference poll; the delegates are chosen by party conventions. The fifteen states and the first year in which they held a presidential primary are as follows:

Florida	1904 (Dem. only until 1956)
Wisconsin	1908
Massachusetts	1912
New York	1912
New Jersey	1912
Pennsylvania	1912
Maryland	1912
Illinois	1912
South Dakota	1912
Nebraska	1912
Oregon	1912
California	1912
New Hampshire	1916
West Virginia	1916
Ohio	1916

Three states recently resumed the holding of presidential primaries. Primaries were held in these states as follows:

Minnesota	1916, 1952, 1956 (repealed 1959)
Indiana	1916–1928, 1956
Montana	1916–1924, 1956 (repealed 1959)

In Indiana and Montana in 1956, as in Maryland, delegates were elected in party conventions and the presidential primary consisted only of a preference poll.

Alabama is the only state in addition to those listed that has held any form of presidential primary in recent years. It enacted legislation in 1923 that was held unconstitutional, but Democratic party authorities held a primary nonetheless for the Democratic national convention of 1924, where Oscar W. Underwood of Alabama, Democratic floor leader of the Senate, was vigorously supported.[2] Alabama delegates to Democratic national conventions have been elected in primaries most of the time since 1924.[3]

Arkansas enacted legislation in 1939 to authorize presidential primaries, to be held at the request of one or more candidates for a presidential nomination and at their expense. It was estimated in 1952 that the normal expense of holding a Democratic primary in Arkansas would be at least $65,000.[4] The law is still in effect, but no presidential primary has been held.

[2] Louise Overacker, *The Presidential Primary* (1926), items indexed under Alabama.
[3] After reviewing available state sources, notably the *Alabama Official and Statistical Register*, Professor Donald S. Strong has concluded that Democratic presidential primaries were held in 1928 and 1932, not in 1936, and in all presidential years from 1940 on. (Letter, March 20, 1958.)
[4] Paul T. David, Malcolm Moos, and Ralph M. Goldman, *Presidential Nominating Politics in 1952* (1954), Vol. 3, pp. 243-44.

[1] All information in Appendix B is given as of August 1959.

C

Experience of States with Presidential Primaries for Election of Delegates

THE STATE presidential primary systems that operate primarily to elect delegates to the national party conventions can be classified in one or another of four categories, as defined in Chapter 10. In this appendix, the salient features of the experience in each state system are briefly noted.[1]

Category One

The ballot *must not* show the delegate's preferences among candidates. Delegates must run on a "no-preference" basis so far as the ballot is concerned. Six states and the District of Columbia use this system.

New York

New York is the prime example of a simple direct-election system for delegates, with no identification of delegates with presidential candidates on the ballot and no presidential preference poll. The delegates may, of course, state their preferences in campaigning. In 1912 the law was optional, applied only to district delegates, and was used only in the Republican party. In a contest among pledged delegates, "a few [Theodore] Roosevelt candidates for district delegates were elected against the opposition of the organization."[2] In 1916 and 1920 the law was compulsory both for delegates at large and for district delegates who were elected separately in their own congressional districts.[3] A delegation pledged to President Woodrow Wilson was elected in 1916, but the delegates ran unpledged on the Republican side in 1916 and in both parties in 1920. After 1920 the law was amended to permit election of the delegates at large by state convention or committee.

The election of district delegates by primary has remained compulsory since 1924. They usually run unpledged and unopposed after nomination by party organizations. Other would-be delegates who favor out-of-state presidential candidates at times campaign but rarely win, and out-of-state candidates rarely involve themselves in delegate selection processes in New York. An incumbent governor who seeks a presi-

[1] The following summaries of experience in the several states are based primarily upon a comparative review of the following materials: Louise Overacker, *The Presidential Primary* (1926), including its appendix tables as well as the items indexed by states; Paul T. David, Malcolm Moos, and Ralph M. Goldman, *Presidential Nominating Politics in 1952* (1954), particularly the relevant state chapters, many of which summarize legislative history and experience in prior years as well as in 1952; a compilation of presidential primary election returns since 1912, prepared by Alice E. Robinson and Ralph M. Goldman of the Brookings Institution staff; a compilation of excerpts from presidential primary laws, compiled by Frances M. Shattuck and Ralph M. Goldman of the Brookings Institution staff; a summary of the 1956 presidential primaries, prepared by Frances M. Shattuck; and recent editions of the Senate documents issued in presidential years on the manner of selecting delegates to national political conventions and the nomination and election of presidential electors.

[2] Overacker, *op. cit.*, p. 42, footnote.
[3] Throughout the remainder of this appendix, it can be assumed that district delegates are elected separately in the respective congressional districts unless the contrary is stated; in California and South Dakota, all delegates are elected at large on statewide slates.

dential nomination may intervene in his own party for the selection of delegate candidates who will support him at the convention. New York delegations usually represent their state effectively at the conventions, but rarely operate under mandates that are express, affirmative, or specific.

Pennsylvania

In its original law of 1906, Pennsylvania provided for the direct election of district delegates only. In 1913 the law was amended: to provide for the state-wide election of delegates at large; to repeal a provision permitting an indication of delegate preferences on the ballot; to add a provision for a presidential preference vote; and to require would-be delegates to indicate on the ballot whether they would or would not promise to support the winner of the preference vote. The legal provisions have since been little changed, except that the compulsory provision for direct election of delegates at large was repealed in 1951 and the method of their selection was left entirely to the state party committees—where in fact it had been performed for many years in both parties under a tacit understanding that agreed slates of delegates at large would run unopposed.

The "promise to support" is the most unusual feature of the Pennsylvania primary, but it has not been effective. Republican organization candidates for delegate who began declaring on the ballot, as early as 1916, that they did not promise to support the popular choice were generally elected nonetheless. Most of the Democratic candidates for delegate in recent decades have "promised to support," but have had little regard for the promise after arriving at the convention. The presidential preference poll has thus been treated in practice as no more than advisory.

Presidential candidates can be entered in the preference poll through a relatively simple form of petition. Their consent is not required, and until 1952 there was some

doubt whether candidates once entered for the poll could withdraw their own names. In 1952, General Douglas MacArthur formally requested withdrawal after petitions had been filed, whereupon one of the petitioners brought suit against the Commonwealth to prevent removal of MacArthur's name. The court ruled that MacArthur had the right to withdraw, on grounds that the voter was not deprived of any rights, since he still had the privilege of voting for MacArthur by write-in; that a person cannot be forced to be a candidate against his will; and that the plaintiff had no property right in MacArthur's candidacy. The court noted the contrary ruling of the Oregon courts in 1916, in *McCamant* v. *Olcott* (156 Pac. 1034), but declined to give it weight.[4]

The Pennsylvania preference poll has produced a number of outcomes that were interesting but in no way decisive: Governor Franklin D. Roosevelt's defeat of the titular leader of his party, Alfred E. Smith, in the preference poll in 1932; President Herbert Hoover's poor showing against Joseph I. France, ex-Senator from Maryland, in 1932; Thomas E. Dewey's strong showing in 1940 and 1944, the wide scattering of Republican preferences in 1948, the strong vote for General Dwight D. Eisenhower in 1952; the write-in vote for Senator Estes Kefauver on the Democratic side in 1952.

Pennsylvania delegates are usually elected unpledged. Their candidate preferences sometimes become known in advance of the election, but rarely seem decisive, although factional contests for delegate seats are more

[4] *Rowland, Jr.,* v. *Smith, Secretary of the Commonwealth,* 83 D and C 99, 63, Dauph. 201.

According to Louise Overacker, writing in 1926, secretaries of state had uniformly permitted candidates to withdraw when so requesting, regardless of whether the state law in question had included any provision for withdrawal. In the Oregon case the courts overruled the state secretary of state, who had withdrawn the name of Charles Evans Hughes at Hughes' request. In a similar case in North Dakota in 1924 the secretary of state was upheld in withdrawing the name of Robert M. La Follette at his request. (Overacker *op. cit.,* pp. 37-40).

common in Pennsylvania than in New York. The state has produced few favorite son candidates, and out-of-state candidates have rarely intervened in delegate contests. Pennsylvania delegations, like New York delegations, have operated mainly on the basis of mandates, if any, that were implied rather than express.

Illinois

Illinois provided for a presidential preference vote in 1912 and for the direct election of delegates in 1913. In the elections of 1916 through 1924, would-be delegates were required to state their presidential preference on the ballot, if their candidate so permitted, or that they had no preference. In 1927 the law was amended to eliminate the expression of the preference on the ballot, and to return the election of delegates at large to the state party conventions. In the elections since 1928 the Illinois system has been substantially the same as that of New York, except for the addition in Illinois of the presidential preference poll.

The preference elections have not been meaningless, but neither have they been important. Candidates who can be expected to run well are frequently entered for the presumed promotional value of a large vote in so important a state. Candidates who cannot expect to run well are seldom entered, and contests of national significance are accordingly rare. Illinois delegates give only perfunctory attention to the preference results in deciding how to vote at the conventions, but it frequently happens that the preference expressed by the voters is in accord with delegate intentions and voting

Illinois delegations usually arrive at the conventions in a position much like that of the Pennsylvania delegations, and for similar reasons. By comparison with New York, Illinois has produced relatively few favorite sons. Out-of-state candidates have sometimes campaigned in the state because of the preference poll. They have rarely made an effort to elect favoring delegates except when the state party organization was prepared to take on the task in their behalf, as the Republican organization did for Taft in 1952.

West Virginia

A presidential primary law was adopted by West Virginia in 1915 (much like the one adopted in Pennsylvania in 1913), with direct election of delegates, a preference poll, and a requirement that would-be delegates announce whether they would support the winner of the poll. The West Virginia primary attracted attention in 1928 when Herbert Hoover was defeated by Senator Guy D. Goff, a favorite son; a contest also occurred on the Democratic side in that year, with Al Smith defeating Senator James E. Reed of Missouri. Thereafter the preference poll was seldom entered by more than a single major candidate in either party, and the "promise to support" feature of the law was repealed in 1939. In 1940 and 1944 the preference poll was marked by frivolous candidacies. In 1948 the Republican poll was carried by Governor Harold E. Stassen of Minnesota, with two little-known candidates as his only opponents. In 1951 the law was amended to require a filing fee of $1,000 for presidential candidates. In 1952 no Democratic candidate filed; Senator Robert A. Taft and Stassen were filed on the Republican side, with Taft winning. In 1956 no one filed for the preference poll in either party.

Candidate affiliations have rarely had much influence on the election of West Virginia delegates; the seats have been contested on the basis of personal and local factional considerations. In 1952, however, a sharp factional fight among West Virginia Republicans led to the election of a mainly pro-Taft delegation, despite the lack of ballot identification.

Alabama

Except in 1936, Alabama delegates to Democratic national conventions have been elected in public primaries since 1924.[5] These elections have been held under a general law prescribing the conditions under which party primaries may be held for any purpose by those parties polling 20 per cent of the vote or more for state-wide offices in the last previous election. Ordinarily only the Democratic party qualifies under this provision, and the Republican party, when it did qualify, showed little disposition to use the statutory machinery. The system is a simple one, with no provision for any form of presidential preference voting, and seems to involve mainly a popularity contest among would-be delegates.

The Alabama delegates rarely carry any express mandate concerning candidates, but may be instructed through the state party machinery on relationships to the national party. In 1948 an attempt was made to pledge the Alabama delegates to walk out of the Democratic national convention if a civil rights plank was adopted. A number of pledged delegates later did so. In 1952, however, the state party committee required all candidates for delegate to execute a pledge to support the nominees of the national convention as a condition for going on the ballot, and the pledge was sustained by the courts.[6]

Nebraska

Since 1912, Nebraska has provided for the direct election of all delegates, with no indication of their preferences on the ballot, and a separate preference poll. Party organization is weak in the state; delegate elections are usually contested but seldom influenced decisively by preferences for presidential candidates. The preference poll is merely advisory, although treated with respect, and it has apparently had some influence on early ballot voting at the conventions.

Presidential candidates could be entered in the preference poll without their consent in the elections of 1912 through 1948, and remained on the ballot unless they objected.[7] Candidates of national stature were usually entered and contests of some interest occurred frequently, which probably helped to give authority to the poll as a guide for delegate action. In 1951 the law was amended to require the written consent of candidates before they could be placed on the ballot; write-in votes were still permitted, however. Taft and Eisenhower ran first and second in the Republican poll in 1952 on a write-in basis, defeating Stassen, who was on the ballot; Senator Estes Kefauver defeated Senator Robert S. Kerr of Oklahoma in a contest regarded as something of a test for both candidates. Both delegations split their votes at the conventions of 1952, with some delegates following the preference poll and others not.

District of Columbia

The presidential primary statute for the District of Columbia was passed in 1955, the only occasion on which Congress has enacted legislation dealing with the form of a presidential primary. The law provides for the direct election of all delegates in the District at large, with no presidential preference features.

The legislative history made it clear that would-be delegates were intended to run as individuals and to be voted on as such, with no provision on the ballot for identifying slates of delegates. But in the resulting situation of long-ballot confusion in 1956, with thirty candidates running for twelve places as Democratic delegates and nine candidates for six Republican places, slates were organized in both parties. Sample ballots identifying the respective slates were widely

[5] See Appendix B.

[6] David, Moos, and Goldman, op. cit., Vol. 3, pp. 196-97. In 1958, Dixiecrat elements were successful in electing a majority of the state party committee that would control arrangements in 1960. See Congressional Quarterly Weekly Report, May 16, 1959, p. 617; June 13, 1959, p. 739.

[7] In 1916, Charles Evans Hughes secured the removal of his name from the ballot. See Overacker, op. cit., p. 38; Merlo J. Pusey, Charles Evans Hughes (1952), Vol. 1, p. 317.

distributed and were taken into the polling places by most voters.

In the Democratic primary, the slate preferring Adlai E. Stevenson won all places in a contest mainly with a Kefauver slate. In the Republican primary, the candidates endorsed by the District Republican state committee were elected over those backed by an insurgent faction led by George P. Lamb, a District of Columbia lawyer.

Category Two

The Ballot *may* show delegate's preference *if* the candidate consents. Delegates may also run on a "no-preference" basis. In 1956 three states used this system.

South Dakota

After a period of experimentation with delegate elections and preference votes, from 1912 to 1928, the present South Dakota law was passed in 1929. Would-be delegates may run only as members of organized slates, all delegates are elected by the state at large, and the ballot can be voted by making a single mark in a circle at the head of the preferred slate.[8] Slates with a presidential candidate preference may so declare on the ballot if they can obtain the consent of their candidate; if consent is not forthcoming (or if the proposed delegation does not yet have a decided preference), the slate may still go on the ballot as a unit on a "no-preference" basis. Both kinds of "no-preference" delegations have appeared repeatedly in South Dakota practice.

The ballot has not carried more than two opposing slates in either party since the introduction of the present system in 1932, but it has produced a number of contests directly involving candidates of national stature. On the Republican side, these have included: in 1936, Senator William E. Borah of Idaho vs. ex-Governor Warren E.

[8] For a sample South Dakota ballot, see David, Moos, and Goldman, *op. cit.*, Vol. 1, p. 177.

Green, which Green won by a narrow margin (the Green delegation voted for Landon at the convention); in 1944, Dewey vs. Stassen, which Dewey won; and in 1952, Robert A. Taft vs. a "no-preference" Eisenhower slate, which Taft won by a hair-thin margin. On the Democratic side: in 1932 a Franklin D. Roosevelt slate won unopposed; in 1948 a Truman slated defeated an opposing slate; in 1952 an Estes Kefauver slate defeated a "no-preference" slate; and in 1956 a Kefauver slate won unopposed.

Massachusetts

Since 1912, Massachusetts has provided for delegate election in primaries. Intermittently, it has also provided for presidential preference votes that have been purely advisory. Organized slates of would-be delegates may be filed as such and are grouped together and receive a preferential position on the ballot, but the district members of slates must be voted on individually in their respective congressional districts, along with other candidates for delegate who file as individuals.[9] Would-be delegates

[9] In saying above that members of a slate are grouped together on the ballot, what is meant is that the candidates for delegate at large on the same slate are listed consecutively, followed by the candidates for district delegate who belong to the same slate and who are running in the district concerned. The ballot is not the same throughout the state; it differs from congressional district to district (and sometimes between smaller units, depending on other offices for which elections are being held), and in each district carries only the candidates for delegate on whom the voters in that district are entitled to vote. This feature is illustrated in the Wisconsin ballot reproduced in David, Moos, and Goldman, *op. cit.*, Vol. 1, p. 179; but in the Massachusetts and the New Jersey ballot, unlike the Wisconsin, the voter must place a mark against each name on the list in voting a paper ballot, or take corresponding action in voting on a machine, rather than put an "x" in the circle at the head of the column where his preferred slate is listed.

The alternative to keeping the members of an organized slate together on the ballot is to list all of the candidates for one category of delegate (at large, or district) alphabetically without regard to their slate affiliations; a further refinement is to rotate the list periodically while printing the ballots and begin at a different point in the alphabet. If the ballot is alphabetical but standardized, and if the voter is allowed to carry a sample ballot into

may state their presidential preference when filing their papers; this in turn appears on the ballot, but only if the preferred candidate gives his consent in writing before close of filing.

Under these provisions the party organizations in the state have usually produced the winning slates, and they have usually run on a no-preference basis. Usually the organizations have not encouraged even preferred candidates to allow their names to be identified with would-be delegates on the ballot. Delegate elections have involved factional strife within the state or locality more often than national candidacies, but a notable exception was the Taft-Eisenhower struggle of 1952. In that year a "no-preference" Eisenhower slate of district delegates defeated most of an identified Taft slate to win twenty-two out of twenty-four district delegates.

New Jersey

Like Massachusetts delegates, New Jersey delegates have been elected in primaries since 1912, with little change in the law since first enacted. A presidential preference vote, purely advisory, was provided from 1912 to 1944 and again in 1952 and 1956. Organized slates may be filed and appear as such on the ballot, but would-be delegates must be voted on individually whether running alone or as members of slates. Slates and individuals preferring a presidential candidate may so indicate on the ballot, but, since 1944, only if the consent of their candidate is endorsed on their filing papers.

New Jersey's system has operated much like that of Massachusetts, with a similarly high degree of influence by the state party organization most of the time. Frequently the organization enters a negotiated slate in which recognition is given to major state party factions. These slates generally are elected on a "no-preference" basis, but have been contested in some instances by preference delegations running with the consent of a willing candidate. A Stassen slate was defeated in 1952; Taft had refrained from entering a slate under the impression that the no-preference organization slate would remain neutral until it reached the convention.

In 1956, Senator Estes Kefauver not only entered the Democratic preference poll, where he was unopposed (as he had also been in 1952), but gave his consent for a complete slate of would-be delegates who ran as his supporters against an uncommitted regular organization slate headed by Governor Robert B. Meyner. Kefauver again won a hollow victory in the preference poll, with 117,000 votes to a write-in 4,000 for Stevenson, but only a single half-vote Kefauver delegate was a winner, the other slate winning 35½ of the 36 delegate votes.

Category Three

Ballot *may* show delegate's preference whether or not the candidate consents. Delegates may also run on a "no-preference" basis. In 1952 and 1956, Oregon, New Hampshire, and Florida were in this category. Oregon, however, also has a preferential poll, the result of which commits the delegates regardless of their stated preference, and is therefore discussed in Appendix D.

New Hampshire

In its original law, passed in 1913 and amended in 1915, New Hampshire provided only for the election of delegates, with no separate presidential preference poll. It authorized the would-be delegates either to pledge themselves to a preferred candidate in their filing papers—whereupon they were identified on the ballot as so pledged—or to run unpledged. In 1949 the law was

the booth with the same physical dimensions as the official ballot (as in the District of Columbia in 1956), slate voting is facilitated somewhat even if officially disapproved.

amended to give would-be delegates three options rather than merely two: (1) they could run as pledged to a candidate, with the ballot so stating, but only with his written consent (which had not previously been required); (2) they could indicate a candidate preference, with the ballot so stating, without giving a pledge or securing consent; or (3) they could run on a "no-preference" basis. Also in 1949, the law was amended to provide a separate presidential preference vote. Candidates could be filed without their consent, but were given an opportunity to object, whereupon they would not be entered on the ballot—provisions under which General Eisenhower permitted his name to stand in 1952 while still on active military duty in Paris.

Of the twenty-two delegations elected under these provisions from 1916 to 1956, seven were elected uncommitted, without facing a committed slate, and another six were committed to an incumbent President without opposition. Presidential candidate interests were directly involved, through ballot identification, in the other nine cases as follows:

Democratic

1932: a Franklin D. Roosevelt slate defeated an Alfred E. Smith slate.

1936: a Roosevelt pledged slate defeated a local factional opponent.

1940: a Roosevelt slate defeated slates committed to James A. Farley and John N. Garner and an unpledged slate, although the Roosevelt slate polled less than half the vote.

1952: an Estes Kefauver slate defeated a Harry S. Truman slate.

1956: a Kefauver pledged slate defeated a slate favoring Adlai Stevenson, entered without his consent.

Republican

1920: a slate pledged to General Leonard Wood defeated one pledged to Senator Hiram W. Johnson of California.

1944: unpledged candidates for delegate ran best; Dewey's men ran better than Wendell Willkie's.

1948: unpledged candidates for delegate again ran best; a Stassen slate made a respectable showing.

1952: an Eisenhower slate defeated Taft and Stassen slates.

Florida

Democratic delegates have been elected in Florida since 1904 under laws that have been repeatedly amended.[10] Florida also made early provision for the holding of preference polls, but—aside from 1912, when Oscar W. Underwood and Woodrow Wilson were listed—until 1952 this feature was seldom used. In 1945 would-be delegates were authorized to indicate their preference on the ballot without securing consent. This produced a primary election in 1948 in which many of the would-be delegates were identified on the ballot as favoring Governor Fielding L. Wright of Mississippi to demonstrate their states rights position, with most of the remainder stating no preference but known to be opposed to Truman. The Dixiecrat extremists won 11½ of the 20 delegate votes. The delegation later voted 19 for Senator Richard B. Russell of Georgia, and 1 for Paul V. McNutt, Ambassador to the Philippines.[11]

In 1952 the Florida primary was the scene of a major contest between Senators Kefauver and Russell. Both were entered in the preference poll, which was considered purely advisory; Russell won. Would-be delegates favoring each and listed as such were on the ballot, but not as organized slates; a plethora of would-be Russell delegates were competing with each other as well as with those favoring Kefauver. In the outcome, the elected delegates at large divided five for Russell and three for Kefauver, the district delegates fourteen for Russell and two for Kefauver.

A new presidential primary law was enacted in 1955, applicable to both major parties and effective in 1956.[12] This law, based on the recommendations of a num-

[10] Manning J. Dauer (and others), "Toward a Model State Presidential Primary Law," *American Political Science Review*, Vol. 50 (March 1956), pp. 138-153.
[11] Based in part on V. O. Key, Jr., *Southern Politics* (1949), p. 338
[12] Dauer, *op. cit.*; Paul T. David, "Specifications for a Model State Presidential Primary Law," Brookings Institution Reprint, No. 11 (April 1956), pp. 1-6.

ber of political scientists, sought to bring together features drawn mainly from the experience of South Dakota, New Hampshire, and Wisconsin. It provided that would-be delegates might run only as members of organized slates, with the state-wide vote controlling in the election of delegates at large and the district vote controlling for district delegates separately in each district. Each slate was authorized to run under the name of its preferred presidential candidate, if it had one; his name was to appear on the ballot above the slate of would-be delegates, which could be voted for by making a single mark at the head of the list. Would-be delegates were not required to give any pledge nor to secure the formal consent of their candidate. If more than one slate preferring the same candidate was filed, the candidate was authorized to choose the one to go on the ballot; otherwise the one filed first was to appear. (Latent in this provision was the candidate's privilege of organizing and filing his own slate if he disapproved of a slate previously organized and filed in his name.) "No-preference" slates were also authorized to file, without restriction on the number of such slates, and could be voted on as units. The provision for a preference vote separate from the election of delegates was repealed.

Under the new law in 1956, on the Democratic side a Stevenson slate defeated a Kefauver slate in the state-wide vote and in five of the eight congressional districts. The primary came late in the preconvention campaigning, and was of major importance to the fortunes of both candidates. On the Republican side, a slate favoring Senator William F. Knowland, filed during the period of uncertainty concerning President Eisenhower's intentions, was defeated by an Eisenhower slate, filed without need for any formal action by the President.

In the early primaries of 1956, Kefauver had scored victories in New Hampshire and Minnesota that seemed likely for a time to end the Stevenson candidacy. Later primaries were relatively inconclusive, until the Oregon primary on May 18, where

Stevenson won; but Florida, on May 29, was a far more important test. Both candidates had committed their prestige in extended periods of active campaigning in Florida, with the even more important California primary to follow a week later. These successive victories of Stevenson's—in Oregon, Florida, and California—were largely responsible for Kefauver's withdrawal before the convention.

In 1959, however, the 1955 law came under heavy attack in the Florida legislature.[13] From a local point of view, the new system as it had operated in 1956 was unsatisfactory in several respects. Public and party officials who had withheld their names from either of the 1956 contesting Democratic slates, presumably because of a reluctance to become associated with either candidate, found it more difficult than usual to make satisfactory arrangements for positions as alternate delegates. Those who did become alternate delegates were seated in the galleries at Chicago, like other alternates, and found access to the convention floor somewhat difficult.

The campaign itself in the state was unsatisfactory to many Florida Democrats who did not agree with the views of either candidate. No Dixiecrat slate had been entered, perhaps because the firmness of Stevenson's views on civil rights had not been fully anticipated, but also because the prospects for electing a no-preference Dixiecrat slate did not seem very good. Not all of the members of the slate actually elected under the Stevenson banner were enthusiastic about their candidate, yet all delegates found themselves much more firmly committed by the nature of the situation than they would have been if elected under the relatively more casual arrangements of 1952.

Leadership in seeking revision of the 1955 law was provided by the chairman of the Democratic state committee. Various efforts were made to devise an amending bill under

[13] The following account of developments in 1959 is based primarily on information supplied by Professor Manning J. Dauer on May 29 and June 22 and 26, 1959.

which the delegations would be unpledged and major public and party officials would receive seats, ex officio, in their party's delegation. When the list grew to include all of the top members of the party hierarchy, all members of the Florida state cabinet, and all members of the Florida congressional delegation, this part of the approach to amendment collapsed of its own weight.

Eventually the legislature enacted a measure reflecting compromise among the forces opposed to the 1955 law. The state party chairman was given a seat, ex officio, as delegate. All other delegates were to be elected in the primary, but with no provision for indicating their candidate preference on the ballot. Two district delegates were to be elected in each of the congressional districts; all other members of the delegation were to be elected at large. A provision was included for a presidential preference poll that any candidate for a presidential nomination could enter, the results to be purely advisory and in no way binding on the delegates.

On June 19, 1959, the amending bill was vetoed by Governor LeRoy Collins. The legislature was already in adjournment, and the veto will stand until the next regular session in 1961 unless there is a special session of the legislature in the meantime, bringing with it, under Florida law, an opportunity to vote to override the veto. In his veto message Governor Collins stated that the system provided by the amending bill was so inferior to the previous system that he could not approve it, and commented as follows:

While I think our present laws governing selection of delegates to the national convention and for the expression by the people of their preference for presidential candidates are inadequate, the proposals embraced in this measure, in my opinion, would take us backward and not forward.

Under the new proposal, each candidate for delegate voted upon (and there doubtless will be more than 20 to be elected) must be selected by the voters individually. There is no limitation on the number who may run, and the people would likely find themselves waiting in lines for hours and badly confused in trying to select from 150 or more candidates. This would likely mean a return to the system of former years of electing candidates for delegates whose primary advantage would be names starting with "A" or "B."

There is no way under the new proposal for the people to be assured of for what or for whom any candidate stands. Under such a system, I think it may be assumed that with widely differing viewpoints a cat-and-dog fight could characterize our delegation when convention time arrives.

The present law includes the distinct advantage of having candidates grouped so that by one vote an elector may approve a whole slate. Of greater importance, the slate approved will either be identified as favoring a specific candidate for President, or clearly identified as being "uninstructed."

The new proposal has been represented to provide more flexibility for our state delegates to the national convention for the purpose of enabling them to make trades, deals and maneuvers.

I grant that certain flexibility is desirable, but I believe the people have a right to know to what candidate a delegate may be committed or, if not committed, the fact that he is uncommitted. The present law would assure this, and the new proposal does not.[14]

Past Practice of Other States

While a number of other states have at one time or another authorized would-be delegates to indicate their candidate preference on the ballot provided the candidate gave his consent or did not object, the number authorizing this practice without consent has been small. Aside from New Hampshire and Oregon, extended experience with this kind of provision seems to have occurred only in New Jersey and Wisconsin.

In New Jersey the provision was used frequently on behalf of an incumbent President, and in rare instances for an out-party candidate who may have been the organization choice—as in 1936, when most of the

[14] From the veto message to the Florida Secretary of State, June 19, 1959, on House Bill 543, as supplied by the Governor's office.

winning Republican delegates had expressed a preference for Governor Landon. In most instances the organization slate seems to have run without commitment on the ballot, and the number of mavericks expressing a preference who ran in opposition was relatively small. Organization control appears to have been strong in both parties during most of the period up to 1944 when a preference could be expressed without securing candidate consent.

The Wisconsin experience from 1912 through 1948 involved the combination of a presidential preference poll with the election of delegates who could freely express their candidate preference on the ballot, and who usually did so. In the early years a number of conflicts occurred between the outcome of the preference poll and the delegate elections. This experience made it clear that the preference poll would be considered only advisory and given little weight by delegates who had been elected after announcing another preference on the ballot. In 1924, for example, William G. McAdoo won the preference poll, which Smith had refused to enter, but an identified McAdoo slate of delegates at large was defeated by an identified Smith slate—a clear case of conflicting mandates, with the Smith mandate seemingly more valid and more likely to be followed, as it was.[15] Thereafter the preference poll sometimes lacked candidates entirely and was used mainly on a write-in basis.

The real contest, when it occurred, was thus between would-be delegates who had identified their candidate preferences on the ballot. Significant contests in the country at large were able to take form on the Wisconsin ballot without regard to candidate initiative or consent. This had noteworthy results for the fortunes of the candidates, as in the Dewey delegation's crushing defeat of a Willkie slate in 1944 in an election that Dewey had indicated he did not wish to enter (see Chapter 5). In 1948, however, with three slates in mixed array on the

ballot—one for Dewey, one for Stassen, and one for General MacArthur—the Stassen slate won all of the delegates at large and most of the district delegates, producing the situation in which it became necessary for Dewey to campaign much more vigorously than he had intended in other states (see Chapter 5). The MacArthur slate ran so well, however, that it alarmed the Stassen supporters. This was one of the factors leading to revision of the Wisconsin law to require the specific approval of a candidate before a slate could use his name.[16]

Category Four

Ballot *must* show delegate's preference for a candidate who has given consent. Delegates *must not* run on a "no-preference" basis. In California, Ohio, and Wisconsin would-be delegates can go on the ballot only with the name of a candidate willing to give his specific consent. Minnesota operated a similar system in 1952 and 1956, but repealed its law in 1959.

California

All California delegates are elected at large on the basis of state-wide slates. The voter votes for a slate by making a single mark against the name of a presidential candidate. In effect, he makes a choice among the candidates—real or alleged and sometimes actually only one in number—who appear on the ballot of his party.

These features, characteristic of the California system almost from the first, have become increasingly rigid as the system evolved. A separate presidential preference poll was held in 1912, but was eliminated thereafter as unnecessary and confusing. Would-be delegates were at first allowed to run either as individuals or as members of slates, and either with or without indications of a presidential preference. After 1924 the opportunity to run on a no-prefer-

[15] Overacker, *op. cit.*, p. 72.

[16] David, Moos, and Goldman, *op. cit.*, Vol. 4, pp. 130-31.

ence basis was eliminated. Would-be delegates were also allowed for many years to indicate their preference on the ballot without securing the formal consent of the candidate, if not repudiated; after 1952 the law was amended to require any delegation running in a candidate's name to obtain his consent in writing. For some years the ballot permitted the voter to vote for delegates either individually or as slates; after 1940 it carried only the names of presidential candidates, omitting the names of would-be delegates and ending any opportunity to vote for them individually. By these various means California has greatly simplified a former long-ballot situation while retaining the election at large of all delegates.

The California system has only occasionally offered the voters an opportunity to provide mandates that are clear, realistic, and valid. In contest cases, the contest in the state seems to have directly reflected the contest in the nation on no more than five occasions in forty-five years: the contest between Theodore Roosevelt, William Howard Taft, and Robert M. La Follette in 1912; between Champ Clark and Woodrow Wilson in 1912; Calvin Coolidge and Hiram W. Johnson in 1924; Franklin D. Roosevelt, John N. Garner, and Alfred E. Smith in 1932; and Adlai E. Stevenson and Estes Kefauver in 1956. In the twelve Republican primaries from 1912 to 1956 the voters were given a choice involving an out-of-state candidate on only three occasions— 1912, 1924, and 1936. The Democrats have offered at least one out-of-state candidate in all of their twelve primaries except two —1920, when an unpledged delegation was elected, and 1924, when the delegation went to William G. McAdoo unopposed.

In eight cases of little or no contest, the situation in the state was generally in accord with that in the nation. In 1928, Herbert Hoover, then Secretary of Commerce, won the California Republican delegation unopposed. Incumbent Presidents won their respective delegations unopposed in 1916, 1932, 1944, 1948, and 1956.

President Franklin D. Roosevelt also won against opposition in 1936 and 1940.

Favorite sons and stand-in candidates have been conspicuous in the primaries in other years, especially in the Republican party. In 1920 a slate supporting Senator Hiram W. Johnson defeated a Herbert Hoover slate, while General Leonard Wood and Frank O. Lowden, who were major candidates, and Senator Warren G. Harding, the eventual nominee, remained aloof. In 1936 a delegation supporting Landon was defeated by one pledged to Earl Warren, then a district attorney and relatively unknown outside California. The Warren delegation, however, voted for Landon on the first ballot at the convention. In 1940 an unopposed Republican delegation was elected in the name of a stand-in candidate, Jerrold L. Seawell, a veteran state legislator. In 1944, 1948, and 1952, Warren won the Republican delegations. He was opposed only in 1952, and then, not by Taft or Eisenhower, but by a delegation headed by Congressman Thomas H. Werdel, whose only function was to enable his slate to qualify for a place on the ballot. On the Democratic side in 1952, Estes Kefauver won the California delegation in a contest with a local stand-in candidate, Attorney General Pat Brown (who six years later was elected governor).

Ohio

The Ohio primary is the most complex and procedurally rigid to be found anywhere in the country. It originated as a simple system for the direct election of district delegates in 1912, but by 1916 the law provided, as it still does, that would-be delegates must state both their first and second choices for President on the ballot. Moreover, they must obtain the written consent of both candidates before they can file their own papers for the election. A serious second choice is never acceptable, because it might seem prejudicial to the first-choice candidate and also because a serious second choice might withdraw before the primary election, invalidating the candidacy of the would-be delegates and their support for the first-choice candidate.

From 1916 through 1944, Ohio also allowed a presidential preference vote in addition to the delegate election; would-be delegates, despite their own formal expression of preference for a willing candidate in order to get on the ballot, were also authorized to file a declaration of intent to be guided by the results of the preference poll. With the disappearance of this poll, the statutory pledging clause has become a dead letter. Ohio delegates make no statutory pledge to support the candidate who authorizes them in writing to use his name, but if he is a serious candidate they become heavily committed and inevitably have a strong mandate to support him.

Ohio differs from California in that district delegates are elected separately in the congressional districts and all would-be delegates appear on the ballot and are voted on as individuals. Dissident factions can find a place on the ballot for relatively small splinter groups of would-be delegates if they can find a willing candidate for President who has enough voter appeal to be useful and who will allow his name to be used—two conditions that are rarely met.[17] A national figure with serious prospects can hardly afford to permit his name to be used for slate-making purposes in Ohio unless he has the active support of the state party organization; or is prepared to do open battle with it; or finds that it is sufficiently disorganized to offer unusual opportunities. Even if invading the state seems worth while, the red tape—especially the technicalities of getting petitions accepted as valid—can present many difficulties to any unwelcome invader, as the

Kefauver managers discovered in 1952.

For these various reasons, contesting delegations have only occasionally been entered in the Ohio primary in recent years, but when they were they have usually involved substantial interests. Ohio Republican delegations running with the consent of favorite son Robert A. Taft were elected in 1940, 1948, and 1952; with the consent of another favorite son, Senator John W. Bricker, in 1944 and 1956. Contesting Stassen delegations were entered in 1948 and 1952, winning nine places out of fifty-three in 1948 and none in 1952. On the Democratic side, where party organization was relatively weaker, organization control was strengthened by White House concurrence from the beginning of the Roosevelt era through 1948. The organization slate was unopposed, although usually placed on the ballot in the name of a stand-in candidate: in 1940, Charles Sawyer, former lieutenant-governor and unsuccessful candidate for governor; in 1944, State Auditor Joseph T. Ferguson; in 1948, Treasurer of the United States William A. Julian. In 1952 the organization slate ran in the name of former Senator Robert J. Bulkley and was opposed by an incomplete Kefauver slate, which polled over 60 per cent of the vote and won precisely half of the seats. In 1956 a favorite son delegation for Governor Frank J. Lausche won 54 of the 58 delegate votes.

Wisconsin

Wisconsin's original law of 1905 provided only for the direct election of delegates. In 1911 the state authorized would-be delegates to indicate their preferences on the ballot (with or without the candidate's consent) and also provided for a separate preference poll. This system continued in effect through 1948; as previously noted, it was similar to the present New Hampshire and Florida systems and had similar consequences for candidates and voters.

Between 1948 and 1952, Wisconsin re-

[17] In 1952 one would-be delegate found a place on the ballot with the consent of Kenneth P. Eisenhauer, an Akron factory worker, whose name in turn was also placed on the ballot as a duly qualified candidate for President under Ohio law. The Eisenhauer delegate was defeated; the genuine Eisenhower permitted no use of his name in Ohio. See David, Moos, and Goldman, *op. cit.*, Vol. 4, p. 19.

vised its system to the form in which it operated in 1952 and 1956. The ballot was streamlined to give the voter a choice between slates of delegates pledged to a specified presidential candidate and could be voted by a single mark against the name of the preferred candidate.[18] But no slate could appear on the ballot without the written consent of its preferred candidate. The state-wide vote controlled the election of delegates at large, while the vote in the congressional districts separately was controlling in the election of district delegates.

Under this system no Stevenson delegation appeared in either year, and Kefauver won the Democratic delegations intact, against local stand-in candidates in 1952 and with no opposition in 1956. There was no Eisenhower delegation in 1952; Taft won twenty-four delegates to Warren's six and Stassen's none. Eisenhower won the delegation in 1956.

As 1960 approached, the Wisconsin primary came under increasing pressure. Local political figures were said to feel that the law gave too much control to the presidential candidates in whose names the slates were filed, and who did not always see fit to recognize party dignitaries with some claim to an ex officio place. The rigidity of the pledging requirement was also irksome, and was held to reduce the state's influence and effectiveness at the convention. On the Democratic side, there was fear of a party-splitting fight in the 1960 primary, but it also developed that supporters of at least two of the Democratic candidates were anxious to have the primary available as an important test of strength. The net effect was to leave the primary law unchanged, for the time being,

but with some likelihood of repeal or amendment after the 1960 struggle was over.[19]

Minnesota

The Minnesota law, as effective in 1952 and 1956, produced an election system similar to that of Wisconsin, with slates of delegates appearing on the ballot under names of presidential candidates to whom they were pledged. Minnesota, however, permitted write-in votes for presidential candidates, and it was held that these could be used to win delegates, even though would-be delegates preferring the candidate had neither appeared on the ballot nor been written in.[20] Eisenhower came close to winning state-wide in 1952 on a write-in basis, and actually did win delegates in two congressional districts, who were then provided by later party convention action.

On the Democratic side in 1952, Senator Hubert H. Humphrey was on the ballot as a favorite son and won the entire delegation against a light write-in vote for Kefauver, who had refused to let a favoring delegation go on the ballot. In 1956 the Democratic primary was noteworthy for the contest between Kefauver and Stevenson, in which Kefauver won 26 of the 30 delegate votes; both candidates were on the ballot and campaigned actively in the state.

The Minnesota law provides that three delegates at large in each party shall be named by the state party conventions, but must be pledged to the presidential candidate winning the state-wide election. This provision permits some inclusion of state party leaders on the delegation, whatever the outcome in the primary.

As enacted in 1949, the Minnesota statute was intended to provide for the use of a favored candidate's name *without* his consent, but this intention was frustrated by the courts, leaving the would-be delegates

---

[18] The law permits would-be "uninstructed" delegates to go on the ballot as individuals. But the form of the Wisconsin system as a whole is calculated to make it easy for slates of delegates to run under the label of a presidential candidate, genuine or otherwise, while many obstacles are placed in the way of individuals seeking to run as uninstructed delegates. A single individual made the attempt in 1952 but withdrew before the election. See David, Moos, and Goldman, *op. cit.,* Vol. 4, pp. 132, 134, 154. For a sample Wisconsin ballot, see *ibid.,* Vol. 1, p. 179.

[19] *Congressional Quarterly Weekly Report,* June 5, 1959, pp. 763-764.
[20] David, Moos, and Goldman, *op. cit.,* Vol. 4, pp. 171-74.

obligated to obtain the candidate's approval. The law had attempted to block the withdrawal of a candidate by permitting it only after an affidavit "stating that he is not a candidate for the nomination of President for the party for which he has been filed and that if nominated by such party he will not accept." In 1952, General MacArthur and Senator Kefauver were both filed without their consent by slates desiring to use their names. Both demanded removal of their names, and both declined to execute the required affidavit. The state attorney general then ruled that a simple request for withdrawal was sufficient, stating:

To require as a condition of withdrawal that the candidate renounce his candidacy is arbitrary and unreasonable and therefore invalid. . . . Minnesota has no power to limit the right of any qualified citizen to continue his candidacy for the presidency in other states as a condition for withdrawal in our state.

In subsequent litigation the ruling was upheld by the state's high court in *Ryan* v. *Holm*, March 14, 1952. The net result was that would-be delegates were required to obtain a candidate's consent, there being no other means of getting on the ballot.[21]

The Minnesota statute of 1949 had an unusual number of drafting deficiencies that made administrative rulings necessary; it was also unpopular with members of both parties who were believers in doctrines of party responsibility and who sought to strengthen state party organization. The state has also had a long commitment to the open primary, in which voters can vote the ballot of either party in a primary in accordance with their interests on the particular occasion—a system with special hazards in a presidential primary, as noted in Chapter 10.

At any rate, the Minnesota presidential primary lost popularity in its own state. A brief and simple act to repeal went through both houses of the state legislature with bipartisan support and was approved by Governor Freeman on March 6, 1959. The effect is to return the selection of delegates to party conventions in both parties.

[21] Entire paragraph based on David, Moos, and Goldman, *op. cit.*, Vol. 4, pp. 162-63, 168-69, 182.

D

Experience of States with Presidential Preference Polls Having Compulsory Effect

THREE STATES— Oregon, Maryland, and Indiana—authorize presidential preference polls which specifically attempt to control the action of delegates. (See Chapter 10.) Montana operated a similar system in 1956, under a law since repealed.

Oregon

In 1910, Oregon invented the idea of a presidential preference poll combined with the separate election of delegates in the same election. In 1915 the law was amended to drop a proportional representation scheme for the election of delegates. Thereafter, the system operated with little further change in the elections of 1916 through 1956. Presidential candidates could be placed on the preference poll ballot at their own request, or by petition; write-in votes were also permitted. Candidates were not allowed to withdraw their names, even when placed on the ballot through petition without their consent. Supreme Court Justice Charles Evans Hughes sought the removal of his name in 1916, but the Oregon courts ruled against him on the ground that the rights of the voters were paramount.[1]

Would-be delegates could file by petition without accepting any formal obligation to follow the outcome of the preference poll, but after 1912 this provision was used on only a single occasion—by a group of Taft

[1] *McCamant* v. *Olcott, Secretary of State,* Supreme Court of Oregon, April 25, 1916 (80 Ore. 246, 156 Pac. 1034), as cited in Louise Overacker, *The Presidential Primary* (1926), p. 38.

supporters in 1952, all of whom were defeated. Other would-be delegates from 1916 to 1956 used a provision of the 1915 amendment for filing "by declaration." They were pledged thereby to use their best efforts to bring about the nomination of the candidate winning the preference poll. They were also permitted to state their own preference on the ballot, but this was done only occasionally from 1916 to 1956, in view of the binding character of the preference poll.

The Oregon primary has produced interesting results on a number of occasions, but the experience is not easily summarized. So far as incumbent Presidents are concerned, they were allowed to win the preference poll of their party unopposed in 1916, 1944, 1948, and 1956. But President Coolidge had to overcome Senator Hiram W. Johnson in 1924; President Hoover, who was not on the ballot, was defeated by ex-Senator Joseph I. France in 1932 (as in several of the advisory polls that year). President Franklin D. Roosevelt was nearly defeated by Senator Borah in the Democratic preference poll in 1936; in 1940 he faced Vice President Garner, but won easily.

As for the occasions when no incumbent President was available, McAdoo won the poll unopposed in 1920 and 1924, and Hoover nearly so in 1928. Borah was a lopsided winner in 1936 in the Republican primary, as was Oregon Senator McNary in 1940, and Dewey in 1944; in all of these instances the competitors, or their supporters, evidently failed to mount effect-tive campaigns. But there were significant Republican contests in 1916, when the reluctant Hughes ran ahead of Senator Albert B. Cummins of Iowa, 2 to 1; in 1920, when Johnson ran ahead of General Wood, Lowden, and Hoover; in 1948, when Dewey defeated Stassen after their famous debate in the state; and in 1952, when Eisenhower ran far ahead of Governor Warren, General MacArthur, and Senator Taft. The Democratic contests were noteworthy in 1928, when Al Smith defeated Senator Thomas J. Walsh; in 1932, when Roosevelt won easily, with Smith not on the ballot; and in 1956, when Stevenson won a hard-fought battle with Kefauver for write-in votes after each had earlier persuaded his respective supporters to refrain from putting him on the ballot.

Victory in Oregon was worth much or little, depending on the circumstances. Dewey's victory of 1948 was an event of major importance in his preconvention campaign; so was the victory of Eisenhower in 1952 and of Stevenson in 1956. But some other victories were lopsided and of little value, because the opposition was perfunctory; it seems unlikely that these had much effect on national opinion, and they did not invariably produce votes at the convention. The France delegation of 1932 gave most of its vote to President Hoover on the first ballot, probably without being released by France, and the Borah delegation of 1936 voted solidly for Landon on the first ballot, probably without being released by Borah.[2]

In general, however, Oregon delegations have usually honored their formal mandate so far as the nomination balloting was concerned, but their support was rarely worth much at the convention for any other purpose. There was little connection between the campaigns by which individual delegates won their seats and the campaigns by which presidential candidates won the pref-

erence poll. The results were apparent in the attitudes of the delegates, even though every Oregon delegation from 1916 to 1956 was pledged to support the candidate who had won in the poll.

In 1957 and 1959, Oregon revised its election laws and made a number of changes in the presidential primary. The major objective, so far as presidential candidates were concerned, was to make it as certain as possible that all of the important candidates for a nomination would be on the ballot in Oregon. In the 1957 changes, the secretary of state was directed to put any candidate on the ballot who had announced his candidacy to the public or had become a candidate in the primary of any other state.[3] This seemed certain to clutter the Oregon ballot with a considerable number of unimportant favorite son candidates, while not necessarily putting candidates on the ballot who were pursuing a strategy of waiting until the convention before announcing.

In the 1959 amendments, the 1957 provisions were repealed and a new formula adopted, under which the Oregon secretary of state was directed, at his own absolute discretion, to put on the ballot all of the candidates for President and Vice President who are "generally advocated or recognized in national news media."[4] The provision for putting candidates on the ballot by petition was retained, although it would be unnecessary to circulate petitions for any candidate the secretary of state agreed to recognize. The provision by which candidates could request a place on the ballot without circulating a petition was repealed. Any candidate may withdraw his name from the ballot, however, by signing a formal affidavit "stating without qualification that he is not now and does not intend to become a candate" for President or Vice President.

Speculation following the enactment of the new Oregon law looked forward to the probability that the names on the ballot in 1960 would include the four senators and

---

[2] Ex-Senator France of Maryland was apparently a front for a pro-Coolidge group and was something of a troublemaker at the 1932 Republican convention. Borah was disgruntled by the platform approved in 1936 and left the convention before the nomination balloting.

[3] State of Oregon, *Election Laws,* 1957-1958, sec. 249.368, p. 34.

[4] ORS 249.368 as amended by Senate Bill No. 280, 1959.

three governors most often mentioned for the Democratic nomination, but would not include Adlai Stevenson, who was expected to file the required affidavit of non-candidacy. A focused race on the Republican side between Vice President Nixon and Governor Nelson A. Rockefeller of New York was anticipated.[5]

The provisions for the direct election of delegates were continued with amendments in 1957 and not further amended in 1959. The little-used procedure for filing "by petition" was eliminated, and all would-be delegates were required to pledge support to the winner of the preference poll. The contents of the pledge, however, were substantially revised; the pledge would no longer be binding after two ballots or in the case of a candidate who received less than 35 per cent of the convention vote.[6] The objective was to give the Oregon delegations greater operating freedom at the conventions when their formal mandate proved unrealistic.

Maryland

Adopted in 1912, the Maryland law has not since been changed in any important respect. It provides for a preference vote at a primary where delegates to *state* conventions are also elected. Each delegate is bound to vote at the state convention of his party in accordance with the preference vote in his own county or Baltimore legislative district. The candidate winning a majority of the county unit votes is then entitled to have the whole state delegation vote for him as a unit at the national convention, as long as in their conscientious judgment there is any possibility of his being nominated.

A presidential candidate might win a majority of the popular vote in the state while still losing a majority of the county unit votes in the state convention, although this has not so far happened in a presidential primary. (It has happened in gubernatorial primaries under the same system.)

The Maryland system has offered contests between presidential candidates in only three of the twelve Republican primaries from 1912 to 1956, and two of the twelve Democratic. On the Republican side, Theodore Roosevelt defeated William Howard Taft in 1912, General Wood defeated Senator Johnson in 1920, and Herbert Hoover defeated ex-Senator France of Maryland in 1932; on the Democratic side, Champ Clark defeated Woodrow Wilson in 1912 and Franklin D. Roosevelt defeated Henry Breckenridge in 1936. The most recent of these cases in an open nominating situation was that of the Wood-Johnson contest of 1920.

In seven other cases, five Republican and two Democratic, a single candidate was entered in the preference poll, with the voter given the alternative under Maryland law of voting for an uninstructed delegation. In this type of contest, Coolidge was victorious in 1924, Hoover in 1928, Dewey in 1940, Eisenhower in 1956, and Kefauver in 1952 and 1956; Wendell Willkie, however, was badly defeated in 1944 in favor of an uninstructed delegation. In the other twelve of the twenty-four primaries, four Republican and eight Democratic, no presidential candidates were on the ballot.

In the instances where a statutory mandate was produced, Maryland delegations have usually given it effect on the first ballot at the convention, but not always thereafter. On critical issues that arise before the nomination balloting, Maryland delegations have shown little regard for the interests of their mandated candidate when they were inconsistent with the personal views of the delegates or the position of the state party organization.

Indiana

From 1916 through 1928 Indiana law provided for a presidential preference poll, the results of which were binding on the delegates, who were elected in state party con-

[5] *Congressional Quarterly Weekly Report,* June 5, 1959, p. 764.
[6] State of Oregon, *Election Laws,* 1957-1958, secs. 249.031, 249.221, pp. 27, 30.

ventions. In the four presidential years when this statute was in effect, it was of no consequence on the Democratic side: President Wilson won unopposed in 1916, an Indiana banker named Evans Woollen won unopposed in 1928, and no one was entered in 1920 and 1924. On the Republican side, a favorite son, Charles W. Fairbanks, former senator and former Vice President, won unopposed in 1916, but contests followed in the other three years. In 1920, Wood, Johnson, Lowden, and Harding divided the vote with no one achieving a majority and with the delegation technically unpledged under the statute as it then stood. Wood apparently received somewhat more support at the convention than might have come to him without the primary. In 1924, Coolidge defeated Johnson, and in 1928, Senator James E. Watson defeated Hoover; both winners received the state's entire vote at the convention.

The Indiana law of 1953 was evidently modeled on the former statute, but attempted less and dealt differently with some contingencies. It authorized presidential candidates to be filed by petition for the preference poll; allowed a mere plurality vote to bind the delegates on behalf of the leading candidate; and bound each district delegate to support the winner of his district and the delegates at large to support the winner of the state-wide vote. On the other hand, it made the instructions binding only on the first ballot at the convention and only if the candidate were still seeking the nomination. Delegates continued to be elected at state party conventions.

The new law was in effect in 1956. Eisenhower won against Lar Daly, a perennial office seeker, on the Republican side; Kefauver won unopposed on the Democratic side, but withdrew before the convention.

Montana

Montana adopted a presidential primary by initiative in 1912 that provided both for a presidential preference vote and for the election of delegates. The legislature re-

pealed this law in 1923, and the repeal was upheld by referendum in 1924. In 1953 the legislature passed a new law that provided for the election of slates of delegates pledged to candidates, a system somewhat similar to Minnesota's. The law was approved in a referendum by a heavy popular vote in 1954, but in 1955 the legislature repealed it and returned the delegate selection to the state party conventions, leaving only a presidential preference vote for the people to decide. Presidential candidates could enter by affidavit or be entered by petition without their consent. Delegates were required by law to support the candidate winning the preference vote until released or until his vote was less than 20 per cent on any ballot.

In 1956 the ballot carried Montana Secretary of State S. C. Arnold and Lar Daly on the Republican side and Kefauver on the Democratic. Arnold was a stand-in for Eisenhower and won; Kefauver won despite write-in votes for Stevenson and other candidates.

In 1959, however, an amending law was passed (approved by Governor Aronson on March 17), by which the relevant sections of Montana law were re-enacted with the presidential preference features omitted.[7]

Past Practice of Other States

Several other states have experimented with preference votes for President while leaving delegate election to the party conventions. Louise Overacker, in her study published in 1926, named Michigan, North Carolina, Vermont, and Illinois as having used this system. She comments:

This type of control has proved ineffective in practically every instance where the popular preference and the sympathy of the state convention have been at variance.[8]

The presidential primaries were short lived in the first three of the states named, and

[7] *Montana Session Laws 1959,* Chapter No. 274.
[8] Overacker, *op. cit.,* p. 61.

Illinois changed to the direct election of delegates after 1912.

For many years the system remained in use in Maryland alone, where it seemed an archaic survival until revived in the recent laws of Indiana and Montana. In 1959, however, a similar plan was strongly advocated by a study committee appointed by the Democratic state chairman in Wisconsin.[9] Alternatives of this kind will apparently remain under study in Wisconsin, along with the possibility of outright repeal of the present law and a return to the convention system of delegate selection.

[9] *Congressional Quarterly Weekly Report,* June 5, 1959, pp. 763-64.

E

State Systems for Electing Delegates in Party Bodies

THE STUDY OF delegate selection in 1952 provides the most substantial body of data on delegate selection by the state party organizations that has ever been collected.[1] It is therefore drawn upon heavily in the pages that follow. Supplementary information for 1956 has been accumulated and included wherever feasible.[2]

As discussed in Chapter 11, the state systems for electing delegates in party bodies can be grouped in three classes and several subclasses. These are discussed below in terms of the states so grouped.

Class 1a

In the Class 1a systems, delegates are elected by state party committees derived

[1] Paul T. David, Malcolm Moos, and Ralph M. Goldman, *Presidential Nominating Politics in 1952* (1954), Vol. 1, pp. 162-73, and relevant state chapters in the other four volumes.

[2] Changes in the laws applicable in 1956 have been noted primarily from the printed item entitled "Manner of Selecting Delegates to National Political Conventions and the Nomination and Election of Presidential Electors," January 1956, compiled under direction of Felton M. Johnston by Richard D. Hupman and Samuel H. Still, Jr., and printed by the Government Printing Office for the use of the Office of the Secretary of the Senate. Although issued quadrennially in recent presidential years, this item is not officially a document or a publication. When available, it is obtainable from the Office of Secretary of the Senate and from senators.

In October 1959 the Republican national committee issued a compilation (prepared by its Research Division) of information relating to delegate selection for 1960. This document, *The Process of Delegate Selection for the Republican National Convention of 1960*, describes the basis for selection and cites pertinent state statutes—where they exist—for both selection of delegates and filing of candidates in presidential primaries.

from primary elections.

In 1952 the state party committee elected the full state delegation in Louisiana, Georgia, and Arkansas on the Democratic side, and in Florida on the Republican. The delegations were elected in Arizona by state party committees meeting as conventions, as noted below. State party committees selected the delegates at large in New York and Pennsylvania. These procedures remained unchanged in 1956 except in Florida, where public primaries were held in both parties.

The differences between election in a state committee and election in a state convention are not necessarily substantial. The committees typically are somewhat smaller than conventions, but often include a hundred members or more. Committees are more likely to be made up exclusively of active party officials with continuing local responsibilities and may thus be somewhat more amenable to organization control. But the states where the party committees select national convention delegates are so few as to provide little basis for generalization.

Louisiana, Georgia, and Arkansas (Democratic party)

In all three of these states the gubernatorial primaries of the Democratic party have been typically the most important elections that are held. Democratic state party committees are constituted through procedures closely related to these primaries.

In Louisiana governors are nominated for four-year terms in primaries early in the presidential year. Members of a state party committee are elected directly in the same primary; usually a majority are supporters of the successful nominee for governor. The committee later names the national convention delegation. The new governor's influence on the choice is usually substantial, but dissident elements may also obtain some representation.

In Georgia governors are elected for a four-year term staggered against the presidential term. County committeemen, who are elected in the off-year primary, elect delegates to a state convention that names the state committee. Customarily the committee is made up of persons acceptable to the incoming governor and follows his lead two years later in naming the national convention delegates.

In Arkansas the system is much the same, although Arkansas governors are elected for only two years. In the off-year primary, members of county conventions are elected, usually as a formality. The county conventions elect members of a state convention, which in turn approves a state committee satisfactory to the incoming governor. Two years later the governor names the slate of national convention delegates and the committee approves.

The Democratic delegations from all three states are seemingly responsive to implied mandates reflecting factional victories in the state-wide contests for governor. In Louisiana these mandates are of the same year; in Georgia and Arkansas they are two years old at the time of the national convention.

New York and Pennsylvania

Incoming state party committees in New York are elected in the same primary with the district delegates to the national convention. The committee meets soon after and approves the slate of delegates at large.

In Pennsylvania the outgoing state party committee is required to name the delegates at large before the date of the primary. In both parties in both states, the slates of delegates at large usually reflect agreement among the leaders and are readily approved.

Class 1b

Delegates of the Class 1b system are elected by state party conventions derived from primary elections. This group of states includes Delaware, Maryland, and Indiana. The system of each state is unique in major ways, but in all of them the state convention delegates can be elected directly by the voters.

Delaware

Delaware is a state which is small enough both geographically and in population to permit the use of relatively simple political arrangements. The members of the state conventions are elected locally throughout the state in what are called "party primaries." Names of candidates for membership in the state convention are filed with local party authorities in advance; when there is no contest, no primary is held. In 1952 only 7 of the 160 Republican state convention seats were contested in the primaries; prior negotiations had led to uncontested compromise choices for the other seats. In the Democratic party no contests occurred that year in the selection of state convention delegates.

Maryland

As noted in Appendix D, Maryland provides an opportunity for a presidential preference poll of mandatory effect in a spring primary at which delegates to the state conventions are elected. These conventions in turn, voting under a county unit system, elect the state's delegates to the national conventions and perform other duties, including nominations for senator. Heated factional conflict has been the rule in the state conventions of both parties in recent years—usually with little direct relationship to presidential candidacies, but frequently reflecting a liberal-conservative split in each party that has had implications for the interests of particular candidates at the national conventions. In 1952, Taft-Eisenhower conflict was acute in the Republican organization, but it was compromised at the state convention by naming Governor Theodore Roosevelt McKeldin as a favorite son and electing a delegation divided between Taft and Eisenhower supporters.

Indiana

Delegates to Indiana state conventions have long been elected from the wards and townships in the spring primary, and the conventions are required to meet within sixty days. The conventions elect national convention delegates. They also nominate party candidates for state treasurer, secretary of state, lieutenant governor, and governor. The voting is done on machines, a feature that appears to be unique in party conventions.[3] Divided votes in the state convention are mainly the result of factional-

[3] The Indiana party conventions are normally held in a large coliseum in Indianapolis, with as many as 2,000 or more delegates present. The main floor of the coliseum is surrounded by a high wall, above which the permanent seats are arranged. The voting machines, about forty in number and of the kind used in local elections, are spaced along this wall, with one machine for approximately each fifty delegates. Voting begins on nominations for the lowest office and continues up the scale to the highest—governor. One office is voted on at a time; the names are set up on each machine and the delegates are queued up past a check-off clerk who determines eligibility. There is no write-in problem, since each candidate for a nomination must post a filing fee ($2,000 for governor), and no name appears unless the filing fee has been paid. The fees are used to defray convention costs. When the delegates have voted, the count is taken by tellers from each machine and presented to the chairman on a written form as he calls the machines by number; the machine totals remain standing until the chairman directs that they be cleared. If no candidate receives a nominating majority, the vote is repeated until some one does.

There is some question whether this system provides more rapid voting than the roll call system if allowance is made for the delays and confusion attendant on the delegates leaving their seats and returning to them.

ism in state nominating contests, but factional divisions may also become involved in the fortunes of national candidates, as occurred in the Taft-Eisenhower struggle of 1952.

Indiana held a presidential preference poll of mandatory effect in the spring primary of 1956, as noted in Appendix D.

Class 1c

Class 1c includes seven states: Michigan, Rhode Island, North Dakota, Wyoming, Arizona, Montana, and, for delegates at large only, Illinois. County conventions are held as an intermediate level of representation in all of these states except Rhode Island, where the intermediate conventions are held in towns and legislative districts.

Michigan

Michigan's selective system is unusual, although its results are similar to those of several other states. The first step in the system occurs at fall primaries in the even-numbered off-year, when party voters elect delegates from the precincts to county conventions. These delegates are usually elected as a matter of routine in a very light vote, two or three write-in votes sometimes proving sufficient. Thereafter the county conventions meet in the year they are elected and the two following years to elect state convention delegates (the first two state conventions select various party officers and nominees for state positions). The third meeting

Both major parties are required by state law to use voting machines. The system, when first installed, may have been intended to prevent the nomination of an organization favorite in one of the major parties. It is said to have had the effect of weakening organizational control over the voting, since it is difficult to know how each delegate votes, even though the machines are in the open and the voting is done in public.

(The foregoing is based primarily on an interview with Niles Jackson of Indiana, Executive Assistant to the Postmaster General, and on information from other Indianians.)

occurs in the spring of the presidential year, and the resulting state convention elects the national convention delegates.

Whatever direct influence the party voters exert in this system mainly reflects factional interests within the state parties. The members of the party hierarchy who will choose the delegates to the national convention are already in office by the time the presidential campaigns become active, so any campaigning on behalf of candidates is directed to them rather than to the voters. In 1952 the Michigan delegations were selected with little direct regard for their candidate preferences, but they were clearly representative of the existing two-party rivalry in the state. Their records at the national conventions were creditable.

Rhode Island

The two major parties form their Rhode Island state conventions differently, but in each case the members are elected as in Michigan—by local party committeemen who were elected in a primary in the previous even-numbered year. In 1952 the Rhode Island Republican delegation was the subject of sharp factional fights, first among the committeemen and later in the convention, with the Eisenhower supporters winning. On the Democratic side, a slate prepared by party leaders was approved by the convention.

North Dakota, Wyoming, and Arizona

In each of these Class 1c states the state conventions are composed of delegates elected by county committees or conventions. These in turn are made up of precinct representatives who were elected in the primaries of the previous even-numbered year. In Arizona the county committees elect large state committees soon after their own election. Technically, it is these state committees that reconvene as state conventions in the spring of the presidential

year; but they may be somewhat reconstituted at that time through new county meetings. In North Dakota and in Wyoming the county committees elect state convention delegates in the spring of the presidential year. In all three states, factional conflict within the organizations is common at county and state levels, and may become somewhat involved in national candidate interests in presidential years. The results were mixed in 1952.

Montana

In 1952 the system in Montana was substantially the same as that described in general for the other Class 1c states. In 1956, under provisions since repealed, Montana conducted a presidential preference poll of compulsory effect, as noted in Appendix D. This was held as part of a spring primary on the first Tuesday in June. Precinct committeemen were elected on the same occasion, as they will continue to be under the amended law. They make up the county committees, which are required to meet as county conventions within fifteen days after the primary to elect delegates to the state party conventions. These in turn are required to meet within another fifteen days to elect national convention delegates. The Montana system thus differs from those previously noted in Class 1c, by the fact that the state party convention's mandate from the voters, although indirect, is of a recent date late in the spring of the presidential election year.

Illinois

District delegates to the national conventions are elected in Illinois in public primaries, as noted in Appendix C. At these primaries, local committeemen are also elected to serve on county committees. They meet shortly after the primary and choose delegates to state party conventions, which in turn elect the delegates at large to the national conventions. Slates of delegates at large were approved with little dissent in both conventions in 1952.

Voter and Candidate Participation in Classes 1b and 1c

In five states—Delaware, Maryland, Indiana, Montana, Illinois—where the systems are built on primaries held in the spring of the presidential year, the voters would appear to have a substantial opportunity to influence the choice of national convention delegates. In Delaware, however, decorum within the party organizations seems to prevent the submission of alternatives to the party voters. In Maryland and Indiana the opportunity is diluted by the complexity of the issues facing the voters and the lack of definite information on the alignments of the numerous candidates for state convention delegate. In Illinois the voters seem willing to leave the problem entirely to the party organizations. In Montana the system may have possibilities not yet realized, despite the layering in of county conventions as an intermediate step.

In the other five states of Class 1c—Michigan, Rhode Island, North Dakota, Wyoming, Arizona—the system of representation is not only indirect through an intermediate layer of delegates but also removed nearly two years in time from the elections in which a few party voters have expressed themselves. These systems provide no opportunity for voter control at the time of decision. They are, however, open to other methods of voter influence. When there is an active contest between candidates, the local party officials may find themselves under direct pressure by more voters than the few who had previously troubled to take part in their election. In the Taft-Eisenhower campaign in Rhode Island in 1952, for example, the competing factions used newspaper advertisements to urge Republican voters to telephone their local committeemen. Many did so, and the results were considered influential at the time.

As a rule, however, candidates for the presidential nominations can find little encouragement for campaigning among the voters in most of these states. Maryland might be an exception, but for the long-term record of avoidance by most out-of-state candidates. In the other states, candidates and their managers necessarily direct their appeals mainly to members of the party organization at the state and county levels. Sometimes local factions within the organizations may align themselves with national candidates, leading to contests at the party conventions and even earlier.

In all of these states, except Delaware, the lowest level of representation consists of local party representatives who have been elected in a publicly administered primary election. Insurgency among the party rank and file, to be effective, must be organized and active enough to express itself by putting up candidates in a kind of primary election that will rarely attract much voter interest. Most of these systems thus seem to be relatively immune to the hazards of seating contests, in spite of the fact that in a number of them the primaries are relatively open to invasion by voters migrating from the other party.

Over a period of years, action in even such low-energy elections may gradually reflect changes in party composition and may lead in turn to profound changes in the make-up of the party organizations, as has occurred in Michigan during the last twenty years.[4] Such processes may perhaps operate more quickly when the relevant primary elections are held in presidential years. But in any case, the first impact of insurgency is absorbed in the slow procedures of a publicly administered election. To be sure, malpractices in the higher levels of the party could conceivably lead to enough disruption to provide a basis for seating contests at the national convention, but this did not occur in any of these states in 1952, and no delegation from any of these states has been involved in a seating contest since 1940.

[4] Stephen B. and Vera H. Sarasohn, *Political Party Patterns in Michigan* (1957).

Class 2

Election of delegates in the Class 2 state systems is by party conventions derived partly from primaries and partly from meetings. In Idaho, Kansas, and Washington, mixed systems provide the representation in state party conventions.

Idaho

State conventions in Idaho are composed of delegates chosen by the county committees, "or otherwise as the county central committee . . . shall prescribe." In the Republican party the county committees apparently choose the delegates directly; in the Democratic, it is customary to call county conventions, but attendance is limited. Members of the county committees are elected by the precincts in primaries of the previous even-numbered year. The system is thus substantially the same as that of North Dakota, Wyoming, and Arizona (Class 1c) and has similar effects.

Kansas

Although Kansas law does little directly to regulate the selection of national convention delegates, it does provide for county committees, made up of precinct committeemen elected in the primary in the previous even-numbered year. In both parties the committees have the option of directly electing delegates to congressional district and state conventions. Alternatively, a county committee may call an open county convention or caucus, to which all party members are invited, to choose the delegates. In 1952 it was reported that this occurred in about half of the counties for which information was available. In Kansas, each party holds conventions in each congressional district, at varying dates. These conventions nominate district delegates to the national convention, subject to ratification in the state convention, which also completes the election of delegates at large.[5]

[5] Governmental Research Center, University of Kansas, *Kansas Voter's Guide 1956*, Pt. 1, pp. 26-36.

Washington

State conventions are composed of delegates selected in county conventions in most counties and in state legislative districts in King County (Seattle). Precinct committeemen, elected in the previous even-numbered year, serve as members of the county conventions in the spring of the presidential year. But several counties allow each precinct to send one delegate in addition to the committeeman. Precinct meetings to elect such representatives seem to be common in some parts of the state; in other parts, the county conventions sometimes operate as mass meetings open to all interested party members. The confusion of these procedures, together with the heat of the Taft-Eisenhower contest in 1952, led to several seating contests at the Republican state convention, and to argument over the use of a unit rule by several large county delegations. A seating contest at the national convention was threatened, but did not occur.

Class 3a

The convention systems of Class 3, which are built on *ad hoc* meetings of the party voters, can, like those built on primaries, be divided into two groups: 3a–those in which the representation in state party conventions is generally direct, and 3b–those in which it is generally indirect. There are also some regional and party differences within the two groups.

Maine, Vermont, and Connecticut

In these three states of Class 3a, the county is of little importance as a unit for political organization. Delegates to state and congressional district conventions are elected directly in town and precinct meetings in Maine, in meetings in the towns in Vermont, and in town and ward meetings and "party primaries" in Connecticut. In all three states Republican voter turnout in the meetings was unusually large in 1952 and the popular mandates were substantial and influential.

Virginia, Kentucky, and Tennessee

In these three states and in both parties, delegates to the state and district conventions seem to be elected as a rule in county mass meetings, or, in the Virginia cities, in equivalent city-wide meetings. The meetings are supposedly open to all party voters of the area, but actual attendance is usually drawn mainly from the ranks of the party organization. County committees sometimes make up the slate of state convention delegates and report it without the formality of convening a public meeting.[6]

Georgia, Alabama, Arkansas, and Louisiana (Republican party)

Primary election procedures are monopolized by the Democratic party in these four states, and are rarely used by the Republicans. Delegates to the Republican state and district conventions are usually elected in county mass meetings open to all party voters. Sometimes these meetings are called county conventions, but they are rarely formed of representatives from smaller units. The active Republicans in the typical rural county would not make much of a meeting even if all were present. Ward or precinct meetings may be held in the cities, either to elect delegates to a county convention or to the state convention directly.

Class 3b

North Carolina, South Carolina, Mississippi, Oklahoma, Texas, Minnesota, Iowa, Missouri, Colorado, Utah, Nevada, and New Mexico constitute the Class 3b systems. In all of these states the normal practice in both parties, required by law in some cases, is to hold local meetings of the party voters in the wards and precincts to elect delegates to county conventions. The county conventions elect delegates to the state and district conventions.

Precinct meetings are usually omitted in either party in areas of party weakness; often there is no precinct chairman to call a meeting. Attendance at precinct meetings in many of these areas is usually small. An estimate from North Carolina in 1952 suggested five to twenty-five persons as a typical range, and the county conventions, although ostensibly delegate bodies, frequently admit and give voting privileges to any party member who has enough interest to attend.

Experience in 1952 in Classes 3a and 3b

All of the processes that begin with *ad hoc* meetings of the party voters in the late winter or spring of the presidential year are relatively open to conflict and voter insurgency when interest in presidential candidates is running high. Such opportunities are reduced when the local meetings are held so early that interest has not yet become active, or when the meetings are called in a manner deliberately calculated to curtail attendance. Early meetings occurred in several states in 1952, and other signs of manipulation were occasionally evident. Procedural deficiencies, however, seemed more often to be the result of carelessness or inefficiency than intent, as in most organizations that rely on voluntary effort.

The sharply focused struggle in 1952 between Taft and Eisenhower supporters led to increased attendance and conflict in Republican local meetings in many states. The consequences were most apparent in the South, where the conflict in Louisiana and Texas led to seating contests at the national convention. Outside of the South, the Taft-Eisenhower struggle was handled with sufficient decorum in the states of this group to prevent any thought of taking seating contests to the national convention.

In the Democratic party in 1952 there were intense factional conflicts in Texas and Mississippi, and seating contests re-

---

[6] For Tennessee, see William Goodman, *Inherited Domain* (1954), pp. 12-14.

sulted. In Virginia the faction loyal to the national party protested organization control and its results, but did not attempt to mount a serious challenge in the county or state meetings. Other forms of factionalism were occasionally noticeable in Democratic meetings outside the South in 1952, but almost never had anything to do with national candidate interests and had few visible consequences for the mandates or behavior of the delegates.

In both parties the candidates for the presidential nominations generally remained aloof from the public proceedings in the states where local party meetings were held in 1952. No instance was found in which any national candidate campaigned in any state before the holding of local party meetings for the purpose of arousing interest, promoting attendance, and developing popular support. In many states, this would have been difficult because of the scattered dates on which meetings were held and the lack of advance information concerning schedules. It would have been possible in Texas, however, where all precinct meetings are held on a single date set by law, and perhaps in a few other states.

F

Analysis of the Results of the Chicago Convention

Shortly after the 1952 Republican convention, the late Senator Robert A. Taft prepared a memorandum on its events as he saw them for some of his preconvention campaign lieutenants. The memorandum, entitled as above by Senator Taft, is published here with the consent of Robert Taft, Jr., his father's executor.[1]

I AM WRITING THIS brief analysis of the result of the 1952 Republican Convention and the several reasons for that result. There is a tendency to lay too much stress on particular circumstances at the Convention and exaggerate the importance of events which made headlines at the moment. I don't want to have any of my supporters blamed for the result and charged with the mistakes which they did not make or which did not really affect the result. I don't want my supporters to feel that there were any serious mistakes of omission and that some striking move would have solved the whole problem.

The result of the Convention came far more from underlying causes which had operated steadily for eight months, and continued to operate at Chicago. First, it was the power of the New York financial interests and a large number of businessmen subject to New York influence, who had selected General Eisenhower as their can-

didate at least a year ago. There was a strong and substantial minority of Taft supporters among business leaders, but they were a minority, particularly in the East.

Second, four-fifths of the influential newspapers in the country were opposed to me continuously and vociferously and many turned themselves into propaganda sheets for my opponent. Of course, this was not true of the McCormick papers, the *Wall Street Journal*, the *Omaha World Herald*, and the *Los Angeles Times*. The *Philadelphia Inquirer*, the Hearst papers, and the Knight papers remained neutral. But most other Republican papers were almost campaign sheets for Eisenhower and were supplemented by the violent support of every New Deal and so-called independent paper. Like the editors, the majority of Republican governors were sold on Eisenhower support, although a majority of Senators and Congressmen were in my favor. However, the governors had far more political influence on delegates.

These underlying causes operated throughout the campaign and at the Convention.

The Convention result, after all, depended far more on the number of delegates than it did on changes of opinion at the Convention, which at so many conventions are likely finally to result in a nomination. A long and intense campaign almost entirely between the supporters of General Eisenhower and myself had lined up nearly all the delegates on one side or the other, except those pledged to Warren, Stassen, and McKeldin. It was a two-man fight.

[1] The copy used here was received through the helpful cooperation of Harold A. Jones of Pasadena, California, in June, 1959. Up to that time the memorandum had not been published, although it is obviously the item referred to by William S. White in *The Taft Story* (1954), p. 182. In late November various newspapers and periodicals published the history of the memorandum and its text. See especially *New York Times*, Nov. 25, 27, 29, 1959.

Going back through the campaign, the primary results were generally favorable to that candidate who had the support of the organization and the newspapers. The primary results were favorable to Eisenhower in the East—in New Hampshire, Massachusetts, Pennsylvania, and New Jersey; and this had a substantial effect on all New England, New York, and Delaware delegates. The primary results were favorable to Taft west of the Alleghenies in West Virginia, Illinois, Wisconsin, and Nebraska. This had a substantial effect, of course, on Indiana, Kentucky, and many other Western States. Where there were no primaries, the Convention results for Eisenhower in Washington, Colorado, and Iowa were more than matched by Taft conventions in many other Western States. The Oregon primary helped Eisenhower on the Pacific Coast.

The influences operating, which I have described above, were such that I had to have a pretty clear majority in order to hold a lot of marginal delegates. We probably would have done better if we had put on a real primary campaign in Pennsylvania, New York, Michigan, Oregon and some other states. The difficulty was the tremendous expense involved in any such program and the lack of time to make an adequate campaign against the newspaper influences. Even in South Dakota we almost lost because the three leading newspapers were for Eisenhower.

The net result, after the primaries were over, provided an estimate of 604 delegates for Taft and about 400 for Eisenhower, with 128 for other candidates and 86 uncommitted, largely in Pennsylvania and New York. But this was never a firm estimate, and we knew that even though this number of delegates had expressed a preference for me they might be persuaded otherwise. In this estimate of 604, we counted on 27 delegates from Michigan who favored me at the time of the Michigan convention and afterwards, 17 from New York, 9 from New Jersey, 28 from Texas, 10 from Louisiana. I saw this number of delegates in New York and New Jersey personally and had definite

statements that they would vote for me. We did not count on Fine's delegates. It was always clear, therefore, that while we had a hard core of 500 delegates, there were others who were subject to persuasion and pressure. The Michigan estimate was particularly uncertain as long as Summerfield tried to hold Michigan as a unit.

To match up possible losses from these delegates, we worked on Governor Fine, Governor McKeldin and numerous uncommitted delegates in New York, New Jersey and other states. We also had assurances of 25 from California if Warren ever released them. In spite of every reasonable effort, we did not persuade McKeldin, Fine or Summerfield. Because of strong pressure by the governors of New York and New Jersey, we lost most of the delegates who had given assurances of support in those states. We did hold 9 votes out of 15 favorable Taft supporters after McKeldin accepted an invitation to nominate Eisenhower. The number of California delegates on the Georgia contest was only 8 instead of 25 because of pressure from the Governor and Senators from California.

By the time the Convention opened, we reduced our estimates in Michigan by 9 discounting Summerfield's defection, Delaware by 3, Oklahoma 2, Virginia 2 and Texas by 6 by reason of the compromise I proposed. These losses were made up by 16 additional contest delegates and gains in Rhode Island, Connecticut, Massachusetts and a few other states, but our estimate of 607 was again based on New York, New Jersey and Michigan delegates, as well as including 50 from the contested states of Georgia, Louisiana and Texas. It was clear, therefore, when the Convention began that if Warren, Stassen and Eisenhower all ganged up on us on preliminary votes, we might not be able to win unless we held on to every vote, or replaced them with additional votes. Neither of these results were we able to achieve.

The first question arose on the change in the rules, contrary to every principle of parliamentary procedure. The whole strategy of the other side was to change the rules and get enough votes to steal all the contested delegates, and it was difficult to see how this could be prevented if the Eisenhower people were supported by the Warren and Stassen forces. They did obtain their support because apparently the Warren and Stassen forces felt that their own success depended on a deadlock, and that this action might bring about a deadlock. It probably would have been better to agree to the rule, but, of course, the loss of votes would make the contest fight more difficult. It was probably a mistake to take a vote because it showed that the combined forces against us controlled the Convention, but even a concession on our part would also have been regarded as a sign of weakness. On the rule vote we held practically all the Taft states, but were unable to withstand the Summerfield pressure in Michigan, the Dewey pressure in New York and the Fine pressure in Pennsylvania. Fine forced his own representative on the Credentials Committee to reverse the stand he had taken after hearing the evidence.

The key vote came on the Georgia contest where we lost the equivalent of 17 votes because of the new rule, but we picked up 9 Taft votes in Maryland and 8 in California in spite of strong pressure from McKeldin and the Governor and Senators from California. On the other hand, we fell below our estimates in New York where all but 4 delegates finally voted against us, and we lost from our estimates 4 in Michigan, 3 in New Jersey, 3 in Nebraska and single votes in other states. We were 38 votes short of winning the Georgia contest, and apparently the same vote would have prevailed in the contest on Texas. Some of this defection may have resulted from the loss of morale on the rules vote, but it seems unlikely. Some Taft delegates couldn't or wouldn't recognize that the Georgia vote was really the first vote on the nomination. Every Eisenhower delegate knew what his job was, and pressure was strong in the states where we had to gain votes.

After the Eisenhower forces, with the assistance of Warren and Stassen, took 39 votes away from us and gave them to Eisenhower, in addition to 11 Louisiana votes lost in the Credentials Committee, our prospective strength on the first ballot fell well below his strength, and he had all the bandwagon advantage which we would otherwise have had. It is hard to see how we could have won the Georgia contest unless we converted Fine or Summerfield or McKeldin, or held our full strength in New York and New Jersey.

I have referred to the underlying forces which operated not only during the campaign, but at the Convention. The truth is that we were up against a tremendous publicity blitz led by four-fifths of the newspapers of the country, and all the magazines. Most of the governors also lent themselves to this propaganda and in states where we did not have a majority we had difficulty in getting any votes at all because of the pressure of the governors. It is remarkable that as many as 500 delegates stood firm against this tremendous pressure, even after the bandwagon was rolling.

The control of the press enabled the Eisenhower people to do many things which otherwise could not have been done. The making of a moral issue out of the Texas case was only possible because every internationalist paper sent special writers to blow up a contest which ordinarily would have excited a few days interest and would have been settled fairly by the National Committee and the Credentials Committee. If there was a moral issue, my suggestion that I be allotted only the district delegates clearly not contested, and that representatives of both sides discuss the whole matter in detail, district by district, certainly should have destroyed that issue. But the press was completely unfair in their treatment of it. Adverse national committeemen frankly admitted that they could not even sit down and talk about the merits of the various Taft contests, "because it would deprive them of the smear issue." The Zweifel people had a sound moral claim that the Democrats had taken over Republican primaries. The only way we could get it before the public at all was by advertisements.

In the same way the Eisenhower press made a moral issue of the change in rules, although it was contrary to all parliamentary procedure, and was admittedly proposed only for this Convention because of the danger of making it a permanent rule.

Also the Eisenhower press, although usually adverse to the growth of television, played up the exclusion of television from the National Committee as though it involved an intention to steal delegates in secret although the proceedings were public and all the American press were present to watch what happened.

It is all very well to say that we should not have permitted these issues to be created, but the alternative was surrender on matters in which we were in the right, and if there had not been these issues the publicity firms would have invented others to be shouted by the pro-Eisenhower press.

A study of the primaries will also show that the metropolitan newspapers had a tremendous effect on the results in the primaries and conventions, far more than they do on general elections. Eisenhower victories were always ballyhooed and Taft victories played down.

My conclusion, therefore, is that we had practically to secure a very substantial majority of the total number of delegates to win, and that the net result of the primaries was to give us a very thin majority, if any.

At one point in the Convention it was suggested that I retire and turn over my delegates to General MacArthur or some other candidate. Any such move, of course, was impossible before the first ballot. It would have been a surrender of principle and a betrayal of thousands of workers and millions of voters who supported me during the eight months campaign. Furthermore, these delegates were built up as Taft delegates, and I had no power to transfer many of them to anybody. It would, of course, have been an indication of weakness and probably would have resulted in the nomination of Eisenhower almost by acclamation. There was no evidence that anyone else had any substantial support in addition to that which I had.

Of course, if a deadlock had been created after the first ballot, I would have been glad to reconsider the whole situation and would have been glad to withdraw in favor of some other candidate holding my general views, if it had been clear that I could not be nominated and that he would have been stronger on the second ballot than I. There was a tentative agreement on the part of the Warren and Stassen forces to recess the Convention after the first ballot.

G

Questionnaire Studies of the Delegates to the 1948 Conventions

TWO QUESTIONNAIRE studies of the delegates of 1948 are drawn on for portions of the data used in Chapter 14. One was made by Charles L. Braucher, then a graduate student at the University of Nebraska, now a member of the faculty of the University of Georgia. The other was made by Daniel W. Tuttle, Jr., who was then teaching at the University of Wyoming and is now a member of the faculty of the University of Hawaii; the Tuttle study was financed in part by a grant of research funds from the University of Wyoming.

The Braucher study was based on a return-postcard inquiry seeking responses from the delegates on nine items of information. The replies were analyzed in a master's thesis in sociology entitled "The Social Composition of the National Political Conventions of 1948," prepared under the supervision of Dr. Paul Meadows, and placed on deposit at the University of Nebraska in 1949. Some of the data were published in an article by Paul Meadows and Charles L. Braucher, "Social Composition of the 1948 National Conventions," *Sociology and Social Research,* Vol. 36 (September-October 1951). Professor Braucher kindly made available a copy of his thesis for use in the preparation of the present study.

The Tuttle study involved a more elaborate questionnaire of some thirty 1948 items, based in turn upon a pilot survey of Republican delegates in 1944. Professor Tuttle in 1951 completed a preliminary analysis of the 1948 replies, and made the analysis

available for use in planning the 1952 study under the auspices of the American Political Science Association, in which he participated. He has since accumulated further information on the delegates of 1952 and is currently completing a study of the conventions of recent years for submission to the University of Minnesota as a doctoral dissertation. He acted as a consultant in the preparation of Chapter 14, and data from his study are used with his permission and that of the Universities of Wyoming and Minnesota.

As in all questionnaire studies relying on voluntary responses by mail, the resulting tabulations may reflect some degree of bias arising out of the self-selection of the respondents. Both investigators received replies from 37 per cent of the Democratic delegates. Professor Braucher received replies from 53 per cent of the Republican delegates on his postcard inquiry; Professor Tuttle from 44 per cent on his longer schedule. On a regional basis, the percentages of response were as follows:

Region	Democratic Delegates		Republican Delegates	
	Braucher Study	Tuttle Study	Braucher Study	Tuttle Study
Northeast	36%	28%	42%	31%
Middle West	46	48	58	49
South	30	36	55	49
West	44	46	60	52
Non-State Areas	9	30	54	47

TABLE 1. AGE DISTRIBUTION OF THE DELEGATES, NATIONAL PARTY CONVENTIONS OF 1948

(in percentages)

Age Group	Democratic Delegates		Republican Delegates	
	Tuttle Study	Braucher Study	Tuttle Study	Braucher Study
10–14	0.17%	—	—	—
15–19	—	0.15%	—	—
20–24	0.17	0.50	—	0.20%
25–29	0.68	0.70	1.27%	1.60
30–34	3.90	5.00	3.59	3.70
35–39	9.15	11.10	6.13	7.80
40–44	13.90	18.00	10.36	12.30
45–49	17.97	17.00	15.64	15.30
50–54	16.27	16.30	20.08	20.40
55–59	13.56	11.40	16.70	15.50
60–64	10.68	8.90	13.11	12.40
65–69	7.80	6.40	8.46	6.20
70–74	3.90	2.70	3.38	2.70
75–79	1.36	1.00	0.63	1.40
80–84	0.34	0.70	0.63	0.50
85–89	0.17	0.15	—	—

TABLE 2. EDUCATIONAL STATUS OF THE DELEGATES, NATIONAL PARTY CONVENTIONS OF 1948

(in percentages)

Years of Education	Democratic Delegates		Republican Delegates	
	Tuttle Study	Braucher Study	Tuttle Study	Braucher Study
4–7	1.2%	1.0%	0.2%	1.0%
8	4.9	3.6	3.0	2.1
9–11	5.9	4.7	4.8	3.1
12	12.1	10.8	12.4	10.2
13–15	21.9	21.6	23.7	22.5
16	23.2	20.6	23.1	25.9
17 or More	30.8	37.7	32.8	35.2

Age

The age distributions of the delegates as reported by the two studies are shown in Table 1. Averages of the percentages from the two studies were used in preparing the chart presented in Chapter 14.

Religion

The Tuttle study is the only known source for comprehensive data on religious affiliations of the delegates. His questionnaire simply asked for "Religious Affiliation: _____ (name of denomination)." He supplied the percentages reported in Chapter 14, but should not be held responsible for the arrangement of the categories or the inferences drawn in the text.

Education

Specific replies on numbers of years of education in grade school, high school, and college or university were obtained by both Braucher and Tuttle. Both supplied their data in a form permitting the recapitulation in Table 2.

Income

The Tuttle questionnaire requested responses on the following income item: "Annual income: under $2,500 ____; $2,500-$3,500 ____; $3,500-$5,000 ____; $5,000-$10,000 ____; $10,000-$25,000 ____; $25,000-$50,000 ____; $50,000-$100,000 ____; over $100,000 ____ (check one)." This part of the form was completed by all but 3 per cent of his respondents. Professor Tuttle made the initial tabulation of the data, and for purposes of the present study, supplied them in the form of tables for each party convention showing the reported number of delegates of each category in each state delegation.

The tabulations included in Chapter 14 were then prepared from Professor Tuttle's data by Richard C. Bain of the Brookings Institution staff, and have been reviewed by Professor Tuttle.

The problems of interpretation for bias arising out of the self-selection of the respondents are especially acute in connection with the income data. Both the Brookings staff and Professor Tuttle have made a number of independent statistical analyses of the basic data and have compared results. A general tendency toward upward bias appears to be somewhat offset by lower reply rates in the case of the high-income states with large metropolitan areas, where the pace of business activity may lead to more than average insensitivity to questionnaires. Areas where party organization tends to become highly professionalized were also among those where rates of return were relatively low.

These questions will be dealt with by Professor Tuttle in his own completed study. Meanwhile, the data presented in Chapter 14 have been included in the present book in the belief that they are sufficiently representative of the actual situation to merit publication and to support the inferences drawn in the chapter.

Occupations

The Braucher and Tuttle studies both asked the responding delegates to state their occupation; on the Tuttle questionnaire, in addition, the delegates were asked to indicate whether their occupation was public or private. The two investigators used somewhat different nomenclature and categories in tabulating the replies, but obtained similar results where comparisons can be made. The data included in Table 14.3 of Chapter 14 are from the Tuttle study, but he should not be held responsible for the arrangement of the categories or the subclassification.

H

Applicability of Small Group Research to Delegation Study

MOST OF THE STATE delegations have some degree of organized life as what the social psychologists call a "small group." Each delegation holds meetings; it is required to reach decisions that can be reported in the form of voting returns and otherwise; and its members usually have a high degree of identification with their state and their delegation as an entity within the convention. Visitors from the state who are closely associated with the delegation, especially those who seem to be admitted to delegation meetings as a matter of right, are a part of the group for some purposes. A "small group" has been defined in scientific research as

> . . . any number of persons engaged in interaction with one another in a single face-to-face meeting or series of such meetings, in which each member receives some impression or perception of each other member distinct enough so that he can, either at the time or in later questioning, give some reaction to each of the others as an individual person, even though it be only to recall that the other was present.[1]

Groups of considerable size can meet these specifications when they involve memberships of high status and long continuity. The convention delegations lack the factor of long continuity except as they come di-

rectly out of highly integrated state party situations. But in view of the factors of travel, housing, and seating together, probably most delegations from all but the largest states have taken on many of the characteristics of a face-to-face group by mid-point in their respective conventions. As such, they lend themselves to various types of research attention designed to achieve a better understanding of their internal leadership, impact of the environment and of external events, group decision-making, and group dynamics generally.[2]

A distinction is sometimes made in the literature of psychology between small groups that are organized and those that are not; an organization is regarded as a special kind of group, but any group with a discernible and continuing leadership may be treated as an organization for some pur-

---

[1] Dorwin Cartwright and Alvin Zander (eds.), *Group Dynamics: Research and Theory* (1953), p. 30. The index of the book carries references to several definitions, all of which tend to emphasize concepts of face-to-face interaction, interdependence and interdependent goals, and identification of members of the group with one another. The quoted definition is by Robert F. Bales.

[2] Inspiration for such research could be drawn from many sources; a wide variety were reviewed some years ago in a compact essay by Edward A. Shils, "The Study of the Primary Group," in Daniel Lerner and Harold D. Lasswell (eds.), *The Policy Sciences* (1951), pp. 44-69. A major attempt to bring conceptual integration to the existing body of research was that by George C. Homans in his book *The Human Group* (1950). Further progress was apparent in the relevant articles in the two-volume *Handbook of Social Psychology* (1954), edited by Gardner Lindzey; the summary therein (Vol. 2, pp. 761-62) of experimental findings on the effects of group size is especially relevant to some of the concerns of the present statement. A recent brief treatment that deserves notice is that by Harold Guetzkow, "Building Models About Small Groups," in Roland Young (ed.), *Approaches to the Study of Politics* (1958), pp. 265-81; the research on decision-making groups to which Guetzkow refers would seem of special relevance for some phases of delegation study.

poses.[3] On this basis, every delegation must be regarded as an organization; but there is undoubtedly a vast difference between the organizational character of such delegations as those of New York, Pennsylvania, Ohio, and Illinois, on the one hand, and the small delegations from Vermont, Delaware, or the Mountain states. The large delegations take on a more formal quality and have less of the face-to-face element, even though they may induce in their members a powerful sense of identification. Even among delegations that are similar in size, however, there are undoubtedly important differences in organizational characteristics, as well as change over a period of time.

Herbert Simon has suggested in some of his recent writing that there is a level of organizational research and theory that deals with "systems that are larger than primary groups, smaller than institutions." He mentions the political club as one example of what he has in mind. He suggests that while many of the same research problems—decision-making, phenomena of power, rationality of behavior, effects of the environment, stability and change, specialization and work assignment—must be studied both in small groups and in organizations, the processes and mechanisms to be studied will not necessarily be the same.[4] This observation seems especially relevant for such *ad hoc* political bodies of intermediate size as the state delegations that are too large or too divided to function readily as a single primary group.[5]

The factors identified in Chapter 15 as of special interest for delegation study (commitment, candidate agreement, factional division, cohesiveness, leadership, ideology) were selected with some regard for small group theory and previous research on small groups, but mainly grow out of what can readily be inferred from ordinary types of political reporting and participant observation. What are here called commitment, candidate agreement, and factional division are aspects of that uniformity of opinion or sentiment with which students of groups have been concerned. Cohesiveness, leadership, and ideology, on the other hand, are all familiar terms in the study of groups and have been used here consistently with other usage so far as possible. The problems of concepts and terminology will need attention in organizing further research.

If more systematic types of delegation study are to be attempted, difficult problems of research strategy will have to be faced. The problems of access will clearly be one center of concern. Experience at the national conventions of 1952 and 1956 suggests that considerable access to delegation meetings and to individual delegates can be obtained by friendly scholars whose political affiliations are known and who come from the state or have active political connections in it. Systematic interviewing, especially interviewing involving a formal schedule of questions, is difficult under the conditions prevailing at the conventions, but simple types of interviewing to obtain indications of cohesiveness and to increase the precision

---

[3] Ralph M. Stogdill, "Leadership, Membership and Organization," as reproduced in Cartwright and Zander (eds.), *op. cit.*, pp. 39-51.

[4] Herbert A. Simon, "Comments on the Theory of Organizations," *American Political Science Review,* Vol. 46 (Dec. 1952), pp. 1130, 1137.

[5] In his mathematical essays recently collected under the title *Models of Man: Social and Rational,* Simon has brought together three of his articles that appear to be of special relevance to the study of delegations and other political groups: "A Formal Theory of Interaction in Social Groups," in which he puts portions of the Homans theory into mathematics; "Mechanisms Involved in Pressures Toward Uniformity in Groups" (with Harold Guetzkow); and "Mechanisms Involved in Group Pressures on Deviate-Members" (also with Guetzkow). Simon introduces these articles with an essay that is consid-

erably more accessible to the non-mathematical reader. In it he discusses, among other things, the relationships between five propositions extracted from previous research: (1) friendliness increases interaction; (2) interaction increases friendliness; (3) cohesiveness tends to produce uniformity of opinion; (4) uniformity of opinion tends to produce cohesiveness; (5) interaction produces uniformity of opinion (under specified conditions). Propositional statements of this kind would seem to provide part of the raw material for an improved theory of the functions served generally by party organizations and by the convention system of nominations in particular. They are obviously relevant to the historic concerns of political science with the processes by which political consensus develops.

with which leadership patterns can be identified would seem readily feasible. Depth interviewing for various purposes would seem most productive if directed primarily to the delegates of experience and political distinction who are not themselves currently holding the posts of active formal leadership, with the attendant demands on their time. The leaders can also be interviewed within limits, but intensive interviewing would probably be most profitable if undertaken before the convention convenes and after it has adjourned.

More important than the problems of access, however, are the problems inherent in defining the goals for which any intensive research should be attempted. The simplest and most concrete goal, although one sufficiently complicated in its achievement, is the development of better descriptions and explanations of how delegations reach their voting decisions. When varying types of delegations have been adequately covered, this type of research can move to the comparative analysis of delegation voting behavior, followed by further attempts to systematize and verify a body of generalized theory on voting in the conventions.

A goal that may seem different but that is also highly relevant to the explanation of group decisions on voting, as well as important for other reasons, is the better description and analysis of the collateral aspects of delegation behavior. This involves such concepts as the amount of "friendliness" or "cohesiveness" within the delegation; the interaction processes by which those qualities are increased or diminished; the communication network within the delegation; the communication network surrounding the delegation; the sources of information, its character and amount; the processes by which the actual leaders of the delegation emerge and become recognized; the intensity of leadership activity; the goals of such activity, especially in the delegation's external relationships; behavior patterns of delegation majorities in relation to minorities; pressures toward uniformity of opinion within the delegation; relationships with the external environment at the convention; relationships with the external environment back home in the state; and so on. Information on these matters will help to explain voting decisions, but may contribute even more to other areas of political information and analysis.

A more remote goal, but one of no small importance, would go on from the kind of thing just indicated into the functions and functioning of state party organizations in relation to presidential politics and the more general aspects of the national party system. For this purpose, delegations could usually be taken as having a central representational relationship to the state party organizations from which they come; in every case, however, the validity of this assumption would have to be examined as a part of the research and in preparation for the interpretation of any relevant findings. It is too early to assess the potentialities of specific delegation research with this kind of orientation, but, if the two previously mentioned goals are actively pursued, the possibilities for applying the findings within a larger setting will undoubtedly become more fully apparent.

INDEX

Index

Acheson, Dean, 109

Adams, John, 11, 13; elected President, 12

Adams, John Quincy, 12n, 15, 56, 159, 222n; elected President, 16

Adams, Sherman, 53, 53n, 368

Advertising Council, 500n

Affirmative mandates, 219

AFL. *See* American Federation of Labor

AFL-CIO Committee on Political Education (COPE), 103, 342

Age, as factor in candidate selection, 138-43, *Table,* 139

Age of delegates, distribution of, 327, 332, 562, *Chart,* 326, *Table,* 561

Agricultural interests: representation of, among 1948 and 1952 delegates, 339-40, 339n-340n; role of, in nominating process, 100-101, 100n

Alabama, 174, 223n, 257; delegate election system, 226, 227, 251, 531-32, 554; presidential primary in, 528

Alaska, 167, 174, 225, 341, 369; advisory preference poll in, 233n

Albert, Carl, 108

Albright, Robert C., 103

Alexander, D. A. S., 67n

Allen, Leo, 68

Alliance, processes of, in national conventions, 437-40; and bargaining considerations, 440; and group affinities, 439; issues as basis for, 438, 439

Alsop, Joseph, 53, 53n, 159n

Alsop, Stewart, 53, 53n

Alternate delegates, 193, 213-14

Alternative vote, in presidential primary elections, 237-38

American Commonwealth, The, 480

American Federation of Labor (AFL), 41, 341n, 342; activity of, in party politics, 102-3

American Heritage Foundation, 288n, 500n

American Institute of Public Opinion (*see also* Gallup Poll), 308-23

American party. *See* Know-Nothing party

American Political Science Association, 226n, 325, 336, 353, 358

Antifederalist party: designation of, as "Republicans," 11; opposition of, to Federalists, 11-12

Antimason party, 17-18, 30; convention precedents established by, 18, 29

Anti-Saloon League, 100

"Anti-Snappers," 76

Appleby, Paul H., 52n

Apportionment rules. *See* Apportionment of votes among the states; Apportionment of votes within the states

Apportionment of votes among the states, 164-92; alternatives to present system, 183-89; apportionment related to the party vote, 178-79; apportionment rules, evolution of, 164-69; apportionment rules (1956, 1960), 169-74, *Tables,* 170-73; bonus votes, 167-68, 169, 174, 179, 182-83, 188, 190, 191; change in, prospects for, 189-92; in conventions of 1960, hypothetical, 188-89, *Table,* 186-87; Democratic apportionment rules, recent changes in, 168-69; Democratic party, variable delegations in, 165; and equal representation of sovereign state units, 176-78, 501; issues in present apportionment systems, 176-83; representation of party voters in 1956 national conventions, *Table,* 180-81; Republican party, history of apportionment rules in, 165-68, 352; reward as an apportionment criterion, 179-83; in state conventions, 178; state power indices in the electoral college, *Table,* 175; voting power under the apportionment, 174-76; voting strength of states (1956), by population groupings, *Table,* 182; voting strength of states and regions in Democratic conventions of 1956 and 1960, *Table,* 170-71; voting strength of states and regions in Republican conventions of 1956 and 1960, *Table,* 172-73

Apportionment of votes within the states, 193-99; all-or-none vs. proportional representation, 197-99; delegates at large, number and uses of, 194; district representation, issue of, 185n, 194-96; districts, methods of apportionment among, 196-97

Arends, Leslie C., 68

Arizona, 37, 182, 552; delegate election system, 251, 551

Arkansas, 341n, 359n, 364; delegate election system, 251, 554; governors, election of, 549; income levels of 1952 delegates from, 334

Army generals, as candidates for nomination, 149, 151, 155, 155n, 157

Arnold, S. C., 546

Aronson, J. Hugo, 546

Arthur, Chester A., 38, 60, 114, 121, 137n, 416, 435

Articles of Confederation, 9

Arvey, Jacob M., 108

Associated Press, 300, 319, 361, 481

Australia, preferential voting in, 237-38, 237n-238n, 315n

Australian Labor Party, 238

569